THE HUMAN SIDE OF ORGANIZATIONS

THE HUMAN SIDE OF ORGANIZATIONS

TENTH EDITION

Dr. Michael Drafke

Professor and Coordinator of Business/Marketing/Management
College of DuPage

PEARSON

Prentice
Hall

Upper Saddle River, New Jersey
Columbus, Ohio

Library of Congress Cataloging-in-Publication Data

Drafke, Michael W.
  The human side of organizations / Michael Drafke. —10th ed.
    p. cm.
  Includes bibliographical references and index.
  ISBN-13: 978-0-13-513974-5 (alk. paper)
  ISBN-10: 0-13-513974-0 (alk. paper)
  1. Psychology, Industrial.   2. Organizational behavior.   3. Interpersonal relations.   I. Title.
  HF5548.8.D68 2009
  658.3—dc22

                                                                        2007033681

Editor in Chief: Vernon Anthony
Acquisitions Editor: Gary Bauer
Editorial Assistant: Kathleen Rowland
Senior Managing Editor: JoEllen Gohr
Operations Specialist: Pat Tonneman
Project Manager: Christina Taylor
Art Director: Diane L. Ernsberger
Cover Designer: Kellyn E. Donnelly
Cover art: Getty One
Director of Marketing: David Gesell
Marketing Manager: Leigh Ann Sims
Director, Image Resource Center: Melinda Patelli
Manager, Rights and Permissions: Zina Arabia
Manager, Visual Research: Beth Brenzel
Manager, Cover Visual Research & Permissions: Karen Sanatar
Image Permission Coordinator: Annette Linder
Printer/Binder: Edwards Brothers
Cover Printer: Phoenix Color Corp./Hagerstown

This book was set in Adobe Garamond Pro by S4Carlisle Publishing Services. It was printed and bound by Edwards Brothers. The cover was printed by Phoenix Color Corp./Hagerstown

---

Pearson Education Ltd.
Pearson Education Singapore Pte. Ltd.
Pearson Education Canada, Ltd.
Pearson Education—apan

Pearson Education Australia Pty. Limited
Pearson Education North Asia Ltd.
Pearson Educación de Mexico, S.A. de C.V.
Pearson Education Malaysia Pte. Ltd.

10 9 8 7 6 5 4 3 2 1
ISBN-13: 978-0-13-513974-5
ISBN-10:   0-13-513974-0

To my wife Kathleen,
my three boys Adam, Erik, and Alex,
to my family,
to members of organizations everywhere,
and to Stan Kossen, author
of the first six editions of this book.

BRIEF CONTENTS

CONTENTS

PREFACE

TO THE INSTRUCTOR

The response to the first nine editions of *The Human Side of Organizations* has been extremely gratifying. Having been adopted by hundreds of colleges in the United States and Canada since its first edition, the text appears to have reached its intended audience. One of the goals of this book has been to avoid overloading students with the multitude of erudite theories that tend to turn off, rather than excite, students facing their first course in organizational behavior, human relations, or industrial psychology. A conscious effort has been made to make this text clear and understandable, something students will want to read, without oversimplifying the subject matter. For this edition the relevance of all content was verified, with changes and numerous additions made as needed. The working environment is changing, and it is more important now than ever before that everyone understand organizational behavior. As organizations change, so must we.

ORGANIZATION OF THE TEXT

The Human Side of Organizations, Tenth Edition, is divided into four parts:

1. **The Basics of Human Relations** Five chapters are designed to help the reader develop insight, sensitivity, and improved understanding of people—both leaders and operating employees—in organizations. Chapters discuss an overview of organizational behavior, the role work plays in our lives, concepts of perception and decision making, and one of the most important areas of all—communication. Two chapters are dedicated to this vital activity, followed by one discussing restrictions suggested by etiquette and ethical concerns.
2. **The Organizational Framework** Five chapters describe the overall structure of organizations and the behavior of managers, groups, and individuals. First the basic element of organizations, jobs, is fully discussed. The various ways organizations are structured are discussed next, followed by the methods used to run (manage) organizations. The last two chapters of this part examine the behavior of groups and individuals.
3. **Inducing Organizational Activity** Three chapters explore factors that induce organization members to act, that is, factors that essentially create momentum in an organization. Motivation theories are explained in the first chapter of this part. The factors that affect job satisfaction and the quality of work life are thoroughly investigated. Change, often the only constant in many organizations, is completely explored.
4. **Strategies for Improving Organizational Behavior and Performance** The previous part discusses factors that essentially create momentum in organizations, whereas this section explores factors for improving organizational behavior and performance and factors that may restrict performance: the role of leadership in organizational behavior, stress factors, and the challenges of globalization, diversity, and the inclusion of all types of workers.

NEW AND UPDATED MATERIALS

This edition incorporates many pedagogical improvements to increase student learning. As always, organizational trends continue to change quite rapidly, so a variety of practical materials have been updated and expanded. Major changes include the following:

- **New Spot Check exercises** ask students to evaluate their comprehension of key concepts as they read through a chapter
- **New student self-assessments**, directly related to the chapter's materials, are in every chapter
- **New skill-building exercises** allow students to apply the chapter materials step-by-step using realistic organizational situations
- **New YouTube™ links** illustrate chapter materials
- **New Personal Point exercises** facilitate personal reflection on chapter concepts
- **The problem-solving** section has been expanded

- **Ethics focus** boxes keying students in to ethical issues have been expanded
- **The ethics and etiquette chapter** appears earlier in the book in response to reviewer requests and the importance of this topic
- **The change management** section has been expanded
- All focus boxes—**Reality Check, A Question of Ethics,** and **A Global Glance**—have been updated
- **Key terms and definitions** appear in the margins
- **Updated Internet addresses** related to key topics appear in the NetNotes
- **Learning objectives** are now directly linked to the questions at the end of each chapter

PEDAGOGY

Goals and Objectives

The overall goals of each chapter and of individual learning objectives are provided at the start of each chapter, presented just as is taught in business and management — broad goals first, followed by specific objectives.

Focus Boxes

Reality Checks bring the work world as it really is into every chapter. **A Question of Ethics** presents ethical questions related to the particular chapter's material. **A Global Glance** looks at an international aspect of a chapter's concepts. **FYI** is a new focus box in every chapter that presents useful hints students can apply in their daily work lives.

Cartoons, Tables, Figures, and Photos

Cartoons such as the extremely popular *Dilbert,* tables, figures, and photos have been included to emphasize key points and enhance student interest in the text matter. The various changes in design are intended to maintain the text's contemporary appearance.

Marginal Notes

A running glossary in the margins and NetNotes have been provided to assist students and faculty. The glossary contains key terms and concepts and their definitions. NetNotes are Internet and World Wide Web sites containing additional information on various topics. Every effort has been made to select valuable and current sites, but please understand that the Web is a dynamic and constantly changing environment.

Spot Checks

Groups of five-question formative tests addressing knowledge and understanding are dispersed throughout each chapter so students may gauge their progress. Answers are provided at the end of each chapter.

Checking for Understanding

These questions cover the major topics of each chapter and test students' comprehension of the material. The questions are directly linked to the learning objectives at the beginning of each chapter.

Self-Assessments

In every chapter, students evaluate their status on topics directly related to the chapter's materials. A summative score allows them to compare their standing, views, or opinions to those of others.

Skill Builds

Skill-building exercises in every chapter allow students to apply the chapter materials step-by-step using realistic organizational situations. Students progress through an organizational situation as it develops, analyze each section, identify the chapter concepts that are involved, and evaluate the correctness of the characters' actions in relation to the chapter concepts.

Applications

A variety of applications are included in each chapter. They are intended to provide students with an opportunity to improve their organizational behavior skills through analysis of realistic situations.

Net-Work

YouTube links increase student engagement by illustrating chapter materials. Each demonstrates a real or a satirical exaggeration of a real organizational situation or type of individual.

Personal Points

Personal Point exercises facilitate student self-reflection on and analysis of each chapter's material. Students create connections between the chapter material and their individual experiences and situations.

Experiential Exercises

Experiential Exercises appear at the end of each chapter. These exercises provide the student with an opportunity to apply specific chapter concepts in teams or individually.

Annotations

The material for the tenth edition has been carefully researched from a variety of current sources. Citation of sources has been greatly expanded for virtually all chapters.

SUPPLEMENTS

Instructor's Manual

The complete Instructor's Resource Manual is written by the author, ensuring complete synergy with the book. It provides lecture notes, video teaching notes, suggested answers to end-of-chapter materials, a test-item file, and overheads. It is available for download at the Instructor Resource Center.

Computerized Test Bank

An electronic version of the test-item file, this supplement allows professors to generate tests automatically or manually, to provide different versions of the same test, and to have easy access to answer keys.

Companion Website

An online resource for distance-learning courses, the Companion Website provides students with extra practice questions, hints for further study, and automatic feedback. Scores and questions can be e-mailed directly to professors. Visit *www.prenhall.com/drafke* for more information and additional resources.

POWERPOINT LECTURE PACKAGE

A PowerPoint Lecture Package contains screens for key concepts in the text, and is available for download from the Instructor's Resource Center.

Online Instructor's Resources

To access supplementary materials online, instructors need to request an instructor access code. Go to **www.prenhall.com**, click the **Instructor Resource Center link**, and then click **Register Today** for an instructor access code. Within 48 hours after registering you will receive a confirming e-mail including an instructor access code. Once you have received your code, go to the site and log on for full instructions on downloading the materials you wish to use.

TO THE READER

This text has been designed with you in mind. It is intended that you understand every aspect of organizational behavior, whether you are a manager or not. Every effort to tell the real story of life in organizations, and not just the theoretical aspect, has been made. I want you to be able to enter any organization prepared for what lies within and to be able to avoid reality shock and many painful learning experiences. I also tried to make this book interesting to read. Therefore, you may find that I am talking directly to you at times, like now. Although this style may seem a little less academic, it is no less serious. I believe that it is more important to write clearly and have interested readers than to succumb to the temptation to use bigger words unnecessarily just to sound important.

Every organization has many sides to it. You are about to explore one of these sides—the human side of organizations. In one sense, an organization exists wherever there are two or more persons with mutual interests. For our purposes, the term *organization* can relate to business organizations, governmental bodies, social organizations, cause-oriented groups, and even family units.

Conflict—Is It Inevitable?

Is conflict inevitable? Not in every instance. Yet, whenever two or more people gather together, potential conflict exists. But do people who make decisions (and who doesn't?) in this problem-beset world have to wait until after a crisis before they act? Wouldn't it be far more desirable if potential discord and organizational problems were anticipated and prevented? Perhaps problems could be prevented far more often if individuals in organizations could develop greater sensitivity toward human problems.

Guard against Simplistic Solutions

Any book on human behavior in organizations shouldn't be a how-to presentation. Wish as heartily as one might, it is unlikely one could come up with 10 simple rules that would enable us to resolve all problems we confront. What should this book be, then? It should be a resource that will help you to develop a keener awareness of and sensitivity toward the needs, sentiments, and attitudes of individuals—including yourself—within organizations, to sharpen your perceptions, and to improve your ability to make effective decisions both on and off the job.

Build a Solid Foundation

I recommend that before you put this book down, you take a quick but careful look at the table of contents. It will give you an idea as to where you'll be going in your reading and also allow you to begin building a framework on which you can attach your newly acquired knowledge.

I also suggest that you take a good look at the learning objectives included at the beginning of each chapter. They are there to assist you. You probably would like to know where you're about to go in a particular chapter; the learning objectives help you find out. They also can serve as a checklist to enable you to see whether you have studied the chapter well.

Key terms have been placed in the margins within the chapters. These terms are defined for you there in order to help you become familiar with them.

This Book Is for You

This text was written with college students in mind. Many of you who read this text may identify with management, although in today's organizations, many of you may not be managers. In either case, it is your responsibility to get along with others (including your boss), as well as to work with individuals, both inside and outside given organizations. Although it may sound a bit trite, the application of good organizational behavior skills is the responsibility of everyone in an organization. I hope that the study of behavior in organizations will assist you in becoming more sensitive to human behavior as well as more successful in your career.

Because this book was written for you, I sincerely hope that you will find studying the tenth edition of *The Human Side of Organizations* beneficial and enjoyable.

Acknowledgments

Special thanks to the reviewers of this text: S. Graham Bourne of Lake-Sumter Community College, Mary Hedberg of Johnson County Community College, Jackie Kroening of Tri-County Technical College, Daniel Montez of South Texas College, and Steve Restad of Anoka Ramsey Community College.

Dr. Michael Drafke

1

Work and Its Place in Life

No other technique for the conduct of life attaches the individual so firmly to reality as laying emphasis on work: for his work at least gives him a secure place in a portion of reality.

Sigmund Freud

When men are employed, they are best contented; for on the days they worked they were good natured and cheerful, and with the consciousness of having done a good day's work, they spent the evening jollily; but on our idle days they were mutinous and quarrelsome.

Benjamin Franklin

Work is the best thing anyone has found to fill up all the time we have.

Anonymous

GOALS

The goals of this chapter are to introduce you to the study of organizational behavior and to describe the elements of the working environment, which is where organizational behavior occurs. You should realize the importance of studying organizational behavior and understand how the physical and mental work environments affect you. You should also begin to understand how you and the way you behave influence others.

OBJECTIVES

When you finish this chapter, you should be able to:

▸ Explain the purpose of the study of organizational behavior.

▸ Trace the history of organizational behavior.

▸ Describe current trends in organizational behavior.

▸ Define work and explain the meaning of work.

▸ Differentiate between work and play.

▸ Explain why people work, and describe the basic philosophy associated with work.

▸ Describe employer theories of the meaning of work.

▸ List and describe the elements of the physical work environment.

▸ Explain how the elements in the physical work environment affect workers.

▸ Differentiate among the caustic coworkers.

▸ List and describe the elements of the mental work environment.

▸ Explain how the elements in the mental work environment affect workers.

▸ Describe your role in the mental work environment.

▸ Compare individual and organizational needs.

ORGANIZATIONS AND HUMAN BEHAVIOR

In effect, an organization exists whenever two or more people have some mutual interest. Organizations often bring far more than two people together for the sake of accomplishing certain goals. When many people are brought together, an infinite number of outcomes are possible. Organizations are truly amazing combinations of human, financial, material, and information resources capable of astounding feats of production, service, coordination, cooperation, precision, and complexity. The mingling of myriad interrelationships and interdependencies can cause conflict and may make it seem impossible for anything at all to be accomplished. Yet people go off to work every day and accomplish their goals and those of the organizations they are a part of, and in so doing they meet the needs of or perform a service for others. The complexities involved can seem overwhelming, and it is easy to spot what does not work. Organizations and work, however, are here to stay. Despite the failures, much gets done well. Learning all we can about how things get done can help us to make sure that even more gets done well and that everyone's needs are satisfied to ever higher degrees.

WHAT IS ORGANIZATIONAL BEHAVIOR?

Organizational Behavior
the actions of people in organizations

Organizational behavior (OB), sometimes referred to as human relations, can be defined as the study of the behavior of people and their relationships in organizations for the purpose of attempting to meld personal needs and objectives with the overall needs and objectives of the organization.

Organizational behavior as a field involves the application of skills garnered from the various behavioral sciences, such as psychology, sociology, and social anthropology. A significant difference exists, however, between OB and other fields. For example, psychology is concerned primarily with the scientific study of the behavior of individuals—why people behave as they do—and sociology emphasizes the scientific study of groups—why groups behave as they do. Social anthropology, a subfield of anthropology, is concerned with why cultures evolve and develop new customs, values, habits, and attitudes.

Organizational behavior is also concerned with the why of people and their groups, but it goes considerably further. In the study of OB, in addition to the why, we want to learn what can be done to anticipate behaviors and to prevent or resolve conflict among organizational members. The goals of an organization and the needs of its members are difficult to satisfy in an atmosphere of irrational or completely unpredictable behavior, or of perpetual conflict.

In other words, our study of OB will be action oriented, emphasizing the development of human relations skills for analyzing behavior in order to understand, anticipate, cope with, and improve behavior. We will also examine behavior and draw conclusions that will apply to many, but not all, people. Rules of behavior that apply to everyone may not exist, but this should not prevent us from attempting to explain the behavior of the many as long as we remember to be alert for the exceptions. In addition, we will examine behavioral trends in order to help reduce and resolve behavioral problems within organizations.

WHAT OB IS NOT

The field of organizational behavior is significant because many problems and conflicts occur regularly among people in organizations. However, the intent of enhanced awareness of human behavior in organizations can easily be misunderstood. Its purpose is not, for example, to enable you to discover techniques for winning friends and influencing people through personality development, nor is it intended to enable you to manipulate people as though they were puppets. Instead, its major objective is to assist you in working more effectively with other people in organizations.

You will soon discover, however, that the study of OB seldom provides the "correct" solutions to human problems, although an understanding of behavioral concepts should assist you in developing better solutions. Individuals who view events as dichotomous, or on a two-valued basis (a right-or-wrong, good-or-bad, one-answer philosophy) are often frustrated when they first confront a human behavior course and find that this narrow approach doesn't work.

A popular cliché is that "working effectively with people is just plain common sense." The application of sound, people-oriented concepts to organizational behavior would seem to be plain common sense, but if this were true, why would there appear to be so much conflict in some organizations? The answer relates to the high degree of interdependence organizational members have with one another. Although organizational members usually share certain common goals, they frequently must compete for limited organizational resources.

Furthermore, value systems among organizational members may differ. Production managers, for example, may see a product primarily from the viewpoint of keeping production costs low, whereas marketing managers may see the same product from the standpoint of requiring features that appeal to the buying public, which may increase the production costs. Even members of the same department—such as those responsible for product development in a razor-manufacturing company—may perceive things differently, some favoring the production and promotion of disposable razors and others favoring nondisposables.

Working effectively with and through people, as you will see to a greater extent as you study this text, goes beyond mere common sense; it also requires an extensive understanding of the needs, values, and perceptions of human beings.

What Is an Organization?

We've already learned that an organization includes two or more people with some mutual interest. There are two other minimum requirements without which you cannot have an organization. All organizations must have cooperation and communication. Even if there are only two people, they must cooperate in order to have an organization. Whether there are 2 or 200,000 people, they must also communicate in order to accomplish the organization's goals. Even if these minimum requirements are met, any two individuals can experience some of the behavioral problems found in larger organizations.

Organizations, however, can be far more complex. If you have ever worked for an organization, you may have noticed something called an organization chart, which is a guide to people's positions and their relationships in the formal organization. The formal organization is the planned or required structure and involves the official lines of authority and responsibility, ranging from the board of directors and president to the operative workers. If you spend time in any organization, you're also likely to notice something called the informal organization, which encompasses the informal interaction that takes place among individuals in any group. The informal organization, or emergent system, involves any natural self-grouping of individuals according to their personalities and needs rather than according to any formal plan. These informal activities and relationships are not found in any company manual or organization chart. They could include cliques, those who cluster around the fax machine, and those who go out together after work for happy hour.

A SMALL DOSE OF OB HISTORY

From a definition of organizations, we will now introduce the study of how people behave in organizations. We needn't delve too deeply into the historical background of OB; however, some significant events are generally recognized as having influenced the greater human awareness that exists today.

INDUSTRIALIZATION—FARMERS LEAVE THE SOIL

The stage was set for concern with organizational behavior at the beginning of industrialization in the mid-1800s, when farmers moved off the land and into towns in hope of improving their situations. Conditions in the early factories left much to be desired. Employees had to work extremely long hours for low pay and were treated more like machines than people. Horrible working conditions persisted until the twentieth century (and some people would argue that such conditions still exist). Before the 1920s and 1930s, managers tended to regard workers merely as factors of production fortunate to be employed.

ALONG CAME TAYLOR, GANTT, AND THE GILBRETHS

Frederick Winslow Taylor entered the organizational scene in the early 1900s. He was concerned principally with efficiency and productivity in organizations and as a result became known as the father of scientific management. Systematically studying ways to improve productivity among steelworkers, he focused on technical efficiency as an organizational goal, maintaining that just as well-designed machinery could be made to operate more efficiently, so could people if their tasks were broken down into simple, repetitive, and specialized activities.[1]

FYI

If at all possible:

- Light your work area so you don't have to strain to see.
- Protect your hearing if necessary.
- Get a small fan, heater, or water garden to help with temperature, humidity, and circulation.
- Select colors and decor that are functional and pleasing.
- Arrange your work area to reduce wasted motion.
- Adjust your work area and equipment to be ergonomically correct.

The studies of Taylor and other proponents of scientific management, such as Henry L. Gantt and Frank B. and Lillian M. Gilbreth, brought needed attention to the human being in organizations and were instrumental in the later development of the field of organizational behavior.

Scientific managers had much to learn about human behavior. Some significant errors in their reasoning included assuming that money was essentially the only reward that motivated workers. They also assumed that workers would always act rationally, which has often proved to be an inaccurate generalization.

Scientific managers also failed to anticipate the resistance that many workers would develop toward standards perceived as unrealistic. Workers were concerned that they would be fired if they didn't attain higher standards. Some workers feared that if they attained these standards, then new and tougher ones would be established. These workers frequently believed that by not attaining new standards, they would discourage managers from imposing higher standards (known as speedups) in the future.

Another shortcoming of scientific management was its failure to recognize the social needs of workers, that is, the need to feel a part of a group. Frequently, scientific managers would isolate workers and place them on a piecework type of compensation. This is not meant to imply, however, that scientific management principles are of no value today. Some of the principles employed by these managers could yield benefits even now, as long as we temper the cold, hard numbers with humane concern for the workers' needs. For example, the study of the motions involved in performing tasks could yield savings by reducing wasted motions or by combining motions that might increase productivity and decrease worker fatigue. Combined with concern for today's better educated, more sophisticated worker, scientific management might prove even more useful than it has in the past.

HOW ABOUT THE HUMAN SIDE OF ORGANIZATIONS?

Excessive concern for production at the expense of the human element brought about numerous organizational problems. As a result, in the 1920s workers formed or joined unions in greater numbers, and some managers became interested in the behavioral, or human, side of organizations.

Some research studies conducted in 1927 are said to have first established OB, then referred to as human relations, as a separate field. They were undertaken at the Hawthorne works of the Western Electric Company in Chicago by the late Elton Mayo (who became known as the father of human relations), F. J. Roethlisberger, and their colleagues at Harvard University.

A series of studies involved altering the work environment of a group of production workers in the Relay Assembly Test Room. During the first study, the level of illumination within the work environment was periodically varied. During a follow-up study, 24 different working conditions were changed, sometimes improved and sometimes worsened. These conditions included rest breaks and workday length. However, to the researchers' amazement, production rates kept climbing and morale improved regardless of the changes made.

Many present-day students of human behavior are somewhat surprised at how basic the results of the study actually were. The researchers discovered that when workers are treated like human beings rather than robots, and when they have feelings of pride and personal worth on their jobs as well as the opportunity to get things off their chests, morale and productivity tend to rise.

THE RISE OF UNIONS

The shock effect of the Great Depression of the 1930s, with almost 25 percent of the U.S. labor force unemployed in 1933, stimulated the cohesiveness and militancy of labor union groups. Managers of the day discovered the need to develop an entirely new style of industrial relations. The judicial and legislative branches of the government began to reverse their previously unsympathetic stance toward collective bargaining. Workers' sit-downs became common practice. In 1937, for example, the General Motors Corporation agreed to recognize the United Automobile Workers after employees had taken over the plant for almost three months.

A union can be defined as an association of workers that has as its major objective the improvement of conditions related to employment. The word *conditions* can represent anything from higher wages to a day off with pay on an employee's birthday. Union activity has long had a significant effect on organizations. Unions have not only had an effect on wages and benefits, but they have also worked hard to improve job safety and working conditions.

THE DECLINE OF UNION MEMBERSHIP

In the last 20 years, union membership has declined, in part because of a decline in the number of factory jobs. Some observers of the labor union scene contend that unions are weaker in the United States primarily because of their success in raising the wages of their members. The difference between union and nonunion wages, for example, is twice as high in the United States as in such countries as Germany, the United Kingdom, and Australia.[2] The high union markup, it is argued, gives U.S. employers the incentive to use hard-line techniques with union officials. Unions generally face less hostility from employers in countries where bargaining takes place for nonmembers as well as for union members.

OB—HERE TO STAY?

At times, the growing awareness of the human side of organizations has approached the proportions of a fad. At other times, a humanistic concern for the employee seems to have done some slipping and sliding because not everyone is convinced of the usefulness of a positive approach to human behavior—after all, fear does motivate.[3] Many people still believe "if you don't like a workplace, just leave. Don't expect the workplace to change just to make you happy." The OB theory that happy workers are productive workers has not been established absolutely. Despite such attitudes, however, too much irreversible change has taken place in our social structure for organizational members to ignore human factors completely.

As we enter the twenty-first century, we see that OB is not yet, nor will it ever be, an absolute science. No magic formulas or lists of 10 simple rules can be applied to specific problems. Human beings can't be poured into test tubes like so many grams of a chemical for the purpose of controlled experiments. Firms that have appeared to be models of excellence during one period have turned out to be failures after a relatively short time. Consequently, there isn't likely to be complete agreement about which behavioral concepts are the most acceptable. A good starting point for understanding organizational behavior is to understand why people work in the first place.

SPOT CHECK

1. The study of the behavior of people and their relationships in organizations is called industrial relations. T F
2. Taylor was primarily concerned with organizational efficiency and productivity. T F
3. The minimum requirements for all organizations are cooperation, collaboration, and communication. T F
4. Maslow is known as the father of human relations. T F
5. The Hawthorne experiments at the Western Electric Company initiated interest in organizational behavior. T F

REALITY CHECK

Does the Physical Work Environment Really Matter?

Wouldn't it be exciting to work in a different spot every day? Wouldn't it be great not to have to find, file, and handle so much paper? Get rid of all the walls and have meetings sitting on a couch? Wouldn't having people check out computers and phones just like library books maximize the utilization of equipment? How about having some chairs mounted on springs or meeting areas made from used amusement park Tilt-A-Whirl cars to add some "fun" to work? Well, all these things, and more, were tried at the Chiat/Day ad agency, and it nearly ruined the firm. CEO Jay Chiat decided to create a totally variable work environment where no one had any personal space, equipment was assigned for the day, paper was not to be used, and people were absolutely forbidden to sit in the same place two days in a row. Chiat wanted a college campus type setting

for creativity, but what he got was a grade-school cafeteria. Probably the biggest problems were that there was no place to put anything and leave it (one person pulled her things around in her child's wagon) and no one could find anyone else. Because no one could be in the same place for more than a day, and there were no rooms to camp out in, many people just went home. This was also part of the plan. Freedom to work anywhere turned into freedom not to work anywhere. One manager lost his entire department for two days. Finally he gave up and went home also. And in the end, that is what Jay Chiat did. Just short of an armed insurrection against this totally open design he sold the agency and retired. So far, not one person who experienced this work environment has been found who will say anything good about the experience.

Source: Warren Berger, "Lost in Space," *Wired,* February 1999, pp. 76–81.

A BASIC QUESTION

The study of organizational behavior, the actions of people in organizations, begins with just this question: Why do people work? Ask most people and they will say that they work for money (and they may think you are a little odd for asking a question with such an obvious answer). During the course of this book, you will find that although money may be a major reason people work, it is not the only reason by far. All the reasons people work and the motivations behind these reasons combine with the reasons of all the other people in an organization to form an amalgam—organizational behavior. In addition, few of the many people who work understand the myriad forces that make up the working environment. Studying organizational behavior can produce such understanding. Studying and understanding organizational behavior can make the difference between a person's being just

---

Knowledgeable Employee

a person who understands the working environment and understands how to be a valuable asset to his or her organization

---

an employee or being a knowledgeable employee. **Knowledgeable employees** understand the working environment and can differentiate between a good working environment and a poor one. Knowledgeable employees know what contributes to their job satisfaction and how to obtain those contributors. Knowledgeable employees know how to cope with change, understand motivation, and communicate effectively. Knowledgeable employees are a valuable asset. They understand their role in the organization. They understand management and the role of the manager. Maybe most important of all, knowledgeable employees are able to work well with others. The person who is just an employee may understand none of these things. Those who have not studied organizational behavior may be frustrated by work; they may not know what work can and cannot reasonably supply; they may not even like work.

Did the last phrase in the previous sentence seem odd? Does it seem unusual to say that some people may not like work, as if most people do like work? Or is it more unusual for people to supposedly dislike something they spend half of their waking hours doing five days of every week? Maybe if people understood what work is and how organizations function, they might like work or at least find work acceptable. To begin the process of understanding, we must first determine what work actually is.

WHAT IS WORK?

Most people know when they are working and when they are playing. They often have difficulty explaining what the difference is, though. Stop here and take a moment to see if you can differentiate between work and play. Write a definition of *work* and of *play* before proceeding.

Some will say that the difference between work and play is that people get paid to work. If payment is the criterion, then mowing one's lawn or dusting one's home can be considered play. So payment cannot be the sole criterion for differentiating between work and play. Some might argue that work is the performance of some task one does not like. Then mowing and dusting would fit with going to work. But many people, if not most, like their work or at least find it tolerable. Therefore, liking or disliking a task is not a criterion for differentiating between work and play. We might next try to examine the task itself, but a professional athlete's work is engaging in sports that nonprofessionals would classify as play. How, then, can we differentiate between work and play?

As shown in Table 1.1, differentiating between work and play requires that three factors be examined:

- the task's purpose
- the attitude of the person performing the task
- the reward or rewards received by the person performing the task [4]

The difference between work and play is in the person and the person's reason for performing a task.

Purpose   Work has a definite purpose. Something is being accomplished when work is being performed. Some resource, material, financial, informational, or human, is being transformed. Play, however, does not have to have a purpose. Sometimes people engage in play for its own sake. At other times play, like work, has an outcome, as when people grow gardens for recreation and also produce food.

TABLE 1.1 DIFFERENTIATING BETWEEN WORK AND PLAY

	Work	Play
Task Purpose	Has a definite purpose	May or may not have a purpose
Personal Attitude	Task viewed as work	Task viewed as play
Task Reward	External and internal	Internal

Attitude   The second criterion to be examined is the attitude of the person performing a task. A task may be work if the person performing it believes it is work. If the person performing a task thinks it is play, then to that person it is play. To a professional athlete, playing baseball feels like work. Therefore, part of the determination of whether a task is work or play resides in the individual.

Reward   The final criterion for whether a task is work or play is whether an internal or an external reward is received for performing the task. External rewards are given for work; internal rewards are received from play. External rewards are given to the task performer from someone else, like an employer. Money may be the most common external reward. Others are promotions, praise, recognition, or status. In contrast, internal rewards (for play) are received from the performance of the task. Internal rewards include curiosity, satisfaction, enjoyment, a sense of achievement, or the meeting of charitable, personal, or philanthropic goals.

WHY PEOPLE WORK

Distinguishing between work and play does not really tell us why people work. Most people would say that they work for money. That is not the only reason, however. People really don't want money; they want the things money can buy. If money is not used (either now or in the future) to purchase the things we want, then we might as well be paid with rocks, and we can pile them up in the corner and look at them. Even those able to accumulate large quantities of money are really doing so because of the status or power that money can provide. Some of them use money for keeping score on how well they are doing. The vast majority of us, however, want money to purchase goods and services so that we may live. Money facilitates transactions. It would be difficult to exchange one's ability to manage others for groceries, gas, clothes, and entertainment. Even someone like an electrician would have a hard time trading electrical work for the necessities of life because there is only so much electrical work another person will need. If people are paid money, they can purchase what they need, and the people they buy from can, in turn, easily buy what they need from others. Now, please don't misunderstand this. Money is important. It is, however, just one part of work, a part that we will see in Chapter 11 is often quite misunderstood.

This still does not answer the question of why people work. A number of explanations have been offered, including this anonymous one: Work is the best thing anyone has found to fill up all the time we have. If you have ever been unemployed, you may be able to attest to this. Not working may seem attractive when you have a job, but most people will tell you that after two or three weeks, unemployment loses its appeal. With little or no cash, you find there is little to do that does not cost money and few companions to do things with because almost everyone else is working. Many unemployed people become depressed, unmotivated, and listless. With no reason to get up the next morning, some people go to bed later and later and get

NetNote

http://www.earthcam.com

Cameras located worldwide in offices, laboratories, and other business settings provide views of physical work environments.

up later and later. Getting up late convinces them that the day has now been wasted and nothing should be started until tomorrow. Procrastination can continue until little or nothing is being accomplished, including looking for a new job. When unemployed, we quickly see that there is more to work than just money.

Other than for money, people work because it is natural, because there are moral and social reasons for working, and to satisfy various human needs. Although this appears to be a short list, there are numerous underlying causes and effects here that will require most of the remainder of this book to explain. This is especially true for the social reasons people work and for the satisfaction of human needs. The natural and moral reasons for work have occupied more than a few volumes in philosophy and psychology.

Douglas McGregor, a historically significant management and motivation theorist, believed that our natural state is to work.[5] To McGregor, life meant activity—activity with a purpose. This activity may consist of work, or it may consist of play, but McGregor believed that the natural state of people is to do something. Essentially, he felt that in activity people were saying, "I am, therefore I work."

In addition to a belief that people are naturally active, Martin Luther believed there are strong moral reasons to work. Luther and his followers considered work a moral and religious duty.[6] Their beliefs eventually evolved into the Protestant work ethic, a version of which lives on in the American Dream. Today people work more to fulfill their own needs and to reach their own goals than to achieve a higher standing in a deity's eyes.[7] Although the moral connections to past beliefs concerning work may have become blurred, social attitudes toward work continue.

The social belief today, as in the past, is that it is far better to be working than to be idle. It is even better to be working hard, for the commonly accepted belief in the United States is that if one works hard and applies all of one's talents, the desired rewards and successes will follow. That this belief is widely held in society creates pressure on people to work and be productive.

Max Weber, a German organization and management theorist of the late 1800s, asked a question that related to McGregor's theory. Weber wondered whether people worked to live or lived to work.[8] Martin Luther or a moralist would suggest that we live in order to work. Many workers today would say that we work in order to live.[9] No matter which view you take, the fact remains that people work. Studies show that most people would continue to work even if they won a lottery or became financially independent in some other way.[10] The ultimate answer to the question of why people work, however, seems to be that work satisfies certain human needs. In the remainder of this book we will examine the needs of humans that can be satisfied through work and how work can satisfy them.

Employer Theories of Work

Just as moralists, theologians, philosophers, unionists, and ordinary people have contemplated the reasons why people work, so have employers. Many employers, when considering the reasons people work, view work in one of the two ways that Weber did. Some believe people live in order to work; others believe that we work in order to live. In the view of some managers, people are here to fulfill the needs of the company.[11] They believe that work is a person's main responsibility in life. Weekends are to rest up for the workweek, and evenings are to rest and prepare for the next day's work. Workers are expected to dedicate themselves to the company, to always put the company and work first, and to always act in the best interests of the company. These are often the same managers who believe that people should leave their personal lives at home, that people should be able to throw a switch in their heads and turn their problems off so that nothing interferes with work. Some believe that by employing people, they own them.[12] Often, the message is that work is of preeminent importance, that the rest of a person's life is a distant second, and that if you don't like it, you should feel free to leave.

At the other end of the spectrum are managers who view work simply as one part of life. They believe that life outside of work is important, is valuable, and greatly affects a person's work performance.[13] These managers are often as concerned for the welfare of their employees' nonwork life as they are for their work life. They may have employee assistance programs to help with work and nonwork problems. They may allow personal days off or mental health days. They realize that personal lives cannot be left at the company's front door. The overall attitude of these managers is concern for the worker, the worker's work and personal life, and the worker's family.

These two views represent the extremes in a continuum of managerial attitudes toward work. Many degrees of opinion lie between them. Some people hold these attitudes about work privately, while others relate their expectations to pay rates. As people are paid more, more dedication is expected of them. As one earns more, more hours are expected to be worked per day and more days are expected to be worked per workweek.[14] Although the convention may be that increased salary justifies higher expectations, some accommodation needs to be made so that workers do not burn out or lose contact with their own families due to career demands.[15] Corporations that do not take into account nonwork factors risk losing some of their most talented new employees, who may choose to go a different route to achieve a balance they feel is more acceptable and humane.[16]

Physical Work Environment

the building, equipment, layout, decor, and other structural elements of the workplace

THE WORKING ENVIRONMENT

In studying organizational behavior, it helps to understand the environment in which the behavior is occurring. The working environment is composed of two main elements: the **physical work environment** and the mental work environment. The physical work environment comprises the building, equipment, layout, decor, and other structural elements of the workplace. The mental work environment comprises the psychological atmosphere created by the work, the management and organizational culture, and the people in the workplace. The physical and mental work environments combine to affect everyone in the organization. However, the working environment affects each person in the organization differently because each person's own behavior influences how others treat that person. In other words, you are part of the mental environment. Your behavior affects the mental work environment, and the mental work environment (consisting of your behavior and that of others in the organization) affects you (see Figure 1.1). It may help to remember the saying "What goes around, comes around." If you act unfriendly, your behavior

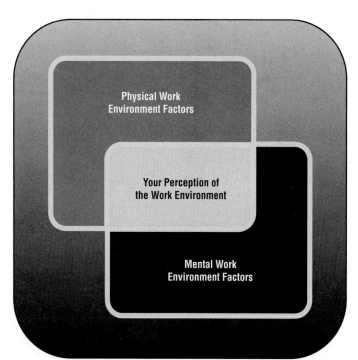

FIGURE 1.1 Physical and mental work environment factors combine to influence you and your perception of the work environment.

13

helps to create an unfriendly mental work environment in which others act unfriendly to you.

THE PHYSICAL WORK ENVIRONMENT

The physical work environment can have a profound effect on people, especially if it is a poor one. A poor physical work environment can decrease efficiency, cause fatigue, decrease morale, decrease productivity, cause lost time, and increase costs, **absenteeism,** and **turnover.**[17] However, many people notice the effects of a poor work environment only after they have been on the job for a while. If you wait to notice a poor physical work environment only after accepting a job rather than before, it may be because you do not know the factors that can adversely affect work or how they will affect you.

The physical factors that affect people in the work environment include light, noise, temperature and humidity, ventilation, color and decor, layout, equipment, supplies, comfort, and safety and security. Knowledge of these factors and proper identification of the source of any problems are the first step toward resolving them. Factors that workers have little or no control over should be scrutinized during the interview tour or before employment (see Table 1.2).

Light   The light from a 40-watt bulb that is two feet away equals 10 footcandles. This is essentially the minimum illumination for most work areas.[18] Of course, this varies greatly with the type of work being performed, with surgery requiring about 500 footcandles.[19] Although there is an upper limit, in general, as illumination increases, so does productivity.[20] In one study, as the light was increased from 2.4 to 11 footcandles, productivity increased 15 percent.[21] The total amount of light is not the only factor of illumination that affects work, however.

In addition to the total amount of light in the work area, the contrast and the **ambient**-to-work-light ratio affects work and productivity. Less illumination is required when the contrast between objects is high (see Figure 1.2). The ambient, or room, light also affects work. Accuracy is greatest when there is a 1-to-1 ratio of

Absenteeism
people missing scheduled workdays

Turnover
the number of people quitting their jobs in a given period, usually one year

Ambient
surroundings, as in the surrounding temperature

TABLE 1.2 WORKER CONTROL OVER FACTORS IN THE PHYSICAL WORK ENVIRONMENT

Factor	Amount of Worker Control
Light	Possibly some
Noise	Possibly some
Temperature	Possibly some
Humidity	Little or none
Ventilation	Little or none
Color and decor	Some
Layout	Little
Equipment	Little
Supplies	Some
Comfort	Possibly some
Safety and security	Little

FIGURE 1.2 WHICH CONTROL IS EASIER TO READ? This figure illustrates the effect of contrast and accuracy. To illustrate the point further, try turning off some lights and reading the two numbers.

16

ambient light to work light.[22] Although room light and work light may be controllable, the color of the light often is not. When the color is controllable (on a computer monitor, for instance), green should be used because it produces less fatigue than other colors.[23]

Noise   Communication and productivity decrease as the noise level increases.[24] People are capable of making some adjustment to a constant noise level, but if the noise exceeds 85 to 90 decibels, productivity will decrease over the course of the workday. Deleterious effects will increase as the frequency or pitch of the noise increases and as the exposure time to the noise increases.[25] When background noise decreases, productivity increases, and worker stress decreases. When the sound level in a work area cannot be decreased, sound-absorbing materials (carpets, draperies, acoustical ceilings) should be used or ear protectors should be worn.

NetNote

http://www.osha.gov
Occupational Safety and Health Administration website.

Temperature and Humidity   Temperature and humidity conditions vary greatly in work environments, and personal tolerances also vary greatly. The maximum comfortable indoor working temperature is about 77 degrees Fahrenheit, and the minimum is about 65 degrees.[26] Some seated workers, however, can tolerate 86 degrees. On the other hand, workers performing physical labor may find 72 degrees the maximum comfortable indoor temperature. For most people, indoor working temperatures below 50 degrees or above 86 degrees can significantly decrease work performance. The ambient (room) temperature that is comfortable is also affected by humidity.

The general comfort zone for humidity is in the range of 40 to 60 percent. Too little humidity can cause problems with static electricity or drying of the nose, sinuses, and throat, which leads to increased chances of contracting colds and the flu. Excess humidity makes higher temperatures more uncomfortable and may cause sensitive equipment to jam or malfunction.

Ventilation   Productivity, morale, and worker health are all affected by the flow of fresh air, or ventilation, in the work area.[27] Ventilation is critical in modern closed work environments. To maintain adequate ambient air quality, room air should change 4 to 10 times per hour.[28] Ventilation should be increased as the amount of harmful or unpleasant substances in the workplace increases. In some areas, ventilation and deodorization may be required.

Color and Decor   Color and decor in the workplace can be used functionally or for aesthetic reasons, or both.[29] In work environments open to the public, the use of color and signage to differentiate various areas can be advantageous. For example, different departments in a hospital might be painted contrasting colors to aid patients and visitors. Color contrast might also be used to differentiate secure and unsecured areas, areas where visitors are and are not allowed, or various levels of safety and danger. Bright or glossy paint is generally preferred, but the effect of the increased glare must be considered. Employees should have as much input as possible into color and decor selection. Although it may not be possible for a large group of people to decide on a color scheme, it may be possible for each person to contribute to the decor. At a minimum, you should be allowed to decorate your own work areas with tasteful personal items. Allowing personalization not only demonstrates a certain humanity on the part of the company, but it also shows an interest in the concerns of each worker and an understanding that work is an integral part of each person's life.[30]

Layout   The main concerns for layout of the work environment are those of minimizing wasted motion and logical grouping of resources.[31] The element being manipulated here is space. Too much space leads people to waste time and energy moving resources.[32] Too little space leads to inefficiency or the inability to perform work properly. Other concerns for layout include social and communication issues.

Equipment   Five factors contributing to the efficiency of the work environment are related to equipment. These are ease of use, maintenance, safety, uniformity, and age. Easy-to-use equipment decreases worker fatigue, decreases time-on-task, and, consequently, increases efficiency.[33] Proper maintenance, the ethical duty of the worker and management, contributes to efficiency by decreasing downtime, but it also contributes to safety. Uniformity of equipment, when possible, decreases errors and increases efficiency by allowing workers to easily share equipment or assignments and by reducing the training required. Although learning to use new equipment takes time, workers often feel they are being supported when equipment is up-to-date.[34]

Logistical
pertaining to the procurement, distribution, maintenance, and replacement of material

Supplies   Logistical supplying of workers is one of the most important functions of organizations. Management must strike a balance between the costs of inventory and the losses that occur when resources are idle. When supplies are inadequate, efficiency and quality decline, and worker frustration increases.[35]

Comfort   Comfort is the cumulative effect of a number of work environment factors. Comfort is part physical and part mental. People should be as physically comfortable as feasible, but the overall work setting should be comfortable, too. You should feel safe and free of unnecessary observation. Increasing comfort levels can reduce stress and increase productivity and job satisfaction.[36]

Security   As a basic need, safety is an issue for virtually all workers. Safety needs range from security from theft of personal possessions to protection from transmittable diseases, electrical hazards, cleaners, chemicals, radiation, and fire, to concerns for air quality. It is insufficient simply to talk about security and safety issues; employees must have confidence that employers are doing everything possible to keep them safe. Employers need written policies, and practices must follow these policies. Fear that stems from safety and security issues inhibits people's ability to work and can erode job satisfaction.

If this information inspires you to investigate new designs for your physical work environment, you should be aware of some additional concerns. First, there needs to be a valid reason to change; otherwise you may do more harm than good by creating confusion or resentment. Second, start with a trial run before rearranging an entire department or company. Third, be brave with the trial design; don't limit the design to what is typical or expected. Fourth, and most important, consider the needs of the people. Tearing out all the walls may seem like a great idea until you try to have private conversations. If some people must work together, place them in close proximity; if others need seclusion, include that in the design.[37]

Sick Buildings   Several well-publicized cases have recently raised concerns about the health of modern buildings and the contributions of numerous factors that individually are of less concern, but when combined may be hazardous .[38] Some of the concerns include toxins from remodeling, cleaning products, pesticides, copiers, printers, fax machines, and even emissions from new office furniture. Ventilation systems may not help as most buildings include sealed windows, and some have vents located near traffic, thus sucking in carbon monoxide. Even removing smokers may not help as many stand just outside the doorway; when the doors open, the building can act like a chimney and suck in the secondhand smoke. How large a concern is this? The EPA says that poor air quality inside buildings is one of the top five risks to our health. Outside specialists are often needed to test building health, pinpoint any problems, and suggest solutions. Correcting indoor work environment problems is not only good for people, but can help companies save money by reducing illnesses and increasing productivity.[39]

THE MENTAL WORK ENVIRONMENT

The **mental or psychological work environment** consists of your aggregate perceptions of four main factors: the work, the **managerial style, coworker influences**, and you. The work consists of 10 factors concerning the actual tasks that make up a particular job. The managerial style consists of the methods managers use to plan, control, organize, and direct the organization. Coworker influences consist of the attitudes, beliefs, and actions of those who work with you. Finally, you, the worker, help shape the mental work environment that affects you.[40]

THE WORK

Whether the work is primarily physical or primarily mental, the actual work a person does affects the mental work environment, as evidenced by 10 factors: work pace, work-pace variety, task duration, task variety, required concentration, required accuracy, error visibility, responsibility level, authority level, and autonomy level. Many of these factors contribute to job stress as well as impacting the mental work environment directly (see Table 1.3).

For many of these factors, there is no correct amount for everyone. Instead, it is important that you understand and examine each factor and determine, for example, what level of autonomy you think you require in a job. Then you must seek out situations that provide the best fit between your absolute needs and those factors you would prefer to be present. Accepting a position that pays well but is a gross

Mental or Psychological Work Environment
a person's aggregate perceptions of the work, managerial style, coworker influences, and the effect the person has on these other factors

Managerial Style
the methods managers use to plan, control, organize, and direct the organization

Coworker Influences
the attitudes, beliefs, and actions of the people with whom one works

TABLE 1.3 COMPONENTS OF THE MENTAL OR PSYCHOLOGICAL WORK ENVIRONMENT AND THEIR TYPICAL EFFECTS ON PEOPLE

Factor	Effect on Workers
Work pace	Stress increases
Work-pace variety	Stress increases
Task duration	Boredom decreases; job satisfaction and performance may increase
Task variety	Interest and motivation can increase
Required concentration	Fatigue and stress increase; accuracy and efficiency decrease
Required accuracy	Stress increases
Error visibility	Stress increases
Responsibility level	Stress increases
Authority level	Stress decreases
Autonomy level	Stress increases

Work Pace
the time required to perform a job task and the time between tasks

Work-Pace Variety
the diversity or differences in the speed or pace of work

Task Duration
the length of time needed to complete one task

Concentration
the fixing of close, undivided attention

mismatch for your mental needs is almost a sure recipe for disaster for you and your employer.

Work Pace   The time required to perform a job task and the time between tasks determine the **work pace.** Fast-paced jobs are those that must be completed in a short amount of time or those with a short interval between tasks. Jobs that must be virtually mistake free and those involving careful or delicate manipulations may be slow paced. Stress typically increases as the pace of the work increases.[41]

Work-Pace Variety   **Work-pace variety** is independent of the work pace itself. A constant work pace, one with little or no work-pace variety, may be present when the pace is fast or when the pace is slower. A constant work pace is often found in assembly-line work and in other areas where time-on-task is well known. In other jobs, the pace is highly variable and is often beyond the control of management and workers. For example, a restaurant is busiest during the traditional mealtimes—morning, noon, and evening. Tollbooths are busiest during the rush hours, which cannot be controlled by toll authority administrators or operators. Typically, as work-pace variability increases, stress also increases.[42]

Task Duration   The length of time needed to complete one task is the **task duration.** As the task duration decreases, boredom can increase. As boredom increases, job satisfaction and performance can decrease.[43] Task duration alone may not be sufficient to affect satisfaction and performance, however. Short task duration combined with a low number of tasks may be required in order to have an impact on satisfaction and performance. For example, teachers must transfer grades from a grade record or spreadsheet to an official grade form. The task duration for recording each grade is very short, about two seconds for each grade. This task is done only at the end of the term, however. Transferring grades three or four times a year may be boring for the few minutes it takes, but there is no overall effect on job satisfaction. If this is all one did, 8 hours a day, 5 days a week, and 50 workweeks a year, then there would be a very significant effect on job satisfaction.

Task Variety   Task variety refers to the number of different tasks a person performs. Typically, as task variety increases, interest in the overall work increases, and as interest increases, motivation increases.[44] There is a limit, however, to the number of tasks that one person can be asked to perform. A balance must be found between having a sufficient number of tasks in a job to maintain people's interest and motivation, and allowing people to specialize enough to become proficient at the tasks. Also, task variety combines with task duration to create an effect on satisfaction and performance. The least desirable situation is typically a job with few tasks, each of short duration. Jobs like this may benefit from expansion of the depth or breadth of tasks or from the sharing of different jobs among two or more people.

Required Concentration   Required **concentration** is the amount of concentration needed to perform the work at hand. Operating heavy or powerful equipment, performing delicate operations, assembling small parts, or making important decisions can demand total concentration. Maintaining a high level of concentration for a long time increases fatigue. High concentration increases stress and, with fatigue, can significantly decrease efficiency and accuracy.[45] To reduce the negative effects of required concentration, high-concentration tasks should be alternated with lower-required-concentration tasks. If this is not possible, then rest periods should be more frequent.

Required Accuracy   Similarly, required **accuracy** is the degree of precision needed for the work at hand. Tasks requiring virtually 100 percent accuracy increase stress levels for most people.[46] Financial transactions, legal proceedings, and medical procedures often require virtually perfect performance every time. Required accuracy can be improved through training, education, and using ergonomically designed equipment and equipment that is in perfect working order.

Error Visibility   When the errors a person makes are highly visible to others, stress increases. **Error visibility** includes the obviousness of the error to managers, coworkers, customers, suppliers, clients, or others. If the error is easy to hide or fix, then stress is minimally affected (there is often some effect, however, as most people do not like to make mistakes even privately). In addition to error visibility contributing to stress, the manner in which coworkers, managers, and others respond to the error can increase or decrease the felt stress. Ignoring an error or providing constructive criticism or advice reduces the stress of making an error. Ridicule, insults, and drawing more attention to an error increase the stress of making a mistake. In addition, the way you handle the mistakes of others can affect the way others handle your mistakes. For example, if you routinely make an issue of other people's mistakes, trying to make them look incompetent or foolish, how do you think they will react when you make a mistake?

Responsibility Level   **Responsibility level** refers to how accountable someone is for obtaining results. Stress generally increases as the responsibility level increases.[47] This is especially true if someone is given responsibility for obtaining certain results but has not been given sufficient authority to achieve these results.

Authority Level   **Authority** means that a person has been given the power or the ability to command resources (human, financial, material, and informational) in order to achieve results. Managers should ensure that the authority level is equal to the responsibility level. People need to be given the ability to command resources (the authority) that is adequate to obtain the results assigned to them (the responsibility). If responsibility exceeds authority, problems and stress typically increase.[48] For example, if you are given the responsibility to make a department more productive but are not given the authority to make needed changes, then you will probably fail and feel angry, bitter, or disappointed.

Autonomy Level   **Autonomy** is the ability of a worker to perform his or her job independently or with minimal supervision. A high level of autonomy (a person working with little or no direction or supervision) is not usually a problem if the person has the required education and training to work autonomously.[49] Sometimes the ability to work autonomously must be earned. A person may have to demonstrate in stages that he or she is capable of working independently before management bestows full trust to work under minimal supervision. At other times managers lack the security to allow people to work autonomously. Although some degree of autonomy is present in most jobs, management theorists like Frederick Herzberg and others believe that a high level of autonomy is a necessary part of virtually every job.[50]

THE MANAGERIAL STYLE

The philosophy, managerial style, or methods that managers use in running the organization so greatly affect the work environment that an entire chapter has been

---

Accuracy
precision or exactness

Error Visibility
the obviousness of an error to others

Responsibility Level
how accountable someone is for obtaining results

Authority
having the power or the ability to command resources in order to achieve results

Autonomy
the ability of a worker to perform his or her job independently or with minimal supervision

devoted to this topic. Chapter 8 is dedicated to the understanding of management styles or theories and the impact these styles have on the organization. In brief, managerial style involves the approach to planning, controlling, organizing, and directing the organization. The level of education, training, and experience the management team has affects all other employees. We will find that virtually everything, from the jobs and tasks people perform, to the size of the workforce, to the level of autonomy and the degree of formality, is controlled by the management team.

COWORKER INFLUENCES

Throughout the remainder of this text, the influence of coworkers will be discussed. For now, a brief introduction will have to suffice. The assumptions coworkers and managers make concerning work greatly affect the degree to which you will be affected by coworkers. For example, behavioral managers (more about this management philosophy in Chapter 8) believe in the social aspects of work; therefore, they attend to the informal organization more than do classical managers. Because a behavioral manager is more likely to intervene in any problems between an individual and coworkers, the impact of these coworkers' attitudes, actions, and beliefs will be accentuated. In addition to the managerial's influence on the coworker portion of the mental work environment, the coworkers themselves greatly affect the mental work environment.

Certainly many coworkers are a pleasure to work with or at least have no negative effect on you. Others range from annoying to injurious. The annoying should be avoided or ignored, but the others, the caustic coworkers, may need to be dealt with. At least seven types have been identified:

- the lazy
- the hothead
- the squealer
- the lone wolf
- the boaster
- the critic
- the blameless

Each of these needs to be handled differently.

Whether hiding, surfing the Internet, talking to others, or just moving slowly, the lazy coworker gets little or nothing accomplished.[51] Give the lazy an assignment and it is unfinished, late, or poorly done. The lazy cannot be depended upon.

Although aggravating, it is better to concentrate on your own performance and avoid the lazy, trusting that eventually the system will catch them. Don't take on the lazy person's work, and avoid being on a team with him or her if possible. If you must be on a team with a lazy coworker, try to ensure that he or she has specific tasks and deadlines that will be visible to management if not completed.

The hothead has great difficulty controlling his or her temper.[52] Hotheads can be overly emotional or are rebels. You should avoid them, but when that is not possible, do not yell back. Remain calm and logical. Later, when the hothead has cooled down, you may approach the person and discuss his or her improper behavior.

The squealer tattles on his or her coworkers to management.[53] The squealer cannot do much harm to others alone, however, as a manager has to be willing to listen for him or her to have much effect. Sometimes squealers report the truth, and sometimes they exaggerate (or even lie), but the events they relate tend to be petty; they are not legitimate whistle-blowers. In any case, two steps are required to deal with a squealer. First, the squealer must be confronted about errors, exaggerations, and lies. Second, the manager who listened must be presented the facts regarding errors and lies. If a squealer knows that others are aware of what he or she is doing, the tattling may stop, and if the manager learns the truth, the manager may stop listening.

The lone wolf may be a recluse or outsider who maintains his or her distance, or he or she may be the office grouch. The lone wolf often chooses the phone, memos, or e-mails over face-to-face communication and is often pessimistic or highly critical.[54] Left on their own, lone wolves may become even more malicious and unsocial. Coping with the lone wolf may involve trying to bring the person into the fold by asking for his or her help. An alternative would be to try to convince the lone wolf to change his or her attitude by explaining how he or she is perceived by others and citing examples.

The boaster is a shameless self-promoter. Boasters not only constantly take credit for actions, ideas, and achievements, but they also tell everyone who will listen how busy they are and how hard they are working.[55] While first in line for recognition, the boaster is last in line for blame. In dealing with a boaster, it is best not to address his or her claims but to ensure that you receive any credit due you. Working independently can help, and while you don't have to turn into a boaster, sometimes you're the only one who will be able to tell your story.

Critics are perfectionist controllers.[56] Critics need to have everything their way and are hypercritical of the ways of others. Critics see things in absolutes: black and white, all good or all bad. Problems arise when critics block the ideas of others or insist on having their way even when it is not the best way. Critic coworkers are mainly a problem in groups or on teams. In these situations, if the critic insists on his or her way, rather than allowing a stalemate to develop, try to have the critic write a minority report and include that with the rest of the group's conclusions.

Last on this list are the blameless. The blameless ensure that all blame is shifted away from them to someone else.[57] Unlike the boasters, the blameless are not looking to take credit or brag, they are simply making sure they cannot be blamed or held accountable for anything that goes wrong. The blameless may act preemptively by opposing something just after it is decided on, or they may express some doubts just before implementation. If everything turns out well the blameless hope no one will remember their opposition, or they may even deny that they had reservations. If things go bad they can say, "I told you so." The blameless may also go so far as to remind managers of the people that supported less successful ventures, excluding themselves of course. To counteract the blameless you may have to document your own position, including your rationale, in case the blame starts to come your way (this is sometimes referred to as "covering yourself").

NetNote

http://stress.about.com/b/a/ 257697.htm
http://stress.about.com/od/ officepolitics/Office_ Politics_and_Dealing_With_ CoWorkers.htm

More annoying coworkers and hints for dealing with them from a stress management site.

Examining the effect of coworkers on the mental work environment introduces the next topic, specifically, your needs in relation to the psychological environment and your coworkers. The important thing is to try to find a match between what you desire in coworkers and what can be provided. If you desire a high level of social interaction with coworkers, then you should seek out jobs and organizations that can provide it. For example, some companies pride themselves on providing social and work interactions. Also, if you desire a high level of interaction on the job, you should focus on organizations that employ teams extensively. You might also avoid working the midnight shift, which typically has fewer workers and less chance for interaction. On the other hand, some people might want to work autonomously. They would seek out jobs and organizations where they could work independently. As with management style, you should try to match your desires with what the situation can provide, or you should modify what you can expect from work. If work cannot provide the social contacts you desire, you could look outside of work to professional and social organizations or volunteer and charitable organizations for these interactions. As you can see, the mental and physical environments are interrelated. Coworkers affect you and the mental environment just as you affect coworkers and the mental environment.[58]

YOU AND THE MENTAL WORK ENVIRONMENT

Many people who complain about work never consider looking in the mirror for another potential source of their problems. Sometimes a manager or coworker may treat you poorly because the manager or coworker is having a bad day. If these are only occasional incidents, they should be forgiven and forgotten. At other times, however, you may receive (or you may perceive to receive) poor treatment because you are having a bad day and are treating others poorly, and they are just responding to you. Possibly the best general advice is to treat people the way you would like to be treated (or as some say, "Treat others the way you would like to see your mother treated"). Other guidelines that may help include:

- not dwelling on the mistakes of others.
- making yourself available to help if needed.
- sharing a little of the workload of a coworker who is having a bad day or is going through a rough period.
- not complaining if a coworker does not do his or her fair share for a day.
- Being available to listen if a coworker needs to talk.
- Not trying to wrest an explanation from a coworker who is unwilling to talk

In applying these guidelines, everyone can benefit. The person having difficulty benefits, and you may earn some understanding when it is you who needs some compassion and empathy. Even given this, some people may not consider themselves a component of the mental work environment.

Some people view the rest of the world as a truly external force. In their view, the world acts upon them; they do not see themselves as an integral part of that world. In their view, they are an innocent beach upon which crash the waves of reality. They see the work environment as the work, the management, and the coworkers—and not themselves. This is quite wrong. How you act contributes greatly to the entire mental work ecosystem.

Perhaps the two most important items to remember regarding your contribution to the mental work environment are (1) not to take other people too seriously, and (2) to remember that most people are human. This not only means understanding that people make mistakes and that anyone can have a bad day, but it also means treating everyone with dignity. It means not looking for hidden meanings in everything people say or do, and it means not being overly concerned about how much or how little someone else is doing.

Why are so many people concerned about how much work others are or are not doing? Maybe it is a habit left over from childhood sibling rivalry over who was going to have to pick up more toys than whom. However, if some of these people spent half as much time working as they do worrying about what others are doing, then there wouldn't be any work left for anyone. The main concern seems to be over some assumed unfairness if the workload is unequal and the fact that everyone is getting paid to work. Some think that they have done a fair day's work if they have done the same amount as others. Their standard is a relative measure of work compared with that of others who are performing a similar job. This is wrong. A fair day's pay is given for a fair day's work. Pay comes from the employer. Employers, however, typically evaluate whether or not a fair day's work was given based on a person's accomplishing what was assigned, not on the completion of work done in comparison with others. The matter, then, is whether a worker has met his or her ethical obligation to the employer to give a fair day's work for a fair day's pay.

To examine the roles in an organization further, look at Figure 1.3. Note that you affect your coworkers and managers, but that they also affect you. If you treat your coworkers to sarcastic, critical remarks, do not be surprised if they are less than friendly with you. If you are constantly whining to management and giving less than a full effort, do not be surprised when managers turn down your requests and applications for promotion. In some respects, the division among the contribution to the mental work environment from coworkers, managers, and you is almost arbitrary. These elements are interrelated. Understanding all of these interrelationships will be a theme running throughout the remainder of this book.

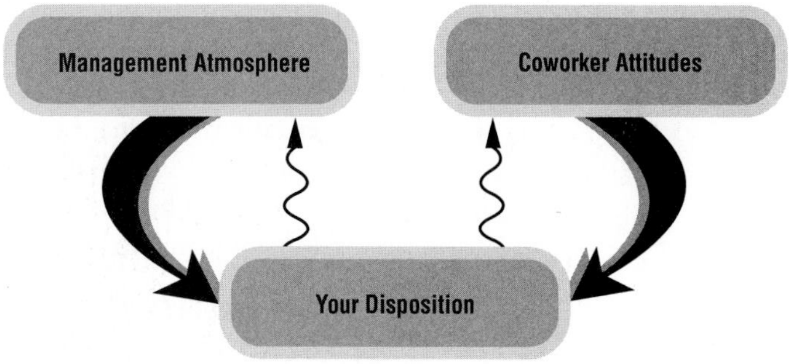

NetNote

*http://www.ergoweb.com/
news/*
http://www.ergonomics.org/
Ergonomic news and
ergonomic resources.

FIGURE 1.3 How you act toward coworkers affects the way they act toward you

INDIVIDUAL AND ORGANIZATIONAL NEEDS

What motivates you to work? Do you think that unless you work, your needs for food, shelter, or a car will go unsatisfied? The income you receive for working helps to satisfy such material needs and wants.

PERSONAL NEEDS AFFECT THE ORGANIZATION

Individuals bring their personal needs to the organizations in which they work. These needs are partially material and economic, partially social and psychological. The personal needs of employees can have significant effects on the organizations themselves. For example, your personal needs strongly influence your motivation and attitude toward your job. Managers especially should attempt to understand human needs because they influence the attitudes and behavior of employees.

ORGANIZATIONS NEED ORDER AND PREDICTABILITY

Try to imagine any organization attempting to accomplish specific goals without some sort of order or guidelines. Freedom for all organizational members to do whatever they want may seem desirable in some situations, but most organizations, however progressive or enlightened, would find survival under such conditions extremely difficult. An organization without some structure can be compared to an airport that has no ground or air control over the airplanes using its facilities. Imagine the chaos that would result.

Almost any well-run organization that you work for is likely to have a set of rules—sometimes called policies, procedures, or guidelines—designed not to restrict creativity but to assist its members in the accomplishment of organizational goals. You are also likely to find that most organizations have some rules that seem reasonable and others that appear ridiculous. Utopia is difficult to find. Because you'll probably never work for an organization that seems absolutely perfect, your next best approach when seeking a position might be to attempt to find one that provides you with a reasonable amount of satisfaction according to your own values. Organizations, like people, have personalities. You probably feel more comfortable around some types of personalities than around others.

Most well-managed organizations will have some order and predictability, referred to as their required system (the formal organization). But regardless of how energetically the management enforces and coordinates formal policies, an emergent system (or informal organization) of behavior related to personal needs will tend to evolve. The needs of workers create many behavioral situations that can't be found in any company manual and should be handled on an individual basis.

ORGANIZATIONAL NEEDS AND VALUES RESULT IN ORGANIZATIONAL CULTURE

Organizations have what is referred to as an organizational culture, consisting of the values that its members, leaders, and employees bring to the work environment. One of the major purposes of this book is to expose you to some modern, people-oriented concepts that, when effectively applied, can assist you in understanding, adapting to, and influencing the culture of organizations.

The application of good organizational behavior skills is the responsibility of everyone in an organization. Managers have the primary responsibility for establishing and maintaining a favorable organizational culture, but workers also have a strong influence over the culture and should share the responsibility for it. More will be discussed on the concept of organizational culture in a later chapter.

WHERE DO WE GO FROM HERE?

We have discussed OB history and provided a foundation for further study by explaining what work is and why people work and by describing the working environment, the place where organizational behavior occurs. We have also mentioned what is to come in some of the other chapters, but let us look at the rest of the book by describing the other chapters in order. Chapter 2 covers perception. Here we will examine the phenomenon that things are not always as they appear. Chapters 3 and and 4 cover one of the most vital and complex aspects of organizational behavior—communication. A thorough examination of the subject will be made so that you will be well equipped to send your message and to understand the messages (verbal and nonverbal) being sent by others.

Chapter 5 prepares you for the subtle but vital skills required to thrive and advance in the business environment. Ethics and etiquette both relate to proper behavior in an organization. The etiquette section is especially valuable; its thorough coverage includes much information that others have learned only after years of experience (and mistakes). Chapter 6 covers jobs, from their creation, to the methods used to evaluate the people performing them, to obtaining a job. Chapter 7 describes formal organizations and the structure that serves as the framework for organizations and the behavior occurring within organizations. Chapter 8 proceeds to the topic of management. The emphasis here is not so much on how to be a manager, but rather on the effect management can have on OB. A reverse look at management is provided in an effort to promote an understanding of how to be managed. Narrowing the focus of OB further, Chapter 9 looks at small-group behavior and the informal organization (the social version of the formal organization). The ultimate focus is provided by Chapter 10, where the individual in the organization is discussed, including the trend toward self-management.

Chapter 11 covers an issue of personal interest to virtually everyone—motivation. Factors that affect motivation are discussed, including self-motivation and the less frequently discussed effects of deadlines and time on motivation. Chapter 12 delves into all the factors affecting job satisfaction and the quality of work life, including trends in hiring temporary workers and downsizing. Chapter 13 examines the one constant in our lives—change. Resistance to change, change methods, and coping with change are thoroughly covered.

Chapter 14 presents leadership, which can apply to managers and nonmanagers alike. Chapter 15 provides an introduction to stress, with the main focus on job-related stress and harmful responses. The last chapter, 16, covers the challenges all organizations and the people in them face—globalization, diversity, older workers, and workers with disabilities.

Throughout the book ethical and global views on each chapter's material are provided. A dose of the real world is found in the Reality Checks, which illustrate what is happening to ordinary people every day. In addition to key terms and their definitions in the margins, review questions, applications, and references, NetNotes offer interesting sites on the Internet and the World Wide Web. These NetNotes provide a starting point for World Wide Web information that supports text material. However, the Web is a dynamic, ever-evolving entity, so if a site has changed or moved, follow it, or use the information to start a search of your own. The FYI feature contains practical information you can use daily.

Finally, and let us be totally honest here, is it really necessary to study organizational behavior? Is this important, or is it just another subject in which a few facts are memorized for a test and then forgotten? Consider this: You will spend more than 40 years (your working life) in an organization of some type. Even if you start your own business and are the only worker, you will have to interact in some fashion with other organizations. Do you want to trust your luck and hope you send the correct message to others, or do you want to learn this material and greatly increase your chances for success? That is what a thorough knowledge of OB can do for you. It can't guarantee success—nothing can—but it can tilt the odds in your favor. Learn the material in this book, and you will gain the benefit of the research and experiences of many others; ignore it, and you stand alone against the expectations and scrutiny of the corporate, organizational world, where one preventable mistake could seriously alter your chance for success.

SUMMARY

Most of us have to work, and if you are going to work you might as well be good at it. In the past it might have been sufficient simply to know how to do the job, but now many more teams, projects, and jobs involve increased interactions with others. Today you not only have to do the job but you also have to know how to act and interact properly. Organizational behavior (OB) examines those actions and behaviors. OB, however, goes beyond explaining why individuals or groups behave as they do and strives to determine what can be done in a positive way about human behavior that may disrupt organizational objectives.

This chapter has presented the history and background of OB. It has explored the meaning of work and differentiated between work and play. It has also introduced some of the reasons why people work (others will be examined in later chapters) and how these reasons affect employers.

The environment where organizational behavior takes place has been described. The physical working environment can and does affect the behavior of those in it. A drab, hot, stale, poorly illuminated, and poorly equipped work environment would depress almost anyone. It would be difficult to achieve and maintain high levels of productivity and creativity in such a place. On the other hand, a bright, comfortable, personalized environment can positively affect moods and output.

The mental work environment can have an impact equal to that of the physical environment. Managers, coworkers, the work itself, and you combine to set the psychological climate of the workplace. Just as the managers, coworkers, and work affect you, your actions and attitudes affect them. Many coworkers are professional, friendly, and good to work with, but a few are caustic and may need special handling. Your actions influence the way others act toward you. Your actions, then, may help to create a positive or negative work environment.

In the end, we work to satisfy our numerous and complex needs. Organizations employ us to satisfy their numerous and complex needs. As much as possible, these sets of needs should coincide. The resulting interplay (and sometimes clash) of the needs of individuals and organizations is expressed as organizational behavior. This behavior is sometimes predictable and understandable, and sometimes not. To enter the world of organizations without a thorough knowledge of OB is to go off to battle only half-armed.

CHECKING FOR UNDERSTANDING

1. What benefits can be derived from studying organizational behavior, given that this study will not provide all the answers?

2. Trace the history of organizational behavior.

3. What are the current trends in organizational behavior?

4. Define work and explain the meaning of work.

5. What is the difference between work and play?

6. Why do people work? List all the reasons.

7. Describe the basic philosophy associated with work.

8. Describe employer theories of the meaning of work.

9. List and describe the elements of the physical work environment.

10. How can each of the elements in the physical work environment affect workers?

11. What are the elements of the mental work environment? Describe each of them.

12. Identify and describe caustic coworkers you have known and how they have affected you.

13. Describe your role in the mental work environment.

14. Compare individual and organizational needs.

15. To accomplish their goals more effectively, should managers attempt to prohibit the emergent, or informal, organization? Explain.

SELF-ASSESSMENT

Answer the following questions regarding your current job and you.

1. The amount of time I have to complete each of my tasks at work is
   a. Less than I like; I feel rushed
   b. Too much; I'm bored
   c. A comfortable amount for me

2. The amount of time I have between tasks is
   a. Not enough; can't catch my breath
   b. I have time to waste
   c. A comfortable amount for me

3. The pace of my work
   a. Varies less than I like
   b. Varies more than I like
   c. Varies as much as I like

4. The amount of time I have to complete each work task is
   a. less than I would prefer
   b. Longer than I need
   c. Right about what I need

5. The number of different work tasks I perform is
   a. less than I like
   b. More then I like
   c. Just right

6. The amount of concentration my work requires is
   a. More than I like
   b. Less than I like
   c. Just right

7. The level of accuracy my work requires on the first try is
   a. Perfect or nearly so for me
   b. High, but there is some time to correct mistakes
   c. Okay; if I make a mistake there is time or an opportunity to fix it

8. If I make a mistake at work
   a. It's obvious to others
   b. It's not seen by many or not a big deal
   c. I'm about the only one who knows

9. If I make a mistake at work
   a. I am really embarrassed
   b. It doesn't bother me a bit
   c. I don't like it but I don't let it get to me

10. The amount of responsibility I have at work is
    a. Greater than I would prefer
    b. Less than I can handle
    c. Just about right

11. The authority I have to command the use of money, people, information, and supplies is
    a. Too little; I need more authority given my responsibilities
    b. I have more authority than responsibility
    c. My authority is about right given my responsibility

12. At work I am supervised
    a. More than I would prefer
    b. Less often than I would like
    c. About the right amount

Add up your number of a, b, and c. answers. Multiply the number of a answers by 1, the number of b's by 2, and c's by 3. Total your score. 29–36 represents a good match between you and your mental work environment; 21–28 signifies a fair match between you and your mental work environment, but with room for improvement; and 12–20 means you may not have the best match between you and your mental work environment at this time.

SKILL BUILD 1

Read the conversation and help these people by answering the Skill Questions as you go. Base your answers on the material in this chapter. Use the terms in this chapter in your answers.

"I just don't see why I have to pay these people more money," Fred said.

"Well, Mr. Birks, I know that you know coins. That's why you are the president of the Numismatic Evaluators of America. But you hired me because I know management, and a good deal of your absenteeism and turnover problems are due to the low pay," Jeffery Foyle replied.

"Absenteeism, turnover—aren't those really the same thing?" Fred Birks asked. "I mean, if someone leaves they are absent, and if they are absent I want them to leave!"

Skill Question 1. Differentiate between absenteeism and turnover (or are they, as Birks said, the same thing?). Whether they are different or the same, what do high absenteeism and high turnover tell us?

"Let's not worry about that now. There are bigger things to be concerned with, like. . . ." Foyle began.

Birks interrupted, "Whatever, I still don't think these people need more money. They would grade coins even if I didn't pay them. Evaluating rare coins is not just a hobby with these people—it's their whole life. They enjoy this and are having fun—so much fun this is really playing for them. They should pay me!"

"Mr. Birks, there is definitely a difference between work and play."

"Oh, then what is it?" Birks asked.

"Well, I don't know exactly how to explain it," responded Foyle.

Skill Question 2. It seems Foyle needs you to help figure out whether the coin graders are working or playing. First, differentiate between work and play in this situation.

Skill Question 3. Draw a conclusion as to whether this is work or play.

"One thing I know is that few people would 'play' indoors when it is 50 degrees Fahrenheit," Foyle continued.

"What? You think it's too cold? Heat is money!" said Birks.

"When your employees wear wool hats and gloves then yes, I say it is too cold in here," Foyle replied.

Skill Question 4. Is it too cold for a job where people sit at a table in order to perform their work? If it is too cold, what temperature should it be?

Skill Question 5. If it is too cold, what temperature should it be?

"Well that's why I divide the work: short jobs, keep them moving. That's the ticket. That should hold their interest, too," Birks declared.

Skill Question 6. What is task duration?

Skill Question 7. What effect can task duration have on workers?

"Actually, I think that contributes to the turnover, too. You personally assign each coin to a grader, and you hand out a sheet with the grading standards on it every time. Yet you only hire qualified graders. They know this stuff backwards and forwards. It's a waste of paper; you are killing a bunch of trees for nothing. They have no freedom to select what they are best at. They have no freedom even to decide what order to do their day's work in. You dole out the work, and they do these little tasks—that gets boring and dissatisfying and then they leave," Foyle said.

Skill Question 8. What is Foyle talking about here? Is Foyle correct about the effect this has?

"They don't all leave. Neuman, Renquist, and Santos have been here awhile," Birks pointed out.

"True," Foyle replied," but where could they go? Neuman runs to you each and every time he thinks someone else has done something wrong. The smallest thing, and he's off to your office. The only people Neuman hasn't done this to is Renquist and Santos. With Renquest he can't because no one seems to know what he does. He's off in that corner behind his walls made of old crates. Sure, he does his work, but he talks to virtually no one, eats alone, leaves alone, and when he does talk he's gruff. Then there is Santos. He has all the others believing he is the greatest coin grader ever. He is constantly telling others how great he is, and if I hear that story about the counterfeit 1913 Liberty Head nickel one more time I'll scream!"

"Forgery," Birks replied calmly.

"What?" Foyle asked.

"It was a forgery, not counterfeit. And I didn't know he was claiming to have found it because I was the one who proved it was a forgery," Birks said.

"What's the difference? He's dysfunctional, period," Foyle said.

"It is a very big difference. A counterfeit coin is meant to fool the public and pass at face value; a forgery is meant to fool collectors and experts and sell for much more. Or did you mean what difference does it make that he said he found this forgery? Well, that is important too. Not just because he lied, but in this business that was a critical find. You see, there are only five known 1913 Liberty Head nickels. None was meant for circulation, and their creation is a bit hazy. At the time only four had been found. If that was the real fifth coin, it would have been worth a lot," Birks explained.

"How much?" Foyle asked.

"Oh, one and a half to two million dollars," Birks replied.

"Whoa! But you see what I mean? You have the three strange rangers, and the rest come and go so often we might as well have a revolving door at the employee entrance. You hired me to help this situation; now let me help," Foyle said, a bit of pleading in his voice.

"I'm still not convinced," Birks replied.

Skill Question 9. Is Neuman a caustic coworker, and if so, what kind is he?

Skill Question 10. What does the chapter suggest can be done with him?

Skill Question 11. Is Renquist a caustic coworker, and if so, what kind is he?

Skill Question 12. What can be done with Renquist?

Skill Question 13. What kind of caustic coworker is Santos?

Skill Question 14. What can be done with Santos?

Skill Question 15. What are your overall recommendations for improving this situation?

APPLICATIONS

1.1 LIFE IN A FAST LANE

Rachel Rubins is the director of an extremely fast-paced local TV news show that reports on the conditions of the stock markets. The show includes two reporters in a studio. One of these is basically a ringmaster, providing commentary on the other reporters' news and the relationship between the various indices, like the DOW, S&P 500, and the Russell. The other in-studio reporter is seated at a desk with a computer covering the NASDAQ and is never in the same shot as the ringmaster. There are also a reporter and camera operator at the New York Stock Exchange, the American Stock Exchange, and the Chicago Board of Options Exchange. Rachel must make split-second decisions on which of the five reporters will be on at any given moment in the eight-hour program. There

are no breaks or lunch away from the control console. If Rachel puts a reporter on the air or takes one off at the wrong time, approximately 250,000 viewers notice.

Rachel has a glass-enclosed control room. Three monitors directly in front of her allow her to see the three offsite reporters while windows allow her to easily see both of the in-studio reporters. A fourth monitor shows what is on the air now. Her control panel is a semicircle so that no control is more than an arm's length away. A PC from 1996, running Windows 95, tries to display market conditions, but it crashes at least once each day; often Rachel just listens to the radio reports from a sister station.

The temperature in Rachel's control room is at least 89 degrees with about 40 percent humidity. She has about eight footcandles of light, all coming from her four black-and-white monitors. The air in the room changes once per hour, and the noise level is about 77 decibels. The control room is locked even while Rachel is working; she can release the lock from her control panel to allow people to enter. Admission to the studio complex is by key only.

Rachel works with three other people as equals on a team, although she is the only one who decides what goes on the air. Greg Gorsky somewhat handles equipment, although officially the team is responsible for everything, not any one team member. Janet Wu assists Rachel, and Tyler Wilder involves himself with program guests. At a team meeting, like the one today, Rachel usually leads the way.

Rachel: I'm concerned with three main items today—guest appearances, the "ringmaster's" upcoming vacation, and equipment failure and replacement. Greg, has there been any progress in getting a new computer?

Greg: I've asked and I get the same answer—if it works, it doesn't need replacing.

Rachel: It's an antique! It doesn't work, it breaks daily, and it can't keep up. I can barely handle what we have, and I really want to upgrade to NASDAQ Level 2. You said you would try.

Greg: And I did. This is not my fault.

Rachel: Fine. I've had it. I'm bringing my laptop from home, which I said I wouldn't do, but I've got wi-fi and I'll get my own information. But if anything happens to it, I'm holding you responsible.

Greg: Forget that noise. This is your decision. This is your responsibility.

Rachel: Well, thanks for all your hard work.

Greg: Hey, I'll do the work, I just wouldn't pay a price for what you do.

Rachel: You mean what the team does.

Greg: Whatever.

Rachel: What about the guests? I need to know *before* the start of the show who is appearing. Finding out an hour before they go on isn't working. Tyler, did you get something worked out with daily guests and a guest replacement for the ringmaster?

Tyler: No. Been busy.

Greg: Doing what?

Tyler: Stuff. I have stuff, stuff I don't have to tell you about.

Jane: I took care of a vacation replacement. I know this is when he likes to go so I just went ahead and found someone.

Rachel: Wow. Well, that was very . . . proactive of you. Thanks.

Tyler: I would've gotten to it.

Greg: What, after you were done talking all afternoon to Connie the "Country Cook"? The only reason you don't talk all day is that she doesn't come in until noon for her evening show.

Tyler: Shut up. I do what I can with what I have and I ain't been fired yet.

Greg: That's because we're a "team" and Janet covers for you.

QUESTIONS

1. List five of the six physical work environment factors Rachel has to deal with. Cite examples. State which are negative and which are acceptable and explain why.

2. What three mental work environment factors does Rachel face in her job? Cite examples. State which are negative and which are acceptable and explain why.

3. Does Rachel have any caustic coworkers? If so, who and what type of caustic coworker is each of them? How should Rachel try to handle them (or herself, if necessary)?

1.2 PAUL'S PROBLEMS

On the way to work today Paul's new car broke down. It is still under warranty, but Paul specifically buys new cars every three years to avoid problems. As he entered the building, he remembered that he was upset with Ike, the security guard. Yesterday, Ike told Paul's boss that Paul arrived at work "at a quarter of nine." Paul's boss took this as meaning 15 minutes after nine, when actually Paul arrived 15 minutes before nine. Paul lost no money, but he is afraid his boss will believe he's not as concerned about his job as he should be.

Paul has never really gone out of his way to help others at work, and now that he needs a little help he is finding that no one is really stepping forward to help him. Paul hasn't even helped when two of his coworkers were so sick they were each in the hospital for over a week. No one asked Paul to help, so he figured, "Why should I? If they need help catching up, they'll say something." They did manage to finish their projects on time by pulling a couple of all-nighters; if they hadn't, Paul surely would have said something. He has even made comments about people not pulling their share of the load when they turn in a report due at 5 P.M. Wednesday at 9 A.M. Thursday. Paul's not one to listen to others complain, though. He always says he is too busy for that kind of thing. Ironically, if someone else is reluctant to talk about something, you can rest assured Paul will pry it out of him or her. He'll nag coworkers until they tell all just to get rid of him.

To top it all off, Paul is unhappy with his job. He likes the actual work, but he blames his unhappiness on the people he works with. As far as he is concerned, they really haven't gone out of the way to make him feel welcome, comfortable, or at ease.

QUESTIONS

1. Identify the cause of Paul's unhappiness.
2. What do you think Paul should do? What advice can you give Paul that can improve his work environment?

NET-WORK

What some people want in a job

http://www.youtube.com/watch?v=BL9fqWqGTX4

Is this person expecting too much, or is he being reasonable? How do his desires compare to yours?

Odd coworkers from the U.K. version of The Office
http://www.youtube.com/watch?v=MDEQ_gsVDsM
Maybe not a caustic coworker, but he is a bit annoying.

PERSONAL POINTS

1. Do you feel you live in order to work or work in order to live? Why? In the future, do you want to live in order to work or work in order to live? Why?

2. Do you view the rest of the world as an external force that acts on you, or do you see yourself as an integral part of the world and as being able to change that world (or at least the parts that you interact with)? Why? How do you think your view will affect your work life?

3. How important is your physical work environment and in what ways is it important?

4. How important is your mental work environment and in what ways is it important?

5. What kind of coworkers do you want and why?

EXPERIENTIAL EXERCISE

Your Physical Environment

Using this form, evaluate your current or most recent physical work environment and job. Concentrate on the area where you spend most of your work time. You may wish to evaluate other areas of the workplace separately. When performing the evaluation, rate how acceptable each factor is to you. Circle VA for Very Acceptable, A for Acceptable, N for Neutral, U for Unacceptable, and VU for Very Unacceptable. In addition to rating each factor, analyze the situation and determine what changes would need to be made in each factor to make it acceptable or very acceptable.

If you plan to remain in the situation you analyzed, determine which of your needed changes are feasible and possible. You may then use the decision-making model from this chapter to decide whether to pursue such changes.

Factor	Acceptable to You	How Would You Change Factor
Light	VA A N U VU	
Noise	VA A N U VU	
Temperature	VA A N U VU	
Humidity	VA A N U VU	
Ventilation	VA A N U VU	
Color and decor	VA A N U VU	
Layout	VA A N U VU	
Equipment	VA A N U VU	
Supplies	VA A N U VU	
Comfort	VA A N U VU	
Safety and security	VA A N U VU	
Work pace	VA A N U VU	
Work-pace variety	VA A N U VU	
Task duration	VA A N U VU	
Task variety	VA A N U VU	
Required concentration	VA A N U VU	
Required accuracy	VA A N U VU	
Error visibility	VA A N U VU	
Responsibility level	VA A N U VU	
Authority level	VA A N U VU	
Autonomy Level	VA A N U VU	

SPOT CHECK ANSWERS

1. F
2. T
3. F
4. F
5. T
6. T
7. F
8. F
9. F
10. F

2 | Perception and Problem Solving

The senses do not give us a picture of the world directly; rather they provide evidence for checking hypotheses about what lies before us.

Professor Richard L. Gregory

There are no facts, only opinions.

Friedrich Nietzsche, paraphrased

GOALS

This chapter examines perception and decision making, aspects of the mental work environment. The main goals include discussing how your view of the world and your reasoning processes can affect your perception of reality. Major applications of your reasoning abilities to creativity and decision making will be covered, along with a model for making more rational decisions.

OBJECTIVES

When you finish this chapter, you should be able to:

- Differentiate between a fact and an inference.
- List the factors that influence what a person sees in a given situation.
- List and describe at least five possible fallacies in logical reasoning.
- Describe the preliminary steps to the problem-solving process.
- Identify the constraints, givens, and goals for problem solving.
- Describe a solution search process and explain the methods for solving problems.

- Identify barriers to problem solving and explain how to overcome them.
- Diagram the nine-step system for decision making and describe each step.
- Explain the nature of intuition in the decision-making process.
- Describe the four pitfalls to effective decision making.
- Describe how creativity can aid the problem-solving and decision-making processes.

INTRODUCTION

Have you noticed that many people tend to be obsessed with finding the correct answer to questions? Quiz shows, for example, have long been a favorite of many television watchers. Question-and-answer parlor games, too, have been perennial best-sellers. However, in the world of organizations, absolute answers are not always found. Information that at one time appeared absolutely correct may turn out to be false. Decisions have to be made daily in organizations. It is important for decision makers to perceive things as they really are in order to make accurate and useful decisions. We must continually be on guard against the tendency to believe that we see the truth in a situation involving human behavior before we've uncovered ample facts. Perhaps the late philosopher-mathematician Bertrand Russell hit the galvanized nail squarely on its round head when he said, "Those who believe themselves to be absolutely right are often absolutely wrong."

In this chapter, we will explore some of the major concepts of **perception** in the hope that an understanding of them will help you to perceive organizational situations more accurately. We will also explore some of the major fallacies in logic, a knowledge of which can aid you in avoiding some of the common pitfalls in perception and decision making. We will also look at a well-known nine-step method for solving organizational problems and making decisions. We will conclude with an overview of the nature of creativity, a characteristic that can also aid substantially in the problem-solving and decision-making processes.

Perception

the process of directly becoming aware through any of the senses

THE IMPORTANCE OF SEEING WHAT'S REALLY THERE

We've all observed how different individuals perceive the same situation dissimilarly. You have merely to take a ride in traffic on a mountain bike to observe some extreme differences in the perceptions of automobile drivers and what they may be thinking about you. Have you ever attended judicial proceedings and observed the pronounced differences in witnesses' perceptions of the same situation?

THERE'S A LOT MORE TO PERCEPTION THAN MEETS THE EYE

There's a human tendency to believe that what we see is the truth. If someone disagrees, it must be the other person who is off base. Many people, however, tend to perceive what they want, or are set to see, regardless of reality.[1] We call this type of perception **mental set.**

Why do we tend to have mental sets? A major reason is that we all possess **perceptual filters.**[2] Each of us has attitudes about people and things. Our attitudes tend to decide for us what parts of our environment we allow our brains to interpret and what parts are filtered out. Because we come from a variety of backgrounds, we tend to view the world through our own set of perceptual filters. Shortly, we will look at some perceptual exercises that help to illustrate how we see what's out there through our own personal filters. Try to keep in mind as you read this chapter that we see with our eyes, but we perceive with our brains. Although we hate to admit it, far too frequently reality is completely different from what we see.

If we are going to confront problems among people objectively, we must attempt to develop the ability to see things as they really are, not as we are set to see them. Because of our deeply ingrained perceptual filters, we aren't going to find doing so

Mental Set

perceiving what we want, regardless of reality

Perceptual Filters

attitudes about people and things

a simple task. A prime (and dreadful-sounding) objective of this chapter is the cleansing and confusing of your mind. You'll see what this statement means as we progress. Take a look at Figure 2.1. This illustration has been around for some years, but it is still useful to prove some perceptual points. What do you see when you look at it? Most observers will see a woman. Approximately how old is the woman? Does she appear young, possibly in her twenties? Or does she look rather old, maybe in her seventies? Or does she seem to be middle-aged? Make a decision before you read further.

About half of those who observe the picture think that the person is a young woman. Others contend that she looks quite old. A few say that she appears middle-aged. Others argue that both an old and a young woman appear in the sketch. Which did you see? Look at the picture again for a few moments to see if your original perception changes. If you saw the young woman, look for the older one. Did you see the older one first? If so, try to see the young one. Both are actually there. If you see only one woman, you may be experiencing some discomfort.

If at first you observed only one woman, what might have been the reason? Could you have been mentally set to see only one? Why did you see only the young (or the older) woman at first? The point is that sometimes we don't immediately see the entire meaning of a situation; accurate perception may take some intense effort. Numerous organizational problems are the result of poor or incomplete perception.

FIGURE 2.1 About how old is she?

PRESET JUDGMENTS

Have you ever known anyone whose mind always seems to be made up on a subject before he or she has gathered enough facts to make an accurate judgment? We're probably all guilty of some inflexibility at times. Here's a short sea story about a sailor who didn't have the opportunity to make the same perceptual mistake twice.

In 1912, the *Titanic* (named after a giant in Greek mythology) was proclaimed to be virtually unsinkable. The ship's builders were so absolutely certain (remember Bertrand Russell's advice?) that it was indestructible that they provided too few lifeboats for the passengers. The world was dismayed when the highly acclaimed vessel failed to complete its first voyage from Southampton, England, to New York. Captain Smith, the Titanic's skipper, apparently set in his perceptions, perceived a small hunk of floating ice that turned out to be a massive submerged iceberg. A fatal gash ended the voyage prematurely. The ship sank and took 1,513 lives with it. How might this incident be related to problems of perception in organizations?

JUDGMENTS SHOULD LEAVE ROOM FOR ERROR

We all must make judgments and decisions in our daily lives without being able to acquire all the facts first, but we should realize that sometimes our picture of reality will be accurate and at other times it will not. Have you ever found yourself making judgments about other people based solely on their clothes? Retail sales personnel have sometimes lost sales and valuable commissions after assuming that a tattered-looking person couldn't afford the goods.

NetNote

http://psychlab1.hanover. edu/Research/

Hanover College psychology department. Includes opportunities to participate in experiments on perception of people and spaces.

Do you tend to judge other people by their handshake? A popular cliché states that a sincere person shakes hands with firmness and strength, not like a dead fish. However, in many cultures, both in the United States and abroad, a firm handshake is an indication of lack of warmth. When dealing with problems of human relationships, make an effort to acquire relevant facts before making up your mind. False assumptions will usually result in false conclusions. Most of your judgments should be flexible and allow room for possible error.

Read the short sentence in the following insert. Have you read it? Okay. Now reread it and count the number of times that the letter *F* appears. How many do you see?

> FINISHED FILES ARE THE RESULT
> OF YEARS OF SCIENTIFIC STUDY
> COMBINED WITH THE EXPERIENCE
> OF MANY YEARS

Did you count three *F*s? Many readers will; others will count four or five; still others will find six. Did you see them all immediately? If not, why not? Did you overlook half the letters? The *F* in the word *of?* Unimportant detail, you may say, but you were specifically requested to count *F*s, weren't you? In a human relations problem, could you afford to overlook 50 percent of the relevant details?

FACT VERSUS INFERENCE

Most of us are impressed by facts. There's nothing wrong with facts. Perhaps they deserve your respect. But are you clear about what a fact really is? Do you know the important distinctions between facts and inferences?

A CONSENSUS DEFINITION

Fact

anything that actually happens, is done, exists, or is strictly true

A **fact** could be defined as anything that we all agree to be true. If the consensus of society is, for example, that the earth is flat, we could say that we have, according to our definition, established the fact that the earth is flat. Quite often a consensus is correct, but occasionally it isn't. For years no one saw anyone fall off the edge of the earth; yet people went right on believing that the earth was flat. The Catholic Church excommunicated the astronomer Galileo for refuting the established facts on the subject of the gravitational attraction of the earth's mass, that is, the law of gravity. So you can see that the consensus definition of a fact can often fall flat on its face, gravitationally speaking.

AN "ACTUAL" FACT

One of *Webster's* definitions of the word *fact* is the "quality of being actual." Without becoming excessively philosophical, when can we say that an event is actual? For example, is it a fact that John, an employee of your organization, is lazy? You may have observed his idleness recently and concluded that he is just plain lazy. But is he actually lazy, or have you only inferred it? Perhaps John has some personal problems that have changed his normal behavior on the job. He may be temporarily idle but not lazy.

Inference

a conclusion reached from information that we know or assume to be true

The point of this discussion is that it is important for you to differentiate between a fact and an **inference**. An inference is a conclusion reached from information that we know or assume to be true. The fine line between fact and inference is difficult to determine, but the distinction is important (see Table 2.1).

TABLE 2.1 THE PRINCIPAL DIFFERENCES BETWEEN FACTS AND INFERENCES

Inferences	Facts
Are made at any time–before, during, and after observation	Are established after observation or experience
Go beyond what you observe	Are confined to what you observe
Represent only some degree of probability	Are as close to certainty as anyone ever gets
Usually generate disagreement	Tend to get agreement
Are unlimited in number	Are limited in number

PROBABILITY SCALE

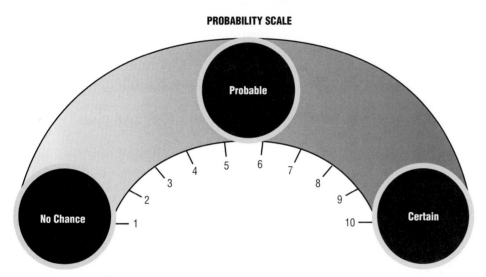

FIGURE 2.2 A probability scale

For example, suppose you are a floor manager in a department store. One of the sales staff anxiously asks to speak with you. She states she knows that one of the other employees on the floor has stolen some money because she saw him take money out of the cash register and put it in his wallet. Is it a fact or an inference that the employee was stealing? Your assumptions as floor manager might significantly influence your action in this case. True, taking money from the cash register and putting it in a wallet are suspicious behaviors, but is there any possibility that such activity could indicate something other than stealing? You can infer that a theft has occurred, but can you logically state your **opinion** as fact? Isn't it also possible that the employee was changing some of his own money?

PROBABILITIES AND CERTAINTIES

Although it may sound strange, we could state that all facts are really inferences with differing degrees of probability. The nearer an inference is to certainty, the closer it is to being a fact. All this may sound a bit philosophical, but perhaps it could be made clearer with the use of a probability scale (see Figure 2.2). For example, we could state that the book you are reading at this moment has been made from poisonous paper. Is such a statement one of fact or inference? Is it possible that if you ripped off a corner of this page and munched on it, you would expire? Certainly it

Opinion
a belief or conclusion held with confidence but not substantiated by positive knowledge or proof

39

is possible, but is it probable? Remember that almost anything can be said to be possible (could occur), but far fewer things are probable (are likely to occur).

Let's look at an example involving probability and certainty. Suppose you are a supervisor of a line of production workers. One afternoon while making your rounds, you observe something strange on the floor beside the workstation of one of your employees, Melvin. On closer scrutiny, you notice that the object on the floor beside Melvin's left running shoe appears to be the remains of a marijuana cigarette, an inference that would rank fairly low on the probability scale. You dutifully pick up the object, smell it, and decide that the possibility of the cigarette's being marijuana has moved up to about 9 on the scale. Should you reprimand Melvin for possession and use of marijuana on the job? You know for a fact that the cigarette is marijuana, but do your past supervisory training and experience tell you whether it is a fact or an inference that the cigarette belongs to Melvin? Where would you place the employee's possession and use on the probability scale? Is it likely that you could convince an objective grievance committee that the cigarette absolutely belonged to Melvin?

REASONABLE DOUBT

Here's an incident based on a true experience uncovered by law enforcement officers associated with Scotland Yard in England. The names of the individuals have been modified.

A law enforcement officer is investigating the burglary of a house that was empty during the previous weekend. The rooms were freshly painted on Friday, so the occupants decided to rent a motel room rather than endure the smell. When they returned home, the owners discovered that a window had been forced open, and expensive pieces of silver and china were missing from a cabinet on the other side of the room from the window. The officer discovered a handprint on the fresh paint next to the cabinet, checked the print, and determined that it belonged to Conroy, a person with a history of convictions for burglary.

Let's assume that we know this was not an inside job—that the occupants of the home were not involved with the crime. Based on your understanding of facts and inferences and the probability scale, would you say that it is a fact or an inference that a burglary occurred in the house? There were visible signs of forced entry—the window had been forced open—and valuable items were missing. Where would you place a point on a probability scale—near 10, close to zero, or somewhere between the two extremes? Most people would probably place a point near 10, indicating that it is a fact a burglary took place, a fairly reasonable assumption.

Here's another question: Is it a fact or an inference that Conroy had been in the room from which the valuable items were taken? Most people will contend that it is a fact that Conroy had been in the room. Although it would seem high on a probability scale that Conroy had been there, such was actually not the situation. Therefore, aren't we actually making an inference in relation to Conroy's presence in the room?

"How could Conroy's handprint have been on the wall if he hadn't been in the room?" you might ask. A good question. Here is what were alleged to have been the "true facts" in the case (except for the individuals' names). Those investigating the burglary learned that a person known as Dirty Larry had attempted to pawn some items stolen from the house in question. After Larry was tracked down and caught with the stolen goods, he explained how Conroy's handprint got on the freshly painted walls.

Larry had previously cased the house and discovered that it would be vacant during the weekend. Larry then saw his past partner in crime, Conroy, and told him about the opportunity. Conroy, however, said that he had decided to go straight; no longer would he participate in such nefarious acts. A violent argument ensued. Larry punched Conroy, who fell backward, hitting his head on a radiator. The blow on the head was fatal. Larry then got an unusually morbid idea. He amputated Conroy's hand, wrapped it in plastic, and took it with him to the site of the burglary, where he touched it to the wall in obvious places. Conroy, as you can now visualize, was never bodily at the scene of the crime. To believe so is an inference, not a fact.

You can see that even in cases where events seem 100 percent certain, we probably should still leave some room for doubt. However, in the world of organizations we don't have an endless amount of time to search for facts. Decisions have to be made. Within limited time, we must somehow attempt to make certainties out of probabilities. Yet we must also remember to be flexible in our thinking and to realize that what we believe to be a fact at this moment could turn out later to be not even a good inference. Leave some room for possible error and be willing to alter your approach when new "facts" are discovered.

THE DETERMINANTS OF PERCEPTION

Numerous factors influence your perception, that is, the way in which you see a particular situation. Among the more significant are:

- hereditary factors
- environmental background and experience
- peer pressure
- projection
- snap judgments
- halo and rusty halo effects
- mental state

HEREDITARY FACTORS

You didn't have much influence in the choice of your parents or grandparents. However, your forebears have had a considerable effect on who and what you are. In science courses you can learn in some detail how hereditary factors influence offspring. For our purposes, however, it's sufficient to understand that in addition to determining things such as the shape of your nose and the size of your feet, your parentage also determines your vision and color acuity. For example, if you are myopic (nearsighted), what you see without your glasses differs from what a person with 20/20 vision sees. Or, like 1 of about 10 American males, you might have a color-weak tendency (popularly called color blindness) and see many objects differently from a person with normal color perception. Your vision and ability to perceive colors may affect your eligibility for particular careers, such as those of airline pilot, commercial artist, or interior decorator.

ENVIRONMENTAL BACKGROUND AND EXPERIENCE

Environment probably has a greater influence on what you see in a given situation than anything else. For example, think about a child who, during her early years, continually hears from her parents such utterances as "Those people are lazy. They don't really want to work," or "You can't trust those people." The child has a good

NetNote

http://www.liquidgeneration.com/Media/Sabotage/Optical_Illusions/
Interesting optical illusions.

chance of emerging into adolescence with a firm belief in such statements. After all, parents do provide children with their needs, determine what is right and wrong, and are practically their complete frame of reference (their models) during the formative stages.

Usually young people will gravitate toward and identify with companions who share common beliefs and interests, and many of their early prejudices will tend to be reinforced. In the organizational world, however, continual agreement among managers or employees can lead to the stagnation of creative ideas. Educational experiences may change some beliefs but conversely can make individuals defensive about their existing beliefs. Did you perchance find yourself becoming defensive when you took any of the perception tests?

The way you perceive any situation is significantly influenced by your past experiences. For example, the next time you see the "How Many Fs?" perception test, you may more quickly perceive what escaped you before. Also, think about how your prior experiences with people in authority affect your present perception. Unfavorable past experiences with bosses can significantly influence how you perceive your present boss.

PEER PRESSURE

The effect that our peers or friends have on what we see is related to environmental experiences. Perception within groups is often different from individual perception. An example of the peer effect took place in a classroom during a discussion of an organizational behavior problem. After most of the students had developed firm opinions on the case, a latecomer entered the classroom. To see if the late-arriving student would be influenced by what she believed to be the attitude of the other students, the professor told her that the class members had considered the behavior of a specific person in the case to be ridiculous, and then the student was asked if she agreed. She responded with an emphatic "Yes!" The professor then confessed that the class had not felt that the behavior was ridiculous. The student then admitted that she hadn't even read the case but thought she should go along with the group. Perhaps our desire for peer acceptance influences our perception more than we sometimes realize. Chapter 9 will explore in greater depth the influence of small groups on the behavior of individuals.

FYI

Watch out for opinions hiding as facts; watch for people who state their opinions as facts.

Just because something works for you, that doesn't mean it will work for others.

What works for many people may not work for you. What works on others may not work on the next person.

When two events occur close together, don't automatically assume that the first event caused the second.

Wanting something doesn't make it happen.

Few things are simply black and white (because few things are simple).

You can't just make a decision; you also have to make it happen; others won't implement it for you.

PROJECTION

"Everyone else cheats on expense accounts, why shouldn't I?" If you haven't already heard that question, chances are that one day you will. Our unconscious tendency is to attribute to others some of our own traits, faults, and motives, a characteristic called **projection.** But think quite seriously about a statement once made by the Dutch philosopher Baruch Spinoza: "When Peter talks about Paul, we often learn more about Peter than we do about Paul."

If you assume, for example, that almost everyone cheats on expense accounts and exams or in politics, might not your assumption be related to your own behavior or values? When approaching human behavior problems, be careful that your perceptions are not clouded by the projection of your own values onto another person.

Projection

the act of attributing to others our own traits, faults, and motives

SNAP JUDGMENTS

Do you know someone who exclaims proudly, "I can size up a person right away"? Most of us from time to time are guilty of making **snap judgments** before we have gathered enough facts to come to valid conclusions.[3] Here's an example of a supervisor named Carla who made a snap judgment at work: An employee, Anne, received a telephone call an hour before quitting time from a doctor saying that her son had just been hit by an automobile and was badly injured. The doctor requested that Anne come to the hospital immediately to be with her son. Anne looked for her boss, Carla, to ask permission to leave, but Anne could not find her. Anxious to see her son, Anne wrote a note informing Carla of the situation and suggesting that an hour's pay be deducted from her wages if necessary. Anne placed the note in Carla's "Incoming" basket.

About 15 minutes later, as Carla was returning from a meeting upstairs, she was stopped by Harry, one of Anne's coworkers, who told Carla that Anne had left work early. Carla was furious. "Why didn't she check with me before she left? I had something important I wanted her to do this afternoon. For that behavior, she is going to be suspended for one week without pay."

Frequently, as in Carla's case, we attempt to solve a problem before we know what the problem actually is.[4] Married couples who have lived together for many years and are still learning about each other hold back a bit. How can you possibly make a valid judgment about a person or a human problem after only a minute or two of exposure to the situation?

Snap Judgments

instant evaluation without the benefit of fact or experience

HALO AND RUSTY HALO EFFECTS

Another human tendency that affects perception has been labeled the **halo effect:** A person is good at one thing and so is assumed to be good at something else.[5] The positive assumption, therefore, creates the halo and is a shortcut. You don't have to think about individuals; you just assume certain people will always do well. For example, you are now a supervisor in a machine shop. Fred, an employee of yours, has been one of the best drill-press operators in your section for over five years. A lathe operator is unexpectedly needed in another section. You recommend Fred, assuming that he will also do well at the lathe. Fred bombs! He may have excelled at one job, but he lacked the necessary skill or training to accomplish the other. Figuratively, you had placed a halo over Fred's head.

Another instance of the halo effect could occur if two people have a violent fistfight on the job, and one is a personal friend with whom you regularly socialize off

Halo Effect

the assumption that because a person is good at one thing, he or she will be good at something else

the job. Watch out for the tendency to place a halo over your friend's head by assuming that the other person must have been the cause of the conflict.

Some supervisors are guilty of what could be termed the rusty halo effect. For example, one of your employees continually makes mistakes. You might place a rusty halo over his head by assuming that he wouldn't do well in any job. One day, when he is the only one around, he answers the phone and talks to an upset customer. He listens and handles the situation well. It turns out that he has a talent for listening and empathizing, so now he is your customer services representative. You found his talent and gave him a chance. You are open-minded enough to perceive people as they really are. Still, always watch out for the tendency to place halos, shiny or rusty, over people's heads.

MENTAL STATE

Your own attitudes, beliefs, and current mental state may also color your perceptions. Attitudes are descriptive thoughts based on knowledge, opinion, or faith. Beliefs are thoughts based on emotion. As such, they may be irrational. Your current mental state refers to your mood, your feelings of stress, how pressured you feel to meet deadlines, and similar factors. For example, let us say that your attitude toward older workers is negative. You believe they are slow and frequently sick. When you see an older coworker cough a few times, you may perceive him or her to be infirm because of your attitude toward all older workers. If, however, the head of human resources for your firm points out to you that in fact the older workers miss fewer days of work, are on time more often, and are generally happier in their jobs than younger workers, your attitude may begin to change.

Beliefs may also impact your perceptions. If you believe that younger workers are, because of their age and fewer years of experience, reckless and irresponsible, you may then perceive any risk taking by younger workers as rash. We are all familiar with how being in a bad mood can affect perception. In these cases, someone simply saying "Hello" may be perceived as just one more irritant set in your path to ensure that you are miserable.

Attitudes and beliefs are often retained for a long time, whereas your current mental state may change a number of times in one day. Beliefs are the most difficult of the three for others to influence because they are based on emotions. Attitudes may be changed by presenting people with new knowledge, or expert opinions, or real-life experiences. Moods may be changed by music, a break, rest, or a vacation. Stress and pressure may be relieved by completing a task, giving the task or responsibility to someone else, or receiving help or additional time to complete the task. Any of these may also affect your perception of other things.

A FEW FALLACIES

In working with case materials or organizational behavior problems, you should make an effort to avoid the following pitfalls in logical thinking:

- the fallacy of composition
- the fallacy of division
- post hoc, ergo propter hoc
- the fallacy of wishing it were so
- two-valued reasoning

We'll now take a brief look at each of these potential roadblocks.

THE FALLACY OF COMPOSITION

"Anybody can go to college if he or she really wants to. I didn't have any money, but I worked nights, lifted myself up by the bootstraps, and got a college degree. If I could do it, anyone can!" Is that assumption necessarily true? What if a person has a large family to support and is living up to or beyond the limits of his or her income? What if a person hasn't had the good fortune to be born with great mental abilities? What about someone who came from an environment that discouraged intellectual growth? The exceptions could go on and on; in fact, the exceptions could become the rule.

"I work because I need the money. Jennifer shouldn't be working here. Her husband makes good money, so she doesn't even have to work." Isn't this person assuming that what is true for one is true for all? Couldn't there be other reasons for working besides the quest for money? How about the need to socialize with others or the need many individuals have to feel that they are making a contribution?

We have a tendency to assume that what is true for one person or situation is true for all persons or situations. If you were to make such an assumption, you might be guilty of employing the **fallacy of composition**, more formally defined as the fallacy of assuming that what is true of a part is, on that account alone, also true of the whole.

Of course, some generalizations are true. For example, if one person were to puncture an artery and then bleed profusely, we would be secure in generalizing that all individuals would experience similar bleeding upon puncturing an artery. On the other hand, let's say you are observing a parade and three rows of tall people are standing in front of you. If you stand on tiptoe, you'll undoubtedly be able to see more of the parade. But if everyone stands on tiptoe, will everyone see better? What is true for you alone isn't necessarily true for all, so be on guard against the use of the fallacy of composition.

Fallacy of Composition
the assumption that what is true of a part is also true of the whole

THE FALLACY OF DIVISION

"Milk is good for everybody, so it certainly would be good for all growing children." Such reasoning is an example of the **fallacy of division**, the assumption that what is true for the whole is necessarily true for each of its parts. A parent, for example, may have learned somewhere that milk is healthful for children and assumes it therefore must be good for his child. However, some children are allergic to dairy products and break out in painful rashes upon ingesting them.

Here's an organizational example of the fallacy of division. Let's look at Jill, a supervisor who recently completed a company-sponsored leadership training program. Jill learned that certain leadership techniques tend to increase the motivation and productivity of workers. If she assumes that results that are true in general will necessarily be true for every one of her subordinates, she may be applying the fallacy of division.

Be careful not to confuse the fallacy of composition with the fallacy of division; they are opposites. The fallacy of composition moves from the specific to the general, and the fallacy of division begins with a general statement and moves to the specific.

Fallacy of Division
the assumption that what is true for the whole is true for each of the parts

POST HOC, ERGO PROPTER HOC (THE FALLACY OF FALSE CAUSE)

The Latin phrase **post hoc, ergo propter hoc** may be translated as "after this, therefore because of this." Another term for this is the fallacy of false cause, the

Post Hoc, Ergo Propter Hoc
the assumption that when one event precedes another, the first caused the second

assumption that when one event precedes another, the first event necessarily causes the second.[6] For example, event A occurs and is followed by event B. If you assume that in every instance event A is the cause of event B, you may be guilty of post hoc reasoning. Say that yesterday evening you took a shower and immediately afterward went outside with your hair still wet and practiced your nollie 180's in the cool night air. This morning you came down with a miserable head cold. Did event A (skateboarding in the cool night air with a wet head) cause event B (the cold)? Not necessarily. What usually causes colds? Cool air? Or is it viruses or germs? Besides, the incubation period for most colds is usually longer than one day. Perhaps you were close to a sneezing friend two days ago.

Here is another example: One of your subordinates is transferred to a different position within your department. Shortly thereafter, the quality and quantity of her work begins to decline. What is the cause? Perhaps it is the transfer, but perhaps it isn't. Additional facts might indicate that she now has personal problems that bear no relationship to her new position. Use caution when making judgments about others. Perhaps there is no correlation between two consecutive events.

One more thing: Don't confuse *post hoc* with *ad hoc*. The latter literally means "for this." In organizations, you frequently encounter an ad hoc committee—one that has been temporarily established to work on a specific task and is therefore sometimes referred to as a task force.

THE FALLACY OF WISHING IT WERE SO

We all tend to believe what we want to believe. If you have a vested interest in and are loyal to the company for which you work, you might believe that its practices are right, regardless of how society perceives certain of its activities. You believe the company is honest, for example, because you want the company to be honest. Sometimes in order to hold onto our assumptions, we ignore or distort reality. When we do that, we subject our logic to the **fallacy of wishing it were so.**

Fallacy of Wishing It Were So

ignoring or distorting reality to hold onto assumptions

Let's look at an organizational example of wishing it were so. You are a manager who has developed a program designed to give your workers a better understanding of the importance of high profits to your firm. You think that, given the information, they, too, will see the importance. You may be in for a surprise the next time the wage contract comes up for renegotiation. Wishing something to be true does not make it so. When you are confronted with organizational behavior problems that present conflicting views, be careful not to substitute hope for logic in deciding what to do.

A QUESTION OF ETHICS

Being Brutally Blunt

American Idol TV show personality Simon Cowell is known for critiquing the performing hopefuls on the show in the most unequivocal terms. While this may generate TV ratings, Mr. Cowell advocates similar bluntness off the air. He also supports everyone starting at the very bottom of his or her organization. In both cases, his reasoning is that this is how he was treated and these were his experiences and they have made

him what he is today. In his opinion, not sugar-coating comments and starting at the ground floor were good for him, so others would benefit from imitating him. What fallacy is this type of thinking? Even if giving an unvarnished opinion is effective in stopping those judged unworthy from continuing their pursuits, is it necessary and ethical to bring people up short in order to make your point?

Source: Simon Cowell, "How to Nurture Talent by Being a Real SOB," Business 2.0, October 2003, p. 68.

TWO-VALUED REASONING

Another pitfall to accurate perception is **two-valued reasoning**, the human tendency to believe that in any situation there is only one correct side. To the person who engages in two-valued reasoning, situations are either right or wrong, good or bad, with no possibilities in between. You may know individuals whose philosophy can be expressed as "We are right, and they are wrong." Once you dig into a problem, however, you frequently discover that there is more to it than just the right side and the wrong one. Organizational problems are seldom clearly divided into entirely right or entirely wrong positions. Be sure to look for those shades of gray in issues that seem to be clearly black or white. Try to apply **multivalued reasoning** to organizational problems; recognize that in most situations, there tend to be more than two sides or two alternatives.

Two-Valued Reasoning
viewing a situation as either right or wrong, good or bad, with no possibilities in between

Multivalued Reasoning
recognizing that there may be more than two sides to a situation

PROBLEM SOLVING

Perception and reasoning are intimately related to problem solving and decision making. How you perceive a situation affects whether or not you think it is a problem requiring a solution. Perception also affects your solution to a problem. Your reasoning approach has an impact on problem solving as well.[7]

Problem solving and decision making have enough in common that some people may not differentiate the two. It might even be possible to reach the same result for a situation using both approaches. Although each deals with problems, each serves a different purpose. Decision making is better suited to situations where alternative solutions need to be identified; problem solving is more for situations where solutions need to be created. Because of this, problem solving is typically a more time-consuming and involved process. Decision making often can follow the steps outlined in the next section exactly with good results, whereas problem solving may have to vary significantly if the problem is more complex or if the solution requires more creativity. While decision making and problem solving may even use some of the same methods, such as brainstorming, decision making is for more routine problems. When a problem is new or lacking readily identifiable alternative solutions, a problem-solving approach is often more effective.

PRELIMINARIES TO PROBLEM SOLVING

A problem is an unresolved question that requires a solution, for example, what should our product be? or, how can we find something other than oil to provide energy for our facilities? or, how can we send more data through our network? These are examples of problems needing a problem-solving approach as alternatives are not readily available. Other problems, like who will work the afternoon shift? or, who will be promoted? or, what short-term investment will yield the greatest return? can be answered with a decision-making model as the alternatives are more apparent to the decision maker. When you encounter a problem, whether a problem-solving or a decision-making model seems best, you have three options: You may accept the problem, you may reject it, or you may question it.

It is not a matter, however, of accepting all situations as problems, or never rejecting them, or always questioning them. What is important is to accept, reject, or question in the right situation. For example, some situations are obviously problems. When the copier and the supply cabinet are out of toner, it is a problem. It may not be a very big problem, and it may be one that is easily solved through a decision-making model by selecting a vendor with quick delivery, but it is a problem. If someone were to come to you and say, "We need to improve quality," should you accept, reject, or question this statement? Quality is important, so this concern should probably not be rejected. Should it be accepted then? No. The correct choice is to question this statement: "What makes you think quality is unacceptable?" If the person responds with, "Half the products coming out of our factories are defective," then you seem to have a problem. If the response is, "For every 1 million products we make, one is defective," and you know the industry standard is one defect for every 100,000 products, then you probably don't have a problem. The point here is that while you shouldn't accept everything you encounter as a problem, you don't have to question everything either. At least, you don't have to question the validity of every problem, but there are still other questions to be asked.

While you may or may not question whether a situation is a valid problem, you should always get to the root of every problem. This requires asking questions, just not the same questions you would use when trying to determine whether you have a real problem or not. Getting to the root of every problem may mean getting down to the original cause or it may mean going back to the original reason a policy, rule, procedure, or decision was made. Not doing so may mean that any new solution has an undesired effect. For example, your insurance company complains to your IT manager that there is a problem with entering new employees into the insurance database. The insurance company complains that your company's job applications don't include information like names of spouses, names of children, and employees' and family members' birthdates. The insurer does not like having to collect that information later. To solve the problem a group redesigns the job application without ever asking why this information wasn't on the forms before. When the new forms arrive the director of human resources sends them all off to the shredder. The new information was never on the original forms because it is illegal to use data like marital status, age, and whether someone has children in hiring decisions. HR was trying to avoid charges of discrimination. Had the form redesign group questioned whether they had a valid problem or not much time, effort, and money would have been saved.

Another, although less common, reason to question problems is that you may really have a solution looking for a problem. Sometimes people have ideas that they want to see used even if the ideas did not result from a problem-solving effort. Sometimes vendors want to sell you solutions for problems you don't have. For example, let's say a software vendor wants to sell you a program that will let you know what every employee is doing every hour; employees will log into the new system and select the category of work they are performing and how close they think they are to completion. That's fine if your employees are widely separated or you have trouble knowing what everyone is doing. But you have 22 people working for you in the same room, all getting their work done, and if you have any doubts about it, you just get up and walk around. You don't have a problem, so you don't need the solution.

The last preliminary step before beginning problem solving is for you to determine whether the problem is worth solving. You should not spend more money solving a problem than the problem is costing you. This doesn't mean only in the short term, though. A $10,000-a-year problem may cost $35,000 to solve, but if that problem would have continued for four or more years, solving it is financially worth it. If, however, it would take 20 years to earn back the cost of replacing an inefficient heating system, and you are moving to a new building in 11 years, then replacing the system is not worth the money. When figuring the financial cost of solving a problem, remember to include the costs of worker time involved, lost production, and even time and money for the problem solvers.

PROBLEM-SOLVING PREPARATION

Once you have decided you have a problem to solve, there are preparations to make before beginning the search for solutions. The preparations are concerned with two main areas: your constraints and goals, and your basis for solving the problem. Your constraints affect the goals you can expect to reach in solving the problem. A basis, or foundation, is needed in order to most effectively begin a solution search.

Constraints   The first question that should be answered in determining the constraints or limits within which a problem is to be solved is, What can and cannot be done? In seeking a solution, what is allowable and what is not? What is possible and what is impossible? Are there laws that limit what can be done? Would certain solutions be unethical? Are some things impossible because of the laws of nature? Will some solutions generate great opposition? For example, gravity and friction are facts that limit solutions. They may be overcome with sufficient force or reduced using certain materials or lubricants, but there are still limits beyond which we cannot go. Or, a solution that results in dumping toxic waste into a river would be unethical even if it were legal and thus limits the options. A union might oppose a reduction in pay to such a degree that a strike would be called that might cost the company more than was to be saved with the reduction. Whatever factors cannot be overcome, circumvented, or violated should be listed in the beginning of the process before possible solutions are created.

Givens   Once the constraints or boundaries of the problem-solving environment are created, the givens should be determined. The givens are the conditions and resources present at the start of the search for solutions. These include, but are not limited to, the information, materials, people, and finances available at the start of the process. For example, it may be a given that your company has a nine percent market share (nine percent of the customers in the market buy your product). It may be a given that you know the date a competitor will release a product that is reportedly superior to yours, but you don't know in what way it will be superior. It may be a given that you do not have the authority to hire any new workers but must use those the company already has. Notice that although givens are not absolutes, like the laws of physics, they are very often additional constraints. However, givens should also include things you *can* do, such as make use of a highly trained and adaptable workforce. So, unlike constraints, givens include resources that may be used in the solution. While many givens are unique to a particular problem, two warrant special mention.

Two givens are present in all problem-solving situations: time and money. Any situation in which time and money are not concerns is not much of a problem. There is always a limit on the amount of money available to solve a problem. That limit may be how much the problem is costing the organization, or it may simply be the limit that has been budgeted. Although it is sometimes possible to exceed a monetary limit, in the beginning it is best not to plan on receiving additional funds. Time is most often viewed in the form of a deadline, which might be flexible or rigid, but there are additional concerns. You should consider how much time you and the others involved have to spend on searching for a solution. Consider your other work commitments and how much time can be given to solving the problem at hand. It is also a good idea to determine, if possible, whether it is more important to get the problem solved by the deadline (even if it means a less than optimal solution) or to achieve the best possible solution (which may mean taking more time).

Goals   With the constraints, givens, deadlines, and budget determined, the goals for the problem solution may be set. Goal setting for problem solving is easier to explain than it is to perform. The basic question to be answered here is, what does the problem solution need to achieve? Often two of the easier goals to set are those for time and money: when must the problem be solved and what is the most that can be spent. Beyond that the task depends on the problem. Is it a goal to have the solution reduce defects, improve morale, increase safety, save money, create sales, or be smaller than a breadbox? Although setting the initial goals is important, it is also important to not let goals become constraints. When solving problems, goals should be reexamined and revised if necessary. It is possible that during the solving of a problem you may be able to exceed your expectations if you are open to that possibility.

PROBLEM-SOLVING KNOWLEDGE

Constraints, givens, and goals establish the environment or framework for the solving of a problem. The next step is to find the answer to this question: Do you have what you need to solve the problem? The answer is key to determining your preparation for the solution search, but the answer may also force you to revise your goals, especially for time and money.

First, consider your point of view. Your point of view might be that of your organization, but then again it might not. Your point of view is different if you are retiring or quitting soon, or if you are an outsider, new, a temp, or acting as a consultant. Once you have determined your point of view, ask if yours is the only point of view. Often it is not. You may need to include other points of view in the solution search. For example, different points of view regarding the solution may be held by others working with you, workers in other departments, upper management, customers, suppliers, governments (federal, foreign, state, and local), and even your own manager. Maybe you are looking at the solution from the point of view of increasing sales while your manager is looking for the solution that will result in a promotion or bonus from him or her. It is not so much a matter of a point of view's being right or wrong as it is a matter of taking into account all points of view relevant to the problem.

After ascertaining the point or points of view involved, you should next determine if you have enough knowledge to solve the problem yourself. If you don't have enough knowledge—and you might not discover this until you start trying to solve the problem—then try to determine who or what you will need to gain that knowledge. Will you need other people and who will that be? Will you need your manager, other managers, your peers, those you manage, or outsiders (like consultants)? Or do you not need other people but need knowledge or training for yourself? Once you have established exactly what knowledge you need, consider where you can obtain it, how long it will take to acquire, and what the cost will be. Having determined the cost and time involved, you may now have to revise your goals.

The next step is to assess the information you will need to solve the problem. First, determine if you have sufficient information on the cause of the problem. Then consider whether you have sufficient information related to the solution. Keep in mind that the solution may require more or different information later. Do not limit the solution according to the information gathered at the beginning. If further information is required, then it should be obtained. On the other hand, you almost never have all the information you could want, so collect what seems necessary and begin the solution search.

SOLUTION SEARCH

The first step in the search for a solution should be to look at the whole problem and determine whether it is a single-part or multipart problem. A single-part problem is one that cannot be divided into separate segments, each needing its own solution. A multipart problem has smaller, separate problems embedded within the main problem. With a single-part problem, you may move on to the next step, which is organizing. With a multipart problem, you must identify the separate sections or parts that have to be addressed and then determine the order in which they need to be solved. In general, you want to work on one problem at a time. If possible, try to work on one part at a time while keeping in mind the interrelations between the parts. For example, if your problem is to negotiate a contract, work on each section by itself instead of all the sections all at once. Keeping in mind the interrelationships may mean ensuring that you have one definition for "a day." You wouldn't want one part of the contract to talk about "days" meaning weekdays but another part to use "days" to mean both weekdays and weekend days.

The second step involves organizing your information. For smaller or more limited problems you may not need to do this, but it can be helpful with large problems and problems for which you have a large amount of information. You may use one of four general methods, of organizing information or devise your own.[8] Of the four general methods, topical order and chronological order are the easiest to use. Topical order involves grouping information by subject or issue. This method can be especially helpful with multipart problems. Placing information in chronological order simply means arranging it by date. The other two methods are analogical order and causal order. Analogical order means grouping information according to similarities. With this method you find common elements and group accordingly: These all deal with quality; these are all related to planning, and so on. Causal order means grouping by cause and effect. If A causes B to happen and C causes D, you would have an AB group and a CD group. If lack of training causes low production, poor quality, service calls, and customer complaints, then all these problems belong in the same group so they are all addressed by the solution.

With your problem or problems defined and your information grouped in the manner that seems most appropriate, it is finally time to search for a solution. At this point *search* is an appropriate word because you don't want to spend time reinventing the wheel. Before you start to create your own solution, you should see if

TABLE 2.2 PROBLEM-SOLVING METHODS

Heuristics	Algorithms	Random Trial and Error	Systematic Trial and Error
What's-Handy	Brainwriting/ Brainstorming	NGT	Delphi Technique

others inside your organization have faced the same or a similar problem as yours. If no one inside the organization has, then you should try looking outside the organization. In either case, if you locate someone who has had the same or a similar problem, see if you can utilize his or her solution. If you can't use the solution as is, see if you can modify it to solve your problem. Even if you can't use or modify the solution, you may be able to use it as a starting point for creating your own.

If you need to create your own solution, there are at least eight methods, listed in Table 2.2, that can be employed in trying to solve a problem: heuristics, algorithms, random trial and error, systematic trial and error, what's-handy, brainwriting and brainstorming, Nominal Group Technique (NGT), and Delphi Technique. Some of these can be used by an individual, some are for groups, and some can be used by both.

A **heuristic** is a rule of thumb, a guide that can be applied and that works most of the time.[9] One of the most well-known heuristics is, "*i* before e, except after *c*." This works much of the time, but not, for example, for the exception *weigh*. If you or someone else has a heuristic that can used to solve your problem, apply it, but then check that the solution is not an exception.

An **algorithm** is a procedure with a specific set of instructions designed to solve certain problems. Algorithms are frequently used in mathematics, linguistics, and computer programming. You are using a very simple, but useful, algorithm when you arrange words or files alphabetically or when you arrange numbers in numerical order. The simplex algorithm is a set of procedures that can be used to solve linear programming problems. Algorithms can be used to determine the total number of workers needed and each person's weekly schedule when the number of workers needed is different each day. There may be algorithms that you can use to solve your problem, or, in solving your problem, you may develop one that can be used later (see NetNote.)

If there are no heuristics or algorithms that can be used, you might attempt to find a solution by **trial and error**. There are two approaches to trial and error: random and systematic. The random approach involves trying whatever comes to mind with the knowledge you already possess, with the givens, and within the constraints of the problem. With the random approach, there is the possibility of repeating trials. Systematic trial and error eliminates the chance of trying something more than once. With the systematic approach, you write down what you will try in various combinations and try each one in order. You cross off the trials that don't work and you keep trying until one does. For example, let us say that you want to increase local sales, and you can afford some cable TV ads. You want to run enough ads to increase sales revenue by more than the ads cost, but of course you don't want to run too many. With random trial and error, you might run 10 ads one day, then 2, then 8, then 13, then 10 again in an attempt to find a number that increases sales. With systematic trial and error, you might start by running 1 ad a day, and then 2, and then 3, and you increase by one everyday until sales increase. You might ask why anyone would try the random approach as it seems so haphazard. Let's say the optimum number of ads for your

Heuristic
a rule of thumb

Algorithm
a procedure and specific set of instructions for solving a certain problem

NetNote

http://en.wikipedia.org/wiki/Algorithm

More information on algorithms from Wikipedia.

Trial and Error
experimenting until a solution is found

situation turns out to be 13 a day. With the random method you would have found a solution on the fourth day, but with the systematic approach it would have taken 13 days. Of course with the random approach, it could have taken, say, 28 or 50 or more days before you tried 13 and found the solution. With the systematic approach, it wasn't going to take fewer than thirteen tries, but it wasn't going to take more, either.

The what's-handy approach involves working with whatever you happen to have on hand to find some kind of solution. Here there would be no attempt to increase knowledge or resources in order to solve a problem; whatever is close and convenient will do. This happens often with human resources. Let's say a small firm needs to develop a website. Using the what's-handy approach, the job is given to someone who already works for the firm. This someone might be the person who is the most qualified of the staff, but that person may not be qualified enough. The solution may be some kind of webpage, but it may not meet the needs of customers, or be easy to use, or compare well with the competition. If possible, the what's-handy approach should probably be avoided.

Brainstorming and brainwriting are often used with groups, and both have been proven to generate a high quantity and high quality of ideas. **Brainstorming** uses a group of people who contribute ideas within the constraints, goals, and givens. This is often done with someone writing the ideas on a whiteboard as people suggest them. The purpose of using the group is that one person's idea may trigger an entirely new idea in another person, an idea neither would have thought of alone. Some people, however, are reluctant to shout out ideas, so one of the most important rules of brainstorming is that the ideas suggested are never evaluated or, worse, ridiculed during the session. All ideas should be measured against the goals after brainstorming has ended. This is often the job of the manager, who may or may not be a part of the brainstorming group.

When using brainwriting, it should precede brainstorming. **Brainwriting** is having individuals write down possible solutions to a problem. The written lists are turned in at the start of a brainstorming session. The ideas are written on a whiteboard anonymously, and then brainstorming, as just described, is conducted to see if other options can be created. Brainwriting serves two purposes. First, it can save time during the brainstorming session, as people arrive with prepared ideas. Second, it ensures everyone's participation. Some people may be inhibited in a brainstorming session because they are new or not a regular member of the group, or they may feel that they do not have enough rank, or they just may be a little shy about their ideas. Brainwriting can even be done in advance by e-mail, with one person collecting all the ideas and compiling a list that starts a later brainstorming session.

Nominal Group Technique (NGT) extends brainwriting and brainstorming. NGT is a three-to-four-step technique for group problem solving (it can also be used for decision making). Once a group is selected, the members engage in brainwriting. The group then meets to share ideas and generate more ideas through brainstorming. In the next step, the group evaluates the ideas and selects the best idea or ideas, sometimes by voting on the alternatives, sometimes by consensus. If several ideas are selected, another round of evaluation is held to make the final selection. NGT can be accomplished through teleconferencing or even with e-mail (although using it with e-mail is a more difficult and slower process). NGT places a large amount of power in the group as it selects the actual solution for the problem.

The **Delphi method** is an approach to group decision making that is useful when group members are separated by time or distance. Instead of meeting, each participant is given a problem or a questionnaire to work on independently. Each person's

Brainstorming
a group generating as many solutions or ideas as possible

Brainwriting
An individual listing as many solutions or ideas as possible

Nominal Group Technique
brainwriting and brainstorming with group evaluation of ideas

Delphi Method
cycles of questionnaires and responses seeking a solution or consensus

analysis and suggestions are then distributed to the other participants without their knowing whose ideas they are reading. Participants then revise their own original decisions and resubmit them to a coordinator. The process can be repeated until a desired conclusion is reached. Although the Delphi method tends to take more time than other group methods, this method helps to avoid some of the negative influences associated with groups, like groupthink (see Chapter 9).

If progress toward a solution is not being made, there are a few actions that can be taken. The first thing to try is to take a break. Put the problem away for a while, do something else, take a walk, get something to eat or drink, maybe even sleep on it and see what comes up the next day. If taking a break fails, try analyzing the alternatives that have been created. Look for the common elements, those that seem to work and those that do not. The analysis may lead to a new approach—"I haven't tried *this* yet!" If this doesn't work, try the exact opposite of what you have been doing; you may surprised how often this yields results. Finally, you might try working the problem backwards. Start at the end, and try to work back toward the beginning. This approach is often quite effective when trying to solve a procedural problem. Rather than asking, "What do I do next?" you start at the end and ask, "What must I do just *before* this?"

Once you find what you think is the best solution to a problem, one that meets all of your goals (or as many as possible), you should review it for unintended consequences. A good solution should not create more or larger problems than it solves. Make sure that your solution is not going to cause more harm than good, that it is not going to do something you never meant it to do. You may also take this time to see if your solution does more good than you thought it might. Maybe you didn't plan for it, but it just happens that the solution will cost less or save more or be faster or take less time. Unexpected benefits may not become apparent until after the solution is implemented, so you should look for them again later on.

BARRIERS TO PROBLEM SOLVING

As if problem solving was not difficult enough, there are several barriers to successfully solving problems that should be avoided: procrastination, framing, catastrophizing, personalization, single-solution syndrome, satisficing, polarization, confirmation bias, fixation, and selective abstraction. Some of these barriers occur before or at the beginning of the problem-solving process, and some occur during the process. Procrastination, framing, catastrophizing, personalization, single-solution syndrome, and satisficing occur at the beginning of problem solving.

Procrastination is delaying without a valid reason. It is a habit, which means it can be broken, but breaking it takes some effort. People procrastinate for a number of reasons, including not wanting to face an unpleasant or complex task, indecision, fear of failure, and lack of confidence (I meant to research other reasons, but I kept putting it off). Essentially, though, procrastination is task avoidance. The desire to avoid the task creates a barrier or wall of inertia that must be surmounted in order to start the task. Avoiding a task can make a person uncomfortable. To diminish the uncomfortable feelings, procrastinators engage in delaying tactics and diversions—organizing, cleaning, "preparing," napping, "research," video games, TV, staring out the window or at the wall. Almost anything will do. Often the delays and diversions use far more time than actually completing the task would. If you are a procrastinator and doubt this, complete a time study. Track the avoidance activities and your on-task time and then compare the two; you may be quite surprised.

To break the habit of procrastination, you must first want to stop. If you don't feel the desire to stop on your own, then you may need to convince yourself that

Procrastination
delaying for no valid reason

you need to stop. Look at the time wasted on avoidance, look at the effect on others (coworkers, managers, family), and if that fails, consider what will happen to you if you procrastinate enough to miss out on a promotion or to lose a job.[10] Once you want to break the habit of procrastination, you will almost certainly have to do it gradually. You first need to start the job early enough in order to complete it. Procrastinators are good at waiting until the last minute to begin, so figure out when you would usually start and double the time before your deadline. If you usually wait until the night before, then start 2 nights before. If you usually leave 5 days for a job, then start 10 days before it is due. Gradually stretch your starting time until you are starting projects when you receive them.

Finding a place to start a task you have been avoiding is another key to breaking procrastination. If the task is large or complex, start by breaking it down into pieces that are manageable, then start on one of the smaller parts. If finding a starting point is difficult, pick one at random. Start somewhere, even if it is not at the beginning. If the problem is not that the job is large, then break it down in time; try 10-minute segments.[11] Set a timer and work for 10 minutes (but you have to work; you can't set the timer and then watch the seconds tick down). After that try another ten, and then another until the job is done. If you need a break, set the timer again for 10 minutes and then return to work when the timer goes off. Gradually reduce the number of breaks until you can work straight through to completion.

Once you learn to start work ahead of time (like when you receive it) and to work through to completion, one task remains in breaking procrastination. Take time to consciously enjoy the feeling of having something completed before it is due. When you complete work ahead of schedule, you should find that you have free time for the activities that used to be avoidance tactics. Now, however, you should be able to enjoy these activities since you are no longer performing them while an undesirable task is hanging over you.

Framing is a barrier that involves the way in which a problem is presented. Consider the following two statements: (1) On any given day about 99 percent of the world's population does not eat at a McDonald's restaurant. (2) On any given day about 1 percent of the world's population eats at a McDonald's restaurant. Which sounds like a bigger problem for McDonald's? Most people would say the first statement is a larger concern because of the way it is framed. Both sentences actually say the same thing, but the first is perceived to be worse. Considering there are about 5 billion people in the world, a restaurant chain with 50 million customers a day is rather amazing, but stated only in the negative (99% *don't* eat there), one might not feel that way. To avoid complications or misunderstanding due to framing, always state the facts, not opinions, and consider stating the reciprocal of the problem, as in the McDonald's case or, for example, "Our turnover rate is 2 percent," along with, "We retain 98 percent of our employees."

Catastrophizing is automatically assuming that the worst is going to happen.[12] For instance, with a downturn in sales—"We're going to go bankrupt!" Staff reductions—"We're all fired!" Restatement of earnings—"We're all going to jail!" Besides needlessly raising blood pressure, assuming the worst leads to extreme solutions, and for people who jump to these assumptions, extreme solutions are about the only ones they come up with. To counteract catastrophizing, apply a liberal dose of realism mixed with an honest assessment of the chances that any one of the various outcomes will occur.

The barrier of **personalization** occurs when a person assumes that a problem is aimed directly at him or her.[13] The person believes the problem involves no one else (rather fitting the popular definition of "paranoia"). Solutions then are those that address the perceived attack on the individual. The solution might also solve the

Framing
a barrier due to the way a problem is presented

Catastrophizing
automatically assuming that the worst is going to happen

Personalization
assuming a problem is aimed directly at you

Single-Solution Syndrome

repeatedly suggesting the same solution for all problems

Satisficing

selecting the first solution that looks acceptable

Polarization

viewing a solution as being at one extreme or the other

Confirmation Bias

retaining only the information that supports a preconceived idea or solution

organization's problem, but there is a great chance that it will not, and it may even work against the organization's goals. A statement of how a problem affects others and the organization as a whole can help neutralize the personalization barrier.

Single-solution syndrome is different from the other barriers. This is a situation where a person has a solution, typically one that did work once before, and now this is the only solution this person advocates. Essentially, it is a one-solution-fits-all-problems situation. Although any solution offered repeatedly as the only option by a particular person falls into this category, some solutions are heard more often than others. For some people the answer to everything is more training. Others may always suggest hiring a consultant: "I remember calling in a consultant in '94 and that cured us right up!" Some favor always having a customer focus group or always doing a marketing survey. An "off-site," or a team seminar, may be suggested as a cure-all for every problem. These ideas are not inherently wrong, but they are wrong when they are applied to the wrong situation. To guard against situation, watch for people who immediately recommend the same solution over and over. You don't necessarily have to reject this one idea, but you do need to carefully check that it will solve the problem at hand.

Satisficing is another barrier that includes a solution; the problem is that it doesn't provide the best solution. **Satisficing** is quickly selecting the first solution that looks acceptable. What this does is to stop the solution search before better solutions can be found. Selecting a solution that looks pretty good may even solve part of the problem, but it may not do the whole job or the best job. Satisficing is an attractive barrier because it appears to save time. Often, more is lost with a less-than-optimal solution than is gained in saved time and effort. To help avoid satisficing, keep the idea-generation step, like brainstorming, separate for the evaluation of ideas. Try to get as complete a list of ideas as possible, and then make sure each one, no matter how extreme, is fairly evaluated.

Satisficing and single-solution syndrome are included with the group of barriers that occur at the beginning of problem solving because even though they supply a solution, they short-circuit the full process. Four other barriers need to be guarded against during the problem-solving process. They are polarization, confirmation bias, fixation, and selective abstraction.

Polarization is when a solution is viewed as being at one extreme or the other—at one pole or the other.[14] A solution is seen as good or bad, win or a loss, perfect or useless. With polarization, there is no middle ground, no shades of gray, just black and white. Granted, some situations are this way. A drug may cure an ailment or have no effect. It is much more common, however, when a product or process doesn't work to find something salvageable, something that can be modified later. So the danger with polarization is that a partial solution will be totally scrapped. To guard against polarization, examine all solutions to see if there is something to be learned even if the overall solution is rejected.

Confirmation bias occurs when a person or group keeps only the information that supports a preconceived notion.[15] What often happens is that an early theory or solution is proposed, then information supporting that theory or solution is kept or accepted as valid, and anything that either does not support the position or that supports another solution is discounted or dismissed. For example, someone may suggest or believe that budget troubles are due to too much overtime. Data are found to support this notion, solutions are created to reduce overtime, and maybe some money is saved. The real problem, however, may have been excess waste, but that information was ignored. The reason money was saved is that less overtime meant less production and so there was less waste. But now there is lower production, fewer products to be sold, and lower income, all because people became attached to the original idea and sought to confirm it rather than performing an objective analysis on all the data looking for all possible causes to the problem.

The **fixation barrier** exists when a person or a group is unable to see a problem from a new perspective. Often these people are living in the past. For example, a band may be focused on making and selling albums on CDs. Customers might prefer to purchase the songs they want over the Internet for a dollar a piece. This might even result in more total sales for the band, but it is fixated on selling CDs. Or, an employer may be fixated on having workers at their individual desks and overlook the solutions of teams or telecommuting. The fixation barrier is another good reason to use groups that engage in brainwriting and brainstorming and to keep idea generation separate from idea evaluation so ideas from many perspectives can be considered.

Fixation Barrier
being unable to see a problem from more than one perspective

Finally, **selective abstraction** occurs when one detail or one part of a problem is focused on and the big picture or overall problem ends up being ignored.[16] Solutions then address only the one detail and often not only fail to solve the whole problem, but create additional problems as well. For example, a worker may complain about always working the afternoon shift because the day-shift workers leave too much of their work unfinished. The unfinished work is then added to the normal afternoon-shift load. Rather than addressing the real problem, management might get distracted by the worker's comment about always working the afternoon shift. A solution for this detail is created, and now all workers are forced to rotate through day and afternoon shifts in order to be fair to everyone. Those on days still leave work for the afternoon shift because this big-picture problem was never addressed. This example points out the importance of listing goals for the problem's solution and then, when you think you have a solution, checking that it meets your goals and that it really solves all of the original problem.

Selective Abstraction
focusing on one detail or one part of a problem and ignoring the big picture

A NINE-STEP DECISION-MAKING SYSTEM: A LOGICAL APPROACH

The start of the previous section mentioned that problem solving and decision making are related. Both are concerned with problems, they can share many of the same methods, and using either might lead to same result. There are also differences though, and a major one is that problem solving is used more for when a solution needs to be invented or created, and decision making is used more for when a solution needs to be identified or crafted. For example, problem solving might be needed to develop a new means of production whereas a decision-making procedure

---

SPOT CHECK

6. Constraints are limits within which a problem is to be solved. T F
7. A procedure with a specific set of instructions designed to solve certain problems is called a heuristic. T F
8. Personalization occurs when a person assumes he or she is the only one capable of solving a particular problem. T F
9. Satisficing is selecting the first solution that looks good. T F
10. Ignoring the big picture in favor of focusing on one detail or one part of a problem is called selective abstraction. T F

can be used to decide who is hired from an applicant pool, who is promoted, or which supplier should receive a contract. One widely followed procedure is the nine-step system depicted in Figure 2.3 and discussed in this section.[17]

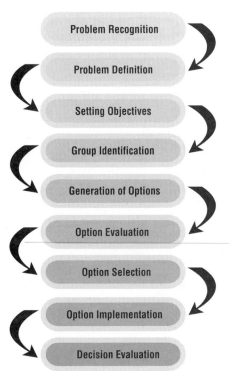

FIGURE 2.3 A nine-step decision-making or problem-solving model

STEP 1: PROBLEM RECOGNITION

Sometimes problems become known all by themselves. Organizations, however, often try to identify problems before they become too serious. In management, controls are often used to identify problems, but just walking around and talking to people can be quite effective, too. Whatever method is used, it is better to take a proactive approach and try to identify problems before they become large and have serious consequences than to wait to react to problems that are finally serious enough to become self-evident.

STEP 2: PROBLEM DEFINITION

What's the problem? Some people dive energetically into their problems like a hungry cougar in quest of breakfast. A far more effective approach to problem solving is first to define the problem. A wise maxim to remember is "A problem well-defined is a problem half-solved."

Defining a problem accurately requires us to be objective, to see the situation as it really is, not as we think it is. Try not to let emotions or overeagerness cloud your perceptual filters. Being too anxious to define a problem, especially before gathering a sufficient number of facts, can result in developing a wonderful solution, but for the wrong situation. Far too often, capable employees have been fired from their jobs or unjustly disciplined because the employer either hastily and wrongly defined a problem or came up with a solution before having a clear definition of the problem. Try your best to avoid the unscientific stance of "Don't confuse me with the facts; my mind's already made up."

In defining a problem, we must strive to differentiate between the symptoms of the problem and the problem itself. We must treat problems, not symptoms. Take the situation of people calling in sick when they are not. Is this a problem, or is it a symptom of something else? In one hospital department, people in certain areas routinely called in sick on Mondays. The result was a mad scramble to reassign people to the understaffed area. Management concluded that the problem was the sick-day compensation and decided not to pay people for sick days. After a little thought, this seemed harsh. What if people really were sick? Management then decided not to pay for the first day a person was out sick, but if someone was very ill and was off for two days, then the hospital would pay for the second day. Absenteeism promptly doubled as more employees remained out for two days instead of one.

The hospital's real problem was never defined. Absenteeism is usually a symptom of something else—the real problem. In this case, the real problem was the scheduling. This hospital would not say no when the schedule was full and a doctor called to add another Monday patient. The hospital should have diverted patients into the Tuesday schedule, or it should have added more staff.

In a more famous (or infamous) case, Coca-Cola failed to define a problem correctly and as a result made the largest marketing blunder since the Ford Edsel. In the mid-1980s, Coke defined one of its problems as the taste of its cola. It was wrong. The real problem was sales. Pepsi was outselling Coke in stores (although Coke was beating Pepsi in fountain restaurant sales), while overall growth of both in the United States was virtually flat. As a result of defining the problem as one of taste rather than sales, Coca-Cola decided to experiment with its highly successful, 99-year-old formula. Its entire line of research was concerned with the taste of one formula compared with another. As a result, Coke came out with New Coke, with a sweeter taste, just like Pepsi. Sales of New Coke were not only poor, but a rebellion began among original Coke drinkers that was so large Coca-Cola had to bring back the original formula—and let New Coke fade into the background. Had Coca-Cola focused on sales rather than taste, this debacle would have been avoided. This emphasizes the point that a mistake in defining the problem may very well render the entire decision useless.

STEP 3: SETTING OBJECTIVES

As you begin your process of decision making, determine what you have to accomplish. Criteria are needed here in order to evaluate the possible alternatives when you reach Step 6. The entire direction of the decision can be altered at this point. In the example of hospital absenteeism, if the objective is to contain costs while reducing Mayhem Mondays, then a more rigid system of scheduling—one that has less-acute patients scheduled for later in the week—may be the solution. If, however, the objective is to provide services to meet even peak demand, then the hospital will have to hire more people and buy more equipment for them.

STEP 4: GROUP IDENTIFICATION

To reduce resistance to the decision, to assist in implementation, and maybe even to assist in the decision-making process, the group or groups being affected must be identified. Once the groups are identified, the impact of the decision on these groups must be taken into account, or representatives of each group must be included in the process. For example, a manager might think that morale would be boosted if the people he or she managed received an hour for lunch instead of 30 minutes. Without taking into account the other groups affected by this decision, the manager may be in for trouble when the rest of the company demands the same treatment.

STEP 5: GENERATION OF OPTIONS

Note that the word *options* is plural. Seldom is there only one solution to a problem. As a wise person once said, "If you have only one alternative to a problem, you have not determined that there is a real problem." Often you will discover after developing alternative recommendations that your second or third solution appears more realistic than your first. Sometimes options that initially seem outrageous actually turn out to be suitable and different enough to actually work.

Options may be developed individually or in groups. Groups often come up with more options than one person can, and sometimes these are better than what an individual can generate alone.[18] However, an individual is faster than a group so if time is short, using a group may be out of the question. It is especially important to separate the generation of options from the evaluation of options when using a group. If options are subject to instant evaluation and criticism, the process may discourage some from participating. What person continues to make suggestions if his or her ideas are immediately shot down?

STEP 6: EVALUATION OF OPTIONS

Compare each option to the criteria established in Step 3. It may be helpful to create a matrix and evaluate each option according to criteria. Table 2.3 shows a sample

NetNote

http://www.mindtools.com/ pages/main/newMN_TED. htm

A variety of problem-solving and decision-making tools and information.

TABLE 2.3 AN EXAMPLE OF AN OPTION EVALUATION MATRIX

	Money	Day Off	Certificate	Lunch	Parking Spot
Do they want this reward?	yes	yes	no	no	yes
Do they feel they have a fair chance to earn this reward?	yes	no	yes	yes	yes
How motivational is it?	4	3	1	2	4
How affordable is it?	1	3	5	4	4

TABLE 2.4 GUIDELINES FOR SELECTING AMONG ALTERNATIVES

What will be the short- and long-term effects of each recommendation on the organization?

What human, financial, and physical resources will be necessary to carry out each alternative?

Will the benefits of my recommendations outweigh their costs?

What support will I need from my boss and employees to implement the best alternative?

Does my chosen alternative relate directly to the problem, or merely to a symptom of the problem?

evaluation matrix for a decision on employee motivational rewards. When evaluating the criteria, you may say yes or no, or you may have to determine how well each option meets the criteria on a scale of 1 to 5, or 1 to 10.

STEP 7: OPTION SELECTION

After evaluating all of your alternatives, choose the recommendation that in your judgment will best accomplish your desired objectives. However, don't forget the concept of situational thinking. You may have to alter your plans during your efforts. Will you be ready for such contingencies? Table 2.4 offers some guidelines that can help in selecting the best solution to a problem.

STEP 8: OPTION IMPLEMENTATION

Putting the decision into action may seem like something so obvious that it need not be stated. Unfortunately, too many people think that making the decision is the end of the task. After all, this is a decision-making model. However, the decision itself really isn't much good unless there are results. You must follow through and ensure that every decision is carried out, or the problem will not be solved.

STEP 9: DECISION EVALUATION

The problem-solving process isn't complete yet. To make sure that your actions accomplish your objectives—that of resolving the problem—you should examine the situation carefully at a later (but not too late) date. If you discover that your objectives have not been accomplished, you may have to study the problem again and apply other alternatives to it. In other words, start the process over.

DECISION MAKING BY INTUITION

Should you ever arrive at conclusions on the basis of feelings rather than logic and facts? Doing so is termed **intuition.** Managers in organizations sometimes make decisions based on the feeling that they know something, that is, without the conscious use of reasoning.

Intuition
the process of reaching conclusions from feelings rather than from logic

Is it wise to make intuitive decisions? Surprisingly, a fairly large number of decisions made on the basis of a hunch are quite successful.[19] However, is their success based solely on chance? Not likely, according to a number of psychologists who contend that many managers whose decisions seem to have been made by intuition alone are in reality drawing subconsciously on their experience and knowledge.[20] Positive and negative past experiences can aid substantially in dealing with present situations.

A caveat is in order, however. Excessive reliance on intuition rather than logic and facts can be hazardous to your decision-making health. For example, hunch decisions that don't work are much more difficult to defend to your associates and your boss than are those based on logic. Further, your moods, emotional states, habits, and prejudices can influence your conclusions, thereby leading you astray. Intuition is best used as a supplement to, rather than as a substitute for, logical means.

PITFALLS TO EFFECTIVE DECISION MAKING

Logical decision-making techniques, when applied properly, can be highly useful in problem solving and decision making. Also useful is knowledge of what to avoid in those activities. Following is a brief discussion of four common pitfalls to which some organizational members succumb, especially those who consistently make bad decisions: making unnecessary decisions, putting out the same fire, not considering the cost, and procrastination. Avoiding these traps should enhance your own problem-solving and decision-making activities.[21]

MAKING UNNECESSARY DECISIONS

In some instances, the best decision you can make is to make no decision at all. Some situations simply work themselves out over time, and unnecessary meddling can possibly create unwise risks. Being able to distinguish those situations requiring action from those that do not is critical. For example, data from checkout-line scanners reveal that sales of a product vary greatly from day to day in any one store. If 70 units are sold in a week, you might think that 10 are sold each day. Scanner data reveal that often 13 units are sold one day and 1 unit the next. Is it necessary to solve the problem of the 1-unit day? At first, some marketing managers thought so. Long-term monitoring revealed that the low-sales days were random. Not being able to predict the occurrence of a low-sale day convinced many managers that no decision was necessary here. Over time, sales averaged out, and this was just one of the unusual variances that are statistically possible.

PUTTING OUT THE SAME FIRE

Have you ever found yourself dealing with similar problems over and over, sometimes as a result of your not having taken care of the problem properly in the first place? Some problems recur unless adequate procedures and policies are established for preventing or dealing with them. By anticipating certain types of problems, you can deal with them more effectively when they do arise. For example, turnover (people quitting) can be a continuing problem if you are not prepared for hiring replacements. Having up-to-date job descriptions and job specifications makes the problem of a vacant position easier to solve.

NOT CONSIDERING THE COST

Sometimes the costs of a particular decision may be far greater than the value of the ultimate result. For example, the decision to buy an expensive mainframe computer would be foolhardy if a few less expensive, strategically located computer work-stations could suffice for the foreseeable future.

A RAPIDLY CHANGING ENVIRONMENT

Decision making is difficult enough, and rapidly changing conditions can greatly increase its difficulty. Four tactics can help. One involves what information you use, another how much information, a third deals with depth of analysis, and the fourth when to give up.[22]

When conditions are changing frequently, or when they are uncertain, you want to use a logical process, but it may also help to include objective and subjective information. Problems with subjective information are that it is often difficult to quantify (turn into some type of number), it can contain bias, and it can be difficult to use in comparisons. It can still be valuable, however. When evaluating alternatives with both objective and subjective information, it may help to have two columns next to each alternative, one for objective information and the other for subjective information. Or, you can add a column to a matrix like the one in Table 2.3 for subjective analysis.

In this decision-making environment you often cannot afford the luxury of collecting huge amounts of information; by the time you do, the decision-making opportunity may have passed. Often you must force yourself to limit how much information you gather to what is absolutely necessary to know and no more. Collect what you need to know, not what would be nice to know.

With time pressures in fast-changing situations, analysis is often shallow. A broader, deeper view can help greatly. A deeper analysis can be obtained by using the 5Y approach which involves asking "why" five times. Asking "why" once generally generates a cursory analysis. Each following "why" compels a wider and more penetrating analysis that is more likely to reach the root cause of the problem and suggest different alternatives.

The fourth factor comes into play after an alternative has been selected and implemented. If the alternative does not appear to be working, it must be abandoned for another rather quickly. Since the environment changes quickly, you do not have the luxury of waiting to see if something will come around. You certainly don't want to stick with an option that isn't working well out of stubborn pride. Better to move on to something else before changing conditions make it too late to successfully respond.

CREATIVITY AND THE INDIVIDUAL

Another concept related to problem solving and decision making is **creativity.** A creative mind can be tremendously effective in helping you develop sound alternatives to difficult problems, and it can be especially useful when dealing with rapidly changing environments and new areas.

NetNote

http://www.creativityatwork. com/

Articles and information on developing creativity.

Creativity

the process of solving a problem or achieving a goal in an original way

Having trouble being creative? Try changing your physical environment—try taking a shower! The physical environment can indirectly function to assist or hinder creativity. The approach in some organizations is to try to change the environment in order to facilitate spontaneous discussions. Sun Microsystems has taken a cue from home parties where people often end up in the kitchen. They created spaces around a company kitchen to encourage and sustain these impromptu meetings.

Creativity is often aided by a private, stress-free place, away from the source of a problem and away from distractions. It turns out that the shower is often a perfect spot. That water is relaxing, and the simple routine of bathing frees the mind for other thoughts. Often these casual thoughts yield nothing but sometimes we do hit upon something useful. A bathtub, whirlpool, or hot tub may be just as good. Surprisingly, if the path is well-known and traffic is not bad, driving can also free the mind for creativity; try turning the radio, tape, or CD off and see what comes to mind.

Source: Dorothy Leonard and Walter Swap, "Igniting Creativity," *Workforce*, October 1999, pp. 87–89; Allison Stein Wellner, "Cleaning Up," *Inc. Magazine*, October 2003, p. 35.

WHAT IS CREATIVITY?

Creative minds of the past have developed a variety of definitions for the term *creativity*. What do you think of when you envision a creative person? Do you picture an oddball in weird clothes who works, lives, and plays in an environment that looks as though a hurricane recently struck? To many people, this is the stereotype of a creative person. But isn't it what individuals accomplish rather than how they look that makes them creative?

What, then, is creativity? Let's say that it's any thinking process that solves a problem or achieves a goal in an original and useful way. But few ideas, if we really think about it, are 100 percent fresh and new. Creative ideas can also result from examining established ideas and methods and building on them. Creativity is also the ability to see useful relationships among dissimilar things. Try, if you will, to think of two objects or ideas that are not directly related, but that could be synthesized into a third useful object or idea.

WHAT CAN HELP YOU BECOME MORE CREATIVE?

You don't need to be a genius to be creative. What you do need is to use your imagination. Forget the rules; they can be overly restrictive.[23] Problem-solving activities are often more effective when you allow your mind to run free, sometimes even letting it go off into what at first appears to be a wild direction.[24] Look for useful relationships among seemingly unrelated objects, and you are likely to develop ideas and solutions to problems that you previously felt incapable of handling. We've already learned how present notions can create barriers to accurate perception. A mentally rigid attitude tends to fog our perceptual filters, making creative activities much more difficult. Most people erect such barriers when approaching the nine-dot challenge illustrated in Figure 2.4. Here is what you're to do with this exercise: Try to draw four straight connecting lines through all nine dots without raising your pen or pencil. Cast off any preconceived notions, give it your best shot, and then check your answer in Figure 2.5.

The creative person is characteristically inquisitive and innovative, able to make new applications of older concepts, and receptive to new ideas. A negative person—someone who thinks a new idea won't work even before it's tried—finds being

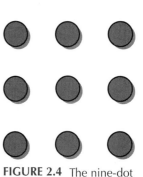

FIGURE 2.4 The nine-dot challenge

creative fairly difficult. Managers should encourage their subordinates to be creative in their activities.

With sufficient desire and practice, most people can improve their creative ability. Why not give it a try? The feeling of having created useful ideas can improve your feelings toward your job and your personal life.

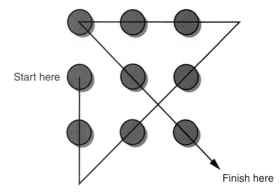

FIGURE 2.5 Solution to the nine-dot challenge Did you restrict yourself with artificial boundaries?

SUMMARY

Perception, by which individuals acquire mental images of their environment, is an important element of organizational behavior. You must be able to perceive OB situations accurately to be effective in preventing or resolving organizational problems. A major purpose of this chapter has been to assist you in developing greater sensitivity of perception. Perception tests reveal that we don't necessarily see an accurate or complete picture of a situation immediately. An awareness and application of certain perceptual concepts, however, can sharpen your ability to see reality.

The differences between fact and inference aren't always clear. Facts can be said to be inferences that appear at higher points on a probability scale. So-called facts may be disproved by new evidence. Flexibility in making judgments is, therefore, essential.

Both heredity and environment influence a person's perception of a given situation. Perception is also affected by pressure from peers, the tendency to project one's own values onto others, snap judgments, and the halo and rusty halo effects.

An awareness of some of the major fallacies in logic can help you avoid some of the common pitfalls in reasoning and perception.

Problem solving and decision making are similar, but each is better suited for certain situations. Problem solving is needed when new solutions need to be devised. Decision making is more useful for when solutions simply need to be identified and evaluated. Decision making should follow a logical model, and with a little practice, the model will become instinctive. There are pitfalls to be aware of, such as, procrastination and not considering costs. Decisions in a rapidly changing industry or situation may require a different approach, which may include the 5Y method.

CHECKING FOR UNDERSTANDING

1. What is the difference between a fact and an inference?

2. What factors influence what a person sees in a given situation?

3. Explain in your own words the meaning of the statement, "False assumptions will usually result in false conclusions." Provide an example.

4. Give two examples of organizational behavior problems that can develop as a result of your perceiving inferences as though they were facts.

5. Explain how heredity and past experience influence perception. How might education alter perception?

6. Would your perception of a politician whom you and three close friends watched on television together be any different if you watched the person alone? Why or why not?

7. Give three examples of the halo and rusty halo effects that you have personally observed.

8. Determine the fallacies in the following statements.
   a. "You're lucky to have an Asian working for you. They're good workers."

b. "We recently hired a graduate of Sage State University, and he is the sloppiest employee I've ever seen. That's the last time I hire anyone from that university."

c. "We never had those types of problems in the Plating Department before we sent Sam Jones, the supervisor, to that management training program. I think we've had quite enough human relations nonsense around here!"

d. "Labor unions are harmful to a free-enterprise system and should be outlawed before it's too late!"

e. "Of course I'm aware that Clarence has had no training or experience in management, but I'm certain that he'll be able to handle that supervisory job. After all, he is my son."

f. "Low tuition is why many students don't do well in college. If we were to raise tuition, students would be willing to study harder and get better grades."

9. List the nine steps in the decision-making model presented in the chapter and explain each step.

10. In the nine-step decision-making model, why is it important to separate generating options from evaluating these options, especially when using a group?

11. Give an example of when the decision to do nothing about a problem in an organizational setting might be the best decision.

12. Explain the nature of intuition in the decision-making process.

13. How would you describe the concept of creativity? What are the characteristics that aid a person in being creative?

14. For which situations is a problem-solving approach better suited and for which is a decision-making model better suited?

15. What can you do if you are a procrastinator and wish to break the habit?

SELF-ASSESSMENT

Part 1

Answer these questions in relation to your work life. SA means Strongly Agree, A is Agree, D is Disagree, and SD is Strongly Disagree.

1. To save time I go with the first solution that looks appealing. *SA A D SD*

2. I feel I have failed if my group or I am not the one to solve a work problem. *SA A D SD*

3. When I hear of a problem I just know it's going to turn out badly. *SA A D SD*

4. I can't get motivated until there is barely enough time to get a job done. *SA A D SD*

5. There are two sides to everything, and only one side is right. *SA A D SD*

6. Everyone wants money, so my employees will be satisfied with money. *SA A D SD*

7. I love getting up early and getting to work early, so when I'm running things, that's what I'll have my people do. *SA A D SD*

8. It is my experience that most stereotypes work, so I apply them to everyone. *SA A D SD*

9. People don't change. If they did well in the past, they'll do well in the future, so I don't waste time checking on them. *SA A D SD*

10. I can size up a person right away. *SA A D SD*

Give yourself 4 points for every SA, 3 for every A, 2 for every D, and 1 for every SD. Total your score for items 1 through 4, then for items 5, 6, and 7, and then for items 8, 9, and 10.

Items 1 through 4

A score of 4 or 5 may mean you have less difficulty with problem-solving barriers; 6–9 indicates some trouble with barriers, and 10–16 means you face increased difficulty from problem-solving barriers.

Items 5, 6, and 7

A score of 3 means you are less susceptible to the fallacies of reasons; 4–8 somewhat susceptible, and 9–12 more susceptible.

Items 8, 9, and 10

A score of 3 means you have fewer problems with the determinants of perception; 4–8 some problems, and 9–12 more problems.

Part 2

For items 1 through 4 identify the barrier to problem solving to which each item refers.

For items 5, 6, and 7 identify the fallacy of reasoning to which each item refers.

For items 8, 9, and 10 identify the determinant of perception to which each item refers.

Review those that you did not score as SD.

SKILL BUILD 2

Answer each Skill Question fully and support your answer with information from the book and the case. Use your own words unless taking support from the case and then use quotation marks.

Bob, Jiayanti, Kwong Lee, and Margarita Barrera are all transportation supervisors for a trucking firm. They are standing around the copy machine discussing a memo Kwong found left in the feed tray that was written by their boss, Homer DePoe.

"Guys," Kwong said, "if none of us knew about this, what does that say about our boss?"

"How does he expect us to meet these new standards if he doesn't tell us?" Jiayanti asked. "That memo is dated *3 months ago*!"

"I don't know, but I'm scared now. My evaluation is in two weeks, and he wanted us to reduce our fuel costs just as gas prices spiked. Even if I stopped all my trucks for the next two weeks I couldn't meet these numbers," Margarita said.

"I'm not worried," Bob said. "My costs have been better the last two weeks, and I think it's because I drink one cup of decaf each morning. You all should too. It works for me so I know it will work for you."

Skill Questions. What fallacy is Bob falling victim to when he tells the other three that decaf helped him so decaf will help them?

Skill Question 1. Name the fallacy.

Skill Question 2. Explain the fallacy in your own words.

Skill Question 3. Show how Bob's claim fits the fallacy you selected.

"Did you switch from regular to decaf?" Kwong asked.

"No. I never drank coffee at all before!" Bob said. "I feel better with the one cup of decaf, so I *do* better and that just has to show up as reduced costs."

Skill Questions. It is a fact that Bob *believes* decaf makes him work better, but is it a fact that the coffee improves his performance? To answer that, start by explaining a couple of terms.

Skill Question 4. What is a fact? (i.e. define "fact")

Skill Question 5. What is an inference?

Skill Question 6. Now explain whether or not it is a fact that one cup of decaf in the morning improves Bob's performance.

"How is it you 'do better'?" Jiayanti asked.

"I don't know, but I'm convinced that decaf is making me work better," Bob said.

"Bob, you're an idiot." Kwong said, "I don't know the name for it, but your thinking is all wrong, and you're wrong again to try to get us to do something even if it did work for you."

"Well how can you argue about facts?" Bob asked.

"*Facts!*" Kwong yelled, "What facts?"

"It's a fact that I believe decaf makes me work better," Bob said stubbornly.

"That is your *opinion*, that it works," Kwong replied.

"It is a *fact* that I believe it works, and you shouldn't argue with facts," Bob said.

"You're wrong again! It may be a fact that you *believe* decaf helps you, but it is your own opinion that decaf actually helps," Kwong argued, "The fact that you believe it does not make your opinion a fact."

What fallacy is Bob falling victim to when he decides that because he drank decaf in the morning his subsequent perception of improved performance was caused by the decaf?

Skill Question 7. Name the fallacy.

Skill Question 8. Explain the fallacy in your own words.

Skill Question 9. Show how Bob's claim fits the fallacy you selected.

"What?" Jiayanti said, "I'm getting confused."

"Who cares about the stupid decaf! We have to do something about meeting these standards. My evaluation may be in just two weeks, but you guys are soon after," Margarita said.

Everyone was quiet for a moment, and then Bob said, "Well, if Mr. DePoe wants these standards met then I'll meet them."

"How? There is no way we can do that even if we all stopped sending trucks out, and we certainly can't do that," Margarita said, exasperated.

"Only one way then," Bob said, "we cheat."

"*What!*" the other three said in unison.

"We massage the numbers," Bob said.

"You mean we lie? We somehow alter the reports?" Jiayanti said.

"Well, you do what you want, but I'm doing something to make those numbers," Bob said.

"No," Kwong said emphatically. "That is not the only way. What we have to do, what we *all* have to do is report our real numbers. If we all have the same results, Mrs. Cassalli will hold DePoe responsible. She's the owner, and she is not going to hold us to a decision DePoe made that we did not know about."

"I don't know," Bob said. "Mr. Depoe *did* make the decision. Now there is a *fact* even you can't argue with. I'm going to fudge the numbers."

"He may have made the decision, but he missed a step. I'm not sure what that is called, but he definitely missed a step," Jiayanti said.

Skill Question 10. This group needs your help. Jiayanti thinks the group cannot be held to Mr. DePoe's decision. Help Jiayanti and the others by finding support for the idea that something is missing in Mr. DePoe's decision process.

"Maybe we can find out what that is called later. Now we need to stick together. Right, Bob?" Margarita said.

"Yeah, Bob. You can stick with the rest of us *or else.*" Kwong said.

"Or what?" said Bob.

"Or we tell Mrs. Cassalli that you falsified reports!" Jiayanti replied.

Skill Question 11. What method are Jiayanti, Kwong, and Margarita using to try to influence Bob to stick with them and create accurate reports even though that means not meeting Mr. DePoe's new standards?

APPLICATIONS

2.1 THE FRIENDLY EXPEDITER

Teresa Gomez has been Section A expediter for 18 months. Her job is to make pickups and deliveries between Section A and other areas of the plant twice daily. Although her exact route is determined by the needs of the sections that she serves, usually she makes 10 stops in four different buildings on each run. Teresa is considered an exceptionally likable and witty woman who often stops to interact and joke with coworkers she encounters on her route. Her coworkers regard her as fun loving and pleasant to deal with, but Eddie Washington, her supervisor, has questions about why she is often late returning from her runs.

One day, Teresa's name came up while Eddie was having lunch in the cafeteria with several other supervisors from some of the sections that she services. "I can sure tell when your expediter, Teresa, is in our area. She's like a traveling comedy show!" remarked one of the supervisors. "Does she do a pretty good job for you?"

"Well," Eddie responded, "she does seem to take longer than necessary to make her runs. She leaves about 9:30 A.M. and doesn't return until almost lunchtime. But she seems to be getting the job done."

"Not on my end, she isn't," said the supervisor from Section B. "We've been waiting for parts to come in from the dock for two days. They claim the parts were sent, but there's no sign of them. No one seems to know what's become of them."

"Maybe she forgot them here in the cafeteria during her breakfast break," laughed another.

"Her breakfast break?" Eddie asked.

"Sure. She stops in the cafeteria every morning while she's here in Building C and has a big breakfast at about 10:00 A.M. I see her here every day when I take my morning coffee break. But don't be too hard on her, Eddie," he continued. "All those expediters are a bit flaky. If they had anything on the ball, they wouldn't be expediting, would they?"

Eddie called Teresa into his office when he returned from lunch. "What's this I hear about you eating breakfast in the cafeteria every morning on your run? Is it true?"

"Well, yes," said Teresa. "I'm over in Building C anyway, so I take my break while I'm over there. I'm in and out in 15 minutes, my allotted break time. It makes more sense to take my break while I'm there than to return and then go all the way back there for a break. Besides, if I don't take a break during my run, I'd have to take it first thing when I arrive or just before lunch, which doesn't make any sense."

"I'll decide what makes sense and what doesn't," Eddie responded angrily. "Your attitude is beginning to be a real problem. Other supervisors are complaining that you disrupt their areas when you come through, and now I hear that the parts you were supposed to have delivered to Section B have never arrived. They were ready two days ago!"

"Those parts for Section B did arrive on the dock. I checked. But I haven't received them for delivery. You can check my delivery registers. If you ask me, they were misplaced somewhere on the dock, and now they're trying to pass the blame off on me."

"Perhaps if you took a more businesslike attitude, these accusations wouldn't arise."

"Look, Eddie, I enjoy my work, sure. But an expediter's job requires that other people stop what they're doing to take delivery or give me things to expedite. I know I get more cooperation from people because of my lighthearted attitude than I would by being hard-nosed.

I think I've taken a creative approach by joking around and being friendly, and I can cite lots of cases where people have gone out of their way to have things ready on time for me, because it's me."

QUESTIONS

1. What perceptual influences have affected Eddie's understanding of the facts in this case? Do you think he sees the facts objectively? Explain.

2. What inferences have been made about Teresa? What examples of fallacies can you find in this case?

3. What do you make of Teresa's claim that she is being creative in her approach to her job?

2.2 THE BROKEN BREAK-IN

Betty Mason owns the Happy Hobby Shoppe in a small suburban town. Betty is on vacation and has left Joe Hanson in charge. Saturday is the shop's biggest day, and Joe has arrived first. As Len and Dan, two of the other three employees, arrive, he stops them at the back door.

"Don't come in and don't touch anything. I've called the police. We've had a break-in!" Joe tells them.

"What are you talking about? What do you mean?" Dan asks.

"When I got here this morning, the back door was closed but unlocked, and Patti's computer was missing. Someone must have broken in and taken it because Len has never failed to lock up. I just don't know how we are going to break this to Mrs. Mason."

"But I didn't lock up last night because I left early; I wasn't feeling well," Len said.

"Well, who did you tell to lock up?" Joe asked.

"Uh, no one. I just figured Dan or Pat would know that whoever left last should lock up. Isn't that just common sense?" Len said.

"Don't look at me, man," Dan said. "Just because I'm the one that messes up 99 percent of the time, that don't mean I did it this time! I wasn't the last to leave, Patti was!"

"Talking about me?" Pat asked, coming up to the group. "What are all you dudes doin' out here?"

"Someone broke in and took your computer and these two think I messed up, but I didn't mess up this time because I left before you," Dan said.

"Did you leave last and did you lock up?" Joe asked.

"I left last and I locked the front door on my way out," Pat said.

"The front door? What about the back door? And why did you go out the front and not the back?" Joe asked.

"Dan went out the back door so I figured he locked it because he was the last who was going to use it. I went out the front because I could get my car closer to the door so I could load my computer," Pat said.

"You took your computer home! What did you do that for?" Joe said, accusingly.

"I didn't take it home; I took it to the computer shop. Mrs. Mason said I could have more memory, a second hard drive, and a CD burner installed," Pat replied.

"So no one locked the back door, no one broke in, and no one stole a computer?" Len asked.

"Looks like it," Dan said, "and it looks like Patti Perfect finally messed up!"

"Shut up, Dan, I did not. *You* should have locked the back door," Pat said.

"Hey, I didn't know what you were up to!" Dan said.

"Well, no one told me about the computer going to the shop, and I think Len should have specifically told someone to lock up," Joe said. "Oh no, here comes Chief Bennett. Even if we don't file a report now he will tell Mrs. Mason and make it sound like we can't be trusted, especially Dan. Bennett thinks you mess up inside and outside the shop. We have to tell Mrs. Mason first. Who's it going to be?"

"Not me!" Len and Dan said together.

"Patti, it has to be you. Mrs. Mason thinks you can do no wrong and this is the first problem you have ever had," Joe said.

"Yeah, man, she'll fire me, but Joe, I think you should tell because she left you in charge," Dan said.

"But I wasn't here. I come in first on weekdays and Len leaves last," Joe said.

"But, I'm still on probation, being the newest, and I really need this job. I haven't worked for 10 months because of the economy. Come on Patti, you do it— take one for the team," Dan said.

"Dan, you're a jerk! What team?" Pat asked.

"Well, it is just the four of us working here, so we are kind of a team. Plus you wouldn't want us, like, mad at you, would you?" Len said.

"Fine, I'll do it! But you dudes owe me—big!" Patti said.

QUESTIONS

1. What are the facts, the inferences (or assumptions), and the opinions in this situation? Support your answer with examples from the situation.

2. What three determinants of perception are present in this case? (Hint: One has two parts that are opposites of each other.) Support your answer with examples from the situation.

NET-WORK

Whose problem is it?

http://www.youtube.com/watch?v=aMIcgT5EJzE&mode=related&search=

Can you solve a problem too quickly?

http://www.workingamerica.org/badboss/?appState=detail_p&story_id=1641

PERSONAL POINTS

1. When listening to others how do you separate opinion from fact? Is this an easy or difficult process for you? How could you improve your ability to differentiate facts and opinions?

2. How susceptible are you to peer pressure and why? Why do you care or not care if your peers accept you?

3. When have you been affected by someone else's use of one of the logical fallacies? What did you do or could you have done about it?

4. How did you feel about problem solving before reading this chapter? Do you feel any differently now? If so, how and why do you feel differently?

5. Are you chronically late? When getting a new assignment, what is your first inclination? Are you not motivated until the absolute last minute? What can you do about this?

EXPERIENTIAL EXERCISE

Divide the class into groups. Each group will analyze the situations that follow. Compare each group's answers to those of the other groups after completing each section. Each group must be prepared to support and defend its answers.

PART 1

Identify each of the following as a *symptom* of a problem, as a *problem* needing a problem-solving approach, or as a *decision* well suited to application of the nine-point decision-making model.

1. A vacancy in a supervisor position.

2. An unexplained decrease in sales.

3. Low morale.

4. Few outside applicants for job vacancies.

5. Your building maintenance contract is about to expire.

6. A new scientific discovery is needed for your next product.

7. Employee health insurance costs keep rising.

8. Which tasks to assign to the 11 workers you supervise.

PART 2

Identify which barrier is interfering with the solution of the problem. What should be done to counteract the barrier?

9. "We have to get this account or we are out of business! I don't care how many accounts we have, it's the next one that counts. You people need to think! *WE NEED THIS!*" Mr. Bellicose roared.

   Jurgen leaned over to Aurore and said, "Not to worry, he's like this right before every account we bid on."

10. ---Original Message---.

    From: Salazaar, Belinda

    Sent: Sat 2/17/2007 2:05 PM

    To: All Staff.

    Subject: Our Budget Problems

    Effective immediately, stop sending me what you think is causing our budget shortfall. I don't want any more information regarding the price of gas, the cost of electricity, lack of security in the warehouse, etc. I knew what the problem was right from the start—you are all paid too much. I have information stating that half of you are receiving pay above the average. I'll be collecting other data on this and adjusting salaries soon.

11. "One hundred and forty-three of the 12,547 truck tires we bought last year will go flat within 24 months of purchase. We have to do something about this; this is a huge problem."

12. "Hey Joe, what are the two boxes for?" Peng asked.

    "I'm going through the suggestions on what to do with the Patterson account. Got tons of ideas to go through. Gonna separate the good from the ugly," Joe replied.
    "You mean the good, the bad, and the ugly, don't you?" Peng asked.
    "What?"
    "Like the movie—the good, the bad, and the ugly. Don't you have good ideas, not good, and maybes?" Peng said.
    "No," Joe said, holding up his two boxes, "Just two. Reminds me of you. Half the time I understand you, the other half I have no idea what you're talkin' about."

PART 3

What problem-solving technique is best suited to each of these situations and why?

13. Adam, Bashir, Jeremy, Luke, and Sam are all managers for a chemical and biological manufacturer. Luke and Bashir work the day shift, Adam and Sam work in the afternoons, and Jeremy works the night shift. Sam and Bashir work in the production division, Luke is a lawyer, Jeremy works in marketing, and Adam is on the research and development team. All five have been assigned to a team charged with creating brand names for four new product lines. Jeremy is the team leader for this effort. What one method should they use and why?

14. Erik, Kunal, and Akanke work in the product development kitchens of a national fast-food chain that will be introducing tacos to the bargain menu. These three need to determine the amount of the taco ingredients that will be used for all tacos. Their goal is a product with acceptable taste for the least cost. Each ingredient will be delivered by a pump dispenser or drop hopper. Both devices can be adjusted in quarter-ounce increments. In addition to a hard-shell (corn) tortilla, these are the ingredients and the least and greatest amount of each they are allowed to use:

    basic, spiced, meat-like substance — from $\frac{1}{2}$ ounce to 2 ounces

    shredded iceberg lettuce—from $\frac{1}{4}$ ounce to 1 ounce

    shredded, economy orange cheese—$\frac{1}{2}$ ounce to $1\frac{3}{4}$ ounces

    chopped common red tomato—$\frac{1}{2}$ ounce to $1\frac{1}{2}$ ounces.

EXPERIENTIAL EXERCISE (Continued)

What one method should the group use and why?

15. It's 6:45 P.M. and Alex, Dana, and Fox have been at it since 8:30 A.M. They have little to show for it except some empty cartons of takeout Chinese that their boss, Walter, allowed them to send out for while they worked through lunch. The coffee (hazelnut)

and tea (Ceylon Kenilworth OP1) are long gone; the group is down to saltines and bottled water. Things started out well, with each contributing ideas of his or her own, and then together they came up with a few more, but things have fizzled since about 2:30. What do they need now and why?

EXPERIENTIAL EXERCISE

We See, But Do We Perceive?

Take a look at the first two illustrations. What do you see?

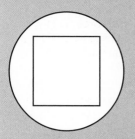
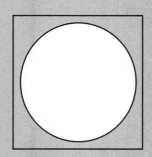
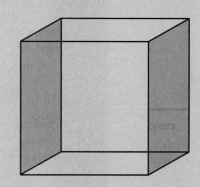

The square in the middle is obviously larger in area than the one on the left, isn't it? How about the circles? Which looks larger in circumference and diameter? The one on the right? Not so! If you measure them, you'll see that they are identical in size. Now take a look at the illustration on the right. What do you see?

You should, if your brain is perceiving accurately, see alternating faces of a box, sometimes viewing it from the front and at other times viewing it from the top. Our brain receives a lot of information at any given time, and it tries to make sense of this information by limiting and organizing sensory input. Our brain, naturally, tries to

help us function, but it sometimes plays tricks on us by creating distortions or inaccuracies in what we see. However, the brain does permit most people to switch back and forth between the sets of images.

QUESTIONS

1. Which was easier for you to perceive accurately—the illustration here or the one in Figure 2.1?

2. How do these exercises relate to the perception challenges you face in everyday life?

SPOT CHECK ANSWERS

1. F
2. T
3. T
4. F
5. F
6. F
7. F
8. F
9. F
10. F

3 | Primary Communications

Making the simple complicated is commonplace. Making the complicated simple, awesomely simple, that's creativity.

Charles Mingus, jazz musician and composer

Never use a little word where a big will suffice.

Michael Drafke

God gave us two ears and only one mouth. In view of the way we use these, it is probably a very good thing that this is not reversed.

Cicero

GOALS

The goal of this chapter is to introduce you to the most important component of organizations—communication. Although you have been communicating all of your life, organizational communication can be different from that with which you are familiar. Just like communicating, the understanding of communication is a two-way street. You need to understand organizational communication in order to fully comprehend the messages of others and to ensure that you send the message you intend and do not accidentally send the wrong message.

OBJECTIVES

When you finish this chapter, you should be able to:

▶ Diagram and explain the basic communication model.

▶ List and explain the five message channels.

▶ List the three components of a message and the contribution each makes to the total message.

▶ Describe the role words play in communicating.

▶ Define and give an example of nonverbal communication.

▶ Describe the six functions of nonverbal communication.

▶ Describe, give examples of, and explain the role of the eight types of nonverbal symbols.

▶ Differentiate between formal and informal communication.

▶ Define and explain the role of upward, downward, and horizontal communication.

▶ Describe and differentiate between male and female communication.

INTRODUCTION

At the height of the downsizing trend, the CEO of a medium-sized company was overheard discussing the annual year-end bonuses with the CFO. Until then, the bonuses had been considered generous given the size of the firm. The individual listening in on the discussion did not hear everything, only that there "needs to be an adjustment in the bonuses this year." The rumor quickly spread that bonuses were being reduced. On hearing this, the CEO sent out a memo stating that he was "appending funds to the annual bonus account." This resulted in another rumor that the CEO was keeping the bonus money for himself. When this reached the CEO, he immediately sent an e-mail stating that he meant that "the annual bonus monies were being augmented." This was interpreted as meaning no one was getting a bonus because the IRS had confiscated the money. Finally, the CEO called a meeting of all employees and inform them that, although he had wanted it to be a surprise, he had to inform them that the firm had had such a good year everyone was getting a bigger bonus!

This awkward experience for what should have been a pleasant surprise helps to illustrate an important concept: Communication can take place in a variety of situations, but for communication to be effective, there must be understanding. One major cause of problems in modern organizations is the lack of effective communication. Frequently, people are positive that they've communicated after transmitting a message in writing. Often supervisors assume that they've communicated when they make oral statements to their subordinates. Naturally, one does have to make certain assumptions in this world to function, but as a famous saying goes, when you assume, you often make an "ass" out of "u" and "me."

Communication is one of the two most basic components of organizations, the other is cooperation. Organizations cannot function effectively when communication skills are lacking among their members. This chapter will therefore consider some of the major facets of communication and will examine the characteristics of words, the need for established feedback mechanisms, and the means of overcoming common barriers to communication. We shall also explore some of the significant aspects of nonverbal communication and the importance of listening.

THE NATURE OF COMMUNICATION

Various forms of communication continually bombard us in our day-to-day activities. Not only are thousands of radio stations and hundreds of television channels attempting to communicate with the nation's citizens each day, but newer forms of communication are now competing for attention. We now can receive calls on our cellular telephones while driving to work and receive printed messages on our portable fax machines while driving home from work. Our voice mail and e-mail systems can receive communications when we are away.

However, are all these sophisticated electronic devices communicating with us when their electrical impulses are functioning and our ears and eyes are tuned in to their messages? Not necessarily. Even though we may hear or see a transmitted message, an essential ingredient of communication is needed to make it effective: understanding.

BASIC COMMUNICATION MODEL

Whether we're talking about a radio station, a fax machine, or e-mail, or about you within your organization, four essential ingredients are necessary for effective communication to take place:

- a sender
- a message
- a receiver (listener)
- feedback

A Two-Way Process   Communication, therefore, can be defined as a two-way process resulting in the transmission of information and understanding between individuals. Note the two-way nature of communication. It's virtually impossible to know for certain how effectively you've communicated without some sort of **feedback**, the process through which the originator of a message learns the response to the message.

For example, if you said to your boss, "Susan, those flowers on your desk sure are fragrant," and she looked up and asked, "Who told you I was pregnant?" have you communicated? Yes, but not as you intended. However, the opportunity to receive instant feedback when you hear Susan's words enables you to correct the misunderstanding. Try to avoid one-way communication as much as possible.

How Messages Are Sent   The basic communication model depicted in Figure 3.1 demonstrates how the elements of communication come together to form a system. The sender of the message is the first step in the process. The sender must encode the message. **Encoding** involves the selection of the words that will be used and their order, the tone, and any accompanying gestures or facial expressions (nonverbal communication). The receiver decodes the message and uses feedback to respond. The message is not only affected by the sender's intent but also by the receiver's interpretation of the message. The **decoding**, or translating, by the receiver is also affected by his or her mood and feelings. In addition to encoding the message, the sender must select the channel that will transmit the message.

The **message channel** is essentially the conduit that will carry the message from the sender to the receiver. There are five message channels:

- face-to-face
- face-to-group
- telephone
- written
- third party

Communication
the exchange of thoughts, messages, or information by speech, signals, writing, or behavior between a sender and a receiver

Feedback
a verbal or nonverbal response by a receiver to the sender's message

Encoding
selecting words and their order for a message by a sender

Decoding
the translation of a message by a receiver

Message Channel
the conduit or medium that will carry a message from the sender to the receiver

FIGURE 3.1 BASIC COMMUNICATION MODEL   The sender encodes the message and selects a channel. The receiver decodes the message and uses feedback to respond.

Each channel carries an inherent amount of **noise**, or interference. This is in addition to the literal noise that may be present, which also interferes with communication. These channels, then, are listed in order of ability to carry the maximum communication, which has three components: verbal, nonverbal, and tonal.[1]

Dr. Albert Merabian has researched interpersonal communication extensively, and he estimates that the majority of a message is composed of **nonverbal communication**. His studies show that 55 percent of the total message sent is composed of factors such as facial expressions, gestures, posture, and territoriality. Next most important is the **tone** used. The tone may indicate that you are being sarcastic, serious, romantic, and so forth. Tone is estimated to account for 38 percent of the total possible message. That leaves just 7 percent for the third component—the verbal part. The **verbal message**—the actual words—might be thought by many as the most important part of any message. In reality, the words themselves are not nearly as important as the tone in which they are spoken and the nonverbal cues that accompany them (Table 3.1). To focus only on the words increases the chance of miscommunication.

Knowing the portion of our total message that each message component contributes allows us to understand the ranking of the five basic message channels (Table 3.2). **Face-to-face communication** is considered the most effective. Face-to-face discussion allows the sender to use 100 percent of the possible message. Face-to-face communication also allows the receiver to give the maximum amount of feedback to the sender. The cycle may continue as needed.

Noise

literally or figuratively, anything that interferes with a message

Nonverbal Communication

nonspoken communication through gestures and expressions

Tone

the pitch of a word used to determine its meaning or to distinguish differences in meaning

Verbal Message

the words used in a message

Face-to-Face Communication

two people conversing while both are present

TABLE 3.1 THE COMPONENTS OF OUR MESSAGES

Message Component	Definition	Percentage of Total Message
Nonverbal	Gestures and expressions	55%
Tonal	Inflection	38%
Verbal	Actual words	7%

TABLE 3.2 COMMUNICATION CHANNELS AND THEIR USES

Communication Channel	When to Use the Channel
Face-to-Face	Whenever possible; for sensitive or confidential communications; when feedback is needed, especially to explain complex or confusing information.
Face-to-Group	When the same important message would be delivered to many, and they might have questions; when input from many areas is needed.
Phone	When something is urgent, so urgent there is no time for face-to-face communication; when the parties are separated, when the message is brief, and an answer or confirmation is needed; when the message can be adequately conveyed without nonverbal communication.
Written	When the message is brief, easy to understand, and must be disseminated to many people, as with an announcement; when documentation is needed; when a reminder message needs to be sent to many.
Third-Party	Rarely, if ever.

Face-to-group communication is second best. Although face-to-group provides many of the same advantages of face-to-face communication, the sender's attention is divided among the audience. If there are 30 members in a group, and each receives equal attention, then the sender can focus on each for just two seconds per minute. In addition, there are also difficulties with feedback. Receivers have less chance to give feedback because of the decreased time the sender has to give each receiver. There is a great chance that an individual's nonverbal feedback will be missed entirely. Also, some people will be reluctant to take the group's time to ask a question, and others may not want to ask for fear of asking what they feel may be a dumb question.

Phone communication is the third best channel. Although you can still use tone with your words, and there is an opportunity for feedback, over half of your potential message is absent. Until videophones become common (cellphones with cameras don't count as you can't see the speaker's face), the nonverbal component will be unavailable when using phones.

Written communication is fourth best because only words are involved. One might try to convey tone by using bold, italic, or underlined words, but much is still missing. A question arises, however. If written channels, memos, faxes, and e-mail are not very good ways to communicate, then why are they used so frequently in organizations? One reason is that people believe if the same message is sent to everyone (as when sending copies of a memo), then everyone receives the same message. However, this is quite often not the case. From the basic communication model, we know that the receiver must decode the message, and much of the decoding interpretation depends on the mood of the receiver. Another reason the same message may not be received by all is that there is limited chance for feedback. Although you might call the sender and ask for an explanation, or you might send him or her a memo or e-mail, you would still be using only a fraction of the total available message, and you still might not gain understanding. This leads to an additional problem.

Written channels can lead to further miscommunication if feedback is delayed or absent and the message is not fully understood. If the message is not complete or understood, then often people will fill in any spaces in an attempt to reach closure. If people don't understand a message, they will contrive understanding for themselves. This is how the phrase "read between the lines" came about. People fill in motivations, reasons, and gaps in a message, which may lead to a rumor. Although a rumor may initially make sense to someone, it often becomes altered or embellished. Messages have a way of taking strange twists as they are communicated from one person to another.

If written channels have such problems, then why are they used at all? One reason is that written messages are often the fastest, easiest, and least time-consuming ways to contact a large number of people. If the message is of less importance, or if it is a simple announcement, then a memo or e-mail is a perfectly acceptable way to get the word out. For example, if Payroll is changing the color of the paychecks, it would be acceptable to send a memo. People want to know this, but it is not really important as long as the bank will still cash the check. Also, it is hard to misinterpret this message. Another example is a meeting announcement. Once a time and place are arranged, it is good form to send a written announcement reminding people of the day, time, and location (including an agenda is also a good idea). Another reason to send a memo is to establish a record of something. A memo or other documentation is often good to have in order to refer to later or to defend your actions.

Face-to-Group Communication
a sender communicating to a group, in person

Phone Communication
communication over a distance with the aid of an electromechanical or electronic device such as a telephone or an intercom

Written Communication
recorded, unspoken messages, such as notes, letters, faxes, or e-mail

NetNote

E-mail Etiquette

http://www.emailreplies.com/

Extensive advice on writing and sending e-mails.

http://www.psychologytoday.com/articles/pto-19920501-000004.html

Effect of electronic communication in the workplace

Third-Party
Communication

communication from
one person to another
through at least one
other person

The last choice for a communication channel is third party. **Third-party communication** means that A tells B to tell C something. Although this often means that A talks face-to-face with B, and B speaks face-to-face with C, this is still a last-resort method. The problem with third-party communication is readily apparent to anyone with siblings or children. Think of this situation: Mother tells Adam to tell his brothers Erik and Alex to pick up their toys. Does Adam walk over to Erik and Alex and say, "Mom asked that you guys pick up your toys, please"? No. Adam runs to his brothers and says, "Ha! Ha! You have to pick up your toys! Mom said! Ha! Ha! You have to clean and I don't have to." With third-party communications, the message encoded by the sender is often re-encoded by the intermediary. To complicate matters further, if any feedback also goes through the third party, it, too, may be changed. The sender cannot be sure of the message sent and cannot be sure of any feedback that is returned.

RESPONSIBILITY FOR EFFECTIVE COMMUNICATION

Paraphrasing

checking the meaning of
a message by restating
the message as it was
perceived

Who has the responsibility for ensuring that effective communication takes place? Both the sender of the message and the receiver share the responsibility. Remember the word *feedback?* One technique for employing feedback to verify or clarify a message is **paraphrasing**. By asking certain questions, the receiver can restate what he or she thought the message was. The sender can do the same to determine whether the receiver actually understood the message. For example, Jill asks Kevin out for a date. Kevin says, "I'm sorta busy that night." Jill asks about the following week. Kevin, as he looks at the tops of his shoes says, "I'm pretty sure I've got this thing that night." Jill and Kevin start clarifying by paraphrasing.

> **Jill:** Are you saying that you don't want to go out with me ever?
> **Kevin:** I never said that!
> **Jill:** Well, that's what it seems like to me!
> **Kevin:** Are you mad now?
> **Jill:** I just want an answer. Now.
> **Kevin:** You don't have to be so pushy!
> **Jill:** Are you saying I'm too aggressive? Can't your delicate male ego deal with women on an equal basis?
> **Kevin:** Are you saying I'm a wimp or that I'm sexist?

REALITY CHECK

When Not to Use E-Mail

E-mail is often useful, but it is not for every occasion. Feedback, even positive, has less effect when given by e-mail. If you send one e-mail and get little or no response, or you get the wrong or an unexpected response, it is probably best to not use another e-mail (if it doesn't work the first time, it's probably time to try something different). Sensitive information should not be delivered in an e-mail. Don't be like one company that decided to try firing people by e-mail. People should never learn of major organizational change by e-mail. If something is big enough to be important or important enough to be big, use face-to-face or face-to-group for the initial announcement. Finally, do not send e-mails when angry; it is too easy to hide behind the computer screen and write things you would never say face-to-face.

Source: Marty Brounstein et al., *Business Communication* (Hoboken, NJ: John Wiley, 2007), pp. 151–153.

Well, things aren't going too well for Jill and Kevin. They are both using paraphrasing ("Are you saying . . . ") to try to understand each other, but neither is really answering the paraphrase directly. Sometimes we don't want to be direct because it is uncomfortable for us. Here, Kevin was trying to conceal the fact that he didn't have the money to take Jill out. He could have saved both of them some trouble by not assuming he was going to pay when Jill was asking him and just explaining his situation. Still, paraphrasing can often clarify miscommunication, although it is not a foolproof method if the other person actually wants to *not* communicate.

In a sense, then, people are often simultaneously producers (senders) and consumers (receivers) of communication. The importance of two-way communication for overcoming misunderstandings can't be overstressed.

WHAT ARE WORDS REALLY LIKE?

We usually expect to have some difficulty when we talk with people whose language is different from ours. Misunderstandings seem likely in such instances. However, we really don't have a completely common language with anybody, whether they are in our country or not. A big part of our communication problem is caused by the characteristics of the symbols we use in much of our daily communication. These verbal symbols are called words and can be used in either oral conversations or printed messages.

ARE WORDS THINGS, OR ARE THEY MERELY WORDS?

If you and I were face-to-face, and I used a word that you didn't understand, the best place for you to find the meaning of the word would, of course, be the dictionary. Or would it? Would a dictionary really tell you what I meant by that word? Not necessarily. Most lexicographers (dictionary authors) contend that the book they prepare is merely a history book, one that shows how some words have been used at particular times and in certain contexts. You can probably think of numerous words that you use daily that are understood but are not in the dictionary.

WORDS AS INEXACT SYMBOLS

Can you write down the meaning of the word *fast?* Think for a moment. Does the word imply motion, as in the case of a fast runner? Or does it imply lack of motion, as in "she stands fast"? Isn't this little four-letter word also related to eating habits, as in the case of a person who fasts during a holiday, such as Lent? What about the expression "He was too fast on the first date"? A complete dictionary will offer at least 50 different meanings of the word *fast*. The same can be said for such words as *wind, wing, run, lie*, and *air*. How, then, can we determine the true meaning of words?

First, you have to discard the notion that words have absolute meanings. The word is not the thing; the word is merely a symbol that represents different things to different people. Words are, in effect, like containers that attempt to transport something to someone else. The true meaning of a word isn't in the word itself or in the way the listener interprets the word. Words in themselves have very imprecise meanings.

The meaning of a word is therefore in the mind of the sender of the word and is carried by the word to the receiver. There are believed to be about 600,000 words in the English language. An educated adult in daily conversation uses about 2,000, of which the 500 most commonly used have 14,000 dictionary definitions. Given these numbers, can we guess the right meaning every time?

Consequently, if we want to discover the meaning of a speaker's words, the only way to be certain is to ask him or her what they mean when we are in doubt. Instead of wondering what the words in a message mean, a better approach is to wonder what the speaker means. A corny story might help to illustrate this point:

"Now," said the village blacksmith to the apprentice, "I'll take this iron out of the fire, lay it on the anvil, and when I nod my head, you hit it." The apprentice did so, and now he's the village blacksmith.

You can lessen the chance of communication failures between you and others by following two rules:

1. Don't assume that everyone knows what you are talking about.
2. Don't assume that you know what others are talking about without asking them questions to make certain.

The blacksmith erroneously made the first assumption, and the imperceptive apprentice made the second.

THE DEVELOPMENT OF NEW MEANINGS

Words develop new meanings with the passage of time. Almost every decade brings forth myriad new meanings for old words. Often the parents of college or high school students can't understand the conversations of their offspring. Many popular songs have contained words with specific meanings only to some listeners. Various ethnic groups have also been a fertile and creative source of new meanings for old words.

WORD INTERPRETATION IS AFFECTED BY DOUBLESPEAK

Which would you rather have happen to you—be "fired" from your job or be "offered a career-change opportunity," be "downsized," "right-sized," "outsourced," "out-placed," or maybe best of all, "dehired"? Which would you prefer—to be "laid

---

REALITY CHECK

Can Shyness Be Changed?

You might be quite happy being an introvert, but if you wish to become at least somewhat more outgoing, there are suggestions you may follow. The most important action to take is to attend situations you wish to avoid. Shy people often feel conditions will be worse than they are. The more you do these things, the more you discover they are not so bad; but start with small challenges at first and gradually face larger ones.

During these new situations, try to talk to more people for a shorter time, rather than attaching yourself to someone with whom you are already comfortable. If you are reluctant to speak out, jot down or make a mental note of points you wish to make. Don't be overcritical of what you say or do. Before speaking, many shy people decide what they were going to say isn't good enough; you'll never really know unless you speak up. After an event, don't be too critical of your social actions. Mistakes you think you made rarely seem so important to others, and your anxiety about them can cause you to make more mistakes. To reduce your anxiety, forget about focusing on how you feel by immersing yourself in the situation. Finding something or someone to focus on can help you forget about your own nervousness.

Lastly, keep in mind that at times, no matter what you do, things will not work out the way you want. This happens to everyone. Try to forget it by focusing on the next time. Remind yourself of this—only 5 to 7 percent of people rate themselves as always outgoing, while 40 to 50 percent of us say that we are inherently shy.

Source: Sharon Stocker, "Don't Be Shy. (Advice for becoming more outgoing)," *Prevention*, August 1997, pp. 96–104; Chuck Green, "Shy-proofing Strategies for the Office," *Chicago Tribune*, September 24, 2003, sec. 6, pp. 1, 4.

off" or to be "excessed" or "transitioned" because the company you've been working for is being "reorganized" or "reengineered" or is engaging in "decruitment" (the opposite of recruitment)? Maybe your employer could offer you a "career alternative enhancement"? If you had participated in the Gulf War or the Iraqi War, would you have preferred to hear that your organization's "massive bombing attacks killed thousands of civilians" or that your "force packages" successfully "visited a site" and "degraded," "neutralized," or "sanitized" targets?

Such is the world of **doublespeak**, a term applied to the use of words that are evasive, ambiguous, or stilted for the purpose of deceiving or confusing the reader or listener. The ethical use of doublespeak is highly questionable, but many organizational managers and politicians make use of it as a means, they hope, of softening the harsh blows of reality and covering up bad news or misleading the public. President Clinton tried doublespeak to explain something (it's hard to tell what) with the often-quoted utterance, "It depends upon what the meaning of 'is' means. If 'is' means 'is' and never has been, that is one thing. If it means 'there is none,' that was a completely true statement."[2] When you hear these phrases, try to uncover the real intent of the sender of the message, although this can be a challenge. Clinton's statement is a good example of an "incomplete success" (read "failure") in terms of clarity.

William Lutz, author of the book *Doublespeak*, has collected numerous examples of the use of doublespeak.[3] He speaks of a place that did not burn but suffered "rapid oxidation." Or there was the company marketing "real counterfeit diamonds." You wouldn't want a junkyard behind your house, but what about a "secondary-fiber business"? Maybe a nice "resource development park," which was actually a proposal for a garbage dump. As you become "chronologically gifted" (i.e., old), maybe you learn the meaning of these terms and phrases, but it seems new ones are constantly being developed.

Like it or not, you may have to learn the meaning behind some organizational doublespeak in order to survive.[4] Your boss may not be a supervisor or manager anymore; he or she may be a "servant-leader." Your "servant-leader" might also be "junior partner" or part of the "coaching staff." You might not be given orders, work, or an assignment; instead you might be "tasked" to "operationalize" "customer-driven" "strategic initiatives." You should probably keep up with the current meaning of these words as they can experience an unplanned paradigm shift at any time (meaning, they can change suddenly).

THE DEVELOPMENT OF NEW WORDS

New words are continually derived as a result of the development of new industries or fields, as in the case of the words *astronaut* and *space shuttle*, which emerged from space exploration, or *DOS*, *PC*, *laptop*, *notebook*, *palmtop*, and the *Net* or the *Web*, which are derived from computer technology. Each trade or profession tends to develop its own specialized or technical language, typically known as jargon.

TONE AFFECTS MEANING

A difference in tone can change the meaning of words. "John, you've been doing a hell of a job around here" is a sentence that could convey praise or blame, depending on the tone of the speaker's voice.

In summary, we should remember six important factors about the meanings of words:

- Words have many meanings.
- Words sometimes have regional meanings.

NetNote

http://www.mwls.co.uk/ jargon.htm

Enter up to three words and click Generate for a free translation into jargon gibberish.

Doublespeak
deliberately ambiguous
or evasive language

- Words develop new meanings.
- Word interpretation is affected by doublespeak.
- New words are continually derived.
- A difference in tone can change the meaning of words.

NONVERBAL COMMUNICATION

As noted earlier, nonverbal communication accounts for 55 percent of the total message we can deliver. It is so powerful that when the verbal and tonal portions conflict with the nonverbal portion, people believe the nonverbal message. This reinforces the old saying "Actions speak louder than words." The following section investigates the details of nonverbal communication.

THE BODY COMMUNICATES

Whether you are conscious of it or not, you're communicating each time you make a gesture or glance at a person. The motions people make with their bodies (or sometimes don't make) often communicate messages. Body language isn't always accurate or effective, but it is communication nonetheless. What would you do if after arriving at your job one morning, you passed a coworker in the hallway who gave you an unusual glance—or at least a glance that appeared to you to be strange. You might wonder for the rest of the day what that glance meant. Some employees seldom greet others when they pass in hallways or work areas. Instead, their faces seem frozen. Sometimes a person might think that a frozen stare is an indication of displeasure.

Once again, a word of warning: Some people are misled by body language. We already are aware that we have plenty of difficulties correctly interpreting the verbal symbols of others, even when we've had training in listening. We can also be easily misled by body language. For example, your listener's crossed arms may not necessarily mean a lack of receptivity to your message. Instead, it could merely mean that the person feels cold.

FUNCTIONS OF NONVERBAL COMMUNICATION

Nonverbal communication (NVC) has six basic functions. Nonverbal communication can accent, complement, contradict, regulate, repeat, or substitute for verbal communication.[5]

When nonverbal communication punctuates verbal communication, the NVC is performing an **accenting** role. Poking a finger into someone's chest is an example of accenting. Punctuating a message with a sweeping motion of the hand at chest level with the palm facing out says that the conversation is over.

Complementing nonverbal communication reinforces the spoken message; complementing NVC would not convey the same message if used alone. The distance between two people is an example of complementing NVC. Standing four feet away from someone might indicate that this person is a stranger. When you stand four feet away from your boss and present her with a formal salutation ("Good morning, Ms. Smith"), then the distance reinforces the message that the boss is of higher rank, and the two of you have an unchallenged authority relationship (more about this later).

Some of the more interesting nonverbal communications are those that contradict the verbal message. **Contradicting** NVC conveys messages that are opposite to the verbal messages. Often this is the way people reveal their true feelings or send the wrong or an unintended message. Even though people say that they are paying

Accenting NVC
punctuating or drawing attention to a verbal message

Complementing NVC
expressions or gestures that support, but could not replace, a verbal message

Contradicting NVC
expressions or gestures that convey a meaning opposite that of a verbal message

attention, if they give less eye contact than they receive (that is, if they look off into the distance rather than at the speaker), they send a contradicting nonverbal message. The message they send is that they are bored or uninterested. When verbal and nonverbal messages conflict, people believe the nonverbal ones.

Regulating nonverbal communication controls the course of a conversation. Raising your hand with the index finger extended indicates that you want the other person to wait a minute or to stop speaking. Tapping a coworker's shoulder twice with your index finger while she is walking away from you indicates that you want her to stop or to wait for you so you can speak to her. Touching someone's arm while he speaks also performs a regulating function by indicating to him that you wish to speak.

A gesture or expression that could be used alone to send the same meaning as the verbal portion of a message is a **repeating** NVC. Note the difference between repeating and complementing nonverbal communication: repeating NVC can stand alone; complementing NVC cannot. For example, rolling your eyes repeats the spoken message of "I don't believe it!" Just rolling your eyes would be as effective, however.

We use **substituting** nonverbal communication to replace a verbal message. This is quite common because sometimes it is not practical or politically wise to state out loud what we are thinking. When two people are in a hurry and pass in a busy hall, they may not have the time to speak to one another, or the crowd may be too large for a spoken word to be heard unless one shouts. Instead, we often substitute an eyebrow flash for a spoken "How you doin', Fred?" We can't talk, but we don't want to be rude to our colleague, so we raise both eyebrows as a silent, substitute salutation. Or you may be standing behind a boss who comes down hard on a coworker for a minor transgression. It would not be politically smart to disagree verbally with this boss, but you also want to let your coworker know that you think the boss is going too far. So you shake your head back and forth in a silent "no" that is unseen by the boss.

Although there are just six functions of nonverbal communication, there are many types and hundreds of examples of these types. Most nonverbal messages are learned automatically, but it is still important to study them, for although many are innate, one can accidentally send an incorrect or overly revealing nonverbal message if one is not knowledgeable and careful.

Regulating NVC
expressions or gestures that control the pace or flow of communication

Repeating NVC
a gesture or expression that can be used alone to send the same meaning as a verbal message

Substituting NVC
a nonverbal cue that replaces a verbal message

Facial expressions and hand gestures repeat a verbal message. Here the woman says, "You need to take care of this" and repeats the word "you" by pointing to the man.

Source: Courtesy of PhotoEdit/Billy E. Barnes.

TYPES OF NONVERBAL SYMBOLS

To be in control of your communication and to always send the message that you want to send, you must first be aware of what types of nonverbal symbols exist. Once you are aware of the types of nonverbal communication that exist, you may focus on the ones that you use. Once you notice the ones you use, you can determine whether they are appropriate or not. Here we will explore the following types of nonverbal communication:

- the eyes
- the face and head
- gestures
- touch
- posture
- territory
- walking
- status symbols

Although all of these are important and they all combine to transmit our total message, some are used more extensively than others. In general, the hands, the face, and especially the eyes are the most expressive.

The Eyes   The eyes may be the single most important area for nonverbal communication. People attend not only to the expressions made with the eyes but also to the amount of eye contact being made. Eye contact is looking at another person's eyes, whether or not that person is looking back into your eyes. In general, Americans give more eye contact than they receive when they are listening.[6] In other words, when two Americans are having a conversation, the listener looks at the speaker for a longer time than the speaker looks at the listener. The American speaker glances at the listener for brief periods and then breaks eye contact. The most common way to break eye contact in the United States is to look diagonally down and to the side.[7] As one person speaks, then listens, then speaks, and then listens, the amount of eye contact given to the other person changes from less, to more, to less, to more again. Although the amount of eye contact varies with one's role, it is always of major importance to our communications.

Eye contact is important when speaking to individuals or when speaking to groups. Maintaining proper eye contact conveys a message of warmth and concern for the listener.[8] When speaking to a group, give some eye contact to each person (or as many as possible) to show interest in the audience members. In business, making eye contact conveys trust and sincerity. Not making eye contact or making the wrong kind of eye contact can send the wrong message or an undesired one.

Eye contact for other than the accepted amount of time can vary from none, to too little, to too much. After reading this section, make a conscious effort to note the eye contact you give others, the eye contact they give you, and the circumstances under which the eye contact is made. For example, if someone fails to make eye contact with you, try to determine why he or she did not. It may be that no eye contact is the perfectly acceptable amount. For example, on the street or in close quarters (in an elevator or while standing in line) or in other situations with strangers, no eye contact is often proper. On the street, anything more than a passing glance can have other meanings (as we shall see in a moment). A concerted effort not to make eye contact on the street can also mean that you do not want to acknowledge someone else's existence (like a beggar).[9] When people you know or work with fail to make eye contact, it could be a signal that they believe they are superior, that they are arrogant, or that they hold you in contempt. Of course, sometimes it just means they are concentrating on a problem or some other thought.

Just as no eye contact is appropriate at some times and not at others, so is a short amount of eye contact. In a room or hall, a short amount of eye contact, two to three seconds, is acceptable.[10] Anything longer can be construed as staring or requires a "hello" or some type of nonverbal substitute. A small amount of eye contact can indicate a withdrawn individual.[11] We may also give less eye contact when asked a question that is embarrassing or one that makes us uncomfortable. When confronted with an accusation, too little eye contact is likely to be perceived as an admission of guilt.[12] However, in some cultures, looking down, and thus giving too little eye contact for Americans, is a sign of respect.

Looking away demonstrates the nonverbal message that what the other person has to say is unimportant.

Source: Courtesy of Getty Images Inc.—Image Bank/Real Life.

Giving too much eye contact, in other words, for longer than the accepted time given the situation, sends different messages depending on the circumstances. When speaking to a large group of people, you may give just about as much eye contact to a person as you wish.[13] Otherwise, staring at someone is a sign of recognition.[14] It is acceptable for friends to look at each other for longer than the situationally acceptable time. If you do not know the person you are staring at, and you both seem to know it, then the message is that you want to know the person (in the case of two people of opposite sexes, or with two women); otherwise, you will make that person feel uneasy (it's not polite to stare).[15] Too much eye contact can also be threatening. This is especially true when a man stares at another man.[16] In a work situation, long eye contact indicates anger or defensiveness.[17] An angry subordinate may stare straight into the eyes of his or her boss when speaking, although normally the subordinate would look away. Prolonged eye contact with the boss can also be a challenge to the boss's authority (meaning you either dispute or reject the boss's authority over you).[18] This situation demonstrates the importance of knowing the message different nonverbal communications send. You would not want to stare at your boss and send a message of anger unless you truly felt that way (and even then you might not want to). Also, as with other levels of eye contact, what is acceptable varies from country to country. Although too much eye contact might be threatening or rude in the United States, in the United Kingdom and in other cultures, too little eye contact would be rude or impolite.

The eyes are extremely important for communication, but they are just one part of the repertoire. The eyes and face combine to send stronger and more varied messages than either one could send separately.

The Face and Head   Research has identified a minimum of 8 eyebrow and forehead positions, a minimum of 8 eye and eyelid positions, and at least 10 positions for the lower face.[19] All of these are used not only in combination, but also in rapid succession. Some of these facial-eye combinations will be described in order to increase your awareness of them.

Working in conjunction with the eyes, the eyebrows are one of the most expressive areas of the face. As mentioned earlier, quickly raising both eyebrows, an eyebrow flash, is a way of acknowledging someone. Raising the eyebrows and widening the eyes indicates surprise, astonishment, or even anger. Showing anger with the eyes and eyebrows can be accomplished by lowering the eyebrows and bringing them closer to the middle of the face. An alternative to this is the ability of some people to lower one eyebrow while simultaneously raising the other. More subtle movements and expressions are also possible, as when people squint ever so slightly to indicate interest in something, as if showing their mental focus through their eyes.

The mouth is also highly expressive. The most well known of all nonverbal cues involving the mouth is the smile. But the mouth is capable of much more, as most of us know. Tightening the mouth can indicate anger. Biting one side of the lower lip can show apprehension. Opening the mouth and leaving it open can indicate surprise. Turning up one corner of the mouth and tightening the cheek on the same side can be just as effective as saying "Oh, sure" to indicate disbelief. Note two things as you review these nonverbal cues. First, they are commonly used in conjunction with eye, eyebrow, and other gestures. Raising the eyebrows, widening the eyes, and opening the mouth combine to indicate surprise. For more expressiveness, we might add movements of the entire head.

The most common head movements are nodding and shaking the head to say yes and no. Nodding the head can mean more than a simple yes. When Ray talks, and Jeannette listens and nods her head, Jeannette is not only saying "Yes," but she is saying "Yes, I understand you."[20] If Jeannette is now speaking, and Ray is listening and nodding his head, then Ray is not only saying "Yes, I understand you," he is also saying that he agrees. Nodding is so important that it can sometimes be used by you to get a positive reaction from someone who is hesitating to agree with your rationale or your sales tactics.[21] You cannot, however, just stand there bobbing your head up and down and hope for results. The nod must be used selectively and in conjunction with a persuasive argument; otherwise, you will look like one of those little dogs or figurines people put in the back windows of their cars. Receiving a head nod is also important and can help you gauge the agreement, or lack thereof, of individuals and

NetNote

http://totalcommunicator. com/

Current and archived communications articles on a variety of topics.

Source: DILBERT: © Scott Adams/Dist. by United Features Syndicate, Inc.

of groups. Receiving a nod is especially helpful when speaking to large groups where other, more subtle NVC is not visible.

The head can be used to convey other messages besides yes, no, and "I understand." Simply turning your head toward someone indicates the start of communication, whereas turning your head away can convey the end. Turning the head up and to one side can be a sign of haughtiness or indignation. Simply rotating the head to turn an ear to someone indicates an increased interest in hearing what that person has to say. Rotating the head with a slight frown indicates that you do not understand or do not agree with something. Tilting the head indicates inquisitiveness. Tilting the head while your arms are crossed in front of your chest indicates that you are skeptical. Add a tightening of the mouth with one corner slightly raised and you can convey displeasure with what the speaker is saying. Again, different areas can be used in combinations to transmit different messages. As with this last example, the hands and arms are often used in combinations for added or more varied effects.

Gestures Adding hand and arm gestures to the NVC mix greatly increases our ability to communicate because hand gestures are almost as expressive as facial gestures.[22] Making a fist indicates anger or tension. Wringing your hands shows nervousness. Hands clasped together in front of you (with the fingers interlaced) can derail a forceful presentation because this gesture is seen as making an appeal or begging.[23] Holding your fingertips together, kissing them, and immediately moving the hand away from the body in an arc is a sign of praise, especially for well-prepared food.[24] Extending the fingers and then touching the index finger to the thumb is the OK, or "Everything is all right," sign. Holding the hand up at elbow height with the fingers extended and together means "halt" or "stop." Holding the bridge of the nose with the thumb, index, and middle fingers indicates fatigue or a depressed reluctance at having to hear about or

Adding hand and arm gestures to the NVC mix greatly increases our ability to communicate. With a simple hand gesture, this person communicates tension.

Source: Courtesy of PhotoEdit/Phil Martin.

87

handle a situation. An index finger pointed at the temple and rotated indicates that you think someone odd or crazy. Sitting back with the fingers separated and the tips of the fingers of both hands touching demonstrates confidence or contemplation.[25] Standing with your palms on your hips with the thumb towards the back indicates confidence or aggressiveness. Poking a finger or object into someone's chest is also an aggressive signal. Hands clasped together behind the back indicates confidence and says "I am in charge." Wagging the index finger back and forth is the same as saying "You were bad" or "You are wrong"; essentially it's an admonition or a warning. Probably the most common hand gesture involving one person is waving hello or good-bye. Other hand gestures involve the arms or two people.

Many hand gestures made during a conversation involve the arms as well as the hands. Holding both hands out with the palms turned up at a 45-degree angle and shrugging the shoulders is telling someone that you don't know something. For example, Mary asks Don where Kassie is, and Don performs this gesture instead of saying "I don't know." Another hand-arm gesture, one that indicates a closed attitude, is crossing both arms in front of your chest. Raising one hand and arm almost level with one's head indicates that the person is strongly emphasizing a point. Raising both hands and arms over the head indicates victory. Other gestures involving the hands and arms are fairly common and well known, but some people use none. Not knowing what to do with their hands, they often put their hands in their pockets. This is not a positive gesture.[26] Worse yet is to have your hands in your pockets and then jingle the coins or keys in them or to put your hands in your suit coat pockets.

Some hand and arm gestures involve two people. The most common of these is the handshake. A proper handshake in the United States is one in which the web at the base of your thumb is in contact with the web at the base of the other person's thumb. There should be a firm grip, the palms should not be sweaty, and the elbow is pumped about three to six times. A weak, limp handshake is a sign of disinterest.[27] When you offer your hand, your fingers should be extended, and your hand should be held vertically. Offering the hand with the palm up is a sign of submissiveness, whereas offering the hand with the palm down is a sign of dominance.[28] The handshake is only slightly different when it involves women—the elbow is pumped less often or not at all, but the hand is not released too quickly. For women, the hand is held for two to three seconds. If a man holds a woman's hand for much longer, it can be taken as a sign of sexual interest.[29] Although the handshake is virtually required during introductions, it is also one of the few forms of touch that is uniformly accepted in business situations.

Touch Strict rules govern acceptable ways to touch in organizations. Touch in general is seen as a sign of caring and concern.[30] In business and in organizations, touch is generally acceptable when it is to the upper back or to the arm.[31] There are other concerns, though, than where the touch occurs. The length of the touch, the amount of pressure used, any movement while touching, the presence of others, the relationship between the people, and the gender of the person initiating the touch are variables in the subtle distinctions between acceptable and unacceptable.[32]

If a man touches a woman, and the touch lasts for more than a few seconds, the touch sends a sexual message. A woman, however, can touch a man for a slightly longer time.[33] To be safe, a man must also use less pressure than a woman.[34] Touching someone and then moving the hand or rubbing the person sends a sexual message too strong for most business situations.[35] Although a brief, light touch to the forearm is acceptable when others are present, almost any touch between a man and woman can have a different or sexual undertone when the two are alone.[36] Touching in hallways, in groups, in meetings, and in public, if done acceptably, can be an asset. Touching between genders in private is often too risky unless both are clear on the meaning. Longtime, close friends and those leaving on long trips may hug, although this is more common with women than men. Another relationship between people that governs touch is rank. People of higher rank can initiate acceptable touch with those of lower rank. In any of these cases, the safest course is to limit touch to handshakes and to the forearm, and only when others are present, and it is appropriate and cannot be misinterpreted.

Posture   It is important to understand postural NVC in order both to send the appropriate message and to interpret the message being sent by others. In recent union contract negotiations, your author was present for the sole purpose of interpreting the nonverbal communications of both sides. From the beginning, the messages were obvious. The workers desperately wanted a contract settlement, and they wanted it soon. Their nonverbal communications revealed their mind-set just as managers' nonverbal cues revealed that they were in no hurry and that they felt that they were

in control. How was all this revealed before one word was spoken? The answer was in the **posture** of the two sides. Both were seated, but the workers leaned forward with arms on the table, and they all gave the chief management negotiator their undivided attention and eye contact. On the other side, the managers all leaned back in their chairs. They were comfortable, they spread out, and many looked around the room rather that at the workers' team. One even arrived late, read the newspaper during the session, and left early! Were the managers as confident as they seemed, or were their attitudes and postures carefully controlled to give them the upper hand?

Postural NVC includes body orientation, arm and leg positions, and sitting positions. Body orientation refers to standing and seated positions. Arm and leg positions often repeat the nonverbal message; we have already discussed some arm positions. Sitting posture not only reveals much about a person, but there are different positions that are expected of people, and to sit otherwise could send the wrong message.

In face-to-face communication, most managers expect those they manage to face them. Turning away from the manager could be seen as defiance or anger. Turning your back on a boss is a strong statement of anger or disagreement. Body orientation also plays a role with groups (see Figure 3.2). If a group allows enough space for others to join easily, the group is displaying an open attitude. If the circle or formation leaves little or no space between people, the group is indicating that it is closed to others (Figure 3.3). If subordinates are listening to a manager, especially

Posture

a characteristic way of positioning one's body

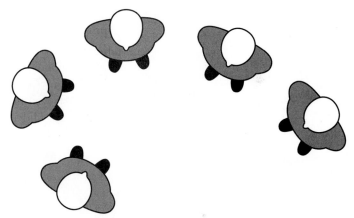

FIGURE 3.2 AN OPEN GROUP The spacing indicates that others may join.

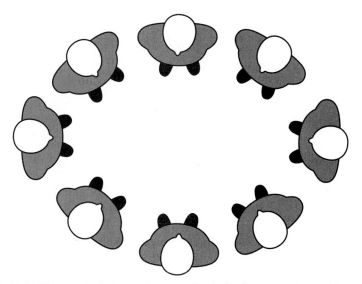

FIGURE 3.3 A CLOSED GROUP The lack of space indicates that others are not free to join.

one who is more than one rank above the subordinates, they often form a "choir" position so that all essentially face the manager (Figure 3.4). If a group is composed of subordinates and managers, the managers closest in rank to the highest ranking person may stand on the same side as the highest ranking person, with those closest in rank standing closest to the high-ranking person's middle position (Figure 3.5).

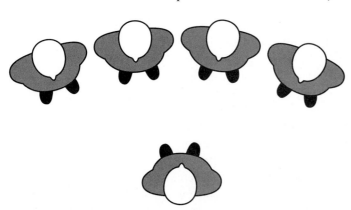

FIGURE 3.4 THE CHOIR ARRANGEMENT The person of higher rank is granted more space, and those of lesser rank face the person of higher rank.

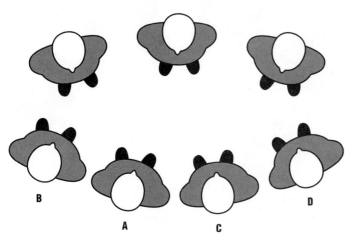

FIGURE 3.5 MODIFIED CHOIR ARRANGEMENT The person with the highest rank (A) is in or near the middle. Those with rank closest to A face the same direction as A. Those with the second highest rank (B and C) stand next to A. Person D stands farther from A because D has a lower rank than B and C.

Arm and leg position can be considered with other postural topics when the arms and legs are in a relatively static position and not moving or gesturing. For instance, when people cross their arms in front of them, they are typically conveying a closed or defensive attitude.[37] Assuming this position as the boss proposes a new idea could be sending a negative "I am not interested" message. A slight variation of this position conveys anger. Standing with your arms crossed in front of you while you tap your index finger on your upper arm indicates anger or impatience.[38] If someone is standing alone and sending this message, it may not be a good idea to approach this person. You also might not want to approach people who are walking with their hands clasped together behind their backs. This posture says that they are in deep thought about something and it may be better not to disturb their contemplation.[39]

Like crossed arms, crossed legs can signal a closed attitude. If someone hangs his or her legs over the arm of a chair, he or she is displaying a very relaxed, casual attitude. When people put their feet up on their desks, they may also be sending a message that they are relaxed or comfortable with the situation. For the most part, legs convey messages when people are sitting. General sitting posture and sitting location also send messages.

General sitting posture often contains a message about the type of authority relationship that exists between two people. If a subordinate accepts or does not dispute the authority of a manager, then an unchallenged authority relationship exists between the two. If the subordinate does not accept or acknowledge the authority of the manager, if the subordinate wants to take the manager's job, or if the subordinate thinks that he or she should be the manager, then the subordinate is challenging the authority relationship of the manager. Sometimes it is not wise to openly confront the manager. Still, the challenge may be revealed in the nonverbal communication of the subordinate. One of the ways the challenge (or lack of challenge) is shown is through general sitting posture.

If a subordinate is not challenging the authority of the manager, then sitting in a particular way can convey this message. A person conveys an unchallenged authority relationship by sitting upright, with his or her back slightly in front of (or away from) the chair back. The person's body is slightly tense, feet together and flat on the floor, and the person gives more eye contact than he or she receives. Deviating from this posture may indicate a challenge to the authority of the manager or that the manager and individual are on such friendly terms that the authority relationship does not need to be reinforced with nonverbal communication. For example, sitting with a slight slouch, the legs crossed, and one arm over the back of the chair sends a challenging nonverbal message to the manager. Sitting posture may show a challenge, or lack of challenge, as does the selection people make in where to sit.

Sitting location combines with a person's general sitting postures to send a message. Figure 3.6 is a diagram of a manager's office. Position A identifies the manager's chair. If you are called into this office and are not challenging the manager's authority, then you will be expected to sit in either chair B or D. You would also sit in the unchallenging body position described previously. Sitting in chair B or D in a relaxed posture shows a slight challenge to the manager's authority position, or it shows that you are so comfortable and on such good terms with the manager that the relationship does not require the same formality as, say, a new employee would be expected to show. Sitting in location C, the couch, is a stronger challenge to the manager's authority. You are deliberately avoiding the expected position, and you leave the manager little choice in his or her sitting location. It would be awkward for the manager to sit in position A and talk over chair B. It is also unlikely that the manager would pull chair B or D over to sit next to you on the couch. Coming to you would be a conciliatory move on the part of the manager. So what is the manager to do? In this situation, most managers will choose to occupy the higher ground—they will stand. In this way, you are forced to look up at the manager, which is a submissive posture. A few might counter your challenge by invading your territory—by sitting next to you on the couch. Still others might immedi-

ately put an end to your rebellion by going to the desk (position A), delaying the start of the discussion, and then ordering you to sit in chair B or D. Managers wishing to deemphasize the authority relationship will meet with people at the round table (position E).

Besides sitting posture and location, there are four other basic ways to challenge a manager with posture. The next highest-level challenge involves standing instead of sitting. To stand or to refuse the invitation to sit conveys anger. The next three combine posture with an invasion of the manager's territory. To stand and lean forward

The man on the left demonstrates the proper subordinate sitting position in an unchallenged authority relationship—upright, back slightly forward from the chair back, slightly tense, attentive.

Source: Courtesy of Merrill Education/Scott Cunningham.

The man on the left is at a meeting with his new manager. He had wanted the management position, but the woman on the right was hired from the outside instead. He hasn't really accepted her as his manager, and on arriving at her office first, he chooses to sit at the head of the table rather than in a chair along the side. He not only denies her the head of the table, but he is not prepared to take notes and is leaning back in his chair in a more relaxed position. What message is he sending to his new manager?

Source: Courtesy of Image State.

with both hands on the manager's desk is the next highest nonverbal challenge. Standing forces the manager to look up at you, or it forces the manager to stand to be on equal ground. Leaning your hands on the manager's desk encroaches on the manager's space or territory. The next highest nonverbal challenge would be to sit on the corner of the manager's desk (although this might be allowed in a long-term and friendly relationship with the manager). The ultimate nonverbal challenge would be to sit in the manager's chair. This is highly challenging, even threatening, and shouldn't be used even as a joke.

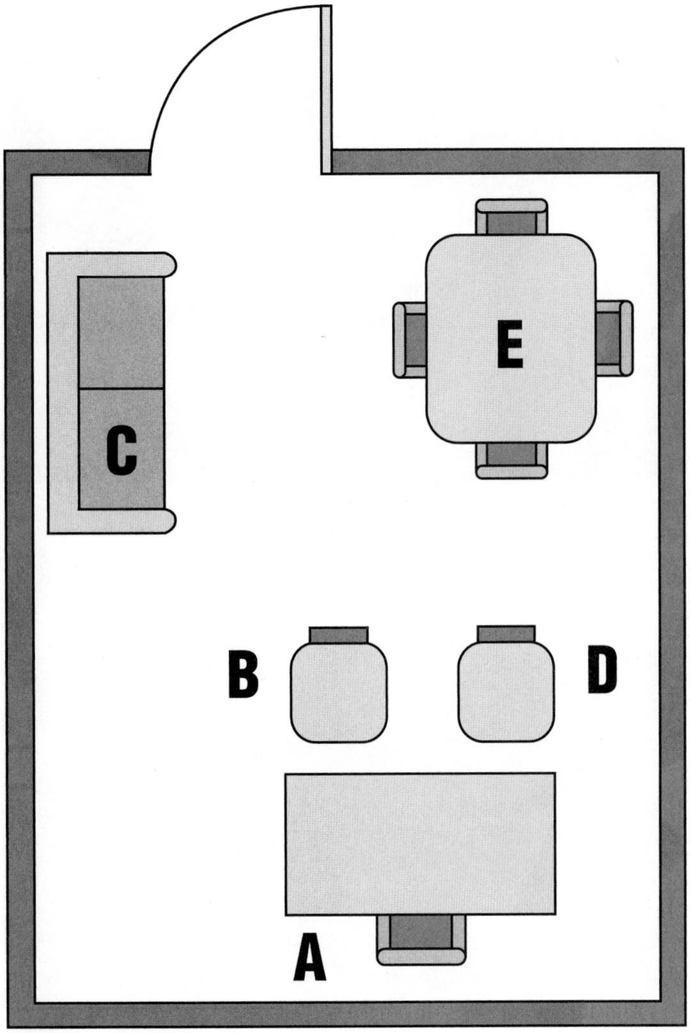

The way space and height are used in office situations can tell us something about the patterns of authority among the various employees. If you observe two department managers, one with office space twice as large as the other, you might safely assume something about their relative authority in the organization. Executive suites are seldom found in the basements of office buildings. In American culture, higher is assumed to be better than lower. Have you ever heard of anyone aspiring to descend the ladder of success?

Just as subordinates may send messages with posture and seating arrangements, so can managers. There have been some strange cases of managers sending nonverbal messages with posture. Some managers make sure that the office chairs are lower than their own chairs; the effect is to force everyone who sits to look up at the manager. Another tactic, albeit a rare one, is for a manager to remove all chairs except his or her own, thus forcing everyone else to stand uncomfortably and virtually ensuring a short stay. The message here is that the manager is far superior and that visitors are not worthy of a chair.

FIGURE 3.6 MANAGER'S OFFICE Given that position A is the manager's desk, sitting in chair B or D will not be construed as a challenge to authority. Location C, the couch, presents a mild challenge because coming to you after you have deliberately avoided the expected position would be a conciliatory move on the manager's part. Managers wishing to deemphasize the authority relationship will meet with associates at the round table (position E).

Territory The way you were raised as a child, how well you know someone, and people's respective ranks all affect the distance you keep between others and yourself (Table 3.3).[40] Americans and others keep a large amount of **territory** between themselves and strangers—typically three and half to four feet. Casual friends or acquaintances can comfortably come to within two to three and half feet of us. Personal friends are kept about one half to two feet away. Intimate friends are allowed within whispering distance, which is less than half a foot.[41] These distances can be observed in public places, such as in a doctor's waiting room. Notice that if possible, people will leave an empty seat between themselves and other patients. Some may even choose to stand if the only open seat is between two strangers. When the comfortable distance is violated, as in a crowded

Territory
the amount of space one commands or the amount of open space around the body that one is comfortable with

TABLE 3.3 TYPICAL COMFORTABLE DISTANCES BETWEEN PEOPLE

Familiarity	Territory (distance from you)
Intimate (spouse, significant other)	6 inches or less
Personal friend (best friend, close friend)	6 to 24 inches
Acquaintance (casual friend, coworker)	24 to 42 inches
Stranger	42 to 48 inches

elevator, people feel uncomfortable. They typically go silent and stare at the floor indicator as if it might skip a few floors that day.

Territoriality also comes into play during meetings at which the location of attendees around the table confers status. The head of the table is typically where the person with the highest rank or status sits.[42] The next highest status individuals sit next to the person with the highest status. Sitting in the middle of a long side of a table will deemphasize a high-ranking individual's power and status. The location of the table itself also conveys status in that the advantage goes to the person owning the table. Attending a meeting at your own company gives you home-court advantage. Within a company, calling someone to your office is an indication of power, and it gives you the advantage. For one thing, you decide whether to answer the phone and allow the conversation to be interrupted. There are times, however, when the better message would be to go to someone else's office or work area. Careful attention is required to avoid sending the wrong message. If it is more convenient to meet in your office, but you wish to deemphasize your power, then choose a lower-status seating arrangement, for example, sit with the others at a round table instead of alone behind your desk.

Managers who do sit behind their desks for meetings often signal their authority by expanding their territory.[43] Expansion of territory includes leaning back in a

Here, the subordinate challenges the manager's authority by leaning on his desk. The manager removes his glasses to essentially say, "I don't see your point," and leans forward to try to reclaim his territory.

Source: Courtesy of Image State.

These men challenge their manager by not sitting down. She responds to the challenge by engaging in delaying tactics—examining her appointment book and making a phone call, forcing them to wait for her.
Source: Courtesy of Photolibrary.com/Graham Monro.

chair with or without extending the legs, putting one's feet up on the desk, or spreading papers and other belongings to claim the desk or table space around one-self. When people expand territory, they convey that they are of higher status or that they feel the authority relationship is unchallenged.

Walking   When we walk, speed, body position, and body orientation all convey nonverbal messages. A brisk pace sends a message of confidence and a sense of purpose.[44] A slower walk sends a message of casualness or of not being very busy. Knowing this, some people have perfected a way of walking so that it appears that they are off to an urgent meeting or are on an important errand when really they are on their way to achieve little. You shouldn't confuse movement with accomplishment. In addition to the speed at which we walk, we also send messages with our bodies.

Body position and orientation combine to send nonverbal messages concerning power and status. A body position with the arms swinging freely indicates a determination to achieve goals.[45] Walking with the hands on the hips is a sign of extreme urgency and a determination to reach one's destination as soon as possible. Walking with the arms crossed in front of one's chest also shows determination and sometimes anger (or maybe the air conditioning is on too high). Walking with the arms clasped behind the back, as mentioned before, conveys thoughtfulness. These walking body positions mainly refer to people walking alone, although they also apply to those walking with others.

Body orientation involves the messages sent through the space between two or more walkers and the direction each one faces. For example, two people of equal status will walk side by side. Two people of unequal status may also walk side by side. When one person walks behind another, the person in back is sending a message that

"Choir" arrangement of professionals. Those of lower rank face the person of higher rank in a semicircle. The person of higher rank is granted more space by the people of lower rank.

Source: Courtesy of Image State.

he or she is of lower status or rank than the person in front. Also, only a person of lower status would walk backward to keep the attention of and maintain eye contact with another person. On the other hand, only a person of higher status would continue to walk forward while someone was trying to talk to him or her.[46]

Status Symbols   Status symbols tend to be visible, nonverbal indicators of an individual's rank in an organization. Items that might appear trivial to an outsider, such as a telephone or wastebasket within easy reach, can have an important influence on the morale of employees. Some executives would prefer a rug on their office floors or a cellular phone in their cars to a pay raise. Any items that people perceive as significant can serve as symbols of status among organizational members. What are some of your favorite status symbols?

Most people understand the various nonverbal messages that are sent, but up to 10 percent do not.[47] The failure to send or interpret nonverbal communication

---

SPOT CHECK

1. The actual words—the verbal message—are the smallest portion of your total message. T F
2. Written communication, such as memos and e-mails, do the best at delivering your total message. T F
3. Nonverbal communication cannot replace verbal communication. T F
4. The eyes may be the single most important area for nonverbal communication. T F
5. Challenging authority cannot be accomplished with nonverbal communication. T F

can adversely affect relations and careers. Poor NVC skills can create anxiety and confusion—anxiety on the part of the person with poor NVC skills and confusion for the people trying to communicate with this person.[48] Fortunately, learning to interpret nonverbal communication messages can correct and reverse the problems poor NVC skills create.

OTHER COMMUNICATION SYMBOLS

INACTIVITY SILENTLY SAYS A LOT

A supervisor is habitually cordial toward her employees each morning as she arrives on the job. She seldom forgets to say hello to anyone. However, one morning she wakes with pressing problems on her mind, problems that demand her immediate thought and attention. As she passes a long-time coworker on that particular morning, her mind might be millions of light-years away, and she hardly notices him.

Only a person of higher status would walk forward while someone was trying to engage him or her in conversation; only a person of lesser authority would walk backward to keep someone's attention.

Source: Courtesy of PhotoEdit/Myrleen Ferguson Cate.

Has she attempted to communicate anything to the coworker? No, not consciously, yet she might have communicated something. The coworker might start wondering, "What did I do? Why didn't she say good morning to me today?" Here, *not* doing something inadvertently sent an unintended message.

Another form of inactivity includes the failure to compliment individuals on the quality of their work. Many employees think that their superiors comment on their performance only when they've done something wrong. You will find that one way to favorably influence fellow employees or subordinates in your organization is to recognize and acknowledge good work when you see it. If you only communicate with the workers when they've done something wrong, they'll soon feel that they're not appreciated in your organization. As V. Wilcox wryly stated, "A pat on the back is only a few vertebrae from a kick in the pants, but is miles ahead in results."

EVEN YOUR VOICE HAS FEELINGS

A person's voice is an important element of communication. Much of what your listeners interpret comes from the sound of your voice. In fact, that's the main thing your listener interprets when you use the telephone. The voice is also a critical part of any face-to-face communication.

Tone, volume, pitch, rate, and inflection all significantly influence how you come across to others. These elements tend to reveal whether or not you're sincerely interested in those with whom you carry on conversations.

We usually aren't very aware of the way our own voice sounds to others. You could gain some personal insights by recording your voice on a tape recorder, preferably by role-playing with another person. A videocassette recorder would be even better because it combines the elements of sound and sight. Such activity could aid you in determining what vocal changes you need to make.

For example, as you listen to a playback of your own voice, does it seem too loud or overpowering? Or is it too soft and difficult to understand? Do you tend to speak in a dull monotone? Do you use adequate inflection and enthusiasm when talking? Is your rate of speech either too fast or too slow? Try to avoid coming across as a fast-talker, the type who tends to be distrusted by his or her audience. Too slow a rate of speech, on the other hand, tends to make holding the listener's attention more difficult. By understanding the strengths and weaknesses in your vocal patterns and by regularly practicing better techniques, you should be able to improve your vocal skills substantially.

THE USE OF TIME

Your attitude toward time and the way you use it may also communicate messages to others. Concerned organizational members seldom arrive late for appointments. Those who do arrive late to work, meetings, or appointments often create a bad impression on those who must wait for them. People who expect you to arrive at a specific time will sometimes postpone other projects in anticipation of your arrival. Any time spent waiting for you is wasted time for them—they could have been doing other things. To avoid this problem, plan to arrive at least 10 minutes before you're scheduled to arrive. If you are traveling by automobile, allow for possible delays, such as those caused by traffic congestion. Struggling through highway traffic when you're late for an appointment can create additional tension and frustration that can do little but detract from your objectives. Those who try to allow precisely the amount of time needed to get to appointments tend to be late because they frequently don't allow for those omnipresent surprise factors.

TYPES OF COMMUNICATION

Have you ever been around newborn babies? They're highly skilled communicators of a sort. At a typical 2:00 A.M. feeding time, infants leave no doubt in their parents' minds as to what the message is: "I'm starved! I want my milk! And I want it now!!" This is another example of one-way communication, a type of communication that is not recommended as effective organizational behavior.

Many types of communication affect you as an organizational member.

A GLOBAL GLANCE

NVC Around the World

Frequently one will hear the statement, "That person has a handshake like a dead fish." A handshake is one of the nonverbal cues (NVCs) we use to communicate. If you travel to different parts of the world, however, you'll quickly discover that not all the world's citizens shake hands like Americans. Nor do all Americans shake hands identically. Remember that some people will make judgments based on your handshake, which to them may communicate something significant.

In many Latin cultures, handshakes are quite soft and gentle, without the vigorous up and down movements common in the United States and Germany. In northern European countries such as Germany, you might suspect that you're in a contest of brute strength with a native handshaker who seems to be testing his or her grip on your hand. In France, if your right hand or arm is occupied holding packages, you may shake hands with your left hand without being regarded as impolite. Some people, while reclining on a Riviera beach, even use their feet!

Various cultural groups in the United States and abroad have different norms regarding touching. For example, some American businesspeople are frequently shocked when they observe the bear-hugging that goes on between businesspeople in Mediterranean cultures. To a Greek businessperson, the lack of a warm hug by an American counterpart could be regarded as a cold or unfriendly gesture.

Formal Communication
the official communication that travels through the structured (formal) organization

Informal Communication

rumors, statements, or reports whose truth cannot be verified by any known authority and which may or may not pertain to the functioning of the organization

Understanding them should enable you to put them to more effective use. The forms of communication that we'll now examine are:

- formal and informal communication
- upward, downward, and horizontal communication

FORMAL AND INFORMAL COMMUNICATION

One way of looking at communication is to consider both its formal and its informal sides. **Formal communication** is the official communication that travels through the structured (formal) organizational network (see Figure 3.7). An example of formal communication would be requesting the purchase of some special equipment through your boss, who would then seek official approval from her or his boss.

Informal communication, on the other hand, is the real workhorse of message networks, one that can either help or hinder an organization's efforts to achieve

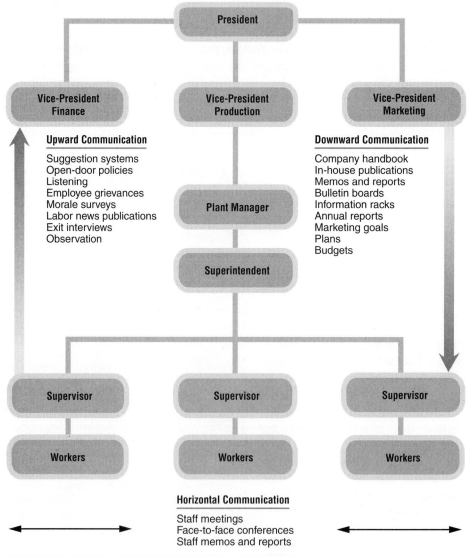

FIGURE 3.7 FORMAL CHANNELS OF COMMUNICATION

its goals. Informal communication travels through a channel often referred to as the grapevine, a network that is usually much quicker than official channels. Wherever there are people, the grapevine is right there with them. The grapevine is the primary means for transmitting rumors, statements, or reports whose truth cannot be verified by any known authority. More simply, rumors are statements that are generally, but not always, incorrect. We'll look at informal communication and the grapevine in more depth in Chapter 4 in relationship to informal groups.

COMMUNICATIONS COME FROM MANY DIRECTIONS

As a member of any organization's work, social, or family group, you must function in a world of symbols. If you were to become a supervisor, you would likely be continually bombarded with questions and situations from all sides. You would receive directives from your bosses, memos from other department heads, and requests and complaints from those you supervise. The nature of the communication coming toward you and radiating outward from you may be upward, downward, or horizontal.

Upward Communication   Let's continue with the example of you as a supervisor. You've probably found that **upward communication** has been a continual problem. This type of communication flows up the organizational structure. Far too many managers think that they know precisely how their subordinates feel about a particular situation. "My people love working here," some bosses may boast. Then, to their complete surprise, someone quits. "I can't understand it," a perplexed manager mutters. "They all seemed so happy here. I can't understand what went wrong."

As you can see in Figure 3.7, some of the principal formal types of upward communication in organizations include suggestion systems, open-door policies, listening, employee grievances, morale surveys, labor news publications, exit interviews, and observation.

Downward Communication   Communication that conveys messages from higher to lower levels of an organization is called **downward communication**; it, too, is difficult at times. Employees typically receive such a tremendous amount of downward communication that they often engage in selective reception, that is, they hear or see the information they are set to hear or see and tune out much of the rest. Anyone who has regularly attempted to convey information to others recognizes how difficult the process is. All groups seem to include a certain number of individuals who fail to get the word. Do you remember our earlier example of how Susan was set to hear the word *pregnant* rather than *fragrant?*

Referring once again to Figure 3.7, you can see that some of the more prevalent forms of downward communication include company handbooks, in-house publications, memos and reports, bulletin boards, information racks, annual reports, marketing goals, plans, and budgets.

The Filter Factor   Unfortunately, one of the most prevalent problems in organizations is the **filtering** of communication. Filtering is the straining out of ingredients essential to understanding as communications rise up to management levels or travel from management down the organizational hierarchy to workers. We'll examine various methods for minimizing some of those difficulties in later sections of

**Upward
Communication**
communication from
workers to managers

**Downward
Communication**
communication from
managers to workers or
from upper management
to middle or lower
management

Filtering
the removal of parts of a
message

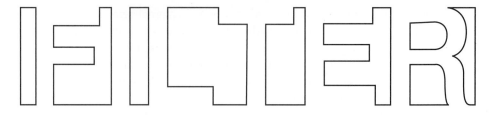

FIGURE 3.8 AN EXAMPLE OF FILTERING Can you read the word?

this chapter. In the meantime, take a look at Figure 3.8 for a graphic example of how our perception tends to filter out certain aspects of communication.

Were you able to read the word in Figure 3.8? If not, go back and fill in the open spaces to prevent the background from confusing your interpretation of the symbol.

Horizontal Communication

communications moving laterally or at the same level in the organization

Horizontal Communication　Often the avenue with the most political content, **horizontal communication** permits managers on the same level to coordinate their activities more effectively. Organizations in which supervisors have little or no opportunity to communicate with other supervisors on the same level often experience such problems as duplicated efforts, ineffective use of resources, lack of coordination, and even destructive interdepartmental rivalry. The political ambitions of peers may be transmitted through horizontal communications. Politics is also often evidenced in the withholding of information from peers, especially as an attempt to control or maintain power.

On the other hand, considerable time and effort can be saved by horizontal communication because teamwork between departments can exist without their members having to refer every matter through a higher level of management. But beware! Horizontal communication, too, can create problems, especially if a bypassed boss feels that his or her decision-making power (authority) has been reduced. It's a good idea to inform your boss of any communication that might affect him or her. If you don't, you could place that person in an uninformed and embarrassing position.

MALE–FEMALE COMMUNICATION DIFFERENCES

In front of you there is a door, large and heavy. Beyond the door is a vast darkness penetrated only occasionally by the faintest light. We are about to open this door ever so slightly. The darkness beyond is the realm of gender differences. Why all the drama? To illustrate that what we explore here is just an introduction into a discipline to which many good and dedicated researchers have devoted their life's work, yet which we have only started to understand. Still, justice could not be done to this book or chapter without mentioning the differences between male and female communications, even if the coverage is not exhaustive.

First, three extremely important comments. One, there are differences in communication styles between the genders.[49] The genders have communication styles in common also, but the differences are worth noting in the interest of creating better understanding. Two, and even more important, men are not better than women at communicating, and women are not better than men at communicating. They are different, and that's it; not better, just different. There may be a tendency for you to believe that your gender, whichever it is, communicates better because that is the communication style you are used to. It is not. Three, gender is only one of numerous ways communication is influenced.[50] The genders have tendencies, but there are many exceptions due to the infinite diversity of humans. Therefore, we will not say that all men and all women communicate in these ways. However, even though we are all individuals, researchers have found tendencies often enough to make their study of them highly valuable. The main problem with both genders is that too often they don't understand how the other gender tends to communicate.

MEN

Men live in a hierarchical world of problem solvers.[51] From the time they are little boys, they play king-of-the-mountain. Encounters are evaluated to determine who is up a status point and who is down a status point. Men do not like being down a point to others.[52] Things that make men think they are down a point include giving them advice when they haven't asked for it, questioning their abilities or competence, and giving them orders.

Giving a man advice when he hasn't asked for it is the same as telling him he is not capable of handling a situation.[53] The advice is taken as criticism by the man and is tantamount to saying that he needs to take immediate corrective action.[54] Essentially, he is being told that he is inferior, and now he is down a status point. He is not happy about this. Questioning a man's ability is like saying, "You can't do this, and I am superior because I can." Give a man an order, and he is definitely down a status point if he obeys. Men react this way mainly because they live in a hierarchical world (still playing king-of-the-mountain) and because men gauge their success according to the results they achieve.[55] Question or take away their achievements, and they consider themselves failures. Given the man's world just described, how is it possible that men are able to work and survive in organizations? Orders and advice are given every day. Why isn't the workplace one huge status and hierarchy battlefield? How can men possibly work together to accomplish anything?

The answer to these questions lies in the way men work together, a way that may seem strange to women. We have said that men constantly assess whether they are up or down a status point in relation to others, and they don't like being down a point. One result is that they jockey for status by challenging one another.[56] In challenging one another, they make statements that are forceful, definite, and unequivocal. A man assesses his status and the correctness of his statements by gauging the feedback he receives. If no one challenges him, then he assumes that he is right and that he has status. He is at the top of the hierarchy. Once the hierarchy is established, the high-status man is expected to give orders and direction to lower-status men. The key to men working together, then, is not the positioning for status; it is that once status is established, the high-status and low-status men accept it. Although men do not like being down in status, once everyone's position is known, they can live with it. If something disrupts the hierarchy, however, the challenge to be top dog may start all over again.

Although status and hierarchy are major concerns for men, other elements of male communication should be examined. Men typically do not talk about a problem unless they need help or advice.[57] Men first contemplate problems alone and ask for input only when they cannot solve the problems themselves.[58] When men encounter someone else's problem, they present a solution because they feel one of their main roles is that of a problem solver, because they measure success by their accomplishments, and because this puts them up a status point. However, they genuinely feel that they are helping, while women often feel they suffer from M.A.D. ("male answer disease").

NetNote

http://www.
psychologytoday
.com/articles/
pto-20040308-000001.html

http://www.
psychologytoday
.com/articles/
pto-20040202-000002.html

Receiving feedback.

When men don't have an answer, or when they are facing increased stress, they become more introverted.[59] When stressed or facing a difficult problem, men can become intensely focused. They withdraw into themselves until the problem is solved or until the stress is reduced. This can be difficult for women to handle because they want to offer help and talk about the problem to the same extent that men do not wish to talk. Men also need to feel needed in order to be motivated.[60] Men tend to give feedback only when things go poorly; when things go well, men tend to say nothing.[61] Also, men take words literally.[62]

The male tendency to take comments literally can be one of the more confusing points in male–female communications. For example, during a meeting, lunchtime approaches, and the following conversation occurs: Maryann, who is hungry, says to Scott, "Do you want something to eat?"

Scott, who is not hungry, takes this literally as a simple dichotomous question. He says, "No," because he wants to keep on working. Is he being insensitive? Now look at the same conversation with just men at the meeting.

David: I'm getting hungry. Let's break for lunch at the Grazing Cow.
Allen: No way am I eatin' rabbit food. We're going to Pizza Mutt.
Scott: Real men don't eat lunch. Let's get back to work.
David, to Scott: No wonder you don't want to eat, with that spare tire.
Scott, to David: You're just jealous because your wife can't cook. Now let's work.
Allen: All right, I'll order in pizza from Lil' Cheeser's, a salad for David, and nothing for you, and we all keep working.

Here, men battle for hierarchical advantage, challenge each other, and solve the problem. When Maryann asked Scott if he wanted something to eat, he answered the literal question. To Maryann, and to many other women, this was the wrong answer. If she had protested that she was hungry and wanted food, Scott would have said that wasn't the question he was asked. To Scott, Maryann should have said, "Can we break now? I want something to eat." Now, Maryann might have thought that is what she said, but Scott would say, "No, you asked if I wanted something to eat, and I didn't. If you said that you wanted to eat, heck, I would have gotten it for you." When women ask something like this, they are typically looking for a conversation. They believe they are taking the other person's feeling into account and that the other person should do the same. If the other person is a woman, then they will typically discuss lunch. If the other person is a man, then he will typically take things literally. This is just one example of how male communication differs from female communication.

NetNote

http://www.princetoninfo.
com/200105/10523s01.html

Gender communication
differences.

WOMEN

We have taken a brief tour of the male communication world, so the next question is what the female communication world is like. Women, unlike men, are not typically concerned with group hierarchies with other women. Women tend to have one close friend or confidant.[63] Women tend to comfort and console one another in their conversations.[64] It is often more important to a woman to share her feelings with another person than it is to achieve a goal with that person.[65] Women relate similar experiences to show support and understanding as opposed to trying to solve a problem as men would.[66] In fact, offering a solution to a woman's concern can be seen as negating or dismissing her feeling.[67]

SPOT CHECK

6. Arriving late to work and meetings will create a good impression on those who have to wait for you; they will think you are very busy. T F
7. Upward communication is relatively easy to achieve. T F
8. Men live in a hierarchical world of problem solvers. T F
9. When men don't have an answer to a problem they tend to feel overwhelmed. T F
10. In high-stress situations, women become more introverted. T F

Women even use different body positioning than men do. When two women converse, they tend to face each other while sharing feelings and experiences. Men tend not to look at each other, sitting as they would at a bar while having a beer. When women converse, they are looking for a sustaining, cultivating relationship.[68] Women want empathy, not solutions.[69] Rather than give orders, women soften and qualify what they say.[70] Women use generalities and metaphors rather than bluntness as a means of softening things and making them less harsh sounding.[71] Women often make suggestions, rather than giving directions.[72] This is not necessarily an advantage in a workplace with men because it is sometimes seen as a sign of weakness or indecision and is not the strong challenge that men look for.[73] On the other hand, women tend to give feedback when things are going well and not just when things are going poorly.[74]

In high-stress situations, women tend to feel overwhelmed.[75] In response to this feeling, they seek out others so that they can emotionally unburden themselves.[76] When frustrated, women tend to use closed words like *all, everything*, and *never* to express how they feel.[77] They do not mean for others to take them literally at these times. Women are typically motivated when they are cared for and respected.[78] Also, women often think out loud rather than turning inward as men do.[79]

MEN AND WOMEN

What are we all to do in light of these differences? The first item on everyone's agenda should be to work toward understanding the other gender's communication style. Read more, learn more, and observe more. For example, some believe that women talk more than men do, whereas studies show there is no difference.[80] On the other hand, watch for perceptions that are true but that are not recommended approaches, such as a male leader's display of anger being seen as effective (angry female leaders, however, are seen as less credible).[81] Second, work to avoid viewing the other gender's style through your own gender's style. Men need to understand that women soften criticism. Women need to understand that men seek to solve problems. Third, watch what you say to others and what their reactions are. Are they receiving the message that you are sending? Fourth, watch what others say to you and notice your reactions to what is said. Are you receiving the message they are sending? Other, more specific suggestions are given in Tables 3.4 and 3.5, but there are two final, general challenges. The challenge for men is to understand women when they talk.[82] The challenge for women is to understand men when they don't talk.[83]

TABLE 3.4 SENDING MESSAGES TO MEN

Suggestions for Talking to Men	Rationale
Ask men, do not order them, to do things.	Ordering men to do things puts them down one status point, but if you ask them, then they are doing you a favor and they are up one status point.
Challenge men when they make declarations, when necessary.	Men establish who is correct according to the challenges they receive.
Don't give men free (unsolicited) advice.	Men solve problems alone. If they need help or advice they will ask.
Ask what you really want to know.	Men take things literally, so don't hint at things.
Don't use closed words.	Men take things literally, and it sounds as if they are being blamed. This only makes them defensive.
Give them the bottom line.	Men see the overall meaning in communications and don't bother with the little details, so don't give them unnecessary ones.
Give praise when warranted.	Men don't often give praise, but they like to receive it.
Don't send men messages when they are working on problems or are stressed.	Men's success is measured by what they achieve, and they achieve things on their own.

TABLE 3.5 SENDING MESSAGES TO WOMEN

Suggestions for Talking to Women	Rationale
Listen.	Women often need simply to share their feelings.
Soften orders and directions; make suggestions.	Women communicate less directly and they often generalize.
Don't give only answers and solutions.	Giving an answer where none was sought negates a woman's feelings; women often want to be nurtured; women often think out loud.
Show empathy and discuss experiences you have had that are similar to hers.	Women view this as support, and they need support rather than answers. A woman's sense of self is largely derived from the quality of her relationships.
Treat her as a respected equal. Give details along with the summary.	Women are motivated when they feel respected. Women are good at seeing details; they look for and expect them.
Look beyond a woman's literal words to find out what she really wants to communicate.	Women speak in generalities and metaphors; they frequently soften their messages.

SUMMARY

Communication, a two-way process imparting information and understanding between individuals, requires a sender, a receiver, and an understood message to be effective. Words facilitate communication but do not themselves have meaning. They are like containers; their meaning is in the user. When in doubt about the meaning of a word, ask the user what he or she means.

A large part of what we communicate is done through nonverbal communication. Although the meaning of many gestures is learned through experience, it is important for organizational communication to be clear. You do not want to send the wrong message unintentionally. To prevent sending the wrong message, it is important to know the meaning of various gestures and to know what NVC people are expecting given the situation.

Men tend to communicate in a certain way, women tend to communicate in a certain way, and these two ways are often different. Although these tendencies do not apply to all men and women, they occur frequently enough in the population to make learning them valuable. Because you are one or the other, and because both are present in the workplace, it is imperative to study and understand the communications of the other gender. It must be remembered that the genders are simply different; one is no better or worse than the other.

Communication failures are reduced when we assume neither that everyone else knows what we are talking about nor that we know what others are talking about without asking them questions to make certain. The meanings of words are not always clear because words often have many meanings, and both new meanings and newly derived words can arise. Meaning can also vary according to region and as a result of double-speak and tone of voice.

Communication in organizations may be classified as upward, downward, and horizontal; formal and informal; and verbal and nonverbal (including body language) forms of communication.

CHECKING FOR UNDERSTANDING

1. List the five message channels and the advantages and disadvantages of each.

2. How would you define communication?

3. What ingredients are necessary for effective communication to take place?

4. Why is communication said to be a two-way process?

5. What are the three components of a message and what contribution does each make to the total message?

6. List and describe the six functions of nonverbal communications.

7. Describe, give examples of, and explain the role of the eight types of nonverbal symbols.

8. What is the difference between formal and informal communication?

9. Define upward, downward, and horizontal communication.

10. What are the differences between male and female communication?

SELF-ASSESSMENT

Think about how you communicate in your organization (with peers, those of higher rank, and those of lower rank). Giving yourself an honest appraisal, select one phrase from column A or B from each numbered pair that best describes how you prefer to communicate assuming all methods of communication are available.

Give yourself 1 point for every odd-numbered pair where you selected a phrase from column A. Give yourself 1 point for every even-numbered pair where you selected a phrase from column B. Total your score.

	Column A	Column B
1.	Face-to-face communication	Phone communication
2.	Communicate the same to everyone	Adjust your communications for cultural differences
3.	Face-to-face communication	Written communication
4.	Arrive late to see someone	Arrive early or on time to see someone
5.	Face-to-face communication	Third-party communication
6.	Make people wait when they come to see you	See people as soon as they arrive
7.	Nonverbal communication	Tone
8.	Written communication	Phone communication
9.	Written communication	Third-party communication
10.	Jargon	Plain language
11.	Nonverbal communication	Verbal communication
12.	Listen while working	Stop work to listen
13.	Tone	Verbal communication
14.	Third-party communication	Phone communication
15.	Paraphrasing	Assuming a message is understood
16.	Speak while working	Stop work to speak
17.	Thinking before speaking	Replying instantly
18.	Walk away while others are still talking to you	Walk away only when conversation is over
19.	Supply upward communication to those of higher rank	Talk about the weather to those of higher rank
20.	Communicate the same to everyone	Adjust your communications for gender differences

Score of:

19–20—excellent communication skills

16–18—generally good communication skills

11–15—adequate communication skills with a few areas that could be improved

6–10—some concern for your communication skills with significant room for improvement

1–5—improvement needed in most areas of communication

SKILL BUILD 3

Mariquita stood waiting patiently outside Vice President Basant Kahn's office while he carried on a rather lengthy phone conversation about his golf game last Sunday. Mariquita had never before been called to Basant's office. Mariquita's boss was Drew Alliana. Drew reported to Zachary Taylor Johnson and then Zach reported to Basant, and Mariquita felt talking to Basant was way, way above her pay grade. Finally, Basant called Mariquita in.

Skill Question 1. What communication symbol is present in the passage above?

Skill Question 2. What is the message being sent to Mariquita?

As Mariquita walked in, Basant went around his desk to his chair and sat down.

"No need to sit, I only have two quick questions," Basant said as he sat down. While Mariquita stood in front of his desk, Basant leaned back in his chair and put his feet up on his desk.

Skill Question 3. There are two different types of nonverbal symbols represented in the passage above. Which one involves Mariquita, what is the symbol, and what part of the passage represents it?

Skill Question 4. Which one involves Basant, what is the symbol, and what part of the passage represents it?

Skill Question 5. What message does Basant's nonverbal symbolism send to Mariquita about their relationship?

"First," Basant started, "did you write the Hamilton report?"

"Yes, sir," Mariquita replied.

"How many pages was it when you sent it to Drew?"

"Sixty-three," Mariquita said.

"Okay, that'll be all," Basant said. Mariquita hesitated just a second and then turned and left.

"Zach, how are you?" Basant said as Zachary Taylor Johnson returned to his office. Zach was surprised to find Basant waiting for him, as Basant usually called people to come see him. Basant extended his hand to Zach with his palm facing slightly down, Zach took the hand, and as he shook Basant's hand he tried to turn their hands vertical but Basant pressed back, not allowing it.

Skill Question 6. What nonverbal symbol is represented in the above paragraph?

Skill Question 7. What message is being sent by whom and to whom?

"What can I do for you?" Zach asked after the handshake.

"I'm concerned with the Hamilton report and others like it," Basant started. "From what I understand that started out at about 60 pages. It then went to Drew Alliana, who turned that 60 pages into about 10 and gave it to you. You gave me one page. Now, I don't know what that is called, but I don't think it's good. I'm going to need more pages on all reports from now on! I want you to see to it!"

Skill Question 8. Basant seems to need your help identifying the problem expressed in the above paragraph. Find the term for this problem, and define the term in your own words.

After Basant left, Zach went to the phone and called Drew.

"Drew, it's Zach. Listen, Basant was just in my office and wants all reports to have more pages."

"What does that mean?" Drew asked.

"Well, he said something about a 60-page report that you turned into 10 for me and I turned into a one-page summary for him. He said he wants more pages on reports from now on," Zach said.

"I'm a little confused, boss," Drew said, "Are you sure he didn't mean for just you to give him more than one page? Or, maybe for me to give you more pages and *then* you give him more pages?"

"That's not what he said," Zach replied. "He said he is going to need more pages on reports."

"Well, how many pages are you going to give him from the reports?" Drew asked.

"One! Don't you see? He said more pages on the reports, not the summaries," Zach said, a little exasperated.

"Gee, boss, I don't see how having more pages in the reports will help when the summaries you write are still one page," Drew said.

"Hey, that's what the man asked for, so that's what he gets. Now let's give it to him—double the size of all reports," and Zach hung up.

Skill Question 9. Is this going to get Basant what he really wants? Why or why not? Hint: The why or why not has something to do with gender communications.

Mariquita did not take the news that her workload had just doubled too well.

"Drew, this is crazy. I'm busy. How can I possibly write twice as many pages on every report? I never get any help at all. I never get any feedback, no one reads all that I write now, and I am never appreciated!"

"Now wait, Mariquita. I helped you on the one report a couple of years ago, and you know I appreciate what you do," Drew replied.

"I don't know that, and there is no help—ever. This is all just too much. I cannot handle this pressure—I'm going to lunch!"

Skill Question 10. Why is Mariquita reacting this way? Hint: Her reaction has to do with gender communications.

Skill Question 11. What organizational communication direction is present throughout this situation?

Skill Question 12. What should have been done differently in order to give Basant what he really wants?

APPLICATIONS

3.1 THE CASE OF THE GREEN WIDGETS

Grayson Stiles is Vice President for Strategic and Tactical Oversight at the Multimore Corporation. Grayson sees one of his managers, Stella Wells, pass his door and calls her in. Stella selects one of the three chairs in front of Grayson's desk. Stella sits with her back straight but not touching the back of her chair. Her hands are folded in her lap, and she is alert and looking at Grayson. Grayson is chasing one of the fish in his large fish tank around with a net trying to catch it.

"Stella, I'd like you to get right over to Derek Phillips over by the loading dock. Tell him my systems have flagged a negative inventory reduction in green widgets. Tell him I think it's a paradigm shift, and I need a truncated procurement status. Tell him to expedite. I want to snare the drift on the downswing. You're dismissed."

Stella leaves while Grayson is still chasing his elusive fish. Stella heads over to the loading dock but is not looking forward to seeing Derek, mostly because she and Derek are competing for the next promotion, but partly because she is not sure what Grayson was talking about. As she reaches the loading dock, she sees Derek and two of his assistants talking to four workers. The four workers are facing Derek and his assistants in a circle where the seven of them are shoulder to shoulder. The group is hanging on Derek's every word. Derek hasn't seen Stella, and she turns and leaves without saying a word.

Three days later, Stella lays a message on Derek's desk while he is out. The message says, "You should probably look at the green widgets, more."

Derek gets the note late that day and increases his order for green widgets.

A week later, among stacks of boxes of green widgets, Grayson screams at Derek: "Why did you order more of these? I told you they were piling up! You should have stopped ordering them completely! If you can't listen, you can forget that promotion."

QUESTIONS

1. Which words, if any, are troublesome in the situation, and what is the trouble?

2. Find the example of one of the six functions of nonverbal communication and identify it.

3. How was Stella's postural NVC in Grayson's office?

4. Were there any problems with communication channels here? If so, what were they?

5. What two reasons can you find for Stella not relaying the message to Derek when she sees him in the group on the loading dock?

6. What gender issues are present in this situation?

7. Of the three people, who is/are at fault for too many green widgets being ordered and why is/are he/she/they at fault?

3.2 THE NEW BOSS AND COMMUNICATION

Lynn has just been hired to head a new department that consists of other new people and some existing employees. Of the existing employees, Mark has the most seniority. There have been two previous department meetings, but these were really "get acquainted" sessions. Today's meeting is the first where the new work arrangements will be discussed. Lynn was specifically hired to implement these new arrangements, which consist mainly of turning the entire department into one cohesive team. Just before Lynn is about to begin the meeting, Mark enters the room.

Mark: Hey! New gal found the meeting room all alone! Well done!

Lynn: Well, I do think it is usually a good gesture for one to arrive a little before any meeting starts.

Mark: Well, you know what I say? If you get there before it's over, you're on time!

Lynn, quietly: That's a very clever little saying. Now. . .

Mark, spreading his papers around him, which eventually take up enough space for at least two people: As you know, I have been with this company longer than anyone else here, and I think it is safe to assume that I know what the top management wants and what this department needs. I have given it careful thought, and what we need to do, and what I shall insist upon by the way, is that we each be given autonomous assignments. By this I mean that we will each be given a separate assignment. In this way we will each be able to focus our talents and we will each be solely accountable for our own work.

Lynn: There are certainly some interesting aspects to this proposal.

Mark, leaning back in his chair, looking at the ceiling: I'm glad you think so. Now I envision someone, probably me, having the primary responsibility for dividing the work up. Of course, I'll keep some for myself, but I'll take the heat if someone misses a deadline.

Lynn, looking at Mark as he looks out the window at a parking lot: I was thinking that there might also be a few other ways to organize things. Maybe we should explore some of them?

Mark, after hesitating to clean some dust off the top of his shoe: Can't see it. Can't see the point.

I got it figured. Figured so well we might all be able to put in 40 hours a week rather than the 56 we have been doing.

Lynn: "Well, it's just that some of the others may have other thoughts or maybe they would be open to other suggestions. We could maybe each write some down, then I could read them to everyone and . . . "

Mark: Since I haven't heard anyone outright say no, I guess I'll get started on those work assignments. Lynn, you run a right quick meeting, I'll try to get you a copy of the assignments after I decide on them.

QUESTIONS

1. What is going on here? What can you learn from the communications here? What do the words tell you? What does the NVC tell you, and which NVC tells you that?

2. Lynn is supposed to be in charge. What communication advice do you have for her?

NET-WORK

Maybe you got the memo, but did you get the message?
http://www.youtube.com/watch?v=qxPaiEiGWsM&mode=related&search=

The importance of NVC. http://www.youtube.com/watch?v=d3yy5elJW2Y

PERSONAL POINTS

1. When you need to communicate with someone, what thought do you give the communication channel you use? When have you chosen a convenient channel rather than the appropriate one and had the message misunderstood? What happened?

2. When has using paraphrasing helped you? When are there times when you should have used paraphrasing and didn't, and what was the result?

3. When have you encountered doublespeak? In what way did doublespeak affect the message being delivered? Have you ever used doublespeak to hide your true meaning, and if so, why did you use it?

4. When have you been provided upward communication, and what was the result? When have you avoided providing upward communication after being asked, and what was the result?

5. When have you experienced miscommunication due to gender differences? How would you now change the communication due to gender to avoid the problem?

EXPERIENTIAL EXERCISE

Variations in Communication

1. Watch a taped movie or television program with the sound turned off and try to determine from the nonverbal cues (NVCs) only what is taking place. Record your observations. Watch the segment a second time with the sound on and check the accuracy of your initial observations.

2. Practice saying the following phrases out loud. Place a different tone on the words each time you say them. Record the number of different meanings you can place on each phrase, and describe how the meaning changes with different tones.

    "Hello."

    "I see."

    "I'm sure you will."

    "Right."

    "Is that so?"

    "I'll call you."

    "What?"

    "Cool."

3. In groups of four, select a topic common to everyone. While two people discuss the topic, the other two observe the nonverbal gestures that are being used and record their observations. After 10 minutes, stop the conversation. Each observer should then review the NVCs used. The NVCs should then be classified as to the functions each performs—accenting, complementing, contradicting, regulating, repeating, or substitution. Reverse roles and repeat the exercise.

SPOT CHECK ANSWERS

1. T
2. F
3. F
4. T
5. F
6. F
7. F
8. T
9. F
10. F

4

Improving Communications and Managing Conflict

No one cares to speak to an unwilling listener. An arrow never lodges in a stone.

St. Jerome

The greatest danger in any [conflict] is that real issues are often clouded by superficial ones, that momentary passions may obscure permanent realities.

Mary Ellen Chase

GOALS

The goals of this chapter are to continue the discussion of communication from the previous chapter and to focus on improving communications. Special emphasis will be placed on improving listening skills and conflict management.

OBJECTIVES

When you finish this chapter, you should be able to:

▶ Identify, describe, and give examples of the 14 barriers to communication.

▶ Explain the importance of listening and identify methods to improve listening.

▶ Describe methods to break down communication barriers.

▶ Describe methods to improve communication.

▶ Identify positive and negative conflicts.

▶ Identify eight methods for managing conflict.

BARRIERS TO EFFECTIVE COMMUNICATION

"I didn't hear you say that." "Oh, is that what you meant?" "Gosh, I'm sorry, I thought you meant . . ." "I'm afraid you must have misunderstood me. What I said was . . ." Unfortunately for the sake of understanding between individuals, these statements are uttered far too frequently within organizations on a typical day. A number of stumbling blocks can trip up effective communication. Understanding the principal communication barriers can assist you in avoiding or overcoming them in the future. These barriers result from 14 factors, as illustrated in Table 4.1.

LYING

Lying
the deliberate deception of others to their detriment or your gain; not telling the truth

Lying, the deliberate deception of others to their detriment or your gain, is an obvious barrier to communication.[1] In some situations lying is a form of aggressive behavior that may lead to workplace violence (see Chapter 16).[2] People seem quite able to lie without instructions, although some are more skilled at it than others. The challenge then becomes one of being able to detect liars. Although no method will detect all liars, certain signs give an indication of whether or not someone is lying. These signals can be divided into two groups: facial indicators and general indicators.

Facial Indicators   The facial indicators of lying include (1) variables involving the eye area and (2) facial expression balance. The eyes can indicate lying through eye contact, blink rate, and pupil dilation.[3] Many people believe that a liar will be unable to maintain eye contact for an extended time. Actually, accomplished liars are quite good at this because eye contact is relatively easy to control consciously. However, blink rate and pupil dilation are a different story. People who are lying may blink more often than people who are telling the truth, and it is difficult to stop the eyes from blinking involuntarily. Pupil dilation is virtually impossible to control. Although it is harder to observe pupil dilation consciously, we are typically attuned to it subconsciously. A high state of emotional arousal causes the pupils to enlarge; when we are unhappy, the pupils constrict.

A lack of facial expression balance can also indicate that someone may be lying. Facial expression balance refers to symmetry of expression on a truthful person's face. When someone is lying, the two sides of the face may not match. Because the liar is using a false facial expression it is more difficult to get it right, the two sides may not exactly match, and a clue is provided that the sender is lying.

Another easily observed indicator is blushing. Some people cannot help but blush when they are lying or hiding something, especially when they are embarrassed or when the lie is a big one. However, not all blushing occurs with lying.

TABLE 4.1   BARRIERS TO COMMUNICATING

Lying	Wasting the thought-speech rate differential
Perceptions	Emotions
Overeagerness to respond	Snap judgments
Closed words	Attacking the individual
Judging	Rank
Credibility gaps	Gatekeepers
Noise	Poor listening

Although this man may tell the person on the other end that he knows what the caller is referring to, his face and hand gestures reveal the truth—he doesn't know.

Source: Courtesy of Photolibrary.com.

Certain people blush just from being talked to. Comparisons between these (and other) indicators and what the person is saying can provide insight into whether or not the person is lying.

General Indicators   Other indicators of lying include sweating, expression duration, expression initiation, and nonverbal communication initiation.[4] As an indicator of lying, sweating is like blushing; both are easy to observe, but many people sweat and blush for reasons other than lying. Expression duration refers to the length of time that an expression is held. One second is the typical duration of an expression of surprise, but liars tend to hold expressions longer than is typical because they must create and hold the expression, rather than have it created and extinguished naturally. Expression initiation refers to the timing of an expression. True emotional expressions occur as words are spoken or even slightly before. Those that are initiated after words are spoken may indicate lying. Further, a nonverbal cue initiated before the spoken words is probably false. A gesture indicating that someone is genuinely mad or upset usually occurs simultaneously with facial expressions and words, and the gestures and facial expressions all match.

Remember: These cues are just an indication that someone may be lying. They do not prove lying.

The indicators mentioned are all physiologic and nonverbal. In addition, lying by exaggeration can effectively deflect attention. Let's say, for example, a coworker asks, "Are you buying personal items with the company's money?" and the person who is presumed guilty responds with, "Sure, that's how I got my car, my wide-screen TV, and my new house." The implication is that the coworker's suggestion is in the same category as the other outrageous claims, when in truth the guilty person was ordering personal items with the firm's money.

PERCEPTIONS

Do you remember our discussion about the many factors that influence our perception? As we learned in Chapter 2, seeing things as they really are rather than as we are set to see them isn't an easy task. Our past experiences, our present moods, our attitudes, our peers, and other factors significantly influence how we interpret a given message. Familiarity with the determinants of perception helps you to recognize that not everyone is likely to interpret your messages in the manner you intend, nor will you necessarily read the messages of others correctly. Once again, remember the importance of feedback in effective communication.

EMOTIONS

We've all seen people in an emotional state who afterward apologized by explaining that they didn't mean their earlier comments. You should try your best to control your emotions because a loss of control often results in a loss of respect by the receivers of your communication. Make every effort to maintain a calm, positive, and friendly atmosphere in your interpersonal relationships, even if others approach you in an excessively hostile manner. Equally important in our conversations with others is that we attempt to avoid causing our listeners to feel either embarrassed or pushed.

OVEREAGERNESS TO RESPOND

Have you ever been around individuals who tend to finish your sentences for you during a pause or interrupt you in the middle of a sentence? How do you feel about such actions? Probably not so great. Yet, do you find that you, too, occasionally interrupt others? One reason we interrupt or finish others' sentences may be related to our ego's need for self-esteem (to be discussed in more detail in Chapter 11). We may feel the need to show others that they're not telling us something we don't already know. In some cases, the inclination to interrupt may be related to our impatience. For example, are you a high-achieving, busy person who often feels short on time? If so, you may find that your intense preoccupation with progressing to something else may create a barrier to effective communication between others and you.

Snap Judgments
drawing a conclusion instantly or with insufficient data

SNAP JUDGMENTS

When people jump to conclusions, they are guilty of making **snap judgments**. Snap judgments can be harmful because they are based on limited information or first impressions.[5] Snap judgments that are positive ("I just met him and he seems very nice") are usually harmless, of course. What is unfortunate is people judging a person's entire character on the basis of a single meeting. A common occasion for snap judgments is during a job interview. Far too often, the decision not to hire someone is made in the first few seconds and is based almost entirely on appearance. Another occasion when snap judgments are made is during a handshake. Some people use snap judgments more than others, and those who do seem especially convinced that there is nothing wrong with instant evaluations. When encountering instant evaluators, ask them how long it took (or is taking) them to select a spouse. If they are so right about instantly evaluating people, then why does it often take people a year or more to decide to get married?

NetNote

Tips for Success.org

www.tipsforsuccess.org/ difficult-people.htm or USA *Transactional Analysis Assoc.*

www.usataa.org/articles-handling-people.html

Advice on handling difficult people.

CLOSED WORDS

"Accounting never gets it right." "All salespeople are liars." "The only thing managers do is go to meetings." "That whole department is useless." These are examples of closed words—inclusive words that eliminate the possibility that there are exceptions to the rule. **Closed words**, like *all, none, never,* and *everyone,* are typically inserted into gross generalizations. Their effect is to create defensiveness in the people who are the subject of the generalization.[6] When talked about in this way, it is understandable that people would say, "Now wait just a minute," and then point out numerous exceptions. Probably the best solution is not to talk negatively about others. If one must, then the facts should be presented as facts rather than as oversimplified generalities that do nothing but create bad feelings.

Closed Words
all-inclusive words that eliminate the possibility that exceptions exist

ATTACKING THE INDIVIDUAL

Attacking the individual involves discussing people or their appearance rather than the real issue.[7] Attacking the individual violates a basic rule of getting along with others: Criticize behavior, not people. When we attack the person, his or her appearance, or his or her accent, we attack something the person cannot change. To focus on the attractiveness or unattractiveness of a speaker while ignoring the speech being made blocks communication and offends the person. This attacks something the speaker cannot change and keeps the critic from receiving a potentially beneficial message. Listen to what people say rather than how they look, dress, or sound when they say it. Remember: If you must criticize, discuss something that can be changed. Don't attack the person's very being; discuss the behavior that you would like to change. Don't say, "I can't stand you," because your coworker smokes. Say, "I would like you not to smoke around me." If you say you hate your coworker, how can he or she do anything about that? How can the person change his or her basic self? If you ask a person to stop the annoying behavior, then however, he or she can easily put the cigarette out.

JUDGING

Judging is a barrier to communication when it replaces a statement of facts.[8] Saying, "The pay at Company X is lousy," is a judgment by the speaker. Saying that Company X only pays $10 an hour tells us something. It is a fact, and we are now free to decide for ourselves whether or not this is lousy. Likewise, telling your boss that your job stinks doesn't say much. How does the boss fix "stinkyness"? However, telling your boss that working from 11:00 P.M. to 7:00 A.M. is ruining your marriage and your family life is something the boss might be able to respond to.

Judging
forming an opinion

Source: DILBERT: © Scott Adams/Dist. by United Features Syndicate, Inc.

You might ask why people judge rather than report facts, since judging is a barrier to communication. Often it is because people don't know exactly what is wrong, so they speak in general terms. To avoid this barrier, try to find out what the problem really is and be specific. Vague, general complaints are unlikely to receive attention.

RANK

Rank
a person's relative status in an organization

A person's **rank** or status in an organization is frequently a major barrier to communication. People are very reluctant to bring a problem to someone of higher rank. Frequently people will ask a colleague how to solve a problem to avoid the potential of looking dumb before the manager. In other cases, people do not want to report transgressors because they do not want to be perceived as a snitch or a squealer. When it comes to other types of communication, in the struggle for power and advancement for instance, men are more likely than women to seek out those of higher rank, but here the motive is more politics than communication.[9] Rank can also be a barrier when it comes to bringing bad news to those of higher rank. This can be deleterious to the health and well-being of an organization because, although it is nice to receive good news, sometimes it is much more important to receive bad news so that action can be taken early.

Rank can also affect downward communication. This is seen at corporate social gatherings where people of different ranks mix. Americans are often uncomfortable with differences in rank. After all, in the United States, all people are created equal. A CEO may be as uncomfortable speaking to a welder on the production line as the welder is when speaking to the head of the company. Consequently, little real communication actually occurs. Instead, people speak around issues or discuss the weather or sports. To avoid this barrier, higher-ranking people must appear approachable, they must listen, they must take action when it is needed, and whether they act or not, they must send feedback to the originator of the

A QUESTION OF ETHICS

You are attending an employee rally at a big-box discount retailer. This store location has been open for one month. The store manager is addressing the entire workforce.

"We are new to this region, to this town, and while we have performed adequately so far I now must ask you to go further, to do more, in order to secure our success. As with any start-up, money is tight, so I am asking you all to help out. For instance, rather than use the employee entrance at the back of the store by the time clocks, couldn't you come in the front door and then go back to punch in? This way, as you walk in you can bring carts in from the lot. As you go through the store you can look around. If something is out of place or messy, fix it up as you go, but don't punch in late! Coming in five minutes early to do these things could really help if we all do it.

"During the day, ask yourself if you really need that break or the whole half hour for lunch. At the end of your shift, after you punch out, take a quick lap around the store on your way out and fix up anything out of place. And I know you all shop here on your days off. While you are doing that take some time to clean or straighten up. Wear your uniform so people know you work and shop here, and then they can ask your help if they need to. Remember, when you help the company, this store, you are really helping yourself."

1. Develop an argument concerning whether or not these are ethical requests.

2. Explain why it is right or wrong to ask employees to work for free, even if for few minutes.

concern. Lower-ranking people should avoid communication barriers by being specific, by having facts to support their claims, and by presenting their message in calm, rational tones. Both higher-ranking and lower-ranking people need to remember all the lessons of communication, especially those involving tone and nonverbal communications.

CREDIBILITY GAPS

Credibility gaps are quite common between managers and workers in organizations. To prevent cynical distrust of the communication that flows throughout an organization, remember that words do not substitute for action. For example, you are a manager and Anne, who reports to you, complains to you about the excessive glare off her computer screen from the sun shining through her office window. She informs you that this makes work extremely difficult, if not impossible. If you promise to remedy the problem but fail to do anything about it, you're likely to discover that Anne will tend not to believe your future statements. Some managers think that a simple statement such as "I'll see what I can do about the problem" will placate their employees. However, when dealing with others, you should be aware that they'll frequently remember the promises you've made. The chasm of disbelief widens with each failure on your part to deliver what you promised.

GATEKEEPERS

In some organizations, there exist barriers to communication called **gatekeepers**. These are individuals who determine what information key decision makers receive. They may or may not be actual decision makers themselves; sometimes they are assistants or secretaries of the person with whom you would like to communicate. Gatekeepers tend to screen information and decide on their own what should be passed on to others. What can you do when confronted with a gatekeeper? Breaking through the gate usually requires a certain degree of political astuteness if it is to be accomplished without creating additional barriers between you and the gatekeeper. Maintain a cordial relationship with gatekeepers. They may become more receptive to you in time. If a gatekeeper continues to be a roadblock, it is advisable to let those whom you would like to contact know that you would like to meet with them. Doing so, however, is not without some risk. You could anger the gatekeeper. Some people overcome the roadblock created by the gatekeeper by writing a memo or e-mail to the person they want to contact, expressing the importance of a meeting. A memo is also sent to the gatekeeper so that he or she will feel included in the communication.

> **Gatekeepers**
> people or devices that control access to another person

NOISE

Loud noise is a fairly obvious barrier to communication. If you are trying to convey some important information to another person, you're likely to experience substantial difficulty if the setting includes noisy machinery or people in the background. Modern, open offices frequently obstruct effective conversations because of the spillover of noise from adjacent offices. Additionally, if you think you might be overheard, you may not communicate freely or fully.

Noise, in the communication process, is broadly interpreted as anything in the sender, the medium of communication, or the receiver that hinders communication. An effective communicator will select a setting that is conducive to effective communication and eliminate or reduce the factors that obstruct the transmission of messages.

NetNote

Listening

hearing and attending to the information that is heard

Verbal Cocoon

a condition of not receiving information or of receiving incorrect or partial information

---

WASTING THE THOUGHT–SPEECH RATE DIFFERENTIAL

How fast can the average person think, and how fast can the average person talk? We think four to six times faster than we can speak, about 600–1,000 words per minute versus 125–150 words per minute.[10] Because we think faster than people speak, we have time during a conversation to contemplate things. If these things are not part of the conversation, then the ability to think faster can be a barrier to communication. To listen more effectively, we should use the rate differential between thought and speech to decode and interpret what is being said to us, rather than waste that time daydreaming.

POOR LISTENING

We frequently misinterpret others because of ineffective **listening** habits. We think of other things while someone speaks to us, or look at other things, or allow distractions to divide our attention. As a result, we sometimes miss the sender's intended meaning. One of the poorest listening habits is to stop listening, not allowing the other person to finish by constantly interrupting with our own message. We'll cover ways to overcome this habit later in this chapter.

THE VERBAL COCOON

Judging from how often important feedback is filtered or misdirected, you might think that some supervisors in organizations are wrapped in a **verbal cocoon** from which they tend not to emerge, especially during their face-to-face interactions. Effective listening is not a simple or passive activity; it requires a concentrated effort and a certain amount of tension. Managers wrapped in a verbal cocoon tend to be nonstop talkers, seldom allowing new ideas to penetrate their encased world. In effect, cocoon listening prevents the penetration of unwanted information.

The cocoon listening problem frequently exists when managers perceive their role as authoritative, one that involves the initiation of action and decision making. To be required to engage in a less conspicuous activity, such as listening, sometimes bruises managers' egos, especially if they feel that they only have control of a situation when they are doing the talking. Such listening habits create a safe, nonthreatening way to avoid the risk of new ideas. However, if you ask satisfied employees what they like most about their supervisors, they frequently say, "I like my boss. My boss listens to me."

Whether you are a manager or a worker, either on or off the job, other individuals may approach you with their personal problems. When they do, is that the time to tell them that you, too, have similar problems? Put yourself in the shoes of the other party. When you have a personal problem that you want to discuss with someone else, do you really want to hear about that person's problem? Does hearing about the other person's problem necessarily make you feel any better? Usually not. Often you're more concerned, consciously or subconsciously, about having the opportunity to get things off your own chest.

Effective listening by organizational members can be a form of preventive maintenance. Just as lubrication can prevent friction and the resulting wear and tear of machinery, so effective listening can prevent friction and problems of human relations from developing in your organizational and personal life. Offering advice to a troubled person is often unnecessary. For people who have complaints or difficulties, the mere act of finding an empathetic listener (one who attempts to put himself or herself into the speaker's shoes) frequently helps them to get things off their chests and possibly to see problems more objectively on their own.

SPOT CHECK

1. Closed words generate defensiveness in the receiver of the message. T F
2. Vague, general complaints to management receive the most attention. T F
3. People are generally willing to bring problems to someone who has higher rank. T F
4. Credibility gaps are quite common between managers and workers in organizations. T F
5. Gatekeepers, when present, determine what information is received by key decision makers. T F

THE IMPORTANCE OF LISTENING

We usually tend to believe that we've understood another person's message merely because we've heard it, a notion that is often many kilometers away from reality. Unfortunately, most people have had little formal training in the area of listening, an important element in effective communication.

Think about your educational experiences. You've had courses in writing, reading, and possibly even speaking. But have you ever had a course in listening? If you're typical of the population, probably not, even though we spend more time in a listening mode than in any of the other processes of communication—speaking, reading, and writing.

A growing number of private organizations and schools have become increasingly aware in recent years of the need for training in listening. Institutions, private firms, and associations have developed a number of training videos and materials to improve listening. The purpose of this section is to present some significant but often ignored concepts designed to develop better listening habits.

EFFECTIVE LISTENING

Management will find it difficult to receive feedback from employees without developing improved techniques of listening. Often rushed and harried supervisors feel that they just can't find enough time to listen to employees. Some supervisors, however, discover that time spent on effective listening can be as valuable as an investment in more efficient equipment and can actually save them more time.

Of course, effective listening habits are important for all organizational members, not only managers. All employees should learn the techniques of better listening to maintain good relationships with those who deal with their organizations. Furthermore, costly accidents and expensive errors can often be avoided when employees listen to their supervisors and coworkers. Effective listening habits can also prevent misunderstandings and rumors from developing in an organization. There are other important reasons for acquiring effective listening habits. Five additional reasons are cited in Table 4.2. Think about how you might employ each of these in your day-to-day activities.

DEVELOPING LISTENING SKILLS

Listening is a skill to be developed. Knowing how to make certain listening responses and how to phrase questions can greatly assist you in conveying to

TABLE 4.2   SIGNIFICANT CONCEPTS RELATED TO LISTENING

People perform better when they know others listen to their opinions and suggestions. Attention paid to small complaints often prevents their blossoming into big grievances.

Managers who don't obtain as many relevant facts as possible often make poor decisions. Managers who jump to conclusions often lose the respect of their subordinates.

Listening requires giving full attention to the speaker; it is impossible to listen intelligently while the mind is preoccupied with something else.

speakers that you are interested, attentive, and wish them to continue. Let's first examine some effective ways to elicit responses from your speakers.

LISTENING RESPONSES

Listening responses should be made quietly and briefly so as not to interfere with a speaker's train of thought. As with any tool, responses can be misused, ineffective, or counterproductive. Responses are likely to be manipulative and unreal if they are not genuinely sincere. Responses are usually made when the speaker pauses. Five types of listening responses are:

- the nod—nodding the head slightly and waiting
- the pause—looking at the speaker expectantly, but without doing or saying anything
- the casual remark—"I see," "Uh-huh," or "Is that so?"
- the echo—repeating the last few words the speaker said
- the mirror—showing you understand by reflecting what has just been said: "You feel that . . ."

PHRASING QUESTIONS

Occasionally, a supervisor may notice that an employee's behavior or work habits have changed significantly. If a dependable employee with a record of good work suddenly starts coming to work drunk or having accidents on the job, the change may be a signal that a personal problem exists. Personal problems that affect an individual's performance on the job should become the concern of the employee's supervisor, who may be able to offer assistance. However, merely asking the worker, "Is there anything wrong, Joe?" will frequently elicit a negative response. There are far more effective ways of phrasing questions to enhance the possibility of receiving a more complete response. Questions may be open or closed. Open questions usually generate better responses than do closed questions.

An **open question** is phrased in such a way that it can't be answered with a simple yes or no. For example, "Joe, I've noticed some changes in your work lately. What seems to be happening?" The questioner who asks an open question, exercises patience, and says nothing until Joe finally responds often discovers that Joe will be far more likely to express his inner feelings about a personal problem.

A **closed question** is phrased in such a way that it can be answered yes or no. Here's an example: "Joe, do you have a problem?" Too frequently the answer to a question phrased this way will be no. Psychiatrists and counselors regularly employ the open-question technique. Can you really imagine a psychiatrist saying to a patient, "Ms. Jones, do you have a problem?"

Open Question

a question requiring more than just a yes or no answer

Closed Question

a question that can be answered yes or no

TABLE 4.3 SOME DOS AND DON'TS OF LISTENING

Do	Don't
Show interest.	Argue.
Express empathy.	Interrupt.
Be silent when silence is needed.	Engage in other activities.
Eliminate distractions by holding telephone calls and choosing a quiet place to talk.	Pass judgment too quickly or in advance.
Allow adequate time for discussion.	Jump to conclusions.
Take note of nonverbal cues.	Let the other person's emotions act too directly on your own.
When you are unsure of what was said, restate what you think you heard in the form of a question.	
When you think that something is missing, ask simple, direct questions to get the necessary information.	

As a supervisor, you could use open questions when trying to discover an employee's attitude about a change in the organization. If you ask, "Betty, do you think the recent change in your duties is fair?" she is likely to say yes because of the natural status barriers between employee and supervisor. However, if you ask, "Betty, how do you feel about the recent changes in your duties?" you will more than likely find out some of her real attitudes. Practice formulating open questions. You may be surprised and pleased with your results. Table 4.3 provides a useful summary of some of the principle dos and don'ts of listening.

HOW TO BREAK DOWN COMMUNICATION BARRIERS

In this chapter, you've learned quite a lot about the nature of communication. These insights are useful, however, only in their application. To be an effective member of any organization, it's essential that you be able to overcome the many communication barriers that continually confront you. In this section, we'll cover some of the major precautions and approaches you can use to minimize communication breakdowns. You can:

- encourage upward communication
- have an open-door policy
- use face-to-face communication when possible
- avoid credibility gaps
- write for understanding
- watch your timing
- be sensitive to the needs and feelings of others
- identify and manage conflict

Too frequently we believe that we've communicated with others only to find ourselves sinking in a sea of misunderstanding and conflict. As has already been stressed in this chapter, feedback—finding out the receiver's response to your communication—helps to reduce misunderstandings. Some of the following recommendations for overcoming communication barriers concern the concept of feedback.

123

ENCOURAGE UPWARD COMMUNICATION

**Upward
Communication**

the sender is on or closer
to the frontlines of the
organization than is the
receiver

To encourage **upward communication**, some organizations have developed formal suggestion systems. This well-intentioned feedback mechanism can be either used or misused. For example, in one of the largest printing plants in the Pacific Northwest, employees passing through a particular corridor of the building could see, very firmly attached to a wall, a wooden box with the words "Employee Suggestions" affixed to its side. The suggestion box looked more like a garbage receptacle than a mechanism for generating feedback. Once, out of curiosity, an employee opened the unlocked lid. Inside the dusty container were unsightly hunks of well-masticated stale chewing gum, along with crumpled old cigarette and gum wrappers. What might the employees have been attempting to suggest to management? The employees seemed to think there was little use in placing anything other than garbage into the box because, as one of the employees said, "Management would only put our suggestions in the wastebasket anyway."

In a related classroom incident, a group of students in a human resources class was studying the communication and motivation chapters. As a small class project, one group devised a suggestion box. The box was adequately constructed and properly labeled. There was only one problem with the box, but it spoke volumes. The students had neglected to include a slot! The box was completely sealed with no method for inserting or retrieving any suggestions. A simple mistake or a Freudian slip?

Some critics of suggestion systems argue that by requiring written suggestions, management may discourage the presentation of useful ideas by employees who lack the inclination or ability to put their suggestions into writing.

However, if management employs a suggestion system, it should give recognition to the submitter, whether or not the idea is accepted, to encourage the flow of useful ideas and employee gripes upward in the chain of command. An employee usually thinks he or she is entitled to know why a suggestion is rejected. Numerous firms provide not only explanations in writing to the employees but also face-to-face discussions of the reasons for the rejection or acceptance of ideas. Others present cash rewards to employees who offer cost-saving ideas. However, employees will soon view a suggestion system as a farce if management does not acknowledge the suggestions.

Let's continue with our discussion of upward communication for the purpose of minimizing communication barriers. Some managers assume that if they haven't personally heard derogatory remarks from employees, there must be little, if any, dissatisfaction with the company's policies and procedures. If much communication

REALITY CHECK

What Managers Should Communicate

To improve communications, managers should disclose things they know that the workers do not know. Information or predictions concerning what the organization will be like and what it will be doing in the future should be shared. Explaining the implications for the organization's operation's, product's, and services' anticipated effect on sales will help workers prepare for any changes. A discussion of what competitors are predicted to do will help

people think of ways to meet any challenges. Communicating the skills people will need in the future will help them focus their training and education efforts in order to acquire those skills, benefiting the workers and the organization.

The manager's position should guide him or her on how far into the future he or she should go. The higher the manager is in the organization, the further ahead the discussion should look. Frontline managers should be talking about the next few months while the CEO should be looking and talking about five or more years ahead.

weren't filtered out so often, many managers would quickly discover what the people they manage really think about them.

HAVE AN OPEN-DOOR POLICY

Aware of the problems of upward communication, many well-meaning managers inform their employees that they believe in an open-door policy and that any time employees want to see them, all they need do is drop in. In too many cases, however, an open-door policy really means that the door is open for managers to walk out. Usually, few workers feel inclined to walk through their boss's door because they sense various psychological or status barriers between the boss and themselves. Even where open-door policies have been announced, many employees have found that upon attempting to walk through the so-called open door, they have been stopped and asked, "Do you have an appointment with Mr. Lockout?"

If managers really want to discover what employees think about the operations of an organization, they must walk through the open portals themselves and engage in some observant exploration. Some organizations, such as Hewlett-Packard, refer to this activity as MBWA, or **management by wandering around**. Wandering around enables managers to make themselves available for informal discussions with employees. Many managers seldom engage in MBWA, instead tending to keep themselves comfortably insulated from their employees.

Management by Wandering Around
random, direct observation of workers

This pessimistic view of open-door policies isn't intended to suggest that they should never be attempted. Some managers are very effective in persuading employees that an open door actually exists. When management's attitude is credible, an open-door policy can be used as an effective tool. For example, at Levi Strauss & Company, the open-door concept has allegedly worked so well that employees refer to it as the "fifth freedom."

USE FACE-TO-FACE COMMUNICATION

Face-to-face communication is believed to be more effective than written orders in reducing misunderstandings because the sender can receive feedback immediately and discover if he or she has been understood. The impersonal character of a memo or letter can be easily misunderstood, especially when information of a negative nature is being conveyed.

For example, while employed as a sales representative for an office products company, Victor discovered that personal meetings with his customers, rather than impersonal written communication, more effectively resolved problems or conflicts that had developed between the customers and his company. By asking open questions and listening empathetically to the answers, Vic regularly discovered that the problems seemed to diminish.

AVOID CREDIBILITY GAPS

A **credibility gap** occurs when communication lacks believability. To prevent others from regarding your statements with cynical distrust, always keep in mind that words do not substitute for actions. Remind yourself that if you want to communicate effectively with and influence others with your messages, you must be able to get them to do the following:

Credibility Gap
communication lacking believability

1. Hear what you say.
2. Believe what you say.
3. Be willing to act on what you say.

Once you have lost your credibility, others are much less inclined to do these three things.

WRITE FOR UNDERSTANDING

Far too frequently, written communication within organizations appear to have been prepared by someone trying not to communicate. A manager with a large insurance company once said that he believed all communication should be delivered with a KISS, which meant "Keep It Simple, Stupid." As employees wrote, they were to chant, "Keep it simple, stupid," as a reminder of one of the goals of their writing. More tactfully, KISS could represent "Keep It Short and Simple." Perhaps you should ask yourself, "What is the major objective of any communication that I desire to make to others?" Communication isn't effective unless there is understanding, which should be a major goal of any communication. Don't overcomplicate your messages. If there was a fire in your office or plant, you wouldn't exclaim, "It is mandatory that we attempt to extinguish the portentous pyrogenation." You would be understood much more readily if you merely shouted, "Let's put out the fire!" And here's a sampling of what one manager actually stated in a letter: "I should be gratified by your willingness to aid in this endeavor." A simpler way to convey the same meaning would be: "I'm glad you want to help."

Written communication, before it can be understood, must attract the attention of those to whom you are aiming it. Imagine seeing this notice tacked to a bulletin board:

> Memorandum to all employees concerning
> regulations and restrictions applicable
> to equitable allocation of vacation
> periods for the year 2009.

Would you expect many employees to spend much of their valuable coffee break perusing such a memo? A simple, readable title would be more apt to attract the attention and understanding of employees, as in the following example:

> Memorandum
> To: All Employees
> From: Personnel Department
> Subject: Vacation Schedules, 2009

Virtually any correspondence can be improved by applying what we'll term the four Cs of written communication. The four Cs stand for complete, concise, correct, and conversational. Use the checklist in Table 4.4 to help determine whether your written communication is likely to accomplish what you want it to. Two books that can help you write clearly are *The Elements of Style* by Strunk and White and *On Writing Well* by William Zinsser.

WATCH YOUR TIMING

One evening, you finally decide to ask your boss for the raise that you think is long overdue. All night you toss and turn in bed, trying to frame the most tactful and persuasive plan to ask for the pay increase. The next morning, however, you observe that your boss appears extremely harried upon her arrival at work and scarcely notices the employees. Nonetheless, your mind is set; your courage is at its peak. You bravely walk through the "open door" of your boss's office and

TABLE 4.4   THE FOUR Cs OF WRITTEN COMMUNICATION

COMPLETE

Have you provided all the necessary facts?

Have you answered all the receiver's questions?

CONCISE

Have you avoided unnecessarily long and complicated words?

Have you said what you wanted in one page or less?

Are your paragraphs short and easy to read?

Have you avoided hiding important information, such as where, when, and at what time a meeting will be held?

CORRECT

Have you checked your correspondence for accuracy?

Are your commitments in agreement with company policy?

Have you checked your grammar, spelling, and punctuation?

Have you eliminated strikeovers and sloppy corrections?

CONVERSATIONAL

Have you written in a friendly, receptive manner?

Will your writing style evoke the response you want?

Have you avoided excessively complicated and flowery phrases?

Have you avoided words and expressions that are likely to antagonize your reader?

Have you put life into your writing through the use of active verbs?

politely but firmly ask for a raise. Suddenly—BANG! You feel as though you're reliving the 1906 San Francisco earthquake. Your boss shouts, "Can't you see I have some important things on my mind?" You realize that you must have picked the wrong time for your question and that you completely forgot to interpret her body language.

Optimum timing is as important as your choice of words, whether you're talking to parents, children, friends, superiors, subordinates, or customers. The best time to attempt to convey important communications face-to-face occurs when your message is competing the least with other situations affecting the listener. However, your message is most likely to be considered and listened to when it provides a solution to a problem affecting the receiver.

BE SENSITIVE TO OTHERS' FEELINGS AND NEEDS

Empathetic speaking and listening are essential for effective communication. Some speakers create communication barriers because they seem to lack the understanding that some words or phrases are perceived as derogatory and offensive to others. Some people, however, think that extreme sensitivity to words is ridiculous. Regardless of how you feel, an important point is to try to know your audience and be sensitive to the needs and feelings of your listeners; otherwise, you may short-circuit important communication networks.

Along the line of concern for the feelings of others, try to remember what we discussed about impatience. Try to develop the ability not to interrupt. Instead, concentrate on listening instead of thinking only of your next response. Most people usually appreciate being listened to. Don't you?

CONFLICT MANAGEMENT

It may seem that whenever two or more people are gathered together, there will be conflict. The causes of organizational conflict are myriad, but research has shown the following to be some of the primary causes: individual differences (in beliefs, knowledge, or values), competition for a promotion, competition for power, a need for autonomy, different perceptions of the organization and its mission, competition for recognition, and personal dislike for others.[11] Not all conflict is negative, however. Depending on how it is managed, conflict can be positive or negative. Whether a conflict is positive or negative is up to the participating individuals. Although not every conflict will be resolved, it is possible to manage many of them so that they can at least be tolerated.[12]

POSITIVE AND NEGATIVE CONFLICT

One of the keys to managing conflict and making it more tolerable is to be able to differentiate conflicts that are negative (or have the potential for becoming negative) from those that are positive. When one or more of the antagonists is dissatisfied with the results, you have a **negative conflict**. A **positive conflict** ends in mutual satisfaction.

Negative Conflict
conflict in which one or more parties will be unsatisfied by the way the conflict ends

Positive Conflict
conflict ending in mutual satisfaction

Negative or potentially negative conflicts have the following characteristics:

- *Feud Mentality.* The conflict pits one group against another (us versus them).
- *Going for Broke.* Each side wants it all. No compromise. This is the way things have to be—our way. Somebody wins and somebody loses, but everyone may feel bad or bitter about the process.
- *Me Syndrome.* The antagonists see only their side of the issue. They can't see that the opposition even has a case to make.
- *You Syndrome.* The conflict is personalized. People are attacked as individuals. Each side criticizes people rather than their behaviors.

Positive conflicts, have these characteristics:

- *Problem-Solving Mentality.* Everyone is at the table to solve the problem, not to fight with each other, even though different sides may have different viewpoints.
- *Going for Mutual Satisfaction.* All sides are trying to work for a solution that everyone can live with and feel satisfied with. Instead of winners and losers, everyone wins. This is different from compromise, which often ends up with everyone feeling equally unhappy.
- *Everyone Syndrome.* Each side recognizes that the other side has legitimate concerns. All concerns are presented, and a solution that takes all of them into account is worked toward by all.
- *Just the Facts.* The discussion centers on the facts of the problem, not on the feelings of the people involved in the conflict.

The first step is to identify the type of conflict involved. If a conflict is negative, try to turn it into a positive conflict. Turn the focus from people and personalities to the core problem. Break down the barriers separating the two sides.[13] Rearrange the seating so one group is not all on one side of the table. If one group is in suits and the other is not, create a uniform dress code. If necessary, have everyone show up ultracasual—shorts and T-shirts. Get out of a conference room. Go outside or to a restaurant. Begin by sharing other things. Pass around pictures of everyone's family, pets, cars, or houses. Eat together, or have everyone bring in a favorite food. Watch a movie—a comedy—together. Do anything to break the conflicting groups down and form one problem-solving group. When everyone views everyone else as fellow human beings, they can begin to see other concerns and mutual needs.

The next step is to draw up rules. No name-calling, no snide remarks under people's breath, no accusations, no dredging up the past, no talking about things that absolutely cannot change. Discuss the facts pertinent to the case, and only those; then set a deadline. Don't allow one side to sit back and try to wait out or wear down the other side. These strategies are essentially for groups to engage in; there are also things that individuals can do to aid in conflict resolution.

GENERAL CONFLICT-RESOLUTION GUIDELINES

As an individual, you can take at least eight actions to help resolve conflicts:[14]

1. Treat others with respect, even if you disagree with them.
2. Be absolutely convinced that everyone has enough in common to make communication and a mutually satisfactory resolution possible.
3. Concentrate on the problem. Avoid ego involvement, name-calling, and closed words.
4. Report facts, not your own value judgments. Use descriptive terms and avoid strong, emotion-filled words.
5. Be very specific. Avoid generalities such as "This is garbage," and "In the broad context of the overall organization, this is an unfeasible outcome."
6. Discuss the issues most open to change and avoid those that have little or no chance of changing.
7. Discuss one issue at a time. Don't bring up unrelated issues; they will just cloud the issue at hand and confuse people.
8. Project a positive image. Walk in totally convinced that things can be worked out.

A GLOBAL GLANCE

Chinese Business Conflict

Singapore has had more than 30 years of rapid economic growth and change that, combined with other cultural factors, has created hard-to-resolve conflicts. Companies in Singapore follow a typical Chinese pattern of organization. This pattern has four distinctions from the pattern of Western organization. In the Chinese pattern, companies are small (10 to 100 people), highly centralized, family run (relying on a patriarch and nepotism), with a high regard for people (paying much attention to others' emotions and to trust). Conflicts come from competition with large, multinational, Western-style businesses. Managers see advantages to the Western-style organizations, but realize that neither the multinationals nor their own system is clearly superior. Much of the conflict in Singaporean firms arises from the clash of generations. In the traditional Chinese system, the patriarch rules over all aspects of the firm. Even though nepotism is accepted, the owner's or boss's children are allowed little say in the firm's affairs. As in other conflicts, the interests of both parties are not clearly stated. Members of the older generation claim not to want to change because their experiences tell them they are correct. Members of the younger generation claim that their superior education tells them that change is needed. The underlying interests are different. The older generation wants to maintain the status quo, while the younger generation wants to change to gain power sooner.

The options available also follow a fairly typical pattern. There are two mutually exclusive options, each presented by a different side. The older generation does not want to change, and the younger generation wants an immediate change to a Western-style system. What may be needed is a new option, a uniquely Singaporean blend of the best of the Chinese and Western systems.

The relationship and communication elements of this conflict are also quite complex. The Chinese system focuses on what is referred to as the Five Relations: sovereign and minister, parent and child, husband and wife, older brother and younger brother, and the relations between friends. Each of these then gives rise to a respective virtue: loyalty, filial piety, faithfulness, care, and sincerity. The state of these relationships before and after the conflict must be accounted for.

The communication method for many Singaporean companies follows the same pattern. The patriarch has complete control, while feeling responsibility for family and workers. This downward-only flow of communication also impedes the communication needed to resolve this conflict. What would you propose to resolve this situation?

Source: Jean Lee, "Culture and Management—A Study of Small Chinese Family Business in Singapore," _Journal of Small Business Management,_ July 1996, pp. 63–67.

Going down the negative path is all too easy for many people; don't join them.[15] If others turn negative, say something like, "I know it's impossible. Now let's figure out how to do it." Be so positive that everything can work out that others have no choice but to join you. Remember that it is easy to let the entire process degrade into a complaint session. If people need that kind of catharsis, let them go off somewhere else, get things off their chests, and return ready to work on the problem.

CONFLICT PERSPECTIVES

In working to resolve a conflict, it is often advantageous to view the conflict from the perspective of the other side. It may be helpful first to write down your position. Then put yourself in the other side's position and write down how you see that side and what your position would now be. Then try a third view, that of a disinterested outsider.[16] Once you have completed this task, try to understand your message as the other side would see it (Figure 4.1).

The other side will see your message as having at least three parts: a demand, a threat, and an offer. The **conflict demand** is what you are asking for. The **conflict threat** is the action that will result if your demand is not met. The **conflict offer** is what you will give the other side if it meets your demand.[17] A simple, common example of these three parts is a union contract negotiation. The union demands money, threatens a strike,

and offers continued work for a certain number of years. From management's perspective, this becomes: The union wants to take our profits, it threatens us with financial ruin if the strike is prolonged, and it offers what we already have (its labor). A personal example might involve your demand for support on a project from a coworker. You threaten to go to the boss if the coworker refuses, and you offer to share the credit when the project is a success. From the perspective of the coworker, this may amount to: You are demanding subservience from me, you threaten me with reprisals from my boss for not adding to my already heavy workload, and you offer more work and less time to spend on my current work.

Conflict Demand
what you are asking for

Conflict Threat
what will happen if your conflict demand is not met

SITUATIONAL ELEMENTS

Conflicts can be broken down into seven components, or situational elements: interests, options, legitimacy, relationships, communication, commitments, and the alternative (Figure 4.2).[18] Although applicable to any conflict, you may wish to reserve analysis of the seven situational elements of conflicts for those times when the stakes are high. Small conflicts, such as when you will be allowed time to use the shared office printer, may not require this level of analysis and concern. However, there are plenty of larger conflicts that do. When first employing this situational analysis, it may be necessary to write everything down step-by-step. With experience, it may be possible to accomplish much of this mentally, further saving time and effort and resulting in even faster conflict resolution.

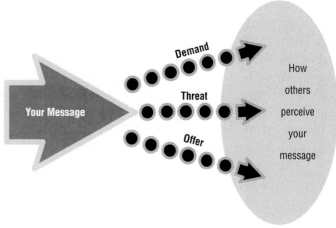

FIGURE 4.1 Your message as seen by the other party in a conflict

Interests   Analyzing **interests** involves looking at the root cause of each demand. Each side views its demand as a solution to a problem. Often the problem remains unstated during the attempts to resolve the conflict. It is often more productive to deal with the problem than with a side's perceived solution to the problem.[19]

Options   The group of perceived solutions to problems that are often unstated by either side yields a set of solutions available for resolving the conflict. Often these options are unacceptable and insufficient to do the job. In view of this, it may be necessary to discard all of the **options** each side separately developed and to jointly create a set of new options.[20] Doing so is easier if the underlying problems or interests have been exposed. With the real motivations stated clearly for all parties to see, it is possible to refocus the conflict from one side versus the other, to both sides versus the problem.

NetNote

Pertinent Information.com

http://www.pertinent.com/ articles/communication/ index.asp

Interpersonal communication articles including e-mail (with a chart on emoticons), getting along with others, handling criticism, and more.

Conflict Offer
what you have to give if your conflict demand is met

Interests
the primary cause of a conflict, often unstated

Options
alternatives that will resolve a conflict

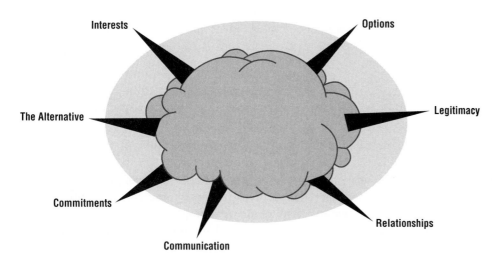

FIGURE 4.2 The seven situational elements of a conflict

Legitimacy
support from a source unrelated to the conflict that an option is fair

Legitimacy   Once a resolution to a conflict has been devised, it may be necessary to add **legitimacy** to the resolution. Neither side in a conflict wishes to be taken advantage of, and the word of the other side that the resolution is fair may be insufficient. In these cases, support from external sources can provide legitimacy and reassurance.[21] External support may be derived from the law, precedent, or statistics. For example, evidence that the rate of inflation is 2 percent and the average salary increase for the industry is 2.25 percent may be sufficient for a union to feel satisfied with a 2.5 percent increase. When people other than those directly involved in the conflict resolution are affected by the results, as is the case in a union contract negotiation, legitimacy may be even more critical as both sides at the negotiating table go back to convince their respective constituencies of the validity of the resolution.

Relationships   A fourth situational element in conflict involves the relationships between the parties. Although it may be important to understand the relationship between the parties during the conflict resolution, it is critical to the success of the resolution to account for the relationships that will exist after the conflict resolution process is complete.[22] It is vital to consider the postconflict level of trust between the parties and what will be present with the proposed resolution. For example, in resolving a conflict over sales quotas, if all trust is lost between the sales manager and the sales staff, how can the manager be confident that the sales staff will do its best to sell the firm's products? Or, after resolving a bitter, emotional conflict over working conditions and perceived sexual harassment with her assistant, will a manager be able to trust her assistant to do his best, return phone calls, and relay all messages accurately? If conflicts are handled with as much concern for the relationships as for the resolution, problems like these may be avoided.

Communication   How the parties involved in a conflict communicate can greatly affect the timely and successful resolution of the conflict.[23] The three main concerns are for clear, direct, and proprietary communication. The need for clear communication involves the presentation of perceptions and interests on the part of both parties. Both parties must state their interests and perceptions of the conflict and its possible solution. Communication will be much less clear if each side is vague or if one side expects the other side to guess at the underlying concerns and interests.

The second and third communication concerns do not involve how things are said; rather, they involve the mechanisms for communicating. Direct communication between the parties is preferred. In organizational disputes, however, you may find that two lawyers representing the different sides talk, and then each reports to his or her respective side. As we saw in Chapter 3, the use of a third party allows for alteration of the message. If possible, both sides should speak face-to-face. This does not mean that a mediator should not be present as well.

Another concern related to the system of dialogue between the parties is whether the discussions are private or public. It is best if the parties are free to speak openly, and that all discussions are proprietary, or confidential. Much counterproductive posturing can occur if both sides play out the conflict resolution in the media.

Commitments   Negotiations can be made difficult by prior commitments and by the commitments that must be made to resolve the current conflict.[24] For example, someone asks you to start a four-week project that requires your full-time attention, but one week ago you committed to and started a five-week project requiring your full-time attention. The prior commitment is blocking resolution of the current conflict. Prior commitments that can make resolving a conflict difficult include those made publicly. If a union commits to its members to obtain a 12 percent raise next year, anything less, no matter how objectively reasonable, may seem like a loss. Current commitments needed to resolve a conflict can also delay resolution. Some people fear ending a conflict because they, and possibly others, must then live with the results. Keeping the negotiations going is an avoidance mechanism that maintains the status quo and holds out the hope (even though it may be a very small hope) that a more favorable resolution may develop. To increase the effectiveness of the resolution process, it is helpful to identify and discuss commitment openly and confidentially early in the process.

Alternatives   The **alternative** is what will happen if the conflict is not resolved. People involved in a conflict often fail to estimate the true cost of not settling the conflict. The tendency is to believe that not resolving a problem will cost you little but will be prohibitively expensive for the other side.[25] For example, a $1-an-hour raise would mean an additional $2,080 per year for a full-time worker. If that worker is currently earning $1,000 per week, a strike of much longer than two weeks means that the worker will actually lose money even if the entire $1-an-hour is received. Assuming that this dollar is the main issue and the company has a good inventory, the alternative to settling the conflict (letting a strike develop) might be better rather than worse for the firm. Other costs of the no-resolution alternative can include destruction of trust and motivation, bitterness, loss of the best workers (immediately or later), and creation of what management theorist Fredrick Herzberg calls a **remembered pain**. Both sides in a conflict must realize the non-monetary costs involved in not resolving conflicts swiftly and satisfactorily.

Alternative
the consequences of not resolving a conflict

A Remembered Pain
an unpleasant or unjust event, real or perceived, that is often passed down from the people originally involved to newcomers

SUMMARY

Barriers continually develop, thus making effective communication more difficult. Among the more common communication barriers are lying, differing perceptions, overeagerness to respond, snap judgments, using closed words, attacking the individual, judging, rank, credibility gaps, gatekeepers, noise, wasting the thought-speech differential, and poor listening habits.

Maybe we were meant to have two ears and one mouth, as if to say that we should listen twice as much as we speak. Yet, how many people have you met who are in constant output mode? They speak and speak but never pause to take in anything. Others hear (the sound reaches their ears), but they do not listen (they do not attend to what they hear). Communication, however, requires at least two people. When one speaks, the other listens, but to be truly effective the roles must reverse. Everyone must listen and listen well in order for communication to occur. Some people listen well naturally, whereas others are simply adequate or inadequate. People in the last two groups should improve their listening skills as much as possible in order to succeed as members of an organization.

Understanding the techniques for overcoming communication barriers can reduce their number. You can improve communication by obtaining feedback, encouraging upward communication, using face-to-face communication when possible, avoiding credibility gaps, writing for understanding, watching your timing, and being sensitive to the needs and feelings of others.

Conflict is inevitable, but it can be managed. To manage conflict, you must first be able to identify the type of conflict you are presented with and then select methods that will reduce or resolve the conflict.

CHECKING FOR UNDERSTANDING

1. What are the facial indicators and general indicators that someone may be lying?

2. How can emotions affect communication?

3. How can an overeagerness to respond affect communication?

4. How can snap judgments affect communication?

5. What response does the use of closed words typically elicit from a message receiver?

6. Fred, a frontline worker, knows of wrongdoing that the company president would be very concerned with. Fred is reluctant to go to the president. Why is he hesitant? What could the company president do to encourage Fred to communicate information, even without knowing that Fred has something to say?

7. What are credibility gaps? How can they affect communication?

8. What role do gatekeepers play in organizational communication?

9. What factors contribute to effective listening?

10. What are verbal cocoons, and how can they affect organizational communication?

11. How can listening skills be improved?

12. List and define the barriers to communication.

13. How can you avoid credibility gaps?

14. What are the characteristics of negative conflicts?

15. What are the characteristics of positive conflicts?

SELF-ASSESSMENT

For each of the following, answer SA for Strongly Agree, A for Agree, D for Disagree, and SD for Strongly Disagree.

1. I feel lying is acceptable if it keeps me from getting into trouble. *SA A D SD*

2. I always know when someone is lying to me. *SA A D SD*

3. Just give me a few seconds and I can tell what a person is like. *SA A D SD*

4. When I disagree with what people are saying I feel it's okay to interrupt them. *SA A D SD*

5. I never let my emotions influence how or what I say. *SA A D SD*

6. I'm *always* right, others are *always* wrong; to admit to less is a sign of weakness. *SA A D SD*

7. If someone speaks with an accent I just can't take them seriously. *SA A D SD*

8. I only talk about the weather to those who outrank me. *SA A D SD*

9. I don't listen to people who are dressed unusually. *SA A D SD*

10. I only discuss facts, not how I value them *SA A D SD*

11. People speak too slowly, but at least that gives me a chance to think. *SA A D SD*

12. I frequently have to ask people to repeat what they just said. *SA A D SD*

13. I nod so people think I'm listening, but I'm really not. *SA A D SD*

14. In a disagreement, if I don't get everything I want, I've lost. *SA A D SD*

15. I'm concerned about me; what anyone else wants is his or her problem. *SA A D SD*

Except for items 5 and 10, give yourself −2 for every SA, −1 for every A, +1 for every D, and +2 for every SD answer. For items 5 and 10 only, give yourself +2 for every SA, +1 for every A, −1 for every D, and −2 for every SD answer. Total your scores. If your total is

27–30, no or almost no barriers are present in your communication. A score of 15–26 indicates there are a few barriers in your communication that you could work on. A score of 0–14 indicates there are some barriers in your communication that you should work on.

A score of 0–15 indicates a significant number of barriers in your communications that need to be addressed. Any score between −16 and −30 indicates all or virtually all barriers are present, and much improvement is needed for you to communicate effectively.

SKILL BUILD 4

Scene 1

"Look, Maalik, all I am saying is that I have never been to one of these in-house training sessions that wasn't dumb, boring, and obvious," Stamos said, "and did you get a look at that presenter? He's stuck in the '80s, man! He was wearing khaki pants, those boating moccasin shoe-things, and a knit shirt with a crocodile on it! How are we supposed to learn anything from someone who looks like that?"

Skill Question 1. Identify the two barriers to communication in the preceding paragraph, list the passage that supports your identification, and define both terms in your own words.

  "But we have not heard him yet," Maalik protested.

  "Well, just the title of the session sounds iffy—'Sexual Harassment: The Legal, Ethical, Moral, and Behavioral Quagmire, An Interpersonal Transactional Analysis.' I mean, come on, what do you have to hear to know this isn't good?" Lani said.

Skill Question 2. Identify the barrier to communication in this section, list the passage that supports your identification, and define the barrier in your own words.

  "I still think we must hear him first before deciding," Maalik said.

  Stamos held up his hand, palm out as if to say "Stop," and then said, "There is more to this, though. Management needs us to go to this, but this is not in our union contract, and they want us to go on our own time. That is not right."

  "That is different than your other concerns," Maalik said. "For these problems you must go to Mr. Wilton."

  "No way," Stamos said, "I'm the union rep and only one-half step above the rank-and-file, frontline workers. Wilton is the vice president of Human Resources. I can't

go to him. Heck, I don't know if I would even recognize him. I've only seen his face twice and from a distance at that!"

Skill Question 3. Identify the barrier to communication in this section and define it in your own words.

Skill Question 4. There are also two different attempts to break down communication barriers here. One seems to be working, and the other does not. Identify each type, including the appropriate passage, identify which is working and which is not, and explain what led you to both conclusions.

  "He does say in our HR Newsletters that we are welcome to come to his office any time, any day," Maalik said.

  "Oh, I think he just says that. He really doesn't mean it! I know people that have gone to see him and he either isn't there or says he's too busy and you need an appointment," Lani said. "If he really meant," he would be more like Ms. Bianco, the director of training. I see her at least three times a week. She's always out and about talking to people. She's approachable."

  "You're right, Ms. Bianco is the one to talk to. I'll see what I can do," Stamos said.

Scene 2

The next day Stamos met with Ms. Bianco to discuss the mandatory sexual harassment training.

  Stamos started, "Ms. Bianco, we have a problem here with this training. Management wants everyone to attend even though I'm not sure it is legit, meaning I'm not sure it is really necessary or even important. Be that as it may, my people work hard and have families and responsibilities after work. The company can't expect them to come back in the evening on their own time for training that is all the company's idea. I mean, I looked into this, and that Wednesday at 7:00 P.M., when this is scheduled for, is a night when some of our people have church, there is flag football and soccer practice going on, and some of our people are not just dropping kids off, they are coaching. Plus, there is a big gymnastics meet. Plus we are done with work at 5:30 P.M. and people would get home and just about have to turn around and come back. So this isn't about not feeling like coming. These are the true details of the situation. There has to be a way to work this out for both sides."

"Well, I'm not sure that upper management realized all this when this was set up," Ms. Bianco replied. "We really expect everyone to go through the two-hour training, but we can't shut down operations for two hours in a row, so we thought it had to be after work."

"There is also the matter of us doing this for free," Stamos said. Ms. Bianco seemed to stiffen at that remark.

"But I have an idea. I mean, if this isn't changed, many, if not most, of the union workers are not going, plain and simple. However, if it is during working hours, so we are getting paid to be there, then I'll guarantee 100 percent participation. Now I know we can't take two hours in a row, but I think we could do half an hour for four days in a row," Stamos said.

"It would cost us more to bring the presenter back for three other days," Ms. Bianco said.

"In exchange for 100 percent attendance and everybody getting what they want?" Stamos said, raising both eyebrows.

Ms. Bianco thought a minute and then said, "I'll see what I can do. I think I can do this."

Skill Question 5. There are only two general types of conflict, positive and negative. Each has four characteristics, but only three are present here. What general type of conflict is present in scene 2 and what are that conflict's three characteristics? Include the name of each of the three conflict characteristics along with the associated passage.

Skill Question 6. List each of the conflict perspectives and specifically identify each in scene 2 of this application.

APPLICATIONS

4.1 THE RETICENT SUBORDINATES

Jennifer O'Keefe is the food-services manager for Wonderworld, a resort hotel and theme park in Orlando, Florida. She sent a memo to her staff two weeks before the usual end-of-the-month staff meeting requesting topics for discussion at the upcoming session. As of two days before the scheduled meeting, none of the employees had submitted any topics, so Jennifer assumed that the meeting might as well be canceled.

QUESTIONS

1. Does the absence of submitted topics necessarily mean that the employees would have nothing to say if the meeting were held as scheduled? Explain.

2. If the meeting were conducted, how might Jennifer elicit comments from her subordinates?

4.2 TRYING TO GET AN ANSWER

Constantine Kouros had gone to Tom Pender's office nine workdays in a row, and every time, Pender's administrative assistant, Mrs. Worth, said Pender was unavailable, then she would look at Kouros, expressionless and blinking rapidly. Kouros was looking for an answer to his request for a raise. This time, he thought he heard a thud behind the closed door to Pender's office, but Mrs. Worth just blinked some more at him, so he left.

Kouros made the rounds in his department, asking how everyone was, seeing if they needed anything. He thought he received the most valuable information from his people this way. Near the end of this trip he ran into Teri Osage, a peer.

"I tried to see Pender again today but he is never available, at least that's what . . ."

"Did you wait?" Osage interrupted.

"Mrs. Worth made it obvious that . . ."

"What is it you want from him?" Osage asked.

"I want to know about my raise. I asked . . ."

"What if Pender doesn't give it to you?" Osage interrupted again.

"I said I would have to leave, and with all the recent retirements he'd be . . ."

"Why should you get a raise? What about me? Why should he give in to you?" Osage asked.

"Because I said I'd take the transfer to Paramiribo," Kouros explained.

"Where?" Osage asked.

"Surinam." Osage stared blankly at him. "South America. Weren't you paying attention when Pender announced it last month?" But Osage had already started walking away.

Pender's a jerk; so is Worth. Osage is useless. It's me against the lot of them, and either I get what I want or I'm out of here, thought Kouros.

QUESTIONS

Support all answers with examples from this situation.

1. What type of conflict is Kouros having with Pender? What are the conflict perspectives in this situation?

2. What barrier to communication is Mrs. Worth? What does Kouros suspect her of and why?

3. How can Kouros's trips around his department be labeled, and what kind of communication is he trying to create?

4. Who, if anyone, is using closed words? List an example.

5. Who has a listening problem? Why do you say so?

NET-WORK

Evaluate these attempts at conflict resolution (from the U.S. and U.K. versions of *The Office*).

http://www.youtube.com/watch?v=wMWuMlbL2FM
http://www.youtube.com/watch?v=KxkhgLRaJs4

PERSONAL POINTS

1. How do you feel about lying? Is it okay to lie a little or to tell little lies? Is there such a thing as a little lie? Who benefits from your always telling the truth, you or others? If others benefit more from your telling the truth, is it then permissible for you to lie?

2. Think of times when you have jumped to a conclusion. When have your snap judgments proved correct and when were they wrong? When you were wrong, did you accept the fact and change your mind, or did you try to justify your initial impression even though it was wrong?

3. How do you communicate with those of higher rank than you? What about those of lower rank? Are you comfortable or uncomfortable speaking with those of different rank and why? If uncomfortable, what can you do to increase your level of comfort?

4. How are your listening skills? Are you easily bored or distracted when others talk to you? What do you think you need to do to improve your listening skills? *How* will you do these things?

5. How do you feel about conflict? How do you handle conflict? When have you analyzed conflicts to determine the type and the perspectives? When *should* you have analyzed conflicts to determine the type and the perspectives? How might these conflicts have ended differently had you analyzed them?

EXPERIENTIAL EXERCISE

This is a group exercise. It may be helpful to conduct part 1 one class period before parts 2 and 3.

PART 1

The class will be divided into three groups. Each group should have five to eight members. An observer will also be needed for each group. If there are many more than 27 students, it may help to divide the class into six groups, each with an observer, and perform the exercise simultaneously with two sets of three groups. To divide the class, the students are instructed to form a line in order from the most influential and persuasive leaders to the less influential and persuasive. The students should be allowed to arrange themselves and to jockey for position until everyone is satisfied that they are in a comfortable place in the influence hierarchy. The students should then count off and record their number for use during part 2.

PART 2

Divide the class into thirds (sixths if a larger class). The lowest number in each group becomes the observer. For example, if there are 25 students, numbers 1 through 8 will be the most influential and persuasive leaders, 9 through 16 will be the middle group, and 17 through 24 will be the less influential group. The students with numbers 8, 16, and 24 will be the observers.

The less influential group will become the top managers of a corporation in need of downsizing. The most influential group will become the frontline workers. The middle group will become the middle managers. The workforce must be reduced by 25 percent.

Of course, no one wants to be fired, so the groups must resolve this conflict.

The observers should try to determine whether any intergroup or intragroup conflicts are positive or negative. The observers should reformulate any requests from their group to the other groups in terms of how the demand, threat, and offer are being made. They should then evaluate the seven situational elements of the conflict. Finally, they record and classify the attempts the groups use to resolve the conflict and report their observations at the end of the exercise.

PART 3

The observers should compare notes and present their findings to all groups. Observations and alternative actions and methods should be discussed. Each group should discuss the reasoning used to produce the actions taken.

Observer's Checklists

Negative Conflict	*Positive Conflict*
Feud mentality	Problem-solving mentality
Going for broke	Going for mutual satisfaction
Me syndrome	Everyone syndrome
You syndrome	Just the facts

GENERAL GUIDELINES

1. Was everyone treated with respect?

2. Did everybody appear convinced that they had enough in common to make communication and a mutually satisfactory resolution possible?

3. Did people concentrate on the problem or become distracted by other issues?

4. Was there ego involvement? Name calling? Were closed words used?

5. Did people report facts or their own value judgments?

6. Did people use descriptive terms or strong, emotion-filled words?

7. Were specifics discussed, or did people speak in generalities?

8. Were the issues most open to change discussed, or did people bring up those that had little or no chance of changing (like why a 25 percent reduction and not 20 percent)?

9. Did people discuss one issue at a time, or were unrelated issues discussed?

10. Was a positive image projected?

    Conflict Perspectives

    The perceived demand
    The perceived threat
    The perceived offer

    Situational Elements

    Interests
    Options
    Legitimacy
    Relationships
    Communication
    Commitments
    The alternative

SPOT CHECK ANSWERS

1. T
2. F
3. F
4. T
5. F
6. T
7. T
8. T
9. T
10. T

5 | Ethics and Etiquette

A young manager, unskilled at hosting, gave a dinner for his customers at a fine New York restaurant. When the wine steward handed him the cork he looked at it in perplexity for several seconds and then made a decision, as all good managers will—he bit off a piece of the end and ate it.

Letitia Baldridge

Behaving like a manager means having command of the whole range of management skills and applying them as they become appropriate.

Herbert Simon

GOALS

The main goal for this chapter is to discuss correct behavior. Ethics and etiquette involve different types of correct behavior, and both are vital to your success because others are constantly evaluating the acceptability of your behavior.

OBJECTIVES

When you finish this chapter, you should be able to:

▶ Define ethics, etiquette, and morality.
▶ Differentiate between ethics and etiquette.
▶ List and explain ethical challenges to business.
▶ Identify the five ethical pressures.
▶ Explain the ethics gaps.
▶ Describe methods for managing ethics.
▶ Define and differentiate philosophies toward business profits.
▶ Explain the ethical concerns for business social responsibility related to employees, consumers, the environment, providing information, assisting special employment groups, and helping small businesses.
▶ Describe socially responsible program guidelines.
▶ Describe office phone, cellular phone, pager, fax machine, copier, and e-mail etiquette.

▶ Describe proper etiquette for shared workspaces.
▶ Describe meeting etiquette.
▶ Explain attire etiquette for men and women.
▶ Explain the advantages and disadvantages of casual business attire.
▶ Describe the etiquette of coming and going.
▶ Describe the etiquette of business dining, including that for ordering, discussing business, using utensils, host and guest etiquette, and proper manners.
▶ Describe the etiquette of business cordiality.
▶ Describe actions that can be taken when others break the rules of etiquette.

THE RIGHT TREATMENT OF OTHERS

Ethics

a set of principles of
right conduct

Etiquette

correct behavior and
practices according to
social convention

Morality

the goodness or badness
of human action or
behavior

Both ethics and etiquette involve behavior and treatment of others. **Ethics** is concerned with a set of moral principles of right conduct. **Etiquette** is concerned with correct behavior and practices according to social convention. To some, these two definitions may sound similar, but the inclusion of moral principles in the definition of ethics is the key to differentiating between the two. **Morality** is concerned with the goodness or badness of human action or behavior.

Etiquette does not include a judgment of whether an action is good or bad, right or wrong. Proper etiquette is concerned with what is accepted by society as proper. For example, it is neither good nor bad to bring food to your mouth with a fork held in your left hand. However, it is not generally accepted as proper etiquette in the United States, although it is in Britain. On the other hand, both cultures acknowledge that stealing is wrong, and there is no proper behavior to accompany it. Both ethics and etiquette transcend the business and organizational worlds, but we will limit the discussion here to the working environment.

The business community has had considerable positive influence on U.S. society, providing jobs and helping to create high levels of living standards for many people. However, well-publicized scandals and some business practices have periodically tarnished its image and adversely affected the public's attitudes toward the business community and its behavior. Such attitudes have fluctuated over the years, at times being highly critical and at other times notably supportive.

Perhaps more important than what attitudes have been in the past, and even than what they currently are, is what they are likely to be in the future. Many business-people today are concerned with the question of ethics and other factors that are apt to mold future attitudes toward business. Many observers of the social scene believe that the way in which business managers perceive and discharge their ethical, legal, and moral responsibilities toward society will significantly influence future public attitudes toward business.

What does the word *ethics* actually mean? Developing a working definition presents little difficulty. Developing illustrations is a more challenging task, as we'll see. Basically, ethics deals with the standards of conduct or morals established by the current and past attitudes and moods of a particular society. In simple terms, business ethics relates to standards of right and wrong.

The most dramatic and damaging ethical violations in recent times occurred around the end of the twentieth and beginning of the twenty-first centuries. Probably one would have had to have been shipwrecked to have missed the media coverage of the debacles of Enron, Tyco, Global Crossing, Worldcom, and others. Ethical standards were ignored, accounting practices were disregarded, other firms were destroyed (once-venerable Arthur Andersen, for example), and it seems a number of laws were broken. The losses were not limited to the theoretical, either, as many thousands, if not millions, of employees and investors lost billions of dollars. We will take a closer look at these events later.

BUSINESS ETHICS: AN OXYMORON?

Accusing all business people of unethical practices would be unfair, but with the events of the last few years it seems there is no shortage of ethically challenged managers and accountants at large firms. Many business managers do maintain consistently high standards of ethical behavior. Nonetheless, business managers must be concerned—as many actually are—with public attitudes because the future of business enterprise, is linked closely to these attitudes. Business managers who ignore public sentiment over time are likely to find that a disenchanted public can exert pressure through its elected representatives, who have started to create regulations, such as Sarbanes-Oxley, that force businesses to display greater social responsibility. There are other important reasons that business has been criticized in recent decades.

ETHICAL PRESSURES

Before looking further into criticisms of businesses and recent gaps in ethical behavior, it will be helpful to examine the five ethical pressures people in businesses and many other organizations face. The pressures come from customers, employees, creditors, competitors, and owners (shareholders in the case of corporations). Customers exert pressure on businesses to produce good products and services at the lowest prices possible (given a certain quality). Employees expect fair treatment and a fair (read "high") wage for the work they perform. Creditors expect their bills to be paid on time. Competitors pressure a business with new or improved products and through their prices. And owners/shareholders and the related investment industries expect the maximum return on their money. Outside analysts even proclaim what performance they expect from a company, and the company's stock price can drop, sometimes dramatically, if the company doesn't "make its numbers."

Effect on Cash   Each of these five pressures places certain demands on a company's money. Customers, in expecting low prices, limit the amount of cash entering a company. In other words, if a company had a monopoly, it could charge whatever it wanted, and that would certainly be more than when customers have alternatives. Employees, wanting maximum pay, pressure companies to give them more cash. But creditors also want their money, and on time. So if a company is a little short of cash, who doesn't get paid? Employees and creditors both want what money there is. The action of competitors exerts pressure to put more money now into marketing, research, and product development. Finally, the owners want as much profit as possible so they can earn money, too (otherwise, why buy a company or its shares?).

Effect on Prices   The five pressures have conflicting influences on the prices a company charges. Employees want prices to increase with the resultant increase in cash going to them in the form of higher wages. Customers pressure companies to lower prices because they don't want to pay more for the product; paying more would give them less money for other things. Creditors want higher prices not only so they get their money, but because maybe next time, they could charge the company more and receive an even greater amount. Suppliers have a harder time charging and making more money if a company can't raise prices to its customers ("you can't get blood out of a turnip"). Competitors' prices prevent a company from charging more because if the competitors' products are less expensive, people are more likely to buy from them. The owners, of course, not only want the current cash, but they also want to see prices increase so that their profits will increase. The net effect is that there are three groups exerting an upward pressure on prices, and two exerting a downward pressure.

Management in the Middle   Certainly you have noticed that these five groups are in conflict over a company's money and, taken together, are trying to push prices both up and down. Management is caught in the middle of a five-way tug-of-war. Worse yet, there is no right or wrong response to these pressures from the perspective of each group; each feels justified in its demand for the cash. What managers have to do is find a balance among all five. Management must decide on prices that

NetNote

Business Ethics

http://www.web-miner.com/ busethics.htm

Links to many business ethics articles.

143

bring in money that pays everyone what seems right. This is much easier to say than it is to do. Employee wages are often negotiated, a supplier raises prices while a competitor lowers them, and customers are bargain hunting while stockholders expect increasing dividends at the end of each quarter. If any one of these five groups starts to exert a disproportionate pressure, management may lose the sense of balance that keeps all five in equilibrium. And just to make sure that management doesn't have it too easy, outside groups and forces that may not have a direct claim on the company treasury, nonetheless still influence, or seek to influence, the managers, their ethics, and the company's activities.

THE EFFECTS OF TECHNOLOGY

Technology, especially in the areas of communications and computers, has had two main effects related to ethics. First, owing most especially to the Internet, more and more has been demanded of workers.[1] This situation has led to a greatly increased level of distress and burnout. Second, the Internet has allowed workers new opportunities to not work, to look for other jobs, or to engage in other non-work-related activities on company time.

The increased opportunities for people to communicate via the Internet, cell phones, voice mail, and so on has made it possible for employers to expect more and more work from people. Check your e-mail at home, call a client in the car, receive and respond to nearly 200 messages per day, and you are more productive—and putting in many more hours—before you know it.[2] Is it ethical, however, to expect people to work more, usually for the same pay, just because they can? The price for increased communication and productivity is often being paid by the workers in the form of unsustainable levels of stress.

The availability of the Internet has also resulted in new ethical pressures for workers and management. With the Web accessible at many workers' desks, it is tempting for them to engage in many activities—checking stock prices, online shopping, even looking for another job. This situation has led some employers to monitor workers' Internet activities, ironically, creating a lack of trust between employee and employer.[3]

A QUESTION OF ETHICS

Ethics and Dow Corning

Dow Corning, a company founded in 1943 by Dow Chemical and Corning Glass to find new uses for silicone (one of the most useful substances around), had a small department that sold silicone breast implants. The implants were not highly profitable, but Dow Corning was doing well overall and only had the two corporate stockholders to answer to. Dow Corning documents show an internal debate on the safety of the company's silicone breast implants, but studies had not proven that the implants were either safe or unsafe. There was concern in the medical community over the safety of the implants, with some doctors believing small amounts of Dow Corning silicone caused a hardening of surrounding tissue at a greater rate than did implants of other manufacturers.

If you had been working for Dow Corning at this time, what would you have done? More importantly, why

would you have done it? Remember: At the time, the implants had not been proven safe or unsafe.

Note: During discovery investigation for a client claiming her implants made her ill, lawyer Dan Bolton found documents, a former employee willing to testify against the company, a few "experts" theorizing that leaking silicone affects the immune system, and a sympathetic jury. Bolton won the case against Dow Corning. Six years later, Bolton represented a similar client, and she was awarded three times the amount the first client received. Publicity caused the second case to ignite a mass tort—a huge class-action suit. Eventually, Dow Corning faced over 20,000 lawsuits and had 480,000 claimants for its settlement offer. This "fatal litigation" caused Dow Corning to file for bankruptcy.

Source: Adapted from Joseph Nocera, "Fatal Litigation," *Fortune,* October 16, 1995, pp. 60–82.

Advances in technology are likely to increase the pressures on both management and workers until some method for establishing limits and balance between work and private life is found.

THE EFFECTS OF ACQUISITIONS AND RESTRUCTURING ACTIVITIES

Some people have developed an antipathy toward business because of the frequent waves of leveraged buyouts (LBOs), mergers, and hostile takeovers. Periods of merger mania have recurred in recent decades, during which smaller or weaker companies have been purchased by larger or more powerful organizations. During these periods, many employees watched with uncertainty as giant companies gobbled up the firms that employed them.

A **leveraged buyout** enables managers to borrow sizable amounts of funds on their firm's equity, which can then be used to purchase equity in other firms. The managers can then sell parts of the acquired businesses at a handsome profit. Most acquiring companies divest portions of their newly acquired assets within a year, often with devastating effects on employees. The motive for breaking an acquired firm into parts is pure profit because the total value of its parts sold separately is usually greater than the value of the entire firm when intact.

Some firms attempt to defend themselves from **hostile takeovers** by establishing employee stock option plans (ESOPs) or by purchasing their own stock on the open market so that would-be acquirers are unable to purchase a controlling share of stock. Other firms that anticipate unfriendly takeovers develop **golden parachute** programs for existing executives whose positions are likely to be terminated after the acquisition. A golden parachute is a severance agreement with executives that guarantees huge payments plus possible benefits, such as stock options, if they lose their jobs as a result of an acquisition. These programs can cost companies many millions of dollars and make top managers even richer; however, there are no golden parachutes for frontline workers or even middle managers. They often simply lose their jobs.[4]

Tremendous amounts of uncertainty and anxiety tend to develop among the employees of the acquired and restructured firms. A recent study found that acquisitions and restructuring activities often fail because companies place too much importance on financial information and spend too little time planning for the stressful effects of change on their staff. Employees typically become uncertain of the future direction of their careers, have decreased productivity and higher turnover and absenteeism, and experience a decrease in trust and motivation.[5] These losses often outweigh the benefits of restructuring and downsizing.

LACK OF SUFFICIENT CONCERN FOR THE ENVIRONMENT

Part of the public's attitude toward the business community has resulted from the latter's reluctance to show concern for the environment unless pressured by government agencies. The public tends to be cynical when it hears business executives talk about their social responsibility but observes what appears to be contrary behavior.

Stirred by reports of acid rain, dirty air, filthy lakes and rivers, global warming, ozone depletion, nuclear and toxic wastes, and the disastrous Exxon Valdez oil spill, the public appears to desire a reversal of the trend of the lax Reagan years by calling for more environmental regulation. Some businesses are concerned about the cost of complying with new regulations, whereas environmentalists argue that the economic cost is well worth it in terms of health-care costs alone. The debate between these two factions is not likely to end soon because businesses sometimes

Leveraged Buyout
borrowing money in order to purchase another company

Hostile Takeover
Company A buying Company B when Company B does not wish to be purchased

Golden Parachute
a severance agreement with executives that guarantees 2 or 3 years of their annual pay plus possible benefits, such as stock purchase options, if they lose their jobs as a result of an acquisition

feel environmentalists have an unrealistic view of what consumers want, and environmentalists accuse businesses of simply being greedy.

AN ETHICS GAP

Greed may be a simple concept, but it can lead to some of the most complex behaviors seen in humans. Greed has certainly divided nations, businesses, friends, and families. It is difficult, however, to argue that greed alone has been the cause of the gigantic gap between ethical standards and the behavior of an alarming number of top businesspeople.[6] Greed seems to be part of the equation when the CEO of a company selling products such as soap and toothpaste earns more than $140 million for one year (based on the standard 40-hour week or 2,080-hour work year, that is, more than $67,000 an hour). Can one person's contribution really be that valuable? Huge compensation also increases the competition among other CEOs to get more money from their companies.[7] Even non-CEOs are making amazingly large salaries. Over the last couple of decades, these amounts have led to a culture in which ever-larger salaries for top people, and only top people, may have caused some to leave their ethics behind. Even this is not the entire story, however.

As greed and other factors combined in recent decades to create a culture that seems to believe that getting into top management means one is entitled to fabulous wealth, other influences were also at work to throw off the balance among the five ethical pressures. Managers, especially top managers, started looking inward, into their companies, and they started to insulate themselves from customers and in most cases the mass of the middle class.[8] Managers began to view themselves as a cut above, supporting the opinion that they not only deserved but were entitled to massive salaries. This would have given them the justification, in their own minds, to do what was necessary to get those salaries.[9] Even thoughts of entitlement coupled with greed might not have been enough for some to abandon their ethics. There was also a confluence of factors around the turn of this century that increased temptation.

In the eighteenth century, Adam Smith (author of *The Wealth of Nations*) saw the dangers of greed and wrote about it in a book about ethics titled *The Theory of Moral Sentiments*.[10] Two centuries of forewarning would seem to be sufficient, but Smith could not have predicted the increased use of teams, the age of the share, stock options, and the Baby Boomers. All four factors, when added to the usual ethical pressures and the changes in top managers and their pay, stretched the ethics of some beyond the breaking point.

Although Smith did see that corporations could become self-serving machines that fed off society rather than contributed to it, he did not foresee the rise of teams. With teams, you get team members. For some people the definition of a good team is "a lot of people doing what I say." The result is that team members are rewarded not for the contribution they make, but for being loyal to the leader.[11] So as the leader goes down an unethical path, the team members follow out of loyalty and the desire for reward.

At about the same time teams became popular, the age of the share arrived. As the focus, form, and function of corporations changed and developed, the belief arose that the main concern should be the price of the corporation's shares. Under this idea the corporation is not there to make goods, or serve society, or supply jobs, but to maximize the price of the shares.[12] In terms of the five traditional ethical pressures, this may sound good to owners and the top managers who represent them, but it might not be so good for the other four groups, especially employees. Related to the share is the rise in popularity of stock options. If the share price is the standard for corporate performance, the reasoning is that top management should not only be judged by the change in share price, but they should also be rewarded with shares. For the company, it works out better to give stock options (the right to buy stock in the future at a set price) rather than actual stock in many cases. Top managers thus had a very personal stake in increasing the price of the shares.

The Baby Boom generation was an incidental contributing factor. As the Boomers got closer to retirement, they started to put some money away. Because they wanted that money to grow, many invested in the stock market, either directly or through retirement accounts. The increased investment led to a desire for investing advice. Much of the advice addressed the future, which led to analysts giving out expectations and companies giving guidance, and this all led to tremendous pressure to meet those expectations and guidance numbers. More than a few companies started taking their quarterly expectations per share, plus a penny (to beat expectations, but not by too much) as a starting point and adjusting their financial reports backward to yield that expected amount plus one cent.[13] This practice produced adjusted earnings, earnings not counting items, and the very popular pro forma earnings.[14] Pro forma financial statements did exist (*pro forma* meaning "according to the form") but were meant for use mainly in business plans to show others how the statements might look if everything went well. Pro forma statements were not meant as a way to adjust a firm's finances. Use of the statements started an erosion of adherence to generally accepted accounting principles (GAAP), which made it much more difficult to compare corporate performance and allowed CEOs and other top managers to camouflage what they were doing.

Summarizing this and putting it differently, in the 1990s and into this century there was not only massive pressure to constantly deliver corporate results that exceeded expectations (due to the age of the share and the large amount of money being invested by Boomers), but there was also the means to make a company look as if it reached expectations even if it didn't (through pro forma–type statements). There were also personal reputations, careers, and fortunes at stake (the CEOs); a mind-set that a large compensation package was a right of being a top manager; and a team mentality to support whatever the top managers proposed. This caused a situation in which CEOs and top managers felt the need to perform or be replaced, and they each had money of their own at stake. The ethics of some people at mutual fund firms such as Putnam and corporations such as Calpine, Tyco, Global Crossing, Worldcom, Arthur Andersen, and, most infamously, Enron, evidently could not hold up to the demands they felt were being made.[15]

The collapse of Enron is certainly going to be one of the most discussed events in business circles and the media for a number of years. Enron also illustrates all of the points just described.[16] Enron's CEO, Ken Lay, was not seen in a bad light, as he often gave to philanthropic causes, but giving to charity is not the same as running a business ethically. Reportedly, he was fixated on the price of Enron shares, and he held many of them himself. His concern carried over to other employees who were swiftly fired if they didn't meet their financial expectations. Employees who were not fired quickly learned to get with the program or suffer the same consequences, reinforcing the inward view of the company. Lay's separation from the commoners and his attitude of entitlement could be seen just before the collapse of Enron in his selling of his own shares while reassuring employees that all was well and that Enron should be promoted among friends and relations. The stunningly complex methods used by Enron's top managers to conceal what was really happening shows the team concerns mentioned before. Also, the loosening of the ethic to use strict accounting enabled them to hide the truth without drawing too much attention to their actions. The Enron case also shows how top managers made out well (until everything imploded) and how employees and investors (many of them Boomers approaching retirement) suffered losses of billions of dollars (maybe more than $100 billion from this scandal alone). The challenge now is how best to prevent this from happening again.

MANAGING ETHICS

While laws, SEC regulations, lawsuits, and the accounting standards board may work to address specific abuses, individuals and organizations can do much to improve and maintain desirable ethics. First, there must be a reason to be ethical, and a definition of ethics must be devised. Second, there must be communication and training. Third, there are ongoing activities that should be undertaken, and fourth, there must be follow-up.

Defining Ethics   Although it might initially seem an odd question, in order to start from the beginning one should ask why anyone should be ethical. To do this, a definition of ethics is needed. Most definitions of ethics mention right and wrong conduct, for example, "a set of principles of right conduct." Now, why should people follow a set of principles of right conduct? Some have argued that people should be ethical because it may cost them (money, a job, a reputation—things mostly related to money, though), or it may cost the company, or because humans are economic and ethical creatures.[17] Reasons concerning money do not work well; such reasoning would suggest that business leaders involved in recent scandals were often ethical to themselves in trying to acquire or retain money. It may be easier to find a reason to be ethical by looking at the opposite: what if no one were ethical? If not for ethics, the world would be chaotic. There would be no right or wrong, no rules, no truth, no trust. There would be no organizations because, as mentioned in Chapter 1, the minimum requirements for an organization are communication and cooperation. Without ethics, nothing that is said can be believed or trusted, as people are only going to be looking out for themselves. With no right or wrong, it is every man for himself, every woman for herself. There goes communication, cooperation, and organizations, and society as a whole, too.

No matter what other reasons one wants to throw in, the basic reason to follow a set of principles of right conduct is that humans, as individuals and together, cannot thrive any other way. We need one another for a society as complex as ours to

---

REALITY CHECK

An Example of Ethical Conduct

Imagine that you work for a company with about $16 billion in annual revenues and that one of your products, which brings in $500 million, might, just might, be harmful to people. What would you do? Oh, by the way, there is no substitute for this product in the world; it is used in industry and many, many homes; and besides losing half a billion dollars if you pull the product, you will incur other charges of $200 million and may have to fire 1,500 workers. Now what do you decide? Most companies would argue the evidence or wait for the government to order them to do something, but not 3M. Minnesota Mining and Manufacturing found that a chemical from its extremely popular product Scotchgard was turning up in some blood samples from different parts of the country. The chemical can change in the cells of mammals, and in high doses can harm animals. There was no evidence that even industrial exposure caused harm in humans, but 3M wasn't taking chances. In a bold example of bravery and ethical behavior, 3M voluntarily pulled the product from the market. This upset many industrial buyers as well as consumers, especially since there is no substitute to be had anywhere. Still, rather than take a very small chance with people and the environment, 3M stopped production of Scotchgard and started researching a safe alternative.

Source: Joseph Weber, "3M's Big Cleanup," *Business Week*, June 5, 2000, pp. 96–98.

function as it does. An individual here or there may be tempted to think that he or she can discard ethics, thinking that "as long as everyone else is ethical I don't have to be." Or, he or she may rationalize it as "I don't have to tell the truth, just so long as everyone else does." Neither of these arguments works. Ethics must apply to everyone. If one person isn't playing by the rules of right and wrong, then others feel justified in not being ethical. Eventually this spreads to everyone, and we are right back to chaos.

With a general definition of ethics and the knowledge that ethics needs to apply to everyone, organizations can draw up a more specific list of what constitutes right conduct. For example, in the medical and allied health professions, the primary ethical principle is that the patient comes first. It would be unethical for a surgical team to leave someone on an operating table saying, "Our favorite unreality show, *America's Idle*, is on. We'll be back in an hour." In education, students come first, so it would be unethical to cancel a class to attend a party or meeting. Other organizations need to establish what right conduct is for their situations. It is not acceptable simply to rely on everyone's knowing right from wrong. Having no policy is giving tacit approval to unethical behavior ("Hey, no one said I couldn't do that!").[18]

Communicating the Ethic   Once ethical conduct has been described, it needs to be widely disseminated and should be accompanied by training. The entire process, as with most organizational endeavors, must start at the top; only then will individuals throughout the organization begin to take the effort seriously.[19] This point is so important that another definition of CEO has been proposed: Rather than chief executive officer it should also stand for chief *ethics* officer.[20]

With all of the attention ethics has received recently, it may be necessary to rephrase some of the guidelines so that people do not dismiss the ethics policy as "been there, done that."[21] Rather than having people ask, "What is the ethical thing to do here?" they may respond better to "What is the right thing to do?" or "If the roles were reversed, how would I want the other person to act?" Another suggestion for reaching people is to use existing online ethics programs. This may be especially useful to small businesses or to large ones that have workers separated geographically or in time (working the midnight shift, for example).

In order to signal to an organization that this is a serious ethics effort, there must be consequences for unethical behavior. As seen in the motivation chapter, one way to signal that something is important is to raise people's level of concern. In other words, it is not as effective just to tell people to do something; they need to know they will be held accountable for their actions. The ethics policy needs to include consequences (punishments) for being unethical. Increasingly, firms are having people sign the policy to acknowledge that they know about it and understand they will be held to it.[22]

Ongoing Activities   The first ongoing activity that should take place may also involve a change of attitude. Upper management must abandon or refrain from adopting a "me first" attitude.[23] What must stop, or never start, is conduct like that of Don Carty who, as president of American Airlines, talked unions into sacrificing more than $1.6 billion and then revealed that upper managers were receiving bonuses and guaranteed pensions.[24] Carty had to resign because of this. For workers and middle managers to believe in the ethics policy, they must know that it applies to everyone.

On an ongoing basis, organization members must demand the truth. While this applies to everyone, it applies especially to top managers. They must demand to be told the true picture—the good and most definitely the bad. They must get the truth from middle managers and workers and not punish them for delivering bad news.[25] If upper managers yell at those who bring bad news, they are reinforcing the idea that employees should never bring bad news, no matter how serious and truthful it is.

Along with seeking the truth, managers need to discover where the ethical risks are in the organization.[26] The identified risks need to be assessed for their potential to lure people toward unethical behavior. Taking a long-term view here is important so that action can be taken before any unethical behavior occurs. A study of the numerous recent ethical failures can point the way toward areas that are potential problems.

Examples of ethical (and unethical) behavior also need to be publicized on an ongoing basis.[27] Communicating examples of ethical behavior serves as a reminder to people and also shows that others are behaving ethically. Discussing unethical behavior, either from inside the company (while considering privacy rights) or outside, demonstrates that the organization remains serious and watchful.

Follow-up   Communicating ethical and unethical behavior might be considered a follow-up activity, but there are others. First, do not allow people to work around the ethics policy.[28] When given a set of rules, some people immediately try to figure out how much they can get away with. Ethical and unethical behavior is not a dichotomy (like black and white, or on and off) but a continuum (black, with many gray shades before coming to white). These people won't know they have gone too far until they cross over into unethical territory, so there can be no stretching the rules. Besides, allowing the rules to be stretched or avoided can send a signal that the ethics policy does not have to be taken seriously.

Enforcement is a critical follow-up activity related to accountability—if one is not held accountable for unethical behavior then it must not be important. When ethical violations are found, they must be dealt with swiftly and by the book (which won't be a problem because consequences were previously established with the policy itself). Some companies have gone so far as to have an ethics officer, sometimes even having people come in from the outside to evaluate ethical conditions.[29]

Whether an internal or external manager or an ethics officer is investigating unethical behavior, he or she should refrain from asking the type of questions that can be answered with a simple yes or no.[30] For example, don't ask, "Did you know about. . . ?" because not only can it be answered with a simple no, but the entire question is wrong. Investigate what the person and the person's boss should have known, when they should have known it, what they did, and what they should have done. When the questions have been answered and the situation dealt with, then learn what you can from what the individuals involved did and could have done, because in the final analysis, all ethical choices are made at the individual level.

ETHICS AND THE INDIVIDUAL

Individuals sometimes have to make difficult choices as members of organizations—difficult because of their potential impact on income and career paths. Imagine, for example, that you work as a sales representative for a steel supply company and that you have called on one of your customers, who wishes to place an unusually large order. This morning you learned that in five days your company intends to make substantial price reductions on the materials that your customer wants to buy. You have at least two options: You can take the order for the materials at today's prices, or you can inform your customer that the price is about to drop, thus saving her or him a considerable amount of money. If you enable your customer to purchase at next week's lower price, your commission, or earnings, would also be substantially lower.

What should you do? For some individuals, the choice would be difficult. But need it be? Presumably your responsibility is not merely to push through one-shot deals. Regular repeat business is far more desirable and profitable to your firm and to you over the long run. If your customer discovers that you sold materials at higher prices than necessary, what will probably be her or his attitude toward you and your company in the future? Ethical company representatives generally learn that they have far more regular, loyal, and profitable accounts when their customers are treated responsibly.

Another situation that could strain your ethical values might be if your boss were to direct you to do something that you believe is either unethical or illegal. For example, say you are an accountant, and your boss asks you to keep a separate set of books—one with padded expense figures—for income tax purposes (a situation similar to the ethical gap cases of the last few years). To say the least, there could be negative consequences whether you fulfill or don't fulfill the request. You are, as they say, caught between a rock and a hard place. When confronted with such dilemmas, you have to make a decision. Do you let your personal financial responsibilities influence or change your decision? What are your alternatives? One alternative is to do as you are directed. However, if you do, you may be as legally responsible (or as criminally negligent) as your boss. Further, your conscience may create unpleasant stress-inducing reactions that could affect other aspects of your life. As seen with Arthur Andersen and Enron, your actions could bring down your firm and maybe others.

A second choice is to refuse to carry out your boss's request, but if you don't do as directed, you also run risks because your boss determines your pay raises and promotions. However, if you are caught, and the chances are fairly good that you will be, how might your career be affected?

A third alternative is to attempt to reason with your boss. In some cases, you may be able to convince him or her to scuttle the decision by stressing the consequences of the illegal activity. You might point out to your boss that you really can't allow yourself to be put into a situation in which you are jeopardizing your career and personal life by breaking the law. You could say something like, "If I broke the law in favor of our company, isn't it likely that I would be the type of individual who would also break the law against our company? Boss, I want you to know that I prefer to deal ethically both for and with our company."

Realistically, such pleas could fall on deaf ears. A fourth alternative that has been used successfully by some organizational members is to merely give the request "lip service"; that is, say, "Okay, boss. I'll do the best I can on that," and then ignore the request. In some cases, the need for such unethical behavior may fade away. Of course, in some cases it won't, and you have to either give your boss more lip service or make a different decision.

The fifth alternative is to go over the boss's head, if that is possible. If your boss is the owner, or the only or top boss, it may not be possible. Even if it is possible to go over the boss's head, it still might not be advisable to do so. In purely ethical terms, and in a perfect world, you are supposed to be able to appeal to a higher authority. But you must carefully weigh this move. You must evaluate your position, your case, your boss's position, your boss's boss's position, and the consequences of not going over the boss's head. Evaluating your position refers to assessing the possibility that you might lose your job or that other things could happen if the appeal fails. In evaluating your case, you must examine the strength and believability of the evidence that you were asked to do something wrong. If it is your word against the boss's, you may have to consider carefully who will be believed, remembering that the boss will get a point or two just because he or she is a boss.

A sixth alternative is the most extreme one. If you find that more positive approaches don't work and that your conscience cannot live with the unethical practices of your boss or firm, then you may have to make the ultimate decision of resigning. Such an act takes a lot of courage. It may adversely affect your financial situation. Others, however, have made such choices and felt better about themselves as a result. You, too, may discover that you can live a far more confident existence if, in your mind, your activities do not border on the unethical or illegal. These scenarios illustrate another point—organizations are not ethical or unethical, individuals are. Each individual must make a personal choice, at times difficult, to be ethical or not. Once having chosen not to be ethical, it can be very difficult to turn back.

TWO PHILOSOPHIES: PROFIT QUEST VERSUS SOCIAL RESPONSIBILITY

How do you feel about profits? Most observers of society today would probably agree that the quest for profits is not in itself an evil activity. However, there exists incomplete agreement as to what degree the maximization of profits should be the concern of business managers. There actually are two principal schools of thought on the subject: the **trustee-of-profit philosophy** and **enlightened self-interest philosophy.**

The classical trustee-of-profit philosophy contends that the corporation's sole responsibility is to produce profits and that any expenditure on corporate social goals amounts to a hidden tax on workers, customers, and shareholders. The second and more modern philosophy, enlightened self-interest, argues that social goals should not be considered as competition for profits but instead as one of the overall goals of management. The two points of view, which typify the opposition that has long prevailed among philosophers, are sometimes referred to as the profit-quest and the social-responsibility approaches. Let's examine each briefly.

THE PROFIT-QUEST APPROACH

Although many families were hit badly by the triple-dip recession of the early 1990s and then again in the economic slowdown at the start of this century, Americans continue to enjoy one of the highest material standards of living in the world. Those who subscribe to the **profit-quest approach** argue that the attainment of such standards has been largely a result of the private (more aptly called mixed) enterprise system in the United States. Although other nations have high standards of living, few offer their citizens as wide a choice of different consumer products as exists in the United States. Trends in other countries—both eastern and western—have frequently emulated developments in U.S. technology and marketing. Americans could survive quite well without DVD or MP3 players, HDTV, laptop computers, DSL and cable modems, picture cell phones, and satellite radio, but the existence of such goods has generally been assured by the consuming public's consistent flow of "dollar votes."

Much of America's wide choice of products and reasonably well-paying jobs has been dependent on the earning of profits by the business community. Reasonable profits themselves—unless you subscribe to Marxian philosophy—aren't necessarily evil. Many past and present social ills in the United States were caused not so much by the making of profits as by what was done with the nation's resources.

However, many corporations seem to have the notion that they aren't obliged to do anything but turn a profit. Some firms profess social concern but, as we have seen, don't appear to mean it. At times, their efforts have seemed merely to be part of a well-publicized public relations fad with little apparent significance.

As the chapter on leadership styles showed, there is more than one philosophy or way of perceiving others; some managers perceive individuals positively, whereas others stress the negative. The same thesis holds true for the way in which business managers perceive the general public vis-à-vis their social responsibilities. Some managers believe that their only concern need be with the quest for profits. "We aren't social workers!" some business leaders exclaim.

Trustee-of-Profit Philosophy

a corporation's sole responsibility is to produce profits, and any expenditure on corporate social goals amounts to a hidden tax on workers, customers, and shareholders

Enlightened Self-Interest Philosophy

social goals are one of the overall goals of management

Profit-Quest Approach

the attainment of a high standard of living is a result of the private (free) enterprise system in the United States

NetNote

Business Ethics

http://www.thecro.com/

Corporate Social Responsibility Report.

THE SOCIAL-RESPONSIBILITY APPROACH

Of course, not all organizations hold an exclusive trustee-of-profit philosophy. For many organizations, **social responsibility,** that is, an attitude of responsibility toward society, is a major concern. Corporate goals still include earning profits, but many executives today also believe that making a good product, offering it at a good price, and earning a decent profit are not enough; many corporations also have a social conscience. Enlightened executives display their social consciences in a variety of ways. In the following section, you will read about the areas of public concern that receive attention from the business community.

Social Responsibility companies are corporate citizens and, as such, accountable for how they affect society

AREAS OF SOCIAL RESPONSIBILITY

We shall now move on to a controversial topic, the special areas of social responsibility that the business community should face. Our list of concerns will be neither complete nor absolute. Keep in mind that issues that seemed almost radical during one era sometimes become commonplace during another. Conversely, issues that were significant during one period become unnecessary during another if the specific problems no longer exist.

The following discussion is intended to illustrate the various types of social responsibilities with which some managers are concerned. The list should be modified as social conditions change. Among current managerial concerns are responsibilities to:

- employees
- consumers
- the environment
- provide information
- assist special employment groups
- help small businesses

RESPONSIBILITY TO EMPLOYEES

One of the primary social responsibilities of an organization should be its own employees, and much of what we've already covered in this text concerns employee relations. From the standpoint of improving the corporate image, employees are exceedingly important because they are an influential communication link to the general public. Information regarding either favorable company practices or the distribution of shoddy products and unfair management tactics will readily be transmitted to the general public through employees' communication networks.

SPOT CHECK

1. Team leaders have been unethical, and sometimes team members follow out of loyalty and the desire for reward. T F
2. Ethics is a set of principles of right conduct. T F
3. If your boss directs you to do something that is unethical, you cannot be held responsible because you were ordered to do it by a person of higher rank. T F
4. The profit-quest approach requires business to do anything necessary in order to earn a profit for the owner or owners. T F
5. The social responsibility approach is only suitable for nonprofit organizations. T F

Some firms have the reputation of being concerned with employees' attitudes, their personal problems, and other factors that influence both on-the-job performance and public attitudes toward the organization. Some companies, for example, encourage employees to further their education by assisting them with the costs of attending night colleges or universities. Others assist employed parents by providing them with day care for their children. As we've already learned, many firms now provide counseling services for employees with such problems as alcoholism, drug abuse, and emotional difficulties. Others provide workshops that offer advice on how to cope during stressful periods of plant closings or relocations. Some companies used to have a long-standing commitment to their employees, either formally or informally, through no-layoff policies. Surplus staff is either retrained and deployed to other departments or reduced through attrition, early retirement, and limitations on hiring when economic conditions require a reduction in personnel. Unfortunately, today only a few organizations are like the National Association of Insurance Commissioners, which tries to maintain a no-layoff policy.[31] Even IBM, which long subscribed to a no-layoff, full-employment policy, has had to abandon the policy during difficult times.

RESPONSIBILITY TO CONSUMERS

A company's customers are its bread and butter. Without customers, there are no revenues and thus no profits. The principle of *caveat emptor* already mentioned is less prevalent today than in the past. Once again, the change resulted in part because an outraged public pressured its elected representatives into passing legislation to protect unwary consumers.

Any company's survival over the long run is highly dependent on its ability to provide consumers with the goods and services they want, at a price they're willing to pay, and of a quality they consider reasonable. Firms that have failed to do so have usually lost business to those that have attempted to satisfy the public's needs. The total quality management movement discussed in Chapter 8 is a positive step in the direction of focusing on customer wants and needs.

Taco Bell Corporation showed its concern for consumers and the community soon after a destructive Los Angeles riot. Many managers decided not to rebuild their destroyed structures, but Taco Bell launched a construction marathon to build a Compton outlet in just 48 hours to replace the $500,000 site that was destroyed during the riots. Calling their efforts "From Rubble to Re-Employment in Two Days," Taco Bell executives agreed to provide some business and job opportunities to minorities during rebuilding. Five of the ten members of the construction consortium were minority-owned contractors, and minorities accounted for 168 of the 255 workers on the job site.[32]

RESPONSIBILITY TO THE ENVIRONMENT

Unfortunately, America's gigantic economy has produced not only an affluent but also an effluent society, one with polluted rivers, foul air, and an urban atmosphere that generates fear, tension, and sometimes misery. Not everyone agrees on the extent to which businesses can afford to be involved with protecting the environment. Some executives contend, for example, that the increased costs resulting from the installation of antipollution devices can price their products out of consumer markets.

Federal legislation requires any company (or individual) that accidentally spills chemicals to report the accident to the Environmental Protection Agency (EPA). Anyone who violates the EPA's spill-reporting requirements faces criminal prosecution and substantial fines.

Is concern for the environment costly? A valid question relates to what additional costs a firm—especially a small firm—can afford and still remain competitive and profitable. However, over the long run, it is doubtful that more stringent environmental concerns and controls will have a significant influence on industry's costs. Historically, some of the most profitable firms have been those most concerned with the environment. Those who oppose such controls principally on the grounds of cost should not overlook an essential point: Society reaps substantial benefit from a pollution-free environment. Of course, a free economy does produce a lot of wealth, and wealth is a social good. But so is health, which is attainable only with the sacrifice of some types of freedoms, such as the freedom to pollute.

Many firms have shown a concern for the environment. Some firms place emphasis on waste prevention and the recycling of waste materials rather than on waste disposal. In fact, so many companies have become involved with recycling activities that the U.S. recycling business became plagued in 1992 by distribution bottlenecks and regional gluts of collected materials. Consequently, more than two dozen large U.S. corporations have formed a voluntary alliance to develop and expand markets for recycled products. The group calls itself the Buy Recycled Business Alliance and includes such companies as McDonald's Corporation, Coca-Cola, Verizon, United States Postal Service, Target, and Wal-Mart. Many member companies have committed senior managers to the effort.[33]

RESPONSIBILITY TO PROVIDE INFORMATION

Another socially beneficial approach taken by some organizations is the dissemination of practical information to the general public or to other businesses. For example, Metropolitan Life Insurance Company has consistently made available free brochures providing information on health and hygiene. Naturally, the longer people live, the longer they will pay insurance premiums to insurance companies such as Metropolitan Life. This factor, however, need not detract from the social usefulness of such efforts.

Another firm, the Kemper Financial Group, has actively distributed free information to companies concerned with establishing drug- and alcohol-abuse programs. Utility companies, too, have provided free counseling on how to insulate houses. Some have also provided low-interest loans to allow home owners to purchase energy-saving items such as solar heating units.

Some companies, however, take an opposite tack, as noted in the section on the ethics gap. In recent years, the trend has been to exclude unfavorable information or hide it in less obvious sections of annual reports. Other techniques include writing down inventory and then reversing the charges later, selling inventory previously written down to $0, the net effect being to inflate earnings on paper.[34] Which is worse, providing misleading information or not providing information at all?

RESPONSIBILITY TO ASSIST SPECIAL EMPLOYMENT GROUPS

Many organizations have shown an awareness of their responsibilities to special employment groups in recent decades. Some firms actively promote their equal employment opportunity hiring practices to increase the proportion of minorities, women, and individuals with mental or physical challenges in their organizations. Others have developed innovations in employment, such as the use of computer terminals at home, so that individuals with disabilities can be gainfully employed.

Many members of special employment groups tend to have less seniority than other employees because many of the former are newer to the workforce. As a result, recessions frequently result in the undoing of much of the progress achieved in the area of equal employment opportunity. Newer employees are usually laid off or discharged during recessions. "Last hired, first fired" has been a well-known expression to many minorities and women during economic recessions. Restructuring activities resulting from hostile takeovers have frequently affected minorities and women in the same manner as recessions.

RESPONSIBILITY TO HELP SMALL BUSINESSES

The concern big businesses have in helping small businesses is partly altruistic and partly self-interest. Altruistically, big businesses may help smaller ones as a way to give something back to the community or as a way of following the social-responsibility belief that what is good for business is good for society. Big businesses may also be acting out of some slef-interest in that there may be a future relationship possible with the small business. The small business might someday become a supplier to the big business; the small business may become a purchaser from the big business; or the two may become partners in some future project or venture.

GUIDE TO SOCIAL ACTION

One of the primary functions of management is that of planning. Yet managers concerned with social programs often neglect this important function. Instead, they too frequently have been involved with putting out fires ignited by disgruntled members of the public.

Social programs developed in a calm and thoughtful atmosphere tend to convey greater sincerity and are more likely to succeed than those hastily conceived in an atmosphere of crisis. Too frequently, pressured and harried executives have developed and employed programs before analyzing their implications, thus creating distrust rather than appreciation and respect in the general public.

Naturally, no magic formulas can guarantee the success of any program, but some approaches tried by various organizations have been effective. The purpose of the following section, therefore, is to offer a set of guidelines (see Table 5.1) that can result in more successes than a helter-skelter approach of haste, indecision, and uncertainty can.

COMMUNITY RELATIONSHIPS

Being an integral component of society, businesses assume certain responsibilities. The number of responsibilities assumed is limited by practicality and choice. For practical reasons, small businesses cannot assume as many responsibilities as large businesses. The main practical limits are money and people. While a small business

---

TABLE 5.1 SUGGESTED GUIDELINES RELATED TO EMPLOYING SOCIALLY RESPONSIBLE PROGRAMS

Management must be committed.
The program should be integrated into regular operations.
The program must be communicated.
The program must be credible.
Participants should be concerned with action.
Failures should not be discouraging.

might commit the same percentage of money and people's effort as a large business, the amounts will be less. This does not mean the efforts of small businesses are any less commendable. The limit of choice is whether or not a business elects to assume community responsibilities. While one small business might choose to become involved in the community, it is understandable when another does not. For example, how much could a three-person business do before its charitable efforts had a negative impact on its commercial efforts?

When businesses become involved in the community, they usually do so because they feel they should. They feel they should because the business affects the community and the community affects the business. Essentially, they have a symbiotic relationship. They respect the rights of their immediate neighbors and other members of the community and expect the same in return. Respecting the rights of the community includes operating facilities safely and in compliance with applicable environmental regulations and taking any additional steps needed to make a positive contribution to the community. Businesses may look for ways to improve the quality of work life in the community, working in partnership with local government, other businesses, and charitable organizations, as well as contributing funds to qualified organizations and projects whose purpose is community betterment. They may also encourage their employees to participate in civic affairs and activities of interest, recognizing that volunteer work is a highly commendable and valuable form of community service. To maximize the success of such programs, there are some additional considerations.

Management Must Be Committed   One of the most important guidelines for social action is that managers—from the chief executive to the supervisors—must have a firm, sincere commitment to a corporation's social programs. This commitment should be part of the ongoing goals and operations of the organization. Spending a few token dollars here or there on temporary programs does not make a company socially responsible in the eyes of the public.

The commitment must be well thought out and above all, consistent and long term. For example, programs that receive funding one year and are put on a bare-bones budget the next will generally turn people off. Consistency should pervade the entire company so that employees in one branch will not be saying or doing one thing while others are saying or doing something else.

The Program Should Be Integrated into Regular Operations   To prevent the appearance of window dressing, no program should be considered separate and apart from an organization's regular operations. A firm sincerely concerned with social responsibility should not grandstand its efforts but should instead attempt to incorporate its obligations to society into the basic structure of the organization.

The Program Must Be Communicated   All levels of an organization must understand the program if it is to be as effective as possible. As we have learned, employees provide a significant communication link with the public, and their misinterpretation of a program can cause untold damage.

Some firms use videotapes, movies, or slides to help explain the objectives of a program as well as details of the employees' responsibilities to it. Company schools are sometimes established so that interested employees can learn about environmental subjects. Public service awards can motivate employees to participate in such programs.

The Program Must Be Credible   Those directing the programs should be concerned with credibility. Few activities will ever be 100 percent successful. Although negative aspects shouldn't be accentuated when company activities are discussed, efforts to gloss over shortcomings may result in the entire program's being mistrusted. In other words, companies should be honest about their programs.

Participants Should Be Concerned with Action   Little is gained by managers who speak eloquently before civic or other groups about the need for social action and yet are not themselves actively and sincerely involved with specific programs. The public can generally see through such rhetoric. Some firms, as we have learned, permit their employees to be genuinely involved by encouraging them to volunteer for work in the community, often on company time. Some firms offer their employees paid sabbaticals; others allow a half day each week for such activities as counseling minority businesses.

Failures Should Not Be Discouraging   As you may know, the Ford Motor Company's Edsel automobile was something of a failure. Undaunted, Ford managers went on to develop two best-sellers, the Mustang and the Maverick. The first version of Microsoft Windows was a rather unspectacular operating system, especially compared with the Macintosh system. Now, Windows dominates the field.

A similar spirit should prevail among those involved with social programs. Not all programs will succeed. Managers, however, should examine the entire picture before deciding that a program has failed and abandoning it. A modification of certain aspects might improve the program's overall effectiveness.

ETIQUETTE

Ethics is often formally addressed in organizations with codes of ethics, ethics training, or both being available, if not required. The other major behavioral topic for this chapter, etiquette, is formally addressed in far fewer organizations. Yet proper etiquette is critical to success in most business arenas. It is often assumed that people are taught etiquette at home or that it is learned through experience or observation. Unfortunately, this is often not the case. Here is a short, but relatively thorough discussion of the main business etiquette concepts.

Etiquette is concerned with correct behavior and practices according to social convention. Business interactions, as we have seen throughout the previous chapters, contain a large social component. Not conforming to etiquette in purely social

---

SPOT CHECK

6. The only responsibility an organization should have to its employees is to give a fair day's pay for a fair day's work. T F
7. Businesses have a responsibility to provide the goods and services consumers want at a fair price for the quality provided. T F
8. Businesses have no responsibility to protect the environment; that is the job of government alone. T F
9. Companies have a responsibility to hide unfavorable information so the value of the company is not adversely affected. T F
10. For any ethical or social responsibility policy to work, management must be committed to it. T F

situations might cause some embarrassment or a loss of social status or invitations to future events. Not conforming to etiquette during business interactions can cause you to lose a sale or not make a deal—or it can cost you a job, an assignment, or a promotion. Whether it is right or not, people often look at your behavior and lack of conformity to etiquette and project this to your ability (or inability) to do a job. Therefore, it is in your best interest to become thoroughly familiar with the behavior that may be expected of you. Although not an exhaustive discussion, we will cover the main points of business etiquette in the following areas:

- office phones, including voice mail and answering machines
- cellular phones, pagers, and fax machines
- copiers
- e-mail
- shared workspaces
- meetings
- attire and grooming
- coming and going
- business dining
- business cordiality
- actions that can be taken when others break the rules of etiquette

The Office Phone   The telephone is one of the most commonly used pieces of office equipment and one of the most vital. Often, it is the first contact a customer, or potential customer, has with an organization. That first impression, whether it is of the organization or of you, sends a powerful message and image to the caller. Answering the phone should always be done in a professional manner (see Table 5.2). You should never answer with just "Hello," or by simply stating your phone or extension number. You should not answer the phone with a nickname because doing so is unprofessional and lacks authority.[35] Nor should you immediately place a caller on hold. If you must place callers on hold, ask their permission and allow them to answer.[36] They may not be able to wait, or there may be an emergency. Try never to leave someone on hold for more than 30 or 40 seconds, but if this becomes necessary, be sure to apologize when you return to the call.[37] If you think someone will be on hold for more than a minute, then offer to call back with the information requested. When you answer a phone and the caller is unknown to you, immediately write down the caller's name.[38] This allows you to address the person by name later in the call, which is far more impressive than having to ask what the caller's name is.

TABLE 5.2 BASIC TELEPHONE ETIQUETTE

Answer the phone in three rings or less.

Answer with your name, your department name, or the company's name.

Make business calls only during normal business hours whenever possible.

Return calls in 24 hours or less. Taking 48 or more hours is considered rude.

Never give personal information about coworkers over the phone.

When someone calls you, do not be the first to hang up.

When you call someone, hang the phone up gently.

When you call, ask the person if he or she has time to talk.

If the phone connection is lost, the caller should be the one to call back.

Never eat while on the phone, and try not to talk to others when you or they are on the phone.[39] If your phone system has call waiting, it is better to finish the first call and then answer the second, rather than interrupting the first to answer the second and then returning to the first. Finish one call; then move on to the next.[40] If you make a call and you get a wrong number, always apologize.[41] If you make a conference call, immediately tell the other parties that you are not the only person on the line. Always ask permission before using a speakerphone, and use it only when necessary, because they are quite annoying to those not on the speaker.[42] Other guidelines for telephone etiquette are found in Table 5.2.[43]

Call-Back Hour

an hour each day, or hours each week, when you will definitely be in to receive and return calls

To facilitate all your calls, create a **call-back hour,** a time for you to return and receive calls without interruption.[44] This is a time when everyone knows that he or she can call and you will be in. Ideally, call-back hour will be the same hour every day. When you are not in to receive a call or the person you called is not in, then you should follow the etiquette rules for voice mail and answering machines.

Most businesses have a voice-mail system or individual answering machines. Both have guidelines for proper usage. For your own system, you should have a brief but informative outgoing message (the message someone calling you will hear). Long outgoing messages, or greetings, are irritating.[45] Likewise, greetings such as "I'm not in; leave a message" are irritating and convey a sense of arrogance—I want to know who you are but I'm not telling you who I am.[46] The greeting should identify you and your company and should invite the person to leave a message. If you have a call-back hour, you might include this as a time when you will definitely be in.[47] If you do not have a call-back hour, then you may wish to change your greeting frequently so you can include call-back times.[48] You may also need to change your message if you travel and are frequently unable to return calls in less than 24 hours. You should check your messages at least twice a day.

When leaving a message on another person's voice mail or answering machine, be brief while including your name, your number, and a time when you can be reached.[49] If your message must be longer, then make sure it is concise and organized. It is often a good idea to plan out a message for every call, just in case the person does not answer. Be sure you include the reason for your call and message; the receiver may not know or remember, and business phones and voice mail should not be used to play guessing games. Use your best business voice, speak slowly, especially with numbers, and get to the point quickly. Do not use voice mail for bad news, sensitive information, confidential information, or complicated information or instructions. Never whine, complain, or leave an angry message—it sounds worse when played back and it can be replayed for the entertainment of others.[50] Finally, don't leave the same message over and over; if one or two fail, then try some other method to contact the person.

Cellular Phones, Pagers, and Fax Machines Technology has extended the power of the phone through cellular phones, pagers (or beepers), and fax machines. Although useful, these devices can also be unreasonably intrusive. To minimize the disturbance to others in the business and work world, all pagers should be the vibrating type rather than the audible type.[51] Even with a vibrating pager, you should not allow meetings or other activities to be interrupted with false emergencies.[52] Pagers, unlike cellular phones, are relatively inexpensive. The cost of airtime for cellular phones dictates that the first rule of etiquette for them should be to use them sparingly. When calling someone on a cellular phone, be as brief as possible, even if this means calling back later on a wired phone. If you have a cellular phone provided by your company, then it becomes your ethical responsibility to minimize your time by restricting calls to only those for clients and company business. You should not talk on a cell phone while walking down the street; in a theater, a restaurant, or a classroom; in a meeting; or in other public places.[53] Remove yourself from the presence of others to make a cellular phone call, and for your own safety and that of others, make sure you can drive and talk on the phone safely and legally before placing a call from your car.

Like cellular phones, fax machines also have a cost factor. The recipient, rather than the sender, pays most of the cost of a fax. Therefore, long documents and unsolicited documents should not be sent by fax.[54] Use overnight delivery for long, urgent documents and third class for junk mail and other unsolicited information. Fax etiquette also calls for the sender to include his or her name and number with the name and number of the intended recipient. If you find someone else's fax on the machine, read the cover page only, place the fax in the recipient's mail, and call the person to let him or her know it is there. Never read another person's fax; it is the same as opening his or her mail.[55]

NetNote

http://clusty.com/search? query=Business+Etiquette& whence=google

Business etiquette resources.

Copiers   Copy machine etiquette is concerned with user order and care of the copier itself. If two people arrive at the copy machine simultaneously, the one with the smaller job should go first. People with a large job should interrupt their copying for those with small jobs (one copy of a few pages, or a few copies of one page).[56] However, if the large job required an involved setup (special paper or reductions or enlargements), then the large job should not be interrupted. Anyone changing the normal setting of the copier should return the machine to a standard configuration—white, 8.5-by-11-inch paper, single copy, single sided, normal darkness, reduction/enlargement at 100 percent (no reduction or enlargement). The paper tray should never be left empty. Low toner should be replaced and jams fixed. If you are unable to do these things, then they should be reported immediately.[57]

E-mail   E-mail is now an essential tool for all businesses, but it is best for shorter messages—two pages is stretching the limit. If you do have a long message, then send it as an attachment, but make sure it is in a form the recipient can open. For example, don't send a Microsoft Word attachment when everyone else is using WordPerfect, or vice versa. These messages should contain nothing that you wouldn't want everyone to know because it is possible for employers to monitor (read) e-mail messages, and it is sometimes possible to retrieve messages that you believe you have deleted.[58] Do not type your entire message in capitals because this makes it appear that you are shouting at the recipients. Typing everything in lower case can make one seem lazy; use standard, letter-form capitalization.

Not all recipients are familiar with Internet abbreviations so do not use them. For example, ask to meet with someone face-to-face rather than saying you want to meet IRL (in real life). Do not assume that everyone reads his or her e-mail frequently. If you need to know that someone received your message, set the return receipt function, which will send you a message when the recipient has accessed your message. You may also be able to set a read message to know when your e-mail has been opened. Always set the priority function carefully. If almost all of your messages are sent at the highest priority when they really are not, then high priority will become meaningless for recipients of your messages. Likewise, do not abuse the broadcast and "cc:" functions. Do not broadcast your every thought to all persons in the company, and do not "cc:" (carbon copy) the CEO or others on every message just to show you are working; it appears as if you are trying to ingratiate yourself with them. Employ "bcc:" (blind carbon copy) to keep multiple recipients from knowing who else is getting your message or to keep the recipients' e-mail addresses private.

Hoteling
temporary workstations; workers move to different locations, sometimes taking their necessities with them on a cart

Shared Workspaces   With the advent of **hoteling,** cubicles, and other shared workspaces, people often come into closer contact than before. Etiquette for shared facilities is concerned with sharing space and sharing computers. In either case, the privacy of others must be respected if you expect others to respect yours. Never read from the desks or computer screens of others.[59] Do not interrupt or disturb others as they work. Keep the shared areas clean. Do not monopolize a shared computer or printer. Do not view, change, or delete other people's files or the software or computer settings.[60] If there is a shared coffee pot, clean and refill it when it is empty and pay your fair share for supplies if that is the custom.[61] If there is a shared water cooler, change the bottle or notify the person responsible and, as with the coffee, pay your fair share. If there is a shared refrigerator, label your items and remove leftover food before it spoils. In general, treat everyone else the way you would want your mother treated.

Meetings   Most meeting etiquette applies to people managing meetings. If you are simply attending a meeting, proper etiquette calls for you to arrive prepared and on time. If you are late, you should apologize but should not offer an excuse.[62] Excuses delay the meeting even more and are often not believed anyway. If you are running a meeting, you are responsible for much more.

REALITY CHECK

Net-Etiquette

With the integration of the Internet, World Wide Web, proprietary networks, intranets, and e-mail into everyday organizational operations, the need for etiquette in these areas is more vital than ever. Here are some general guidelines :-)

1. Remember that you are communicating with a real person on the other end of the wire—a person who can be hurt, insulted, or offended; just because you can't be seen doesn't mean you can be rude.
2. Check your spelling and grammar. People place more value on what you say if it is said correctly.
3. Use proper salutations when e-mailing someone you do not know well.
4. Use the subject line for e-mails and don't open e-mail with suspicious subject lines.
5. Reply to original e-mails with the original message so people know what you are referring to.
6. Don't send large, unsolicited attachments; they clog e-mail systems.

7. Avoid raving, rambling, or flaming—if you must do any of these, save them for when you are on your own time.
8. Do not send or receive personal messages at work unless you are absolutely positive your employer allows this.
9. Watch the humor; people are trying to work and you may accidentally offend others.
10. Do not visit Internet sites with questionable morals (you know what this means) from work; people have been fired for this.
11. E-mails should be short; instant messages at work (IM) should be really brief (and urgent).
12. When sending an IM, always ask if you are interrupting (as you would do on the phone).
13. Set your IM availability if your system allows this.
14. Use a professional screen name at work; "partyanimal247" is not a good idea (the same goes for e-mail addresses).
15. There are still a few people new to all this so be kind; you were once new too.

Sources: Shari Caudron, "On the Contrary: Virtual Manners," *Workforce,* February 2000, pp. 31–33; Grant Crowell, "You Lose Business When You Miss Manners," *Inc.*, September 2001; Anne Stuart, "IM Etiquette 101," *Inc.*, June 2002.

Before calling a meeting, you are responsible for determining if the meeting is necessary. The question to be answered is whether your objectives can be achieved through a means other than a meeting. If you must call a meeting, then it is your responsibility to prepare and distribute an agenda, giving everyone sufficient advance notice. The agenda needs to include the date, time, location, and purpose of the meeting. The number of people may vary, according to the purpose of the meeting. Five or six people is often the effective limit for problem-solving meetings, whereas ten or fewer may attend a problem-identification meeting. Adequate facilities must be obtained, including sufficient space, lighting, and ventilation, with minimum noise and interference. The projected length of the meeting should be included in the agenda, and every effort should be made to finish on time or early. Break time is typically required for meetings lasting longer than 90 minutes.[63]

It is proper for you to arrive first to a meeting you have called. You should arrive early enough to review the arrangements, ensuring that everything is prepared, that any food or equipment has arrived, and that all of the equipment is working properly. The more high-technology equipment being used, the earlier you should arrive, especially if you are unfamiliar with the equipment's operation. You are responsible for starting the meeting on time, ensuring that everyone participates, taking minutes or arranging for them to be taken by someone else, keeping the discussion relevant (according to the agenda), and ending on time. Meetings should take precedence over phone calls. If some people need to be present for only part of the meeting, it is acceptable to allow them to present their material and leave.[64]

After the meeting, you are responsible for returning the room to its premeeting condition or having this done by others and for seeing that the minutes are typed and distributed to those in attendance in addition to those unable to attend.[65]

Videoconferencing Videoconferencing, although still a meeting of sorts, is different enough to have its own etiquette. Seating is vital. If people are too close together, the arrangements look careless, and it becomes difficult for the camera operator to obtain individual shots. The background should not detract from the conference nor should any objects in or around the table. The most critical guidelines for a successful videoconference concern instructions to the participants. They must be carefully instructed in dress, behavior, and speech etiquette because the camera amplifies and exaggerates everything. Acceptable dress is conservative business attire in navy or gray, with a pale blue shirt. Dress should match the audience, even if your firm dresses casually. Makeup should also be conservative; men should not have a five-o'clock shadow. Nonverbal communication must be greatly moderated because the camera will exaggerate looks of boredom, disbelief, or disagreement. Nail biting, pencil or foot tapping, and other nervous habits must be controlled. The best approach is to maintain a poker face, a neutral but alert expression of interest. Proper etiquette calls for participants to face the camera, which may require instructions if multiple cameras are used so that everyone knows which is currently on. Interrupting or overly loud talking is not acceptable during a videoconference, nor is leaving early. It is often helpful, if time permits, to rehearse and tape the conference, providing each participant with a copy for analysis.[66]

ATTIRE AND GROOMING

You only have one opportunity to make a first impression, and your attire and grooming will account for most of the impression you make. Attire and grooming are still critical after the first impression, however. While business casual dress is accepted in many corporate settings, if you wish to advance, and sometimes even if

Videoconferencing
a meeting conducted with video and audio connections, with the two groups in separate geographic locations

you just wish to remain with an organization, you need to look as though you belong. The guidelines that follow refer to attire and grooming for the typical business situation. Here, conservative and safe dress is described. Over time, you may be able to modify your dress as you observe what the top officials in the organization wear. Matching their attire can be very important for advancement. If 80 percent dress a certain way, then you should too. If there is a wide variety in the way upper management dresses, then select clothes that flatter you, leaning to the conservative and traditional. In all cases, clothes should be well coordinated, well tailored, and well maintained.[67]

Attire for Men Well-dressed men wear suits for business. Everything about the suit is coordinated, meaning that articles that should match are precisely matched, whereas articles that contrast do so obviously. For example, all of your leathers (shoes and belts) must match.[68] However, you do not wear a striped suit with a striped tie and a striped shirt. At most, two of these three may be striped, and it is safer to have just one of the three striped and the other two a solid color; a navy blue suit with a white shirt and a rep (diagonally striped) tie is always acceptable. Or a navy suit with white pinstripes, a white shirt, and a maroon tie with small white polka dots would be fine for all business occasions. Business suits should be wool, although a wool-polyester blend that is at least 45 percent wool can be acceptable. It may be possible to wear a cotton or linen suit in warm climates, but these wrinkle easily. Suits should be blue or gray; solids, pinstripes, and chalk stripes are acceptable.[69] Dark plaids may be used, especially plaids that are nearly invisible. If you ever have the slightest doubt about whether a color or plaid is too loud, do not buy it. Your doubt or hesitation is a warning to yourself—one you should listen to.

The shirt should be cotton, which is cooler than other materials but does tend to wrinkle. A cotton-polyester blend will wrinkle less but is not as cool; the blend should be more than 50 percent cotton.[70] The shirt may be solid white or striped. The stripes may range from pinstripes up to one-sixteenth of an inch wide. Occasionally a blue or very pale pastel shirt may be acceptable. All business shirts are long sleeved.

The selection of a tie can make or break a suit. Business ties are silk and are worn with no tie tack or with a simple one. The tie may be a solid color, but more often some design is included. Initially, select conservative ties, which are accepted everywhere. As with other aspects of attire, once you have observed the accepted customs of top managers and clients, you may be able to deviate from the strict conservative look. In any event, you may safely select a coordinated polka-dot tie (your shirt color should match the color of the dots). A rep tie (a diagonally striped tie) is another fine choice, as are ties with a repeating diamond pattern and the extremely versatile paisley.[71]

The remainder of business attire includes some items about which choices can be made and some set items. For example, the color of your socks must match the color of your pants, not your shoes. You may choose between lace-up shoes and a dressy slip-on, as long as they are conservative, black leather.[72] A freer choice is available when selecting between a belt or braces (suspenders). Braces are more comfortable for sitting, hold the trousers at a consistent height, hold pleated trousers better, and allow for personal discretion in selecting a color or pattern. Belts seem less "yuppie-ish," allow men to wear their trousers under their stomachs more easily, and do not have straps that may slip off your shoulder or feel uncomfortable in hot weather. If a belt is selected, then it should have a simple, conservative buckle.

Attire for Women   Women should follow a similar conservative pattern, at least until becoming more familiar with the attire of top management. If the top female managers dress a little less conservatively, then you may also. You should start, however, with the basic skirted business suit; a blazer-cut jacket and matching skirt, or a dress with jacket.[73] The skirt should reach to just at or below the knee, a length that is always acceptable and shows that you are not just trying to keep up with the current fashion. Typically, no vest is worn with this basic business attire, and a scarf is optional. Ties should be avoided because they make it seem as if you are trying to imitate male attire. The first choices for the suit material are wool or linen.[74] A second choice is any synthetic that imitates wool or linen well. Solids, tweeds, and plaids are acceptable, but pinstripes should be avoided because they, too, can be seen as an attempt to imitate male attire.[75]

In general, women have more color choices for business wear than men, although many of the same colors can be worn by both. The most conservative choices, which are the better ones to start with, include medium gray, dark gray, medium blue, navy, deep maroon, and camel.[76]

The blouse that accompanies the skirted business suit should be simple—free of frills, patterns, or unusual collars. The collar should be equivalent to that of a man's shirt worn with the top button open. The first choices for the blouse material are cotton or silk, with the second choice being any synthetic that successfully imitates cotton or silk. The blouse should be of a solid color and may be white, any shade range between beige and tan, any blue, any brown, maroon, light gray, or pink. The blouse must contrast and coordinate with the color of the suit.[77]

Other items include shoes, which should be plain pumps in blue, black, deep brown, or gray.[78] The shoes must be coordinated with the suit. Neutral or skin-tone panty hose should be worn with a business suit.[79] Makeup should be subtle to the point that people think you are wearing none, and any perfume should be light. Whenever feasible, a businesswoman should carry an attaché case, rather than a purse or handbag.[80] Jewelry should be simple and tasteful, never overdone.

Casual Attire   Some workplaces have instituted a **casual day,** often Fridays, when the official or unofficial dress code is relaxed or abandoned. This is not necessarily a

Casual Day
a day of the week on which the dress code is relaxed or suspended

---

REALITY CHECK

The Clothes Must Fit, in More Ways than One

Not all professions or industries follow the attire-for-advancement rules. Health-care professions have their own codes that, although not requiring suits, are still professional. Computer firms have an altogether different code. Here, a suit sends one of two messages: (1) You are a nontechnical person, or (2) you are on a job interview. The former is far worse. A typical business suit can signify that you are a marketer and thus nontechnical, or a member of the Finance Department, in which case you are not only nontechnical, but you should be feared and avoided. In organizations where it is common for people with the brightest minds to wear the same T-shirts and jeans for days, just a clean T-shirt can be considered dressed up. Even a shirt and tie are rare. One computer programmer went too far and worked in the nude. If he was being polite, he kept his keyboard strategically located in his lap. If you had an interview for a technical position at a firm like Microsoft, Apple, or Intel, what should you wear? To show that you were seriously concerned about the job, but also that you fit in with the culture, you might wear a suit one day and a T-shirt and jeans for the second day. After obtaining the job, the extreme casual look is standard, even for seminar presentations.

Source: Adapted from Michael Hyman, *PC Roadkill* (Foster City, CA: IDG Books, 1995), pp. 12, 33.

blessing. Even though the standards of attire are supposedly lowered, what you wear will still be scrutinized. Now, instead of business wear and casual wear, you may need attire that falls in between these two—something that is now being called business casual. Also, often the dress restrictions are eased only for those with no client contact. This means that people must check the calendar (to see if it is a casual day) and their schedules (to see if they have outside appointments) before getting dressed in the morning. Casual dress may bring other problems as well. In many companies, workers have taken the casual concept too far coming to work in sweatsuits, shorts, and spandex, and causing the companies to limit or eliminate casual work dress. Another drawback to casual dress, say some, is that it also leads to casual attitudes. One firm found that the sales staff felt that casual day was a "no sales call" day; instead of getting one relaxed dress day, the firm got one less workday. The policy was soon reversed. If you are permitted to, and you decide to participate in casual business dress, then it may be best to begin with sportscoats and sweaters and slacks before trying a T-shirt and blue jeans. It may also help to consult a local men's or women's business clothes store or upscale department store such as Nordstrom for ideas on appropriate casual business wear. As with regular business attire, start conservatively, observe what others wear and their reaction to what you wear, and do not push the casual limits too far.[81]

Grooming   The perfect attire, impeccably tailored and coordinated, can be completely destroyed by poor grooming habits. Successful business grooming begins with cleanliness and moderation.[82] Hair must be neat, trimmed, organized, clean, and away from the face. If you wear glasses, they should be clean and fit well and should not be hanging from chains. Teeth should be clean, breath fresh. Fingernails should be clean and trimmed. Any scents should be lightly applied. As a final check, all buttons and zippers should be checked and all shoelaces tied. In general, avoid trying to follow the latest trends in hairstyles, makeup, and other grooming unless you are sure that they will be accepted by clients, coworkers, and management.[83]

COMING AND GOING

In the bustling world of business, there is much coming and going, and there is etiquette for doing this properly. Whether entering or exiting doors, elevators, escalators, or staircases, those in the business world should follow certain guidelines. In some ways, the etiquette is simpler today than in the past. For example, when it comes to opening doors, the general rule today is that whoever reaches the door first should open it for others. It no longer matters whether this is a man or a woman. There are three main exceptions, however. First, a younger person should hold the door for a significantly older person. Second, a customer or client should never have to hold or open a door. Third, anyone needing assistance should have the door held, as a courtesy.[84] For instance, a woman should open the door for a man carrying two 10-ream boxes of copier paper, even if he arrives slightly before she does. If a group arrives at a revolving door, then the host or first to arrive goes first, pushing to help the others.[85] Upon reaching automatic doors, the first to arrive goes through, yielding to the elderly, people with bulky packages, and people with disabilities.

The rules are similar for elevators, stairs, and escalators. Before entering an elevator, allow those already on to exit. First arrivals enter first, except for a host or those with disabilities. Those nearest the door exit first or move to allow others to exit. A host allows a guest or client to enter and exit first, holding the door open for him or her. The person nearest the controls should hold the "door open" button until all have entered or exited. On stairs and escalators, the host or first arrivals ascend or descend first.[86]

Introductions   With all of the coming and going in business, there are numerous opportunities to meet new people and to introduce peers, managers, and acquaintances to them. The rules of etiquette call for you to mention the person with the highest rank and introduce others to him or her.[87] For example, upon reaching a group of middle managers with the new CEO, Ms. Little, you would say, "Ms. Little, I would like to introduce Ms. Eipers, Mr. Davis, and Mr. Henness." If people are of equal status, then introduce the younger people to the older ones.[88] Other rules for introductions include always standing during introductions and always shaking hands. If you have forgotten someone's name, apologize and ask him or her—never guess. If someone is introducing you and having difficulty with your name, interject and help him or her. Always address people by their titles and last name until they invite you to call them by their first name.

Business Cards   Business card etiquette is more relaxed in the United States than in many other countries. In Japan, the business card and your title on it are very important. In some professions in the United States, business cards are more common than in others. Most sales people carry and use business cards. To be proper, exchange business cards before a business meeting, but at the end of a one-on-one meeting. If you are visiting someone else's office, you should present your card first. For a sales call, the presentation should be at the start of the meeting. Never distribute cards at purely social events.[89]

DINING

In some industries and professions, business is conducted during meals. For the unprepared, this can be a tense affair. Variations occur, depending on the situation and location, but we will at least cover the basics here. Some general rules of etiquette will be discussed along with rules for ordering, eating and drinking, host and guest rules, and manners.

The first general rule of business dining is to remember that the food is not the central issue. The whole purpose for the business lunch is business. Second, business is properly discussed after everyone has placed an order.[90] Don't appear overeager and begin talking shop before everyone has had a chance to look at the menu and order. This delays the meal, and the pause after ordering is a natural time to change the subject to business. When you do start to discuss business, do not speak so loudly that those at other tables hear you.

Ordering a business lunch or dinner has a set of rules all its own. To indicate that you are ready to order, close your menu and place it on the table.[91] Because the main reason for the meal is to conduct business, order foods that will not interfere with the discussion and will be easy to eat.[92] Do not order foods such as lobster, clams in the shells, or corn on the cob. Furthermore, guests should not order the most expensive item on the menu unless invited to do so by the host.[93] Guests should also not order a first course unless others do. Because alcoholic drinks are often not part of a business lunch, guests should wait to see what the host does, and if alcohol is ordered, it should be consumed in moderation (one, maybe two drinks). You should not drink at all, however, if you are trying to close a sale or deal.[94]

Once the food arrives, the trouble really begins for some people. First, if it is a buffet lunch, do not pile your plate high with food. Remember: The real purpose is to conduct business, not to graze like cattle. Buffet or not, the next step is to decide which silverware to use. The first major point is to use silverware for virtually everything, even french fries and chicken. Next, in general, start using the utensils on the outside of the setting first. For example, if there is a salad with the meal, the salad fork is typically the left-most utensil. If you drop a piece of silverware, leave it on the floor and quietly ask the waiter for a replacement.[95]

Once you have the correct utensil, remember the basic rules. With soup, move the spoon away from you while in the bowl and then toward you to eat the soup, eating silently from the side of the spoon.[96] When cutting foods, hold the fork in your left hand at a 45-degree angle from the plate, cutting one or two pieces of food at a time. Do not hold the fork vertically in your fist and saw your food as if playing a bass fiddle.[97] After cutting, there are two acceptable methods for bringing the food to your mouth. The more common method in the United States is to set the knife down (placing it across the top of the plate), switch the fork from the left hand to the right, and bring the food to the mouth with the right hand. The fork must then be switched back to the left hand for additional cutting. The other method is to leave the fork in the left hand and bring the food to the mouth with it after cutting. Not everything is cut, however. Do not cut bread or rolls; instead, break off a piece, butter it if you wish, and eat it. To signal that you have finished eating, place your knife and fork diagonally across the plate. If coffee is served do not blow on it, simply let it sit until cool enough to drink.[98]

There are rules of etiquette for both host and guest during business dining, starting with who pays. In general, the person issuing the invitation to lunch or dinner (or even breakfast) pays the bill. During the ordering, the host should allow the guest to order first by telling the wait staff to "allow my guest to order first." This also signals to the wait staff that you are the one to receive the bill. An even more discrete method is for a host to arrive early enough to sign an open charge slip, instructing the staff to add a gratuity (possibly even 20 percent in this case). With this method, when the meal and business are complete, the entire payment scene is avoided, and you have given the impression of being important enough to have some type of standing account with the establishment. Another subtle signal a host can provide is to mention items that "look good" on the menu. This gives the guest an indication of what the host is considering and a price range that is comfortable to all. As a guest, etiquette calls for you not to order a first course or a dessert unless others do and to wait to eat until the host begins.[99]

A GLOBAL GLANCE

There Is Much More to Knowing the Language than Learning the Words

When going to other countries to conduct business, you must not only learn the verbal and nonverbal language, you must learn about the culture and the etiquette in order to be successful. You must prepare thoroughly. At the least, you must examine a book such as Roger Axtell's *Do's and Taboo's Around the World.* If possible, you should talk to others conducting business in the same country as well as people from that country who are living in your area. Here are some examples of varying customs: The Japanese rarely say no. When they mean no, they say something like "Maybe," or "That would be difficult." In many other countries, the business card is much more important than it is in the United States. You should add your highest college degree and your title when conducting business in Africa, South America, Japan, and Europe. If you work for an older firm, you would include the year of the firm's founding for business cards to be used in the Netherlands, Britain, and Germany.

Gifts are often exchanged in other countries even for business purposes, but the custom of when and what to give varies widely. Gift giving requires careful research and consideration. People in some countries value well-made U.S. products, whereas others value commodities that are difficult to obtain in their own country.

Dining for business purposes can also vary greatly across countries. Rules governing etiquette and conversation can differ widely. In Japan, long dining and entertainment experiences are considered part of becoming acquainted. In the United Kingdom, business is not typically discussed during meals. Wherever you go, follow your host's lead; when in doubt, don't say anything; and do your homework before you ever leave the United States.

Source: Adapted from Marjorie Whigham-Desit, "Business Etiquette Overseas," *Black Enterprise,* October 1995, pp. 142–144.

Finally, some general guidelines for good manners. Do not place your elbows on the table while you eat. Say please and thank you often. Do not eat until everyone at your table has been served. If you must leave during a meal, place your napkin on your chair. Because it makes people uncomfortable, do not send food back unless it is completely unfit to eat. To send something back runs the risk of making you look pretentious or of insulting your host. If the occasion arises for you to reciprocate with an invitation, you must do so at a restaurant of similar quality.[100]

CORDIALITY

There are times when business dealings seem to cross a line into the social world. At these times, etiquette is important so that the correct mix of the two worlds is maintained. For these occasions, to promote cordiality, that mix should contain more social content and a little less business. Three areas appear to need special guidance: writing thank-you notes, gift giving, and the office Christmas party.

Thank-You Notes   Thank-you notes can serve two main purposes: to simply thank someone for what he or she has done, or to thank someone and send a business message. In either case, the note also serves to keep your name on the mind of the recipient. Thank-you notes should be sent:

- when you have received a gift
- after special lunches or dinners (such as the first one at which you are a guest or one at a special restaurant)
- to recognize a special favor or performance above and beyond the call of duty
- after the first sale or at the close of a large sale or a large deal

Thank-you notes can be especially effective today because they are less common than in the past, but they must be sent within 24 hours of the incident that prompts you to write one. A good thank-you note is brief, simple, and personalized. The note should be handwritten, if you can write legibly, on good quality, 5-by-7-inch

---

FYI

If you can't do the time, don't do the crime. If you think you can be grossly unethical and not get caught, talk to the top people at Enron, Worldcom, Global Crossing, and the like (but you may have to visit a prison to do so).

Organizations are not ethical or unethical; the individuals are. If you are being pressured to be unethical, resist. If everyone else in the organization is engaged in unethical behavior, leave.

There may be numerous pressures that tempt one to be unethical; often the key is to find an ethical balance among these pressures.

Proper etiquette is no substitute for job competence, but improper etiquette can overshadow even brilliant performance; it can break a deal, a sale, or a career.

When in doubt about proper etiquette, do as the host does.

Learn to dress properly. When new or in doubt, start conservatively until you learn the limits for the situation.

Neat, clean, inexpensive clothes that fit properly are preferable to sloppy, wrinkled, poor-fitting clothes even if they are expensive.

Learn how to dine properly in a formal setting, even if you do so infrequently.

paper. The message should be organized into three parts. The first part should thank the person for the specific incident. If you need to conduct any business through the note, that should constitute the second part. The third part, if needed, should promise a specific follow-up: a phone call, information that you are including with the note, or information that you will send later.[101]

Gifts   Another way to say thank you or to recognize someone is to give a gift. There are cautious rules of business etiquette regarding gift giving, however. A manager may give a subordinate a gift, but gifts should not travel up the chain of command because this is viewed as ingratiation. A client's gift must never be able to be interpreted as an attempt to bribe or influence decision making. Gifts should cost less than $25 (the limit for deducting the cost of a business gift). Client gifts should be useful and should take the receiver's personality into account. Subordinate gifts should not be related to work. For example, a compact disc would be suitable for a music lover, or a bookstore gift certificate would be appreciated by a reader. Brand-name gifts are best, but no personal items (perfume, clothes) should be selected as gifts. A carefully selected gift is always more meaningful than cash.[102]

Christmas Parties   Gifts are often given around the Christmas/New Year holidays, often at the time of the office Christmas party. The party itself has rules of etiquette to be followed if you wish to maintain your dignity, respect, and relations with your managers, peers, or subordinates. To be safe you should:[103]

- limit your consumption of alcohol for your own safety and to make following the remainder of these guidelines easier
- not try to be the life of the party
- not flirt
- not divulge secrets or violate confidences
- remember your position—don't be overly familiar with your manager or subordinates
- refrain from discussing work; after all, it is a party

WHEN OTHERS BREAK THE RULES

When someone breaks a less important rule of etiquette, like wearing colors that do not coordinate or eating with the wrong fork, it is often best to ignore the incident. If no real harm is done, then do not embarrass the person. For the breaking of more important rules or for blunders that can damage client and other important relations, then discreetly mention the situation to the person in private. In fact, most violations of the rules of etiquette should be handled directly and in private. For example, if a man calls a woman "sweetie" or "honey," she should tell him in private that she does not appreciate being referred to in this manner.[104] Never answer an offensive remark with one of your own. Instead, tell the person whose jokes ridicule other groups that such humor makes you uncomfortable.[105]

During a job interview, if the interviewer asks you how you will get to work or who will care for your children if you get this job (which is an illegal question), then you should answer the hidden question the interviewer is really asking.[106] He or she doesn't really care how you get to work or who cares for your children; what the interviewer really wants to know is whether you will be at work each day, on time. Assure the interviewer that you will and, if possible, offer the evidence that you have, for instance, never missed a day of work for the last three years.

To many people, smoking is a sensitive topic. Only after you have privately approached a person smoking in the no-smoking lounge should you consider enlisting the help of a manager or others. You should remember the rules of etiquette even if those around you do not.

SUMMARY

Organizational leaders have done little in the past to modify the many erroneous concepts and prejudices about business held by the general public. Business ethics and trust in management have taken a severe beating recently. In far too many instances, management has been reluctant to talk about its problems candidly, and as a result, the public frequently feels that business has something to hide. Annual reports, for example, have customarily been filled with puffery, window dressing, and glad tidings, instead of honest appraisals of things as they really are.

Management must learn that talk alone will not convince a skeptical general public of the desirability of private organizations. True, zealots have at times thrown uninformed and biased rhetorical rocks at the business community. In the long run, however, management will fail to get its message across by fighting rhetoric with rhetoric. To quote an old cliché, "You can try to fight fire with fire, but firefighters usually use water."

The general public also has certain responsibilities. Rather than being blindly and emotionally prejudiced against business in general, it should strive to become better informed about the actual activities of the business community and to realize that many organizational contributions toward society cannot be made unless firms are able to earn reasonable profits.

The solutions needn't involve a battle between business and the general public. Instead, business leaders must establish long-term commitments to social action. Too often, programs have been ill conceived, hastily adopted, and then hastily dropped. Management must be willing not only to anticipate the need for change but also to employ programs with foresight before it is pushed up against the corporate wall, as it has been during some turbulent periods of the past. Some citizens have argued that aggressive and hostile attacks on business are the only effective way to get its attention. The public must be convinced otherwise, not through the use of clever managerial rhetoric or propaganda campaigns in the mass media, but by a display of sincere concern for the well-being of American society.

Management should profoundly examine the ethical aspects of all its actions. The temptation is sometimes great to pursue ethically questionable practices because they benefit the cash-flow or profit positions of a company. The long-run effects of such actions, however, not only could be disastrous but could ultimately sound the death knell of U.S. private enterprise. As one Bank of America official has asserted, "In the long pull, nobody can expect to make profits—or have any meaningful use for profits—if our society is racked by tensions."

Etiquette is also concerned with the way people treat one another, but in a different way than ethics. Etiquette often comes into play because of the problem of intangibility. In many business situations, people are being asked to commit to something that cannot be sensed, that is intangible. For example, in the case of agreeing to purchase services, the service cannot be sensed before it is performed. People are uncomfortable with intangibility, so they look for assurances that quality is present. They take other actions as an indication of quality. If someone cannot or does not conform to proper etiquette, they reason, then maybe his or her services will not conform to standards as they should. To some, poor etiquette equals poor service in business dealings, and this equals no sale.

Etiquette is involved with the treatment of coworkers, too. If it is not enough for some people to treat others right because it is good in and of itself, then they may need to be reminded that if they wish others to treat them well, they have to treat others well. There are numerous rules of etiquette, but their number should not deter you from trying to learn them and put them into practice. For example, someone has to hang up the phone first. Etiquette helps us avoid an awkward moment here. Etiquette helps guide our selection of clothing so that we avoid being overdressed or underdressed. Etiquette for the office and workspaces helps avoid conflicts and enables the organization to run more smoothly. In general, etiquette helps make our efforts less clumsy and less embarrassing. There is an underlying logic to most etiquette: If you strive to remember the reason, you may be better able to remember the rule.

CHECKING FOR UNDERSTANDING

1. What five ethical pressures face managers?

2. What forces came together at the time of the ethics gap?

3. What can people do to manage and improve business ethics?

4. Explain how the profit-quest and social-responsibility philosophies differ regarding the public responsibilities of business organizations.

5. Explain the following statement: "The actual dollars-and-cents value of social-responsibility programs is difficult to determine."

6. What are some of the major social responsibilities managers are concerned with? How do you feel about these concerns?

7. What are the probable long-run consequences of business organizations' ignoring their responsibilities to the general public?

8. Why is the commitment of senior management toward any organizational program essential for its success?

9. Describe office phone, cellular phone, pager, fax machine, copier, and e-mail etiquette.

10. Describe proper etiquette for shared workspaces.

11. Describe meeting etiquette.

12. Describe attire etiquette for men and women, and explain the advantages and disadvantages of casual business attire.

13. Describe the etiquette of coming and going.

14. Describe the etiquette of business dining, including that for ordering, discussing business, using utensils, host and guest etiquette, and proper manners.

15. Describe the etiquette of business cordiality.

16. What actions can be taken when others break the rules of etiquette?

SELF-ASSESSMENT

For each of the following situations answer P if you Probably would do it, M if you Might do it, and D if you Doubt you would do it.

1. If asked to do something unethical by someone of higher rank, I would quit.   *P   M   D*

2. If asked to do something unethical by someone of higher rank, I would ignore the request. *P   M   D*

3. If my boss asked me to do something unethical, I would go over his or her head and report him or her.   *P   M   D*

4. If my company had a product that just might be harmful to some people, I would stop selling it. *P   M   D*

5. At work I would follow this philosophy: I don't have to tell the truth just so long as everyone else does.   *P   M   D*

6. I would significantly adjust my department's earnings to keep me from getting in trouble. *P   M   D*

7. I would ask team members to act in unethical ways if it was the only way to complete our tasks. *P   M   D*

8. If my company was dumping toxic waste, I would report it to the authorities.   *P   M   D*

9. As CEO, I would accept an unusually large salary even if it meant workers were fired in order for the company to afford my salary.   *P   M   D*

10. I would pay creditors more slowly than promised if it meant my company made a little more money.   *P   M   D*

For all items except 4 and 8, score 2 points for every D, 1 point for every M, and zero for every P. For items 4 and 8 score 2 points for each P, 1 point for each M, and zero for each D. Total your score. A score of 17–20 represents very ethical positions on these items; 10–16 represents mostly ethical positions; 9 or less represents less ethical positions.

SKILL BUILD 5

Penny needs your help. Penny, the lead accounts payable clerk, arrived late to the Macadame X-mas Party, which was always a tastefully catered affair. She was sampling the hors d'oeuvres when she noticed a slight commotion on the other side of the room. She saw a man dressed in a red sport coat, white shirt, a tie like a Christmas tree with a tiny blinking light at the top, red shorts, black over-the-calf hose, and black wing-tip shoes. It was Warren, one of the sales reps.

Skill Question 1. Are there any violations of the etiquette for attire and grooming here, and if so, what are they?

Warren had obviously over subscribed to the spiked punch and had just tipped over a large bowl of cold shrimp and ice. He didn't even make an attempt to pick it up; instead, he was heading in Penny's direction.

Skill Question 2. Is there a violation of etiquette, and if so, what is it?

"Penny," Warren shouted, "hey, if you had been born with a little more they woulda called you Nickel!" and with that he almost fell to the floor with laughter. After a minute he said, "Oh, I'm jus' kiddin'. Here, looks at this, I bought you sumpin'" and he handed Penny a long, narrow box.

Penny opened the box to find a silver watch, worth at least $100, she thought. "Why, Warren? What's this for? And what are you supposed to be?" she asked.

Skill Question 3. Is there a violation of etiquette, and if so, what is it?

"For? Ish for you. Got a gold one for my boss, if I could only find him. And, ah, be? I'm a self," Warren said.

Skill Question 4. Is there a violation of etiquette, and if so, what is it?

"You're yourself?" Penny replied.

"What? Myself? No, A self—a cross between Santa and an elf—a S-ELF? You likes the watch though?" Warren asked.

"I don't see why you would give this to me," Penny said, since she and Warren hardly saw each other on the job and never off the job.

"Jus' need you to do a leetle favor. She, I mean see, I gots thish bill from . . . ah, calls on my shell phone, I mean cell phone. Lotsa calls. Big bill. Hava look she, I *mean* see," and Warren handed Penny a crumpled bill.

"Wow, $1837.28! In *one* month. How did you do that?" Penny said, stunned.

"Clients, all clients," Warren replied.

"How could you have called your clients this much? What, were you on the phone with them 24-7?"

"No, no, I didn't call them. They didn't call me. They kept wanting to borrow my phone. Shed, I mean said they had to check things. You know, like in Shingapore and Shidney, stuff . . . like . . . business . . ." Warren said, his voice trailing off as he slowly looked around the room, distracted.

Skill Question 5. Is there a violation of etiquette, and if so, what is it?

"Well I can't pay all of this. No one is allowed to file for more than $75 of cell-phone reimbursement per month," Penny explained.

"Got to pay it all, got to," Warren said, "that's last month's bill. The phone company has been all over me cuz this month, it's even bigger bill. Bigger. Gotta pay, though. All bish-ness related. They clients, they expect it. Say I owes it to them. Parta closin' the deals."

"There is no way I'm going to believe that your clients feel they are entitled to run up a sales rep's cell-phone bill," Penny said.

"Do you believe my phone company ish after me?" Warren asked.

"Yes."

"Then believe you need to pay that whole bill," Warren said.

"Sorry, not without authorization, and plenty of it."

"Once my bosh she's, sees, this watch, he'll author-ish it," Warren said as he stumbled off.

After the holiday break, Warren sent the bill to Penny with a Post-It note saying, "OK to pay."

Penny tried calling Warren, but when she finally got him he put her on hold for 15 minutes; that's when she gave up and hung up. Then she e-mailed him. The first four times her e-mail was returned because Warren's mailbox was full. When she did get through, he replied with a seven-page explanation that didn't answer her question. Finally, she went to see him.

Skill Question 6. What are the three problems with etiquette here?

"Warren, about that cell-phone bill . . ." Penny started.

"Oh, you want this month's now? It's just a little higher," Warren said.

"No! I'm not paying last month's either! You get $75 for last month, and $75 for this month *if* you file the proper forms. And did you know your cell-phone company called *me* asking for payment? You can't tell them the company is paying all of it! What's wrong with you?"

Skill Question 7. There are five ethical pressures. Which two does Penny face? Support each answer. What should Penny do about each?

"Look, I don't make enough to pay all that and I can't ask the clients who made the calls to pay, or I lose the accounts. If I lose the accounts, the company loses the accounts, and those are big. So if you value this company and your own job you will find a way to pay those bills."

Skill Question 8. Warren faces which four of the five ethical pressures? Support each answer. What should Warren do about his ethical pressures?

APPLICATIONS

5.1 IF AT FIRST YOU DON'T SUCCEED, LIE, LIE, AGAIN

Olinda reached the copy machine with only a minute or two to spare before the big meeting. Felicia was already there, and she appeared to be in no great hurry.

"Felicia," Olinda said politely, "may I ask how many copies you will be making?"

Felicia turned slowly and said, "I am making seven sets," and then turned back toward the copier.

"Of how many pages?" Olinda asked.

Without looking at Olinda, Felicia replied, "Eighteen. For the Woodston meeting."

"That's not for two weeks!" Olinda exclaimed. "I need to make four copies of one page for the meeting starting right now. May I interrupt you?"

"No," Felicia replied.

Olinda was late for the meeting.

Mr. Jefferies, the general manager, looked at Olinda and said, "I was telling the others that the thank-you note I was going to write to the old man on behalf of all of us for the great Christmas gifts will have to wait for a couple more weeks. We have big problems. Sales of our Xlypod MP3 players are going nowhere, and I don't get it. Who wouldn't want a personal music device shaped like a tiny xylophone? Well, whatever. Collin and I have a plan."

"We have an absolutely huge number of Xlypods in inventory," Collin Flitch, assistant GM explained, "What we are going to do is store them with that place that uses empty semi trailers."

"The Wandering Warehouse?" Sankar, the IT manager, asked. "How will that help?"

"We book the stored units as sales. They are out of the building so who will know?" Flitch said.

"We can't do that," Olinda said.

"Well no, not like that," Mr. Jefferies said. "You see, we don't have the money to pay the Wandering Warehouse. So what we do is store just enough Xlypods in each semi so that if sold at full retail, they cover the cost of their storage. When the Wandering Warehouse starts crying for money, we tell them to keep the Xlypods and sell them. They get their money, and we won't really be lying because they will be sold."

"But then we are out the money, and I don't get my commission," Arkady, the company salesman, said.

"What commission?" Flitch said, "If you sold product we wouldn't have this problem. But you don't get sales because of the way you dress. Look at that suit. You look like an investment banker. We are trying to sell a hip, cool product to young managers running music stores and websites. You need to look like them to connect, don't you know that?"

"Whoa, you are both right," Mr. Jefferies said. "Arkady, you dress like my grandfather, and Collin, this will create an even bigger money problem than we have now."

"I have that worked out," Flitch said. "We can save some money by using all those Model 13 headphones. You know, the ones with the RCA plugs that are a little too narrow. They are sitting in storage doing nothing and will save some money."

"They fall out of the Xlypods with the slightest pull. People will complain," Olinda pointed out.

"They won't all complain," Flitch said. "Some will go out and buy phones on their own.

"And the others?" Sankar asked.

"I'm having our toll-free number modified so it puts people on hold but never forwards the call to Customer Service."

Sankar and Olinda just stared at him incredulously.

"That won't take care of everything," Mr. Jefferies said. "There will need to be some belt-tightening. Workers will be cut back to minimum wage."

"For many that is half of what they get now!" Olinda said.

"I know, but the government won't let us go less than minimum wage," Flitch said.

"I can't stay here for minimum wage," Sankar said.

"Oh, I just mean workers, not management," Mr. Jefferies said. "Our pay stays the same."

"Well, not taking a cut is nice, but the workers will be upset, and Jabulani, our most vital engineer, was promised a raise."

"Got it covered," Mr Jefferies said. "We will pretend to take a cut but cover that, plus raises for Jabulani and everyone above his level, with money from petty cash."

"There is not nearly enough in petty cash," Arkady said

"Not to worry, I'll get the old man to sign for more," Mr. Jefferies explained.

"He won't do it," Sankar said.

"He won't know. I'll have him sign a check for petty cash for one hundred dollars, but I'll leave space and add the word 'thousand' after the one hundred later. No problem," Jefferies claimed.

"Isn't this going to push the company to the breaking point?" Sankar asked.

"Pretty close," Mr. Jefferies said. "However, I have a golden parachute, and if things get bad enough we will be bought out. So I'll be fine. So what do I really care?"

"That parachute, I've seen it; it would bankrupt us even with a buyout," Flitch said.

"Not my problem," Jefferies said. "Well, I think we are done here."

With that, Jefferies, Flitch, and Arkady got up and left.

Olinda sat there staring at her unused copies, and then she looked at Sankar. "Do you believe it?"

"I think I'm still trying to interpret it all," Sankar said.

"I guess we shouldn't be too surprised," Olinda said. She stared at the copies again and after a moment said, "You know, I always thought we should have had an ethics policy. Jefferies and Flitch certainly seem to need something along those lines."

"Oh, we do have a policy, have had it for over a year. The old man wrote it. Did a nice job, too."

"What? I missed it," Olinda said.

"No, you didn't. I said we have a policy. The old man never sent it around," Sankar said. "I think once he wrote it, he felt it was all common sense so there was no point in handing it out."

"Too bad. Doesn't seem to be much sense around here, common or otherwise."

QUESTIONS

1–4. Four of the five main ethical pressures are present here. List them, numbering them 1 through 4, and cite sections of the application supporting your answer with each one. Explain whether each is being handled ethically or unethically and support your position.

5. Does Jefferies think he has an ethical dilemma with his golden parachute? Should he have an ethical dilemma with it? Why or why not?

6. What, if anything, is wrong with the ethical policy in this application? Cite a section or sections of the application that support your answer, and state how the problem should be corrected.

7–10. There are four violations of etiquette in this application. List them, numbering them 7 through 10, cite sections of the application supporting your choice with each one, and explain what the violation is.

5.2 JUDGMENT CALLS

What do you do or say, if anything, in each of these situations, and why?

1. A colleague, an amateur pilot, shows up at a critical meeting with some Japanese executives wearing a tie adorned with pictures of a P51D-Mustang escorting a B-29 Superfortress (the Mustang is a World War II fighter, and the Superfortress is the type of plane that dropped the atomic bombs on Japan at the end of World War II).

2. You know you only have $110 left before you hit the limit on your credit card, and you have $8 in your wallet. You are the host to three clients. One has just announced that he is considering the lobster dinner for $40. The other two clients nod their heads.

3. While waiting outside a meeting room, you notice that the next middle manager making a presentation is rehearsing what he will say. The pants zipper of his blue suit is open, and part of his white shirt is protruding.

4. Your firm has a no-smoking policy in all its buildings. One of your coworkers consistently smokes in the bathroom, usually just before you have to go in there.

5. During an initial lunch with some important potential customers, your boss made a spectacle of herself. The potential customer's managers spent most of the time watching her as she talked about how dumb your company's suppliers are and how all managers are like those in *Dilbert*. She used her fingers to wipe her mouth and kept her napkin on the table to wipe her fingers on. She used a salad fork to stab the chicken out of the chicken soup and wrapped her tea bag around her desert spoon to wring the last drops of tea from it. At the end, she asked for a doggie bag because she "might want a little something later." She says she can't wait for the next meeting, which may make or break the whole deal.

6. You are the executive vice president of marketing. As you return to your office from a meeting, you notice that your secretary is on the phone. When you get to your desk, you see that one line on your phone is lit (the one your secretary is on), and one is blinking—someone is on hold. You pick up the blinking line, and you get an earful. It is your biggest retail customer. She has called twice, once letting the phone ring 13 times before hanging up and a second time letting it ring 16 times before your secretary picked up the phone. Your secretary then put your customer on hold for eight and a half minutes. No one got back to your customer until you picked up the line. When you ask, your secretary says that she was talking to her boyfriend, with whom she is on the verge of breaking up. What do you say to or do for your customer, and why? What do you say to or do about your secretary, and why?

NET-WORK

Office equipment etiquette (from the U.K. version of *The Office*)

http://www.youtube.com/watch?v=UbrDuyN3Vrg

Why people shouldn't drink at the office holiday party

http://www.youtube.com/watch?v=QRtvyO_RL0k

PERSONAL POINTS

1. What are your personal ethical standards?

2. What would you do if you were told to make your numbers or lose your job, and you knew the only way to make your numbers was to greatly falsify them?

3. Which of the five ethical pressures have you faced, and what did you do? What will you do differently if you face them again?

4. Explain how you would feel it you were working harder with the result that your CEO was getting more money? Is this situation ethical or unethical and why?

5. What rules of etiquette have you not been following? What should you do to change this behavior? Do you believe not following a rule of etiquette has affected a job or your career, and if so, how?

EXPERIENTIAL EXERCISE

Ethics

This exercise works through the ethics development process. If working individually, select your current job, or if you are not currently employed, select a previous job in which ethical conduct was a significant concern. If working in a group, select one group member's current job, or if no one is currently working, select someone's previous job in which ethical conduct was a significant conern. Do *not* obtain a copy of or duplicate an existing ethics policy.

STEP 1

Create a specific list of what constitutes ethical conduct for the workplace that you or your group has selected. List major operations or situations in which the people in the organization face ethically challenging situations. Describe right conduct for each operation or situation listed. Develop consequences for violating the guidelines for ethical conduct you have created. Remember that the punishment must fit the crime; it would not be fair to fire people for minor violations, nor would it be proper to give someone a verbal warning for cooking the books to the point of bankrupting the company.

STEP 2

Devise a method for communicating the descriptions of ethical conduct developed in step 1. Be specific as to how each group in the organization will learn about ethics and the ethical conduct guidelines you have developed. Where will ethical training begin? Who must support it? How must the ethics policies be supported? Rephrase the description of ethical conduct in terms of what the right thing to do is rather than what the ethical thing to do is. How will you verify individual awareness and commitment to the ethical standards you developed?

STEP 3

Describe the ongoing activities the organization's members must perform in order to demand truth and obtain the true picture (the good and the bad) of the organization's condition without punishing people for delivering bad news.

Describe the ongoing activities needed to discover where the long-term and short-term ethical risks are in the organization. Include examples of what these risks might be.

Describe how examples of ethical and unethical behavior will be publicized on an ongoing basis without violating any privacy rights of those involved in unethical behavior.

STEP 4

How will you prevent people from working around the ethics policy? What enforcement activities will you need, and how will they be related to accountability? How will you handle ethical violations? If there is an ethical violation, what questions will be asked about the situation, and how will you implement what is learned from the situation?

STEP 5

If possible, and after completing steps 1 through 4, obtain the ethics policies and procedures from the workplace you selected as the basis for this assignment and compare what you have developed with the actual policy. Identify differences and evaluate them for effectiveness. Which version of the different sections do you prefer and why?

SPOT CHECK ANSWERS

1. T
2. T
3. F
4. F
5. F
6. F
7. T
8. F
9. F
10. T

6 Jobs, from Design to Appraisal

When your work speaks for itself, don't interrupt.

Henry J. Kaiser

If we face a recession, we should not lay off employees; the company should sacrifice a profit. It's management's risk and management's responsibility. Employees are not guilty, why should they suffer?

Akio Morita

GOALS

The goal of this chapter is to give everyone, from job designers to job holders, an awareness of how organizations describe work in the form of jobs. An understanding of the process and the results of job design, from job analysis to performance appraisal, should be basic knowledge for all because your job defines your basic role within an organization.

OBJECTIVES

When you finish this chapter, you should be able to:

▶ Explain what constitutes a job.
▶ Differentiate employment at will from job contracts.
▶ List and describe several job trends.
▶ List strategies for career management.
▶ Describe and create strategies for finding a job.
▶ Describe the advantages and disadvantages of specialization.
▶ Compare and contrast current trends in job design.
▶ Describe a job analysis.
▶ Differentiate and appraise job descriptions and job specifications.

▶ List and describe the principal types of interviewing styles.
▶ Summarize the suggestions for conducting and participating in interviews.
▶ Differentiate among the types of interviews.
▶ Appraise performance appraisals.
▶ Describe and identify appraisal threats.
▶ Describe and create appraisal responses.
▶ Create strategies to deal with losing a job.

WHAT IS A JOB?

To many people, a job is an identity. To managers, a job is a collection of tasks. In this chapter, we will concentrate first on the managerial view of what constitutes a job. We will analyze the job and its components in order to understand the motivations and goals of those creating and filling jobs. To begin with, we must know to whom the jobs belong.

In the past, this question probably did not need to be answered. Historically, jobs were perceived as the property of employers. The legal term for this is employment at will. This means that people are hired and retained according to the will of the employer. It also means that both the employer and the employee are free to separate at any time with no advance warning. In the past, this has been more of an advantage for employers than for employees. Because of the questionable practices of some employers, courts began to modify employment at will with the concepts of an implied contract and wrongful discharge.

Unless there is a written contract or union agreement, people are employed at the will of the employer. Some courts have held that an implied contract could be in effect if an employer gives a person written or oral promises, such as "As long as you do your job, you'll have a job with us."[1] An employee handbook could be construed as creating an implied contract if it specifies the length of employment or states that one cannot be fired without just cause. Although an implied contract can be written or oral, it is much more difficult to prove that any oral contract exists, especially if there are no witnesses. Still, implied contracts do offer employees some protection from unscrupulous employers.

Protections have also been granted to people held to have been discharged improperly. The concept of wrongful discharge, the improper or illegal firing of someone, protects employees from being fired on a whim or in violation of a law. Examples of wrongful discharge include being fired for serving on a jury, for refusing to break a law, or for reporting safety violations. Wrongful discharge protection can also be sought if you are fired in violation of the Civil Rights Act, the National Labor Relations Act, the Fair Labor Standards Act, the Occupational Safety and Health Act, or the Americans with Disabilities Act. The Civil Rights Act prohibits firings based on discrimination. You can't be fired because of factors such as gender, race, religion, age, marital status, color, ancestry, or national origin. The National Labor Relations Act covers workers' rights to unionize. The Fair Labor Standards Act concerns wage, hour, and overtime laws. Safety in the workplace is covered under the Occupational Safety and Health Act. Rules concerning workers with disabilities and accommodations employers must make for them are addressed in the Americans with Disabilities Act.

Wrongful discharge protection and implied contracts do not make jobs the property of employees, but they move in this direction. Lawsuits to recover lost jobs and laws requiring a 60-day notification of workers before plant closings are further attempts to classify jobs as the property of employees.[2] The question today is whether employees will have any such property to claim.

Headlines and front pages carry numerous stories on the loss of jobs. One story claims that the job has been eliminated. According to some, there will be work in the future, but not the traditional job as we know it. Reportedly, firms can no longer afford vast cadres of jobholders. Instead, everyone will be a consultant or independent contractor. People will take themselves and their skills from one employer to another as they work on a series of projects. There will be no set hours and no vacations.

People will work until the project is done. A vacation will be any period in which a person can't find work. Some people might get hired in the traditional

NetNote

U.S. Department of Labor Bureau of Labor Statistics

http://stats.bls.gov

U.S. Bureau of Labor Statistics site for labor data and publications. Information on the economy, too.

A QUESTION OF ETHICS

People: Assets or Liabilities

Virtually anytime a company announces layoffs, its stock price rises. In the view of many, a large expense has been reduced. Are workers an expense, or are they assets? If workers are an expense, then why not eliminate all of them? Must companies endure the drain on resources that having employees imposes on them? Isn't it the duty of every company to make the most money possible? To do this means that costs must be minimized, including the costs of having people on the payroll.

Is it ethical, however, to view human beings as liabilities? Are they merely expenses to be employed and unemployed at the discretion of some other people (managers) acting on behalf of a vague group of faceless people known as stockholders? Is it ethical to tell a person who has given 25 years of good service to a company, "You are an expense we no longer desire to support. Go and try to find other work at 50 years of age"? Is it ethical to expect people to be loyal to the firm and to work hard, but then to outsource their work to others when they finally start to make some money?

In academia, professors are viewed more as assets than liabilities. They are given tenure, which means that once you have proven yourself, you essentially have lifetime employment (barring some gross act of misconduct). The value of tenure is now being debated as many schools consider the idea of downsizing (maybe for no other reason than because business is doing it). Maybe this is the wrong way to go. Instead of schools pressing to limit or eliminate tenure, maybe workers should be looking to introduce tenure to business.

1. Is it ethical to treat people as liabilities? Why or why not?

2. How would jobs change if people were considered assets? What are the ethical obligations a company and its management have toward stockholders?

3. Is it ethical to downsize people to save some money? To avoid paying higher salaries?

4. What happens to the work that downsized workers were doing? If 20 percent of the workforce is released, does that mean the company does 20 percent less work? Is it ethical to expect those not laid off (at least this time) to perform more work?

sense, but they, too, will be assigned to projects and will constantly need to acquire new skills. This world of freelancers supposedly will have less emphasis on education (which apparently is outdated soon after it is acquired) and experience (simply many years of repeating the same uninspired actions). The necessary skills will be simply the desire, assets, and ability (education and skills?) to do work and the attitude and ability to work with others. These types of definite and dire predictions may sell magazines and newspapers, but for many reasons, jobs probably will continue to exist.[3]

Certainly some jobs in the future will be as just described. However, not all jobs will be eliminated in favor of consultants and temporary workers. One reason goes back to the original rationale for creating jobs: there are jobs that are done repetitively, that take advantage of experience and the learning curve, and that would disrupt operations if left unperformed. Also, imagine what would happen if a firm could not find independents when it needed them. The no-job scenario seems to assume that workers will be standing in line waiting for employers to beckon them in, but will the independents that the companies need be available exactly when the companies need them? When a company has its own workers, it can depend on them, and, as will be seen in the performance appraisal section of this chapter, dependability is important to managers. Budgeting is also important and would be much more difficult in a jobless environment. How is budgeting affected when the independents demand twice what they earned last time because their expertise is in demand? What happens when one firm hires an expert to do some work that gives the company a competitive advantage, only to have a competitor immediately hire the same expert to do the same work? The Japanese have answers to these concerns and not in the form of masses of contract workers.

THE JAPANESE WAY

The Japanese answer to the job question is lifetime employment. With a few exceptions that began surfacing in the mid-1990s, the Japanese essentially require large companies to provide lifetime employment for their employees. They see only one major disadvantage—not being able to lay off workers to cut costs immediately—but they work around this by withholding semiannual bonuses if necessary. The Japanese see many advantages that argue against a no-jobs world. Although a number of U.S. firms believe that they can't afford to keep workers, the Japanese would say you can't afford not to keep workers and to keep them for life. One of their two main reasons for keeping employees for life is that this aligns the employee's future with that of the company.[4] When you are going to stay somewhere for life (like a tenured college professor), you tend to be very concerned about the health of the organization (or at least the health of your department). What do contract workers think? Temporary workers have little motivation to be concerned about the organization.[5] (See *Doonesbury*, p. 389.) Their focus is the work they are hired to perform, rather than on the long-range viability of the company. In Japan, workers work late and welcome changes like automation—what's good for the company is good for them.[6]

The other main reason for the Japanese lifetime employment policy in corporations is to decrease competition for other firms' workers. Because all large firms accept the system, which includes not trying to steal another firm's workers, there are cost savings involved. In a no-job world, competition for top workers could get expensive (just look at the free-agent athlete market in the United States). A company with lifetime employees has an incentive to invest in training and in research and development (R&D). Why invest in people and R&D in a no-job world when the temporary workers can walk out the door with it and take it to the competition? Lifetime employment also provides an incentive to train workers. The workers will be with the firm long enough for the firm to reap the benefits of skills and management training; the workers won't train and then run off to a different position with someone else.[7] Why train in a no-job world where workers are disposable anyway? Either no-job firms will be followers rather than leaders, or there will be a two-tier system. The two tiers would be one group of longer-term workers who had access to proprietary information (employees, but without rigidly defined jobs) and temporary workers who performed less sensitive jobs. Still, it will be difficult to keep information out of even temp workers' hands in this computer and information age.

The Japanese view is much closer to the wants of U.S. workers. The top five job characteristics important to U.S. workers are:

1. health insurance and benefits
2. interesting work
3. job security
4. the chance to learn new skills
5. yearly vacations

Companies attempting to give workers what they want have found that it is often less expensive to do so and retain workers than to withhold what is important and constantly replace them.[8]

CURRENT JOB TRENDS

What will the job world be like in the future? Although no one knows for sure, the reality probably lies between the extremes of work but no jobs, and lifetime

NetNote

Benefits Link

http://www.benefitslink.com

Mostly a site for employers for information on benefit packages, but some information for individuals participating in a benefit plan.

employment. Some firms may divest themselves of most nonessential (frontline) functions and hire other firms to perform support functions (the ultimate form of specialization?). Other firms may find a competitive advantage in keeping a loyal, long-term workforce. Many firms will probably fall somewhere in between. Some may keep a few support functions, whereas others may prefer the control provided by keeping many of these areas.

At least six job trends deserve watching:

- flexible work hours
- telecommuting
- computer usage
- self-management
- educational requirements
- outsourcing

Work hours, **telecommuting,** and computer usage are somewhat interrelated. Computers make telecommuting feasible. Telecommuting (working from a home office with a phone, fax, or computer link to the company) erodes the concept of set work hours. Computers make global communication easier, which pushes firms to operate 24 hours a day, which further influences work hours. Businesses will make much greater use of computers in general, with special emphasis on networks and the Internet or World Wide Web. People will spend longer hours at their computers and be more productive from them, especially as computers are linked with communications and information systems.[9] With increased computer capability, there are fewer reasons for all of a company's employees to be in one location. Telecommuting will continue to increase as we continue the twenty-first century.[10]

With less time in the office, there is no need for every person to have his or her own office or desk, so companies have created the practice of **hoteling,** sharing desks and office equipment as needed.[11] Telecommuting, the global marketplace,

Telecommuting
working outside of an office, often at home, and communicating and transmitting information by phone, fax, or modem

Hoteling
workers sharing desks and office equipment, not having a permanent desk or work area

REALITY CHECK

Jobs—Going or Coming?

Late at night your Internet connection goes down, so you call tech support; the helpful person who answers the phone may be in India. The Indian tech rep wants another number you can be reached at in case the connection is lost, so you give him your cell phone number; the high-tech chip in that cell phone may have been designed in China. More and more high-paying, white-collar jobs are leaving the United States and Europe and going to developing countries at a cost savings of 50 to 60 percent. Some estimates are that over 3 million of these desirable jobs will leave the United States alone by 2015. Add that to the 2 million jobs lost from 2001 to the beginning of 2004, and employment prospects for good jobs start to look pretty grim. Some people, however, are worried about just the opposite, not too few jobs, but too few workers.

Just at the time when it seems that good jobs are evaporating, another major event is set to increase job openings by a much greater amount. The Baby Boom generation has started to retire. This will create a large number of both skilled and unskilled jobs. The projected loss to developing countries of over 3 million jobs will be offset by U.S retirements creating over 5 million skilled-worker jobs by 2010 and 14 million by 2020. Add in openings in unskilled positions, and 7 million workers will be needed by 2010, 21 million by 2020. The net effect should be plenty of jobs in the United States from the Baby Boomer retirement, yet low prices from the movement of jobs offshore where wages are much lower.

Source: Pete Engardio, Aaron Bernstein, and Manjeet Kripalani, "Is Your Job Next?" *Business Week*, February 3, 2003, pp. 50–60; Paul Kaihla, "The Coming Job Boom," *Business 2.0*, September 2003, pp. 97–104.

NetNote

Knowledge Worker

someone who contributes value to a product or service through what he or she knows

Outsourcing

moving work that was being performed by employees to workers or contractors who are outside the firm

Downsizing

reducing the size of the workforce; firing people

Reengineering

redesigning the way work is performed; often accompanied by restructuring the formal organization

Contingent Worker

a person hired temporarily, often with no benefits

reengineering, and increased competition have caused employers to expand and rearrange hours.[12] Atypical and expanded hours have compelled some employers, such as Toyota, to supply night care in addition to day care.[13]

The freedom (or self-reliance) offered by computers, telecommuting, and other developments influences management styles and dictates the educational level required of workers and managers. Although management has yet to adapt fully to the rapidly changing work world, one trend is beginning to stand out. More and more, firms are turning to teams, team management, and self-management.[14] (These developments are so important that a major portion of Chapter 9 is dedicated to teams, and a major portion of Chapter 10 covers self-management.) These developments all increase the need for more education on the part of workers. In fact, many people will need to continue their education throughout their life just to remain competitive; further education will be needed if they wish to advance.[15] The **knowledge worker** will be the major source of productivity and will be discussed in greater detail in the next section on career management. Although pressure for education for life will continue, with the accompanying stress to meet family needs, this stress may be minimal compared with the stress created by outsourcing.

Outsourcing, downsizing, reengineering, and other related terms all refer to eliminating workers and having others (different firms or the same people hired back temporarily and with no benefits) perform the work. As long as this trend continues, the stress of losing a job, finding another, changing careers, and trying to exist as a **contingent worker** will dominate some job types and industries.[16]

CAREER MANAGEMENT

In the past, companies frequently took an active role in developing employees to help the company and to advance their careers. This phenomenon is less common now, and in the future it may not exist.[17] In the future, workers will be responsible for their own careers, and some will spend much of their work lives as independent contractors and consultants. You will have to determine what work is in demand, maintain your skills, know what companies need, and know how to find work.

In the last era of business, production ruled. Mass production raised living standards and provided blue-collar workers with middle-class wages. In the computer age, the knowledge worker will be in highest demand.[18] One need only look at representative products from these eras to see the differences. In the previous era, the quintessential product was the automobile, and about half the cost of producing the car was labor. The vital product of the computer age is the computer chip. Labor costs are 1 percent or less of the total cost of the chip. The key ingredient of products and services in the future will be knowledge, not labor. Knowledge work is more difficult to value—current accounting systems are inadequate in this regard—but valuation of such work is vital.[19] Knowledge will provide the competitive advantage once afforded by mass production. Knowledge workers will receive the major rewards from companies, and companies will expend greater efforts to retain them.[20]

Although the knowledge worker will be one of the most important factors in the future, every worker will need certain basic skills. The basics still include:

- technical and business skills
- interpersonal skills
- reading, writing, and arithmetic skills
- listening skills
- problem-solving skills

- learning skills
- self-management skills

Most of these have been basic requirements for some time now, although a few are new or newly recognized as being needed.

TECHNICAL AND BUSINESS SKILLS

People will always need basic **technical skills,** the skills needed to perform the job, in order to stay employed and to advance. In addition to technical skills, you will have an advantage if you have skills in the business areas of finance and accounting, computers, marketing, outsourcing, team building, and diversity.[21] Finance and accounting skills are needed to understand the basic unit of all business—money. Anyone combining one field (for example, marketing) with finance and accounting will be ahead of those with just a single field. If you are studying accounting, keep in mind ways to value knowledge and knowledge work.[22] Computer skills certainly will play a part in most fields. Marketing helps companies give customers what they want. No matter what, every organization is selling and marketing something—so know how to do it right. Outsourcing will be prevalent enough to warrant knowing how to hire and manage nonemployee workers. Because team building will be even more prevalent than outsourcing, it is important to learn how to work in teams and how to form and increase the cohesiveness of teams (see Chapter 9). All of this work will be conducted in an environment that is increasingly diverse in terms of minorities, gender, abilities, country of origin, and age. Learn to treat diversity as an asset and not as a liability.

INTERPERSONAL SKILLS

Technical skills along will probably be insufficient for success in the future; achievers will need **interpersonal skills** as well. Even now, some companies try to measure not only employee IQ (intelligence quotient) but also employee EQ (emotional quotient). Essentially, your EQ is your ability to control your emotions and to perceive emotions in others. It is one thing to be able to engineer a gene or a microchip—that's IQ. It is another thing to be able to manage the social and personal elements of what is appropriate at work—that's EQ (see Chapters 7, 8, 9, and 10). Both skills are needed—the knowledge to do the work, and the ability to control your emotions, to empathize, and to self-motivate (the three parts of the EQ).[23]

LEARNING, COMMUNICATING, AND PROBLEM-SOLVING SKILLS

Although EQ skills are just now being recognized and measured, other skill requirements are quite old. For many years, businesses have needed people with what used to be called the three Rs: reading, 'riting, and 'rithmetic. Reading, writing, and arithmetic are still important, and we can add to this list problem solving, listening skills, and knowing how to learn.[24] We might group these into learning, communicating, and problem-solving skills in the future. People will need to be able to read (from a book or information on the Internet), listen, and learn in order to stay competitive in the future. Writing and listening will be needed with speaking and presenting skills in order to communicate effectively. Arithmetic, computational, and other skills, such as pattern recognition (the ability to see patterns that have occurred or have been experienced before), are needed to solve problems—a vital function today and for the future. Working in very busy situations can enhance pattern recognition

NetNote

Women's Career and Education

http://career-education. womendiary.net/

Career advice site geared toward women.

Technical Skills
skills needed to perform the tasks in a job

Interpersonal Skills
the ability to communicate and work cooperatively with others

and learning. Experiences are compressed into a shorter time when an organization is busy.[25] For example, if one particular exception occurs in every 100 cases, then it is better to spend one year at a firm handling 100 cases a year than it is to spend four years with a firm doing 20 cases a year and risk never seeing this exception.

SELF-MANAGEMENT SKILLS

With the tendency in organizations toward less hierarchy and fewer managers, people have to be able to manage themselves.[26] More people will have to be self-motivating, self-monitoring, and self-evaluating. A key component of **self-management** is the ability to differentiate between what is important and must be done immediately, and what is unimportant and should be dropped.[27] With self-management also comes the responsibility to manage your own time and your own career (see Chapter 10).

FINDING A JOB

Of course, before any of these skills can be used, one must have a job (or at least employment, an assignment, or a project). The first rule for job searching is to start early.[28] Find the careers that need people (see Table 6.1) and find out where the jobs are (see Table 6.2). In general, technicians and other knowledge workers will be in demand.[29] Technicians are going to want recognition for their efforts, but they will also be in a good position to get it.[30] Once you decide on a career, get some experience in that field, preferably with a company you want to work for after graduation. Some major employers currently set one-third of their new jobs aside for their interns; this figure may increase to one-half. Other firms make offers only to their

---

Self-Management

the ability to manage yourself, to differentiate between what is important and must be done immediately and what is unimportant and can wait; includes self-motivation, self-monitoring, and self-evaluation

---

NetNote

Various Job Sites

http://www.monster.com/
http://www.career.com/
http://www.jobs.com/

TABLE 6.1 OCCUPATIONAL GROUPS PROJECTED TO HAVE THE HIGHEST NUMBER OF JOB OPENINGS THROUGH THE YEAR 2014

1. Retail sales	6. Waiters and waitresses
2. Registered nurses	7. Food preparation and serving workers
3. Postsecondary teachers	8. Home health aides
4. Customer service representatives	9. Nurse aides, orderlies, & attendants
5. Janitors and cleaners	10. General & operations managers

Source: U.S. Bureau of Labor Statistics, www.bls.gov, *Occupational Outlook Handbook 2006–07.*

TABLE 6.2 TOP 10 AREAS PROJECTED TO HAVE THE HIGHEST EMPLOYMENT GROWTH RATE FOR 2003–2013

Las Vegas, Nevada	Orlando, Florida
West Palm Beach, Florida	Fort Lauderdale, Florida
Riverside, California	Phoenix, Arizona
Jacksonville, Florida	Tampa, Florida
Raleigh-Durham, North Carolina	Sacramento, California

Source: Paula Kaihla, "The Coming Job Boom," *Business 2.0,* September 2003, pp. 97–104.

interns.[31] Even for first-year college students, it is not too early to start gaining a foothold in the world of work.

As graduation approaches, job seekers will have to go to the employers, rather than waiting for employers to find them (especially when looking for work with small to midsize companies). Networking is also valuable for getting the job you want.[32] Many jobs are filled by someone who heard about the opening through word of mouth. Without becoming annoying, use contacts as a source of information in two ways: to pass information about jobs to you and to send out information to others that you are available. Next, put together a professional-looking resume, tailor a cover letter for each employer, and work to get an interview.

To save stamps, shoe leather, or both, you can locate job openings or information on the Internet. Look on home pages for job listings or human resource listings or to get an address for your mailing list. Web sites can also be used to learn about an industry and to learn about individual company histories; both can be useful in an interview.

During an interview, demonstrate that you have an interest in the company.[33] Learn everything you can about the firm so that when the interview committee says, "Do you have any questions?" you can reply with verifying questions. "Isn't the company opening a new production facility in Malaysia next year, and Ms. Smith, aren't you being promoted to manage that?" So few people do this that it is an excellent way to differentiate yourself from the masses. Remember though, that if it were easy, everyone would do it. Maybe you should treat the interview as your final final exam; you pass if you get the job of your choice, so prepare with the same intensity you would for testing.

Once you have work, remember that many hierarchies have been demolished, which means fewer traditional advancement paths and fewer managers to watch out for your development.[34] You will have to assume responsibility for managing your career. This means working on broader, transferable skills, keeping up with the skills of coworkers, and constantly upgrading your skills.[35]

In the future, people will identify themselves much more by the skills they have and the work they do ("I design distribution systems") rather than by the company for which they do the work ("I work for Acme Brands").[36] Develop a career plan with goals and objectives, and include goals for keeping your visibility high and for maintaining good relations with bosses.[37] Staying on good terms with the boss helps, but you must also be on good terms with team members.[38] Both requirements underscore the need for interpersonal, or people, skills and a thorough knowledge of organizational behavior.[39] Changes in the working environment and changes in your career mean that you must also learn to adapt and cope with change (see Chapter 13). To obtain and retain a job, you should not only know what a job is but also how jobs are designed and described and especially how your job performance is appraised.

SPOT CHECK

1. The use of knowledge workers will decline in the near future. T F
2. Technical skills are those needed to perform a particular job. T F
3. Networking means getting other people to get you the job you want. T F
4. Career plans are obsolete as the future is much more uncertain than ever before. T F
5. During an interview, demonstrating that you have an interest in the company will make you appear overeager. T F

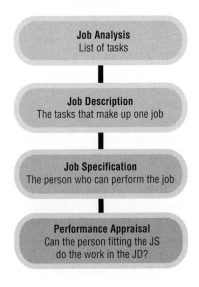

Job Design

the process of defining the work that needs to be done, dividing the work into jobs, describing the jobs, and describing the people capable of performing the jobs

Job Analysis

creating a list of what tasks need to be performed in order to complete a job

Job Characteristics Model

job design that considers task variety, identity, and significance; autonomy; and feedback factors

Task Variety

the assortment of skills a person needs to perform the tasks in a job

Task Identity

how closely the work is related to a finished product

Task Significance

the effect one person's work has on the work of others

JOB DESIGN

Job design is the term used to refer to the process of defining the work that needs to be done, dividing the work into jobs, describing the jobs, and describing the person capable of performing the jobs. Once someone is hired, performance is measured to ensure that the person described in the job specification is doing the work listed in the job description. The sequence is depicted in Figure 6.1.

JOB ANALYSIS

The first step in job design is the **job analysis.** This involves gathering information and creating a list of what tasks need to be performed in order to complete a job. If jobs already exist, then the job analysis often begins with observing what workers are doing. If new jobs are involved, then individual tasks have to be conceived, often by starting at the last operation and determining what must be done just before that. The end result is a list of tasks. One task then becomes a job, or tasks are grouped to form jobs. Grouping of tasks is common but often requires a detailed analysis first.

JOB CHARACTERISTICS MODEL

Several methods for analyzing tasks and designing jobs exist, including simply combining tasks that seem to go together (this is often not the best way to design jobs, however). As an organized method of job design, the **job characteristics model** by Hackman and Oldman has seen widespread use since its development about 20 years ago. This model examines five factors in designing jobs: task variety, task identity, task significance, autonomy, and job-related feedback.[40]

Task variety refers to the assortment of skills a person needs in order to perform the tasks in a job. As task variety increases, more training, education, and experience may be required of the person, but the job might be less boring, also. **Task identity** refers to how closely the work is related to a finished product. The closer the work is to the product's completion, the more the worker is able to identify with the product and the tasks, and the more involved he or she is in seeing that the job is performed well. **Task significance** refers to the effect one person's work has on others. A person is typically less likely to perform a task poorly if doing so will create difficulties for others. If others will not be affected, the person may care less about performing well.

Autonomy is concerned with how free an individual is to perform tasks and control work. Lower levels of autonomy can increase stress. The last factor is feedback, which is the direct reception of job information. **Feedback** provides the person with information on the quantity and quality of work and can be motivational.

DIFFICULTY LEVEL

In addition to these five factors, a job designer must consider the difficulty level involved in performing tasks.[41] Considering these six factors may make job design seem like an extremely difficult task, which it sometimes is. However, sometimes a factor or factors may be fixed and beyond the control of the designer. For example, a task may be so difficult that only a highly skilled person can perform that task and only that task. Such a situation effectively limits task variety. A professional photographer, for instance, needs a high level of skills, but there is not a wide variety of those skills. A manager of frontline workers needs planning, organizing, motivating, budgeting, hiring, conflict resolving, and other skills, including technical knowledge related to the work his or her people are performing.

Task significance and autonomy may also be defined by the work itself. One person's work may inherently greatly affect others, as it does on an assembly line. Autonomy may be limited because the work pace cannot be controlled or because the methods the person uses are dictated by the process. An electrician has little freedom if the work is to be safe and conform to the National Electric Code. Feedback is another factor that is inherent in some jobs but must come from different sources in others. The photographer knows when the film is developed how successful he or she is, as do physicians when patients leave cured or a salesperson when a deal is closed. An office assistant, however, may need feedback from others in order to know that he or she is answering phones, typing, taking messages, and filing at the desired level.

A THREE-FACTOR MODEL

The job characteristics model has been used often in the 20 years since its development, but a new model may be needed for the workplace. At least two have been proposed for use in high-technology, computer-based industries. One model, developed by Dean and Snell, examines three elements of a job: task variety, task complexity, and task interdependence.[42] In this model, task variety is used in virtually the same way as in the job characteristics model. When a job involves solving problems, applying alternatives, or using extensive technical knowledge, it is seen as having a large amount of task complexity. The third factor, **task interdependence**, refers to the lack of barriers between departments or tasks that were previously distinct. In applying this model, the advanced manufacturing environments of today are seen as having high task variety because many jobs include the performance of a large number of tasks with a large amount of problem solving. Increased demand for problem solving, plus an increase in the use of technical knowledge, conceptual skills, and analytical skills, places advanced manufacturing jobs high on the scale for task complexity as well. The integrated nature of these systems and the collaboration required of the workers mean that these jobs also have a high level of task interdependence.

THE CPOS MODEL

The **CPOS model** for job design explores job components in greater detail than other models and with more attention to the psychological aspects of advanced

Autonomy

the freedom workers have to perform tasks and control their work

Feedback

the direct reception of job information; information on the quantity and quality of one's work

Task Interdependence

the lack of barriers between departments or between tasks

CPOS Model

job design that considers cognitive demands, production responsibilities, operator control, and social interactions

Cognitive Demands
the mental requirements of a job

Production Responsibility
the responsibility a worker has for expensive equipment and increased productivity

Operator Control
the control workers have over the timing of work, the methods used, and the boundaries

Boundary Control
a worker's responsibility for primary and secondary tasks needed to complete work

Social Interaction
the social contacts and social support involved in a job

Social Contacts
the quantity of interactions a person has with others while on the job

Social Support
the quality of interactions a person has with others while on the job

technological work.[43] The factors in the CPOS model are cognitive demands, production responsibilities, operator control, and social interactions.

Cognitive demands refer to the mental requirements of a job, such as the number of systems a person must know how to operate or the number of problems a person must solve. An increase in cognitive demands is similar in effect to increases in task significance and variety in the job characteristics model.

Production responsibility, which is similar to task significance in the job characteristics model, involves the responsibility a worker has for expensive equipment and increased productivity. Production responsibility increases if an error made by a worker would be costly in terms of time, money, or quality. Too great an increase in production responsibility may increase a worker's stress level and decrease job satisfaction.

Operator control is similar to autonomy in the job characteristic model. Advanced technology may lead to less control on the part of workers because these systems dictate procedures. Operator control in the CPOS model differs from autonomy in that it specifies three subtypes of control. Here, control consists of the worker's ability to vary the timing of work, the methods used, and the boundaries. The manufacturing process frequently dictates timing and methods, which decreases operator control. **Boundary control** involves a worker's responsibility for both primary and secondary tasks needed to complete work, rather than for just primary tasks. For example, if you have to acquire materials, assemble a unit, test a unit, and then clean the work area, the boundaries around these four jobs have been blurred. You have less boundary control than if your job involved only assembling the unit.

Last in the CPOS model is **social interaction**, which refers to the social contacts and support involved in a job. **Social contacts** are the quantity of interactions a person has with others while on the job. **Social support** refers to the quality of those interactions. Higher levels of equipment monitoring can reduce the social contacts of a job. However, advanced technology does not appear to affect the social-support aspect of these jobs. All of these factors have been found to affect job satisfaction, and increased social support has been found to decrease the adverse effects of high levels of equipment monitoring and production responsibility. In other words, support from coworkers and work friends can offset some of the ill effects higher job demands can make on you.

WORK EFFECTIVENESS

In addition to these factors (and those covered in Chapter 1), the work effectiveness of a job needs to be considered. **Work effectiveness** is the integration of tasks and jobs in order to carry out the mission of the company in meeting the needs of customers.[44] The key here is to design jobs that are satisfying, increase productivity, lower costs, and, maybe most important of all, serve the needs of customers. Jobs

---

SPOT CHECK

6. A job analysis reveals the time needed to complete a task or job. T F
7. Autonomy is concerned with how free an individual is to perform tasks and control work. T F
8. Task variety refers to the number of different people needed to perform a job. T F
9. Task interdependence means there are fewer barriers between departments or tasks than before. T F
10. Social contacts are the number of individuals a person can go to for help on the job. T F

must not only accomplish tasks, but they must accomplish tasks that meet the needs of the customers. If jobs or tasks do not ultimately contribute to serving customers, then maybe they need not be performed. Tasks may not have to serve the needs of customers directly, but one should be able to draw some connection. For example, a training department may not train customers, but better training of frontline workers may reduce errors or increase quality, which does benefit customers by holding costs and pricing down and providing a better product.

Using one of the three models discussed here or combining elements to form your own can aid in the design or the understanding of a job. Tasks can be combined into jobs so that each characteristic is balanced or set at a level that provides growth and job satisfaction for the worker, cost savings for the employer, and the desired quality and service levels for the customers. The number of tasks constituting a job, however, is also dependent upon the management philosophy and the degree of specialization needed and desired.

SPECIALIZATION

Specialization, or the division of labor into separate tasks, is at the heart of modern working conditions. Virtually all jobs use specialization, but the degree of specialization varies. Classical managers believe in a high degree of specialization. In the ultimate form, one worker performs one task. Jobs that cannot be performed by machines, require few skills, and are performed frequently are often highly specialized. In the past, jobs were often highly specialized because workers did not have the ability to perform more than a few tasks adequately or because managers assumed workers could not handle more than a few tasks. Today, many jobs are less specialized, and workers are given more tasks because managers have found that people can do more when asked. Also, workers are less bored when they have more tasks to perform.

Boredom is a significant disadvantage to specialization. People want interesting work. That was second on the list of desirable job characteristics (whereas high pay was 11th). Boredom decreases job satisfaction, decreases alertness, and can increase the injury rate. To counteract boredom, managers try **job enlargement,** adding more tasks to a job. They also employ **job enrichment,** adding more worker involvement to a job (sometimes by letting people inspect their own work). They have also tried job sharing, having two or more people trade jobs.[45] All of these actions are designed to offset boredom from specialization, but there are so many advantages to specialization that we are not about to abandon it any time soon.

Specialization offers five significant advantages:

- time compression
- large-job feasibility
- training time
- expertise in problem solving
- efficiency

Time Compression   It is possible for someone to build a house alone, but it takes a long time. A group of workers will compress this time drastically. Also although it is possible for someone to build a house alone, it is not possible for one person alone to build the Sears Tower or any other large building. The time needed to complete such a job exceeds many lifetimes.

Large-Job Feasibility   Specialization makes large jobs feasible. Think of all the knowledge you would have to acquire to build a house alone: excavating, concrete

Work Effectiveness
the integration of tasks and jobs in order to carry out the mission of the company in meeting the needs of customers

NetNote

Employee Productivity Site

http://www.accel-team.com/ work_design/
Job design history to today.

http://www.accel-team.com/ job_interviews/index.html
Job interviews and job analysis.

Specialization
the division of work into separate tasks

Job Enlargement
adding more tasks at the same difficulty level to a job

Job Enrichment
adding more worker involvement to a job

work, carpentry, plumbing, electricity. The training for any one of these fields would take years, to say nothing of the years of experience needed after training in order to perform even one of them well.

Training Time   You could learn enough to build a house, but for a specialized job the training time is much shorter and typically involves greater depth in the job's tasks. Training for an all-inclusive job could stretch into years, and if the trained worker quit, employers might have to wait years again for a replacement to be trained.

Expertise   Being a jack of all trades and master of none means you would perform certain tasks infrequently. With specialization, tasks are performed frequently. Therefore, something that might be problematic to the generalist would be considered routine by the specialist. The specialist has more expertise and therefore can solve more problems than the generalist because the specialist has seen more and performed more and has experience with even rare situations.

Efficiency   The sum total of specialization is efficiency. Specialized workers get more work done because they have perfected techniques for accomplishing the same few tasks over many repetitions (they have advanced along the learning curve).

Although the advantages of specialization are many, and it is used in virtually all jobs, there is no one correct amount of specialization. The trick for managers is to use enough specialization to reap the benefits but to include enough diversity of tasks so that boredom is minimized. Once this has been accomplished, the job should be formally outlined and the requirements for people capable of performing the job described.

JOB DESCRIPTIONS AND JOB SPECIFICATIONS

Job Description

a written outline of the tasks that constitute a job and other items related to depicting a job

Job Specification

a written description of the characteristics required of a person that will enable him or her to perform the job

A **job description** outlines the work and related items that constitute a job. A **job specification** describes the characteristics required of a person that will enable him or her to perform the job. The impetus for these documents and the distinction between them result mainly from two management principles: the technical competence principle and the separation principle. Both principles are from Max Weber's list of management principles and are among the earliest attempts at recording an organized system of management and organization theory.[46] The technical competence principle states that the most qualified person should be hired for every job. The separation principle says that the position one fills is separate from the individual filling it. If you leave a firm, your position (along with the responsibilities, authority, desk, chairs, and other equipment) still exists and remains with the firm. As a result of these two principles, we have job descriptions to explain the position and job specifications to describe the person that can do the job and the technical specifications he or she should have.

Although there is no one correct way to write job descriptions, most of them have certain elements in common. When you ask to see a job description, for instance during a job interview, you can expect to find:

- a narrative description of the job
- the reporting relationship
- advancement order
- responsibilities

- duties
- tools and equipment
- working conditions

The narrative description is an overview of what the job entails and how it relates to other jobs in the department or in the organization's processes. The reporting relationship describes the location of this position in the organizational chart, clarifying what position this position reports to. Some job descriptions include the order of advancement, which may describe positions that lead to the current one and the position that could follow. For example, a supervisor's advancement order might say "Promotion from: frontline worker. Promotion to: manager."

Responsibilities are essentially duties carrying additional significance that the person is expected to complete without guidance. Examples are being responsible for a cash drawer, opening a business for the day, or having others report to this position. **Duties** often constitute the main portion of a job description; this area lists the tasks to be performed. The tools and equipment section lists and describes what needs to be operated while performing the job. Finally, the section on working conditions lists the hours and days to be worked, vacations, holidays, and the amount of travel, if any. If a firm does not have a written job description for a job you are applying for, be sure to ask questions that will provide you with the same information.

Although employees and prospective employees commonly view the job description, the job specification is less often seen. Job specifications are used more often by the human resources department and by managers to recruit workers and to evaluate applicants. Once a person meeting the specification is hired for the job, there is less need to see the specification. Job specifications typically address four areas:

- education
- experience
- skills
- abilities

Education refers to the formal education and any training needed to perform a job—for example, a high school diploma or GED and certification as a master mechanic, or a bachelor's degree in marketing. **Experience** refers to the amount of prior experience performing the same job. For example, an accounting manager may need five years of accounting experience and two years of supervisory experience. An **entry-level** (starting) **position** is one that requires no previous experience. **Skills** are learned or acquired capabilities. Typing is an excellent example of a skill; no one is born able to type. **Abilities,** on the other hand, are essentially physiologic aptitudes. Abilities would include the use of both arms or both legs or the ability to lift 50 pounds from the floor to a shelf four feet up, 30 times an hour for eight hours. After finding a person who meets the job specifications, a performance appraisal is needed to measure the work output against the job description.

Responsibilities
duties carrying additional significance that the person is expected to complete without guidance

Duties
individual tasks to be performed in a job

Education
the formal education and training needed to perform a job

Experience
the amount of prior time performing the same work that is required for a position

Entry-Level Position
a position requiring no previous experience

Skills
learned or acquired capabilities

Abilities
physiologic aptitudes; inherent capabilities

SPOT CHECK

11. Specialization is is the division of labor into separate tasks. T F
12. Job enlargement means adding more worker involvement to a job. T F
13. Job enrichment is adding more tasks to a job. T F
14. A job description outlines the work that constitutes a particular job. T F
15. A job specification describes the person needed to perform a job. T F

TRYING TO OBTAIN A JOB—THE INTERVIEW

Another aspect of small-group behavior that receives considerable attention in management literature is the process of interviewing. For our purposes, **interviewing** can be defined as the act of consultation between a manager and a present or past employee or an applicant for employment. Most employees, whether managers or associates, are often involved in this form of interpersonal behavior because interviews are used for a variety of purposes in organizations. The principal types of interviews are:

- employment—to observe applicants for job openings
- appraisal—to review an employee's performance
- counseling—to aid employees with personal problems
- disciplinary—to discuss an employee's substandard behavior or performance
- grievance—to discuss an employee's complaints
- morale surveys—to discover employee attitudes
- exit—to assess reasons for employee terminations

STYLES OF INTERVIEWING

The particular style of interview employed generally depends on the nature of the interview and the experience of the manager. As with most activities, interviewers (as well as interviewees) should alter their styles to suit the particular situation. The most commonly used styles include the structured, unstructured, group, and stress styles of interviewing.

Structured (Directive) Interviews   A **structured,** or **directive, interview** is one that usually follows a predetermined pattern. Frequently, a specific set of questions taken from a detailed form are asked of the interviewee. The form is a guide to what questions should be asked, and it helps keep the interview on track. Some interview forms include two sets of questions: (1) the specific questions to be asked during the interview, and (2) questions not asked by the interviewer but intended to help him or her interpret the significance of the interviewee's answers. These latter questions usually appear directly below the primary questions and are often highlighted in a different color to make them distinguishable. Some types of interviews— employment or disciplinary, for example—lend themselves to a fair degree of structure by their very nature because interviewers usually know the specific ground they want to cover. Other types of interviews, such as counseling or grievance, are typically less structured.

Unstructured (Nondirective) Interviews   An **unstructured,** or **nondirective, interview** is one that attempts to avoid influencing the interviewee's remarks. Often a broad, general question is asked, and the interviewee is encouraged to answer in some depth. "How would you describe the perfect boss?" and "How did the problem between you and Cathy start?" are examples of such an open question. During an unstructured interview, the interviewee tends to feel freer to express attitudes, desires, emotions, and problems. With certain types of interviews, such as grievance or counseling, the unstructured approach often serves as a beneficial safety valve by which employees can vent pressures or complaints. Inherent in such interviews, however, is the danger of getting sidetracked and wasting time on unrelated topics, especially if the interviewee has a tendency to ramble.

Interviewing
consultation between a manager and an applicant for employment

---

Structured (Directive) Interview
an interview that follows a predetermined pattern

Unstructured (Nondirective) Interview
an interview that attempts to avoid influencing the interviewee's remarks

---

Group Interviews Another technique, the **group interview,** is adaptable to a variety of situations. In one variation, several managers, or members of a board or panel, observe, challenge, and pool their impressions of the interviewee. Applicants for positions with a high degree of responsibility, such as sales or executive trainees, may be subjected to group interviews. Some governmental jobs also require applicants for available positions or aspirants for promotion to go before a board or panel of interviewers.

In another variation of the group interview, several managers question and observe candidates for a particular position as a group. The group being interviewed may be questioned, observed, and assessed by the executive panel as the candidates interact with one another.

Performing well during a group or panel interview may be dependent on five key factors: staying calm, making key points, practicing answers, dividing your attention, and repeating questions.[47] Some group interviews are deliberately designed to expose candidates to high pressure; even when they are not, these interviews generate plenty of stress simply because the candidate is outnumbered and being asked numerous questions. It is important to remain as calm as possible. In order to help stay calm, you should commit your resume to memory. This can increase your confidence and can help you avoid leaving out important points. To further help you stay calm, you should practice answers to common interview questions ("What are your career goals?" "What do you know about our firm?") while visualizing a group of grumpy executives sitting before you. While you are answering, make eye contact with everyone conducting the interview so that no one feels ignored. Finally, to show that you have been attentive, repeat and paraphrase the questions you are asked (which can also help you when multipart or multiple questions are being asked).

Group Interview

a committee or group
conducting an interview

Stress, or Situational, Interviews The **stress interview,** or situational interview, places the interviewee in a tense, often realistic situation to see how he or she responds to stress.[48] The theory underlying this approach is that during stress, the true personality of the interviewee tends to emerge. It is debatable, however, whether a person has one true personality. Most individuals tend to react differently at different times to similar situations, depending on their moods at the particular moment.

Managers who use the stress technique believe that by introducing tension into the interview the applicant can be observed in circumstances other than artificial, courtship-style-behavior situations. Job situations in which a customer is right, and the interviewee's department or colleague is wrong may be used to see what words will be used (or what lies told). A radical approach for inducing stress into an interview is for the interviewer to indicate that the applicant is obviously unfit and shouldn't be wasting the interviewer's time. The interviewer then observes the response of the applicant.

An inherent danger in this approach is that the applicant might develop a negative attitude toward the organization and interviewer that may be difficult to shake off later. A further danger is the possibility of a civil rights complaint of bias in hiring by a disgruntled applicant. The introduction of artificial stress also runs the risk of producing false results because applicants may be unwilling to challenge someone in an interview, especially when they perceive the interviewers as having most, if not all, of the power. To see how people react under actual job stress, some employers pay the most promising applicants for one-half or one full day of work. The applicants are then observed under real and relevant stress-inducing situations.

Stress Interview

an interview in which
the interviewee is placed
in a high-tension or
abusive situation

TYPES OF INTERVIEWERS

Just as there are different types of interviews, there are different general types of interviewers. Each has a particular style and is looking for information in a particular way, and there is a way that interviewees should respond to each. Five general types can be identified: the investigator, the shopper, the adjudicator, the talker, and the skeptic.[49]

The investigator is searching for clues—clues to the interviewee's past, personality, or feelings. The investigator wants to probe beneath the surface and may try to twist what the interviewee says in order to see what is there or to see the interviewee's reaction. The investigator is not only listening but is watching closely, so an interviewee must watch what he or she says and try to control nonverbal communications. While you shouldn't say anything negative in any interview, you especially do not want to do this with an investigator as your comments may be turned against you.

The shopper is out in the marketplace looking for the best product. The shopper will often come right out and tell the interviewee what the company is looking for and then spend the rest of the interview determining how well he or she meets those needs. The shopper essentially follows a consumer buying pattern: The shopper has a list of what is wanted, seeks the features each interviewee has, and finds the person who best matches what the company wants. In this case, you need to cite evidence that demonstrates how well you meet the company needs.

The adjudicator seeks the worthy. Adjudicators pass judgment over interviewees and their fitness to be a member of a profession or to join the club (i.e., the company). A problem here is that most of what an interviewee should do when meeting with an adjudicator needs to occur before it is known that the interviewer is an adjudicator. With this type, an interviewee should arrive early. His or her appearance must be perfect for the situation. Advance preparation is needed so the interviewee can show interest in, and knowledge of, the company. Fortunately, these are all things that should be done before all interviews anyway. With an adjudicator, an interviewee would not want to say what he or she is, for example, a systems analyst; instead, the interviewee would want to describe what he or she can do.[50]

The talker reverses the typical interview situation. Interviewers usually want the interviewee to do almost all of the talking. Instead, this type of interviewer does the vast majority of talking. Talkers may discuss themselves or the company, which is not, by itself, bad, but it does not allow the interviewee the chance to make his or her points. The interviewee may learn whether the company is right for him or her, but the talker may not learn enough about the interviewee to make the best decision. With a talker, try to answer any questions and then ask one of your own that needs only a yes or no answer. For example, "Yes, I have moderated teleconferences before. Do you do many?"

"Yes."

"Great, because I really enjoy preparing for them. Do you hold any over more than three time zones?"

"Yes."

"Well those are more difficult, but fortunately I have done many like that. Do you ever do any with less than four weeks notice?"

The fifth general type is the skeptic. The skeptic is suspicious of all applicants; the better an applicant appears, the more suspicious the skeptic becomes. Some skeptics wonder why anyone would want to work at their company because they have been burned before by people who looked promising but didn't work out or left quickly for something better. Skeptical interviewers may appear not only doubtful, but uninterested or even hostile. To the interviewee, the situation may seem hopeless, causing him or her to stop trying and thus fulfilling the skeptic's opinion. Such circumstances can cause the company to miss out on good people. To salvage the situation, you could try to find out what is bothering the skeptic. You could ask if this is a particularly bad day and offer to reschedule. This may shake the skeptic out of his or her bad mood. Or, you may ask if the skeptical interviewer has had a particular problem with past new hires and then give examples of how you do not behave that way.

GUIDELINES FOR CONDUCTING INTERVIEWS

Regardless of the type of interview, the manager should have patience, knowledge of questioning and listening techniques, an awareness of and sensitivity toward nonverbal communication, and a basic liking and respect for people. Some types of interviews, such as disciplinary interviews, tend to be more effective when they take place out of earshot of others to prevent embarrassing the employee.

Although many managers go along with the suggestion that they should criticize in private and praise in public, the procedures of some companies and the contracts of some labor agreements require that a third party be present during any disciplinary interview. In the case of company policy, the purpose is to provide a witness in the event that the employee makes false accusations at a later time. Some union officials believe that a third party witness who is a union member is useful to help protect the employee against unfair treatment. In general, however, the technique employed by the interviewer is far more critical than its setting to the interview's success.

The following is a list of some guidelines for conducting more effective interviews:

1. Plan ahead. Know why you are there and what you want to accomplish. What do you want to find out?
2. Know something in advance about the person whom you are interviewing. Look at the person's application, personnel file, or any other relevant information before the interview.
3. Watch out for your own biases. Your task is to obtain information or provide assistance, not to feed your own ego.
4. Try to help the interviewee relax and feel confident enough to communicate with you.
5. Don't make the mistake of doing all the talking; encourage the interviewee to talk. You shouldn't be doing more than 25 to 30 percent of the talking.
6. Practice the concepts of good listening and phrasing questions.
7. Avoid questions that are likely to produce a biased answer, such as "How did you get along with your former coworkers?"
8. Don't fight the clock. Try to arrange for enough time to conduct the interview so that the session does not become tense.
9. Control the interview. Some small talk may help to relax the person you are interviewing, but in general, attempt to guide the interview in the direction of your objectives.
10. Never argue. Arguments usually prevent the attainment of your objectives.
11. Look beyond the employee's words. Is there an ulterior meaning that has not surfaced?
12. Maintain your alertness at the end of the interview. Much can be learned after the first good-bye.

GUIDELINES FOR BEING INTERVIEWED

We've just examined the interviewing process mainly as a tool of management. But almost everyone—both workers and managers—is interviewed periodically. So let's step now into the shoes of the person on the receiving end of an interview. How might you improve your image when being interviewed? The following guidelines could help:

1. Prepare answers for common interview questions (e.g., "Why do you want to work here?" "Where do you see yourself five years from now?").
2. Be prompt. Arriving late is getting off to a very bad start.
3. Make certain that your appearance is appropriate for the particular situation.
4. Bring something to do (like a book or job-related magazine) in case you have to wait to be interviewed and to help you relax.
5. Don't be overanxious to answer questions. Give complete, but brief, responses. Don't ramble.
6. Listen carefully to the interviewer. If you don't understand a question, don't fake the answer. Ask for clarification.
7. Don't overreact to questions. They may merely be a part of a stress interview intended to test your ability to handle difficult situations.
8. Be certain to take with you any background, reference, support, or statistical material you might need.
9. Be polite and courteous throughout the interview. Don't forget to thank the interviewer for his or her time, shake hands, and say good-bye.

Once you are successful at obtaining a job you need to be concerned about your performance and how it will be measured.

PERFORMANCE APPRAISALS

Performance Appraisal

a measurement to determine if the person meeting the job specification is performing the work in the job description

A **performance appraisal** is used to determine if the person meeting the job specification is able to perform the work in the job description. If a worker is found to be performing poorly, the tendency may be to blame the person. However, other factors may explain a poor performance appraisal. True, maybe the employee is not doing well. Another possibility, however, is that the rater, or evaluator, did a poor job. Maybe the job specification asks for the wrong kind of person—one with too little experience, perhaps. Maybe the job description is outdated, or the performance evaluation is inadequate. Never be a passive participant when you are evaluated. You can take several actions before, during, and after the evaluation.

SPOT CHECK

16. A structured, or directive, interview has a specific set of questions that the interviewee must answer in writing. T F
17. A nondirective interview attempts to avoid influencing the interviewee's remarks. T F
18. The shopper interviewer is searching for clues. T F
19. The talker type of interviewer does the vast majority of speaking. T F
20. If an interviewee prepares answers to common interview questions, he or she will appear disorganized. T F

KNOW HOW YOU WILL BE EVALUATED

Your first action should be to read and understand the evaluation process and the instrument to be used. The best time to see the evaluation form is either before you take the job or at least during the first few days of employment. It is vital that you find out what the job is and how your success at performing the job will be determined. If you don't know what the evaluation will cover, how can you work toward obtaining a good rating on it? Asking to see an evaluation form during the interview may set you apart from all the applicants that don't bother to do so. If a prospective employer does not have a written evaluation, then you have learned something valuable. With nothing in writing, how will the employer decide whether or not to retain you? The interview is the time to ask so that you can decide whether you want to work under those conditions. Even if an employer does not have a written evaluation, many managers commonly use certain criteria. These criteria might not be explicitly mentioned on the evaluation form, but they are usually present in every appraisal. The common criteria are:

- attitude
- compatibility
- dependability
- knowledge
- efficiency
- organization

Each of these criteria commonly colors a **rater's** opinion of the ratee.

Attitude   Perhaps the vaguest of these six items is **attitude.** Although we might be able to agree on which people have bad attitudes, it is harder to rate people with great, excellent, or average attitudes. A bad attitude may be commonly agreed upon as one that is negative with regard to the work, the employer, coworkers, and so forth. Although we might agree on what constitutes a bad attitude, what can be done about it? Is a bad attitude a problem or merely a symptom of a different problem? If you categorize it as a problem, what can be done about it? The answer is nothing. We can't do anything directly about a bad attitude because it is really a symptom of some other problem. However, we might be able to do something about that underlying problem, which may then improve a person's attitude. Then again, it may be something personal that we can't do anything about. Whether we can do something or not, attitude is second in importance only to dependability in many rater's minds.

Compatibility   In an era of teams, work groups, and matrix organizations (more about this in Chapters 7 and 9), **compatibility** with coworkers is more important than ever. The ability to work well with others can enhance your performance appraisal and your chances for receiving key assignments and promotions. Compatibility is a criterion that influences evaluations whether or not it is explicitly mentioned.

Dependability   **Dependability** may be the single most important evaluation criterion, given that the person has adequate job knowledge. Managers consistently mention dependability as critical to a good evaluation. Some managers admit that they would prefer a dependable average worker to a superstar with erratic attendance. It doesn't matter how great you are if you are not there or can't be counted on to meet deadlines. Dependability may appear on some evaluations, or it may be counted with attendance, tardiness, or ability to complete work on time. Once again, even if not mentioned explicitly, it is on the minds of raters.

Rater
a person who evaluates or rates others

Attitude
a state of mind or a feeling; a person's disposition

Compatibility
the ability to work well with others

Dependability
reliability, especially in being present for work or completing work on time

Knowledge   Job knowledge is important for obvious reasons. No matter what other personality traits you have, and even if you are there every day with a great attitude, if you can't do the work, the evaluation must reflect that. Maintaining job knowledge is a challenge we all face, but it is one that must be met to stay with one's current job, much less advance.

Efficiency and Organization   Efficiency and organization are related, but not identical. Although it is difficult to be efficient without being organized, it is entirely possible to be organized and completely inefficient. How? Some people spend so much time getting organized that they never get any work done. These people may have clean offices, a clear desk, and tidy files, but they have spent so much time color coordinating files and ensuring that the one-third cut tabs on their files all go in order, that the day is spent, and it is time to go home. These people may even look busy, but watch what they are doing, and you may catch someone with printed labels on his or her blank floppy disks. Some degree of organization is good for efficiency, but organization should be the means to an end. The goal is to be organized so that you can be efficient. The goal is not simply to be organized.

These factors underlie virtually all evaluations, and they should receive your attention. These, along with doing the tasks assigned, are general concerns for working people. There are other actions, in addition to doing the job well, that should be taken in preparation for a performance appraisal.

PRE-EVALUATION PROCEDURES

All evaluations review the past and establish a worker's current status. The better evaluations also look toward the future. You should ensure that this future component is part of your evaluation. Too often people do little more than present themselves for judgment. This being done, they say little and leave, relieved to have completed the whole process. Managers often have the same apprehensions and feelings of relief. To maximize the value of the evaluation, you should prepare for it to the same degree or even to a greater degree than the manager does. If you become involved in the evaluation rather than leaving it all to your rater, then the evaluation can become an important tool for advancing your career.

To move your career along you need to have good evaluations and plans for the future. The plans move your career from a condition of waiting for someone to notice you are doing well (a risky proposition) to a situation where you are taking active measures to fulfill your goals. The first step in being actively involved in the evaluation process is to prepare yourself by following the guidelines for a good evaluation. Before the formal evaluation, take the time to evaluate your own performance candidly. Summarize what you have and have not done and how well you have done your job. State your current situation. From this, plan for your future so that you accomplish your goals and objectives. The difficult part in all of this is to be objective with yourself. Remember that we are all inherently biased toward ourselves. Most people create excuses, rationalize poor performance, blame others, or downplay the importance and impact of any failures. Resist this. Look at what you have done as if everything were performed by someone else. What rating would you give that person?

In reviewing your current situation, start with your last evaluation. Identify all the areas in which you improved, all the areas in which your performance was satisfactory (your performance was adequate last time, but you haven't become any better or worse), and all those areas still needing improvement. Then, list all of your accomplishments since the last evaluation. Next, look for the causes of your performance—not only why you did poorly or why you just maintained your adequateness, but also why you did well. Remember: It is not necessarily bad to make mistakes, but it is bad not to learn from your mistakes. A mistake is doing something wrong once; a failure is doing that thing wrong twice. Once you have analyzed your successes and mistakes, there are two things to do. First, learn from your experiences. Find out why you did well so you can duplicate that performance; learn why you did poorly so you can correct the situation or avoid making the mistakes again. The second thing to do is to examine your current status.

Consider three perspectives when examining your current status. Consider your current situation in relation to your last evaluation, your employment, and your career. Although your manager may be most concerned with your performance since your last evaluation, it may be advantageous for you to remind him or her of what you have accomplished since you were hired, rather than just what you have done during the most recent evaluation period. Managers like to see progress and improvement. Someone with no experience may have a huge potential for improvement because this person is functioning at a relatively low level. There is no place for rookies to go but up. Veterans may show very little improvement, but this may be because they have worked themselves up to such a high level that little improvement is possible. One should not be judged solely on how much one has improved. Raters should also take into consideration what level of performance has been attained in the past. You may need to be the one to mention your total accomplishments since being hired in addition to your accomplishments since the last evaluation. Looking at your career may hold more meaning for you than for your manager, but what better time to assess where you are with your plans for where you want to be than at an evaluation?

In fact, planning for your future actually may be the most valuable portion of the evaluation. Why? You can do nothing about the past, but you can do something about the future. Future plans give you the chance to identify growth and improvement opportunities. Growth refers to expanding into new areas. Improvement refers to being more successful at tasks you currently do not perform well. A manager may dwell on the need for improvement. To advance your career, you may need to introduce growth and expansion into new areas and introduce new responsibilities into your goals.

Goals are needed as an aid in developing your career and in reaching your full potential. Review previous goals. Eliminate those that have been achieved, possibly revise those that have not been achieved, and add necessary new ones. A common goal is to change job responsibilities or to earn a promotion. Either one leads to an important question, and the performance appraisal is a natural time to ask it. The question is, "If I applied for promotion today, is there anything that would prevent me from getting it?" First, this shows that you are thinking about advancement, and that is almost always taken as a good sign (unless, of course, it is your manager's job you are asking about, and he or she has no intention of leaving it). Second, the answer identifies areas for you to work on. For instance, suppose you wish to become a manager next year. You ask if you would get the job now, and your boss says, "No, you would need a management course and a managerial accounting course, and you need to complete the management mentoring program on the job." Better to find this out while there is time to do something about it, rather than be turned down for these reasons when a position opens. Third, you have planted the idea in your manager's mind. He or she can now guide you and will know that there is at least one person from the inside enthusiastically interested in moving up.

Preparing for the evaluation interview is another way to demonstrate enthusiasm. Few people prepare for their own evaluations, and the fact that you did shows that you are concerned and that you are interested in your work. It shows that you

NetNote

The Quorum Group

http://www.jbrau.com/qg-8. html

Evaluation problems.

believe you have a career, rather than just a job. Preparing reflects positively on you and, at the least, will not hurt you. However, preparing is no guarantee that everything in the evaluation will go smoothly. You need to watch for a number of possible threats to your appraisal and take the necessary actions if you notice them occurring.

APPRAISAL THREATS

Some managers do not enjoy conducting performance appraisals, especially when the ratings are low. Others have had little or no training in rating people. Even with training, rating workers is difficult to do correctly, and appraisal threats increase the difficulty. Appraisal threats are conscious or subconscious rater biases. These biases are:

- the halo effect
- the Hawthorne effect
- recency
- uniformity
- vagueness
- conflict avoidance
- distance
- trait measurement
- personal bias
- cost concerns

These biases can significantly decrease the accuracy of an evaluation. Incorrect evaluations can rob the worker of compensation, recognition, advancement, or the chance to correct deficiencies before being fired.

The Halo Effect   One of the most well-known threats to the accuracy of appraisals is the **halo effect.** In the classic situation, a person is given a good rating solely because all previous evaluations have been good.[51] Maybe the manager was pressed for time or not paying attention. In any case, a good evaluation is given on faith and the hope that the previously good worker is not in a slump. Although giving another good evaluation to someone with a history of them is the typical meaning of the halo effect, it is possible for this to work in reverse. With a reverse halo effect, a poor rating is given to someone who has had a series of poor evaluations, even if the employee has improved. Once again, the assumption is that history is repeating itself. In both cases, this could be the year that the person broke the pattern, so everyone should be evaluated as if the current evaluation is the first evaluation.

The Hawthorne Effect   Another threat to appraisals is the **Hawthorne effect,** which says that the act of measuring something changes that thing, so one can never exactly predict anything that relies on observation alone.[52] In other words, if you observe people to evaluate them, they will change their behavior (for additional proof of this watch local TV news programs during any of the sweeps or rating months). Because people change their behavior when they are observed, we don't really know what their typical performance is, and not knowing that, we can't really predict if it will continue in the future. Although this sounds like an argument against all evaluations, we must also be practical. Some idea of how people work is better than none, and we must strive to make the measurements that are taken as accurate as possible.

Recency   A relatively common, though often unintentional, threat to appraisal accuracy is **recency**—workers are only evaluated on their recent performance,

---

The Halo Effect
giving a person a good rating solely because all previous evaluations have been good

---

The Hawthorne Effect
the change in behavior people exhibit because they are being observed or evaluated

---

Recency
evaluating workers only on their most recent performance, instead of on the entire rating period

---

instead of the entire rating period.[53] The problem is compounded by annual evaluations, large departments, and busy raters. What can happen is that the Human Resources Department notices that Steven is up for his annual review. The HR department sends Steven's boss, Amy, an evaluation and a memo about a month before Steven's anniversary date. Amy has been so busy and has so many workers that she hasn't been watching all of them all the time. Now she starts to observe Steven's work. If it is good, he will get a good rating, even if his performance during the other eleven months was terrible. If his work during the last month is bad, he will get a low rating even if his efforts during the rest of the year were excellent. If workers know managers are prone to this problem, they may increase their efforts just before their anniversary date so that they receive a better rating.

Uniformity   **Uniformity** is a particularly bad appraisal threat because of its effect after the evaluation. With the uniformity appraisal threat, everyone in a team or department is given the same evaluation regardless of effort. Maybe the manager gives everyone an excellent rating, or everyone gets an average or low evaluation.[54] In any of these cases, the evaluations are inaccurate, and motivation is seriously affected. When everyone is rated the same despite differing achievements, there is a serious demotivating effect. The better performers may give up trying to excel because even if they do, they will receive the same rating as the low performers. The better performers will ask themselves, "Why should I work hard when I can take it easy and get the same evaluation?" Whether they like it or not, people must get the rating that they have earned. A manager is not doing poor performers a favor, and the better performers are being treated unfairly when everyone receives the same score.

Uniformity raises other complications for managers and subordinates. In addition to being unfair, if managers rate everyone high or average, they will have a much more difficult time if they later try to fire someone who deserves to be released. The worker can point to all the high or satisfactory ratings in the past to strengthen the case for being retained. Problems exist for workers, too. When upper management sees that everyone in a department is rated average or below, those workers may be passed over for advancement or raises. If the "everyone is equal" manager leaves, and a new manager who is not subject to uniformity starts accurate evaluations, those who were high or average may see a sudden, severe drop in their ratings. It is in everyone's best interest, then, that people be rated according to individual effort, with high, average, and low performers rewarded accordingly.

Vagueness   Unlike uniformity, **vagueness** essentially affects just the evaluation, but it does a disservice to the person being evaluated nonetheless. Vagueness is using

Uniformity
rating everyone in a team or department the same

Vagueness
failing to be specific

DILBERT

Source: DILBERT: © Scott Adams/Dist. by United Features Syndicate, Inc.

words like *poor, bad, frequently,* or *often.* Examples are: "Her work is generally poor," "He takes frequent rest breaks," "She is late often," or "He has a bad attitude toward taking directions." These criticisms leave the worker with few opportunities to correct a problem.[55] How many times is frequent or often? What constitutes "too often"? How much does the person have to change before something is acceptable? How does one correct poorness or badness? If such vagueness appears on your evaluation, ask the rater to be specific. If told that you are late by five minutes twice a week and that only twice a month is acceptable, you can work to correct that. If your defect rate is 6 percent when the average is 1 percent, then the problem can be discerned, action taken, and results monitored and known to all. Vagueness can also be unfair to high performers. If a manager tells you that you have done a good job, you might want to ask what constitutes good and how well you did in objective terms.

Conflict Avoidance

giving an evaluation that is higher than the person deserves in order to avoid a confrontation

Conflict Avoidance   **Conflict avoidance** is a conscious decision on the part of a rater to give an evaluation that is higher than the person deserves in order to avoid a confrontation. Some people are very bold, bold enough to go on the offensive during an evaluation if they think it will be low. Others are very argumentative and will scrutinize every word and debate every point. These kinds of people engage in this behavior whether or not it is justified. It is easy to see why a manager might think, "It's not worth the time or stress, and a low evaluation won't change this person anyway. I'll give a rating the person can live with and get on to other work." This just avoids the problem; it does not solve it.

Distance

the rater is more than one organizational level above the ratee; the rater is not the immediate supervisor or manager

Distance   The **distance** between the rater and the person being rated can be a problem when it is so great that the rater has no real idea or firsthand knowledge of the person's performance.[56] Some total top down systems, in which everyone above the worker performs an evaluation, can have this problem. Sometimes your immediate supervisor isn't the rater. If your department manager rather than your area supervisor does the evaluation but has little or no contact with you, how accurate can the rating be, and on what can it be based? If information comes to the manager through the supervisor, there may be problems with third-party communication (as seen in Chapter 3). The direct supervisor should perform the evaluation, and the supervisor should have regular and frequent contact with the worker in order to have sufficient information on which to form an opinion.

Trait Measurement

the evaluation of one's personality

Trait Measurement   The problem with **trait measurement** is that it is an evaluation not of one's work, but of one's personality. There are a number of problems here. For one, extroverts tend to receive higher ratings than introverts. Tall people are often rated higher than short people. Attractive people and thin people tend to be rated higher than those considered less attractive or obese. Conformists may be rated higher than those who raise objections, even if the objections are legitimate. Also, we tend to give higher ratings to people who are like ourselves.[57] Performance appraisals should be measured using objective criteria based on how well people complete their work, not on personality or physical traits that have no impact on the job.

Personal Bias

the personal preferences, likes, or dislikes of a rater

Personal Bias   Almost everyone has some **personal bias**, but good evaluators do not let their personal feelings taint the appraisal. Personal bias may involve a difference of opinion over what is important on the job and what the job description states.[58] For example, one manager's main concern may be punctuality. Come in on time and you will be rated high on everything. Another manager may have a penchant for excessive neatness, while another requires everyone to do things his or her way only, and they rate people accordingly. Other biases can arise from attitudes about gender, race, color, religion, age, politics, or even sports interests or willingness to contribute to the evaluator's favorite charity.[59] Once again, people need to be evaluated using measurable, objective criteria based on how well they complete their work.

Cost Concerns   The final appraisal threat to be discussed is cost concerns, which may lead a rater to give workers lower ratings than they deserve. The goal here is to save money by not giving merit raises. One manager (who is no longer a manager) had a system for this. Just before a person's evaluation, she would severely criticize the person's work. This was to justify a rating so low that no merit pay was warranted. She then gave a 1 percent or 2 percent raise, "even though you don't deserve one," in an attempt to placate the worker and garner some favor with him or her. Finally, so that workers would not quit, she praised them about a month after the evaluation for their "improvement," saying, "See, my way worked!" After four years of this, everyone in the department knew of her tactics and eventually quit en masse. The manager was finally fired, and some, but not all, of the workers returned.

APPRAISAL RESPONSES

The only appraisals that require a response are those that are inaccurate, not necessarily those that are negative. You may find it very difficult to evaluate your appraisal objectively when it is negative, but you must do so before you consider a response (see Figure 6.2). Before making any response to a negative evaluation,

FIGURE 6.2   WHY IS THE PERFORMANCE APPRAISAL POOR? Poor work? Poor rater? Incorrect job description? Incorrect job specification? Poor evaluation instrument?

verbal or otherwise, go off to a quiet place, review the evaluation, and ask yourself, "Is any of this inaccurate?" Resist the urge to rationalize. If your work has been off lately because you are tired from working a second job, don't rationalize it by saying, "It is not my fault. I need the money. If they paid me more, I wouldn't need two jobs and then my work would improve." Employers need to see good work first; then you may see more money, not vice versa. If the poor evaluation is accurate, and you want to improve, you must analyze the situation and determine why you did poorly. Does the reason have something to do with a lack of training, a misinterpretation of the job description, or poor equipment? Is it something in your personal life? Is it a temporary change or will it continue indefinitely? Once you have determined what caused the low rating, you can take the next step.

Having determined the cause of the poor rating, you can work to correct it. Maybe you need more training, more experience, more supervision, clearer instructions, more practice, more time, or more authority. Or maybe you need a new job or career. Whatever it is, make sure that it will solve the problem, and then take your suggestions to the boss (see Table 6.3). At the least, this shows you are concerned, motivated, and have the desire to improve your performance, all of which will impress most managers. However, once you talk about improving, and the employer has provided the training or whatever else you claim you need, you must work hard to actually improve.

Contesting an Evaluation It is possible that a poor appraisal is inaccurate as a result of an appraisal threat or the rater's inexperience or lack of training. If you are sure that your low evaluation is undeserved, you must decide if and how you should respond. The decision to appeal a poor evaluation is not necessarily automatic; in the real world, you must always consider the political environment in addition to what is right and wrong. The first step is to decide whether the cost of appealing an evaluation is worth the possible gain. If it is a minor point, with little or no impact and little or no potential gain, then it is probably best

TABLE 6.3 POSSIBLE RESPONSES TO A POOR EVALUATION

Causes of Negative Evaluation	Possible Actions
Insufficient training	Ask for more training from employer. Obtain additional education on your own.
Lack of communication	Prepare written list of confusing points and issues and meet with rater to discuss them.
Misunderstanding or lack of a job description	Request a revised job description or obtain the same information if job descriptions do not exist.
Unknown criteria used	Ask for a copy of the performance appraisal. Ask for specific behaviors that workers can exhibit that will earn a higher evaluation.
Ability deficit	Improve skills through more education and additional practice. Consider a different career.
Personal problems	Resolve them. Meet with the rater to discuss the resolution; commit to and deliver better performance in the immediate future.
Rater error	Consider not appealing (weigh the political costs, the gain, and the likelihood of success). Question, don't accuse. Mention the specific appraisal threat involved. For example, "I felt my low evaluation might be based on the last three weeks, which I admit were not good, but the rest of the year I was at least average. Could you reconsider my rating with this in mind?"

to let it go. If the war is unwinnable, don't go into battle. Even if you have just cause, the evaluator has an advantage—if upper management trusts the person enough to evaluate others in the first place, then it probably will trust the evaluator's opinion over yours. If you are convinced that an appeal is worth the potential gain and risk, then you may follow one of two paths: an informal path or a formal one.

An informal protest of an evaluation carries less risk than a formal one and is a good place to start. If you try an informal protest first, you can always make a formal protest later if it doesn't work. However, once you start a formal protest, there usually is no way to make it informal. An informal appeal involves speaking to the rater rather unofficially. Start by asking a question, maybe on break, in the hall, at lunch, or after work. Maybe something like this: "I was going over part 2 of my evaluation and was wondering if you could take another look at it. I guess I was a little surprised and confused by how low it was." This approach is less threatening, and if a mistake was made, the rater can make a correction without losing face. In a formal protest, some raters may dig in their heels for fear they may look foolish in front of their boss if they admit to having made a mistake.

The steps for formally contesting an appraisal are probably outlined by the company's Human Resources department or in your employee handbook. Follow the procedure to the letter. If there is no procedure, go to the rater first and then to the rater's boss or to human resources. Whatever route needs to be taken, you will have to prove that you are correct.[60] If you appeal an evaluation based only on your word or interpretation versus that of the rater, the rater will almost always win. To prove your case, you need evidence, which means you must start collecting information before you appeal. Care is needed here; the evidence may prove that the initial low rating was correct. If you think you might ever be evaluated inaccurately, collect information throughout the evaluation period to ensure it is available for an appeal.

Once you have evidence, you need to organize it into a presentation.[61] Put your information in chronological order, or group it in some other way, but make it easy to understand and present. Put the presentation together in as professional and logical a manner as possible. Then:

- remain calm and rational
- practice your statement
- avoid accusations or making the rater feel the need to be defensive
- follow the conflict-management guidelines from Chapter 4
- remain calm and rational

It is critical to remain calm and rational. The more businesslike you sound and appear, the more credible you will seem. Anger, screaming, and yelling will not help your cause. State your case in objective, nonthreatening terms, answer questions, and leave a written copy of your rationale. Ask for a date by which you can expect a reply, and follow up if needed. If you hear nothing by the designated date, ask the next day. If necessary, pursue the matter further, but carefully evaluate the risks before going over someone's head.

LOSING A JOB

Losing a job is a major concern for many workers. At least 37 percent are very concerned that they may lose their jobs.[62] Losing a job is not viewed negatively today unless the individual has committed major mistakes.[63] When the phrase "losing a job" is used you may immediately think of being fired, but you may be the one to decide it is time to leave. Some reasons for leaving may be more obvious to you than others. For example, if your current job does not require you to fully use your skills, or if you are not learning, are not being paid equitably, or must violate your principles, it may be time to move on. At other times you may be unable to pinpoint a cause. If you hate the thought of going in to work, are unhappy because of your work, or have physical or mental symptoms of distress (ulcers, headache, sleep problems, depression, etc.), then finding the exact cause may be of less concern than removing yourself from the situation.[64]

If you do lose a job, for whatever reason, you then have about three choices: (1) give up working, (2) find another job, (3) find another career. Before you decide on your next move, make sure you get all you can from your current (soon to be previous) employer. Many employers offer some type of **severance package** (pay and benefits to assist workers who are fired) and **outplacement services** (assistance in finding another job). The questions are, "Is it a good package?" and "Is it the best package you can get?" Much depends on your position in the company. If you are low in the organizational structure, and management makes a mass announcement and offers a standard package to your peers, you may not get far trying to negotiate. If management starts private negotiations with you, you have a better position. In any case, how much severance pay should you get? For lower positions, one to two weeks for every year of seniority is common. Two weeks per year is acceptable. If you negotiate, ask for four and be happy if they give you three weeks per year of seniority. If you have received bonuses in the past, a good company will pay them but doesn't have to. If you have a chance to receive stock options, keep them or negotiate for them even if it means less cash. Finally, stay as long as possible (until you have another job, if you can), and maximize the use of employer facilities, such as offices, phones, office equipment, and outplacement services.

Once you have your best severance deal, you have three choices: give up work, look for another job in the same field, or change careers. Few people consciously choose giving up work as an option when they lose a job. The danger is that it becomes a

Severance Package
pay and benefits to assist workers who are fired

Outplacement Services
assistance for fired workers in finding another job

FYI

Identify where you want your career to go and what it will take to get there.

Always ask to see the job description and performance appraisal before taking a job.

Always prepare for an interview; have answers for typical questions and have questions prepared that demonstrate your knowledge and interest in the employer.

Honestly assess your job performance weekly.

Many managers do not enjoy performance appraisals or have not been trained in conducting them; don't let this adversely affect you, and watch for appraisal threats.

Carefully plan any challenge to a poor performance appraisal; make sure the challenge is worth the risk and make sure you can support your claims.

choice by default. After even a few weeks of unemployment, it is easy to sink into a pit of inactivity. Oh, not working sounds great when one has a job; there seem to be so many things that one could do. The problem is that everything except the library costs money, something the unemployed have a limited supply of. At first, you rush out early Saturday afternoon to get the Sunday paper so you can read the job listings as soon as possible; on Sunday you put resumes in the mail; on Monday you make phone calls. If after a few weeks you still have no job, a negative way of thinking can take over. Soon you don't even look at the job ads until late Monday morning, and when you do look you say to yourself, "All the good jobs are taken already. I'll wait until next week." Even the days are wasted. You have no reason to do anything because there is always tomorrow, and endless tomorrows after that. You can't even decide when to go to bed because you don't have to be up by any particular time the next day.

To avoid this situation, try to go from one job to another. Try not to quit one job until another is definite. If that is not possible, do whatever you can to find another job fast. You might volunteer at a charitable organization in order to maintain a joblike schedule and make new contacts. Do what you can to avoid the dark side of joblessness. The second option on losing a job is to find another like it. Use any network you are part of, and utilize the full capabilities of any outplacement services available.[65]

Avoid any employment agency that wants job seekers to pay it. Use an agency that will be paid by the employer. Additional resources are the career guidance office at your alma mater and state agencies. Be prepared to relocate, compromise, or take a reduction in pay if you don't find work quickly. You may also have opportunities to go to work for yourself doing your old work as an independent agent (sometimes with your previous employer).[66] Or you can look toward the third option.

Increasingly, people are opting to change careers after losing a job. Some take the severance pay and start a business, often in an attempt to say good-bye to the corporate world forever. Others go to work for other companies in a new field. The most successful career changers try new jobs more in tune with their character than their old job was (which they may have just fallen into straight from college rather than selected). Another possibility is not necessarily to make a complete change, but rather to use what you know and can do well in a new way.[67] A good presenter might change to teaching, or an academic researcher might try marketing research. Try to select something you want to do, which will maximize your chances of job satisfaction. Although the economic realities of life often interfere with our desires, keep in mind what can happen if you take a job just for the money: If your job makes you miserable for 8 hours a day, it will probably make you miserable for the other 16.

A GLOBAL GLANCE

Getting Fired in the Great White North

To fire someone in Canada, one can't simply tell him or her to take off! Canada does not have employment at will as the United States does. Canadian courts have held that workers must either be warned they are about to be fired so they have time to find another job, or they must be paid to leave. The amount of warning or pay is not fixed; it depends on the person's age, skill, and seniority. Those with more of any of these three factors are entitled to more notice or more severance pay. While many employers choose to pay workers upon firing, they must still handle the situation in the least traumatic manner for the worker—or risk having to pay even more money. Not providing a reference for a fired worker or unfounded charges of poor performance are also upsetting and can cost employers more money again. Even distressful events in a worker's personal life are taken into account lest a firing increase a worker's burden beyond his or her tolerance.

Source: Jorge Talbot, "Canada's Rule of Employee Respect," *Workforce*, May 2003, p. 15.

SUMMARY

This chapter has explored one of the basic units of organizations—the job. The factors that constitute a job were explained, and the difference between an employment agreement and job contracts was explained. Because most jobs are created on the principle of specialization, the advantages and disadvantages were listed.

With the future of the traditional job in question, current trends in job design and career management were explored. This included a comparison of U.S. job trends with the desires of U.S. workers and an examination of the Japanese tradition in its large businesses. Future job trends were also explored.

The methods for creating a job were included so that you know how your job was developed and also to assist you when searching for a job. The job design sequence from job analysis, to job description, to job specification was explained. Maybe of most importance to many, obtaining a job was explored. We examined the structured, unstructured, group, and stress types of interviews. An understanding of effective interview behavior can be helpful to both managers and workers, along with responses for various types of interviewers.

The last step in the job design sequence, the performance appraisal, measures whether the person described by the job specification is performing the job listed in the job description. This area is important to everyone; it is also an area susceptible to inaccuracy. In order to be a more completely informed employee and in case you someday need to defend yourself, appraisal threats and appraisal responses were presented.

Finally, because of the possibility of job loss, strategies for managing and coping with this situation were covered.

CHECKING FOR UNDERSTANDING

1. What is a job? Explain what a job comprises.

2. What is the difference between employment agreements and job contracts?

3. What is career management?

4. What are the current trends in job design?

5. What are the advantages and disadvantages of specialization?

6. What is a job analysis? How is a job analysis conducted for a new position? How is a job analysis conducted for an existing position?

7. List and define the five components of the job characteristics model of job design.

8. How does task difficulty fit into job design?

9. Explain the three-factor model of job design.

10. List the components of the CPOS model of job design and explain each component.

11. What is work effectiveness?

12. What is a job description, and what information should you find contained in one? Be specific.

13. What is a job specification and what information should you find contained in one? Be specific.

14. What are the different types of interviewers?

15. What threats to accurate appraisals exist? Explain each in your own words.

SELF-ASSESSMENT

Emotional IQ

For each item answer SA for Strongly Agree, A for Agree, U for Unknown/Undecided, D for Disagree, and SD for Strongly Disagree.

1. I know what my strengths are. *SA   A   U   D   SD*

2. I am confident that my capabilities will allow me to get the job done. *SA   A   U   D   SD*

3. Others believe in my honesty.
   SA   A   U   D   SD

4. Life involves frequent change; I can handle that.
   SA   A   U   D   SD

5. I am quick to anger.   *SA   A   U   D   SD*

6. I am in control of how well I perform.   *SA   A   U   D   SD*

7. My colleagues trust me.   *SA   A   U   D   SD*

8. I am constantly trying to improve myself in ways large and small.   *SA   A   U   D   SD*

9. I stay with a job or problem until it is finished.
   SA   A   U   D   SD

10. When I fail, it is someone else's fault.   *SA   A   U   D   SD*

11. I am aware of the needs and feelings of others.
    SA   A   U   D   SD

12. I know my limitations.   *SA   A   U   D   SD*

13. My colleagues would say that I am a leader.   *SA   A   U   D   SD*

14. I'll help others when I see they need it.   *SA   A   U   D   SD*

15. I have difficulty controlling my emotions.   *SA   A   U   D   SD*

16. I can detect the power relationships in groups.
    SA   A   U   D   SD

17. My colleagues would say I am a good listener.
    SA   A   U   D   SD

18. I work to turn disagreements into positive, rather than negative, conflicts.   *SA   A   U   D   SD*

19. I understand the needs and feelings of others.
    SA   A   U   D   SD

20. New ideas annoy me.   *SA   A   U   D   SD*

For all items except 5, 10, 15, and 20, score 2 points for every SA, 1 for every A, 0 for any Us, −1 for every D, and −2 for every SD. For items 5, 10, 15, and 20, score −2 points for every SA, −1 for every A, 0 for any Us, 1 for every D, and 2 for every SD. Total your score.

A score of 31–40 indicates a high emotional IQ; from 10–30 indicates a moderate emotional IQ with some room for development. A score of 9−−19 indicates room for significant emotional IQ improvement. A score of −20−−40 indicates a low emotional IQ.

SKILL BUILD 6

FEBRUARY

Larry and Juanita are team leaders at an animal-feed production facility. They often collaborate and cooperate with each other, as they are today on filling an opening on Larry's team.

"Juanita, have you thought about these interviews that are coming up for my vacancy?" Larry asked.

"Just yesterday, actually. I drew up a list of what I think you should look for. Check it out," Juanita replied as she gave Larry a handwritten list.

After looking it over, Larry said, "This looks okay. I made a list, too, with all of my talking points, all the things I want to mention." Larry handed the list to Juanita.

"Oh my. This is quite a list. The interviews are scheduled for half an hour each. When will the applicant get a chance to talk?"

"I don't expect much talk from an applicant," Larry replied, "I need to see how well the person listens, you know, to see how he—or she—follows directions and takes orders. That's the main thing for me—will the person listen? You know what they say, 'When the mouth goes open, the ears slam shut!' I need to know the person will hear me when it is important."

Skill Question 1. What type of interviewer is Larry? Explain his type in your own words.

Skill Question 2. What type of interviewer is Juanita? Explain her type in your own words.

AUGUST

"Juanita," Larry called, as he jogged to catch up to her. "Hey, you remember that Dillon guy I hired last February? You sat in on the interviews?"

"Oh sure. Did he work out?"

"Terrible! I did his evaluation last week, and he's really a nervous type. He's hinky," Larry said.

"'Hinky'? What does that mean?" Juanita said.

"You know, like jittery but not so shaky. He was looking here and there; seemed unsure of himself, almost self-conscious."

"And this is news to you?" Juanita asked.

"Well, I kind of forgot to check up on him. I mean, once he got going, maybe the beginning of March, it didn't seem necessary. Then I remembered last week it was almost the end of his probation so I spent a couple of days with him," Larry explained.

"What do you mean you spent a couple of days with him?" Juanita asked.

"You know, I *spent* a couple, as in two, days with him. All day. Followed him everywhere almost and watched his every move. Took notes the whole time," Larry said.

"And what did you come up with after all this?" Juanita asked.

"I just told you," Larry said, glancing at a printout of Dillon's evaluation. "Was a little late. Dressed okay enough. Kind of nervous and hinky."

Skill Question 3. Juanita seems to need your help identifying the problems with Larry's evaluation of Dillon. There are three problems; identify them, explain what they are in your own words, and support each with examples from this scenario.

"That's *it?*," Juanita said, shocked.

"I think it sums it up nicely," Larry said defensively.

"Well, I'm not sure what to call that whole process, but I think you have a few problems there," Juanita replied.

"I already typed it up," Larry protested, waving his piece of paper at Juanita. "And I already made plans for replacing him. I think I'll add some things to the job

though. Nothing any harder than is there now, just more variety."

Skill Question 4. Larry and Juanita both need your help with the changes they are talking about for the position currently held by Dillon. What term explains what Larry is talking about? After you identify this concept, explain what it is in your own words.

"How is that going to help? Besides, if you add things, *you* won't be able to remember all the stuff that person is supposed to do," Juanita said. "Why don't you make some kind of a list of everything that job is supposed to be? There must be some kind of example to follow somewhere."

"You know, that's not a bad idea! Maybe I could also have a list of what the person to be hired is like. You know, what we want them to know or have done before, how much they have to lift and such," Larry said excitedly. "This could help every time we hire someone. We wouldn't have to reinvent the wheel every time. I'm going to start on this right after I talk to Dillon."

Skill Question 5. What two concepts are Juanita and Larry talking about here? After you identify both concepts, list what is typically found in both of the documents Juanita and Larry are talking about producing.

Larry's talk with Dillon did not go well, to say the least. Dillon argued a little about how the evaluation wasn't fair, or long enough, and that Larry's comments didn't really say anything—certainly nothing Dillon could use to try and improve himself. Larry said it really didn't matter because Larry was going to talk to his boss about letting Dillon go when his boss returned from vacation next week.

Skill Question 6. Dillon is so unhappy that he is planning on protesting his evaluation. List the steps in the process he should follow and how he should behave. Note: Your answer cannot be something like, "He should go to the Human Resources Department and follow their procedures." Detail is needed.

APPLICATIONS

6.1 APPRAISAL TIME

Fred is your boss. Over the last two years, he has had many new duties assigned to him. Many of these duties require him to create extensive plans. As a result, he is not around much. In fact, he is so pressed for time that his boss, Natalie, conducted your annual performance review last week. It did not go well. Natalie came to see you twice in the two weeks before your review. Prior to that, you weren't really sure what she looked like. She then said things like "I would like you to try harder" and "I think you need to do better." She also said that she had heard you were late returning from lunch a few times. Still, she said that she would give you about the same marks she gave everyone else this year. She had little choice, she said, because there was no money for merit increases, and any "excellent" ratings would warrant an increase according to company policies. She also said that she would try to put all this in writing, but it has been two weeks, and you have seen nothing yet. You think you have had one of your better years because your productivity increased 12.37 percent. How should you respond? Create a detailed plan of what you will do. What performance appraisal threats exist here?

6.2 DON'T LET THE SCREEN DOOR HIT YOU ON THE WAY OUT

Your company, Amalgamated Malgams, has had a great year. Still, everyone seems to be downsizing lately, so the CEO decided that she would, too. You have been with the firm for eight years and have worked your way up to vice president of operations. You were given the word in person that you would be leaving, but so many people were being told the same thing that day that you were given an appointment for a second meeting to describe your severance package. The VP mentioned a willingness to give you one week's severance pay, but your termination date hasn't been determined yet, and the whole restructuring is to be complete in six months. Stock options or cash were hinted at, but the VP wanted to speak to you about this at the second meeting.

QUESTIONS

1. How will you proceed? Draw up a list of the minimum you will accept and another list of what you really want. Then draw up a list that you will present at the second meeting.

   Between the first and second downsizing meetings, a friend of yours arranged for you to interview at his brother-in-law's partnership for a job you would be perfect for. Your friend tells you that his brother-in-law has hired five people in the last year for the job you are suited for. Two never even started; they used his job offer as a way to get a raise where they were working at the time. The other three sounded good, maybe even overqualified, and sure enough, they all left within months when they found something else. The brother-in-law is bitter about this. Your friend is not sure what the other partner is like.

   You arrive on time and looking sharp. On meeting the partners, the brother-in-law doesn't even say hello or shake hands. The other partner starts out with, "You were fired from your last job?"

   You reply, "Actually, a large number of people were released in a typical downsizing."

   "So your previous employer thought you were worthless?"

2. What type of interviewer is the brother-in-law? How should you respond to him? What type is the partner? How should you respond to him?

NET-WORK

Management Isn't Easy—A Performance Appraisal from the U.K. version of *The Office*

http://www.youtube.com/watch?v=I9LLZJFBWdc&mode=related&search=

Ever have a job interview that seemed to go like this? From *Monty Python*

http://www.youtube.com/watch?v=mkj4wm6infy

PERSONAL POINTS

1. What are your career plans and goals? If you don't have any, start writing them (they don't have to be perfect; you can always change them later). Describe any elements such as flexible work hours and telecommuting that you think you will need.

2. Describe your job needs in regard to task variety, task identity, task significance, autonomy, and feedback. How will you ensure future jobs contain the degree of each you feel you need?

3. Describe the social interaction you feel you need on the job. What will you do if a job you otherwise like does not provide the social interaction you feel you need?

4. If you had an interview right now, how would you answer the more common interview questions? How will you answer these questions differently at your next job interview?

5. Describe what you did to prepare for your last performance appraisal. If you did nothing, describe how you should have prepared. For how many of your job evaluations have you presented yourself for judgment? How did that work out for you? How would you want your evaluations to be different than they are now? How much do they focus on your job or career development?

EXPERIENTIAL EXERCISE

Designing a Job

For your current job, or a previous job, perform a job analysis. Once this is complete, draft a job description. Have at least four sections: responsibilities, tasks, tools and equipment, and working conditions.

Next, create a job specification. Again, use at least four sections: education, experience, skill, and abilities.

Finally, create a performance evaluation that will measure whether the person described by the job specification is performing the job listed in the job description. If possible, compare your documents to those of your employer. Where are the differences? Why are there differences? Which do you think is more accurate?

SPOT CHECK ANSWERS

1. F
2. T
3. F
4. F
5. F
6. F
7. T
8. F
9. T
10. F
11. T
12. F
13. F
14. T
15. T
16. F
17. T
18. F
19. T
20. F

7 Formal Organizations: How People Organize

Take my assets—but leave me my organization and in five years I'll have it all back.

Alfred Sloan, Jr.

If it's not broken, don't fix it.

Anonymous

Just because it works, it doesn't mean it's right.

Anonymous

GOALS

The main goal of this chapter is to introduce you to the structure of organizations. The different organizations, the guidelines for forming them, and their characteristics help to create the surrounding in which organizational behavior occurs. It can be a great advantage to your work life to understand the structure of any organization to which you belong.

OBJECTIVES

When you finish this chapter, you should be able to:

▶ Define the hierarchical structure principle.

▶ Define the unity of command principle.

▶ Differentiate between line and staff departments.

▶ Explain the division of labor principle as it applies to formal organizations.

▶ Describe the span of control principle.

▶ Define the positional power principle.

▶ Define the rules principle.

▶ Identify the features and functions of an organization chart.

▶ Describe the characteristics of functional, geographic, customer, product, matrix, horizontal, learning, virtual, and developing organizational structures.

▶ Differentiate among functional, geographic, customer, product, matrix, horizontal, learning, virtual, and developing organizational structures.

▶ Identify the advantages and disadvantages of functional, geographic, customer, product, matrix, horizontal, learning, virtual, and developing organizational structures.

▶ Describe liberation management.

▶ Define reengineering and the concept of core competency design.

▶ Explain the reasons for using organizational structures.

▶ Discuss issues related to organization size.

INTRODUCTION

Many small firms have organizational structures without having a printed organization chart. With or without a chart, the need for control, giving direction, orderly decision making, and overall coordination requires some type of organizational structure. Even a sole proprietorship with one employee has an organizational structure. You can tell much from a company's organizational structure and from the presence of and adherence to its formal organization chart. Because virtually everyone either works for or with organizations having formal structures, it is important to thoroughly understand them and how they function.

FORMAL ORGANIZATIONS: RELEVANT MANAGEMENT PRINCIPLES

Understanding formal organizations begins with reviewing and introducing applicable management principles and with outlining the features of formal organizations, and the charts that depict them. Seven management principles govern or influence organizational structures and the way they function:

1. Hierarchical structure principle
2. Unity of command principle
3. Line and staff principle
4. Division of labor principle
5. Span of control principle
6. Positional power principle
7. Rules principle

The first five are closely related to the features and design of a formal organization. The last two are more closely related to the way the formal organization functions.

HIERARCHICAL STRUCTURE PRINCIPLE

The hierarchical structure principle states that a structure or chain of command is needed in order to provide direction and control for the individuals and the organization as a whole.[1] Both control and direction begin at the top of a pyramid-shaped structure (see Figure 7.1). Hierarchies are very powerful structures for the collection and dissemination of information. They are effective mechanisms for control, being especially useful when exacting standards must be met. They are especially well suited to controlling large numbers of people and can be effective at coordinating them. Hierarchies are also relatively easy to understand, and most people are fairly adept at being able to at least survive in them.

Hierarchies have limitations: regimentation, the tendency not to be creative, a strict adherence to rules. However, they help mobilize large numbers of people to perform complex tasks. The trend in certain companies is to redefine, downsize, or even seemingly eliminate hierarchies, but hierarchies still have their uses. The pyramid shape of a hierarchy is further defined for management purposes by the unity of command principle.

UNITY OF COMMAND PRINCIPLE

Responsible for much of the look of traditional organization charts, the unity of command principle is one of the easiest management principles to understand,

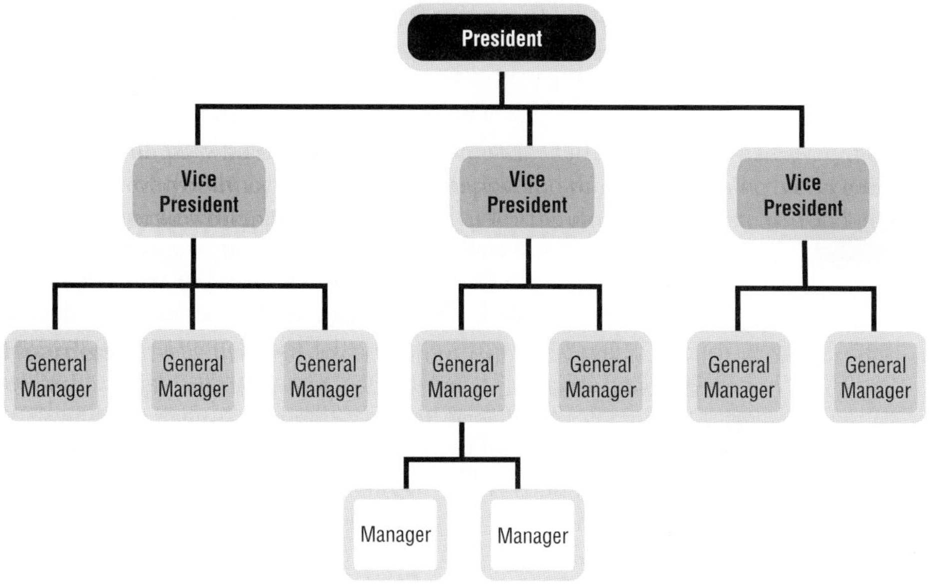

FIGURE 7.1 PYRAMID ORGANIZATIONAL STRUCTURE Control and direction begin at the top.

and it is one of the more important. The unity of command principle states that each worker should have only one manager.[2] No one should be placed in the position of having to choose which of two equal managers to obey. Note in Figure 7.2 that in order to be in compliance with the unity of command principle, the line leading up from each position should lead to only one manager. The reciprocal of the unity of command principle should never occur, however. A manager should never have only one subordinate (what would the manager do—sit and watch one person all day?). Although the unity of command principle is sometimes broken (as in a two-person partnership), roles should be defined in order to avoid forcing workers into a no-win situation. For example, if two managers of equal power were each to give someone conflicting orders, that person's behavior would be wrong no matter which order was followed. Organizations cannot maintain control, accomplish work, and be efficient if this type of conflict is prevalent.

LINE AND STAFF PRINCIPLE

Some departments in an organization directly perform or are directly related to the primary functions of the business. Other departments merely support the areas that are directly related to the functioning of the business. The **line and staff principle** governs the relationship between these two types of departments. Line departments are directly related to the function of the business. A company's sales department, for example, is always a line department because selling is what all organizations do (or they cease to exist). Marketing and production departments are also directly related to the business. Staff departments, by contrast, support the line departments. Staff departments assist the line departments in reaching the goals and objectives of the organization. Organizations might be able to survive solely with line departments; as we will see, virtual organizations try to do this. However, organizations composed solely of staff departments could not survive. Sometimes you must know the business to decide whether a department is line or staff. In most firms, the accounting department is a staff

Line and Staff Principle

line departments are directly related to the function of the business; staff departments support the line departments; staff departments cannot be superordinate to line departments

department; in the accounting firm of Arthur Andersen, however, accounting is a line department because accounting services are one of that organization's primary products.

The purpose of the line and staff principle is to guide the organization structure. Any reporting relationship between line and staff is permitted except that a line department may not report to a staff department. Line can report to line, staff to staff, and staff to line, but line never reports to staff. The rationale is that because line departments are directly related to carrying out the objectives of the organization, their considerations must come first. In addition, the support staff cannot direct the line departments; to do so would be like putting the cart before the horse.

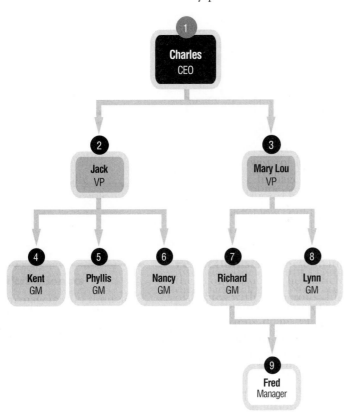

FIGURE 7.2 A BASIC ORGANIZATION CHART   Jack, Kent, Phyllis, and Nancy form one department. Mary Lou, Richard, Lynn, and Fred form another. According to this chart, if Richard wants to speak with Nancy, he must send a memo to Mary Lou; she sends one to Charles, who sends it to Jack, who sends it to Nancy. In real life, Richard just picks up the phone, but for formal communications, the formal organization often must be followed. Can you find the violation of a management principle in this chart?

DIVISION OF LABOR PRINCIPLE

As discussed in Chapter 6, dividing the work into specialized areas can increase efficiency. The division of labor, or specialization, makes possible increased expertise, faster training, the completion of large jobs, and the compression of time (jobs are completed in less time). Through specialization, the labor is divided, and the tasks are then grouped into jobs. These jobs constitute the positions in the formal organization and the corresponding boxes on the organization chart. Management can be viewed as an extension of the **division of labor principle** because the supervisory, planning, and other managerial functions are separated from the technical or production tasks. If carried too far, the division of labor principle can disrupt organizations and result in inefficiency when boredom reduces effectiveness and causes negative repercussions among the workers.

Divison of Labor Principle

dividing a job into tasks and assigning them to different people

Span of Control Principle

the number of people a manager has under his or her direct control

SPAN OF CONTROL PRINCIPLE

The **span of control principle** provides guidance for determining the number of people assigned to a manager.[3] The span of control is the number of people a manager has under his or her direct control. The number of people that a manager has varies because each situation is different. Some span of control guidelines pertain more to the overall structure of a formal organization, whereas others are related more to the span of control of individual managers. An important general guideline is that the span of control becomes smaller as one moves closer to the top of the organization chart. The higher one goes, the fewer people one directly manages because top managers are directly responsible for middle managers but only indirectly responsible for all those reporting to the middle managers.

Eight factors affect the span of control of an individual manager:

- worker autonomy
- exceptions to the rules
- group coordination
- worker dispersion
- task similarity
- worker reassignment
- manager planning
- manager capabilities

Complete knowledge and application of these guidelines is not required unless you will be a manager; however, you should be aware of these factors in order to understand the forces exerted on a manager with too large a span of control and the effect on you and others.

Worker autonomy affects span of control. As people are able to work more autonomously, a manager's span of control can increase. That is, a manager can supervise more people if those people are self-directed and self-managed. Worker autonomy can be increased in a number of ways. In general, the better trained and better educated people are in their field, the more autonomy they can be granted. Likewise, the more experience (in the field) and the more seniority (time at the current job) people have, the wider the span of control can be.

The greater the degree of specialization, the greater the span of control. If workers are performing the same simple task over and over, a manager could supervise relatively more of them than if they were performing relatively complex tasks. The span can also increase if there are routines or rules to guide the workers. One reason accountants can work autonomously is because they have rules, the *Generally Accepted Accounting Procedures*, to guide them.

Although rules and procedures can allow the span of control to be larger, the number of **exceptions to the rules** modifies this guideline. The establishment of rules is actually the application of another management principle. The exception principle states that managers should handle only the exceptions to the rules. It is a sign of good management when the frontline workers are trained and trusted to handle the routines in the workplace. This frees the manager for other tasks. Some professions, such as law enforcement and insurance claims adjustment, might have more exceptions than, say, a factory assembly line. When the nature of the work creates more exceptions that a manager must handle, then the span of control should be smaller.

The nature of the work itself and the people performing it also affect four other factors. The first is **group coordination.** If the work group needs to be coordinated by a manager, similar to the way an orchestra needs a conductor, then the span of control must be smaller. The second factor is **worker dispersion.** If people are spread over a large area (their physical dispersion is increased), the span of control decreases because it is easier to supervise people who are all in the same location.

The third factor is **task similarity.** If workers are performing similar tasks, then the span of control can increase. It is easier to supervise people who are all doing the same work than to supervise people who are all performing different tasks. Fourth is **worker reassignment.** If workers are being grouped and regrouped frequently, so that Lynn and Ron work together one day, Ron and Kelly work together the next day, and Lynn, Ron, and Kelly all work together the third day, then the span of control can be affected. The effect is based on a mathematical formula that gives the number of interrelationships that exist between a manager and the workers for all

NetNote

U.S. Department of Justice

http://www.usdoj.gov/dojorg.htm

Examine the organization chart for the U.S. Department of Justice. Notice any violations of organizational design principles?

Worker Autonomy
the functioning of workers under little or no supervision

Exceptions to the Rules
unusual or infrequent occurrences not covered by procedures

Group Coordination
teamwork or orchestration required in order for a group to perform its work

Worker Dispersion
the physical space or distance between workers

Task Similarity
the degree to which the tasks workers perform are alike

Worker Reassignment
the frequent regrouping of workers

TABLE 7.1 THE NUMBER OF RELATIONSHIPS A MANAGER MUST KEEP IN MIND WHEN ASSIGNING PEOPLE TO GROUPS USING THE GRAICUNIS METHOD

$$n(2^{n-1} + n - 1)$$

Where n = the number of subordinates.

For example, the number of relationships between 1 manager and 4 workers is:

$$4(2^{4-1} + 4 - 1) = 4(2^3 + 3) = 4(8 + 3) = 4 * 11 = 44$$

possible combinations (see Table 7.1). This formula takes into account that two or three individuals may work well together, but add a fourth and the result may be two groups of two that do not work well together. Note also that the number of interrelationships increases dramatically as the number of people involved increases. These interrelationships must be considered by the manager when making work assignments. Although it may seem impossible to keep all these relationships in mind when the number of employees is large, managers work around problems by keeping work groups relatively constant. Also, many employees work with others because they believe they have to, even if they don't like them.

The final two factors affecting span of control are related to the manager's job and the manager. One factor is **manager planning.** If a manager's job contains a greater than normal amount of planning, then that manager's span of control must be smaller. The more time managers must spend planning, the less time they have for supervising people. The last factor is **manager capabilities.** The more experience, education, and seniority managers have, the greater the span of control they can proficiently handle.

POSITIONAL POWER PRINCIPLE

The **positional power principle** states that organizations are most effective when power is vested in the position and not in the person occupying the position. If power were vested in the individual, then the individual could use the power for his or her own gain. With power residing in the position, power is given or withheld when people are hired or fired. This principle also reinforces the importance of the positions in an organization chart. Each box represents a position in the organization. Each position exists whether or not it is filled at the time, and each position carries with it a certain amount of power, certain duties, and a measure of responsibility.

RULES PRINCIPLE

The last principle related to organizational structure is the **rules principle,** which says that organizations need strict rules for the conduct of the people in the organization. These rules ensure orderly operations and continuity. Because owners, managers, and workers come and go, continuity is maintained through the organizational structure and the rules that support it.

THE ORGANIZATION CHART

The seven management principles (hierarchical structure, unity of command, line and staff, division of labor, span of control, positional power, and rules) form the

Manager Planning

the amount of planning, strategy creation, or scheduling a manager must perform

Manager Capabilities

the experience, education, seniority, and proficiency a manager possesses

Positional Power Principle

power is vested in the position, not in the person occupying the position

Rules Principle

organizations need strict rules for the conduct of the people in the organization to ensure orderly operations and continuity

SPOT CHECK

1. The unity of command principle states that each manager should supervise one worker. T F
2. According to the line and staff principle, a line department may report to a staff department. T F
3. The division of labor, or specialization, principle makes possible increased expertise and faster training. T F
4. All eight factors that affect the span of control of an individual manager, plus the calculated number of relationships, should be considered together when determining the number of workers for each manager. T F
5. In almost all organizations when people retire or are fired, their position, or box, in the organization leaves with them. T F

basis for an organization and an organizational structure. The resultant structure is often depicted in an **organization chart.** Although the organizational structure and the formal organization chart may have a number of different forms, the basic structure is similar for all but the newest organization types. Much can be learned, then, from examining the organization chart. Figure 7.2 depicts a generic version of the more traditional structures. The boxes represent positions in the company; these positions may or may not be filled at any given time, but the position remains with the firm. The arrowed lines represent the formal reporting lines or lines of communication, and the lines and boxes represent the chain of command. Groups of boxes represent departments. The level of a box denotes relative status. From the number of levels, one can determine whether the organization is tall or flat. The span of control can also be determined, and this gives an indication of where the power is distributed and what emphasis is placed on control. In addition, the titles indicate the organizational style that is used—organization by function, geography, customer, product, matrix, or some other form.

Organization Chart
the graphic depiction of the formal organization

NetNote

Organizational Design Guidelines

http://www.mapnp.org/ library/org_thry/design.htm

Large amount of information on organizational design, including profit and nonprofit organizations, legal forms of organizations, organizational life cycles, and related topics.

ORGANIZATIONAL STYLES

Organizations typically are divided into a number of departments. The process of grouping an organization's human resources in this way is called departmentalization. One of the most common methods of **departmentalization** is by function, but companies also can be organized by geography, customer, product, or matrix; in a horizontal style; as a learning organization; as a virtual corporation; or in one of the new and still developing forms. Each style has certain characteristics, advantages, and disadvantages. There is no one best way to organize; if there were, all companies would use it. In fact, most firms use more than one method, as we will see.

Departmentalization
the process of grouping human resources within an organization

FUNCTIONAL ORGANIZATIONS

Functional organizations form departments by grouping similar activities and those performing similar jobs.[4] Often the departments are formed along professional or occupational lines. Figure 7.3 shows a functional organization. Other departments might include Finance, Bookkeeping, Accounts Receivable, Accounts Payable, Payroll, Billing, Training, Marketing, Advertising, Public Relations, Legal Affairs, Mergers and Acquisitions, Quality Control, Shipping, and Receiving. Small and medium-size organizations are often functional organizations. This method of departmentalization is sufficient when the firm is highly specialized and has relatively few products.[5]

Functional Organization
departmentalization by similar activities and jobs

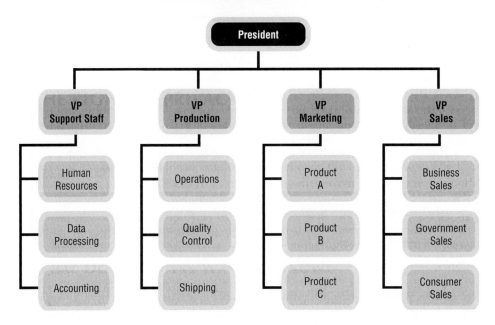

FIGURE 7.3 A FUNCTIONAL ORGANIZATION Organization by function is very common at the higher levels. This company is organized by function at the top, but within different departments it is organized by function, product, or customer, which is also common.

Functional designs are useful when control and uniformity are required, because they are typically centralized, with decision making located at the top of the organization. The major advantages of a functional design include efficiency, centralized control, minimal duplication of effort, more uniform policy administration within functions and job types, and maintenance of the power, status, and communications of the major functions. Retaining the power and status of the functions can be important because many people identify themselves by their profession ("I am a corporate trainer") rather than by their company ("I work for Pearson Prentice Hall") or the project they are currently working on ("I write drill-and-practice lessons for customer relations trainees"). Maintaining functional communications can be important for problem solving within a function. A few accountants might meet informally at the water cooler and end up solving a problem.

One disadvantage of functional organizations is that functional managers usually have limited views of how the total business operates. This limits the managers' ability to be promoted to higher levels because they only know how one area operates. To counteract this limitation, some organizations play "musical chairs" with managers, constantly rotating them so they can acquire broader knowledge. Another disadvantage of functional organizations is that success is often measured by accomplishing one small function, no matter how the rest of the organization does or how satisfied the customers are. Also, coordination of all the functions can be difficult, especially as the organization grows. Finally, people may be more loyal to their function than to the firm and more concerned with territorial disputes (turf battles) with other departments than with satisfying customer needs. Although functional organizations work well when matched to the right situation, special situations may benefit from other methods of departmentalization.[6]

GEOGRAPHIC ORGANIZATIONS

When facilities located physically close to customers would be beneficial, then departmentalization by geography may be advantageous. Figure 7.4 is an example of a geographic organization. Departmentalization varies depending on the company but could be by city, county, state, region, or country. Having coordinated activities

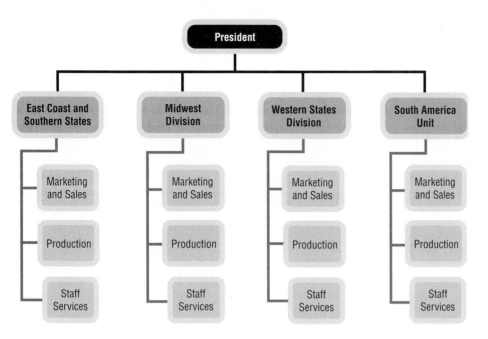

within a region is a major benefit for **geographic organizations.** Imagine a department store with outlets in the Midwest, the West, and Hawaii. Clothing purchases would vary greatly in the Midwest and West as seasons change, whereas those in Hawaii would not vary by season. The major disadvantage to a geographic organization is duplication of effort. For example, a firm might need one person to manage payroll in one location, one and a half people in another, and one-half of a person in a third. Therefore, if organized by function, it could hire three full-time people. If organized by geography, it might need four full-time people: one, two, and one.

Geographic Organization
departmentalization by physical location or territory

CUSTOMER ORGANIZATIONS

When customers need the utmost in service, or when they have different needs, then departmentalization by customer can be used.[7] Figure 7.5 depicts a customer organization. **Customer organizations** can be seen in service industries, as when a bank has groups working with individual, corporate, and government accounts. The primary advantages to organization by customer include a close relationship with the customer, attention to customer needs, and the assignment of specific people to work with each customer. One disadvantage is duplication of effort. Also, product knowledge is a difficulty because each customer representative or group of representatives must be familiar with all of the firm's products and services.

Customer Organization
departmentalization by customer or industry served

PRODUCT ORGANIZATIONS

When product knowledge is vital, or when products are widely varied, then **product organization** is advantageous, as seen in Figure 7.6. For firms like General Electric, whose products include light bulbs, jet aircraft engines, and medical-imaging equipment, and which has service divisions, such as G.E. Capital Auto Leasing, and owns the NBC broadcast network, organizing by product is almost required. The lack of commonality in firms like this rules out many of the other departmentalization forms. The major advantage to product organization is that each unit or department is focused on a particular product. Disadvantages include duplication of effort and the possibility that one customer may be serviced by more than one department,

Product Organization
departmentalization by product or service

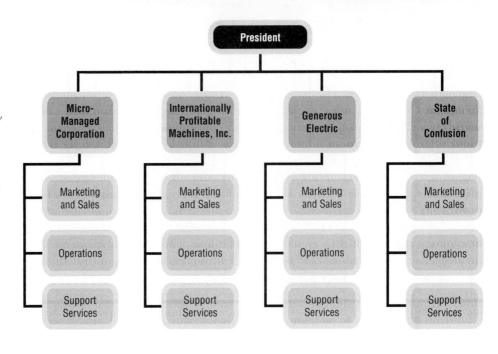

FIGURE 7.5 A CUSTOMER ORGANIZATION CAN BE IMPORTANT WHEN A FIRM HAS A FEW LARGE CUSTOMERS, SUCH AS LARGE CORPORATIONS OR STATE GOVERNMENTS, NEEDING SPECIAL ATTENTION   One disadvantage is duplication of effort, seen here in the functional organization with each customer.

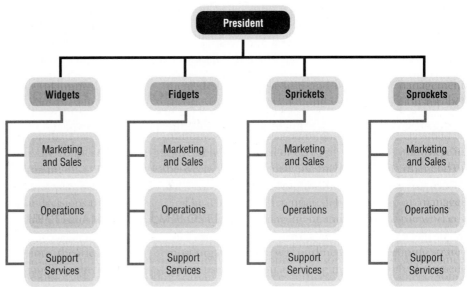

FIGURE 7.6 A PRODUCT ORGANIZATION CAN BE IMPORTANT WHEN PRODUCTS ARE VASTLY DIFFERENT   Duplication of effort is a disadvantage, as the functional organization with each product line demonstrates.

with representatives from each. When customers have needs, they may not take the time to differentiate between the responsibilities of the representatives. Because of the duplication of effort, providing a uniform appearance and a consistent effort to customers may be difficult.

MATRIX ORGANIZATIONS

One of the more recent developments in organizational design is the **matrix organization** (Figure 7.7). Matrix organizations violate the unity of command principle by assigning people to functional departments and to projects. Workers report to the functional department head and the project manager. This unique aspect of matrix organizations holds the potential for great conflict, so everyone in

---

Matrix Organization

an organization consisting of functional departments and cross-functional project teams

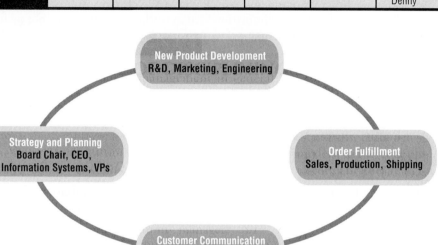

	Finance	Marketing	Sales	Research & Development	Production	Distribution
New Product #101	Freda	Max	Sandra	Renee, Dave	Pete	
Growth Product #99	Francisco	Melissa, Mark	Sam, Sunanda, Sid		Paula, Pat	Dan
Established Product #1			Sophie, Sang Lee		Pete, Patrice	Dawn, Don, Denise, Denny

FIGURE 7.7 A PORTION OF A MATRIX ORGANIZATION CHART Functional departments are listed across the top. Projects are listed down the extreme left. People from each department are periodically assigned to different projects. Some projects may use people from all departments, whereas others may use people from only a few.

New Product Development
R&D, Marketing, Engineering

Strategy and Planning
Board Chair, CEO,
Information Systems, VPs

Order Fulfillment
Sales, Production, Shipping

Customer Communication
Marketing, Advertising,
Customer Service

FIGURE 7.8 A HORIZONTAL ORGANIZATION Note the flat structure. Organization is according to processes that must be completed to serve customers. Examples of the activities carried out in each process are in bold.

the organization must accept this structure and agree to work together. For technologically oriented firms and those in highly competitive, rapidly changing markets, matrix organization provides advantages in speed and the ability to handle complex issues.[8] With the many different viewpoints brought to a project by the people from the various departments, problems can be identified and dealt with early. One additional feature of matrix organization can be an advantage or disadvantage depending on your point of view. Project assignments are for a limited time. For some people, the change of work and the chance to meet and work with different people is considered an advantage. For others, the change can be seen as disruptive.

HORIZONTAL ORGANIZATIONS

Some companies, like AT&T, General Electric, Motorola, and Xerox, are trying structures that are on the leading edge of organizational evolution. Their approach is the **horizontal organization** (Figure 7.8). Unlike the organizations described thus far, which are hierarchies or based on functional departments, horizontal organizations are virtually flat, and departmentalization is based on the core processes essential to meeting the needs of the customer.[9]

Seven key characteristics differentiate horizontal organizations from other types of organizations. First, the organization is divided into core processes, and each process has a manager or team leader. This person in effect takes ownership for the ac-

Horizontal Organization
virtually flat organization, departmentalized around the core processes needed to meet the needs of customers

complishment of the process. Second, the organization is flat because tasks that do not add value for the customer have been eliminated. Third, teams are used almost exclusively, which tends to eliminate the practice of identifying people by a traditional functional area and provides further impetus for flattening the organization. Fourth, performance is measured and rewarded by customer satisfaction, rather than stock price or completion of some narrow functional task. Fifth, team effort and success earns team rewards. Sixth, the customer, rather than the internal workings of the functional departments, is the central focus for everyone. Seventh, an open-book management system is used so that all employees have access to all the information the firm has in order to enable them to complete their process and serve the customer.

The advantages of horizontal organization include increased efficiency, faster process times, faster customer response, and the reduction or elimination of boundaries.[10] In theory, boundary elimination focuses workers on customers, not on functional hierarchies, and drastically reduces the number of times work is passed from department to department. Each transaction between departments is not only time-consuming but is also another chance for work to fall between the cracks. The primary disadvantage of horizontal organization relates to difficulties in making the transition to this structure.

LEARNING ORGANIZATIONS

Learning organizations are difficult to explain and even more challenging to diagram. Essentially, a learning organization is a philosophy, a way to operate an organization, rather than a structure or a design. Learning organizations focus on improving learning and the way knowledge is disseminated throughout the organization.[11] Notice that the focus is on *improving* learning and *improving* the way knowledge is spread. In a sense, all organizations are learning organizations; however, some are much better at learning and sharing knowledge than others.[12]

Three concepts in learning organization theory are key to improving learning and sharing knowledge. The first is that the whole organization is more important than the parts because the parts are interrelated in constituting the whole. Therefore, we cannot repair just individual parts because a change in one affects the others (because they are all interrelated). If change is in order, the whole organization, rather than just small parts, needs to be examined and changed. Second, all people are interrelated and are defined by the people around them. People are not to be treated as disposable items but as part of a team because the team helps define the individuals in it. Third, language describes reality, but it is not actually reality. This means that we can have different descriptions of the same reality, and none of them is ultimately or inherently correct.[13] This notion is similar to part of Friedrich Nietzsche's philosophy—there are no facts, only opinions. The basic characteristics of learning organizations can then be described according to the way organizations learn and the way the learning is passed on to others in the organization. The people in learning organizations continuously question their beliefs, produce knowledge as opposed to simply performing tasks, and transmit the useful knowledge so that it is not just sent, but received.[14]

Learning organizations use the act of learning to reach company goals and objectives, to avoid failure (repeatedly making the same mistakes), to learn from what goes wrong as well as what goes right, and to share information.[15] They are as concerned with how learning occurs as they are with what is learned.

Communities of Practice   In learning organizations, much learning takes place in groups called **communities of practice**. A community of practice is an informal

---

NetNote

Learning Organizations

http://home.nycap.rr.com/klarsen/learnorg/

A paper discussing teams and learning organizations.

Learning Organization

organization focused on improving learning and how knowledge is disseminated throughout the firm

---

Community of Practice

an informal group that is cohesive because it faces and tries to solve a common set of problems

---

group that is cohesive because it faces a common set of problems.[16] Some communities of practice exist within an organization, and some are outside it. They are concerned solely with solving common problems or improving a situation, and they share information in an informal manner. Information is spread on breaks as much as any other way, and people do not claim ownership or try to benefit personally from a tip or hint. Furthermore, communities of practice apparently have no bosses, and people freely enter and exit the group, depending on whether they have something to offer. A curious phenomenon is that attempting to manage communities of practice can cause them to disperse.[17]

Although communities of practice are beneficial, some managers worry that people drawn in from outside the company may learn too much about the operation. However, current research shows that although people in communities of practice share information, they do not reveal everything, and what is revealed is usually an even trade for what is learned. In the end, more study is needed on communities of practice and learning organizations in order to more fully assess their functioning and value.

Virtual Corporations   A **virtual corporation** is an organizational structure composed of highly specialized firms or pieces of firms that join to form a new entity in order to complete a specific task (see Figure 7.9). Virtual corporations may consist of a venture capital firm, an entrepreneur, a manufacturer, a distributor, and a retail store chain that form what appears to be a new company in order to bring to market a new product. An example might be a fad product, like a child's action figure from a movie. A virtual corporation might be formed to exploit very high demand that is also short-lived. When popularity wanes, the corporation dissolves. During this time, parts of the firms involved might be involved in similar, dissimilar, or rival markets with the same partners or with others.

The characteristic that differentiates virtual corporations from joint ventures or alliances is the degree of sharing involved. Virtual corporations are held together by information, which is shared more openly than in other forms of business cooperation. The ultimate form of the virtual organization is the hollow organization,

Virtual Corporation

a structure comprising highly specialized firms or pieces of firms joined to form a new entity in order to complete a specific task

A QUESTION OF ETHICS

Non-Work-Related Learning

On the face of it, learning organizations sound great. Everyone teaches everyone something; everyone is continually learning and continually developing. How could there possibly be an ethical question here? Well, some learning organizations have really taken this concept to heart. In order to advance, and in a few cases in order to be considered adequate, employees are required to learn constantly. Some organizations are not concerned about whether the material that is learned is related to your work or career. Learning anything can fulfill the company requirements. Is this right? Should a company be able to tell workers that they are expected to learn something, anything, so long as they learn? Does forcing people to learn

and improve show a sense of commitment and concern for them (after all, what could it hurt)? Or is it an invasion of privacy (don't we have a right to be as educated or uneducated as we like)? Consider these questions:

1. Is it, or is it not, ethical to require workers to continue learning job-related material? Why or why not?

2. Is it, or is it not, ethical to require workers to learn material that isn't related to their jobs? Why or why not?

3. Is it ethical to require learning of any type in order to earn promotion in a company? Why or why not?

4. Is it ethical to require learning of any type in order to keep one's job? Why or why not?

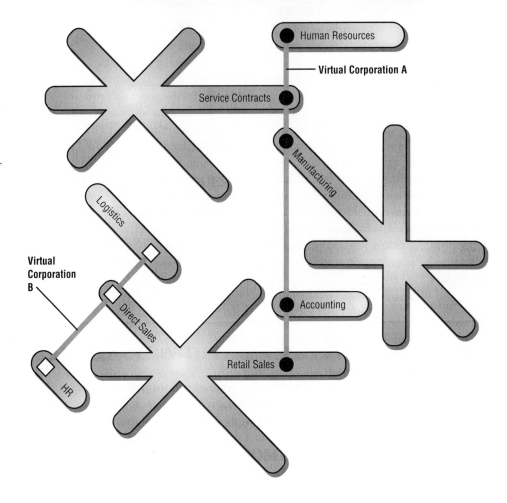

FIGURE 7.9 VIRTUAL CORPORATIONS Each diagram represents a corporation. Some reach out in many directions; others reach out in only a couple of directions. The lines represent the virtual corporations that are formed for specific efforts.

which consists of a core of top-level business officers who contract, outsource, and create virtual organizations for everything.[18]

Virtual corporations are flexible, quick to react, and very lean, and they concentrate all efforts on performing one or just a few functions extremely well. However, they are dependent on others for key elements needed to make the entire virtual corporation work, they are constantly forming and reforming with different partners, and they may lack the size needed to launch products on a national or global scale. Furthermore, their success is highly dependent on the ability to find partners that are dependable.

DEVELOPING ORGANIZATIONAL STRUCTURES

This last section covers a group of organizational structures that are still developing. Some involve new methods of departmentalizing, others provide a different way of thinking about organizations, and still others offer methods for redesigning existing structures. Liberation management organizations, pizza-shaped charts, and molecular charts represent new and different methods of departmentalization. Upside-down pyramids and cloverleaf designs are essentially conceptualizations or new views of structures, rather than new structures themselves. We will also consider the topics of reengineering and core competencies, which are ways to redesign existing structures, whatever they might be.

NetNote

Virtual Corporations

http://www.ve-forum.org/

Information on virtual enterprises and network organizations.

LIBERATION MANAGEMENT

Of the developing structures, the most extensively explained in the literature is Tom Peters's **liberation management** organization. Liberation management organizations are small, about 50 people, or comprise clusters of small, autonomous units.[19] Each unit or each team within a unit is entirely self-sufficient. The 50-person units or teams hire and fire people, complete performance appraisals, and even perform accounting, budgeting, and planning functions. The units or teams are highly focused. They often do only one thing, but they do it very, very well.[20] For example, Tightflex is a liberation-management-style firm that produces custom-made hoses for aircraft. The units are project based, as in matrix organizations, but very nimble—they are able to respond to customer needs and market conditions almost instantaneously.[21]

Liberation Management
small organizations comprising clusters of small, autonomous units

The key elements in operating a liberation management organization include trust, knowledge, information, and empowerment. People are trusted to get the job done by performing whatever tasks are necessary; some liberation management firms have no job descriptions whatsoever. Liberation management organizations follow some of the precepts of learning organizations in that learning is seen as vital in the rapidly changing markets in which liberation management organizations are found. Information is vital also. The better the information, the faster the organizations can respond and the better they can serve their customers. In order to get the job done, quickly serve customer needs, and respond rapidly, the people must be empowered to do whatever is needed, and because of the fast-moving environment, they must be trusted to make a few mistakes (from which they must then learn).

Egalitarian Designs
nonhierarchical organizational structures in which functions are related but are not superordinate to each other

The advantages of liberation management organizations are that they can survive today's hectic pace and global competition while adapting for the uncertain future. They are fast, responsive, and dedicated to giving customers what they want. They are accountable because each small unit or team is a profit center.[22] The disadvantages stem mainly from difficulties in forming the organizations and in maintaining control.

EGALITARIAN DESIGNS

Molecular organizations and pizza-shaped organizations are still in the developmental stages. In a molecular organization (Figure 7.10), major functions are linked, and support units surround each. The pizza-shaped organization (Figure 7.11) views major functions and support functions as interdependent units. Both **egalitarian designs** attempt to depict a nonhierarchical structure in which functions are related, but none is more important than the others. These completely flat organizations deemphasize power and control and attempt to show that organizations are one system of connected, interdependent units. The move toward classlessness harkens back to a sole proprietorship in which one person

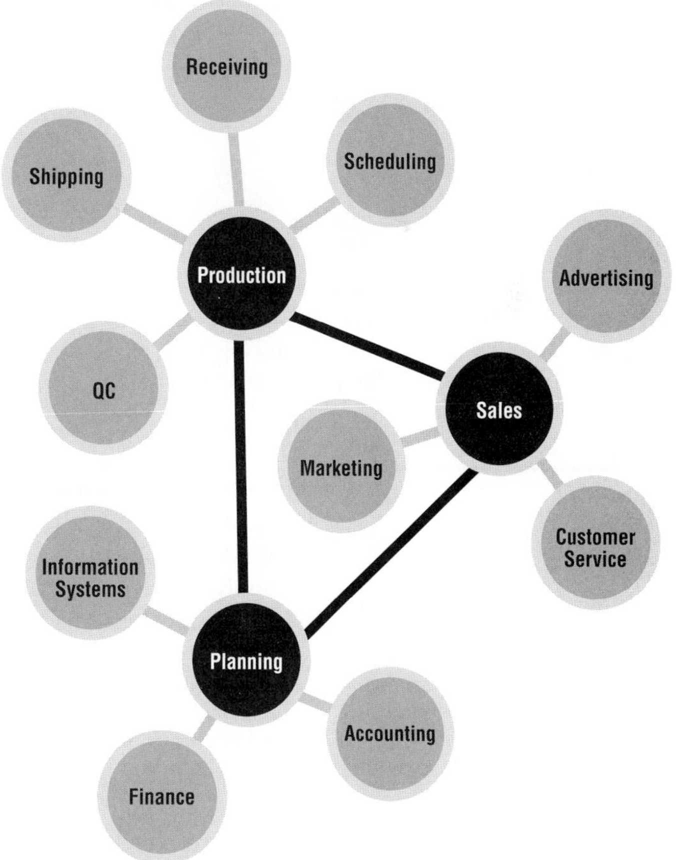

FIGURE 7.10 A MOLECULAR ORGANIZATION AS VIEWED FROM ABOVE   Major functions are linked, and each is surrounded by supporting units.

231

Upside-Down Pyramid Organization

a hierarchical chart inverted to emphasize the importance of frontline workers

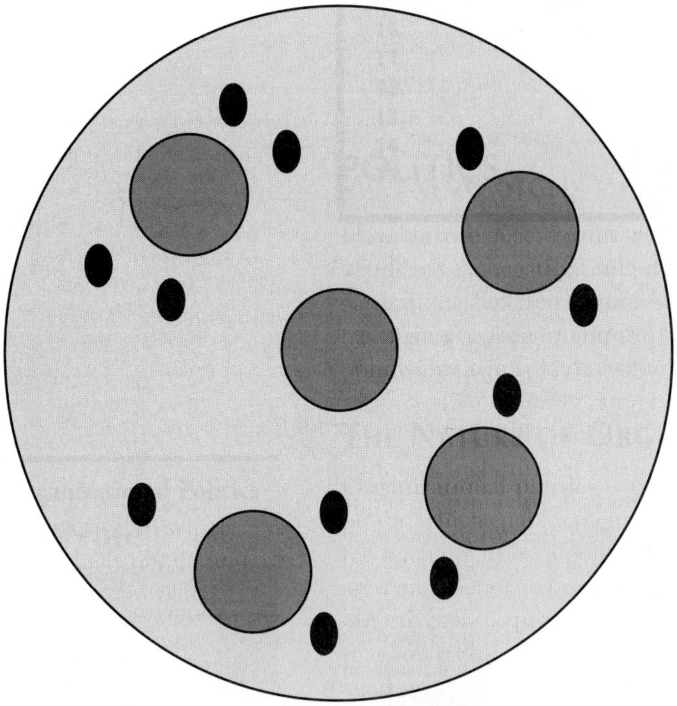

FIGURE 7.11 A PIZZA-SHAPED ORGANIZATION The pepperoni represent major functions, and the black olives represent support functions. The pepperoni in the middle represents the CEO.

Cloverleaf Organization

internal and external contingencies come together to accomplish goals

Reengineering

redesigning an organization to focus on processes rather than functional areas

does everything and everything is geared toward satisfying the customers. When the job grows, more people may be needed, but they are all vital in serving the one goal—customer satisfaction. These forms recognize that someone (like a president or board) needs to set priorities and that there are decision makers, but they are all on the same level. In a way, these organizations strive for a more rational environment; decisions are made for logical reasons and not because of the personal goals or whims of a particular person who just happens to have the title of manager.[23]

Advantages and disadvantages of egalitarian structures like molecular and pizza-shaped organizations are difficult to list because these designs are so new. They sound attractive in theory, but reality may be quite different. Power and structure may be absent from the organizational diagram, but that doesn't mean people won't try to create a hierarchy as they grab power for personal reasons.

CONCEPTUAL DESIGNS

Whereas egalitarian designs like the molecular and pizza-shaped structures combine structure with a philosophy concerning how organizations should function, upside-down pyramids and cloverleaf designs are more conceptual than actual.[24] The **upside-down pyramid** organization (Figure 7.12) is, on paper, a hierarchy turned on its head. Although technically a different structure, the point being made is psychological. Upside-down pyramids are trying to make the point to frontline workers that they come first. These acknowledge that very often the most important people are those doing the real work and coming in contact with customers. One questions, then, why these most important frontline workers don't receive the largest rewards, but perhaps this is at least a start toward recognition for frontline workers in organizations.

A **cloverleaf organization** (Figure 7.13) doesn't place frontline workers at the organizational forefront; instead, the cloverleaf attempts to show how different internal and external contingents come together to accomplish goals. The emphasis here is on some groups that are sometimes forgotten, like part-time workers and outside contractors. Like upside-down pyramids, the purpose is more to benefit the thinking of the people in the contingents than it is to demonstrate their workings and relations.

REDESIGNS

Two other topics, **reengineering** and core competency organizations, are related to organizational structure in that they seek more to redesign existing structures than to create new ones. Reengineering is a well-established method for redesigning not only organizational structures but also jobs and management operations.[25] The very basics of reengineering include redesigning work to focus on processes, rather than pigeonholing work into numerous restrictive job descriptions based on functional areas. Reengineering questions every activity, and if an activity is not adding

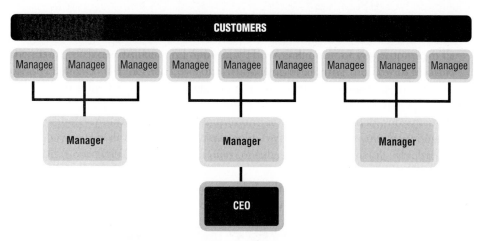

FIGURE 7.12 AN UPSIDE-DOWN PYRAMID ORGANIZATION Frontline workers are at the top, along with the customers served by the firm.

value to the product or the service, it is eliminated. Although the main goal of reengineering is not to reduce the size of the workforce, this does sometimes happen. A redesign around core competencies, on the other hand, frequently leads to a smaller workforce.

A **core competency design** concentrates on what an organization does best and eliminates everything else.[26] Many of the eliminated functions still need to be performed, but they are done by resources outside the organization. For example, colleges are in the business of transmitting knowledge. Teaching and learning should be core competencies for them. Excluded would be writing payroll checks, feeding and housing students, or mowing the lawns. In a core competency redesign, these functions would be divested from the college. A payroll firm, a food-service firm, a dormitory-management firm, and a landscaping and grounds maintenance firm would be hired. In other words, core competency firms concentrate expertise in what they do best, and they eliminate distractions from the pursuit of core success. They then engage other firms with expertise in those eliminated areas to complete their work.

The advantage of reengineering and core competency designs is a more efficient organization that delivers greater customer satisfaction. Applying them, however, often leads to downsizing. Core competency organizations face an added risk: The competencies may be so narrowly defined that all of the firm's eggs are placed into one basket.

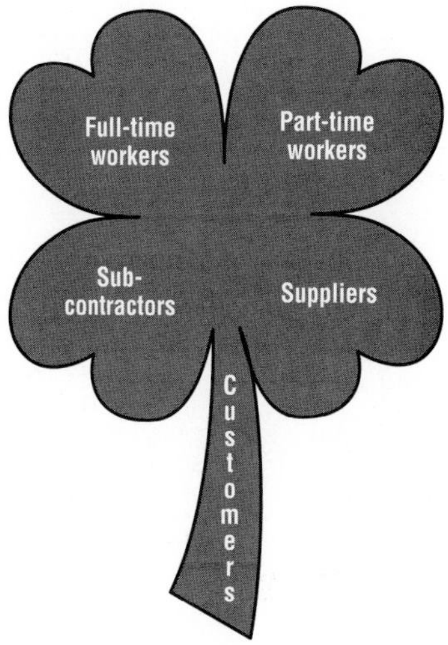

DOWNSIZING AND REVISION

Companies periodically change, as just described, and recently many of those changes have included firings or layoffs. Often the restructuring or revision is in response to a crisis or is an attempt to elevate sagging stock prices.[27] Unfortunately, recent research shows that this is often a case of too little, too late. Especially with **downsizing**, many firms are seeing negative effects with few, if any, positive ones.[28] The negative effects include poorer corporate performance, longer hours for those not fired, a severe decline in morale, and increased anger, confusion, fear, and interpersonal conflicts.[29] Unless downsizing is combined with careful reengineering and is not undertaken as a last-ditch effort, its positive effects are often limited to a temporary increase in profits. Some mature, stable industries might not require radical change. In addition, when considering eliminating people and positions, reasons still exist to retain people rather than outsource all services.[30] For example, employees are present all the time. They have a feel for the pulse or atmospheric pressure in the organization.

FIGURE 7.13 A CLOVERLEAF ORGANIZATION Major constituencies come together to provide products or services for customers.

Core Competency Design
an organizational structure reduced to the functions it performs best

Downsizing
reducing the size of an organization, with or without reengineering or restructuring

Outsources

nonemployees
performing work for an
organization

Employees are immersed in the corporate culture; they do not need to study it or be told it. **Outsources** (nonemployees who perform work for the organization) lack this insider knowledge. Also, outsources feel the need to supply answers, but they tailor their response to the person who hired them (and may hire them again). Finally, outsources have increased anxiety levels from not always knowing when or from whom the next job is coming.

FYI

Know whether you are in a line or staff position; remember that staff supports the line functions.

Span of control factors illustrate many of the difficulties in management; determine how each impacts you.

Look for communities of practice and join them for help in solving problems.

Even in egalitarian organizations many individuals may try to grab power and create their own informal hierarchies.

Remember that reengineering is not supposed to be synonymous with downsizing; it is supposed to redesign work and eliminate meaningless activities.

Even though outsourcing and core competencies sound like great ideas, they entail a loss of some control to and an increase in dependence on the providers of the outsourced functions.

SPOT CHECK

6. Functional organizations form departments by grouping similar activities and those performing similar jobs. T F
7. Matrix organizations violate the unity of command principle. T F
8. Horizontal organizations are virtually flat. T F
9. Egalitarian designs are nonhierarchical. T F
10. Reengineering is really nothing more than a synonym for *downsizing*. T F

SUMMARY

Formal organizations help to maintain order and facilitate communication within collections of people. Certain management principles aid in the creation of formal organizations and the charts that represent them. The traditional methods of organizing consist of the functional, geographic, product, and customer methods. Matrix organizations have become more popular in an attempt to improve firms in highly technical and highly competitive markets. In response to the need for knowledge and information as a result of increased global competition, new organizational forms have been developed. Newer forms include horizontal, learning, virtual, and other structures.

Numerous organizational structures exist because there is no one right method for all organizations. Each structure may be right for some situations and wrong for others. Much, but not all, of the appropriateness of a structure depends on how fast the market changes and how flexible the company must be. Many of the traditional methods are still in use, and some of the newer ones have not been held to the test of time. As structures evolve, there is a trend toward smaller organizations, but downsizing alone is probably not an effective strategy. Reengineering, with its rethinking of the work process, can work, but simply cutting workers often means releasing many valuable employees.

CHECKING FOR UNDERSTANDING

1. What is the hierarchical structure principle?

2. What is the unity of command principle?

3. Differentiate between line and staff departments.

4. Explain the division of labor principle as it applies to formal organizations.

5. What is the span of control principle?

6. What is the positional power principle?

7. Define the rules principle.

8. What do the boxes on an organization chart represent?

9. What do the lines that connect the boxes on an organization chart represent?

10. Describe the characteristics of, and differentiate among, functional, geographic, customer, product, and matrix organizational structures.

11. Describe the features of horizontal, learning, virtual, liberation management, and egalitarian organizational structures.

12. List the advantages and disadvantages of functional, geographic, customer, product, and matrix organization structures.

13. List the advantages and disadvantages of horizontal, learning, virtual, liberation management, and egalitarian organization structures.

14. What is reengineering, and what is its goal?

15. Explain the concept of core competency design.

SELF-ASSESSMENT

For each of these following statements select SA for Strongly Agree, A for Agree, D for Disagree, and SD for Strongly Disagree.

1. I want a hierarchy with very few levels. *SA   A   D   SD*

2. Each person should have only one supervisor or manager to report to directly.
SA   A   D   SD

3. The line and staff departments must be distinct.
SA   A   D   SD

4. A high degree of specialization is necessary.
SA   A   D   SD

5. The span of control principle is small/narrow.
SA   A   D   SD

6. Strict, explicit, written rules are needed.
SA   A   D   SD

7. Workers need a high degree of autonomy.
SA A D SD

8. Ideally, workers will be located close together for better control. *SA A D SD*

9. Only workers with similar tasks can be grouped together. *SA A D SD*

10. A functional organizational design is best. *SA A D SD*

For all items except 1 and 7, score 4 points for every SA, 3 points for every A, 2 points for every D, and 1 point for every SD. For 1 and 7, score 1 point for every SA, 2 points for every A, 3 points for every D, and 4 points for every SD. Total your score. A score of 10–19 indicates a preference for less traditional organizational designs. A score of 20–30 indicates no preference or that you are undecided. A score of 31–40 indicates a preference for more traditional organizational designs.

SKILL BUILD 7

Shafira is a newly hired supervisor for Hi-Tech Industries, which, despite its impressive name, is a relatively new company started by the father and son team of Art and Van Delaney. Van, the father, has retired now that the company has grown way past the entrepreneurial phase and is well established. Up until now everything has been rather loose and open, everyone doing whatever was needed. Now the company is so big that this loose and open style has become a liability. Things are either unfinished or turn into rush jobs; there is confusion and a general lack of accountability. So Art, whose experience and education is solely in the plastic injection-molding business that is the mainstay of Hi-Tech, has decided to do some reorganizing and wants to talk about his ideas to Shafira (she is the company's only employee with any formal management education—one college class in supervision).

Shafira really needs your help. Hardly any of what Art is asking was covered in that one class she had. Go through the chapter, find the terms and concepts that apply to this situation; and answer the skill questions.

"Okay, Shafira, see what you think of this. First, I want to sell off those areas that are not directly related to injection molding. I want to focus; to concentrate. I think those other areas that we acquired along the way are a distraction," Art said.

Skill Question 1. What developing organizational structure concept is Art talking about?

"Next," Art continued, "we need regulations. Most of the people, especially the new, have no idea how we handle certain things, and there is nowhere for them to go to find out except to other people, and that takes time and wastes time."

Skill Question 2. What management principle is involved here? Should it be used and why or why not?

"Next, we will end up with some people doing the main job of the company, injection molding, but we will still have a few support areas. I say, let birds of a feather flock together. Injection-molding people need their own groups and support people their own, and the support people need to know that the injection-molding people come first—they are supporting the rest of us," Art continued.

Skill Question 3. What management principle is involved here? How should this principle be properly applied?

Skill Question 4. An organizational style seems to be suggesting itself by the situation Art is describing. Which one is it, and what in the situation supports your choice?

"Then, we have to divide some of this work. It seems to me that we have three types of jobs here. Those that are too big for one person, those that can be handled by just one person alone, and those that don't take someone all day to do. So I say we divide up the too-big-for-one-person jobs, assign those that one person can do, and then group the little jobs into something that would fill a person's day. I'm especially concerned that we divide up those big jobs," Art explained.

Skill Question 5. What management principle is involved here? Should it be used and why or why not?

"I also figure we need about seven groups and I think there are about 13 people, besides yourself, that would make good supervisors. So we let each group have two supervisors, kinda spread the work a bit. Watcha think so far?" Art asked.

"Well, I'm not sure about the rest, but somehow I don't think that last part about two supervisors for each group would work. Two supervisors for a group might be confusing to the workers," Shafira said.

Skill Question 6. What management principle, other than span of control, is involved here? Should it be used as Art describes and why or why not?

"And a few more things, most of our people can work on their own, you know, without anybody really looking over their shoulder. See what that's called and how it affects the groupings," Art said.

Skill Question 7. What span of control factor is involved here? Explain this factor. Given the situation, should the span of control be larger or should it be smaller than usual?

"And maybe, "Art went on, "the fact that each group that does a different task works together in its own room and that, unfortunately, those rooms are just barely big enough, so every group is pretty close together—that must be called something and must affect the supervising."

Skill Question 8. What span of control factor is involved here? Explain this factor. Given the situation, should the span of control be larger or should it be smaller than usual?

"Oh, and each person in a group of workers does the exact same thing as everyone else in that group—maybe that matters?" Art asked.

Skill Question 9. What span of control factor is involved here? Using your own words, define this factor. Given the situation, should the span of control be larger or should it be smaller than usual?

"Just one more thing, you are the only person with any real supervising experience, besides me, so see if having supervisors who are untrained and inexperienced makes a difference—okay?"

Skill Question 10. What span of control factor is involved here? Using your own words, define this factor. Given the situation, should the span of control be larger or should it be smaller than usual?

Skill Question 11. Altogether, there are four span of control factors involved here. Taking into account all four, in general can the span of control be larger or should it be smaller? Why?

7.1 AN ORGANIZATIONAL EYE CHART

Hickory Handles, Inc., is a 150-year-old firm that manufactures hickory ax handles. On the next page is the company's functional organization chart. Examine it carefully and identify the violations of organizational principles.

7.2 REORGANIZING THE REORGANIZATION

Mel Whiteshirt is the vice president of finance for Hickory Handles, Inc. (see their organization chart). Mel has been with the firm for nearly 40 years. Recently, he called together the 11 people who report to him and made these remarks: "My son is away at Ivy League University, and he sent some articles home for me to read. Mostly they were about ways to organize people. So I got to thinking, things have been pretty much the same here at HH for as long as I can remember. I think it is time for a change. We need to close the loops. There needs to be a paradigm shift to more of a learning organization. We need to put the Finance Department's customers first and become more process than product oriented. I want to invert the pyramid in a molecular manner and reengineer our financial core competencies. What I want you to do is draw the new organization I just described and integrate that with the rest of the company, which, by the way, does not seem to share my vision and will not be changing."

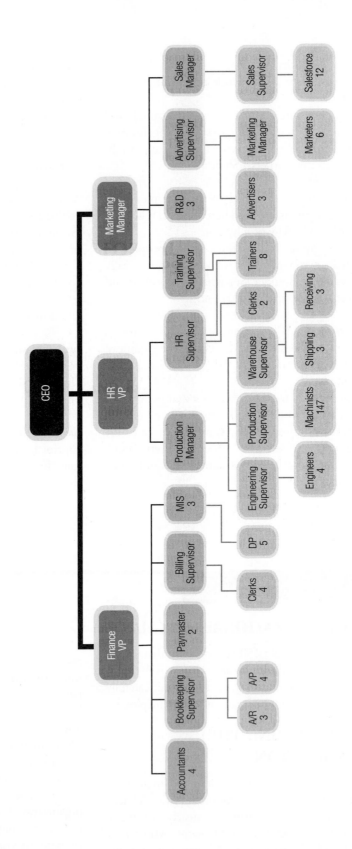

QUESTIONS

1. Attempt to draw the new Finance Department and the Hickory Handles organization chart as Mr. Whiteshirt has described it.

2. What problems exist with Mr. Whiteshirt's concept?

7.3 REORGANIZING DOCT-CO

Darius, Grace, Corky, and Sam have pooled their money to buy a failing business—Doct-co. Doct-co supplies a number of different services to other companies, including billing, payroll, employee manuals, custom job descriptions, and performance appraisals. The four co-owners are brainstorming reorganization ideas.

Darius: Okay, we know this company is in trouble so I call for radical actions. First thing, no more chain of command. I think this was a big problem. Everyone should be equal. Number two, we bring in all new managers right out of college. Obviously the old ones did not know what to do. If we give them each plenty of people, they'll rise to the occasion. Third, everyone gets cross-trained so anyone can do any job. Makes us more flexible.

Sam: I like that last one, and to keep them sharp we give each person a different job every day, completely random.

Grace: Yes, and we make them spread out so they are independent and not asking others for help — no one is allowed to work at the same workstation or next to the same people two days in the same week. We do the same with our support teams.

I don't want the client contacters thinking they're somehow more important.

Corky: I don't know, I think we need to group teams according to the services we provide.

Grace: If anything, it should be according to the clients they serve.

Corky: Word. And all managers report to the four of us, and we each talk to each manager; keep us informed of what's going down.

Sam: And any of them can't cut it, we get a bunch of dudes in India to take their jobs.

QUESTIONS

1. Which three chapter concepts is Darius proposing? Define each and cite your evidence from this discussion. Which two would be violating organizational principles? Explain how.

2. Which three chapter concepts is Grace proposing? Define each and cite your evidence from this discussion. Which two would be violating organizational principles? Explain how.

3. Which two chapter concepts is Corky proposing? Define each and cite your evidence from this discussion. Which one would be violating organizational principles? Explain how.

4. Which two chapter concepts is Sam proposing? Define each and cite your evidence from this discussion. Which one would be violating organizational principles? Explain how.

NET-WORK

What is the hierarchy? Who is in charge of whom? From the U.K. version of *The Office*

http://www.youtube.com/watch?v=17nMqvRE3Lk

PERSONAL POINTS

1. In what type of hierarchical structure do you think you want to work and why? Before acceping a job, how would you determine the type of hiearchy that the organization is using?

2. Would you rather work in a line or staff department and why? Is your current career in a line or staff area? What will you do if your answers to these two questions are different?

3. What degree of division of labor do you want in your job and why? Before accepting a job, how

would you determine the degree of specialization present in the position?

4. How would feel about working in a matrix organization, given that you would essentially have two bosses?

5. How would you feel about working in an egalitarian organization as a frontline worker? What if you were a manager? What challenges would you face as a frontline worker in an egalitarian organization? As a manager? How would you handle the challenges?

EXPERIENTIAL EXERCISE

Organizing Human Resources

Your task is to create an organization chart for a publishing company. In doing so, you must decide how the company will be departmentalized, you must select the correct structure, and you must select an appropriate span of control for each area. The situation in each city is different, and it is constantly changing. Competition is stiff. Each city unit must be able to respond quickly.

Proceed as follows:

1. Using the information provided in the breakdown that follows, group the departments. So you don't forget anybody, start at the top of the list. Write down "Accounting." Look at the next department. If you want it to be in the same group as Accounting, then write it down and move to the next department. Go through all the departments in order. If a department does not fit with a group you have already started, then begin a new group. Keep placing departments into groups by adding to existing groups or by creating new ones until you reach the bottom of the list. When you are done, you may have some small groups that can be combined with other small groups. For example, you may end up with a group called Staff Services or Support Services in which all of the small groups of staff functions can be placed.

2. Decide on a method of organization. This may require further grouping. For example, if you organize by geography, you would next group the

	Number of People		
	NY	Chicago	Divide These However You Wish
Accounting			15
Accounts Payable	6	5	
Accounts Receivable	6	6	
Advertising	4	3	
Billing	3	3	
Binders	10	10	
Customer Service			8
Data Processing			28
Editors			
Acquisitions	3	3	
Developmental	12	3	
Front Matter	5	2	
Line	27	23	
Managing	3	2	
External Affairs			1
Finance	3		
Human Resources	7	4	
Legal		2	
Marketing	6	6	
Management Information		5	

EXPERIENTIAL EXERCISE (Continued)

	Number of People		
	NY	Chicago	Divide These However You Wish
Payroll	8	8	
Printers	48	42	
Purchasing			8
Quality Control	6	6	
Receptionists	3	2	
Sales	12	8	
Shipping	28	23	
Switchboard Operators	5	2	
Typesetters	12	9	

departments by city. Remember that many organizations use more than one method, like function at the top of the chart and then geography in the lower levels.

3. Draw a formal organization chart. In this case it is probably best to start at the bottom of the chart and work up. For example, if two departments are related, and one has 26 people and the other 10, you may divide the 26 into two groups of 13, each with a supervisor. The group of 10 is given a supervisor, and the three supervisors then report to one manager.

SPOT CHECK ANSWERS

1. F
2. F
3. T
4. T
5. F
6. T
7. T
8. T
9. T
10. F

8

Understanding Management

If you ask managers what they do, they will most likely tell you that they plan, organize, coordinate, and control. Then watch what they do. Don't be surprised if you can't relate what you see to those four words.

Henry Mintzberg

By working faithfully eight hours a day, you may eventually get to be boss and work twelve hours a day.

Robert Frost

GOALS

The main goal of this chapter is to improve relations and increase understanding between managers and those being managed. Although ambitious, this can be quite important because most employed people report to someone else. By examining the role of management, especially from the perspective of those being managed, it is hoped that a beginning can be made in changing attitudes of managers and workers from an adversarial (us against them) attitude to the realization that everyone is—or at least should be—on the same side.

OBJECTIVES

When you finish this chapter, you should be able to:

- Describe management's role in an organization.
- List and define the four functions of management.
- List and define the four resources of management.
- Describe the managerial working environment.
- List and describe the types of decisions managers make.
- Define management principles and describe their effect on the working environment.

- List and describe the characteristics of classical management.
- List and describe the characteristics of behavioral management.
- Explain the management continuum.
- Differentiate between good management and poor management.
- Describe the worker's role in an organization.
- List and describe the steps in the total quality management process.
- Describe strategies for coping with being managed.

COPING WITH MANAGEMENT

Unless you work for yourself and by yourself, you are involved with management. Either you are a manager or you are being managed, and you could be in both situations. Some people learn to survive in organizations and cope with management on their own. Many learn the ropes the hard way: by making mistakes and suffering consequences. Our goal here is to help you avoid the pain of learning by accident, to equip you with the knowledge needed to work with managers and do more than survive—to excel. To begin, we look at one of the most frequently asked questions concerning managers: "What does the boss do?"

Ask many people what the boss does and the most common first response is, "Nothing." If pressed, some will say that their boss goes to meetings or that the boss sits at a desk. However, most still feel that it all adds up to nothing. This, then, makes management one of the best jobs around if one likes no work and good pay. Of course, top managers and company owners must be rather dim to pay middle managers and supervisors for doing nothing.

The idea that managers do nothing is especially prevalent in professions where supervisors and managers are promoted up from the frontline workers. Here the view is often that the manager is just another person who could be helping with the work if he or she wanted to. Instead, the boss chooses to do nothing. Well, managers must do something, so why do people believe that they don't? One of the reasons is that managers rarely, if ever, explain what it is that they do. They rarely explain that, even if they used to be a frontline worker, management is a different career.

This chapter will explain the management field so that people being managed can differentiate between management's role and the role of frontline workers. Basic management principles and the two main approaches to managing will be discussed. The role of frontline workers will be examined, and good management and poor management will be differentiated. The overall goal will be to show how managers and those being managed fit into the overall organization.

THE ROLE OF MANAGEMENT

Semantically, the terms *management* and *manager* add to the misconceptions about who does the "real work" in an organization. In most organizations, there are managers and there are workers. If workers work, then what do managers do? Not work? Of course managers work, but it is a different kind of work. To move from a frontline position to management is really a career change. Still, *manager* and *worker* are often the terms used. Right from the start, a line seems to be drawn—one that seems to establish a win-lose or lose-lose conflict. Other terms could be substituted, but some are even worse. Take superiors and subordinates, for example. *Superiors* obviously makes those people sound better than others, and *subordinates* makes it sound as if those lowly people should bow to their superiors. *Boss* sounds like someone constantly giving orders, and *employee* doesn't quite work because both managers and those being managed are essentially employees. It may be time for different terms. Some companies now refer to people as associates. This does not, however, differentiate between a manager and someone being managed. Maybe we should refer to those being managed as **managees.**[1] At least this term carries no inferior or negative connotations and does not imply that one group works and the other doesn't.

Management is a career unto itself. Unfortunately, this may be news to as many managers as it is to workers! We tend to assume that someone able to perform a

Managees
those being managed

job well will be able to manage people doing that job. The ability to weld, for example, is in no way related to the ability to manage other welders. Still, good welders are given jobs as welding supervisors and managers, often with little training or education. Some new managers realize the need for management education and seek to learn about it on their own. Others seem to believe that because they were given a management job, they inherently must know how to manage. Management education is critical in order to learn from the successes and failures of past managers and to understand just what the job of managing entails.

Manager
one who plans, controls, organizes, and directs resources

MANAGEMENT FUNCTIONS AND RESOURCES

The job of managing involves four main functions and four main resources (see Figure 8.1). A **manager** plans, controls, organizes, and directs an organization's financial, informational, material, and human resources (see Figure 8.2). This gives managers 16 areas to study for the performance of one general job. Managers must plan, control, organize, and direct financial resources and plan, control, organize, and direct informational resources, and so forth. Although this results in 16 areas, managers do not typically divide their time this way. Instead, they must pull together these 16 areas, make sense of them, and perform the one job of managing. In addition, any one of these 16 areas may develop problems and require that time be diverted from the others. For example, a manager may set aside Monday morning to plan financial resources (work on next year's budget). When Monday arrives, a high number of absentees may force the manager to drop the budget and organize human resources instead. It is almost impossible, however, to describe the job of management or to learn managing by looking at the job as a single unit. Instead, management is easier to understand if we divide it into the four functions and four resources.

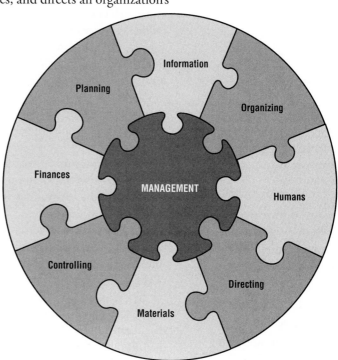

FIGURE 8.1 IN THE JOB OF MANAGING, FOUR MAIN ORGANIZATIONAL RESOURCES COMBINE WITH FOUR MAIN MANAGERIAL FUNCTIONS

Management's Job	Planning	Controlling	Organizing	Directing
Human Resources	Plan HR	Control HR	Organize HR	Direct HR
Financial Resources	Plan Finances	Control Finances	Organize Finances	Direct Finances
Material Resources	Plan Materials	Control Materials	Organize Materials	Direct Materials
Information Resources	Plan Information	Control Information	Organize Information	Direct Information

FIGURE 8.2 FOUR ORGANIZATIONAL RESOURCES COMBINE WITH FOUR MANAGERIAL FUNCTIONS TO DELINEATE MANAGEMENT'S JOB IN A MANNER THAT FACILITATES LEARNING   In practice, a manager may be called on at any time to perform one of these 16 interrelated functions. For example, a manager might need information on salaries for human resources in order to plan for the future.

NetNote

Free Management Library

http://www. managementhelp.org/

Access to a large amount of management information on many (75) topics.

Planning
establishing the destination and the route that a business will take

Controlling
supervising, disciplining, evaluating, and managing the change of the four managerial resources

Organizing
grouping the four resources

Directing
leading and motivating

Leadership
providing a vision for attaining the organization's goals and showing people the path or direction for realizing that vision

Motivating
giving people a reason to work; providing incentive and moving people to action

Four Functions **Planning** is considered the most basic management function. The other three areas need planning questions answered before they are addressed. Planning involves establishing both the destination and the route for the business. Planning involves everything from setting company goals and objectives to establishing standard operating procedures. Plans are created for the long term (five or more years), the intermediate term (more than one year but less than five years), and the short term (one year or less).

The planning process essentially begins with the company purpose and the mission or vision statement. The purpose and mission change infrequently, whereas goals and objectives change at least yearly. Goals are rather broad statements of direction. It is acceptable to say that one corporate goal is to increase sales next year. With this goal, the sales manager may establish objectives. Although goals are general statements, objectives are more specific. Objectives must be measurable, they must contain a verb (an action word), and they must mention time. An objective might be the following: Increase sales by 15 percent by the end of the first quarter. This is measurable (we can calculate 15 percent), it is an action (selling), and it describes a time limit (the end of the quarter, March 31). In some organizations, workers are asked for opinions concerning planning, but it is management's job to finalize plans and priorities.

Controlling entails supervising, disciplining, evaluating, and managing the change of the four managerial resources. Controlling activities include evaluating the performance of equipment and people, analyzing the usefulness of information, measuring the performance of financial resources, measuring errors and reject rates, and changing resources that are not working well. In essence, controlling is ensuring that actual performance matches the specifications. Workers may be involved in carrying out the controlling effort, but it is management's job to design the control and the controlling systems.

The **organizing** function of management involves the grouping of the four resources. Managers group people, information, and equipment and allocate money to them in order to meet the goals and objectives of the organization. One of the most noticeable results of organizing is the formal organization as depicted by the organization chart. Organizing also involves coordinating departmental operations, grouping human resources on a permanent and daily basis, and staffing the organization (hiring, promoting, and firing). On a larger scale, organizing includes the reorganization of the organization, which includes the buying or selling of entire companies and subsidiaries, and the resizing (typically downsizing) of the whole organization. On a smaller scale, organizing entails the scheduling of work shifts, work hours, and breaks.

Directing consists of two difficult tasks: leading and motivating. **Leadership** entails providing a vision for obtaining the organization's goals and showing people the path or direction for realizing that vision. Motivating involves giving people a reason to work. **Motivating** is a complex and important task (so much so that it will be discussed in depth in Chapter 11). Adding to the complexity is that there is no one way to motivate everyone. The tasks involved in motivating range from providing rewards to providing a work environment conducive to self-management.

Although these are the four main functions of management, other managerial activities span all of them. Three of the most important are communicating, decision making, and representation. Communication, as discussed in Chapter 3, occurs in four directions: upward communication to higher management, downward communication to workers, lateral communication to other managers at the same level, and external communication to areas outside the organization. Decision making, as introduced in Chapter 2 and expanded upon later in this chapter, is

A QUESTION OF ETHICS

Relationships with Managers

In the past, a large measure of the relationship between a manager and a worker involved trust. People dedicated their lives to an employer and trusted that the employer would manage their career, employ them for life, and provide for them during retirement. This scenario no longer exists in many organizations, yet workers still believe that this is important. Nearly 90 percent of workers say that being able to trust management is very important; fewer than 40 percent believe they can. Does this matter? Is there a price to pay for abandoning trust? It seems that there is.

Research has shown that an absence of trust can impede decision making, reduce productivity, and interfere with innovation and interpersonal relations. In the absence of trust, people become cynical, suspicious of others, and distrustful of coworkers. This can cause people to withhold information or present overly optimistic reports and projections. People become defensive, and stress levels increase. In addition, companies often overlook symptoms of low trust or are very slow to recognize them.

In order to build or increase trust, companies have to be fair, they have to strive to do the right thing, and they have to care about things other than just making money, like employee and customer relations. They must communicate and be open. But with the competition and pressures facing companies, is trust between managers and workers possible, or even desirable?

1. What is the relationship between trust and ethics? Is it ethical to contribute to a distrustful work environment?

2. Is it possible to have trust between a company and customers or workers in a competitive business environment?

3. Is the present really different from the past as far as trust and ethics are concerned, or do some companies just use this as an excuse? Explain.

4. Considering the negative effects that low levels of trust can have on the work environment, do managers have an ethical duty to owners and shareholders to maintain a trusting relationship between management and workers?

Source: Frank Sonnenberg, "Trust Me . . . Trust Me Not," *Industry Week,* August 16, 1993, pp. 22–27.

---

another major function of management, to such an extent that managers have been called professional decision makers. The third major area involves representing the department to other departments and areas. Here the manager serves as a spokesperson, liaison, and promoter of the department. All of this—the planning, controlling, organizing, directing, communicating, decision making, and representing—concerns the four resources of management.

Four Resources   Management must use human, financial, material, and informational resources to accomplish the organization's goals and objectives. Of the four, the **human resources** (the people who work at a firm) often receive the most attention and are typically the most difficult to manage. This is because humans are by far the most complex and often the least predictable resources. The most marvelous and amazing machines and systems are toys compared with the human body and mind. Often the very abilities that make humans so valuable—such as creativity, adaptability, and the ability to work independently—are the ones that make them so difficult to manage. For comparison, money does not become depressed when its value decreases. Machines do not become upset and go on strike when there is talk of their being replaced. Supplies do not have bad hair days. Humans, however, must be dealt with carefully.

The other three resources are somewhat easier to understand and manage. **Financial resources** are money and things that act like or can be converted into money (like stocks, bonds, and accounts receivable). Money can be invested and its performance evaluated using accounting and financial skills. **Material resources** are all the items needed for the production of goods and services.

Human Resources
the people working at a firm

Financial Resources
money and things that act like or can be converted into money (like stocks, bonds, and accounts receivable)

Material Resources
the items needed for the production of goods and services (like supplies, equipment, and raw materials)

247

Supplies, equipment, and raw materials are the main categories of materials. **Informational resources,** the firm's collection of knowledge, facts, data, or intelligence, are becoming ever more important and abundant. This is good news and bad news. More and better information can lead to greater customer satisfaction and better decision making. But the availability of more information also means that it is more difficult to keep current with developments and that it is becoming increasingly easier to become inundated by information. The challenge for managers is to receive as much useful information as possible, rather than as much information as is available.

Managing any one of these three resources may be easier than managing people, but this is not to suggest that managing these resources is easy. The difficulty is especially apparent when we consider that the four resources must be coordinated under the four functions. By now you have probably begun to see that there is more to management than doing nothing or going to meetings. The four functions interact with the four resources to produce 16 facets of what must be one cohesive whole in order to operate properly. In the process of managing these 16 facets, managers use decision-making and communication skills to represent their areas to two different environments—the internal environment and the external environment, which are discussed in the next section.

THE INTERNAL AND EXTERNAL ENVIRONMENTS

Managers must contend with two different environments. One is the internal environment of the organization; the other is the world outside the organization, which is referred to as the external environment. The **external management environment** comprises the entities in direct contact with the company, combined with the major forces of the population and society. Entities that have regular contact with the organization include governments (local, state, federal, and foreign), competitors, suppliers, financial institutions, and, of course, customers. The major forces of the population and society include demographic changes, environmental concerns, concerns of the public, social trends, concerns of special interest groups, technological change, legal and political trends, and the press or the media. Managers must take these forces and trends into account as they oversee operations in the internal environment.

The **internal management environment** consists of the company or organization itself. It comprises the mental and physical working environments described in Chapter 1, in addition to the overall social and political forces in the firm. A particular manager, therefore, when considering a decision, must be concerned with its effect on subordinates, higher managers, and managers of other departments who are at the same level. The manager must consider effects on the social and political relations among those above, below, and at the same level as his or her position. For example, it may be perfectly logical that Pam and Brian take over Walter's area when he retires. Pam and Brian may not be able to state this openly, however, because three other managers, Jason, David, and Adam, all want Walter's department. Jason wants it because his department is being automated, and he believes that power is related to the number of people working for you rather than the amount of work being completed. David wants Walter's department because he wants to expand his operation, and he needs Walter's budget. Adam wants it because he is bored and is looking for a change. Jason, David, and Adam are the company founder's grandsons, so how do Pam and Brian proceed? The nine-point decision-making model presented in Chapter 2 can assist them in solving their problem.

DECISION MAKING

Managers are sometimes referred to as professional decision makers as a way of demonstrating the importance of making decisions. Decision making spans the range of managerial functions, and managers are expected to make decisions in as rational a manner as possible. In Chapter 2 a nine-step decision-making model was presented as a method for obtaining rational decisions on a regular basis. (The model is included here in Figure 8.3 for your reference.) The nine-step model does not, however, mention the many other types of decisions that are made by managers—the decisions that are not purely rational, as far as the organization is concerned. We must take into account political, personal, social, and temporal influences on decision making. There are eight general classes of decisions, some of which have subclasses (see Table 8.1).

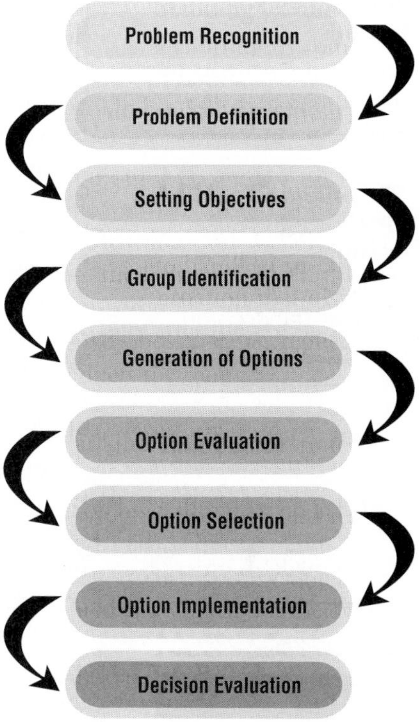

Rational Decisions   Managers are not expected to make perfect decisions, but they are expected to make **rational decisions**—decisions based on reason and following a logical system.[2] Managers are not supposed to base their decisions on emotion or personal preference, although they sometimes rely on intuition.[3] Rational decisions, as we shall see, are not always made. Even when they are, it may be difficult for others to see the rationale in the rational decision. You may cope better with a manager's decisions if you see the logic, and in order to see the logic, it helps to put yourself in the place of the decision maker. When the rationale cannot be determined in this way, try classifying the decision according to one of the following less rational types.

Problem Recognition

Problem Definition

Setting Objectives

Group Identification

Generation of Options

Option Evaluation

Option Selection

Option Implementation

Decision Evaluation

FIGURE 8.3 THE NINE-STEP DECISION-MAKING OR PROBLEM-SOLVING MODEL

Political Decisions   Many decisions are **political decisions** to some degree, but when the main concern is the political impact of a decision, then it leaves the rational arena and can be placed into one of five political classes, which consist of politically popular, personal political, superior's political, politically rewarding, and politically punishing decisions.[4]

A **politically popular decision** is one that is made in order to satisfy the majority of those involved.[5] These decisions are not always the best possible. They may even be unfair, but they do satisfy most of those involved.

A **personal political decision** is one that benefits the decision maker or the decision maker's career.[6] What is best for the department, division, or organization is disregarded as the decision maker's agenda is advanced. This agenda may include a desire for power, control, advancement, transfer, or a move to another organization. It is difficult for anyone adversely affected by a personal political decision to accept the situation. Sometimes the only consolation available is the knowledge that the decision was political and not due to some failing on the part of those adversely affected.

Rational Decisions

decisions based on reason and following a logical system

Political Decisions

decisions for which the main concern is political impact

Politically Popular Decision

decision made in order to satisfy the majority of the people involved

---

TABLE 8.1 THE EIGHT GENERAL TYPES OF DECISIONS

Rational Decisions	Political Decisions	Temporal Decisions	Emotional Decisions
Economic Decisions	Risk-Based Decisions	Conflict-Based Decisions	Buck-Passing Decisions

Personal Political Decision

decision that benefits the decision maker or the decision maker's career

Superior's Political Decision

a decision made mainly to benefit the decision maker's boss or bosses rather than the decision maker

Politically Rewarding Decision

decision made in order to repay a favor

Politically Punishing Decision

decision made in order to exact revenge or to inflict a penalty

Temporal Decisions

decisions in which time plays a major role

Emergency Temporal Decision

decision made during a crisis

Quick Temporal Decision

decision made in a short amount of time, but not during a crisis

Delayed Decision

decision taking a longer amount of time than is needed

A **superior's political decision** is one that is made mainly to benefit the decision maker's boss rather than the decision maker.[7] For example, suppose a vice president and network manager agree that new computers are needed for a local area network. The vice president wants a brand of computers that is adequate, but not the best available for the money, because the vendor offers help with minicomputers. The vice president wants the minicomputer support because the manager for the mini is weak in this area but is a very good friend of the VP. The network manager is then forced to purchase and work with mediocre computers to satisfy the VP's political needs. This may be difficult to live with, and again, about the only thing the network staff can do is to realize that it was not their manager's decision.

A **politically rewarding decision** is one that is made in order to repay a favor.[8] For example, say last year Sumit supported Andrea in a budget battle. This year, even though Andrea has some needs, she supports Sumit's department in order to return the previous year's favor. Politically rewarding decisions are sometimes made in promotion decisions when someone is advanced or given a prime assignment not because of merit or ability, but because the person has supported the boss or the boss's causes in the past.

A **politically punishing decision** is the opposite of a politically rewarding decision. Here, someone is being punished for political reasons.[9] This can occur when someone has failed to support a manager or perhaps has embarrassed the manager in front of top managers or a client, or when some indiscretion is beyond the reach of existing disciplinary policies.[10] If the violator cannot be punished officially, he or she is punished in another manner. It is even possible to be punished for performing a job too well. If the top performer is seen as a threat to take the manager's job, the manager may make a decision that prevents this from happening.

Temporal Decisions   Time is a factor in most decisions; in temporal decisions, time is the main factor influencing the decision maker. Some **temporal decisions** are based on having too little time, whereas others involve long periods of time.[11] Temporal decisions fall into five categories, with subcategories in each. Emergency and quick decisions occur in a short amount of time; delayed, barrier, and nondecisions occur over a long period of time.

An **emergency temporal decision** is made in a crisis situation.[12] Because of the high pressure and the short amount of time, these decisions may not be the best ones possible. If everyone could make good, fast decisions, they would. In actuality, good decisions that can be reached quickly are often easy decisions. Decisions in a crisis are often not easy, so it is no surprise that some are less than ideal. Given the situation, it is usually best to forgive poor decisions made in an emergency or crisis situation.[13]

A decision made instantly in a nonemergency situation is classified as a **quick temporal decision**.[14] These can also be poorly made decisions if adequate information is not gathered. Sometimes quick decisions are made out of impatience. At other times they are made under pressure. For example, a subordinate may pressure a manager for a fast decision, and the subordinate may get it, but it may not be the one that was hoped for. In general, managers should not be pushed to make fast decisions; the cautious nature of many may cause them to say no when a yes is desired. If it appears that a manager is about to make a hasty decision, you may volunteer to come back in a day or two so that the manager has time to contemplate the situation and make the decision you hope for.

A **delayed decision** is one that has been postponed for longer than the amount of time needed to make it. Sometimes decision makers deliberately delay a decision in the hope that the situation will resolve itself or the person requesting the decision will forget about the issue and not come back.[15] If you suspect that this is happening to you, it may be necessary to remind the person that the decision is still needed. You may ask for a date or a time by which the decision will be made. If possible, try to get a specific time or make an appointment rather than allowing the decision maker to say that he or she will get to it in a couple of days. Some managers may become annoyed if you inquire too often about a decision; others may give you the answer you want just to keep you from constantly coming in to ask about the decision. Here, prior experience or advice from others may guide you in the frequency of your inquiries and the interval between them.

A **barrier decision** is another delayed decision. In this type, decision making is delayed or avoided by constantly adding new conditions or barriers that must be met before the decision can be made.[16] For example, say you approach your manager with an idea that requires a decision. The manager may introduce a barrier by asking you to put the request in writing. After you write down your idea and ask for a decision, the manager next asks for a cost analysis. When that condition is met, the manager asks for an impact statement on how the decision affects other departments. If you do that, then the manager has to wait for the next department-head meeting. This is followed by a request for more research. Each of these conditions is a barrier to making the decision. The idea is not to test your endurance, but to say no without having to say the word. The manager is secretly hoping to wear you down to the point at which you stop asking for the decision.

The last type of decision involving a long period of time is the **nondecision**. Here, decision makers never make an actual decision. They just never seem to find the time, either from conscious effort to ignore the decision or because the decision is so unimportant to them that they just keep forgetting about it. Not making a decision is actually just another way of saying no without having to speak the word.[17] You may be tempted to press for a decision, but doing so may result in simply annoying the person enough for him or her to actually say no. An alternative that may work is to say that if you don't hear from the person by a certain date, then you will view that as a yes and proceed from there. If you are dealing with a peer or someone with less or only slightly more status and power than you, this might work. However, if the person has significantly more power and status than you, then you might take the opposite approach and say that if you do not receive a reply by a certain date, you will treat that as a no.

Emotional Decisions

Emotional decisions, which are based on subjective feelings, can be divided into two main types: those arising from anger and those arising from affective responses.[18] Feelings form the foundation for both types of emotional decisions. In these cases, rational, logical thought is replaced with sentiments.

An **angry emotional decision** is often obvious to any witnesses but difficult to detect when you are not present at the time the decision is made.[19] The anger may, or may not, be directed at you. Sometimes the decision maker is actually angry at the situation, a boss, a spouse, or the latest sports results. Whatever the cause, anger creates a poor decision-making environment. If an anger-based decision was made that punishes you unjustly, then you may be able to file a grievance or complaint with the decision maker's manager or with the human resources department. If an anger-based decision adversely affects you, but the decision maker was angry at something or someone else, then it is better to wait until the decision maker calms down. Then return and calmly ask that the decision be reconsidered.

Barrier Decision
decision taking a long time because of the continued addition of new conditions or barriers

Nondecision
never actually making a decision; saying no by saying nothing

Emotional Decisions
decisions based on subjective feelings

Angry Emotional Decision
decision based on feelings of rage or hostility

An **affective emotional decision** is based on sentiment, instinct, gut reaction, or some other subjective criterion.[20] Decisions based on liking one person over another are affective; if they adversely affect you, then you may wish to ask the decision maker to tell you on what basis the decision was made. There should be a logical, rational reason for each decision. Even if the decision was between two equally attractive alternatives and the decision maker tossed a coin, you should be told this. As with any inquiry to a superior that has the potential to look like a challenge, you should consider the politics involved in pressing for an answer. What you may gain if the decision is reversed should be weighed against what you may lose from appearing to challenge someone. In other words, you may gain so little and lose so much that an inquiry cannot be risked.

Economic Decisions Decisions based solely on a concern for money can be categorized as **economic decisions**.[21] Money is objective. When one option is less expensive than another, it is sometimes easier to accept a decision to take the cheaper route. The decision to spend less may not be popular or even wise, but it is hard to argue against less spending, especially in lean times. Even though people might accept the numerical facts that one option is less expensive than others, they may not accept the ramifications of an economic decision. This is often the case when the decision adversely affects you or your work economically. At least knowing that the decision was based on economics and not on some failure on your part may provide you with some comfort.

Risk-Based Decisions Decisions involving the chance of loss or injury are **risk-based decisions.** The extremes of risk (extremely low and extremely high) can be of special concern to decision makers.[22] Sometimes decision makers are willing to make decisions as long as there is little chance of failure or if failure would not be highly visible to superiors or those outside the department.[23] When working with people who are willing to make only a **low-risk decision,** you must show how you have accounted for any risks or how you have at least reduced risks to an acceptable level.

Affective Emotional Decision
decision based on sentiment, instinct, gut reaction, or a similar subjective criterion

Economic Decisions
decisions based solely on a concern for money or cost

Risk-Based Decisions
decisions involving the extreme chance of loss or injury

Low-Risk Decision
decision involving little chance of visible failure

FYI

Becoming a manager involves entering a new profession; prepare for it as much as you would for entry into any other completely different profession.

It is easy to be a bad manager; it takes a great deal of effort to be a good manager, but the rewards are greater.

Always be aware of the political implications of your actions and the actions of others.

Write out each step in making rational decisions; soon it will become second nature, and you won't have to write the steps out.

Use the right tool for the right job—be classical when you have to; be behavioral when you need to; be able to blend the two when necessary.

There can still be a great deal of benefit from a time and motion study; just because it is an old idea doesn't mean it is a bad one.

Managers and workers have an equal chance at being incompetent—don't be either.

At the other extreme are decision makers willing to make a **high-risk decision.**[24] High-risk decisions involve a significant chance for failure, large loss, or high visibility. Decision makers willing to make high-risk decisions are often decisive, but a few will back up their decisions with a scapegoat. Beware if you are asked to make a high-risk decision or to play a highly visible role in a decision-making process when it is not normal for you to do so. Sometimes this new opportunity is just that, your first opportunity to demonstrate your abilities. However, it could also be that you are being positioned to take the blame for a failure. When there is no clear reason for you to be trusted with a high-risk decision, you should consider what your position will be should everything fail completely. If no one else will be taking any blame, then maybe it will all be left for you.

Conflict-Based Decisions

Many decisions contain some potential for causing or avoiding conflict. **Conflict-based decisions** are those predominately based on whether they cause or avoid conflict.[25] Some decisions minimize conflict and are made in order to keep the peace or to reduce stress for the decision maker.[26] Sometimes there is a personal aspect to decisions that minimize conflict.[27] A decision may go against a person because he or she is the least likely to complain. For example, let's say Tom is the new person and still on probation. An assignment arises that no one wants. Giving it to one of the more senior workers would cause many complaints. To avoid the conflict, the assignment is given to Tom, who is in no position to complain. On other occasions, a decision maker may select an option because it will cause conflict rather than avoid it. For example, assignments may be given in the hope that the resulting conflict will cause some undesirable people to quit, thus avoiding the difficulty of having to fire them.[28] Also, some managers believe that a certain amount of conflict keeps subordinates more alert. If the conflict level is lower than they believe is adequate, they make a decision that introduces additional conflict.[29] It is debatable whether this tactic actually works.

Buck-Passing Decisions

Decisions sent to another person to make are called **buck-passing decisions.**[30] Let's say Larry is the assistant director of training. As such, he is supposed to select new training materials, some of which are interactive CDs. Not wanting to make the decision, he says that the CDs must be compatible with the computer systems at the firm and that the decision is up to the director of computer services or his boss, the director of training. It is legitimate to send a decision to another person when you lack the authority, power, or command of the resources involved. However, to pass a decision to another when it concerns your area is passing the buck, especially when it is an unpleasant, unpopular, or risky decision. This can be self-defeating. If others are going to make your decisions, why does the organization need you?

COPING WITH DECISIONS

Decisions made by others and affecting you range from those that are exceedingly in your favor to those that are very detrimental. Decisions between the favorable end and the middle of the scale are easy to accept. The closer the decision gets to the detrimental end, the more coping is needed. Sometimes the coping is mere acceptance of the decision; much depends on the extent of the decision's impact and its nearness to the extreme detrimental end of the range. When people are powerless to change a decision, then acceptance may give way to other coping mechanisms, such as escapism, amnesia, and anger.

High-Risk Decision
decision involving a strong chance for failure, loss, or high visibility

Conflict-Based Decisions
decisions based on whether they cause or avoid conflict

Buck-Passing Decisions
decisions passed along to another person

Escapism

running away from or avoiding a threat; can manifest itself as tardiness, absenteeism, turnover, or request for transfer

Amnesia

forgetting about decisions one does not like

Escapism   **Escapism** is an ancient response to danger in which an organism runs away from the threat. In the wake of a detrimental workplace decision, escapism can manifest itself as tardiness, absenteeism, turnover, or a request for a transfer. Tardiness and absenteeism are minor escapes and could simply be considered protests. Any message these protests send to the decision maker or manager might be missed, however, because there are many causes of tardiness and absenteeism other than trying to escape a decision. Requesting a transfer or quitting are actions that also send messages, but they eliminate any reason for changing the decision that caused the action. Transferring and quitting would be drastic actions if the causal decision concerned a minor matter, but they both may be legitimate actions if the decision causes changes that you just can't live with. Still, such drastic moves should always be carefully considered first.

Amnesia   In the workplace, **amnesia** allows people to forget about decisions they do not like or agree with. In order to cope with the situation, they actively or passively forget about the decision. Active amnesia occurs when a person consciously decides not to think about an adverse decision again. Passive amnesia occurs when people have so little concern for the decision that they unconsciously stop thinking about it. This does not mean that the person disobeys the decision; this just means that he or she will not think about it further. For example, if a person does not receive a particular job, he or she may make a conscious decision not to dwell on this and never to think about it again. As an example of passive amnesia, consider a decision to throw out the modern-style office furniture and purchase traditional wood furniture. Some people keep a desk so covered with work that it matters not what supports it. They forget the decision and keep right on working. In practice, these are not bad coping mechanisms if you can employ them.

Anger   Anger, the choice of many, is not always a bad method of coping with certain decisions. Everything is dependent, however, on the type of anger. If a decision makes you angry for a short time, and you release the anger by talking about it with someone or through a vigorous workout at the health club, then this is not the worst method for coming to terms with a disturbing decision. However, if the anger lingers, if it is always there just below the surface, if it continues for a long time and begins to cause poor job performance, or if it begins to negatively affect relations outside of work, then it is a poor choice for a coping mechanism. In this case, one should try to employ one of the other coping mechanisms or talk to someone who can help. Consider the importance of the decision that you are trying to cope with, and ask yourself if it is worth getting upset over. Before answering, ask two other questions: "If I do get upset, will anyone notice?" and "If I do get upset, will anything change?" If either answer is no, then why upset only yourself (see Chapter 15 on stress), or why get worked up when nothing will change?

SPOT CHECK

1. Leadership consists of directing and motivating. T F
2. Managers are expected to make perfect decisions. T F
3. A barrier decision is an attempt to delay decision making. T F
4. A nondecision is just another way of saying no. T F
5. Tardiness and absenteeism are smaller methods of escape. T F

MANAGEMENT PRINCIPLES

Managers do not typically wish to make decisions or take actions that will cause subordinates problems or force them to use some coping mechanism to survive. In order to help managers, a number of principles have been developed. To understand managers and organizations, it is important to understand the management principles that guide them:

- the division of labor principle
- the separation principle
- the technical competence principle
- the hierarchy principle
- the authority principle
- the unity of command principle
- the unity of direction principle

Four of these principles were discussed in Chapter 7. The division of labor principle says that there are great advantages to dividing work up into smaller parts. Specifically, people gain greater expertise, are more efficient, can compress time, can accomplish large jobs, and are faster to train when using specialization. The separation principle says that a person is separate from the position the person holds, and the technical competence principle says that only people having the competence to perform the job should be hired. The hierarchy principle says that the organization should have separate levels with the larger span of control among the lower levels. These principles, along with the next three, present an excellent introduction to management thought and how organizations function.

Authority Principle   The **authority principle** says that managers have the right to direct people toward the accomplishment of the organization's goals.[31] In directing people, managers may issue written orders or simply ask them to do something. In any case, it is the managers who ultimately decide who will do what, when, where, and how. Although managers are given the right to direct others, they also have the responsibility for getting the tasks accomplished. Failure to accomplish the tasks is also the manager's responsibility. In fact, much of the stress of being a manager comes from being responsible.

Unity of Command Principle   The **unity of command principle** states that each person should have only one boss.[32] In this case, unity refers to a unit, or one, rather than something being united or in agreement. In practical terms, this means that no one should ever be placed in a position of having to decide which of two equal bosses to obey. Directions should, therefore, come from one immediate supervisor or manager because having two equal bosses will ensure that the person is wrong when the bosses give conflicting orders. When learning of this principle, some people insist that they have two bosses. Some are right and some are wrong. The ones who are wrong often miss a point: They have two bosses of unequal authority. Many people have a supervisor, and the supervisor has a manager, and sometimes they give conflicting orders. This is not a violation of the unity of command principle because the manager has more authority than the supervisor, so one does what the manager says. Some people actually do have two bosses of equal authority, as seen in some partnerships. If a firm has two full partners, they each have equal power. To avoid the kind of problems that can come from violating the unity of command principle, the two partners might divide the work or the people

Authority Principle
managers have the right to direct workers toward the accomplishment of the organization's goals

Unity of Command Principle
each person should have only one boss

who report to them, as is the case in larger firms. Most larger corporations follow the unity of command principle because it works perfectly with hierarchies. Matrix organizations, however, violate the principle outright and can only do so if everyone in the organization agrees to work around this problem.

Unity of Direction Principle
similar tasks and tasks working toward the same organizational goal should be grouped together

Unity of Direction Principle   The **unity of direction principle** states that similar tasks should be grouped together and that tasks working toward the same organizational goal should be grouped together.[33] In many organizations, this means putting all the accountants together, putting all the people working in Chicago under one manager, or putting all the people producing and selling widgets in one group. Some of the newer forms of organization (see Chapter 7) may define the groups differently, but they are still using this principle. Whether a company has departments for sales, operations, and human resources or departments for order fulfillment and logistics, the idea is to group resources in the best way possible in order to fulfill the organization's goals.

In analyzing these principles, we see that they are mainly concerned with organizing, staffing, and controlling. Organization is accomplished by using the authority, hierarchy, unity of command, and unity of direction principles to create a chain of command that gives each person only one manager, gives the managers authority to direct the resources, and groups similar tasks together. The hierarchy is then staffed using the division of labor principle, the separation principle, and the technical competence principle to define the work, define the relationship between the work and the worker, and define the person needed to do the work. Control is maintained by using the authority, hierarchy, and unity of command principles to define who has the authority and ultimate responsibility for completing the work, who reports to whom, and who controls whom. How all of this is done varies greatly in different firms, although there are just two main schools of management thought: classical and behavioral.

FROM CLASSICAL TO BEHAVIORAL MANAGEMENT

The two main theories concerning how to manage are often referred to as the classical school of management thought and the behavioral school of management. They are not dichotomous, however. These two philosophies are actually two ends of a continuum with many variations in between. Some managers are very classical, some are somewhat classical, some are partly classical and partly behavioral, and others are somewhat behavioral or very behavioral. Classical management was developed first and is still used today, whereas behavioral management evolved from classical management around the 1930s.

CLASSICAL MANAGEMENT

The classical system of management was actually hundreds of years in the making. It began to develop during the Industrial Revolution in the 1700s. Then, for the first time, large numbers of people were brought together to work for someone else, with someone else's tools. Prior to the Industrial Revolution, people worked as farmers, merchants, or artisans. They worked alone, with families or very small groups, or in guilds. Very little management was needed because there was very little to manage. With the Industrial Revolution, a method was needed to organize and coordinate larger numbers of people and resources. Classical management developed partly out of necessity and partly from example.

Managers who feel, for whatever reason, that they are losing control of a situation may resort to a more classical, autocratic approach. In an attempt to regain control they start to issue more commands. They may try to scare people into obedience by threatening them, or they may embarrass or degrade workers in front of others. While this behavior may result in short-term compliance, it also creates angry and defensive workers. If the situation is serious enough, workers may need to seek help from Human Resources. Meetings with workers, the manager, and HR professionals have been found to help improve relations under these circumstances.

Source: Paul Falcone, "Communication Breakdown (Improving Supervisor-Employee Relations)," _HR Focus_, September 1998, p. 8.

Command Systems   In casting about for guidance, early managers found only two examples for organizing large numbers of people: the churches and the armed forces. Both of these are autocratic, or command, systems. **Command systems** are designed as hierarchies with narrow spans of control and with an emphasis on downward communication and strict adherence to rules. These two examples are only part of the reason classical management developed as a command system. Besides having two autocratic systems as examples, it was necessary for early owners and managers to use a command system for another reason. In the extreme, then as today, command systems function by the managers telling the subordinates what to do and the subordinates' doing it. Period. Subordinates are not asked for their opinions, and their feelings are not taken into account. Subordinates are there to work, and the bosses take care of everything else. In the early days, this structure was almost required because the managers often were the only ones who knew how things operated.

It may help to imagine those days as they were and not as life is today. At the start of the Industrial Revolution, a new way of work was emerging. The workers were not familiar with it, and the managers were only a little familiar with it. Before the advent of factories, people worked essentially from sunrise to sunset. With the factory system, people went to work, and when work was done people had some time for themselves. Today we call this leisure time, although given the hours and the work of the early Industrial Revolution, it is doubtful that workers of that time would have called their after-work time leisure time. While the working conditions were new, so was the work. Training for this new work had not been invented, and what schooling people had did not prepare them for this new environment. Learning took place on the job from the bosses' directions or from taking orders. For managers, the most expedient approach was to tell people what to do and have them obey. The workers knew little, so discussing the matter would have been somewhat of a waste of time. An autocracy, or dictatorship, seemed quick, easy, and effective.

Eventually, the classical method evolved to the point that the system could be written down and taught to others. This started to happen during the late 1800s and early 1900s in the United States, France, and Germany.

Three people are generally credited with being the first to write about management theory, although the many unnamed managers that came before them certainly deserve some credit. Still, Frederick Taylor in the United States, Henri Fayol in France, and Max Weber in Germany each synthesized the body of management knowledge into principles and theories that others could learn and use. Other early contributors to classical management include Henry Gantt, Frank

Command Systems
hierarchies with strict adherence to rules

NetNote

"A Message to Garcia"

http://www.birdsnest.com/garcia.htm

Read this essay on workers from almost 100 years ago. Does it still apply today?

and Lillian Gilbreth, and even Henry Ford (who proved the need for managers and management by not having any).[34] As classical management is described, keep in mind that other command systems served as models, a command system seemed to be the most straightforward way for getting people to do things, and the workforce was less educated and less experienced than it is today.

Time–Motion Studies
research involving the time and motions required to complete a task

Time and Motion Studies One of the prime goals of classical management is to improve productivity. To do this, early managers often focused on motion studies and **time–motion studies.** For example, most people know that they should lift heavy objects by using their legs and not their backs, but they do not know that this is a result of early classical management studies. Taylor found that workers got more done with fewer injuries when lifting with the legs. This was good for the company as well as for the workers because the more they did, the more Taylor paid them. Classical managers also found that workers accomplished more if they did not work 8 consecutive hours. At first, this may seem counterintuitive. How can someone get more done by sitting down and not working? Classical studies found that rest breaks increased productivity and that without breaks, workers became so fatigued that they lost more productivity by working tired than they did by not working during the breaks. Other classical studies looked for wasted movements. Many of the time and motion studies looked for ways to increase productivity by sequencing and combining movements in order to keep them at a minimum.

The result of all the study on performing a task was often referred to as "the one best way." Classical managers believed that their methods produced the single most productive way to complete tasks. Once this was determined, all workers were to use the one best way.

The attitude that all workers are to use the management's way is indicative of the autocratic nature of classical management. With this system, managers issue explicit instructions—whether giving a quick order or in outlining work procedures. Classical management derives its authority from the owner, and managers retain all of this authority. Authority is not delegated to subordinates. This is due partly to managers' believing that they act for the owner and partly because they assume subordinates are lazy and do not want responsibility. This assumption encourages tight controls and close supervision, the belief being that, left on their own, people will find a shady tree and sit under it.

Classical Motivation The assumption that people do not want to work also affected classical motivation theories. Classical managers motivate through two main mechanisms—fear and money. Threatening people with the loss of their jobs is fairly common and is used because it is assumed that people do not like work but need a paycheck. In addition, if the only reason people do work is for money, then money becomes the prime motivator. The message, then, is twofold: (1) to make more money, work faster, and (2) do what management says, or lose your job and your money. Further, because people are assumed to be lazy and to dislike work, there is no sense in managers' worrying about worker attitudes or morale. Classical managers believe that attitudes and morale will be poor anyway because people really don't want to work and the money should make up for it. The entire system sharply divides managers from subordinates, and the emphasis is on the managers.

Fear is still used today.[35] New managers and those uneducated in management theory and technique are especially susceptible to believing that fear is the way to control people and get the most work out of them. In difficult economic times, this belief becomes even more prevalent and can be coupled with greatly increased workloads.

Classical management is manager-centric. In other words, it is focused on the manager. Success is derived from the skill of the manager in getting the mostly expendable workers to do the work as fast as possible. Social interactions among people interfere with work, and managers should not permit it. Managers have the authority, and they tightly control it through a chain of command that emphasizes downward communication (one doesn't need upward communication because, presumably, the subordinates do not want to be involved anyway). In some situations, classical managers even presumed to tell subordinates what their needs were. If all of this sounds rather unappealing, remember that in the beginning, many jobs consisted of being human machines. Henry Ford supposedly lamented, "Why do I get a whole person when all I want is a pair of hands?"

For some, it seems that classical management is a self-fulfilling prophecy. Many years after Taylor, Fayol, and Weber, management theorist Chris Argyris claimed that classical management makes people unmotivated, and by not involving workers, it creates an attitude of "I don't want to be involved" even if managers ask, which they don't.

Around the 1920s and 1930s, workers started rebelling against severely autocratic company owners. As a result of workers' rejecting this style of management, and some managers' feeling the classical method mishandled the human aspects of work, two changes started to appear. Workers, in ever-increasing numbers, worked toward unionization, and some managers developed a new way of managing.

BEHAVIORAL MANAGEMENT

Behavioral management, which recognizes the human, social needs in the workplace, developed from classical management in an effort to address the human side of the working environment. The spark for this new way of managing began as a series of failed and flawed classical management productivity studies. The **Hawthorne studies** took place in the assembly room of the Hawthorne plant of the Western Electric Company in Cicero, Illinois, and were supposed to test the effect of several changes in the working environment on productivity. The study was set up as an experiment with a control group (for which nothing environmental would change) and an experimental group (for which one factor at a time was designed to change). The first environmental factor to be tested was lighting; the two groups were moved to separate rooms. When the lighting was increased in the experimental room, productivity increased. The productivity in the control group, where nothing changed, also increased. This was unexpected. Next, the lights in the experimental room were turned down, the lights in the control room stayed the same, and productivity in both rooms went up. In fact, when any of the factors were changed in the experimental group, productivity increased. Furthermore, productivity increased in the control group even though nothing had changed. It seemed a good time to call in the scholars.

Elton Mayo, an Australian professor at Harvard University, led a team that investigated the Hawthorne studies. The team concluded that something other than environmental factors was influencing the workers. What they decided was that social factors were involved in the productivity increases. The problem was that the experimental design was flawed. In the scientific method, only one factor at a time is supposed to change. Here, at least four major factors changed. First, the workers were initially in a large assembly room but were placed into smaller rooms so that the environmental factors could be controlled. Second, there were so many people in the main assembly room that the individual workers did not really identify themselves as being part of a unit. The people in the study's control and experimental

**Behavioral
Management**
management system that
recognizes the human
social needs in the
workplace

The Hawthorne Studies
research into effects of
changes in the working
environment on
productivity that led to
the development of
behavioral management

groups were placed in small, easily identifiable groups of six. Third, the workers knew they were being observed and measured. Recall the Hawthorne effect from Chapter 6. When people know they are being observed, they often change their behavior. Not only did the workers know they were being observed, but they felt that they were doing something important. The work mattered to them, and they were more concerned about their output. Fourth, the environmental factors changed, which the original study designers thought was the only thing being changed.

Now for the first time, managers thought they had proof that there was more to work than the work itself. Behavioralism, or participative management, became some managers' answer to classical management's mishandling of the human aspects of work.[36] The Hawthorne experiments seemed to prove that people did want to become involved with work. After these studies, some managers began a radical rethinking of how frontline workers should be managed. Managers started to believe that everyone in the company was capable of contributing. Over the years, behavioral management has been further developed by W. Edwards Deming, Fredrick Herzberg, and others to mean that management:

- is concerned with the economic and the social aspects of work
- acknowledges the worker's ability to contribute ideas and labor to the organization
- allows worker autonomy
- tries to make work more interesting
- tries to make work a learning experience
- emphasizes upward and downward communication
- recognizes the formal and the informal (social) organization
- views the manager as a leader of a team, rather than a boss
- views people as wanting to work and capable of liking work
- sees many motivators other than money

NetNote

The W. Edwards Deming Institute

http://www.deming.org/

Teachings, publications, and information on the Deming Institute.

Behavioral managers are more likely to listen to and act on subordinate concerns. Communication and participation receive emphasis. Where a classical manager will make a decision alone, a totally behavioral manager will allow the subordinates to make the decision. Even a partially behavioral manager will give workers a part in all but emergency decisions (when time is of the essence). In general, behavioral managers are concerned with the whole person rather than just his or her hands.

Concern for people extends to concern for the whole individual, according to behavioral managers. Behavioralists understand that people have lives outside the workplace. They understand that sometimes personal life interferes with work and that people cannot check their emotional bags at the time clock. Possibly the greatest difference between behavioralists and classicalists can be found in the focus of the theories. Classical management is centered on the manager; behavioral management is focused on the worker. A behavioral manager believes that his or her job is to lead and to ensure that the workers have everything they need to do a good job. All of this does not mean that behavioral managers are not involved or not concerned with getting the job done.

Sometimes people think that behavioral managers are concerned with making people feel good and not with getting the job done. This is not true. Behavioral managers simply differ in the way they get the job done. Behavioral managers still have controls, rules, and an organization chart. However, their communication style, their human relations skills, and their approach to decision making, which includes everyone differ greatly from those of classical managers.

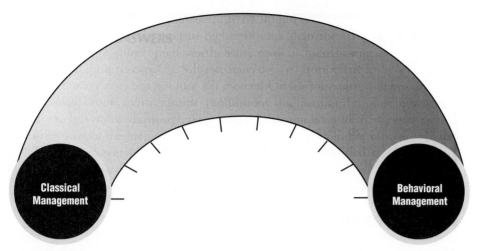

FIGURE 8.4 THE MANAGERIAL SPECTRUM   Managers are not simply either classical or behavioral; many variations exist between the two extremes.

THE MANAGEMENT CONTINUUM

Some managers strictly follow the extreme classical view of management, whereas other managers are firm believers in a totally behavioral approach. These are really just extremes along a **management continuum** (Figure 8.4). Most managers fall somewhere between the two extremes. Why are some managers at one end, some at the other, and many in between? One reason is that there is no one best way to manage. Situations and people vary. The choice of a method varies with the manager, the manager's training, the organization, the situation, and the workers. Some managers seem capable of being only classical or only behavioral managers. It seems to be part of their personal nature to be one or the other, and they probably couldn't switch even if they wanted to. Other managers have never been trained or educated in management so they really have no choice but to stay with what they have. As with the earliest managers, this usually means being a classical manager. At times, managers must use behavioral techniques because the organization does. It is almost impossible to be the only behavioral manager in a classically run organization. Other organizations may be predominantly behavioral, but certain departments or situations may require classical management. Ditchdiggers are not typically managed behaviorally. They are told to dig so far, so wide, and so deep and not to hit each other with the shovel. There is not much room for discussion. Finally, some people can be managed behaviorally and others classically.

It can be difficult for people to cope with a situation in which some people are treated classically and others behaviorally, but sometimes this is justified. For example, behavioral management requires trust between the manager and the worker. When an employee is new, a manager may use a more classical approach because the person has not earned the manager's trust yet. Something like the reverse can be true when a new manager comes into a department. In other situations, some people may fit the assumptions of the classical system. Maybe one employee is a little lazy or has a tendency to procrastinate. Even a strongly behavioral manager may think that closer supervision of this person is justified. Some people may have a difficult time reconciling different treatment for different people. The fact is, people are very different, and sometimes they abuse freedoms and bring closer scrutiny upon themselves. In the end, there is no one right or wrong way; some ways are appropriate for one situation but not necessarily for another.

**Management
Continuum**

the range of managerial philosophies from classical to behavioral management

THE WORKER'S ROLE

Management's role is to act on behalf of the owner or owners when the situation is too complex for one person or, as in the case of corporations, when there are many owners. Where do the workers fit into an organization? There would not be a need for a formal organization without workers, and no need for managers. Of course, no work would be done, and there would be very little organizational behavior without an organization full of people. Due to the size and complexity of many modern tasks, there are many roles to fulfill—planner, organizer, director, controller, and worker. Let's consider the role of the frontline worker, the person who has no other people to manage. **Frontline workers** perform the individual tasks that form the basis of the organization. It might be possible for organizations to exist without managers, although they might not work well. However, it is not possible for organizations to accomplish their long-term goals without frontline workers.

Frontline Worker
someone with no one to manage

DOING THE BEST JOB

Frontline workers perform the technical tasks of their profession. Their duty is to perform these tasks to the best of their abilities and at an acceptable level while using the least possible amount of the organization's resources. The phrase "to the best of their abilities" requires further discussion. A good worker does at least an adequate job, but if this person can do better, even better than others in the department, then he or she should do so. In other words, people should give their best performance, not just the bare minimum.

The three main reasons people should contribute their best performance are (1) it is essential for society, (2) it is part of the work ethic, and (3) to do otherwise would be bad for the individual. If everyone did less than his or her best, if we all did the absolute minimum, then our society would first stagnate and then collapse. Because we have created a society in which everyone depends on everyone else and everyone benefits from the progress society as a whole makes, doing less affects society and each individual—we all have less to share and then we each have less to receive. Doing our best is also part of our work ethic.[37] The unspoken contract with owners and managers is: "A fair day's work for a fair day's pay." Less than a fair day's work is bad for the organization and bad for the individual if he or she is fired. The third reason also affects the individual. Hard work is how people get ahead. Doing one's best is not only ethically right, but there are personal reasons for it as well. To move to the next level, one first has to do well where one is.

Is it unreasonable to expect people to give their best constantly? No, it would be unreasonable to expect people to be perfect all the time. Expecting people to give their best means that we understand that some days will be better than others. It is the striving to give their best that is important.[38] The new thinking could be summarized as "Do your best, even if you make mistakes, but don't be a failure." Mistakes are errors, and if you don't make some, you probably are not working hard enough or taking enough risks. Failure, on the other hand, is not learning from your mistakes, that is, making the same mistake over and over.

Part of the worker's role is to do the technical parts of his or her job as well as possible. Another part of the role is to cope with managers.

TOTAL QUALITY MANAGEMENT (TQM)

TQM is an ongoing process, one that requires everyone in an organization to be motivated toward the goal of continuous improvement and to be oriented toward meeting the needs of customers. In simple terms, TQM involves focusing all of a company's energies on improving the quality of its activities. The key elements of a TQM include a supportive culture, benchmarks and standards, strategies and training, and continuity.

TQM
an organization's efforts to maximize product and service quality

A supportive organizational culture begins with full support from the highest organizational levels and must include everyone down to the lowest levels.[39] Top management must initiate, communicate, and support the effort. The values of the employees and the culture as a whole must be dedicated to continuously improving quality for the ultimate arbiters of TQM's success—the customers.

To provide quality, customer quality standards must be determined, but competitor quality standards must also be known. Benchmarking is the continuous process of obtaining accurate information about how competitors handle similar quality problems by comparing products, services, and practices with industry leaders. Benchmarking has become a popular way of identifying organizational weaknesses, setting realistic targets, and improving performance. Benchmarking should lead to the establishment of realistic quality standards that employees are expected to meet.[40]

After standards are set, strategies for attaining the standards and training programs must be developed. It is important to develop quality standards that help close any gaps between what current quality levels are and what they should be. For example, a software firm may find that many customers have difficulty utilizing certain commands because they prefer not to use the print manual. A TQM objective would be to make it easier for end users to find explanations of the software's commands. The strategy is to develop easier-to-access "Help" commands that clearly explain the hardest-to-understand functions. Training in TQM concepts, team building, problem solving, and statistical methods is then needed to execute this strategy.

As TQM is an ongoing process, continuity of the effort is needed. Establishing continuous improvement teams (CITs), an outgrowth of quality circles, and measuring and monitoring performance are ways to maintain continuity. CITs are generally established first among middle managers, followed by the development of teams for assistant managers and supervisors. Team members meet on a regular basis and are empowered with responsibility for identifying, analyzing, and establishing objectives for solving current quality and productivity problems.

Statistical process control (SPC) is often used in measuring the progress of the TQM effort. SPC involves the use of statistical techniques that aid in analyzing a process and its output and in determining the activities necessary for improvement (i.e., for eliminating any gaps). It also supports the monitoring of the TQM process. Here it is especially important for employees to receive feedback regarding their activities. Providing feedback not only communicates results but helps maintain employee interest and enthusiasm in the process. If successful, TQM enables organizations to continue to meet or beat customer expectations, which is the major purpose of the entire process.

COPING WITH MANAGEMENT

Little coping is needed when you have good managers, but let's postpone our discussion of good management for the moment and consider the types of managers who can hurt people and careers. Of course, many managers are average or adequate, and coping with them really means little more than understanding the duties and responsibilities of a manager and a subordinate as outlined in the first part of this chapter. Your coping skills will be needed most often for those managers who deliberately or negligently harm others and their organizations.

The two general types of poor managers are those who are incompetent and those who are malicious. **Incompetent managers** are unable to fulfill their duties owing to a lack of ability or to a psychological deficiency.[41] Malicious managers are those who cause some type of suffering for others, typically emotional or psychological suffering.[42] The difference between these two is similar to the difference between being passive and being active. Incompetent managers passively have a negative effect on subordinates; more harm is caused by what they don't do. **Malicious managers** actively do things to embarrass, berate, or harass people. Malicious managers cause harm by what they do, not by what they don't do. It is important to be able to identify and cope with both types of poor managers because more of them are found in the workplace than most of us would like.

Incompetent Managers The incompetent manager is a victim of the Peter Principle or a psychological deficiency. The Peter Principle states that people are promoted to their level of incompetence. In other words, when people do well in a job, they are rewarded with a promotion. If they do well in the next job, they are promoted again. The cycle repeats itself until they are placed in a job that they can't perform. Then they are demoted, moved laterally, or fired. The level at which the Peter Principle applies is different for each person. Some people reach competence with an entry-level position; others reach it after 10 promotions.

Some managers are incompetent not because of a lack of ability but because of an apparent psychological defect. The only result of their actions that they foresee is failure. They are unable to decide because they are convinced that whatever they choose will be wrong. Several warning signs can identify the psychologically challenged incompetent manager:[43]

- denial
- playing it by the numbers
- buck passing
- abdication
- obfuscation
- delaying tactics
- escaping

It is important to be alert to these warnings signs, for it is difficult to do a good job, much less progress, with an incompetent manager.

Managers using **denial** will insist that there are no problems. Problems brought to their attention either don't exist, will go away by themselves, or were solved long ago. If there are no problems, no decision needs to be made or action taken. Managers **playing it by the numbers** always consult the rule book. If the answer is in the

---

Incompetent Managers

managers unable to fulfill their duties owing to a lack of ability or to a psychological deficiency

---

Malicious Managers

managers who cause emotional or psychological suffering

Denial

insistence that no problems exist

Playing It by the Numbers

doing only what the rules cover

---

book, then they do not have to devise any solutions, and if the problem is not in the book, then it is not a problem. This attitude can often be seen in the firmly entrenched, and dysfunctional, bureaucratic mind.

Buck passing—passing a problem along to someone else—is a strong sign of incompetence, but it may also be a characteristic of new managers. Sometimes a manager has not been managing long or is so new to the organization that he or she really doesn't know the answer and must pass the decision along. If the manager is experienced, then buck passing can be a sign of incompetence. The issue may be passed to other areas or departments, or it may be passed up to the manager's manager. In either case, the incompetent manager can never seem to decide anything on his or her own authority.

An incompetent manager who can't give a problem to another manager may try giving it to a subordinate. Whereas buck passing removes the decision from one manager to another, **abdication** passes authority off to others with less power or with no official power. Abdication can involve passing authority to a committee, to subordinates, or to a third party. Passing authority to subordinates may look like participative management, but a behavioral manager acts as a group leader, not as an absent leader. When unable to form a committee and when unable to have subordinates make decisions, the abdicator may bring in consultants.[44] (See Table 8.2 for what to do if consultants are called in.)[45] Whatever form of abdication is chosen, there are two goals: avoid making the decision, and ensure that there is someone else to blame if things go wrong.

Some incompetent managers use **obfuscation**, clouding and confusing the issue to the point that people walk away too embarrassed to admit they are confused, or they give up in frustration. If the problem cannot be clouded or given to someone else, then the incompetent manager may try to delay any involvement. Managers have a number of effective **delaying tactics.** One reason many of them are effective is that sometimes there are valid excuses for waiting. However, delaying tactics become warning signs of incompetence when they constantly recur. One common delaying tactic is to ask for the problem in writing. This works quite often. Sometimes people are reluctant to create evidence that they are afraid may be used against them, or they may believe that writing the incident down will be a waste of time because nothing will happen anyway (which with incompetent managers is usually true). Not putting the problem in writing in this case reinforces the manager's mental problems because the manager can now rationalize the avoidance of decision making by saying that it couldn't have been much of a problem if the individual wasn't willing to put it in writing.

Caution is another delaying tactic used by incompetent managers. Here the manager always warns others, "We better not move too quickly. Slow and steady wins the race." Another form of using caution to delay is to wait for new technology.

Buck Passing
passing a problem along to someone else

Abdication
passing authority to others

Obfuscation
clouding and confusing issues

Delaying Tactics
maneuvers that postpone

TABLE 8.2 ACTIONS TO TAKE IF CONSULTANTS ARE CALLED IN

Try to figure out why consultants were called in.

Do not be defensive or sarcastic, and do not make jokes.

Answer and help them, but watch what you say about your bosses.

Give them your ideas, even if the boss didn't like them.

If a company-consultant team is formed, try to get on it. You'll be on the inside and in a better position to look out for yourself.

But because technology is always improving, the manager is always waiting and never has to decide. Another delaying tactic involves insisting that problems must be handled on a first-come, first-served basis. Because this manager still has his or her first problem to decide, this in effect bars all future decisions until the past ones are decided. Sometimes the problem is insufficient information. Therefore, the situation will have to be studied and some research done. Of course the information is never gathered, or there is always more to get.

The final signal that a manager may be incompetent is **escaping,** or running away from the entire situation. Some managers escape by leaving for a business trip, going home, arranging to be too busy or always in a meeting, or going on vacation. In one situation involving an abusive health care worker, the day finally came when physicians, an outside agency, coworkers, and a particularly spineless manager were to present a large volume of information, and the worker was to be fired. As the appointed hour on a Wednesday afternoon came, all were gathered except the manager. After several minutes of this high-tension atmosphere, the manager's secretary came in to announce that the manager had just called to say he had decided to take an unannounced vacation day. About two months after the abusive worker was fired, many of the same people and some top administrators gathered for the firing of this manager (for this and other acts of incompetence). The event was somewhat anticlimactic because the manager this time had taken an unannounced personal day.

Malicious Managers   Incompetent managers are just one type of generally poor managers; other bad managers can actually be classified as malicious. Malicious managers actively cause harm or distress to others. Typically this is mental distress, but sometimes sexual or physical harassment is involved.[46] These managers can be classified by the manner in which the maliciousness manifests itself. Some of the mostly unsuccessful malicious managers are:[47]

- clueless
- split personalities
- grumps
- hoarders
- spineless

Four other types are often highly successful, but their tactics are typically unnecessarily harsh or stressful. These types can be classified as:[48]

- workaholics
- players of mind games
- perfectionists
- intimidators

If you are being managed, learn to differentiate among the types because your responses should differ accordingly.

Clueless Managers   These managers are living in the dark ages.[49] They have missed or ignored behavioral management, women's rights, diversity and minority rights, and the Americans with Disabilities Act. **Clueless managers** may stun you with behavior so out of date that you have no immediate response. Sexual advances; stereotypical comments concerning race, gender or ability; and a lack of any sense of what is appropriate in the workplace are symptoms of managerial cluelessness. Typically, the clueless manager is consistently clueless, whereas the split-personality manager is unpredictable.

Escaping
running away from a situation

NetNote

Workingamerica.org
http://www.workingamerica.org/badboss/?appState=listStories_p&ord=random
Anecdotes about bad bosses.

Clueless Managers
managers displaying outdated behavior

Split-Personality Managers and Grumps   Split-personality managers have two faces, a good side and a bad side, and workers never know which to expect.[50] The disturbing aspect to their behavior is that their mood can change from day to day or even from hour to hour. Many consider the split-personality types to be more difficult than **grumps,** who are always in a bad mood.[51] Grumps seem to hate everything and almost everybody, never appear to be happy, and think that nothing is ever going to improve or to work properly. However, at least grumps are consistent. You know what you are getting when you have to talk with one. People fear the unknown, and the split-personality types touch this fear because of their unpredictability.

Hoarders   These managers are overprotective. They jealousy guard all of their "possessions"—especially their budgets, position, and power. **Hoarders** watch others suspiciously and may even resort to spying on them.[52] Of course, just because you are paranoid doesn't mean that they are not out to get you; sometimes people really are trying to move you out. The difference between people responding to typical office politics and the hoarders of the corporate world, however, is that there is no real reason to be suspicious and certainly no reason to go snooping around someone else's office.

Spineless Managers   These managers choose to avoid issues and deny problems, and they are quite adept at it. To avoid being held accountable later, **spineless managers** avoid taking a stand or expressing a strong opinion.[53] These managers seem to walk around holding their breath, fearful that someone might ask them a pointed question. Once, during a heated discussion involving much yelling and gesturing, two people who were arguing turned to a third colleague, each looking for support. The colleague was almost totally spineless even though the outcome of the argument was going to affect him directly. Instead of choosing sides, offering a compromise, or even offering a third option, he just stood there staring at the floor. After more than a few moments with no response, the two who had been arguing looked at him, looked at each other, looked at him again, and looked at each other once more. Finally, one said, "Hello? Anyone home?" The entire argument stopped cold while Mr. Spineless stared at the floor. Ultimately the two settled the argument, and things broke up. Later, Mr. Spineless said that he was so shocked to see the other two yelling that he couldn't respond. The problem was that he couldn't decide who was going to win, and rather than take a chance or try to figure out who was right, he pretended that his brain had locked up on him.

Because of their insecurities, the spineless will not commit to things and will not direct people in what to do. As with the other signs of maliciousness, this one is self-evident. Because this behavior is seen, the incompetence of spineless managers eventually is exposed, and few last long in any one place. This is not to say that they can't, for reasons strange and bizarre, be found in upper management. They can. However, you would not find as many of these as you would the next four types.

Some successful managers can still be classified as malicious. This is so because when dealing with other people, sometimes it's not whether you win or lose; it's how you play the game. Some extremely malicious people (Hitler, Attila the Hun, Stalin) had what they would argue was some degree of success. We typically reject a Machiavellian world in which anything goes in the name of winning (winning meaning that the individual gets what he or she wants regardless of what happens to others). The ends do not justify the means. An example of one who sometimes succeeds is the workaholic manager.

Workaholic Managers   These managers are the first to arrive and the last to leave. They often work on Saturdays, Sundays, and holidays. This would be fine,

Split-Personality Managers
managers who display two contrasting personalities

Grumps
managers who are constantly in a bad mood

Hoarders
managers who accumulate and guard resources, believing people are plotting to take their power or territory

Spineless Managers
managers who avoid decisions so that they avoid being held accountable later

NetNote

Dilbert.com
http://www.unitedmedia.com/comics/dilbert/

Dilbert Zone—check out the Web site for this popular cartoon about work.

Workaholic Managers
managers who work virtually all the time and expect equal dedication from others

Players of Mind Games
managers who take pleasure in psychologically aggravating people

Perfectionists
managers who think all work must be completely without defect or error

Intimidators
managers who bully

except that most **workaholic managers** expect their people to do the same.[54] One workaholic manager put cots in the workplace to remind people that their 12- to 14-hour workdays could be worse—they could be 24-hour workdays. Worse yet, workaholic managers seem to travel in groups.[55] Entire organizations can be composed of these workaholics, so it is important to know whether or not you can fit in with these people before making a major commitment to what is essentially an entire lifestyle.

Players of Mind Games   These managers constitute another group. These malicious managers take perverse pleasure in psychologically aggravating people. For **players of mind games,** it is not enough to yell; it is what they yell or say. The comments work on people's emotions, doubts, and self-esteem. The mind games may involve twists of logic and reason designed to confound and confuse others. Some of these managers have no tact or no patience, or they have to keep other people off balance. The common thread is that the attacks and mental mind twists are personal: "How could you send that letter? That's not English! Didn't you ever learn to write? You must be a worm!" And that is a mild example.[56]

Perfectionists   These managers seem to think that everyone must share in their compulsion. The malicious **perfectionist** with power often victimizes subordinates with numerous, highly detailed questions that it is unlikely any one person could answer.[57] Other perfectionists may make completely unreasonable demands of subordinates and then berate them publicly for not being able to complete the task. One perfectionist who sometimes screams at people with veins popping out of his head and fists banging on the desk until they leave in tears has a sign on the wall saying, "Be realistic. Demand the impossible."[58] Although we should strive to do the job right, perfectionists' standards are unrealistically high, and they perceive anything less, no matter how close to perfect it comes, as failure. In school, these people consider missing one item on a test with 50 or 100 questions failure. It is not just their high standards that stress other people, but rather the anything-less-is-totally-unacceptable attitude that accompanies them that seems to push these people into the poor manager category.

Intimidators   The final general type of malicious manager exhibits behavior that is often seen in other types. Whether as a means to push their perfectionist ideals or as part of mind games or to make up for their own deficiencies or mental inadequacies, some managers may become **intimidators.** Intimidators do not lead (at least not in the typical way), they do not persuade, they do not request. Instead, they bully people. They yell, insult, or scream to get what they want. Some intimidators return work they don't like torn into tiny pieces.[59] Others throw things, make people stay in meetings past midnight, withhold paychecks, or keep people waiting simply to demonstrate their power.[60] A few even work with a partner. While one plays the bad guy, screams and yells and stomps out of the room, the other plays the good guy, staying behind and remaining calm so as to smooth over the intimidation of the one playing the bad guy.[61] Intimidators are not just intelligent or tough; they can be either or both, and they want to display their power and position. Maybe they like to be bullies; maybe they can't think of another, more civil way to act; or maybe they don't believe other tactics will work. In any case, they and the other malicious and incompetent managers need to be dealt with.

Coping Strategies   Once you have identified the incompetent or malicious manager's type, you can choose the coping strategy that has the best chance of success. First, the responses to the specific types will be presented, followed by some general strategies. Note that the presentation covers actions you can take. There are other actions that some people do take that carry substantially greater risk and may have significantly less chance of resolving the issues. For example, some people may be tempted to sabotage the company, or get the bad boss fired, or come up with some other idea for vengeance, but these actions cannot be recommended. Even the idea of just taking it is not much of an answer. If people can simply tolerate the bad boss, they will. These strategies are for people who cannot or will not tolerate bad management.

When a clueless manager steps out of the Stone Age with an out-of-line remark or action, you must establish the limits of this behavior that you will tolerate. These managers need to be politely, yet firmly, educated on behavior in the twenty-first century.[62] Split-personality managers should be confronted about the bad side when the good side is facing you; they are more likely to listen when not in psycho mode. You need to take control calmly when the good side is showing, just as you need to take control with a grump. Grump bosses have given up, so you need to take charge. With a grump, you need to develop and present the answers. A grump won't act without insistence from others, because grumps have given up. Remember that they think things are going to fail before they start, so they feel no need to act.

The paranoid hoarder types might need to be dealt with in two stages. In the first stage, you question the boss and address basic trust. For example, if you catch the paranoid boss going through your things or excessively checking your work, discuss the issue in relation to how you feel.[63] Say something like, "I feel that you don't trust me.

269

What can I do to help or reassure you?" Showing the boss that you are aware of his or her behavior may induce change. Some may not change, and then you may have to go to the human resources department. Going to HR is your second choice, however; directly confronting any person you have conflict with is almost always the best choice.

You must also take control, in a way, when dealing with a spineless boss. With a spineless boss, you must offer specific options. It is important to offer more than one option. Offering one option lets the spineless boss just say no. Giving the spineless boss forced options makes him or her choose. Another option for dealing with the spineless boss is to give him or her a deadline for making a decision. It cannot be an ordinary deadline, though. With the spineless boss, you must give a deadline with a default option. The boss either selects an option by a certain date or you will enact a default option. For example, "I need a decision on the Smith account. If I don't hear from you by the 5th, I'll assume it's a go." If this sounds strong, remember that we are talking about a spineless boss, someone who excels at not making decisions, and this is affecting you. An anxiety attack may be the only thing that can get the spineless to grow some vertebrae.[64]

When faced with a workaholic, you must set limits (similar to handling the clueless). You must set the boundaries between work and the rest of your life.[65] Where this limit is can vary drastically with the job and the salary. Certain professions have hours falling outside the Monday through Friday, 9:00 A.M. to 5:00 P.M. block, so investigate this well before embarking on a career. Salary can also affect employer expectations. If the employer is paying you $250,000 a year, you have to expect to work more than 40 hours a week. If the career and the pay are accompanied by long days and weekend work, and if this is not for you, it is probably time to change jobs.

Mind gamers, perfectionists, and intimidators are all handled in a similar fashion. Of course, the easy advice is just to do things exactly the way they want them done. Frequently, these types make unreasonable and even impossible demands. If this is the case, remember that often they are playing a game—one that requires two players. Avoiding play can be difficult, but you can try to minimize contact with them and try to get from them specific objectives that can be completed. Also, stay calm. Some of these types seem to engage in behavior designed to upset you. To get upset is to play their game. As difficult as it might be, strive to maintain your calm and do not blame yourself. Sometimes people try to cope by looking for a reason for the actions of these types of managers. Looking at the manager or owner as a superior, some may feel that they brought the situation upon themselves.[66] When dealing with malicious or incompetent managers, keep in mind that they are the problem, not you.

What if these suggestions fail or the boss is not in one of these categories? What are your options? General actions include trying to accept the situation the way it is, talking to the boss, talking to the human resources department, talking to the boss's boss, and leaving.[67] Trying to accept the situation may not be the best solution, especially if you get tired of taking ulcer and colitis medications. As mentioned when discussing actions for specific types, talking to the boss may work if you follow certain guidelines.[68] First, stay calm. Subordinates will almost always lose in an argument with a boss, and when you lose your cool, you lose your credibility. Second, discuss the boss's behavior, not the boss. Do not attack the boss; instead, point out how the boss's actions are preventing you from completing your work. Third, be specific. If things are unacceptable, what is the boss supposed to do? How can she or he fix unacceptability? You must describe specific actions that will make the situation acceptable. Fourth, present facts, not opinions. Opinions, even if they are specific, can't replace facts.

If talking to the boss does not work, you may have to consider one of the other options. Each one carries some risk, however. If the company has a human resources department, you can try talking to a person there. Understand that a boss, even an incompetent or malicious one, will be in a stronger position just because he or she is a boss. You will need specific facts and evidence, and as many people to support your story as possible. Specific HR policies on harassment and behavior will also help. If this doesn't work or there is no HR department, then you can consider talking to the boss's boss if there is one. If the malicious or incompetent boss is the boss, then you have to choose another option. If your boss does have a boss, then you must consider the risks involved. If your boss and his or her boss are close, you will have a much more difficult job on your hands. Even if they are not close, you will have to evaluate the chance that the boss will retaliate and you could be worse off than before.

Given the risks associated with these last options, you may have to give serious thought to the final option, which is leaving. Leaving the situation really gives you two options. You could request a transfer, thus leaving the situation but maintaining your seniority with the organization. If this is not feasible, the last resort is to quit. Try not to leave before having another job to go to, but if this is what is needed in order to live a normal life, then you may have to do it. Life is too short to waste it with a boss from hell.

Good Managers The rather frightening picture of managers painted so far might leave you wondering if there are any good managers. Actually, most managers are at least adequate, and some are quite good. A number of companies, such as Disney, Saturn, and FedEx, seem to attract and hold good managers and share their insights with others.[69] Some of the most well-respected individual managers are listed in Table 8.3.

Good management starts, but certainly does not end, with some level of productivity and profitability. **Productivity** is the amount of goods or services a person produces in a given time. **Profitability** is the amount that revenues exceed expenses.[70] Without productivity and profitability, firms fail, and managers and workers are out of work. Good managers get the job done and constantly work to improve productivity and ensure profitability.[71] Management cannot be considered good when the only focus is on productivity and profits, however. Good management must go beyond profits to service three main groups—stockholders, customers, and employees. To focus only on the bottom line often means placing stockholders far above customers and employees. When management is concerned about all three, then success follows, which benefits all three groups.[72]

Productivity
the amount of goods or services created in a given time

Profitability
the amount that revenues exceed expenses

TABLE 8.3 SOME OF THE BEST MANAGERS AND THEIR COMPANIES

Manager	Company
Rose Marie Bravo	Burberry
William McGuire	United Health Group
Arthur Levinson	Genentech
George David	United Technologies
James McNerney	3M
Jonathon Grayer	Kaplan
Vivek Paul	Wipro
Ken Thompson	Wachovia
Steve Jobs	Pixar
Orin Smith	Starbucks

Source: "The Best Managers," *Business Week*, January 12, 2004, pp. 56–66.

After a concern for stockholders, customers, and employees, good management consists of:

- a concern for job basics
- workplace assessment and a concern for worker attitudes
- problem detection and correction
- an environment of trust
- a concern for social interactions
- valuing diversity
- empowerment
- providing recognition
- clear communications
- a clear overview of the business

An organization may not have all of these factors present, but it could still be regarded as having good management if most of these were present.

A concern for workplace basics is a fundamental prerequisite to determine if good management is being practiced. Workplace basics include reimbursement, respectful treatment, and interesting work.[73] Reimbursement includes salary and benefits. In an age when companies downsize to avoid paying benefits, there are still firms that value people. Some of these firms provide good wages and full benefits and find that they are not just profitable but highly competitive.[74] Respectful treatment includes treating everyone as having worth to the firm and not releasing people at the first sign of a decline.[75] Interesting work means that, as much as possible, people are given the chance to grow, to learn about the job, and to advance.[76] All three address the most basic tenets of work. Good managers strive to maximize each of these, realizing that it is more cost-effective in the long run to keep a well-maintained workforce than it is to take the cheaper route in the short term and pay out more in high turnover costs in the long run.[77]

Good managers are not only concerned about workplace basics; they are concerned about the working environment, too. In addition to the physical and mental environments discussed in Chapter 1, good managers are concerned with workplace assessment, worker attitudes, problem detection and correction, and creating an environment of trust.[78] Concern for the working environment includes measuring the characteristics of the environment (through climate studies and worker satisfaction studies) and continually monitoring these characteristics. Once problems are detected, the well-managed firm moves quickly to correct the situation. Good managers use these and other efforts to create an atmosphere of mutual trust. One of these other efforts is the use of open-book management. In open-book

NetNote

Psychology Today

http://www.psychologytoday. com/articles/pto-19930501- 000012.html

Article on good bosses.

management, everyone is taught how to follow the company's performance, and everyone is given free access to all financial information.[79] In the open environment, everyone's opinion is valued and given in an attempt to improve the organization so that the three main constituencies benefit.

In harmony with these ideals, good managers are concerned for the social interactions on the job; they value diversity and empower workers with the freedom to do their jobs to the best of their abilities. One of the reasons people work is for social interaction. Good managers recognize this and, as much as is practical, cultivate it.[80] Not only do good managers sanction social interactions, but they also realize that people can find ways around restrictions on interactions. Why not work with workers rather than against them? (See "Reality Check: No Talking in the Graveyard.") In addition, not endorsing social interactions would be counter to an open, concerned environment. This would also be true for not valuing diversity and empowerment. In an open environment concerned with giving workers what they need to accomplish the job for the good of the organization, it would be unthinkable to say that only a certain group can be open and only this group will be listened to. Good managers value all opinions and encourage opinions to be presented in a clear, direct, and nonthreatening manner.[81]

With a great focus on people, and a great effort and acceptance of responsibility expected of them, workers need feedback in order to know how well they are performing. The recognition and feedback must be monetary and psychological and must be given to teams and individuals.[82] Feedback ideally comes from the work itself; the worker should be able to tell whether or not a good job has been done. Recognition comes from others, including peers and managers.[83] The feedback does not always have to be expensive and can include Employee of the Month awards and dinner for the employee and his or her spouse (to recognize that sacrifices are often made at home also).[84]

The better managers are often wise enough to know when *not* to follow the example of their previous boss, realizing that their styles and the methods of the past may not be applicable today. A good manager today knows how to probe for occasions to help the whole organization to succeed.[85] These managers may ask workers, "What keeps you from doing a better job?" or "What's preventing you from doing your best work?" Note the difference between these questions and "How's it going?" Rather than an answer of "Okay," the first two questions require an

REALITY CHECK

No Talking in the Graveyard

The Union Oil Refinery in Lemont, Illinois, maintained a large tank farm—rows of oil storage tanks, with levees surrounding each tank to hold the oil should the tank burst. The tank farm was created partly by excavating an old graveyard. The relatives of the people in two of the graves could not be located, so the graves remained on a hill almost as high as the tanks. In summer, college students managed by some very classical managers maintained the grounds around the tanks. Due to erosion from rain, teams of three student workers were constantly raking the levees. There was a

no-talking policy on the levees. Evidently the managers thought that their workers could not talk and rake at the proper rate. The managers never stayed out in the sun long, but they would occasionally drive up to enforce the proper distance between rakers. Unfortunately for them, the rakers could see them coming for two miles off, so they would spread out when they saw the dust cloud from the manager-laden truck approaching. The height of the antisocial rules concerned the graveyard, which was properly maintained at all times. The managers would never climb the 70 stairs to the top, but each week, as two people carried a lawn mower up the stairs to the little plot of grass, they were reminded that no talking was allowed in the graveyard either.

explanation. A good manager will take that explanation and work to remove barriers and improve conditions and performance.

All these considerations would be insignificant if managers failed to possess other characteristics. Good managers must be able to communicate their ideas, requirements, and expectations of their subordinates clearly, and good managers must have a clear understanding of how the organization as a whole functions.[86] If managers cannot communicate, and in the context of good management this includes upward, downward, and horizontal communication, then all the efforts just listed will be for nothing. Good managers communicate often, in person, and clearly, and this is one of the most important keys to success.[87] Lastly, if managers fail to grasp the big picture, if they do not understand how all of the areas are integrated and interrelated, they will not be able to maintain the success and growth of the organization.[88] Managers must be able to plan, organize, control, and direct the financial, informational, and material resources with the human resources to ensure the long-term success of the firm and to be considered good management.

SUMMARY

This chapter explored the role of management and the relationship between managers and workers with the hope that understanding management and the role of managers will lead to better relations and increased unity.

In describing management's role in an organization, the four functions of management (planning, controlling, organizing, and directing) were presented along with the four resources managers must handle (human, financial, material, and informational). The interrelationship among these areas results in 16 facets of the same managerial working environment.

Because decision making is a major part of the managerial function, the major types of decisions that managers must make were presented. Here again, the effort was directed toward understanding the situation managers are in, rather then delving into theories of how decisions are made. By understanding the type of decision a manager has made, you may be able to cope with any negative effects from that decision.

Principles of management not pertaining to formal organizational structures (which were in Chapter 7) were defined and their effect on the working environment described. Classical and behavioral management theories were described along with the relationship between them; they are two ends of a management continuum. A few managers might actually be classified as extremely behavioral or classical; most are somewhere in between, and some may use methods from either end of the continuum as needed for the situation or the person.

The chapter differentiated between good management and poor management and described the worker's role in an organization. TQM, now an integral part of most organizations, was outlined. Finally, coping strategies to use when you are being managed were discussed.

CHECKING FOR UNDERSTANDING

1. Describe management's role in organizations.
2. List and define the four functions of management.
3. List and define the four resources of management.
4. Describe the managerial working environment.
5. Define the management principles and their effect on the working environment.
6. List and describe the types of decisions managers make.
7. List and describe the characteristics of classical management.
8. List and describe the characteristics of behavioral management.
9. What is the significance of the management continuum?

10. How can we differentiate between good management and poor management?

11. What are the steps in the TQM process?

12. Describe strategies for coping with being managed.

13. Why is it important for you as a subordinate to do the best job you can?

14. What is the difference between productivity and profitability?

15. Top management has called in a consultant for the area you work in. What action should you take to protect yourself and your interests?

SELF-ASSESSMENT

How do you feel about management in general? Select SA for Strongly Agree, A for Agree, U for Undecided, D for Disagree, and SD for Strongly Disagree.

1. Managers perform work vital to the organization. *SA A U D SD*

2. Managers don't work; they go to meetings. *SA A U D SD*

3. I resent taking orders from my manager. *SA A U D SD*

4. Managers expect perfection from workers. *SA A U D SD*

5. Managers motivate me. *SA A U D SD*

6. Managers are only concerned about saving money. *SA A U D SD*

7. Managers make logical decisions for the good of the organization. *SA A U D SD*

8. Managers expect workers to be workaholics. *SA A U D SD*

9. Managers are more knowledgeable than workers are. *SA A U D SD*

10. Most managers are incompetent. *SA A U D SD*

11. Managers give a fair day's work for a fair day's pay. *SA A U D SD*

12. Managers expect loyalty but give none in return. *SA A U D SD*

13. A manager is more like a coach than a boss. *SA A U D SD*

14. A manager's decisions mainly benefit him or her personally. *SA A U D SD*

15. Managers care about workers. *SA A U D SD*

For all odd-numbered items score 2 for every SA, 1 for every S, 0 for every U, −1 for every D, and −2 for every SD.

For all even-numbered items score −2 for every SA, −1 for every S, 0 for every U, 1 for every D, and 2 for every SD.

Total your score. A score of 19–30 indicates a very positive view of managers and management, 7–18 a positive view, from −6–6 an undecided or mixed view, −7–−18 a less favorable view, and −19–−30 a very unfavorable view.

SKILL BUILD 8

Andrea seems to need some help analyzing this situation. Use the course materials for this chapter to help her identify what is going on.

Frank Pierce leaned back in his chair with his elbows bent and on the armrests, the fingertips of both hands touching each other. He looked at Andrea Jackson, did not invite her to sit, and then looked away and gazed out his side window. After a few seconds passed he spoke.

"And what would the newest of our managers possibly want with me?"

"I understand that you are the head of IT, correct?" Andrea asked.

"Yes. Yes, I am," Frank replied.

"Well, I have to combine three departments that were separate into one department of teams, so I need to know certain things, and Human Resources said that while they have collected what I need you are the one to talk to about getting what I want from the database. Is that right?" Andrea said.

Skill Question 1. What is Andrea trying to do, that is, what management function is she trying to perform?

Skill Question 2. Define that function in your own words.

Skill Question 3. What management resource is she trying to get from Frank Pierce?

Skill Question 4. Define that resource in your own words.

"Maybe. I think first I need to know how you will arrange everyone," Frank said.

"Teams, like I said," Andrea replied.

"Yes, I know, but how will you run them? How will they be controlled?" Frank persisted.

"I don't really see how that matters to you," Andrea said, a little frustrated.

"A database can be very tricky. One must know the parameters of the paradigm. The constraints of the construct. The perimeter of the periphery, so to speak. Otherwise the interrogation of the database may lack perspicuity."

Andrea just stared at Frank.

Skill Question 5. Which incompetent manager tactic is Frank using here? (*Hint*: The answer is *not* delaying tactic.)

"You see," Frank said, "this is just what I am talking about. You don't really understand these things, while I do. This is why you must elucidate."

"Do you mean that I plan to form teams of people who will learn as part of their job, so that they grow? That they will receive feedback and recognition and be freer to do their jobs so that they have a chance to like their work? That I see them as being motivated by things other than just money? That I plan to be a team leader rather than boss them around? Is that what you mean?" Andrea said, annoyed at having to explain herself.

Skill Question 6. What style of management is Andrea proposing to use?

Skill Question 7. How did this style of management come about (after what event)?

"It is, as I feared," Frank replied, "completely the wrong way to go about it. You can't control people that way. Managers have an inherent right to control subordinates. That right must be exercised regularly and vigorously for, like any muscle, it will weaken and be useless without exercise. You must tell these people what to do, every step of the way. Your job is to find out what your workers are doing and make them stop, for without your constant presence they are surely slacking off. Without a firm hand I'm afraid anything I can provide you from the database will be wasted."

Skill Question 8. Frank Pierce is basically lecturing Andrea on how he thinks a department should be run. What one management *principle* is he basing his management ideas on?

Skill Question 9. What *style* of management is Frank telling Andrea to use?

Skill Question 10. How did this style of management come about?

"Are you refusing?" Andrea asked, incredulous.

"Let us say that I prefer not embark upon efforts that will fuel future failure," Frank replied coolly.

At this, Andrea lost it a bit, "Listen, you jerk, I am managing a frontline department vital to this organization. *You* are in a staff, a *supporting*, position, and it is *your* job to provide me with what I need to do *my* job. *Got it*?"

"Even if I wanted to, and your tone hardly provides the proper incentive, I can't," Frank replied calmly.

"*Why not?*" Andrea yelled, obviously mad and frustrated.

"Because you do not have the right forms. A form is needed for all requests *and* that form must go through proper channels. We can't have just anyone walk in here asking for things, now can we. You need a Form 54, Request for Database Penetration on Behalf of Non-IT Personnel. You will also need a Form 22, Authorization to View an IT Database Extraction by Non-IT Personnel," Frank explained.

Skill Question 11. Based on everything he has said so far, what type of malicious manager is Frank?

"What? Look, I already talked to my boss, Donghai Wu, and he said this wouldn't be a problem," Andrea said, even more frustrated.

"Well, this is my department, and in my department we do things properly, by the procedure manual, not by vague recollections of dubious conversations. Without those forms I'm afraid I just can't help you. Now, I have other matters to attend to. If you do get those forms please come back and we can talk again," Frank said, and he turned his chair around to face away from Andrea.

Skill Question 12. Which incompetent manager tactic is Frank using here? (*Hint*: The answer is not delaying tactic, nor is it the same one he used earlier.)

Andrea was so mad it took her about 20 minutes to calm down and start looking for Donghai Wu.

"Andrea," Donghai said cheerily, "how are things going so far?"

"Most things are going fine, but do you remember telling me how I could get some HR materials from the IT department?" Andrea asked.

"I did?" Donghai replied.

"Yes, remember? I need to form all those people from the three old departments into teams? It was just yesterday!"

"Hmmm. Not ringing any bells really," Donghai said.

"But, this is the only thing I have asked you for!" Andrea said, astounded.

"Getting something from IT, huh? Something from Frank Pierce? See, he's a tough customer. I try not to deal with him," Donghai said.

"Okay, you may not want to deal with him, but you said I could," Andrea persisted.

"Dunno. Kinda hazy," Donghai replied.

Skill Question 13. Donghai Wu is initially using what method to cope with decisions? (*Hint*: What he is doing is not something a good manager would use to cope with decisions.)

"All right, whatever. He said I need a couple of forms filled out anyway, so I'll ask you now, can I get those?" Andrea said.

"Oh, gee. That might upset Frank Pierce, and upsetting him could cause our VP, Bill Carter, to look badly upon us or at least to look badly on my boss, Stefany Cleveland. See, she is working on a promotion and really wants to keep all the wheels from squeaking. See, if Ms. Cleveland is unhappy, that's not good for us and our careers, is it? Isn't there some other way?"

"Sure," Andrea said.

Skill Question 14. What type of decision is Donghai Wu making? This is a little tricky because it is a decision-making method that he is using in order to justify *not* making a decision. So to find the type of decision look at *why* he is not making the decision.

"Ms. Cleveland? I'm Andrea Jackson, the new manager? We met during orientation?" Andrea said, after spending an hour tracking Stefany down.

"Oh. Yes. Is there something I can do for you?" Stefany said.

"Actually, there is. I'm trying to get some HR reports from IT, and it seems I need some forms completed and thought you might tell me how to get those," Andrea explained.

Stefany stared at Andrea for a few seconds and finally said, "My dear, I couldn't possibly make such a decision. You would have to talk to someone else." Then she turned and walked away.

Skill Question 15. What type of decision-making tactic does Stefany Cleveland use on Andrea?

APPLICATIONS

8.1 WHOM TO GO TO?

Lenny and Carlton are supervisors with a big problem—they need to find a manager to make a major decision. Lenny and Carlton have a vital project that needs the right combination of workers and sufficient money to be completed successfully. Unfortunately for them, supervisors in their company do not have the authority to reassign people, nor do they have access to budgets. Lenny and Carlton have eight managers they might go to, but need to select the one that will give them the best chance of a good decision.

Lenny: I'm not excited about going to Walter Brenner, there's no sense to it. We might as well go right to his boss because that's where we'll end up. The last time Brenner made a decision on his own Nixon was president.

Carlton: Sue Teeson will make us put it in writing, then she'll want 10 copies, then she'll make us rewrite it, copy it again, then on different paper, and, well, you know what she is like.

Lenny: Yeah, and then she would make us have a bake sale to get the money. What about Dave Hall?

Carlton: What's in it for him? First thing he'll want to know. He only decides things if they make him look good.

Lenny: Zondra Jones-Creighton, now she's not like any of them.

Carlton: She has a lot on her plate. In fact, I think she has about 10 plates—all full. You know she has been the first one here and the last to leave for the last two years? Might be tough for her to squeeze us in. Diana Waters looks busy, but is she really?

Lenny: Heck no, she's just trying to keep people from catching up with her. Even if we did talk to her, she'd duck out on vacation until we found someone else. What about Lamont Williams? He'd make time for us, or anybody. If there are other problems, he'll find them and fix them. He won't give us any more money than we absolutely need, though.

Carlton: Yeah, but he won't give us any less either. He gives credit where credit is due, too.

Lenny: True. Although, we catch Sheila Hills on a good day, and we might get whatever we want.

Carlton: What are the odds of that? Not better than 50/50, I'd say. She might take care of this, and she might take our heads off, and there's no way of knowing beforehand which it will be. What about Mark Preeda? I don't know him too well.

Lenny: They call him "The Twister" because he'll twist your brain or leave you twistin' in the wind.

We mess with him, and by the time we get done, we'll be paying for this out of our own pockets and feeling about two inches tall. Then he'll rip us again if we can't change those two inches into microns in our heads!

QUESTIONS

1. Lenny and Carlton's problem involves which one of the four functions of management?

2. What two managerial resources are involved here?

3. There are eight managers. Three make particular kinds of decisions. Who are they, and what type of decisions do they make? One shows signs of being an incompetent manager. Who is this, and what incompetent behaviors does this person show? Three appear to be malicious; who are they and what type are they? That leaves one—the best choice. Who is it? Give evidence from the situation to support each of your answers.

8.2 INCOMPETENT MANAGERS: THEIR SIGNS AND SYMPTOMS

Incompetent managers may display one or more signs or symptoms of their incompetence. It is vital for you to be able to identify these managers from these signs and symptoms. Define each of these and explain them in your own words. What exactly will you look for?

1. denial

2. playing it by the numbers

3. buck passing

4. obfuscation

5. abdication

6. delaying tactics

7. escaping

NET-WORK

A classical or behavioral manager—you be the judge.

http://www.youtube.com/watch?v=6EU1P-lsjlk&mode=related&search=

What exactly does this manager want? How can the minimum not also be acceptable?

http://www.youtube.com/watch?v=-1Kj4-23ly4

PERSONAL POINTS

1. Which of the various decisions have you made or which can you see yourself having to make? What could you have done or what could you do to avoid the decisions?

2. How do you feel about the classical system of management? When might you use it or when would you not use it?

3. How do you feel about behavioral management? When might you use it or when would you not use it?

4. Given your choice, where do you want to be on the management continuum and why? Would you want to be in one spot or be able to manage at any point, and why?

5. Are you now or have you ever been one of the types of incompetent or malicious managers and why? Do you now or have you ever had a manager that was a type of incompetent or malicious manager? What did you do about him or her? Knowing what you now know, what would you do about him or her?

EXPERIENTIAL EXERCISE

The Middle Manager's Quandary

This exercise requires a group of at least four subordinates, a middle manager, and a top manager (typically the course professor).

1. The top manager (professor) should take the subordinates out of the room and instruct them in preparation for the exercise. The subordinates are told that as far as they are concerned, they are working as fast as they can, their quality is perfectly acceptable, and there is no way they can work any overtime. They are free to use whatever excuses or explanations they want as long as they stick to these points and do not compromise or give in.

2. The top manager (professor) should leave the subordinates outside the room for the moment and instruct the middle manager in front of the remainder of the class. The middle manager is told (by the professor acting as top manager) that in the top manager's opinion, the quality of this group of workers must improve, they must work faster, and they need to work at least eight hours of overtime per week (paid at time-and-a-half, of course). Also, the company cannot afford to fire these people because replacements are not available, which is also why the company cannot just hire more people to increase production. While the middle manager contemplates his or her methods, the top manager (professor) should retrieve the subordinates. The department meeting between the middle manager and the subordinates may now begin.

3. Of course, if all play their parts, there will be an impasse. After the meeting has gone on for a few minutes, the top manager should request a progress report. As no progress is likely to be evident, the top manager should remind the middle manager that it may be necessary to replace him or her if he or she cannot get the job done and get the subordinates to agree to the company's desires. After one or two of these reminders, it may actually be necessary to replace the middle manager (or the middle manager may quit). When picking the original middle manager and any replacements, the professor should try to select people who are convinced they will be (or are) great managers or who think management is easy or unnecessary.

4. In the end, the professor should reveal the situation and instructions given the subordinates. Point out that, although the subordinates were told to be unyielding, the situation is still quite realistic, and it illustrates the middle manager's quandary, which is how to satisfy the needs of the subordinates and the demands of upper management. Middle managers are often caught just like this—between a rock and a hard place. This exercise can be very effective because being the middle manager is a good experience for those who think they have all the answers. It is also interesting to note the approach the middle manager takes in trying to persuade the unyielding subordinates.

SPOT CHECK ANSWERS

1. F
2. F
3. T
4. T
5. T
6. T
7. F
8. T
9. F
10. T
11. T
12. T
13. T
14. F
15. F

9

Small Groups and the Informal Organization

The problem facing almost all leaders in the future will be how to develop their organization's social architecture so that it actually generates intellectual capital.

Warren Bennis

Groups, like individuals, have shortcomings. Groups can bring out the worst as well as the best in people.

Irving L. Janis

GOALS

This chapter will discuss the power, influence, and inner working of informal groups, small groups, and teams. The use of groups and teams is increasing in the workplace, and the behavior exhibited by the people in them can be complex. This behavior can also have a profound effect on you and how you feel about your job.

A large body of theory related to the dynamics of group behavior has developed. Our approach here will not be to explore each theory in depth but, instead, to try to glean from past research those ideas that can be applied in a practical manner to the everyday organizational behavior of small work groups in which you may be participating now or in the future.

OBJECTIVES

When you finish this chapter, you should be able to:

▶ Describe the purpose and nature of formal and informal groups.

▶ Describe group-member characteristics.

▶ List and describe factors affecting group attractiveness and cohesion.

▶ Identify the types of group-member behavior associated with small groups.

▶ Explain how informal groups utilize the grapevine.

▶ Describe methods for conducting effective meetings.

▶ List, describe, and differentiate between two group formation models.

▶ List and describe methods for maximizing team efforts.

GROUPS

Most people are members of a wide variety of groups, such as household, school, social, religious, and work groups. Being a member of a group or groups is usually a basic part of our lives because, for the most part, humans are social creatures. According to Maslow's hierarchy of needs principle, social belonging follows immediately after the need for safety and the physiologic needs for food, shelter, clothing, and water. Although one reason groups exist is that they are part of our basic nature, there are other reasons as well.

WHAT IS A GROUP?

Group
two or more individuals who interact

Do you remember reading in Chapter 1 that whenever two or more people are together, there is in effect an organization? The same premise also applies to our meaning of the term **group.** Although not all scholars agree on the precise definition of a group, for our purposes we'll define the term as two or more individuals who interact personally or through communication networks. Groups usually share (or are supposed to share) similar goals, experiences, or needs.

Based on our definition, then, a husband and wife, an assembly team in a factory, and the members of a large multinational corporation could all be considered groups. Although it is apparent that groups vary in size, our principal focus in this chapter will be on the behavior and problems associated with smaller groups, those that interact on a face-to-face basis rather than through official interoffice or interdivisional communication networks.

GROUP FORMATION

What causes people to join groups? Years ago, social scientists believed that people were a lot like sheep and therefore had a flock instinct not unlike that of their woolly, four-legged cousins. Most social scientists today reject this theory and believe that people tend to join groups for reasons such as those cited in Figure 9.1. We'll look briefly at each of these factors.

Security Have you ever noticed that when you're home alone at night, you feel somewhat different than when you're there with someone else? Do the squeaks and creaks in the dark recesses of the house sound much louder and spookier when you're alone? Does the presence of another person (or even a pet) tend to give you a greater feeling of security? The need for security is an important reason people form groups such as neighborhood watch groups, unions, rifle associations, industrial cartels, medical associations, and so on.

In an organizational setting, forming a buying committee could enable individuals who are responsible for making organizational purchases to feel more secure. A buying committee is an ongoing, established group whose function is to determine the best sources for the organization's purchases. Each member of the committee may feel more secure in his or her buying decisions because the responsibility for a bad decision is shared with others. No single member of the group is solely responsible for the group's actions.

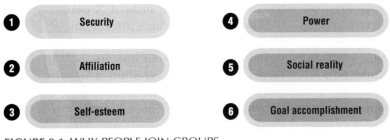

FIGURE 9.1 WHY PEOPLE JOIN GROUPS

Affiliation   Don't you generally prefer to be with other people who share your interests and values? This tendency, **affiliation,** is another reason why people generally want to be a part of a group. Some people join computer support groups to share ideas, knowledge, and software. Some people join Edsel owner clubs to share their feelings of owning a "successful failure." Managers sometimes join service groups, such as Kiwanis, to be able to exchange ideas (and business cards) with other managers in the locality. Engineers may join engineering societies, insurance risk managers may join associations of risk managers, procurement managers may join associations to share ideas on purchasing. Some organizational members may affiliate with others at work on an informal basis, perhaps regularly eating lunch together or playing softball together on company teams. People tend to affiliate more with groups that they join voluntarily than with groups to which they are formally assigned.

Self-Esteem   Membership in some groups tends to affect its members' feelings of **self-esteem,** or worth. For example, imagine being a part of the management team of a company on the verge of bankruptcy, alleged by the popular press to be responsible for the mismanagement of its resources. Wouldn't your feelings toward yourself, as well as those of others toward you, be higher if instead you worked for a high-technology company that was considered one of the most innovative, progressive, and profitable in the industry? Membership in certain groups can therefore provide individuals with good feelings about themselves that they might otherwise lack.

Power   "In numbers there is strength" advises an old adage. Being a member of a group, therefore, helps individuals to acquire strength—that is, power—which is difficult if not impossible to attain alone. Power is defined as the possession of control, authority, or influence over others. Membership in a union or employee association, for example, provides workers with influence—the bargaining strength—that they lack as individual employees.

Social Reality   Another purpose of groups is to establish and test **social reality.** For example, when several individuals have similar attitudes about perceived unfair treatment by their boss, they tend to feel more secure in their beliefs because of the consensus of opinion that develops. The group members create their own reality, regardless of how accurate their perception of the situation may be.

Goal Accomplishment   Mountain climbers, basketball players, and astronauts—like the members of any work unit—generally function in groups. The group enables its members to accomplish their goals more readily because of the variety of skills and knowledge that can be collectively provided.

GROUP SYNERGY

In basic mathematics, we learn the concept of **synergy,** that the whole of an object is equal to the sum of its parts. With group relationships, however, the whole is often greater than the sum of its parts. This concept is termed **synergism,** the interaction of two or more independent parts, the effects of which are different from those that would be attained by each part individually.

A group has more information than any of its individual members. Thus problems that require the use of knowledge should give groups an advantage over individuals. Even if one member of the group (for example, the leader)

Affiliation
being with other people who share your interests and values

Self-Esteem
having pride in yourself, self-respect; a feeling of self-worth

Social Reality
security in one's beliefs due to support or consensus of opinion from colleagues

Synergy
a whole that is greater than the sum of its parts

Synergism
the interaction of two or more independent parts, the effects of which are different from that which would be attained by each individually

knows much more than anyone else, the limited unique knowledge of lesser-informed individuals could serve to fill in some gaps in knowledge. For example, a skilled machinist might contribute to an engineer's problem solving, and an ordinary worker might supply information on how a new machine might be received by workers.

Let's look at the synergistic effect that two separate departments, sales and manufacturing, can have on customer satisfaction. Some salespeople promise customers that their purchases will be delivered by a certain date and that the quality of the finished product will be of a particular standard. If the manufacturing department cooperates by meeting deadlines and quality standards, customer satisfaction is maintained or enhanced. Of course, if such cooperation and coordination are lacking, the synergistic effect on customers' attitudes will be adversely affected.

THE NATURE OF FORMAL AND INFORMAL GROUPS

Groups tend to be a basic part of organizational life. Regardless of the type of group we might discuss, most work groups have split personalities. They have their formal role and their informal, or social, role. Let's examine the principal differences between the two.

FORMAL GROUPS AND ROLES

Formal Groups
required systems formed by management

Required Systems
a group positioned and coordinated by management for attaining organizational goals

Most **formal groups** are **required systems.** Required systems consist of individuals who are positioned and coordinated by management for the purpose of attaining predetermined organizational goals and objectives. Let's say, for example, that you own a bicycle and roller-skate sales and rental shop and employ five people to help you achieve your planned objectives. Your organization will typically have some sort of formal structure to achieve your goals of selling bicycles and roller skates, providing service, and making a profit.

Formal systems provide some degree of order and predictability in an organization. You assume, for example, based on your planning, that Suzy, Joe, and Karen—your staff of salespersons—will be on the job promptly at 9:00 A.M. each morning, as will Frank and Ernestine, both service repair workers. Your work group couldn't function as effectively without a formal—that is, required, planned, or orderly—system.

Formal organizations, then, exist for a variety of reasons. Basically, formal groups assist people to:

- accomplish goals much less haphazardly than in informal groups
- coordinate the activities or functions of the organization
- establish logical authority relationships among people and positions
- apply the concepts of specialization and division of labor
- create more group cohesion as a result of a common set of goals

INFORMAL GROUPS

In Chapter 10 we'll examine concepts related to human needs and motivation, concepts that are significant to the topic of small-group behavior, especially to its informal aspects. Let's return for a moment to your bicycle and roller-skate sales and service shop. Whether you are what your employees consider to be a good or a bad boss has little effect on the existence of an informal organization. You, as owner-manager of the shop, can create a formal work group, but you cannot eliminate an informal one as long as you have an organization. The **informal groups,** or social groups, emerge in one form or another, regardless of your personal wishes, although you can influence their activities and behavior.

Informal Groups
social groups that emerge spontaneously without the assistance or consent of formal groups

WHY DO INFORMAL GROUPS EMERGE?

We've already discussed the reasons groups generally form, as well as the major purposes of formal groups. Many of the same reasons apply to informal groups. Don't informal groups also have goals and objectives? Don't most individuals have various sorts of psychological and social needs that require satisfying? However, the required systems seldom satisfy all individual and social needs, so informal groups come galloping to the rescue. But what, exactly, are informal groups, and are they a good or a bad thing?

Although the formal organization described in Chapter 7 represents the way things are supposed to be, the informal organization is the way things really are.[1] The informal organization represents the social relations in the organization and the true way that power is distributed. The informal organization takes into account who likes and dislikes whom, who is effective and knowledgeable and who is not, who is related to, dating, or having an affair with whom, and which people are outspoken or have more charisma or personal power. The informal organization exists in tandem with, and in spite of, the formal organization. Although it is common to diagram formal organizations, it is much less common to diagram informal organizations. One reason is that the informal organization changes frequently. Another reason is that informal organization diagrams can be quite complex (see Figure 9.2).[2]

Informal organizations will always exist; there is no known way to totally eliminate them. Sometimes they are good (working toward organization goals), and sometimes they are bad (working against organization goals). One of the ways informal organizations aid formal organizations is in the informal organization's ability to close gaps in the structure. If a person is missing from the formal organization,

REALITY CHECK

Informal Talk

It used to be water-cooler or hallway talk, but whatever name is used, informal conversations can be useful in bonding relationships among coworkers, superiors, or subordinates. In fact, informal conversations are often equally important as formal communications. There are three guidelines for maximizing the effectiveness of informal conversations, involving the person, the time, and the topic.

Some people are more receptive to small talk than others. It is important to select someone who is open to informal conversations; otherwise your attempts may be viewed as an annoying waste of time. Even when you have found someone to have an informal chat with, pay close attention to his or her nonverbal communication. Know when to end the conversation so you are not keeping the other person from other tasks. This overlaps with the second guideline: choosing the best time for small talk. Consider the other person's temperament and situation that day so you know when it is acceptable to start an informal conversation. Third, select an appropriate topic. General topics about last weekend, family, or the big game are safer than topics about one's work or personal interests. Less safe are topics like politics and religion. Remember that the value of these conversations is in bringing people together, not splitting them apart. Used effectively, informal conversations can increase group cohesiveness and trust and keep you in touch with others.

Source: Diana Booher, "Making a Big Deal Out of Small Talk," *Business Credit,* May 1999, p. 8.

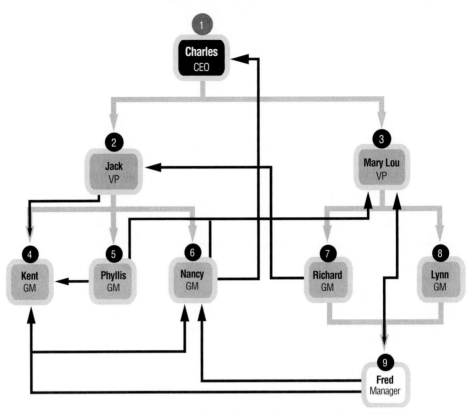

FIGURE 9.2 CONTACT CHART DEPICTING THE FORMAL ORGANIZATION (THE WAY THINGS ARE SUPPOSED TO BE) WITH GRAY LINES AND THE INFORMAL ORGANIZATION (THE WAY THINGS REALLY ARE) WITH BLACK LINES   This shows who actually speaks with whom about work-related issues.

the informal organization can compensate, or work around, the void. On many occasions, the informal organization provides the speed needed to accomplish objectives quickly; waiting to go through formal channels would sometimes mean that opportunities would be missed. On the other hand, the informal organization can work against the goals of the organization when it influences people to work slower, when it wastes time fretting over false rumors, or when informal organization cliques fight over power and members.

There is little doubt that informal groups sometimes create problems for organizations. They can transmit false information (rumors) through the grapevine, resist change, cause excessive conformity to group norms, and sometimes even develop goals that conflict with those of the formal organization. The members of the group may ostracize or exclude an employee from social interaction. For example, a person whose work pace is faster than the norm for a particular group might be looked upon as a "ratebuster" who is trying to show up the other group members. The group will inform the overachiever of the going rate and encourage the person to conform. If conformity is not forthcoming, additional and sometimes stronger methods of persuasion will be applied.

The informal organization can, however, perform a variety of positive and useful functions. As already mentioned, informal groups help the individual members satisfy psychological and social needs. In large plants and offices, a person could feel like merely an employee number instead of a human being if it were not for the opportunity to socialize and interact with other members of the group.

GROUP BEHAVIOR

Groups are dynamic. Managers often express amazement at the strange behavior of some employees when they are grouped together. It's important to realize, however, that all sorts of factors can influence behavior in groups, such as the membership of the group itself, the cohesiveness of the group, the work environment, and the grapevine as a means of informal communication among group members. First, we will examine the characteristics of group members.

GROUP-MEMBER CHARACTERISTICS

Groups, as we know, are a lot like individuals. Both groups and individuals have distinct needs, personalities, and beliefs about what constitutes acceptable, or so-called normal, behavior. But individuals often undergo a kind of metamorphosis when they become part of a group, and their concepts of what ought to be may be altered along with their personalities.

Individuals also have roles to play in the group. These roles are assumed or assigned in every group. One person, and sometimes more than one, leads. Some people are followers, some contribute, and some just seem to watch. Often there is a secretary, or recorder. Some people play **devil's advocate,** meaning that they argue against their own beliefs or against the group consensus in order to probe for holes in the logic. Any weakness in the group's position can then be corrected, so a devil's advocate is actually trying to help the group. However, certain people will argue against what everyone else thinks simply because they like to argue or because they wish to delay the process. Because such people have their own reasons, which typically have little or nothing to do with helping the group, they often succeed in simply blocking the group's efforts. If blockers do not cause trouble for the group, sometimes the roles themselves cause problems.

Group roles cause problems in three main ways. The problems may stem from **role conflict,** ambiguity, or overload.[3] Role conflict can occur when your group role does not match your other roles. For example, Beth is a vice president assigned to a social committee made up of middle managers and frontline workers. Beth's outside role is as a leader and autonomous decision maker. For this committee, a frontline worker is selected leader, and Beth must make decisions in conjunction with the others. Conflict can occur especially within strong leaders when they are not in leadership positions.

Role ambiguity can occur when there is confusion over the roles and their boundaries. This sometimes happens with leaderless teams. As in the situation with Beth, sometimes it is assumed that the highest-ranking person is in charge. A leaderless team might be proposed as a way to equalize everyone, at least within the

Devil's Advocate
one who argues against the consensus in order to probe for weakness in the position

Role Conflict
differences between one's group role and one's other roles

Role Ambiguity
confusion over roles in a group and their boundaries

Role Overload

group or team assignments too great for a person

Group Standards

social norms; behavior acceptable to a group

Group Cohesion

an emotional attraction and closeness that members have for one another and for the group

Group Attractiveness

the ability to generate interest in others or the ability to entice others to join a group

group or team. Some must lead, if for no other reason than to ensure that roles are clear.[4] Things can easily fall between the cracks when roles are ambiguous, as when each person assumes the others will call the next meeting and no one does.

A related problem is **role overload.** If, in the effort to make the roles less ambiguous, all working roles are assigned to one (or a few) of the members, then he, she, or they can suffer from role overload. When the group or team assignment is too great for the person, the resultant role overload increases stress levels. The increase in stress can then cause a decrease in performance or withdrawal from the team.

If role problems are avoided or solved, then most groups or teams consciously or subconsciously set group norms. These **group standards,** known as social norms, have a powerful influence over the group member who wants to be accepted by peers. A shy, quiet office worker who seldom asserts himself when alone in an unfamiliar crowd may suddenly become boisterous and obnoxious when with friends. Most of us have read about or observed the antisocial activities of youth gangs, who as individuals alone would seldom behave in such a manner.

Some years ago, Solomon Asch conducted an experiment, now referred to as the Asch conformity studies,[5] that helps to illustrate how people tend to conform to group standards as a means of being accepted. Asch gathered several groups of eight people to participate in the experiment. The eight people sat in a row and were asked to judge the length of various lines. However, seven members of each group had been previously instructed by Asch to conspire against the remaining one. They were told to state the wrong answers in a confident manner two-thirds of the time. The subjects of the experiment in each group had to make their choices last. About 40 percent of the time, the unknowing individuals went along with the incorrect decisions of the group, admittedly because they didn't want to look silly in front of their peers, not because they believed the group's answers.

GROUP COHESION

Another common characteristic of group behavior is an emotional attraction and closeness, or **group cohesion** that members have for one another and their group. One way to tell that groups are becoming cohesive is when members stop saying "I" and start saying "we." Groups provide the mechanism for giving people a sense of identity and unity, something referred to as a feeling of belonging.

Some groups are highly cohesive. Their members stick closely together in spite of pressures to reduce their emotional ties. Other groups consist of members who couldn't care less about unity, solidarity, or group cohesiveness. They don't really feel part of a team. These people are merely a collection of individuals who may officially be members of the group but whose needs are not satisfied by the personal interaction with the group's other members.

At least seven factors initially attract people to informal and formal groups and teams. These are the same factors that increase team or group cohesion. There are also at least seven factors that decrease **group attractiveness** and cohesion. Both types of factors are listed in Table 9.1.

Factors That Increase Group Attractiveness and Cohesion As the prestige and status of a team or group increases, the attractiveness and cohesion of the team or group increases. If others admire or look up to the members of a team, or if the team wields significant amounts of power, then people will want to join the team and those on it will be more tightly knit. When a group is known for having members who cooperate and work well together, and when group membership increases the number of opportunities one has for interacting with others, then the group will

TABLE 9.1 GROUP ATTRACTIVENESS AND COHESION FACTORS

Factors That Increase Group Attractiveness and Cohesion	Factors That Decrease Group Attractiveness and Cohesion
Prestige	Group or group work has an unfavorable image
High status and power	Unreasonable demands made of members
Increased interactions with others	Disagreement over group norms
Members cooperate with each other	Competition to belong to other groups
Members face a common threat	Group and individual goals are dissimilar
Members are similar to one another	Gaining admission is too difficult
Small group size	Individual had previous unpleasant experience with the group or a group member

appear more attractive to join. This is especially true if the members themselves have high status or are people the individual wishes to interact with. When group members are cooperative, the group will be more cohesive as members strive to maintain their positive relations and try to increase interactions. When group members are similar, attractiveness and cohesion increase—people tend to choose to be with others who are like them. People also like to be with others who face the same threat they do, and often this common threat is the supervisor or management in general. While these factors increase cohesion, they also increase attractiveness. As attractiveness increases, more people wish to join. Group size, however, is inversely related to attractiveness and cohesion. Smaller groups are more attractive and cohesive. As attractiveness and cohesion increase, more people wish to join, but larger size decreases attractiveness and cohesion. There are seven other factors that work more directly to decrease attractiveness and cohesion.

Factors That Decrease Group Attractiveness and Cohesion   If a group's image is unfavorable, possibly because the work being performed is seen as too difficult or unpopular, then attraction to the group and cohesion among the group members will be low. This will also be true if the amount of work the team has to perform is regarded as excessive. Disagreement among the group members over group norms, the group's mission, or team outcomes will decrease attractiveness and cohesion. Attractiveness and cohesion will also decrease if people have many alternative groups they can belong to. If the group's goals are significantly different from the goals of the individual, then the individual will not be attracted to the group. Likewise, if the group members find that the group's goals and their goals diverge, then cohesiveness will decrease. If a person has had an unpleasant experience or relationship with a team, or team member, then attractiveness will decrease. Finally, if admission to the group is seen as being too difficult, then the attractiveness of the group decreases. However, if it is so easy to join a group that everyone does, then attractiveness will increase due to easy admission, and cohesion will decrease because the group will not be as small. Additionally, prestige and status, which are greatly influenced by exclusivity, will decline. What status is there in something anyone and everyone can acquire easily?

Group cohesion can be tricky. Individuals, for example, may develop cohesiveness either in harmony or in conflict with the goals of the formal organization. Subgroups or cliques may form within a group. Even in this age of management efforts toward diversity, certain members of a group may develop cohesion against other group members and ostracize them based on their gender, race, age, or physical characteristics.

NetNote

United States Department of Labor News

http://stats.bls.gov/news. release/ecopro.toc.htm

U.S. Bureau of Labor Statistics site for news releases. Topics include economic, workforce, employment, and occupation facts and projections. The news releases are easy to read and quick to download or print.

Some groups may be reluctant to accept new members. They view anyone who is not a part of their established group as an outsider. If you are assigned to a department where such cohesion exists, what should you do? Some authorities suggest that you recognize this as a natural process in many group situations and that you be patient about winning acceptance by the group's members.[6]

Some groups have informal initiation rituals that may range from giving new persons less desirable work to pulling pranks on them or giving them a bit of a hard time.[7] In many cases, this is not mean-spirited but serves a purpose. Established group members judge the new person's ability to take a joke as a sign of how willing the new person is to accept direction and instruction from experienced coworkers. In situations where coworkers are highly dependent on each other, not listening to those with more experience may be physically dangerous.

Group cohesiveness is also important when the group faces a common threat. The threat may come from other individuals, groups, management, or the work itself. When the threat is not from poor management, a high level of group cohesion can improve management-worker relations. Highly cohesive groups are more likely to quickly rally together for the group's defense. Group members are also more likely to commiserate with one another and in general enjoy increased job satisfaction.[8]

WORK ARRANGEMENT INFLUENCE ON INFORMAL GROUPS

Studies made by Michael Argyle indicate that the formal arrangement of the physical work flow influences the nature of the informal group. According to Argyle, employees who work side by side on assembly lines seem not to develop a group feeling; they tend to feel isolated from their coworkers. Such a lack of group cohesion, Argyle contends, can provoke absenteeism and unfavorably affect job satisfaction, turnover, and productivity.[9] All of these factors, of course, can have adverse effects on the quality of the work done. To overcome such problems, some firms have restructured their assembly lines to include worker teams or quality circles. Some firms have also designed office layouts that create more interdependency and effectiveness of employees. Such factors as the location of desks influence group members' ability to satisfy belonging needs as well as their status in the group.

A BALANCE BETWEEN TASK AND MAINTENANCE ACTIVITIES

Groups, as we know, are formed to accomplish goals. A balance between two types of activities—task and maintenance—is essential if the group's goals are to be accomplished.

Task activities are specific behaviors that directly affect goal accomplishment. Processing letters or operating a fax machine are task activities. **Maintenance activities** are related to the social and emotional needs that employees bring to the job, for example, the need to clown around or joke from time to time. Any effort by a manager to squelch the satisfaction of such needs can upset the balance between the two factors and adversely affect the group's performance.

CULTURAL DIVERSITY IN GROUPS

In an earlier period, white male corporate culture was the norm in the United States, but the workplace is becoming less a melting pot and more a mosaic. According to the Bureau of Labor Statistics,[10] women will constitute nearly half the U.S. workforce—47 percent through 2012, up from 43.3 percent in 1982. African Americans will represent 12.4 percent of the workforce, up from 10.2 percent in 1982. Hispanics will make up 15 percent, compared with 6.1 percent in 1982. Asian representation will

Task Activities
behaviors that directly affect goal accomplishment

Maintenance Activities
behaviors related to social and emotional needs

more than double to 6 percent by 2012 (up from the 1982 level of 2.5 percent). Consequently, work groups of the future will increasingly reflect what is referred to as **cultural diversity,** which means that group members will be even more varied in their beliefs, value systems, behavior patterns, and thought characteristics.

This diversity can influence the cohesiveness of groups because of the mind-set and prejudices some group members have toward others. For example, behavior common to one culture may appear exaggerated when performed by members of another culture. If a white male pounds on a table to emphasize a point, he may seem merely assertive to other white males. If an African American male pounds on a table to emphasize a point, white males may perceive him as aggressive and hostile.[11]

Furthermore, members of different cultures frequently have different ways of responding to certain behavior. For example, some ethnic groups tend to react negatively toward structure. Others may interpret eye contact as intimidating. Additionally, diversity also exists within each culture. For example, any cultural group has members who dislike being praised in front of their peers and others who don't mind at all. Such diversity can actually enrich the effectiveness of groups when properly handled. Chapter 16 deals more with such diverse groups as ethnic minorities, women, people with disabilities, and the aging.

Cultural Diversity
variety in beliefs, value systems, behavior patterns, and thought characteristics

INFORMAL GROUPS AND THE GRAPEVINE

In Chapter 3 we learned that informal communication travels through a channel typically referred to as the grapevine, the real workhorse of message networks. We also learned that the grapevine is the means for transmitting rumors, statements whose truth cannot be verified by any known authority. The grapevine has a significant effect on any organization and should, therefore, be well understood by organizational members.

THE NATURE OF THE GRAPEVINE

The **grapevine,** as part of the emergent, or informal, organization, exists out of the personal needs of employees. Let's now find out what grapevines are really like.

Grapevine
the informal communication channel

Grapevine Communication Is Fast   First let's think about how formal communication is developed. Ideas have to be crystallized, organized, and frequently put into writing. They then have to be transmitted to others, often through the various layers of the formal organization. However, informal messages traveling through the informal organization—that is, the grapevine—are fast. They need not travel through a formal hierarchy. Professor Keith Davis, well known for his extensive research in the area of informal communication, has expressed the following about the grapevine:

> Being flexible and personal, it spreads information faster than most management communications systems. With the rapidity of a burning power train, the grapevine

---

SPOT CHECK

   6. Devil's advocates hurt groups and need to be stopped. T F
   7. Role conflict is when people are unsure of their position or responsibility. T F
   8. Group standards are standard, or the same, for all groups. T F
   9. A small group size increases a group's attractiveness. T F
  10. Initiation rituals serve no real purpose. T F

filters out of the woodwork, past the manager's office, through the locker rooms, and along the corridors. Its speed makes it quite difficult for management to stop undesirable rumors or to release significant news in time to prevent rumor formation.[12]

Grapevine Communication Is Oral   Unlike most formal communications, messages transmitted through the grapevine are generally oral rather than written. This factor contributes to the speed at which they travel. The grapevine is also an excellent means for managers to transmit information that they prefer to be off the record.

Grapevine Communication Thrives on Insecurity   Another feature of grapevine communication is its tendency to be used more extensively by organizational members when they feel insecure about various situations. For example, out-of-the-ordinary information, such as an impending plant relocation or closure, or a company restructuring, often causes organizational members to be extremely active on the grapevine, typically transmitting rumors in the process.

Grapevine Communication Fills in the Gaps   Rumors tend to fly through the informal organization when organizational members lack facts. For example, take the case of an employee, Michael, who injured his finger on a machine this morning. Harriet, who works near Michael, merely told Shayne during a coffee break that Michael was hurt while working on his machine but failed to give Shayne any details. Shayne, in turn, told three other persons that Michael had received a serious injury on the job, and within half an hour the rumor spread that Michael was critically injured and not expected to survive. You can see, therefore, that managers must attempt to influence the grapevine and rumor mill by making certain that employees have accurate facts. One effort to do this is through open-book management (described in Chapter 6).

Grapevine Communication Is Extensive When People Relate to the Situation
If organizational members have no interest in, or don't relate to, the information traveling through the grapevine, they are unlikely to pass it to others. Of course, the converse holds true. If the 6 o'clock news reports there will be a significant cutback in defense spending during the next year, engineers and others who work for companies in defense-related industries will relate to such news. They may deduce that their companies are likely to require substantially fewer engineering activities in the future, and, therefore, some of the staff is certain to be laid off. Rumors related to "impending layoffs" could start spreading among engineers throughout many organizations.

CHAINS REQUIRED FOR GRAPEVINE COMMUNICATION

How does the grapevine actually work? What are the typical networks through which informal messages pass from person to person? Four generally accepted patterns, or chains, characterize the grapevine, as depicted in Figure 9.3.

Single-Strand Chain   The simplest, and least common, pattern of grapevine communication, is termed the **single-strand chain,** which is the transmission of informal messages from one person to the next person in the chain. For example, Marilena recently walked by a manager's office and overheard someone say that a key senior executive was likely to be dismissed in the near future. Marilena, in turn, passes the information on to Jeremy, who tells Cameron, who relates it to Stan, who tells Jan, and so on.

Single-Strand Chain

the transmission of informal messages from one person to the next

---

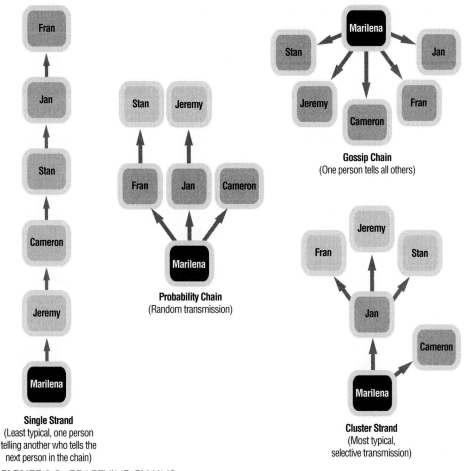

FIGURE 9.3 GRAPEVINE CHAINS

Gossip Chain A second grapevine network is termed the **gossip chain.** As with the single strand, the gossip chain is not particularly common because it exists in those rare instances in which only one person passes the information on to everyone else.

Probability Chain Substantially more common than the two grapevine networks already discussed is the **probability chain,** which exists when information flows through the informal organization on a random, or unpredictable, basis. Referring again to Figure 9.3, the first person, Marilena, passes the message by chance to Fran, Jan, and Cameron. Then Fran and Jan randomly pass the message on to Jeremy and Stan.

Cluster Chain By far the most common grapevine network is the **cluster chain,** in which individuals are selective regarding whom they pass information to. For example, an individual may tell something to one or more persons, who may merely keep the information to themselves or pass it on to a few other persons. As you can observe in Figure 9.3, Marilena tells Cameron and Jan. Cameron, however, does not pass the information on, but Jan, in turn, tells three others. Because of the tendency for an individual to pass information to more than one person, we can see that it often takes very few persons to transmit a rumor to a large number of people. Those who pass information on in a cluster fashion are often selective in their approach.

Gossip Chain

one person passing information to another

Probability Chain

information flowing through the informal organization on a random basis

Cluster Chain

individuals selectively passing on information

They may tell others not to tell anyone else. If anyone abuses their confidence, he or she may not become privy to certain informal communication in the future.

A fairly useful rule to follow is this: Don't tell anyone anything that you do not want passed on to others. Saying to your receiver, for example, "Be sure not to repeat what I told you," is no assurance of confidentiality. Many people on the receiving end of so-called private information tend to promise not to tell anyone else, but later they do pass on the information, telling these people not to tell anyone else.

MANAGEMENT AND THE GRAPEVINE

The grapevine cannot be eliminated, but some managers do try to influence it. They should, however, recognize that the grapevine provides the organization with substantial benefits.[13] For example, it provides people with a release of tensions, an outlet for pent-up emotions. The mere opportunity for employees to get things off their chests informally often eliminates the likelihood of explosive reactions later. In addition, the grapevine provides management with feedback, an opportunity to find out how employees feel about the organization.

Rumors, however, frequently become a thorn in the side of organizations in which trust is lacking between managers and their associates. Whereas rumors may be difficult to eliminate entirely, their frequency tends to be reduced in organizations where people are kept well informed and whose managers see to it that credibility gaps are rare. Managers have to be sensitive to incorrect rumors so that they can be squelched before causing damage to the morale of organizational members.

MEETINGS

Meetings in organizations are common, necessary, and almost universally disliked. Some are called in order to exchange information. Others are for group decision making and problem solving (see Chapter 2). Although many decisions are made as a result of one-to-one interaction between two individuals, a considerable amount of decision making in today's organizations takes place in meetings. Because of the prevalence and importance of meetings, their group dynamics and characteristics deserve careful study.

PLANNED AND UNPLANNED AGENDAS

When managers call meetings for the purpose of providing information or for finding solutions to specific problems, they generally have a good idea of what should be covered during the meeting. In other words, they typically have a **planned agenda.** The planned agenda is useful in that it serves to guide the group's activities toward a preestablished goal. A planned agenda can help conserve scarce and valuable time.

Although an agenda may be planned, one of the potential pitfalls of any meeting is the possibility that a **hidden agenda** will surface. A group member's hidden agenda is basically the attitudes and feelings that he or she brings to the meeting. The hidden agenda may be planned in advance of the meeting, or it may emerge spontaneously as the result of a disagreement with ideas expressed or a distrust of the people conducting the session. In some instances, the person with the hidden agenda, either consciously or subconsciously, tries to place obstacles in the path of the planned agenda. A chairperson should weigh the validity of any hidden agendas that crop up and try to prevent them from sidetracking a meeting too far from its original purpose.

Planned Agenda

the items proposed to be covered in a meeting

Hidden Agenda

the attitudes and feelings a person brings to a meeting; a person's secret objective

FORMING A COMMITTEE

In some organizations, difficult decisions are often referred to committee, either an ongoing **standing committee** or an **ad hoc committee** established to handle a specific situation. A committee can be defined as a group of two or more persons who officially meet together for the purpose of considering issues or problems related to the organization. In some instances, an ad hoc committee is referred to as a **task force**.

Occasionally a manager who is trying to gain a high profile and establish a track record forms a task force as a setup. To attract attention, the manager establishes a task force to study a problem the answers to which she or he already has. The true intent of such a task force is for the manager to push her or his idea to gain recognition for future personal benefit, such as a promotion or pay raise.

Many people, however, hold the view that committees, when properly administered, are useful. They believe that committees can result in better decision making because, as with brainstorming, two heads can be more effective than one. They also argue that a greater input of ideas can occur in committee meetings, with one idea perhaps rising out of others. Further, several people with different types of knowledge, abilities, and experience might be able to see more facets of a particular problem than could one person.

DEFICIENCIES IN GROUP DECISION MAKING

Although creative ideas do result frequently from group decision making, there are inherent dangers to the process that one should continually guard against. Such dangers are itemized in Figure 9.4. Let's look briefly at each.

Wasters of Time   If meetings are not well planned, they are potential time wasters. A manager and his or her subordinates can find much of their time wasted through discussions of trivia, topics that do little to further the organization's goals and objectives. One critic of committees, the late Dutch American historian Hendrik van Loon, had this to say about committees:

> Nothing is ever accomplished by a committee unless it consists of three members, one of whom happens to be sick and another absent.

Diluted Responsibility   Another danger inherent in the use of group decision making by committees is that it tends to lead to **diluted responsibility**. Because decisions are arrived at by group consensus, no one person can be blamed for a bad decision.

Standing Committee
a continuous committee; it does not disperse or end its activities

Ad Hoc Committee
a committee established to handle a specific situation that dissolves after the task is accomplished

Task Force
a temporary grouping of individuals and resources for the accomplishment of a specific objective

NetNote

Meeting Advice

http://www.fin.ucar.edu/hr/ staff_dev/mtg_man/ conducting.html

http://www.nwlink.com/ ~donclark/leader/leadmet. html

Diluted Responsibility
the sharing of responsibility to the point that accountability is difficult to ascertain

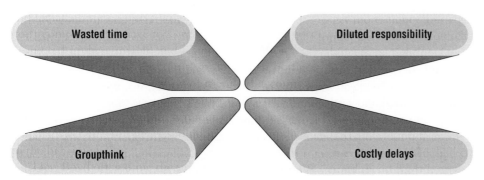

FIGURE 9.4 Dangers inherent in the group decision-making process

Antisynergy Synergy is present when a group produces more than the individuals in the group would have if they worked alone. Synergy is the goal of groups and is cited as one of their main advantages. Groups do not always achieve synergy, however, and the cause, ironically, is related to there being a group in the first place. Because of diluted responsibility, there are other people to rely on, and because some people put forth less effort than others when working by themselves, groups can sometimes produce less than if the group members had worked alone.[14] When people who put out greater effort work with those who put out less, sometimes everyone works to the higher level and sometimes to the lower level. There can be times when those who normally work hard feel they are being taken advantage of, and they may decrease their efforts (an application of the equity theory in Chapter 11). At other times people may feel they can skate or cruise—they can do less because others will make up for it. To prevent **antisynergy**, managers and team leaders need to have individual as well as group accountability. Individual effort must be identified and measured as well as the group results.

Groupthink A further potential problem of group decision making lies in what has been called **groupthink**, the process of deriving negative results from group decision-making efforts as a result of in-group pressures.[15] We've already discussed the nature of group cohesion. Oddly enough, it can actually contribute to poor group decision making. Some groups become so cohesive that their tendency to agree interferes with critical thinking. People do tend to be influenced by their peers. Therefore, the attitudes and influence of some group members, especially those with status, can sway an entire group into pursuing an undesirable course of action. Such closely knit groups can be said to suffer from the illusion of unanimity: No one wants to break up the cohesiveness of the group. The group members become the victims of groupthink.

Group leaders sometimes encourage groupthink at meetings, particularly when they've arrived at specific decisions before the meeting even begins. The other members are there merely to rubber-stamp predetermined decisions. Group leaders may also assume that silence on the part of the participants means consent to or agreement with decisions actually made unilaterally by the leader.

Costly Delays Group decision making can also result in costly delays. Other tasks must be neglected while committee members are in session, and sometimes important members arrive late or are absent altogether. There also tends to be more indecisiveness rather than candid and creative thought among committee members as they try to arrive at reasonable decisions and conclusions. The German philosopher Friedrich Nietzsche long ago warned about group behavior, stating that "madness is the exception in individuals but the rule in groups." In far too many cases, he seems to have been right.

AVOIDING MEETING PITFALLS

In spite of the many potential pitfalls inherent in group decision making, it is likely to continue playing an important role in many organizations. When its limitations are recognized and sessions are properly planned, group decision making can lead to good ideas. Let's look briefly at some suggestions about holding meetings that can reduce some of the potential problems associated with group decision making.

Have a Good Reason Managers spend a large amount of their time attending meetings, some of which are a waste of time. To avoid wasting time, meetings should

---

Antisynergy
groups producing less than if the group members had worked alone

---

Groupthink
negative results from group decision making due to intragroup pressures; suppression of dissent within a group

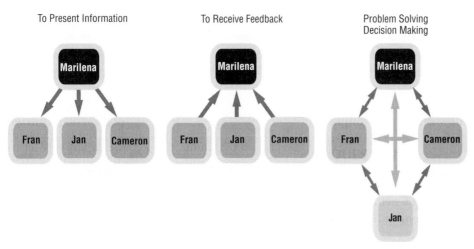

FIGURE 9.5 TYPICAL REASONS FOR CONDUCTING MEETINGS

be called only when there's a good reason to have one.[16] Some meetings appear to be called more out of habit than necessity. ("Why did I call a meeting? Because we always have meetings on Fridays, that's why.") Why call a meeting if you don't have a specific agenda? When you have the responsibility for calling meetings, be certain that you have a planned agenda, which can go a long way toward preventing considerable scarce and valuable time from being eaten up needlessly. As can be viewed in Figure 9.5, meetings are generally held for any of the following three reasons:

1. to present information to the attendees
2. to receive feedback from the attendees
3. to solve problems and make decisions

Make sure that a meeting is really necessary, however. With teleconferencing, e-mail, and videoconferencing, many meetings might be held just as well (and less expensively) using electronic means. In addition, when you have drawn up a reason and an agenda for the meeting, review them. If the issues can be handled in a memo, then do it that way and save people a lot of time. Remember the communications lessons of Chapter 3. There is nothing wrong with a good memo when it is used appropriately.

Respect Time   Try to avoid scheduling open-ended meetings; they tend to drag on and on due to the lack of time pressures. Instead, establish precise times for meetings to begin and end. Let participants know that you expect them to arrive at meetings promptly because waiting for participants can waste considerable time. Be sure to start meetings on time because if participants know from experience that your meetings always begin 15 minutes late, they may think that there is no particular reason for them to be there on time. When planning the length of a meeting, take a lesson from seminar planners. Their rule is that the brain can only absorb what the butt can endure. If a meeting must go so long that people's bottoms are in danger of going numb, then plan some breaks and some moving about into the schedule. On the other hand, if it looks like less time will be needed than you thought, never underestimate the value of ending early—it's like giving people a gift of time.

Be Creatively Brief   Some managers schedule meetings just before lunch—say, 11:00 A.M. to noon—or during the hour just prior to quitting time. The theory

NetNote

infoteam

http://www.fastcompany.com/online/02/meetings.html

The seven sins of deadly meetings. An article on how to run meetings.

behind this scheduling is that participants usually aren't eager to sit in a meeting during their lunch hour or on their own time. One manager keeps his meetings short by conducting them in a room with no chairs. He believes that the less comfortable the setting of a meeting, the more quickly participants will want to take care of the business at hand.

Recognize the Effect of Physical Settings　The layout of the meeting room, that is, who sits where, can significantly affect the influence of some individuals on others in attendance. For example, those who sit at the ends of the conference table are frequently perceived as having more power and influence than those who sit on the sides. People sitting side by side tend to have more difficulty seeing and communicating with each other. Tables designed so that everyone appears to be in an equal position, such as round tables, tend to encourage the free flow of ideas and discourage the domination of a meeting by one individual. Also consider meeting somewhere new and different, maybe even away from the workplace.

Clarify the Responsibilities of Attendees　In many instances, you're likely to be responsible for attending but not organizing or conducting a meeting. In such a case, you still have certain responsibilities. You can help make meetings flow more smoothly and waste less time if you do the following:

1. Obtain an agenda of the meeting. Find out the meeting's objectives before attending it.
2. Prepare for the meeting. Obtain information that can enhance the meeting's outcome.
3. Participate at the meeting. Your ideas can build on those of other participants and contribute toward accomplishing the meeting's objectives.
4. Decide on a follow-up action. During meetings, determine what your follow-up responsibilities are and decide when you will accomplish them.
5. Confirm follow-up action. Explain to the chairperson your understanding of your follow-up responsibilities to avoid going off in useless directions.

Other tips, hints, and rules for better meetings:[17]

- Never call a "memo meeting." If what you have to meet about could be covered in an e-mail or a memo, then write one. Meetings are for problem solving, question-and-answer sessions, and collaboration.
- To get the problem solving or collaboration started faster, give people something to work on before the meeting and between meetings.
- Make sure the people running meetings know how to; if they don't, get them the training they need to run meetings well.
- Remember, the agenda is not etched in stone. If the meeting goes out of order or off on a different *but useful* path, let it.
- Summarize what was accomplished so everyone is clear on where things stand.
- People can often benefit from having a block of time to work, so consider declaring a meeting-free day. Monday is a good choice as people can prepare for the meetings later in the week without ruining their weekends.

Meetings will be with us for the foreseeable future, but they don't have to be something everyone dreads. With preparation, consideration for human needs, some variety, and maybe even some tasteful humor, you may find that people are achieving results rather than stabbing themselves in the thigh with their pens to stay awake.

TEAMWORK

At its best, teamwork may be the key to increased competitive advantage and increased productivity. At its worst, it can be defined as "a lot of people doing what I say," or it can even induce paralysis. Why all the talk and writing about teams and teamwork then? One major reason is the increased complexity of creating goods and services.[18] Teams also have many of the advantages (and disadvantages) of groups, such as greater creativity and more numerous alternatives for problem solving. Teams are somewhat different from groups, although some people use the terms interchangeably. Groups and committees are collections of people. Often they are selected to be representative of larger groups. The members of **teams,** on the other hand, are selected based on the knowledge and expertise each brings to the team. Teams have other characteristics as well.

Teams have some characteristics in common with groups and some that are different. Teams have the following traits:

- are difficult to start and must be managed in order to start quickly
- need individuals in order to succeed
- may not work well with the existing organization
- need clear direction
- need leaders

Although teams can also be very useful, they are not the answer to everything.[19] There is still plenty to be said for highly capable individuals working on their own. As with many things, individual work, groups, and teams can work well in the proper situation and fail in the wrong situation.

MODELS OF TEAM DEVELOPMENT

One of the characteristics teams share with groups is the stages each passes through on the way to productivity. There are at least two models of group or team development, one involving less management than the other. In the somewhat more traditional model of group development, the group or team is less managed and passes through four stages: forming, storming, norming, and performing.[20] **Forming** is basically members meeting and greeting. To work well, the team should clarify its goals and set rules for how the team will function. This phase can be shorter if a clear purpose is provided to the team. In the **storming** phase, conflict ensues over

NetNote

Psychology Today
http://www.psychologytoday.com/articles/pto-20030916-000002.html
Teamwork and you.

Teams
groups whose members are selected based on the variety of knowledge and expertise each possesses

Forming
group members becoming acquainted with each other

Storming
conflict over the direction a team will take and over leadership

---

FYI

Know why people join groups and use these factors to attract the best to your teams.

Know your role in each group and don't take on more roles than you can handle.

Join committees and teams carefully; avoid do-nothing groups.

Listen to the grapevine but beware; much is exaggeration or simply wrong.

Always have an agenda for a meeting.

Come prepared for every meeting.

Prepare activities to move your teams through the development process to performing as fast as possible.

Norming

cohesion and communication as a team agrees on its direction and leadership

Performing

a team working on the assigned task

Focusing

a team learning, stating, establishing, determining, or clarifying its goals

Leveling

performance remaining steady

NetNote

Teamwork Tips

http://humanresources.about.com/od/involvementteams/a/twelve_tip_team.htm

Guidelines for developing effective teams.

Charge

a mission or goal a team is to work toward

the direction the team will take and over leadership. Some organization occurs, although if the team is big, there can be a massive turf fight as different cliques jockey for power and influence. One way to try to reduce storming is for management to assign a leader to the team. If the team survives storming, then cohesion and communication can take over in the **norming** phase. Finally, the team begins to work in earnest in the **performing** stage. This is one popular model, but there is at least one alternative.

John Beck and Neil Yeager, of the Charter Oak Consulting Group, have modified the traditional model of forming, storming, norming, and performing to "forming, focusing, performing, and leveling."[21] One of the first things one notices is that there is no storming phase. According to the Beck-Yeager model, storming does not have to occur. Beck and Yeager claim that many teams form, clarify the work needed, and start in on the assignment. Beck and Yeager believe that storming can be a self-fulfilling prophecy; having learned the traditional model, people storm because they expect it to happen. The modified model states that immediately after forming, teams can move to **focusing**.[22] In focusing, the teams learn, state, establish, determine, or clarify the goals and objectives of the team. Once everyone knows what is to be accomplished, the group moves to performing. During performing, the work is divided and people begin. It is here that Beck and Yeager make another important point. Much teamwork is not performed as a team. Much is done by individuals and later combined with the work of the others in the team.[23] Without regular meetings to keep the work on the team members' minds, to check progress, combine information, and solve problems, productivity may stagnate in a **leveling** stage. The leveling stage of this model is just one way that teams can fail.

Although teams are popular and can be effective, they can also fail. However, managers, team leaders, and team members can take actions that will make teams more effective and reduce the risk of failure. Because many of these actions can reduce or eliminate the storming phase of the more traditional team development model, the discussion here will follow the Beck and Yeager model. In either case, the actions will still help a group or team to become productive.

Before beginning the forming stage, it is important to understand that teams are difficult to form.[24] One cannot just throw some people together and consistently produce a team. That may work sometimes, but far too often it will result in a group, not a team, and a rather ineffective group at that. Team members must be carefully selected to ensure compatibility and to ensure that each person is bringing something to the party.[25] Teams are also not naturally self-directing.[26] Teams need to be given a **charge**—a mission or goal. The charge needs to be well defined, or the team should be directed to define it as soon as possible.[27] An explicit and narrowed mission will help to eliminate or reduce disagreements (the storming phase of the traditional model).[28] Establishing a leader or leaders is also important; the role exists and will be filled by someone. The decision is whether to let the team argue about it, to appoint a leader, or to provide an orderly and quick method for deciding on leadership.[29] The establishment of leaders by appointing them places this step in the forming stage; otherwise, leadership establishment resides in the focusing stage.

In the focusing stage, the criteria for success must be established and the time horizon, or duration of the team's existence, should be determined.[30] A clear method for making decisions must be established.[31] This could mean that the leader decides, or that the members vote, or that consensus must be reached. The decision-making process should be defined and be clear as another step toward eliminating storming. Further defining of the work to be completed (the objectives) and a division of work are also needed in focusing, along with the establishment of accountability.[32] It must be remembered that people cannot be allowed to hide behind the team or behind other members. Individuals are accountable even when they are members of a team.[33] Once the tasks to be performed have been decided or established, and once the team members have been given their assignments, the group can move to performing.

To gain the maximum benefit from the team, an agenda of when tasks will be performed is needed.[34] To enable the members to perform their tasks to the fullest extent, the team members should be located in close proximity to one another.[35] Some companies physically relocate people for team assignments. At least one firm uses portable equipment that people wheel to team locations every day. Members need to communicate with one another in person and on a regular basis.[36] In addition to individual and spontaneous conversations, team meetings are needed. To maximize team performance, the meetings need to be organized and well managed,[37] as discussed earlier in this chapter.

A QUESTION OF ETHICS

Construction or Obstruction

A team was formed to create new performance appraisals for the frontline workers of an organization. The team was to be composed of about four middle managers and about four union members. Both sides agreed to ignore that fact, however, and devise a developmental, rather than judgmental, performance appraisal. At the first meeting, Tammie arrived late, a behavior she repeated often. Once she did arrive, she would doodle. This was noticeable to all the others on the team because it was not casual doodling; Tammie became very involved in creating patterns using different color pens. During the course of the team's work, Tammie had a tendency to go to one team member to complain about another, rather than talk directly to the person she had a problem with. Tammie had been with the firm for a number of years, and she never seemed to run out of grievances from the past concerning almost every performance measure that had ever been introduced. She was adept at making cynical comments just loudly enough

for only those sitting close to her to hear. Many of these ridiculed or insulted the people sitting just beyond the range of her voice. She also seemed to relish playing "he said, she said." Here she would make a vague comment, and when someone paraphrased her to see if her meaning was understood, she would deny that the paraphrase was what she meant. But others never could get her to say exactly what she did mean. These incidents usually ended with her saying, "Well, people will hear what they want to hear."

1. Was it ethical for Tammie to agree to work on this team? Why or why not?

2. What is Tammie's real agenda—what is she really trying to do?

3. Is it ethical for the team leader not to do something about Tammie and her actions? Why or why not?

4. Which of Tammie's actions are unethical and why?

Source: Minda Zetlin, "Helps and Hinders: The Habits of Successful Teams," *Getting Results,* September 1996, pp. 5–6.

SUMMARY

Everyone is a member of various small groups. Organizational members should try to gain an understanding of the working of group behavior, both formal and informal, because of its significant influence over them. Managers, too, have an influence over the small group. Work groups strongly influence the behavior and performance of their members in either positive or negative ways. Groups as well as individuals function more effectively when a balance exists between task and maintenance activities.

Informal groups often use the grapevine for their informal communications. Although the grapevine can be used to spread harmful rumors, it can also be utilized in ways that benefit the organization. Group decision making has its advantages and disadvantages. Managers who conduct meetings will accomplish goals more readily with planned agendas. Teamwork is increasing in popularity. Used correctly it can be beneficial; however, too many teams can result in less being accomplished. It is also possible for teams to take more time to complete work than a capable individual would.

CHECKING FOR UNDERSTANDING

1. Evaluate the following statement: "Formal groups, by their very nature, restrict our freedom. This would be a far better world in which to live and work if formal groups didn't exist."

2. It has been said that informal groups help individuals satisfy their psychological and social needs. How might an informal group have the reverse effect, that is, create dissatisfaction in an individual group member?

3. Describe group member characteristics.

4. List, describe, and differentiate between two group formation models.

5. What are social norms? In what ways might they make a supervisor's job easier? More difficult?

6. List and describe methods for maximizing team efforts.

7. What factors increase group cohesion?

8. Describe methods for conducting effective meetings.

9. What are the major characteristics of the grapevine?

10. Explain how informal groups utilize the grapevine.

11. Summarize the advantages and deficiencies of group decision making.

12. Is group decision making better than individual decision making? Explain.

13. What is antisynergy and what can be done to counteract it?

SELF-ASSESSMENT

Answer each of the following questions according to your behavior in a group or on a team. Answer SA for strongly agree, A for agree, D for disagree, and SD for strongly disagree.

1. I never seem to know what I'm supposed to be doing when I'm on a team or in a group. *SA A D SD*

2. I'll accept whatever group or team role I receive. *SA A D SD*

3. I tend to take on many group tasks to the point that I often feel overwhelmed. *SA A D SD*

4. I work for unity among all group or team members. *SA A D SD*

5. If others in the group or on the team want to, I let them do my work for me.
SA   A   D   SD

6. I work to have clear group or team goals and rules.   *SA   A   D   SD*

7. I go with whatever the group majority opinion is.   *SA   A   D   SD*

8. I strive to get to the real work, the reason the group or team was formed.   *SA   A   D   SD*

9. If need be I'll fight to be in charge of almost all groups or teams I'm on.   *SA   A   D   SD*

10. The schedules of others are not my concern; we stay until the group or team work is done.   *SA   A   D   SD*

For items 2, 4, 6, and 8 score +2 for every SA, +1 for every A, −1 for every D, and −2 for every SD. For items 1, 3, 5, 7, 9, and 10 score −2 for every SA, −1 for every A, +1 for every D, and +2 for every SD. Total your score. A score of 10–20 indicates good group/team skills; 1–9 indicates acceptable group/team skills but some improvement could be made; 0−−9 indicates there is much improvement to make in group/team skills, and −10−−20 indicates poor group/team skills with improvement needed in all areas of teamwork and good group performance.

SKILL BUILD 9

Birmingham Bristle is a manufacturer of high-quality paintbrushes for hardware stores and professional building painters (their smallest brush is a one-inch trim brush). Lakshmi, Valsilisa, Javier, and Dwayne work at four consecutive workstations on the assembly line. Dwayne is the newest worker. Having just finished his third month, he is now a union member like the others, who have been there about five years each. Even though Dwayne is new, he, like the others, feels threatened by their boss, Merl. Other workers under Merl do not share this threatened feeling, just these four who happen to be on the last four assembly stations (which are closest to and in direct view of Merl's office). Due to the nature of their work and family obligations, these four workers are never able to be together. They do talk during the course of a day, as Lakshmi has to go between his station and Valsilisa's, Valsilisa must go between hers and Javier's, and Javier must go between his and Dwayne's. Dwayne, being last on the line, does not leave his station except for breaks and lunch, and then one of the others takes his station for that time.

Skill Question 1. What classification of group is that formed by Lakshmi, Valsilisa, Javier, and Dwayne? How did you reach this conclusion?

Still, they do manage to communicate, enough so that a rumor has passed from one to another that Merl intends to fire one or more of them and that Merl plans to use information collected from one of the group against the one or more to be fired. For this reason Lakshmi, Valsilisa, and Javier feel the four of them really need to stick together. They are, however, reluctant to admit Dwayne without Dwayne first proving himself to them. The three have had Javier tell Dwayne that he must prove himself the same way they had to when they started—he must file a grievance against Merl. This won't be easy because Dwayne has to find something, no matter how weak or lame, about something Merl has done to him to make a formal complaint about. The three don't even care if Dwayne wins or loses the grievance; he just needs to file it.

Skill Question 2. What group formation concept explains Lakshmi, Valsilisa, Javier, and Dwayne banding together as a worker group?

Skill Question 3. What group attractiveness and cohesiveness factor is driving Lakshmi, Valsilisa, Javier, and Dwayne to be in the group?

Skill Question 4. What group attractiveness and cohesiveness concept explains Lakshmi, Valsilisa, and Javier wanting Dwayne to make the gesture of filing some kind of formal grievance against Merl before letting him into the group? Why do the three want Dwayne to do this (what is the point, since they don't care if he wins or loses)?

Skill Question 5. Analyze the workplace communication system between Lakshmi, Valsilisa, Javier, and Dwayne. What type of grapevine do they have going?

Merl has gotten some idea that something is up with Lakshmi, Valsilisa, Javier, and Dwayne, but he is not sure what. He isn't even sure how they communicate or why they would band together. He has asked for a meeting of fellow supervisors Salar, Ed, and Claudine. He asked them each beforehand to write down their ideas on what he can do about these four workers.

Skill Question 6. What classification of group is that formed by Salar, Ed, Claudine, and Merl? How did you reach this conclusion?

Skill Question 7. What term explains Merl's having the other three supervisors write down some ideas before their first meeting?

Skill Question 8. Is this technique generally a good idea for meetings or a bad idea? Why is it good or why is it bad?

This was Merl's agenda for the first meeting:

Take attendance
Collect written idea papers
Check schedules for future meetings
Set next meeting

Skill Question 9. Looking at the agenda, what kind of a meeting is this (*Hint:* Find a term from the book), and is this kind of meeting generally a good thing or a bad thing? Why is it considered good or why is it bad?

The group was less than thrilled at meeting for 30 minutes to accomplish these four little items. At a second meeting, Merl handed out a list of ideas compiled from the three individual lists he collected at the first meeting. He had added no ideas of his own. After handing out the list, Merl asked the three to come up with other ideas after reviewing the list. He wrote down their few new ideas but added none of his own. For the next meeting he asked the three to come up with possible solutions for him.

Skill Question 10. What technique did Merl use in the second meeting?

Skill Question 11. Is this technique generally a good idea or a bad idea? Why is it considered good or why is it bad?

At the third meeting there were no real ideas for Merl other than "wait and see what happens." Merl is frustrated with the group, especially since the four of them had worked so well together a year ago when they created a successful Total Quality Management program. At that time the four of them all came in prepared and with good ideas that just got better after they worked on them as a group. This time around Merl is actually thinking he could have done better by himself.

Skill Question 12. What concept could explain Merl's group doing well with the TQM project but doing so little in helping him that Merl thinks he would be better off without them?

Skill Question 13–15. Finally, look at Merl's meetings. Focus on the chapter section concerning clarifying the responsibilities of the attendees. Merl does do some things right, but he has missed some points here too. Make a list of at least three suggestions you have from this section that could improve his meetings.

PERSONAL POINTS

1. Would you rather work alone or as part of group and why? When would you rather work alone and why?

2. When and why have you joined informal groups at work?

3. Do you listen to or spread gossip at work and why? How much of what you hear through the grapevine do you believe and why?

4. Have you ever succumbed to antisynergy and why? If not, have you seen others who have? How was this dealt with?

5. How do you feel about meetings? Why? What would improve them? Have you ever thought of bringing a fork to meetings to poke yourself with in order to stay awake? Why not?

APPLICATIONS

9.1 THE HATCHET COMMISSION

Chikako Nakayama called the group to order for its first meeting, "I would like to welcome you to the start-up of the Career Transition Team . . ."

"You mean 'The Hatchet Commission' since everyone knows we were given no power to decide which 25 percent of the employees are fired," Jayne Davis said.

"If I may," Glenn Bergerman interjected, "one advantage to being in this group is we know none of us will be among that 25 percent."

"You may snicker, but before your company bought mine, I was president of Deutsche Papier. Now I am not even in charge of this committee," lamented Otto Kolb.

"Would you like to be our recorder or liaison to the Leadership Committee?" asked Chikako.

"No," Kolb replied.

No one else wanted the jobs, either.

"Well, I guess I can try to lead, record, and be liaison, although I'm not sure how I will do all three at once. What about some ground rules—meeting times, place, arriving on time, leaving early, and so on?" Chikako asked.

"A counterpoint, if I may," Bergerman offered. "If we get all formal with these things might we be tempted to be less formal with the selection of 'separatees' if you will. Maybe we should allow a little latitude, especially as everyone else will hate us just for being on this team anyway."

"I don't know that we have to deal with this now," Otto said sullenly.

Jayne leaned over to Otto and said to him alone, "You may have a problem with being here, but at least you have that. I don't know what is going on or what I am supposed to do—I've never been on a team before, much less one with a despised task. The job is unclear. I'm just hazy on the whole thing!"

"How will we let people know who isn't on the lay-off list?" Otto asked.

"Just tell my administrative assistant; one word to him, and he'll blab it to everyone in the company personally!" Glenn proclaimed.

And so it went. Chikako seemed stuck with all the work other than talking; she even tried giving the leadership of the team to someone else, but nobody wanted it. Glenn had a "counterpoint," as he called it, for almost everything. Otto seemed to want to take charge, but then knew he shouldn't, and Jayne kept repeating, "I'm so confused." In the end, Chikako was still the undisputed leader, but they never did get to the ice-breaker activity she had planned.

QUESTIONS

1. Who is the devil's advocate and what makes you believe that?

2. Who has role ambiguity, role conflict, and role overload? Support your answers with examples.

3. What one factor increases the cohesiveness and attractiveness of this group, and what two factors decrease the cohesiveness and attractiveness? Support your answers with examples.

4. What group member characteristic is the group *not* agreeing on, which is also decreasing group attractiveness and cohesiveness? What group development stage is the group in? Support your answers with examples.

5. What type of grapevine chain was proposed to disseminate information?

9.2 TEAM SPIRIT

Bob Boston has a little problem. He was supposed to put together a team to design a Web site for the entire company, Kankakee Knutson Valves, Inc. Obviously, the company is already behind in the rush to get on the Web, and Bob's group hasn't done much to help. It's not that Bob didn't assemble a team. Six months ago he selected Camille from the Computer Support Department; Martin from Marketing; Prajesh from Production; Simone from Sales; and Ivan Ivanovich from Inventory and Logistics. Bob selected these people because he knew they had not worked together before and he hoped this meant there would be no bad feelings from previous experiences. Bob also figured he would let the group democratically select a leader, decide on a working arrangement, and devise a Web site as the team saw fit. With the different backgrounds and the expertise each person possessed, Bob was sure he would have a top-notch Web site in record time.

Two months after telling each person he or she was assigned to the team, nothing had been done. The team had not even met. When Bob found this out, he brought everyone together and asked them why they had not started. They told Bob that because they didn't know each other, no one wanted to step on anyone else's toes by taking charge and calling the team together. After Bob stood looking like a deer caught in the headlights for a while, Martin said they could meet in his department tomorrow because he had the largest conference room and access to a computer. They all agreed on that and little else.

Once they started meeting, Camille, Martin, and Simone all wanted to be in charge. They each had reasons that sounded good and no one was willing to let any of the others take over. Prajesh and Ivan didn't care who was in charge, as long as it wasn't either of them. That was just the beginning, though. Prajesh didn't really care about the Web site, saying he didn't see as it

had much to do with production. Ivan wanted the Web site to be used only by KKV's suppliers and distributors. Martin and Simone wanted the Web site dedicated to customers only. Camille said that because she was the only one in the group who could actually create Web pages, it should just be an informational site that described the company and the products in general and provided the company phone numbers. Besides, Camille said, she had other projects and that was about all she was willing to do. They have been arguing about this for four months now.

QUESTIONS

1. What team selection mistakes did Bob make?

2. What should Bob have done with the team two months before the first meeting?

3. What should Bob have done before the first meeting the team had without him?

4. What should Bob do now?

NET-WORK

Anatomy of a 4+ hour game programmer's meeting

http://www.youtube.com/watch?v=lmjhCFrOpPg

FedEx commercial about group member roles. Exaggerated? Not by much.

http://www.youtube.com/watch?v=6hKWM5Z1zds

EXPERIENTIAL EXERCISE

Examining Formal Work Arrangements

During the next week or so, observe carefully in one of the departments where you work the formal arrangement of the physical work flow. (If you are not currently employed, ask an acquaintance to arrange for you to visit his or her office or plant.) How does the arrangement contribute to, or detract from, employee feelings of group cohesiveness? Are employees able to interact with each other based on the location of workstations or desks? How does the existing layout affect the status of the group members?

SPOT CHECK ANSWERS

1. F
2. F
3. F
4. T
5. T
6. F
7. F
8. F
9. T
10. F
11. T
12. T
13. T
14. T
15. F

10 | Individuals and Self-Management

Never tell people how to do things. Tell them what to do and they will surprise you with their ingenuity.

General George S. Patton

You control your life by controlling your time.

Hyrum W. Smith, Creator of the Franklin Day Planner

GOALS

The main goal of this chapter is to explore the role of the individual in organizations. We will explore what organizations expect from individuals and how individuals are often treated. Your responsibilities, both the more traditional ones (like time management) and the newer ones (like self-management), are presented in order to decrease the reality shock many experience on their first jobs.

OBJECTIVES

When you finish this chapter, you should be able to:

▶ Explain why a certain degree of conformity among organizational members is desirable.

▶ Explain conformity as it relates to privacy, company resources, off-the-job activities, workplace affairs, attire, and smoking.

▶ Define the general types of individuals you may have to adjust to and explain how to deal with each.

▶ Evaluate the three general areas in which many employers believe that they have the right to know.

▶ Describe sound concepts for disciplining employees.

▶ Summarize some typical challenges that individuals may have with themselves in organizations.

▶ Describe the nature and purpose of organizational politics.

▶ Define influence strategies and ways to influence others.

▶ List, define, and explain the concepts and components of self-management.

▶ List, define, and explain time-management techniques.

INTRODUCTION

All people share some similarities, yet each individual has a distinctive personality and a set of values established long before joining a formal work organization. Although they may go along with current fads and trends, most individuals seem to enjoy, and even need, feelings of uniqueness. Few people want to be treated impersonally, as if they were just numbers or members of a faceless mass.

The successes of participative management help to substantiate the need individuals have for a feeling of personal contribution and involvement. Most of us want to believe that others value our individual opinions.

Do you have to give up some individuality upon becoming a member of a work group? What happens when your philosophy and needs seem not to meld with those of the organization? To what extent do employees have the right to privacy? How should discipline be applied when a person's behavior deviates from accepted organizational standards? What are some of the typical challenges faced by individuals whose personal aspirations exceed their capabilities? What can you do when promoted to a position in which the demands exceed your present skill level? Should errors ever be admitted, or are they better covered up? Does an individual member of an organization have to be political to achieve personal goals? What are some of the typical political activities that take place in organizations?

The answers to these important questions, which can help you understand some of the critical issues and challenges you might be facing now or in the future, will be discussed in this chapter. Like the previous chapter, this chapter provides you with information that can assist your own adjustment to organizational life.

THE QUESTION OF CONFORMITY

Is there room for nonconformity in organizations? Many organizational members are intensely individualistic, yet they continue to be cooperative and capable members of their work groups. Other employees find it difficult to conform to the standards of their organizations and seem to be miserable in their jobs.

Is conformity necessary for organizational members? If it is, then to what degree does an organization have the right to expect—or even require—you to conform? For example, as an organizational member, should you be told what to think, what to wear, and what to do? Or should you have the right to do whatever you believe is right whenever you want?

PROBLEMS OF INDIVIDUALISM

One of the difficulties besetting individuals is that of reconciling the desire for being one's self with the necessity of being an effective team member of an organization. Organizational members are generally expected to match their own personal cultures with the culture of their employer and subscribe to philosophies of the organizations for which they work. Robert N. Hilkert, a banker, once expressed an attitude that still commonly prevails in organizations:

> Our decisions are contained within the framework of our philosophy. By "our philosophy" I mean that of the institution we serve and that which is our own, provided that our personal philosophy does not for long conflict with that of the institution's which we serve. If we cannot live with the philosophy of our employer, and if we cannot bring our employer around to ours, then our days in that organization are numbered. We must decide whether to leave before we are requested to do so.[1]

At first glance, Mr. Hilkert's philosophy may seem somewhat crass. However, regardless of your personal reaction to his words, it's important for you to remember that organizations have unique personalities and values. Some organizations follow the general practice of aggressively introducing new products and establishing new programs. Others take a wait-and-see approach, preferring to let competitors take risks. Some firms are highly structured and expect rules to be followed to the letter, whereas others are relatively informal, allowing considerable variation in practices and procedures. No single type of organization serves as the model for all others.

Because organizations differ, before accepting a position with a particular organization, you should attempt to "know thyself" and "thy organization." Do you know what sort of culture exists in the organization you are considering for a career position? Are your expectations toward the organization realistic? If not, you may soon discover that philosophically the relationship is incompatible.

DEALING WITH INDIVIDUALS

Previous chapters have included a discussion of caustic coworkers and malicious managers, but there are other types of individuals found in organizations that are not bad; they just may take a little getting used to. At least nine types are distinct enough to merit mentioning:

- the angry
- the attitude problem
- the distraught
- the entitled
- the gossip
- the legend
- the literal
- the never available
- the powerless

They may be bosses, subordinates, or coworkers, and although they might be annoying, most are not a threat or major problem.

The angry are either mad all of the time, or they become upset or irate quickly and often.[2] The angry may get mad and then not talk to others, but many yell, berate coworkers, or even throw things. The frequency of outburst differentiates those going through a temporary rough time and those who are chronically aggressive. Work or nonwork factors may trigger an outburst. Having a couple of outbursts is not cause for concern when they are out of character, but being angry every few weeks should be more alarming. It indicates the need for the person to find other ways to vent his or her emotions. If you are confronted with an angry outburst, do not yell back or become defensive. Tell the angry person you cannot continue until he or she calms down, and if that fails, just walk away and discuss things later.

Someone with an attitude problem is unhappy and shares this with others.[3] According to these people, everything stinks, nothing is good enough, things were better before or someplace else, nobody knows anything, or nothing is worth trying. People who have a bad attitude should be management's concern, as negativity can be contagious. Once the negativity starts, it can expand, so that one person complaining about one thing can grow to many people complaining about many things. Another aspect may involve you as an individual. If possible, avoid these people, and if they can't be avoided, try to resist any urge to join them, lest you start to become like them. You may choose to suggest that if things are all that bad for them, then maybe it is time they move on (or else quit complaining all the time).

The distraught bring all of their personal and emotional problems with them wherever they go.[4] They talk about their boyfriends, girlfriends, husbands, wives, parents, siblings, relatives, neighbors, or soap opera characters and lament for them all. To them it seems that everything is upsetting to the point that they just don't seem to know how they can go on. As with the angry, if someone is upset over personal events a few times, this is understandable, and often he or she just needs someone to talk to. If the worry and distress are constant, then it is better not to listen, so your time is not wasted and he or she is not encouraged.

The entitled feel they are owed an income just for showing up in the morning. If anyone wants them to work as well, that is going to cost something extra.[5] When asked to do something, their response is often a variation of "What's in it for me?" There are two main methods for dealing with these individuals. One is to ask for their help. Sometimes this is effective because now the person can feel as if he or she is doing you a favor (also see male communications in Chapter 3). If this is unacceptable to you, then you might explain how your request is simply asking the entitled to do his or her fair share. Explain what others are doing and what you are doing and that he or she needs to contribute the same. In case the entitled person is going to become an underperformer, you might want to document what he or she was to do and when you discussed the situation.

While many people exchange major news occasionally, gossips are more concerned about gathering and spreading rumors than about working.[6] Gossips can be major time wasters as they either want information from you or want to tell you the latest story. Another problem is that half of all gossip is not true, and you rarely know which half. While many people pass on what they hear, gossips do far less work and spend far more time spreading the latest scandal around. Avoid gossips if you can, and if you can't, then show no interest in what they are saying and never give them any information that they can spread.

To hear the legend talk, he or she is the Almighty's gift to the organization.[7] Amazingly productive, always right, marvelously good looking—it is a wonder anyone else is needed. The legend's ego is so large it is difficult to get it through the door and even more difficult to be in the same room with it. Even if you voice sarcastic agreement, the legend will not notice; your comment will be taken as a compliment. Mostly you can just roll your eyes and try to endure the legend's ego, but if the legend tries to take credit for your work, then you need to document your contributions and ensure that you receive recognition when it is necessary.

The literal can only do exactly as they are told.[8] If told to bring their sales reports to the evaluation meeting, they will bring the sales reports but not the call reports. When you say you need all reports to perform an evaluation, they will point out that you said *sales* reports, not sales *and* call reports. Some people are literal all the time, but in others being literal may be a sign of protest or resistance to unwanted change (see Chapter 13). When being literal causes damage or loss to the organization, it is called malicious compliance—doing exactly as one is told while knowing that doing so is wrong or will cause harm. While the literal require explicit and detailed instructions, malicious compliance is a symptom of larger problems requiring the attention of management.

The never available are busy, very busy, so busy, can't talk, gotta go. They always seem to be on the way to an important meeting or off on a trip.[9] When attending a meeting, they may arrive late or leave early or both. While they may look busy, the never available never seem to have time for much work. Two problems can surround these individuals. First, because they are so busy they may try to delegate their work to you either blatantly or by not doing their share. Second, you may not get answers when you need them. In the first case, do not accept any of the never-available person's work. Explain that you also are busy and that right now your plate is full. In the second case, get an appointment, get a deadline, and if that fails, send a written message stating that if you do not hear from him or her by a specific date you will go ahead with what you feel is proper.

The last of the annoying individuals are the powerless. The powerless actually have some power; they just don't think they do, or they are afraid to use it.[10] The powerless do not take sides or make decisions. They don't solve problems, and they don't intervene. The powerless might be willing to administrate (perform routine, no-risk tasks), but they are not leaders. They might listen to you or even pat you on the back, but they will not defend you or support anything controversial. To deal with this kind of person, start with "what if" scenarios and theoretical situations, then move to the real request. Or, start out with a small request or just the mention of a situation one day, then move to larger requests another day. If a powerless person absolutely refuses to take risks, see if it is possible for you to do so (as long as you get the credit for the successes also).

IS CONFORMITY A SELLOUT?

How do you feel about conformity? Is conforming to an organization's standards akin to selling out? Most of us probably want to retain our individuality. Yet the word *conformity* might have connotations that are somewhat harsher than reality. Don't we voluntarily conform to many things each day out of need and our own interest in survival? For example, not conforming to the directive of a one-way sign on a road could result in the loss of your life. Not conforming to no-smoking rules near combustible or explosive materials could do the same. Perhaps conforming to organizational standards is also related in certain ways to our survival.

Of course, the likelihood that you'll be willing to conform to and approve of everything about a particular organization is slight. What are your alternatives when your values differ from those of the organization? In the extreme, you could quit, but that's not always a practicable solution. You might try to change the organization's standards, but you may discover that some standards in organizations change slowly and that your efforts are largely unappreciated. You can also continue to work with the organization and maintain a negative attitude that makes your organizational life miserable.

A more useful approach than either quitting or being perpetually negative might be to ask yourself some important questions: In general, do I like my job? Does it ordinarily satisfy my basic needs as well as my ego needs? Do my desired opportunities for advancement exist in this organization? Will I necessarily find a better job elsewhere? If you conclude that, in general, the advantages of your job outweigh the disadvantages, perhaps you should attempt to adjust your standards to those of the organization.

TYPES OF CONFORMITY

Areas of conformity can be classified in a variety of ways. For example, conformity can be categorized as either legitimate or nonlegitimate. It can concern either thoughts or behavior and can involve either on-the-job or off-the-job situations. Each of these sets of factors relates to the other.

Most of us are willing to conform in areas that to us seem legitimate. For example, we probably would agree that we should conform to the practice of honesty—that it would be wrong for us to steal our employer's money. On the other hand, we would probably disagree with a company practice that forced us to vote for a particular candidate or to attend a particular church.

What, then, makes conformity standards on and off the job legitimate or non-legitimate? Frequently, their legitimacy is gauged by how job related the standards of conformity are. For example, arriving to work on time is a fairly clear-cut, job-related standard of legitimate conformity. Not punching your boss in the nose when he or she turns down your request for a raise is another. Many other routine types of activities are also typically accepted as necessary for the organization to function effectively.

The legitimacy of some areas, however, is far less clear, especially when they involve the personal values of an employee. Let's examine five of these areas separately: the use or misuse of company resources, off-the-job activities, workplace affairs, standards of appearance, and smoking.

CAN I DO WHAT I WANT WITH COMPANY RESOURCES?

You probably recall from Chapter 2 that not everyone perceives situations in the same fashion. Some employees, for example, will "borrow" company equipment or supplies, such as pencils, pens, and paper, for use at home. Others misuse company computers by infringing on copyrights through the copying of proprietary software for personal use.

Do you perceive these actions as legitimate? Would you approve of such actions if you were the owner of a company whose employees used your firm's materials for their personal gain? Not very likely. Yet some employees have rationalized their behavior by saying that the items they take are insignificant and that the company will never miss them. Others may assert: "I've worked here for a long time; the company owes it to me. Besides, the company can afford it better than I can." Such rationalizations, however, fail to make the activities legitimate.

After experiencing excessive occurrences of employee theft of company information, some organizations have established policies related to computer use by employees. The firms have also attempted to restrict employee access to certain types of information. Formal policies, it is believed, tend to discourage employees from using company property, such as computers, for personal purposes, such as creating betting pools or preparing resumes for themselves and friends.

Some companies have purchased expensive monitoring systems that enable them to know which employees are misusing computers and telephones. Unfortunately, such activities smack of Big Brotherism to some observers who feel it is an invasion of employees' privacy, a topic we will discuss later. Nonetheless, courts have usually ruled in favor of employers because the employees' activities involved the misuse of company property. Some companies, apparently concerned with the privacy issue, attempt to give employees advance notice of a computer audit; others realize that such audits can be very disruptive to work and the working environment.[11]

SPOT CHECK

1. When confronted with the angry coworker's outburst, do not yell back. T F
2. When dealing with a chronically distraught coworker, do not listen, so your time is not wasted and he or she is not encouraged. T F
3. Spreading rumors almost always helps the organization. T F
4. To help with an unavailable coworker, get an appointment, a deadline, or set your own. T F
5. When dealing with the powerless, start with "what if" scenarios. T F

WHAT I DO ON MY OWN TIME IS WHOSE BUSINESS?

Employees in some fields must regularly be on call. Although they may not be required to be physically present at the workplace, they must be available when needed. Medical doctors, for example, make arrangements to be on call periodically—such as every third weekend—so that medical attention can be provided to the patient whose own doctor is unavailable. Customer-service representatives with some manufacturing companies, such as a manufacturer of computer mainframes, are on call periodically to ensure that assistance will be available if a customer's computer malfunctions.

Suppose that your job responsibilities require you to be on call occasionally. One evening when you are on call, you and your spouse are entertaining friends at your home. It should be fairly apparent that during your on-call period you really aren't free to do anything you might desire. For example, if your beeper warns you to call your company and you're told that you have to make a quick trip to the office of an important customer, you certainly wouldn't enhance your company's image by arriving at the customer's site intoxicated.

But what if your position doesn't require you to be on call? Are you then free to do whatever you want on your own time? Although the line between what you can and can't do off the job isn't always clear-cut, many managers would contend that you shouldn't engage in behavior away from the job that would be damaging to the organization that pays your salary. It's important for you to know the boundaries of behavior that are acceptable to your particular employer, recognizing, of course, that not all companies adhere to the same standards of acceptability and unacceptability.

Let's take one more example: You are an office systems salesperson who calls principally on major accounts in a particular territory. You've worked in the same territory for five years, and you've discovered that you can meet your sales quota without having to work full-time. Although you could probably expand your sales volume by putting in a full day's work, you've decided to use your "spare time" to operate your own business on the side. You've heard that many doctors have tropical fish tanks in their waiting rooms to entertain their waiting patients, so you've decided to start your own business and to spend two hours of each working day calling on doctors' offices to promote your line of tropical fish and aquarium supplies. You are meeting the sales quota agreed upon with your primary employer. Therefore, is it legitimate for you to carry on a business on the side? Most sales managers would contend that such behavior is outside the boundaries of legitimacy. They would be more likely to believe that your full allegiance during a normal working day must be to your primary employer.

WHAT'S WRONG WITH WORKPLACE AFFAIRS?

Nobody should tell you whom you may date, right? The answer "right" to that question would certainly appear to be logical. Unfortunately, however, workplace affairs—the dating or romancing between two adults employed in the same work situation—can create challenges for supervisors attempting to maintain productivity standards and morale.

In general, two types of affairs can exist in the workplace, each of which may have adverse effects on productivity and morale. One type of workplace affair occurs when either one or both persons are married to someone else. The two individuals discover a mutual attraction and begin dating. The second type exists when two unmarried individuals working in the same department share common interests and begin dating.

Should the supervisor put an emphatic stop to such departmental liaisons? Not according to many companies. A recent survey found that 88 percent of the companies had no policy against workplace affairs, and more than 90 percent of the

NetNote

The Office

http://www.bbc.co.uk/comedy/theoffice/

The British view of dealing with coworkers (and an odd boss) from the hit TV series. Needs to be watched several times to catch all the nuances.

12 percent that did have a policy said it only concerned manager-worker dating.[12] Some have found that office romances are less troublesome than parent-offspring working relationships. Still, some believe that the supervisor does have an obligation to become involved when workplace affairs cause productivity to decline or morale of other employees to suffer.

How can such workplace entanglements affect productivity? One way may occur when the lovers spend an inordinate amount of work time concentrating on each other rather than on their job responsibilities. Further, coworkers who observe the lovebirds consuming company time planning their upcoming weekend together at Lake Tahoe may become upset at having to carry their workload.

Another potential problem exists when one or the other is married and a spouse discovers the romantic link, as frequently happens. Many disgruntled mates have been known to create havoc on the work scene either by perpetually telephoning the department or by furiously bursting onto the work site in person.

Supervisors whose departments experience workplace affairs should remember that their major concern should be with job performance, not personal lives. Prior to any interviews with the participants, the supervisor should carefully document any adverse job-related effects the romance has caused. If performance or morale has deteriorated, the supervisor should hold separate interviews with each party and concentrate on performance, not on the affair. The supervisor should stress that the affair is the business of the participants, but that productivity and morale are the responsibility of everyone in the department. The participants should be given ample time to clear up productivity problems on their own. Previously announced disciplinary action may have to be taken if improvement is not forthcoming.

CAN'T I WEAR WHAT I LIKE?

To what extent should we have to conform to an organization's standards of appearance? Shouldn't we be free to dress and look however we want as long as we're carrying out our job responsibilities? After all, it has long been suggested that a book should never be judged by its cover, so why should human beings be judged by their clothing?

Progressive thinkers might believe that their personal appearance should be nobody's business but their own. Ideally, perhaps they're right. As we saw in Chapter 3 and Chapter 5, appearance is an important part of nonverbal communications, and when a person's NVC conflicts with his or her spoken words, people believe what they see. Although blue jeans and a T-shirt may be more comfortable, the image is not what we expect from many professionals. Research reveals that a large part of the impact a person makes on others is based on appearances and that appearance can also affect pay. In general, good-looking and well-dressed people earn more than those of average appearance, who earn more than those who appear plain.[13]

Some companies have fairly stringent employee dress codes that emphasize a neutral look, one that tends not to detract from any message employees may present to members of the public.

Some employees, in their intense desire to be free, actually tend to imprison themselves by conforming to what may be their own unrealistic standards. The desire for freedom or nonconformity can become so much of a fetish that it actually prevents some persons from opening doors of opportunity that might otherwise be there for them.

Of course, no hard and fast rules for dress can apply to every situation. What might be an acceptable standard of dress in Manhattan's financial district might seem bizarre in the small town of Twin Forks, Montana. Some organizations prefer that their employees—especially those who contact customers—conform to a relatively conservative image. Others are fairly loose in their standards of dress. Certain standards tend to persist over time, such as dressing in a low-key manner that tends not to draw undue attention to your appearance. However, each organization has its own expectations about what constitutes sound standards.

BUT THERE ARE INDIVIDUAL DIFFERENCES

There are some organizational hazards associated with assuming that everyone's behavior and values in an organization should conform to a predetermined and precise set of standards. An excessively homogeneous atmosphere, for example, can squelch creative ideas. Furthermore, not all employees share the same types of self-image and aspirations.

For example, managers are sometimes guilty of unrealistic role expectations of certain employees. Some managers may be surprised when an employee refuses an offer to be promoted to a supervisory position. But does everyone necessarily want to become a manager?

To illustrate, let's look at Jim. He has worked for 14 years in a branch office of a large bank. He knows the technical aspects of his job better than most of the other employees and has a personal style with the public that enhances the bank's image. Each time promotional opportunities have arisen, however, Jim has turned them down. Some of his coworkers have difficulty understanding Jim's attitude. Each individual has different needs, however. Only Jim himself really knows why he doesn't want a promotion. Perhaps he is confident in his present position and believes he would lose some of his feelings of security if he became a manager.

Regardless of Jim's personal motives, if he is carrying out his job responsibilities satisfactorily, is there any particular reason for not permitting him to remain in his present position? Some companies give special recognition to individual contributors, such as Jim, as a means of helping to satisfy some of their ego needs.

A SMOKE-FREE ENVIRONMENT

In a free society, shouldn't those who want to smoke have the right to do so? Although freedom is a revered concept in the United States, passive smoking—breathing cigarette smoke wafting through the air—tends to restrict the freedom of nonsmokers. It also tends to have an adverse effect on the health of smokers and nonsmokers alike.

For example, smoking leads to about 400,000 U.S. deaths a year.[14] An Environmental Protection Agency (EPA) study involving lung-capacity tests on 2,100 people examined over a 10-year period indicated that the effects of long-term exposure to environmental tobacco smoke on the lungs of nonsmokers were about the same as the effects of smoking 1 to 10 cigarettes a day. The EPA also emphasized that "substantial evidence shows nonsmokers are at risk of cancer from secondary tobacco smoke." The American Heart Association (AHA) has also declared that passive tobacco smoke is a major risk factor for heart disease. AHA studies report that exposure to secondhand smoke raises the risk of dying from heart disease 30 percent and causes more than 50,000 deaths a year. The AHA has found that environmental tobacco smoke is one of the leading sources of indoor pollution.[15]

Studies by the EPA indicate that secondhand smoke is also extremely hazardous to children. EPA researchers said, "Exposure to secondhand tobacco smoke accounts for thousands of serious respiratory ailments, such as pneumonia, bronchitis and emphysema, in young children, especially infants."[16] With smoking being the leading preventable cause of death and disease in the United States, it should not come as a surprise that an increasing number of firms have adopted smoking policies in recent years.

THE RIGHT TO PRIVACY

To what extent does the individual in an organization have the right to privacy? Opinions differ. What an employee may perceive as an invasion of the right of privacy may be believed by an employer to be merely the right to know. The U.S. Constitution protects citizens from intrusion by the government, but it says nothing about employment situations. A growing concern related to personal rights has developed as a result of employers' expanding their activities in the area of what they believe they have the right to know about employees.

WHAT DO EMPLOYERS WANT TO KNOW?

The Human Resource Management Association surveyed its members and asked what activities they believed their companies had the right to engage in to uncover necessary information about employees. The three general activities most reported were (1) employee testing, (2) collection of information, and (3) surveillance.[17] The box "A Question of Ethics: The Boss Is Watching!" summarizes some of the principal findings of the report. The section that follows briefly examines each of these three major activities.

TESTING EMPLOYEES

Possibly the most common test is also among the oldest and least controversial. The Myers-Briggs Type Indicator (MBTI) is more than 60 years old, and yet most major corporations use it in some way. The MBTI is used to place people in four categories from pairs of opposites: extroversion/introversion, sensate/intuitive, thinking/feeling, and judging/perceiving. The MBTI may help demonstrate decision-making tendencies, but some companies use it for hiring, which it was not meant for. While other psychological and personality tests are also used, they all should be used with caution.

A QUESTION OF ETHICS

The Boss Is Watching!

Sheribel F. Rothenberg, a Chicago lawyer who specializes in employment matters for both employees and employers, believes that increased instances of invasion of workers' privacy are a sign of the times. Rothenberg says, "Rights of privacy are being eroded across the board." He adds, "I think it's open season for employers."

Although not everyone would agree with Rothenberg's negative tone, a recent study by the Human Resource Management Association seems to assert that the employers of its members are increasingly exercising their right to know about employees and job applicants.

What's your opinion? Do you think employers should be permitted to use such devices as polygraphs, integrity tests, credit checks, spotters, and HIV examinations as tools in the employment process? Is such activity a legitimate way to ensure that employees meet organizational standards and fit into the organization's culture, or are such techniques an invasion of employee privacy? What do you think?

Source: Adapted from Carol Kleiman, "What Privacy Rights Do Workers Have? Very Few," *San Francisco Examiner*, September 15, 1991, p. 2-B; Donald McNerney, "Workplace Privacy," *HRFocus*, December 1994, pp. 1–5.

Other employer tests that are common and accepted by companies and workers alike are skills tests. Skills testing measures worker or job-applicant performance on job tasks. Maybe the most well known is the typing test. Tests exist for many if not most job skills, but they can be expensive. Related to individual skill tests are those conducted by licensing and accrediting bodies or states, as is the case for nurses and allied health professionals, lawyers and doctors, or car and truck drivers. Urinalysis and saliva testing for the detection of drug and alcohol use are becoming more common in an effort to create a drug-free work environment.

LIE-DETECTOR TESTS

An area of concern related to the privacy issue has been whether an employer should have the legitimate right to require individuals to take a polygraph, or lie-detector, test, as a condition of employment. Because of their widespread abuse and questionable reliability, pressure against polygraph tests began to build during the late 1980s. As a result, legislation was passed to make illegal the use of polygraphs by private-sector companies as a tool for employee screening or dismissals. The bill, called the Employee Polygraph Protection Act of 1988, has certain exceptions. Employers can ask an employee to submit to a polygraph test only when they reasonably suspect that the employee was involved in a workplace theft or other incident causing economic loss to the employer.

The act also permits the use of lie-detector tests on government employees, utility workers directly involved in the production and transmission of electrical power, many private security company employees, pharmaceutical workers handling controlled substances such as prescription drugs that are addictive, and people working in child-care centers.

Integrity Tests Now barred from using lie-detector tests to screen employees, some firms have turned to various types of **integrity tests** as alternatives. One of these is a pencil-and-paper honesty test, which seeks to gauge integrity through multiple-choice questions on ethical dilemmas. Critics of this approach claim that the tests gather private information rather than job-related information.[18] Another criticism is that the tests do not accomplish their objectives. The Office for Technology Assessment found that integrity tests were correct 2 percent of the time and incorrect 58 percent of the time, whereas the University of Iowa found that they were able to predict undesirable job behavior.[19] Questions that have appeared on pencil-and-paper tests include:

1. Do you always tell the truth?
2. What would you do if you observed your boss stealing company supplies?
3. Did you ever make a false insurance claim?
4. Have you ever gotten really angry at someone for being unfair to you?
5. Do you blush often?

A person who says "No, I never have" to number 4 is probably distorting the answers to other questions, according to users of such questions. Question 5 is said to be a type of question thrown in as a change of pace.

Graphology Testing Some employers have turned to the use of **graphology testing,** which is the analysis of handwriting. Supporters of graphology testing contend that it can be used as a means of character testing. Of course, as with any employment tests, employers may be required to prove that graphology tests are valid and job related.

Integrity Tests
honesty tests seeking to gauge integrity through questions on ethical dilemmas

Graphology Testing
handwriting analysis

HIV Testing Another area of controversy related to the right of privacy is **HIV testing,** that is, examining employees for HIV, the AIDS virus.[20] Testing specifically for HIV by private companies is not yet common, although detection may occur during a physical examination. Ericsson, the Swedish electrical multinational, tests managers who must travel to other countries where the HIV risk is great because HIV infection impairs resistance to other diseases. In the United Kingdom, companies such as Unilever test managers recruited in high-risk areas on the grounds that they may travel to countries that require a negative HIV test before a work permit is granted.

A fear expressed by some authorities related to HIV testing concerns the stigmatization and ostracism that often follow revelation of HIV-positive status. Likewise, HIV tests do not guarantee that applicants are or will remain HIV free; the most commonly used tests detect only antibodies, and these may take months or longer to appear after a person becomes infected.

COLLECTION OF INFORMATION

Employers may desire a wide variety of information ranging from criminal records to psychiatric history. An increasingly prevalent method of looking into the private lives of present employees or applicants for jobs is a technique that employees may never even know is being used—credit checks. As an alternative to the use of polygraph tests, many employers routinely run credit checks on applicants for employment, contending that they are a good measurement of a person's integrity. Employers who use credit records argue that the way an applicant handles bills, loans, and other financial obligations helps predict whether he or she is likely to steal, sell company secrets, or otherwise act irresponsibly on the job.

Nordstrom Incorporated, a department store chain, runs credit checks on finalists for sensitive jobs in its security, financial, and credit departments. Abbott Laboratories, a Chicago-based maker of medical supplies, evaluates credit reports as "part of the routine reference-checking on everybody," according to Ellen Walvoord, director of corporate communications. She adds, "If a person had serious financial problems as revealed in their credit report, it could affect their suitability for certain positions."[21]

SURVEILLANCE OF EMPLOYEES

Almost 60 percent of the company representatives polled in the Human Resources Management Association survey cited earlier approve of some types of surveillance of employees, even including searching employees' offices, desks, or lockers. Some of the methods of surveillance are fairly sophisticated, as can be seen by the discussion that follows.

Workplace Monitoring According to information revealed during a Senate Labor and Human Resources Committee employment and productivity subcommittee hearing, about 10 million U.S. workers are affected by **workplace monitoring;** that is, they are monitored by covert electronic surveillance devices at job sites across the United States, often without their knowledge or permission.

Spies Some employers have resorted to hiring spotters who spy on employees as a means of checking on employee integrity. Employers say that such monitoring enables them to better train employees, measure productivity, and ensure that proper procedures are followed. Three Chicago hotels—the Palmer House, the O'Hare Hilton, and the Westin—formerly hired spotters who acted as employees but spied

---

HIV Testing
examining employees for HIV, the AIDS virus

Workplace Monitoring
observation of workplace behavior, with or without the individual's knowledge or permission

on workers for drug use, theft, and other rule- or law-breaking acts. The hotels have since ceased the practice because of union pressure.[22]

ACCESS TO PERSONNEL RECORDS

Should employees have the right to see their own personnel records? An increasing number of organizations now permit their employees to have access to the files. Do employees also have the right to place limitations on the access that third parties have to such records? The trend appears to be in the direction of greater rights of privacy regarding third-party access to information in employee records.

Some states have passed legislation giving employees the right to see their personnel files, and some, such as Connecticut, also restrict release of the contents of these files to outsiders. Apparently goaded by the Business Roundtable and the Department of Commerce, many firms have adopted formal privacy policies on their own.

THE CHALLENGE OF DISCIPLINING EMPLOYEES

An activity that affects individuals and their behavior in organizations is disciplinary action. Traditionally, discipline has been considered a negative activity aimed at punishing employees who fail to meet organizational standards. Although in some cases punitive actions may be unavoidable, a more modern managerial philosophy looks at discipline as a constructive opportunity to correct rather than to punish a person's behavior.

THE NATURE OF DISCIPLINE

The word **discipline** stems from Latin and means teaching or learning. Because most employees don't intentionally deviate from a manager's standards, perhaps managers need the Latin approach of attempting to modify, improve, or correct employee behavior. After all, isn't your concern as a manager to return the situation to normal as rapidly as possible? Managers who attack the employee rather than the situation generally find that their troubles intensify.

> **Discipline**
> attempting to modify, improve, or correct employee behavior

PROGRESSIVE DISCIPLINE

Many managers employ a form of **progressive discipline,** an approach that follows the philosophy that the severity of disciplinary measures requiring some degree of punishment should increase each time an employee must be disciplined. Typically, the first stage of progressive discipline is an oral warning, followed by a written warning for the next infraction. The third step may be a disciplinary layoff. The ultimate in discipline—the last step—is discharge, which should only be considered after all reasonable efforts at correcting the employee's behavior have failed. Some authorities contend that discharge should not be considered a part of the disciplinary process but is actually the result of the failure to have disciplined in an effective manner.

> **Progressive Discipline**
> the severity of disciplinary measures requiring punishment should increase each time an employee must be disciplined

CAN YOU DOCUMENT IT?

Once again, the importance of full documentation related to any disciplinary measures can't be overstressed as a means of protecting managers and their companies against false charges by a disgruntled employee. Also important is that disciplinary measures be applied in a consistent fashion throughout every department of an organization to avoid employees' charges of discrimination or unfair treatment. Remember to document even positive accomplishments of employees. Documentation of both positive and negative employee performance assists you in preparing formal performance reviews. Trying to maintain an incident file in your mind, especially considering all the other information vying for brain space, is indeed a difficult task.

DO IT IN PRIVATE

As we will see in Chapter 11, people have a need for self-esteem. The manner in which managers discipline workers will significantly influence how well this need is satisfied. For example, has your boss ever chewed you out in front of your coworkers? If so, how did it feel? Such experiences can seriously damage a person's feeling of self-worth. The embarrassment of being disciplined in front of peers can act as a demotivating force on an employee. A general guideline, therefore, is to try to obtain a physical setting for discussing problems with employees that will result in a positive, rather than negative, outcome.

JUST LIKE A RED-HOT STOVE!

In these modern times when microwave ovens are so common, there may be some individuals who aren't familiar with stoves. Nonetheless, as a further means of reducing troubles associated with disciplinary action, it is sometimes recommended that managers employ what has been termed the **red-hot stove method**, a concept that equates disciplinary action with touching a hot stove. Think of what happens when a person touches a red-hot stove. The person near the object receives ample warning (the redness of the stove). The discipline is immediate (the person receives immediate feedback). The discipline is consistent (everyone who touches it is treated equally—he or she gets burned). The discipline is unemotional (a stove doesn't lose its temper). Finally, the discipline is impersonal (the severity of the discipline depends on how much or how long the person touched the stove, not on the personality or characteristics of the person who touched it).

Red-Hot Stove Method
discipline that is immediate, consistent, unemotional, and impersonal

SITUATIONAL DISCIPLINE SHOULD BE APPLIED

Of course, managers should be consistent and treat everyone equitably when administering disciplinary action. However, in some circumstances, the nicely laid out four steps of the progressive disciplinary model might not apply. For example, numerous fire departments have strict rules related to reporting to work drunk. If a firefighter abuses the rule, the disciplinary act is one of immediate dismissal. This type of discipline, therefore, tends to take the form of a penalty. It does have the effect of discouraging firefighters from being intoxicated during working hours. In general, the major factors that should be considered in determining the disciplinary action needed are:

- seriousness of the offense
- past record of the employee
- elapsed time since the last offense
- circumstances surrounding the particular case
- company practices in similar past cases

ENFORCING RULES

Disciplinary measures, whether corrective or punitive, are usually taken as a result of nonstandard performance; that is, an employee has failed to meet planned organizational objectives. Is it really fair to discipline a person who has not been given the opportunity to learn an organization's standards? Managers are expected to enforce rules, which can be defined as statements of precisely what activity or conduct is or is not to be engaged in. An illustration of a rule is "Coffee breaks are not to exceed 15 minutes and are to begin at 10:15 A.M. and 2:15 P.M. daily."

Managers are likely to have trouble enforcing rules that don't make sense to employees. Rules should continually be reevaluated to ascertain whether they are applicable to changing organizational conditions. Employees tend to lose respect for rules that either seem illogical and out-of-date or are not enforced. Also, rules must be communicated to and understood by the employees. Rules should always be enforced equitably, promptly, and consistently or they will lose their effectiveness. For instance, suppose a firm has a company parking lot with special places nearer to the plant for senior executives of the organization. For the past six months, about 10 operating employees have parked regularly in the reserved spaces, but management has said nothing to them. On one particularly dreary, rainy Monday morning, an executive arrived at the parking lot a bit late and couldn't find a parking space near the plant. He became enraged at the prospect of becoming soaked by the downpour. On discovering that workers' cars occupied two of the reserved spaces, he determined who they were and suspended them for two days without pay for the infraction of the rules.

The punished pair could become hostile for a number of reasons and might even submit a grievance to their union steward if there is one. The rule hadn't been enforced previously, so the workers had reason to believe that the rule, in effect, didn't exist. Also, the punished individuals were only 2 of about 10 persons who had used the executive spaces during the past six months, yet the others weren't disciplined. Was it fair to enforce the rule without advance notice after it had been ignored for six months? Morale problems and labor unrest could develop from what might seem like an insignificant event.

FIRING PEOPLE

Employees should be dismissed only as a last resort, after other reasonable efforts at correction or discipline, such as additional training, oral warnings, or suspensions, have failed. Some traditional managers believe that if a person has done something serious enough to warrant discipline, he or she should be fired immediately. A more constructive and modern attitude is that the situation or employee's behavior should be corrected rather than the employee punished.

Sometimes, however, employees must be dismissed, especially during economic recessions when organizational restructuring activities take place to cut costs. In such cases, some organizations have attempted to assist the discharged employees in obtaining employment elsewhere by inviting prospective employers to job fairs for the purpose of interviewing the employees. Outplacement consultants are sometimes used to assist discharged executives. There is no simple way to fire employees, but some useful tips can make dismissal somewhat easier on people:

1. Come directly to the point. Don't beat around the bush and be so tactful that the employee doesn't really understand your intentions.
2. Timing is extremely important. The bad news will probably be less disastrous if presented to the employee late in the working day. To save the employee unnecessary embarrassment, be certain that other employees do not overhear you. Consider the individual's personal situation. Can your decision be postponed in the event of a serious family illness? Can your decision be timed to avoid sentimental holidays, such as Christmas or the employee's birthday or personal anniversary?

3. Let the employee know why he or she is being dismissed. The dismissal may be necessitated by cost-cutting measures rather than the employee's own performance. By informing the employee of the reason, you will help eliminate feelings of self-doubt. An employee fired for a negative reason can benefit from knowing what types of behavior should be avoided in the future. Also, be certain to have factual documentation to support your decision to discharge an employee.

4. Don't encourage retaliation during the termination interview by losing your temper, even if the employee becomes belligerent. Angry employees will occasionally attempt to take revenge against you or the organization.

5. Allow time for the terminated employee to respond, but maintain control of the interview.

6. Terminate the employment as soon as possible after the decision to fire has been made. Often, even if two weeks' notice is mandatory, immediate dismissal with two weeks' salary paid in advance is preferable to retaining the employee for the two weeks. Employees are frequently not very productive during their last days with an organization and, if disgruntled about the firing, can sow the seeds of discontent among other employees.

CHALLENGES WITH ONE'S SELF

When we experience problems, our tendency is to look for external causes. We often feel more secure if we can convince ourselves that someone or something else can be blamed for any troubles we've experienced. Unfortunately, however, such attitudes are sometimes out of tune with reality.

A more effective approach is first to satisfy ourselves that we aren't the cause of the problems before we blame others. For example, suppose the job performance of Harriet, one of your employees, has recently deteriorated. Your immediate reaction might be to assume that she is entirely the cause of her changed behavior. However, could the reprimand that you gave her last week in front of her peers have had a

---

REALITY CHECK

Recovering from a Mistake

You have made a mistake. Not large enough to be fired, but big enough that you need some damage control. What can you do to get back in everyone's good graces? Assess, rebuild, communicate (ARC). First, assess your mistake. Find out how it happened and determine what you can do so that it never happens again. Second, rebuild your image. Ensure that everything else you do is perfect. You may consider taking on additional tasks, especially unpopular ones, but beware of taking on so much that you run short of time and consequently do many things but none of them well. Also ensure that your punctuality is perfect. Arrive a little early to work and meetings; stay a little later at the end of work. Third, keep the lines of communication open. Don't shy away from people, especially your boss. Maintain a consistent level of professional communication, greeting people as before, reporting your accomplishments, and so on. You especially want your boss to know about things you have done and done correctly, but you should be careful how you accomplish this. The trick is to keep the boss aware without making it look like you are essentially running around saying, "Look! I did this right and this right and this right, and doesn't this make up for the mistake I made?" Remember that many managers will tolerate a mistake, but not failures—a mistake being doing something wrong and failure meaning repeating a mistake and not learning from it. If you make a mistake fix it, learn from it, and move on.

Source: Adapted from Sheri Eng, "Get Out of the Doghouse," *Chicago Tribune*, October 18, 1998, sec. 6, p. 3.

demotivating effect on her? By first looking within yourself, you may discover the true causes of some problems.

WANTS BEYOND CAPABILITIES

Not everyone has the aptitude to become a neurosurgeon. The desire to pursue a particular profession isn't usually sufficient in itself. Let's take a look at the hypothetical case of a young man named Bob whose father happens to be a well-known neurosurgeon. Bob and his family have for some time assumed that he would follow in Dad's footsteps. Although bright in many ways, Bob unfortunately lacks the aptitude and abilities to be a surgeon. Bob, however, refuses to recognize his limitations and, because of family connections, has been accepted by a medical school. Bob is highly motivated, a factor that sometimes offsets lesser ability, but in his case motivation fails to get him through medical school. Bob flunks out.

What has occurred in Bob's case is a problem that sometimes develops when an individual's aspirations are greater than his or her capabilities. Although many management skills can be developed, not everyone has the capability, for example, to direct and coordinate a division of a large corporation. Frustration often results when a person fails to heed the admonishment "Know thyself" sufficiently and believes that he or she has capabilities that don't exist. However, in cases where potential capabilities do exist, individuals with a blind faith in themselves have sometimes dived in and succeeded where excessive caution might have caused them to seek lower-level opportunities.

THE PETER PRINCIPLE

Problems can also develop for individuals whose higher-order, or ego, needs are quite strong. Let's take the case of Heidi, who has performed well in every position that she has ever held in her firm. If Heidi has done a reasonable job, the chances are fairly good that she'll be promoted to a higher level. If she does well in the higher position, then she'll probably be promoted over time to an even more responsible position.

Can you visualize what might occur? Heidi has performed admirably in position A. As a result, she is promoted to position B. After an outstanding and conscientious performance in position B, Heidi is promoted to position C. She now discovers that she is grappling for her very existence in position C. She is the quintessential example of the **Peter Principle.** She finds that she can't perform as well as she did in her previous positions, so she is likely either to remain in position C indefinitely, be demoted, or be terminated.

Peter Principle
being promoted to one's level of incompetence

Who knows? Perhaps one day you will be promoted to a position in which you feel insecure. If so, what should you do? Resign? Try to avoid your boss and your associates? Or pursue a more positive approach? Whenever you feel somewhat insecure in a new position, you might first try to discover what your deficiencies actually are and then develop a specific plan and timetable for overcoming them. Perhaps your only deficiency is a temporary feeling of uncertainty about your ability to perform your new job, which is a normal reaction when a person is faced with new challenges. You certainly needn't be destined for a lifetime of feeling insecure solely because of a promotion.

FEAR OF ADMITTING ERRORS

Managers shouldn't make mistakes, should they? If you agree, you have crowned managers with undeserved, glistening, golden halos. Managers, too, are human and will make mistakes occasionally, although naturally they can't afford to err excessively.

Managers also have egos and, like most individuals in organizations, may be embarrassed when they make errors in judgment. If an office manager purchased a large quantity of the wrong size toner, he or she might become excessively defensive and try either to cover up the mistake or to pass the buck. However, for good managers, as a sign on the late president Harry S Truman's desk candidly stated, "The buck stops here."

Individuals in organizations, whether leaders or followers, will generally earn far more respect by admitting when they are wrong or don't know something. Attempts at concealment generally fail in the long run. However, some employees are mentally set to believe that their managers should know everything, and some managers seem to believe that there is no room for error among their associates. Perhaps such individuals would benefit from exposure to the realities of human fallibility.

POLITICS

How do you react to the phrase "the need to play organizational politics"? The words have a negative tone, don't they? Yet many managers, especially in larger organizations, believe that politics is a way of organizational life, and many managers have failed in their attempts to rise in the organizational hierarchy because they were politically inept.

THE NATURE OF ORGANIZATIONAL POLITICS

Organizational Politics
the manner in which individuals obtain and hold onto power

Organizational politics is the manner in which individuals obtain and hold onto power, which enables them to influence events and other people. Organizations differ. Each has its own political philosophy, just as national political parties do. If you are a member of an organizational political group, you will accomplish more of your objectives by acquiring the political skills necessary to gain and maintain the power that you require. Jeffrey Pfeffer, author of *Managing with Power*, contends that managers who want to succeed, and often even survive, must learn the craft of politics. Pfeffer states, "To get things done, you need power—more power than those whose opposition you must overcome—and thus it is imperative to understand where power comes from and how these sources of power can be developed."[23]

Political activities aren't necessarily complex or abstract, nor should they be dysfunctional for the organization. They include such behavior as not embarrassing your boss, willingly accepting certain assignments and invitations, compromising and trading off decision-making activities and resources where necessary, and having close relationships with others who have power in the organization. Regardless of your own personal views on the need to play politics in organizations, a certain degree of political astuteness is essential for those who aspire to rise in many organizations.

Yes-Person
someone willing to tell the boss whatever it is that she or he likes to hear

One caveat: Guard against allowing your support for the boss to get out of control. Unqualified, unswerving support could turn you into a **yes-person,** someone who is willing to tell the boss whatever it is that she or he likes to hear. The subject of the yes-person has been studied at the University of Chicago by economist Candice Prendergast, who found that the more subjective the measure of a person's contribution to the organization, the more likely it is that the person will develop into a yes-person. Prendergast found the same tendencies in groups, reinforcing the need to be alert to groupthink. In groups, yes-people develop because group members tend to alter their comments to mimic the sentiments of the others. These groups will consequently produce fewer ideas as a group than they would individually. Even the flatter organizations of recent years add to the creation of a yes-person because workers have more contact with the few managers left and are then able to know the manager's likes, dislikes, and opinions. The overall effect of yes-people is to decrease efficiency and increase costs by withholding or altering the flow of information in the organization.[24]

You have probably noticed that your boss is anything but an invincible, godlike figure who never makes a mistake. On the contrary, you have probably observed that bosses have insecurities and human frailties like everyone else. Because your boss occasionally goofs, you could find your own confidence beginning to sag, which might make you less supportive of him or her. However, is it realistic (or politically astute) for you to expect the impossible from your boss? If we believe that bosses aren't supposed to make errors, then our expectations are probably out of tune with reality.

INFLUENCE STRATEGIES

Individuals in organizations frequently need to influence others. It may be as a member of the formal or the informal organization. Or, it may be as a manager or leader, or as a worker. Whatever the reasons, there are eight influence strategies people have been found to use: reason, assertiveness, coalitions, negotiation, debt collection, sanctions, ingratiation, or appeals to a higher authority.

Reason is typically regarded as the most effective influence strategy because it has a positive effect on how others view the user and the user's chances for advancement.[25] This is true whether the user is a manager or a frontline worker.[26] Reason involves using facts and logic to influence others. A rational appeal may be that a certain alternative would save more money, last longer, operate faster, produce higher quality, or increase sales. A reasoned appeal is usually objective but may also include a moral argument, for example, that option A is less hazardous to the environment than is option B.[27]

Assertiveness is a confrontational method.[28] It may entail demanding or ordering compliance. Some start out with this method, but others may turn to it after other methods fail.[29] Using assertiveness may seem simple and direct and might appeal to those choosing or wishing to challenge authority, but it can cause resentment and may reduce the user's chance for advancement within the organization.[30]

Forming a **coalition** is an attempt to influence by getting others to agree with or support your position, believing there is power in numbers.[31] The idea is that a large number of people supporting an idea will be persuasive by showing the acceptability of the idea, the consensus of the coalition, or how many people will be adversely affected if the coalition does not get its way. For example, if 9 out of 10 workers in one department want a change, what can the manager do, fire all 9 of them?

Another method that is often well regarded and recommended by many has actually been shown to negatively impact the user. **Negotiation** involves bargaining for what one wants.[32] Managers do not, however, appreciate constant deal making with those who report to them, and the quid pro quo ("this for that" or "I'll do something for you if you do this for me") bargaining can hurt one's chances for promotion.[33] Another form of negotiation involves asking someone to do you a favor, which you will repay later. Some people make this offer, however, with no real intention of upholding their end of the bargain. In general, negotiation is probably best saved for when it is the only influence strategy available.

Debt collection may or may not be associated with negotiation. **Debt collection** involves calling in a favor in order to influence others.[34] Debt collection may be part of a quid pro quo arrangement or it may be that the person being asked to return the favor was unaware that any debt was owed. For example, Fred may tell Ned to

Reason
using facts and logic to influence others

Assertiveness
demanding or ordering others to comply

Coalition
gathering others to support your idea

Negotiation
bargaining for what you want

Debt Collection
influencing others by having them return a favor

go ahead and ask for more capital items on Ned's budget for this year. The following year, Fred may remind Ned that he offered no resistance to Ned's requests last year, nor did he ask for any capital expenditures. Because of that "favor," Fred expects Ned not to compete with him for capital funds this year.

Sanctions involve using threats or punishment to influence others. It may work but, like assertiveness, can also create resentment.[35] The sanctions may be vague threats ("It's in your best interest to do what I ask"), or they may be specific. The sanctions might also be a threat to withhold something ("If you don't sign the contract now, I won't be able to include the discount") or a threat to do something ("If you don't volunteer for my charity drive, I'll have to switch you to the night shift").

Ingratiation is a very common strategy that many people firmly believe to be useful and effective in influencing others.[36] **Ingratiation** may involve flattery, groveling, doing personal favors for someone, and other such methods to curry favor. Some people are quite susceptible to even blatant forms of ingratiation, but, although it may make them like the ingratiator, the use of this method may also prevent the ingratiator from being advanced.[37]

Some that try to influence others may try an **appeal to a higher authority.** This typically involves skipping a level in the organization chart. The idea is that if a higher-ranking person agrees, the lower-ranking person cannot then disagree.[38] This is typically true. This is also typically dangerous. Very few people who have been skipped over will casually accept this. This is especially true if the first-level manager said no initially and then had his or her opinion forcibly changed by his or her boss. Jumping over or going around someone is politically the most dangerous strategy and can only be recommended when the person being skipped over has done something illegal or unethical.

INFLUENCING OTHERS

Although there are eight influence strategies, there are only three main types of influencers. **Influencers** actively try to persuade others. Some try a rational approach, some the ingratiation approach, and others the never-ending approach. **Rational influencers** are the most successful in terms of persuading others and in advancing their careers.[39] Rational influencers always use reason as their main strategy. Often they use only reason but if necessary they may add coalition or negotiation to their rational appeal. **Ingratiators** typically use only ingratiation, which sometimes influences but typically does not help the ingratiator's career.[40]

Those using the **never-ending approach** may employ all eight influence strategies. Many believe that the never-ending approach is *the* method to ensure you get your way and you get ahead. The never-ending approach means never accepting no as an answer. With this approach, if one strategy fails, you try another.[41] You keep on trying until you get what you want. If assertion doesn't work, try sanctions. If that fails, get a coalition together or appeal to a higher authority. Basically, do what it takes to get your way. This may be popular on TV or be viewed as how real movers and shakers get things done, but those using the never-ending approach are often left behind in their careers.[42] As the saying goes, "there is no I in team," and constantly pushing for what you want may be seen as a lack of maturity and an unwillingness to accept direction and decisions from others.

SELLING YOUR IDEAS

Selling—another form of influence—is basically the art of persuading others to buy (accept) an idea, product, or service. Many people react negatively to the

---

Sanctions

using threats or punishment to influence others

Ingratiation

complimenting or flattering others to gain influence

Appeal to a Higher Authority

skipping over someone and going to a higher-ranking person

NetNote

Marwell & Schmidt

http://www. workingpsychology.com/ marwell.html

Influence strategies and their variations.

Influencers

people who actively try to persuade others

Rational Influencers

those using reason to influence people

Ingratiators

those using ingratiation or flattery to influence others

Never-Ending Approach

endlessly seeking influence with any or all of the eight strategies

---

concept of selling, but if you think about it, haven't you been selling all your life? From childhood on, haven't you been trying to persuade others to go along with your point of view? If you have any children, haven't they consistently and untiringly tried to persuade you to buy them the latest in stylish garments or electronic games? Learning the basics of selling can help foster your own organizational activities and opportunities with your boss as well as your peers. Let's examine two guidelines for attempting to sell your point of view to others in the organization.

Focus on Benefits, Not Features　If you are trying to sell your boss or your peers on an idea, don't focus solely on yourself, although your own features are certainly important. When attempting to sell an idea, you should demonstrate how the other person and the organization are going to benefit from the idea, that is, how it will satisfy their wants and needs. Remember: people don't want quarter-inch drills; they want quarter-inch holes.

Would a printer salesperson, for example, be likely to say to a prospective customer, "If you buy this color laser printer-fax-copier-scanner unit with telephone and voice mail, my husband and I will be able to afford that trip to Martinique that we've been longing for"? Not likely. The salesperson would first try to find out what was important to the prospective buyer and then relate her product's features to the customer's needs. Can you see how this approach could help you sell your boss on giving you a raise, a larger budget, or more help?

Test the Waters First　Another approach to selling your ideas to your boss or a peer is to use what has been termed the trial-balloon approach.[43] You might, for example, merely say to the other person, "I got an idea the other day that I'd like to share with you." You briefly discuss the idea and then possibly change the subject. What you've done is planted a seed that might very well grow. If instead you had pushed for an on-the-spot decision, you might have received immediate resistance. People frequently develop negative attitudes toward new ideas that require adjustments in their thinking or behavior. After they have had the chance to mull over the ideas without the pressure of having to make an immediate decision, they frequently become more receptive.

SELF-MANAGEMENT

The business trends of downsizing, empowerment, and Total Quality Management (TQM) have led to another development—**self-management.** Downsizing has left fewer managers in many companies, yet someone has to manage. Part of empowering people includes giving them the power to control their working environments. Combine these two trends with the responsibility for quality in a TQM program, and a logical conclusion is to let people manage themselves. This is not always easy, however. If self-management were easy, businesses would have promoted and instituted it long ago. Self-management not only requires a commitment from management; it also requires extensive training and familiarity with the different components of self-management.

Something as different as self-management requires the support of top management in order for it to succeed. Self-management must also be used under the right circumstances. For example, self-management is not a solution to a problem; it is a means for allowing people to devise their own solutions.[44] Self-management is similar to a calculator in this respect. Although a calculator does not solve problems by

Self-Management
people organizing, controlling, and directing their own work

Companies like SAS go out of their way to care for employees and their families, even providing tutors for dependents having trouble with school. What does SAS get for this? Turnover is very low—4 percent in an industry that usually has a 20 percent rate. Loyalty to the company is very high. Just a few of the benefits include on-site day care where parents can have lunch with their children, massages, a lactation room for mothers who are breast-feeding, two company artists to create original art for the walls, and a strict 5:00 P.M. quitting time. Company founder James Goodnight believes the productivity drop after eight hours of work is so great that longer days are not worth the effort and that having families together for dinner is worth it. Maybe most important to traditionalists, SAS is not losing money. It is saving approximately $75 million per year on turnover costs alone, not to mention incalculable amounts earned in employee goodwill.

Another dramatic example of concern for individuals is the story of Malden Mills and its owner, Aaron Feuerstein. In December 1995, Malden Mills was almost completely burned to the ground. The 3,000 employees were sure that the 70-year-old Feuerstein would not reopen the plant, putting them out of work and almost certainly destroying two Massachusetts towns. To the surprise of many, Feuerstein not only rebuilt the mill, he paid the salaries of the workers during the three months of construction. The key to understanding why Feuerstein did this comes from the man himself. "I consider our workers an asset, not an expense," he stated.

Critics said that Feuerstein was old-fashioned and out of step with modern business practices. Feuerstein countered by saying that he could have replaced his current workers with contract employees earning less than half what he paid, "But that breaks the spirit and trust of the employees."

How did Malden Mills employees respond to this treatment? Before the fire, they produced 130,000 yards of fabric per week for L.L. Bean and Patagonia. After the fire, ingenious and loyal workers figured out ways to increase production to 230,000 yards per week. Said Feuerstein, "They were willing to work 25 hours a day." What goes around, comes around!

Source: Malden Mills information is adapted from Michael Ryan, "They Call Their Boss a Hero," *Parade*, September 8, 1996, pp. 4–5; SAS Industries information is adapted from Michelle Conlin, Kathy Moore, and Ann States, "Photo Essay: SAS," *Business Week*, June 19, 2000, pp. 192–201.

itself, it does provide the means to add, subtract, multiply, divide, and more. Because self-management entails the sharing of responsibility, confidence, and trust between managers and workers, everyone must have free access to all the information necessary to do a job (open-book management), and everyone must be working toward a common goal.[45]

In order to employ self-management, top managers must delegate authority, power, and responsibility down the organization chart.[46] This must be accomplished in such a manner that the employees believe in the transfer and in its permanence. A major step in self-management is to allow workers to learn from their mistakes.[47] If workers are empowered and self-managing so that they may succeed, then they must also have the power to fail from time to time without being unduly reprimanded or fired.[48] As will be seen in the next chapter on motivation, recognition is also important, as it is in all other work efforts.

Training is possibly the most important item for implementing self-management. Workers and managers must have a thorough understanding of what is expected of them, and new workers must be carefully selected and trained in self-management techniques.[49] Such training involves the different components of self-management and some general training. The general training could cover general problem identification and problem-solving strategies.[50] The company mission and vision must be presented, and everyone must share in the vision in order to be successful.[51] It is also critical that a perception of ownership be created with everyone.

When a feeling of **ownership** has been created with workers, they feel responsible for the company, and they have pride in their work just as if they owned the business themselves.[52] When a feeling of ownership is present, managers and workers believe that they are on the same side. They care for company property as they would their own property, and they make each product as if they were making it for themselves. Creating a feeling of ownership in employees is not easy; it requires management that empowers people, management that trusts people and can be trusted, and an open environment where information and ideas flow freely. Conversely, it is easy to destroy feelings of ownership (which may take years to create) with just one broken promise. Many companies seem to find it easier to treat people as disposable resources than to expend the extra effort required to create and maintain an environment of bidirectional loyalty and trust. In fact, does any company try this? Some large corporations, like Levi Strauss, Motorola, FedEx, Xerox, Wal-Mart, and Nordstrom, do, as well as some medium and small firms (see "Reality Check: Concern for Individuals"). Creating a feeling of ownership is an extremely important step that enables the different components of self-management to work successfully.

Ownership
workers feeling responsible for the company and having pride in their work just as if they owned the business themselves

Self-Direction
the individual setting his or her own goals and objectives

THE COMPONENTS OF SELF-MANAGEMENT

As illustrated by Figure 10.1, self-management has five main components. To be self-managing you must be self-directing, you must apply job redesign to your work, and you must be self-controlling, self-monitoring and reporting, and self-rewarding. Although your work must still be integrated with the mission of the company and the products and services of your coworkers, the application of self-management techniques can make you as self-sufficient as is feasible. The five components of self-management must also be integrated with one another, but they are also described here in roughly the same order in which they would be performed.

Self-direction consists of the individual setting his or her own goals and objectives.[53] Individual goals and objectives must be consistent with the mission of the company, the company's goals and

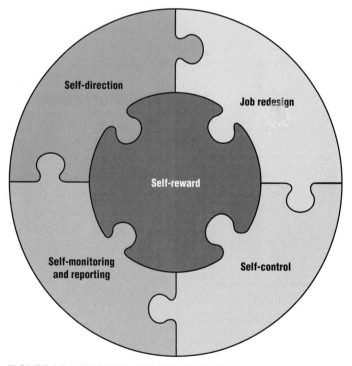

FIGURE 10.1 THE FIVE COMPONENTS OF SELF-MANAGEMENT The process begins with self-direction and proceeds clockwise, ending with self-reward. However, the process repeats and is ongoing, so the components are closely interrelated.

Goals

general statements of what needs to be accomplished

Objectives

specific statements of work to be accomplished, containing a verb and a time parameter and capable of being measured

Job Redesign

an individual proposing changes to his or her work, to the work flow, or to the work systems

Self-Control

the regulation of work by the individual

Self-Monitoring

the individual's ascertaining how well he or she is doing

Self-Observation

the individual monitors and records his or her activities and gathers information regarding his or her performance

Self-Assessment

the evaluation of the information gathered during self-observation

objectives, and the individual's position in the company. What is the difference between goals and objectives? **Goals** are general statements of what needs to be accomplished. **Objectives** are more specific. Objectives must contain a verb and a time parameter, and they must be measurable. Each goal will have one or more objectives accompanying it. For example, let's say that your goal is to obtain a new widget press. Your first objective may be to list the 10 main specifications that will be required of a new widget press by the end of the week. The verb describing the action you will take is to list, the time is by the end of the week, and the objective is measurable because at the end of the week you will have a written list of 10, or 12, or 3 specifications, in which case you will have met, exceeded, or failed to attain your objective. The purpose of self-direction is to accomplish your work (and the company's) in an orderly, proficient manner, on time, as opposed to floundering in chaos while reacting to one self-generated crisis after another.[54]

Self-direction is conducted within the framework of the individual's position, but the actual work often is restructured. Setting goals and objectives through self-direction sometimes indicates a need for job redesign. In this component of self-management, the individual proposes changes to his or her work, to the work flow, or to the work systems.[55] For example, workers at FedEx proposed changes to their billing system that saved the company more than $2 million per year.[56] At Levi Strauss, individuals decide when to advance to the next step in a procedure and which steps need to be examined for refinements and improvements to be made.[57] The power to consider and conduct **job redesign** is consistent with the ideas behind self-management and empowerment. How can you manage yourself without the ability to change what you do? How better to contribute to the creation of a sense of ownership than to give people the power (and create in them the interest and concern) to change their own working environment? The next step in the process of self-management, self-control, follows self-direction and any resultant job change from that initial step.

Self-control refers to the regulation of work by the individual.[58] With self-control, the individual sets the pace and schedules the work that needs to be accomplished in order to meet his or her goals and objectives. Here tasks are prioritized, large tasks are analyzed and divided into manageable units, deadlines are established, and resources are allocated. One of the most important of these resources is time. Time management is not unique to self-management, however, and it is such a large and important topic that it is discussed later in its own section.

Once the individual sets his or her own goals and establishes a schedule, the next step involves **self-monitoring** and reporting. The overall goal of this component of self-management is for the individual to ascertain how well he or she is doing without having to ask the manager.[59] Self-monitoring includes **self-observation** and **self-assessment.** Reporting involves self-assessment and **documentation.** In self-observation, the individual monitors and records his or her activities, gathering information regarding his or her performance toward the completion of goals and objectives.[60] Self-assessment involves the evaluation of the information gathered during self-observation.[61] Here it is just as important for the self-managed individual to understand why things work as it is to understand why things sometimes do not work. We should know why things work so we can repeat successful strategies. We should understand why things do not work so that we can change our behavior in the future. Finally, in documentation, the individual uses the results of the self-assessment to report on his or her own progress. Much of this documentation is for the use of the self-managed person. The self-monitoring and reporting component isn't sent to a manager who then passes judgment on the individual and doles out rewards. That could (and almost certainly would) lead to exaggeration of one's achievements and withholding of one's failures. In self-management, self-monitoring and reporting lead to the self-rewarding component.

In the **self-rewarding** component of self-management, the individual receives or denies rewards that he or she has established for the completion of specific goals.[62] The rewards range from being able to take a break after completion of a small task to leaving work on time or being able to take a vacation in July.[63] The key point is that it is the individual who sets and administers the reward. Although self-rewarding theoretically includes denial of rewards and even punishment, there is some feeling that punishments are much less effective than rewards for changing behaviors.[64] As mentioned earlier, training is needed in these five major components before people can manage themselves. Additionally, organizations can take certain steps when trying to implement self-management.

IMPLEMENTING SELF-MANAGEMENT

At least 10 actions by organizations can increase the chances that self-management will succeed. First, organizations can carefully hire or select individuals for self-management positions.[65] The people must fit the organization and must be sufficiently motivated to manage themselves. Second, it is imperative that the nature, purpose, culture, goals, and objectives of the organization be communicated.[66] In order to match individual goals to company goals, the individual must have a clear understanding of the company goals. Third, in addition to having a clear understanding of the company goals, each self-managed individual must have a clear understanding of the job he or she is to perform.[67]

The fourth step organizations can take to support the move to self-management is to ensure that all self-managed workers understand the immediate and long-term benefits to them (for example, realization of their personal career goals).[68] Organizations should not assume that the self-managed will automatically discern all of the benefits or that they will see each as a benefit to them. The fifth step is also an example of something some might consider a benefit and others might not. In self-management, everyone should have input into decision making.[69] Some may see the chance to be involved in decision making as an advantage, whereas others may see it as a chore.

The sixth action organizations can take is to remove barriers to self-management.[70] If everything that is not self-management is removed, then what is left should contribute to self-management's success. For example, if no time is being allocated for self-direction or self-monitoring, then that barrier must be removed. Time must be made for these activities or the entire system will fail. If a manager is still supervising in the old, autocratic way, then that manager may have to be removed or retrained to be in tune with the new system. The seventh action is to provide coaching along the way.[71] Although some changes can be implemented quickly and easily, self-management isn't one of them. Self-management is different enough to require training, implementation, reinforcement, and patience.

The eighth action is also a long-term one. People who are self-managing need to continue to improve their basic work skills and their self-management skills.[72] The ninth action involves self-managed teams. If at all possible, all team members should be relocated so that they are in close proximity to one another.[73] Some office furniture manufacturers produce special team office furniture to provide privacy and a central meeting area. Finally, the tenth action that can be taken to support the development of self-management is to ensure that everyone receives a fair return.[74] This refers not just to a fair distribution among those

Documentation
the individual's uses the results of the self-assessment to report on his or her progress

Self-Rewarding
the individual receiving or denying rewards that he or she has established for the completion of specific goals

NetNote

University of Victoria Counselling Services

http://www.coun.uvic.ca/learn/program/hndouts/slfman.html

A checklist for self-management.

NetNote

Microsoft

http://office.microsoft.com/en-us/outlook/default.aspx

Outlook 200 product page, Microsoft's program for time and self-management and more.

who are self-managing but also to a fair distribution from cost savings and productivity gains among workers, customers, and shareholders (or owners).

With these actions, and support from those who will be self-managed, significant increases in productivity and job satisfaction can be realized. However, self-management and other forms of management may owe much of their success or failure to how well or how poorly people manage one key resource—time.

TIME MANAGEMENT

Time is the one resource that we all possess in an equal amount. How we spend the limited time we have can be the factor that separates the more successful from the less successful. There are really two kinds of time: There is time that is well spent and time that is poorly spent. Notice we did not say that the two types of time are time for work and wasted time, or productive time and nonproductive time. These differentiations might lead you to think that if you are not working, you are automatically wasting time, or that if you are watching television, you are not being productive. The distinction here is that it is not necessarily the activity that wastes time but the underlying reason for undertaking an activity that determines whether the time is well spent or poorly spent. For example, watching television is not necessarily time poorly spent, and we are not just referring to watching educational programs. Everyone needs a break once in a while, and if a comedy provides a good laugh or a music video entertains you, then this is time well spent. The same may be said of reading, watching your children play, watching a sunrise or sunset, or playing video games. If these provide a brief escape or a contrast to stress, then the time is well spent. If, however, all that one accomplishes is watching TV or playing video games or counting the bubbles in one's beer, then this is time poorly spent. A momentary escape is one thing; taking a permanent vacation from reality is another. In other words, do not think that you must work yourself to death to spend your time wisely. We all must make some time for our families and ourselves; to do so most effectively, we should manage our time and work smarter, not harder.

The advice "Work smarter, not harder" has been around for some time. Instead of working faster or longer, it means you use time more efficiently so that you get more accomplished in the same amount of time. For example, in one four-year period, I wrote two books, edited a state medical journal, changed careers, completed all of my doctoral degree courses, had three children (no twins or triplets), single-handedly restored a 90-year-old Victorian house, and did all the little day-to-day things that always seem to arise. How did I do it (besides not sleeping for those four years)? With a schedule like that, there is no room for time poorly spent. Time management is the way to accomplish much in a short amount of time, and once you learn how to spend your time most wisely, the lesson tends to stay with you for life.

In the workplace (and in life), time management is important not only to accomplish more of the things that you wish and need to do but also to control the many activities and pressures that try to waste your time. Good time management, especially in the workplace, also affects productivity and self-esteem. Wise management of your time can increase your productivity, and increased productivity can increase your self-esteem.[75] Some of the problems people encounter while trying to manage their time include interruptions, not delegating work that others should be performing, wasting time with the telephone, attending nonproductive meetings, and being preoccupied by many little items rather than the one big one that counts.[76] It seems as though everyone is busy, and for some it is fashionable, even a sign of high status, to have no time (often meaning, "I do not have time I wish to

NetNote

Palmsource

http://www.palm.com/us/

Palm computer site—check out a device for time and self-management.

spend on you"). Is it really good or a sign of high status to have no spare time? Or is it a sign of poor time management? Given that time management can provide us with more time to spend as we wish and can decrease stress, which in turn improves health, it is difficult to see how being too busy is good or desirable.[77] How, then, does one go about managing time and spending it more wisely?

WORKING SMARTER: CREATING A TIME-MANAGEMENT SYSTEM

To begin with, any method that assists you in accomplishing your goals and objectives is good. No one way is best.[78] Some systems are good for some people but useless for others. Even if you have a system already, the information here and in other sources may help you refine it. One thing is certain, however: Whether you use a yellow legal pad, sticky notes, a pocket calendar, a desk calendar, an appointment book, an expensive day planner, a computer scheduler, or a palmtop computer, almost any system is better than no system.

To help you choose or create a time-management system, we will first present a method for measuring how your time is currently being spent. This will be followed by specific practical tips, a discussion of lists, document management, and a discussion on handling big jobs. First, however, a cautionary note: Do not devise a system that takes more time to use than the amount of time it saves you. If, after you learn a system, you find yourself dedicating large amounts of time to writing and rewriting lists, setting priorities, and making different lists, then maybe it is time to consider a simpler system.

One method for determining how you are spending your time is to use a **time log**.[79] A time log is a sheet (or series of sheets) on which you record how you spend your time each day (see Figure 10.2 for two sample sheets). When starting a time log, you should first write down your activities in order to determine which categories would be most useful to you. Recording the time spent on each category should be done for at least one week, although you may have to use the log for two, three, four, or more weeks, depending on your situation.[80] Once the time logs have been completed, the numbers are totaled and the percentage of time spent in each area is calculated. This information must then be combined with other information, such as which tasks are not being completed on time. Once you know how your time is being spent and what is not getting done, you may employ some of the following techniques to gain more control over your time.

YOUR PEAK TIME

One of the first steps you can take as a person, student, or worker is to find that time of the day when you are performing at your best. This is your peak time. Some people are early-morning types. They arise and are ready to take on the day. Others don't function well early in the day (with some feeling that anything before noon is early). I found that my **peak time** is between 7:00 P.M. and midnight. If you are not sure when your peak times are, you may need to develop awareness for the signs of peak and nonpeak times. If difficult tasks consistently seem easier and are completed faster in the morning, then morning is probably your peak time. If you stare at a report or read a sentence over and over and still can't remember what it says, if you tend to slump forward so that your forehead bounces off your desk, or if you find your coworkers checking to see if you still have a pulse at 5:30 P.M. every day, then this is probably not a peak time for you. Whatever your peak times are, find them and try to adjust your schedule so that you perform more demanding tasks

Time Log
a sheet (or series of sheets) on which people record how they spend their time each day

Peak Time
the time of the day when you are performing at your best

Date _____	Planning	Controlling	Organizing	Directing
Human Resources				
Financial Resources				
Material Resources				
Informational Resources				

Date _____	Office	Phone	Fax	Internet	LAN	Walk-ins	Meetings
Scheduling	30						
Planning	45						
Budgeting	15		15				
Problem Solving	30	45				15	15
Report Writing	45						
Data Gathering		15	15	30	45		15
Analyzing	45					15	60
Putting Out Fires		60	15		45	90	15

FIGURE 10.2 TWO SAMPLE TIME LOGS   The one on top is a relatively simple log for a manager. The one on the bottom is more detailed and demonstrates how a time log might be completed. Note that you may use increments of 15 minutes or 10 minutes or whatever length is easiest. Just remember that a time log should help you gain control over how you spend your time—it is not supposed to consume all of your time.

during those times.[81] At work, for example, you might schedule routine tasks, meetings, and phone calls for nonpeak times. You then save your peak times for more demanding tasks, like analyzing, writing, computations, and creative work.

TWELVE PRACTICAL TIME-MANAGEMENT TECHNIQUES

Once you know your peak times, it is time to start to work. There are still some questions, though. When do you do what work? How long will it take? In what order should the work be completed? Here, we will look at 12 ways to help you answer these questions. To start with, you will need some method of keeping track of time.

1. Find a calendar and time schedule that works for you and doesn't take more time than it is worth to use. You can choose from a wide variety of products or devise your own system. Some people simply take a legal pad and write a list of things to do that day or week and then allocate times for each task. Others use desk calendars, pocket calendars, or appointment books costing only a few dollars. A few people opt for $100 to $200 systems like the leatherbound Filofax. There are a number of software packages, such as Microsoft's Outlook or Lotus Organizer, for use on computers. There are palmtops and PDAs (personal digital assistants)—handheld computers, some of which are capable of running word-processing and spreadsheet software, too. Many cell

phones include calendars, and some are essentially a combination PDA and cell phone. Whatever your choice, you need a system, you need to make using it a habit, and it must work well and easily for you. Once you have your system of choice, it is time to start scheduling.

2. Schedule recurring events at the start of a time period. If you have a staff meeting every two weeks on Friday for the whole year, then start at the beginning of the year and schedule it in. Or start at the beginning of the quarter or the month, or whatever time period works for you.

3. If you have to prepare for a deadline or a meeting, work backward from the due date and give yourself plenty of warning to begin the task. Do this carefully, remembering Murphy's Law ("Anything that can go wrong, will go wrong"). If it will take two days to prepare for a meeting, you may need four or six days' warning. This is in case other things arise or you become ill or have to take a trip.

4. Look ahead—especially on Fridays, during busy times, and anytime you find you have a few extra moments. Sometimes it helps just to start thinking about upcoming work. At other times you might be able to get an early start on your work. Anything you can do to get ahead of schedule helps because, again, you never know what might come up unexpectedly.

5. A very important time-management technique is that, once recurring meetings are scheduled, you can block out certain times for particular kinds of tasks.[82] You may want to block out a call-back hour, a time when you will return phone messages, and mention it on your outgoing voice-mail message. You may block out times to do your work, times when you are unavailable for calls or walk-ins (people who walk in to see you without calling first or having an appointment) unless they are true emergencies. Also consider times when walk-ins are welcome—true **open-door times.** Don't forget to block out times for yourself. Schedule lunch and even breaks if you must. Block out time for family and vacations if you must. Then, stick to this schedule. Eventually others will learn that you are unavailable from 10:00 to 11:30 A.M. each day, but that it is all right to stop in from 1:00 to 2:00 P.M.

6. A technique of major concern for those of us who are professional procrastinators is "Don't do it." **Procrastination** is dangerous, especially for those who seem to get motivated only when there is barely enough time to finish before the deadline (see Chapter 2). Hard-line procrastinators, those who collate and staple a term paper in the car on the way to class while also eating dinner, know who they are. They also know that procrastination is a difficult habit to break. Procrastination is really a method of scheduling for those who need the special motivation of an impending deadline in order to hear the call to action.[83] The downside to procrastination is that one could figure wrong and not have enough time, or something could happen (Murphy's Law again) so that there is insufficient time. To counteract procrastination, one can set earlier deadlines and try to meet them. Unfortunately for chronic procrastinators, they know the deadline is artificial, so some ignore it anyway. In addition to the tendency to procrastinate, other people often threaten your time schedule. Besides setting a time for walk-ins, you may find the remaining techniques helpful for managing your time with others.

7. Whenever possible, if you have to meet with other people, go to their office as opposed to having them come to you.[84] This way, you can leave when you are finished. When people come to your office, they may linger, and it is difficult to find a polite way to ask them to leave.

Open-Door Times
times when walk-ins are welcome

Procrastination
waiting until the last possible moment to perform a task

8. A technique for formal meetings is, if you have a choice, to attend only those meetings that affect or interest you.[85] Few things are more frustrating than having work to do while stuck in a meeting that doesn't affect you or one with business that could have been handled in a memo or e-mail.

9. A technique that can apply to meetings, when you go to someone's office, when someone walks in to see you, or when you are on the phone is to set a time limit, just as you would for any other task.[86] If you have only 5 minutes and some issue requires 25 minutes, then inform the person or persons and reschedule for when you do have time.

10. Do not let people make their emergencies your emergencies. If someone procrastinated or forgot to talk to you earlier, don't let that person destroy your schedule because of it. Protect your work blocks and your lunch blocks, breaking them only for true emergencies, not for those caused unnecessarily by others' poor time-management skills or laziness. If they must wait, then they must. Failure to plan on their part does not constitute an emergency on your part.

11. Sometimes it is difficult to stay on schedule, especially when you are spending a long time on one task or one type of task. An important time-management technique is to take periodic breaks. This may seem counterintuitive: How can you get more done by taking some time to do nothing? The answer is found in the difference between the quantity of time dedicated to a project and the quality of that time. The quantity of time spent on a task increases as the quality decreases. If your quality of work is declining, take a break. When you do, you should contrast your activities. If you are sitting at a desk, your break should not be spent at the desk or even sitting down. It is better to spend the break walking around; this is often more effective than caffeine at reawakening your brain cells.

12. The last time technique concerns priorities. Not all tasks are created equal. You will need to set priorities according to some system. Some people assign priorities to tasks of 1, 2, 3, or A, B, C.[87] An alternative could be dividing tasks into those that need to be completed immediately, soon, eventually, and if you have time someday. The particulars are not as important as the act of prioritizing. Whatever method you use, you must differentiate between tasks that must be performed immediately, those that can wait a little while, those that can wait a long time, and those tasks that need to be sent to others or discarded. Once you establish broad categories and place tasks into them, you may have to go through each category and place those tasks in order. After establishing priorities, you can estimate times, schedule tasks, and start to work. Table 10.1 recaps the 12 time-management tips.

TABLE 10.1 TIME-MANAGEMENT TIPS

Find a calendar and time schedule that works for you.	Schedule recurring events at the start of a time period.
Work backward from deadlines.	Start thinking about upcoming work early.
Block out times for particular types of tasks.	Don't procrastinate.
Go to other people's offices for meetings.	Attend only those meetings that affect or interest you.
Set a time limit for meetings and conversations.	Don't let people make their emergencies your emergencies.
Take periodic breaks.	Set priorities.

FYI

Find a way to cope with those who take a little getting used to.

When new to an organization, conform. Test the limits of nonconformity, if you must, slowly and carefully.

Never waste company resources. The money saved might be used for salaries; if it's wasted, it definitely can't be used for salaries.

Document disciplinary actions for your own protection.

Be aware of the Peter Principle; just because someone offers you a promotion and thinks you can handle the job, it doesn't mean you really can. Know your capabilities and limitations.

Use logic to influence others.

Learn to manage yourself. Even in organizations that don't currently use it, the skills are personally valuable.

Master time.

LISTS

Some people are dedicated to making lists.[88] Sometimes the lists are made instead of, rather than as a way of, prioritizing, and at other times the lists are made in conjunction with prioritizing. Some software programs and palmtop computers have built-in "To Do" lists, and items that are not crossed off are automatically forwarded to the next day. Whether you prioritize separately or not, once the list is made, the next question is which item do you do first? Some people start at the top and simply work through the list. Others do the tasks they like first and the ones they don't like last. On the other hand, some reverse this, saving the jobs they like as a reward for completing the ones they dislike. Some people like to do all the little tasks first so that they see some progress; others want to dive right into the big job to get it behind them.

Any of these methods can work as long as high-priority work is getting done, but if someone is using one of these methods to procrastinate and escape necessary work, then that person is wasting time, not managing it. Remember, too, that the whole point of time management is to ensure that you have the time to complete the things that you need and want to get done. Spending a large amount of time writing and rewriting lists can defeat the whole purpose, and it just creates more paperwork.

PAPER HANDLING

Business executives report that they waste an average of six weeks a year looking for lost documents.[89] The general advice for document management is to handle documents as few times as possible—preferably just once.[90] One way to do this is to use the **FRAT** system when you receive documents or mail. FRAT stands for file it, refer it, act on it, or trash it. The first time you handle a document, decide what to do with it and then do it. If it is a record for your files or a meeting notice, then file it. Or mark the meeting on your schedule and then file it in the folder for that meeting or activity. If the document is not one that is to be filed, then see if it can be referred or delegated to someone else. If the document is something you must attend to, then prioritize it and find a time to work on it. If the mail or document does not fit any of these three categories, then you can probably trash it, but check one more time before you do. With this system, you can minimize the time spent

FRAT

File it, refer it, act on it, or trash it—a system of document handling

Pile People

those who place things in different stacks and remember where in their many piles a document is located

File People

those who place papers in files

on handling paperwork. The paper you do handle may benefit from some special treatment to further ensure that it can be found easily and that it is in the right place at the right time.

Once you decide to keep a piece of paper, you will need to find it again. The two basic systems for accomplishing this are files and piles.[91] **Pile people** place things in different stacks, and most seem to have the innate ability to remember where in their many piles a document is located (or at least they know the general direction in which to start looking). **File people** place papers in files. Some use the standard manila folder, and others have elaborate systems with colors, tags, labels, and titles in alphabetical order. Then there are the many people in between who use some files and some piles. Whichever system you prefer, having special files or piles can help. Urgent, high-priority work can be kept in your only red folder or in a special pile or bin. Outgoing documents and mail can be kept in another folder or bin. Other special colors, boxes, bins, or even sticky notes can be used to identify and differentiate your papers.

BIG JOBS

Throughout this discussion of time management and tasks, prioritizing, and scheduling, it may have seemed as if all jobs are accomplished rather quickly and the main problem is prioritizing and finding time to work. But what about the really big job, like writing this book? How does one even start a job that is too large to conceive of or to contemplate all at once? There are two keys to accomplishing large projects. The first key is to start. In order to complete a large project, you must first cross a barrier. Once you begin the project and have crossed this barrier, the project seems easier to handle. You may find that what is depressing is the thought of doing the project, not the actual performing of the activity. You must start in order to finish, even if you have to force yourself to start in a very small way.

The second key is to divide the large, overwhelming project into a series of manageable portions. Don't think of the entire project; think of the portion you can complete this week, today, or by the end of this hour. For example, no one sets out to write a whole book all at once. A chapter at a time may be contemplated and researched. Then the chapter is divided into sections. Sometimes the reading for just one section is done. Next the writing of the section may be planned, and then each paragraph is written. Sometimes it seems that one paragraph is all that can be managed. At other times page after page is written in one sitting. Through it all, it seems best not to even think about the end of paragraphs, much less a whole book. One just keeps writing, and one day the last topic is complete (and then you get to rewrite it). If you limit your view to what you can accomplish during the current work session, then by constantly chipping away at the whole, you, too, will eventually find yourself at the end of large projects.

SPOT CHECK

11. The peak performing time for everyone is early morning. T F

12. If you have to prepare for a deadline or a meeting, work backward from the due date to give yourself time to begin the task. T F

13. To manage time, if you have to meet with other people, go to their office. T F

14. Do not let people make their emergencies your emergencies. T F

15. To get more done and better manage your time, skip all breaks. T F

SUMMARY

A certain degree of conformity is necessary in most organizations to provide predictability and stability and to accomplish organizational goals. Most employees whose individual philosophy differs markedly from that of their employers must make some significant choices. They have to decide whether to quit, to try to change the organization, to continue working but with a negative attitude, or to try to adapt to the organization's standards.

Conformity can be classified as legitimate or nonlegitimate. Employees can be asked to conform in the way they think and in the way they behave. The concepts of conformity also apply to both on- and off-the-job activities. Efforts by managers to create a conforming atmosphere should not overlook individual differences. The right to privacy and management's use of tests, collected information, and surveillance of employees are also issues facing employees in the workplace today.

Besides having to conform, you may have to adjust to the people you work with. Some, as seen in Chapter 1, are caustic coworkers, but others, as seen in this chapter, just require a little getting used to.

Leaders face the challenge from time to time of having to discipline some employees. Following accepted guidelines tends to make the task more effective. Individuals in organizations often have problems associated with their own attitudes and activities. For instance, their wants may exceed their capabilities, they may become dissatisfied after achieving goals, they may discover that they have gotten in over their heads, they may have difficulty admitting errors, and they may occasionally face ethical dilemmas.

Playing politics appears to be a basic part of contemporary organizational life and is not necessarily a negative set of activities, except when its presence hinders the organization and its members. One of the more common activities in organizations involves trying to influence others. Although there are different methods, the most consistently reliable method is to be rational.

Self-management is growing in popularity, and according to some, virtually everyone in the future will be required to self-manage. Either with or without self-management, time-management skills will be needed. Time management not only aids in the accomplishment of routine tasks, but it can be the key to working smarter, not harder.

CHECKING FOR UNDERSTANDING

1. Should an individual member of an organization be expected to conform to all of its standards and policies? Explain.

2. What are the potential dangers to organizations that encourage excessive conformity among employees?

3. What is the difference between the literal and those with an attitude problem? How should each be handled?

4. Should your manager have any right to tell you what you can't do on your own, off-the-job, time? Why or why not?

5. Should workplace affairs between consenting adults be permitted? Explain.

6. Do you think that employee testing, credit checks, and the use of surveillance techniques, as described in the chapter, invade the privacy of employees? Explain your position.

7. Should employees be permitted to have access to their own personnel records? Explain. How do you feel about third-party access?

8. What is the purpose and nature of the progressive disciplinary process?

9. What is the significance of the red-hot-stove rule?

10. What is meant by the term *organizational politics*? Do you think that it is a favorable part of organizational life?

11. Why is it considered politically astute to be supportive of your boss?

12. There are rational influencers, ingratiators, and those using the never-ending approach. Which

would be better to be and why? Which one should you avoid and why?

13. List and define the components of self-management.

14. List and explain the 12 time-management guidelines from this chapter.

15. Which of the 12 time-management guidelines are you currently using? How can you implement the ones you are not currently using?

SELF-ASSESSMENT

The following questions refer to your behavior when you are trying to influence others at work. Answer SA for strongly agree, A for agree, D for disagree, and SD for strongly disagree.

1. I never stop trying. *SA A D SD*

2. To get what you want you have to threaten people. *SA A D SD*

3. I get other people on my side; they can't say no to all of us. *SA A D SD*

4. My philosophy is you have to give a little to get a little, but I drive a hard bargain. *SA A D SD*

5. I always use a rational approach. *SA A D SD*

6. Get your boss's boss to agree with you; then your boss can't say no. *SA A D SD*

7. I do favors beforehand so other people owe me when I want something. *SA A D SD*

8. I demand that others give me what I want. *SA A D SD*

9. If you want something from others tell them how great they are (whether it is true or not). *SA A D SD*

10. I never let something drop no matter how many nos I get. *SA A D SD*

For all items except 5, score −2 for every SA, −1 for every A, +1 for every D, and +2 for every SD. For item 5 score +2 for every SA, +1 for every A, −1 for every D, and −2 for every SD. A score of 11–20 indicates a very effective influence style, 1–10 an effective influence style, 0–−10 a less effective influence style, and −11–−20 a much less effective influence style that may also be annoying to those you are trying to influence.

SKILL BUILD 10

"You must be Juliet, the new ex-pat from France. I'm Jack, Jack Johnson."

"Very nice to meet you, Jack," Juliet replied, extending her hand.

"Your English is excellent; you are from France, aren't you?" Jack asked, taking her hand. Juliet shook his hand quickly and let go.

"Yes, I was born in a small town on the Cotentin peninsula and have come from the Paris office. I spent much time in England and learned most of my English there. Where are you from?" Juliet asked.

"Born? Birmingham, Alabama, but I'm from our Atlanta office. I'm here to show you around. Introduce you to people. Mr. Boyd, our boss, is, um . . . busy. Let's start with the team room. You get your own desk, but not your own office. All our desks are in the same room so we just call it the team room," Jack explained as he started down the hall.

Jack led Juliet through a door into a windowless room with six desks. Four had the rest of the team seated behind them; one had nothing on it at all.

Before Jack could say anything, Jamal stood up and said, "Well, well, you are *definitely* going to want to sit next to me. The rest of these bums can't hold a candle to me. As I am the heir apparent, you will want to be extra nice to me too."

Skill Question 1. Juliet needs your help interpreting all she has seen and heard so far. Start out by helping her to deal with this individual. Classify Jamal and explain what type of individual he is.

Skill Question 2. What advice from the chapter can you find to give Juliet in dealing with Jamal's type?

Juliet looked at Jamal and then at Jack and then back to Jamal. Before she could speak, Jack said, "All right, back off, Jamal. If you were twice as smart as you think you are, you still wouldn't be nothin'."

"Don't mind him," Jamal said to Juliet, "poor Jack isn't a fantast like I am."

"Say what? What do you mean I ain't fantastic like you?" Jack said.

"Not fantastic–a fantast. It's like, a dreamer, a visionary," Jamal explained, as if speaking to a child.

"You're dreaming all right," Jack said.

"I'm not dreaming about how smart I am. I was just selected to join Nensa, the organization for smarter people," Jamal said.

"Don't you mean Mensa, with an *M*? And don't you need, like, 140 IQ to get in?" Jack asked.

"No, I mean Nensa, with an *N*. We're one better than Mensa. And you need 110 IQ or more to get in," Jamal said.

"What? That's less; 110 is less than 140, and 110 is still in the average range, isn't it?" Jack said.

"We let more people in this way. That's why we're better. Anyway, my dear," Jamal said to Juliet, "You can rely on me to help you in every way possible to rise above the slightly above average to be with me."

"Whatever," Jack said, "Mr. Boyd said he was too busy to take her around so he asked me, not you. Try to remember that."

"Everybody, this is Juliet. She was just transferred from Paris. Let's all try to help her get settled—except for Jamal the superstar, who I'm sure will be too busy inflating his own high opinion of himself," Jack said, getting a laugh from everyone else. "Juliet, that's Gene, Chloe, and Estavan."

Gene stood and marched right over to Jack, Juliet, and Jamal, "Listen, this is *your* job, Jack. You want help, don't come to me, I have my own problems. I just got promoted up here myself, and it's not easy. As for you Jamal, I want the Pasco account, so don't even bother asking about it. I never get any of the good accounts, and I'm demanding this one no matter what you say."

"Forget it, Gene, you are way out of your league," Jamal answered. "You never should have come up here to the big time."

"Hey, Boyd offered me the promotion, and I had to take it. Now he's never around to help me. What good

is he?" Gene said angrily. "You're *not* going to mess with me on this one, Jamal!"

Skill Question 3. What kind in influence strategy does Gene use with Jamal?

"What I am not going to do is argue with you. Especially in front of this lovely lady from France. I'll just go right to Mr. Boyd with this, and we'll see who he wants handling Pasco—the best there is, meaning me, or someone in way too deep already. If that doesn't work, I go right to Boyd's boss," Jamal replied confidently as he turned and left the room.

Skill Question 4. What kind of influence strategy does Jamal talk about using?

Estavan took his feet off his desk and sat up in his chair. He looked at Juliet and said, "Don't pay attention to Jamal and don't let Gene get to you; he's always mad about something." Gene grunted and walked out the door.

Skill Question 5. What type of individual is Gene?

Skill Question 6. What advice can you give to Juliet in handling or reacting to Gene's type?

Skill Question 7. What principle from this chapter applies to Gene and what *should* Gene have done to prevent it from applying or happening to him?

Estavan continued, "This can be a real sweet deal. Let those guys argue over who gets the big accounts. Who cares? The bigger the account, the more the work. They want me to take on those high-maintenance accounts, they need to pay me something extra. There are plenty of small fry to pick up, and as far as I am concerned, that's all my salary covers. What do you get for handling the big ones? More big accounts and more work. If you do enough they promote you and what do you get? *More* work. Sure, you get more money, but you'll never have time to spend it. Nope. You knock yourself out if you want, but until I see something right now for the effort I'm good with what I got. You can have my share of the work, and you are welcome to it. Besides, if I really wanted the Pasco account, I could get it in a minute. If I could ever find my old buddy Boyd, he'd give it to me. Boyd and I go way back, and I've saved his bacon from the fire enough times that he owes me. If I ever asked, he'd come across with the goods. But until then I'll just keep the cruise control on. I don't want to end up a basket case like Chloe."

That said, Estavan got up and left the room, but Chloe yelled after him, "I am *not* a basket case!"

Skill Question 8. What type of individual is Estavan?

Skill Question 9. What suggestions can you give to Juliet for handling Estavan's type?

Skill Question 10. What kind of influence strategy does Estavan talk about using?

Turning to Juliet, Chloe said, "It's nice to meet you. From France, huh. My name's French, but I'm not. I'm just American, and I'm not a basket case, I just got problems, cuz, like, I've tried not sleeping and napping and getting up the same time every day, but nothing works because I'm really a night, person, well, evening at least because that's when I wake up, I mean, I'm awake, it's just that I don't think as well until it's, like, seven at night and that's when I used to work, from like three in the afternoon to eleven-thirty, but then, like the one time I see Mr. Boyd, he switches me to this day stuff, and like getting here at seven in the morning is just so wrong, so I'm like ready to pull my hair out because I walk around like hazy all day, and then at home at night I like have all this energy, but I can't work cuz of this day shift, and like everything I need is here, and I try to make notes and bring stuff back, but the notes make no sense cuz I don't have my stuff and I go to meetings an' feel like I'm going to burst, you know, and like sometimes I just cry or at least I want to, but nothing comes, and so I end up sounding like a sad puppy, and I like just do *not* know what to do!"

Chloe abruptly stopped talking and stood there looking at Juliet for 10 long seconds and then turned and went back to her desk, sat down, and put her head down on her desk.

Skill Question 11. What type of individual is Chloe?

Skill Question 12. What time-management principle is Chloe aware of but unable to utilize in her current job?

Skill Question 13. What advice from the chapter can you give Juliet for dealing with Chloe and why should Juliet follow the advice?

Juliet looked at Jack, and Jack just gave her half of a smile and said sarcastically, "Any concerns?"

"Just one," Juliet replied. "Is Mr. Boyd really difficult to see?"

"You hit on the only obviously important piece of information in all that. Yes, I'm afraid he is. In fact, we see him so rarely that when we do we call it a live sighting."

"Does he have other people to supervise?" Juliet asked.

"Nope, we're it. And before you ask, no, we have no idea what he does or where he gets off to. We just deal with it. Now, did you pick all the other lessons to be learned from this?" Jack asked.

Skill Question 14. What type of individual is Mr. Boyd?

Skill Question 15. What advice can you give Juliet for getting answers to the questions she will have from Mr. Boyd himself?

APPLICATIONS

10.1 A REBEL WITH OR WITHOUT A CAUSE?

Randy Kaufman has been a sales representative for the PhotoMade Office Products Company for the past nine months. Although he has generally attained or surpassed his monthly sales quotas, Randy seems to be experiencing some difficulty in adjusting to organizational life.

Randy has never been much of a conformist. While in college, he was generally outspoken in opposing U.S. foreign policies. He continually bragged that he would go to prison before he would fight an "imperialistic war" in such places as Iraq or Somalia. During holiday dinners, such as Thanksgiving, he typically argued with some of his relatives about a wide variety of issues. His caustic, somewhat combative manner of discussing issues tended to alienate others.

Randy is accountable to Terry Titeship, the district sales manager. Titeship follows a practice of applying close controls on his sales staff. For control purposes, the sales representatives are required to submit the following reports:

1. Monthly sales projection, submitted monthly
2. Weekly sales projection, submitted weekly
3. Production sheets, submitted weekly, that indicate the following:
   a. Number of telephone survey calls
   b. Number of telephone appointment calls
   c. Number of actual product demonstrations
   d. Number of cold calls on prospects
   e. Number of leads obtained
   f. Monthly goals report projecting sales and describing methods for achievement (partially overlaps number 1)
4. A weekly planner, indicating scheduled product demonstrations
5. A hot-list report, summarizing past activity with a listing of prospects that are likely to make a purchase within the next 60 days, submitted daily
6. A postproduct demonstration report, submitted at the end of each day

In addition, the sales representatives are required to report to the office each morning at 8:00 and spend a minimum of two hours on the telephone making survey calls and setting up appointments. They are required to check back into the office between 4:00 and 5:00 each afternoon. They aren't permitted to leave the office before 5:15 P.M. The sales representatives must prepare paperwork and sales proposals on their own time, that is, not during official working hours. They also are required to attend evening meetings lasting until 10:00, for which they receive no compensation. Because they work on a straight commission, their earnings depend solely on their sales.

Most of the sales representatives in the office think that the paperwork demanded by Titeship is greater than that imposed on sales representatives at other companies. However, they comply with Titeship's requirements, complaining only to one another and to their spouses rather than to Titeship.

Randy, however, has been complaining quite openly both to Titeship and to others in the office. Titeship has frequently warned Randy that his negative attitude must change and that his complaints are damaging to the morale of the other employees. Randy's behavior, however, has not changed. This morning Randy was given a written warning that placed him on probation. He was told that he would be discharged if his attitude did not improve substantially during the next 2 months.

QUESTIONS

1. In your opinion, are the demands for conformity that Titeship has placed on his salesforce legitimate or nonlegitimate? Explain.

2. How do you feel about Titeship's decision to place Randy on probation?

3. What are some of the choices of action available to Randy in relation to the standards that he has found difficult to accept?

10.2 GETTING THINGS DONE

"Khalid, I'm not getting my contracts typed up in time. I told you that if you were going to let Sunda work at home I wanted the keystroke-monitoring program installed on her computer. Did you do it?"

"Mr. Mortenson, I know I am new to this country and this unit of the company, but I am in charge of word processing, and you are in charge of legal affairs. We are equals on the organization chart, and I do not think you can just order me on how to do my job, sir."

"Look, Khalid, I'll tell whomever what to do and how to do it when it affects me! You get that software installed!"

"I do not think I can do that. Sunda is using *her* computer in *her* home. That program would be invading her privacies. Besides, that type of thing is a task for the HR department."

"Hey, I talked to Danny Danco in HR. Maybe you don't know what he is like. He won't do anything without getting something in return. He figures he's given his fair day's work by showing up on time. If you don't do what I say, I'm talking to our VP, Ms. Pamir, and there will be trouble for you, pal."

"I am not saying you or Sunda is right or wrong; I just think it is difficult as it is not really my area," Khalid replied.

"Ah, you're useless," Mortenson said as he stormed out of Khalid's office.

In Vice President Pamir's office, Mortenson had the same manner, but a different tone.

"June, you said you owed me for taking care of the Pender incident for you, and now I want you to take care of this new guy, Khalid, for me. I told him what needed to be done, and he just whines that he can't do it. We can call things even between us if you put the fear of me in him," Mortenson said. Ten minutes later, Khalid and Ms. Pamir were alone in her office.

"Khalid, Jim Mortenson was here before telling me about what happened. I'm suspending you without pay for two days and ordering you to clear things up for Jim," Ms. Pamir said.

Khalid was shocked, but finally said, "With all due respect, Ms. Pamir, I have been with this company for 11 years, just not in this unit, and I know of no disciplinary procedure that starts with a suspension."

"I'm calling it insubordination."

"But that starts with a verbal warning, and there are four other steps before reaching a one-day suspension," Khalid said.

"So you read the Employee Handbook! I use the red-hot poker method and you just got jabbed. Now go and get to work."

When Khalid returned, he called Sunda and found her completely disorganized. She was spending much of her time planning and arranging her work before starting on it. Then when she did begin, she often started

with the contracts that were needed last, figuring she had the most time to do them and if they didn't get done she was safe. She often started one contract and then switched to another. She said she had no idea she was doing anything wrong because she had no idea of what was the right way to work at home.

QUESTIONS

Support your answers with examples from the application.

1. What issue was Mortenson trying to force Khalid to act on?

2. What two influence strategies did Mortenson use with Khalid and what other strategy did he use on Ms. Pamir?

3. What kind of person did Khalid consider himself to be and what kind is Danco?

4. What disciplinary concept does Ms. Pamir's red-hot-poker method *not* use? What one smaller part of Ms. Pamir's disciplinary action was at least done properly with Khalid?

5. Based on what Khalid found out, what two chapter concepts could Sunda benefit from?

NET-WORK

What type of caustic coworker is this?

http://www.youtube.com/watch?v=Unf14TLuQSw

Time Management

http://www.youtube.com/watch?v=1rFMWRYnT18&mode=related&search=

http://www.youtube.com/watch?v=SLROb9yR1SI&mode=related&search=

PERSONAL POINTS

1. How do you feel about conforming to an organization's desires? If you feel a need to be nonconformist, how could you do this outside of work instead?

2. How do you handle mistakes made at work? If you could improve your handling of mistakes, how would you do that?

3. If you were self-managed, how would you overcome temptations to seriously underperform (i.e., to slack off)?

4. How are your time-management skills? How often is your work late or finished at the last minute? How late are you for appointments? How will you survive the work environment when dependabilty is one of the most valued qualities in an employee?

5. What is your peak time for work? How will you match this to your job?

EXPERIENTIAL EXERCISE

Declining Ethics?

Read the following paragraph:

> The younger generation has views somewhat like those of the young student, Raskolnikov, in Dostoevsky's classic novel *Crime and Punishment,* who believed that "[t]he end justifies the means." As long as Raskolnikov achieved his goals, he thought it mattered little what he did in pursuing them. Many young people in the United States have been equated with this student. Many observers see them as the least morally anchored generation ever and assert that their only consideration is winning and "looking out for numero uno." As with Raskolnikov, they are willing to do whatever it takes to accomplish their own personal goals.

ACTIVITY

Show the paragraph to at least 10 young people under 25 years of age. Ask them an open question, such as, "What is your reaction to these comments?" Did the young people interviewed agree or disagree with the views presented? If they disagreed, what were their reasons for disagreeing? What did your informal survey tell you about the current values of some young people? How do you personally feel about their responses?

HOW WILLING ARE YOU TO CONFORM?

Read the statements below. Then rank on a 0 to 10 scale your degree of acceptance of the statements related to your career or job, with zero representing a complete lack of willingness to conform to the requirements of the statement and 10 a complete willingness. After you have finished

ranking the statements, get together with four or five class members and compare responses. Ask each other why the particular statement was ranked in a particular way.

1. I would willingly wear a dark, somber-looking suit on the job.
2. I would willingly get my hair cut each week (if a man) or have my hair styled professionally twice a month (if a woman).
3. If requested by my boss, I would be willing to make up a phony invoice.
4. I would be willing to play on the company volleyball team even if I did not like playing volleyball.
5. If requested by my boss, I would be willing to stop dating a coworker.
6. A person unwilling to accept a promotion should not be allowed to maintain his or her job with an organization.
7. A ban on smoking in the workplace is acceptable to me.
8. Employers have the right to use secret video cameras to monitor employees.
9. A person must play politics to succeed on the job.
10. My boss has the right to control my behavior off the job.

SPOT CHECK ANSWERS

1. T
2. T
3. F
4. T
5. T
6. T
7. F
8. F
9. F
10. F
11. F
12. T
13. T
14. T
15. F

11 | Motivation and Morale

One of the greatest discoveries you can make, one of the great surprises, is to find you can do what you were afraid you couldn't do.

Henry Ford

An honest man is one who knows that he can't consume more than he has produced.

Ayn Rand

GOALS

The goals of this chapter directly affect all organizational members. The discussion of motivation is meant to examine and explain major motivational theories as they may be applied by or to you. Morale is also a part of the daily work environment. A better understanding of both may enable you to participate in and respond to motivational and morale-building efforts in a manner more beneficial to you.

OBJECTIVES

When you finish this chapter, you should be able to:

▶ Explain the importance of understanding the concepts of needs and motivation.

▶ Describe a basic model of motivation.

▶ Explain the nature of four common learned needs.

▶ Differentiate among the motivational theories of Maslow, Alderfer, and Herzberg.

▶ List and define the four principal techniques of reinforcement used in behavior-modification activities.

▶ Describe expectancy theory.

▶ Describe equity theory.

▶ Describe Hunter's intrinsic/extrinsic theory.

▶ Describe how time and importance affect motivation.

▶ Describe the special role money plays in motivating people.

▶ Describe actions you can take when you are not motivated.

▶ List and describe the principal factors that influence morale.

▶ Recognize the major warning signs of poor morale.

▶ Describe the various methods for measuring or evaluating morale.

WHY LEARN ABOUT MOTIVATION?

Theories of motivation were devised in an attempt to explain the behavior of people. As you are either a manager or a worker (or will be soon), you have a vested interest in understanding motivation in order to (1) motivate others, (2) understand how others are trying to motivate you, or (3) enable you to better participate in your own motivational effort or the efforts of others trying to motivate you. Understanding the motivational theories allows you to identify the motivational efforts managers are trying to apply. This will help you identify the assumptions the manager is operating under and enable you to coordinate your motivationally related requests. Knowing and identifying a manager's motivational methods also help you decide whether or not the manager's efforts match your needs.

THE IMPORTANCE OF NEEDS AND MOTIVATION

Need
a lack of something
required

All of us have needs. Although we might be able to survive without such gadgets as video telephones and digital compact disc players with random-access programming, we wouldn't survive for long without food, drink, sleep, air to breathe, and appropriate atmospheric conditions. A **need,** in effect, gives a person a feeling of deprivation, that something is missing from his or her life, at least at the moment. The missing things may be physiological (food and drink), security (medical insurance), social (friends), or psychological (self-esteem, status, and feeling of achievement). When you are deprived of various things, something to drink, for example, you feel a type of tension that moves (motivates) you to engage in activity intended to quench (satisfy) your thirst. Certain types of deprivation on the job can also influence your attitude—that is, morale—at the workplace, a topic that will be covered in a later section of this chapter.

NetNote

Mental Health Net Motivation

http://www.mentalhelp.net/poc/view_doc.php?type=doc&id=9824&cn=353

A psychological view of motivation.

NEEDS AND MOTIVATION

An awareness of the concept of needs, important for various reasons, is especially important for a greater understanding of your own behavior and the behavior of others with whom and through whom you work. If you ever become a manager or supervisor, you'll discover that an understanding of the needs of your associates will greatly facilitate your attempts to motivate them. Employees and family members also can benefit from a knowledge of needs concepts.

Needs are also called motives because they move or motivate us to act. **Motivation** means the various drives within, or environmental forces surrounding, individuals that stimulate them to behave in a specific manner.

Motivation
an incentive to act

IF YOU ARE A MANAGER

Managers get things done with and through people, and an understanding of concepts of motivation and human needs is essential if management is to be effective in accomplishing organizational goals with and through its associates. Managers should attempt to avoid the all too common mistake of assuming that everyone is motivated by the same incentives. One person, for example, might feel motivated by the opportunity to have more responsibility on the job; others may be frightened at the mere mention of such a prospect. It is essential, therefore, that managers who want to establish and maintain an organizational climate that motivates employees continually remind themselves that different employees have different mixes of needs, wants, and goals.

Classical managers believe that most people dislike work and will be best motivated by fear and financial reward. Such managers believe that since most individuals must work, they will respond more productively when the fear of suspension, demotion, or dismissal hangs over their heads. Fear can motivate in the short run, but often in the long run it merely motivates individuals to seek employment elsewhere. Fear can also create people who are overly cautious, are yes-people, or seek revenge.

The behavioral management approach to motivational management makes greater use of positive environmental factors, such as recognition, status, and empowerment, than of the negative factors preferred by the classical manager. Behavioral managers also recognize that they can have a significant effect on creating an environment that provides employees with positive expectations for accomplishing the outcomes (rewards) they desire. Managers who fail to recognize such environmental factors frequently have morale problems among their employees.

IF YOU ARE A WORKER

How can you as an employee benefit from an understanding of needs and motivational concepts? The knowledge of what motivates a particular type of behavior can enhance your understanding of yourself and others. You should find that you become less irritated with the behavior of others when you're able to understand it. You may find it easier to solve problems between you and your boss or your coworkers if you have a better understanding of what motivates people.

A MOTIVATION MODEL

Look at Figure 11.1, a model of the motivation process. As you can see on the left side of the model, a felt need creates tensions. Tensions motivate a person to make an effort to reduce or eliminate the tensions. The individual's past and present environmental experiences influence the direction that effort takes. Any person's environment tends to shape his or her needs. In this model, **expectations** influence effort. A person may not even bother to make an effort if he or she believes desired outcomes are unlikely or impossible. Managers, however, can influence employee expectations in a variety of ways, such as by offering incentives and establishing goals jointly.

Continuing with our examination of the motivation model, ability then blends with the person's effort and results in a certain level of **performance**. Unfortunately, however, performance alone doesn't always enable individuals to satisfy their needs

Expectations
the prospect of success or gain

Performance
completion of a task or tasks; taking action in accordance with requirements

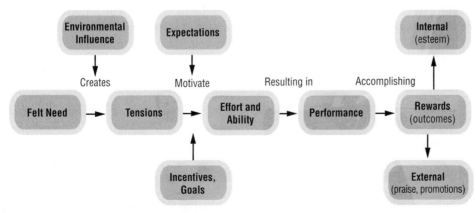

FIGURE 11.1 A MOTIVATIONAL MODEL

Rewards, or Outcomes
satisfying returns or
results for performance
of a required behavior

and attain their wants, especially when their skill levels are deficient or their prior training is inadequate.

On the far right portion of the model are the **rewards, or outcomes,** that result from achieving the motivated activity. Outcomes may be derived from the person's external environment and take the form of praise, promotions, or financial rewards from the boss. An external environmental outcome could also be approval from one's peers. Outcomes can also come from the internal environment, such as the personal feeling of self-esteem or achievement resulting from accomplishing a goal. Of course, outcomes are not always positive. When negative, they tend to result in employee dissatisfaction.

CAN YOU LEARN TO NEED NEEDS?

We are motivated to satisfy many of our needs in quite a natural manner. For example, we don't have to learn how to sleep when we're tired. Nor do we have to learn to eat or drink when we are hungry or thirsty. Yet certain needs emerge from the cultural environment of which we are a part. Four commonly accepted learned needs are (1) approval, (2) achievement, (3) competence, and (4) power. Keep in mind that these are learned needs and, as a result, can vary substantially in intensity among different individuals.

THE NEED FOR APPROVAL

Approval
official consent or
confirmation

We learn early in life to behave in a certain way with our parents, and later with our peers, in order to obtain their **approval.** As already suggested, people vary in the intensity of their approval needs, but researchers Crowne and Marlowe discovered that people who have a high need for approval tend to be more likely to conform to group standards. They learn more rapidly when consistent approval is given for correct performance than when nothing is said. They also tend to experience difficulty acting in an independent, self-assertive fashion because they fear disapproval.[1] Can you visualize how these characteristics might influence the manner in which a manager assigns tasks to his or her associates?

THE NEED FOR ACHIEVEMENT

Achievement
feeling that you've
accomplished a goal

Why do some people seem to have such strong desires to achieve while others seem content with mediocre accomplishments? The answer relates to **achievement** needs, which also vary with the individual. Psychologists contend that the achievement need, as with most learned needs, is developed quite early in life. People whose parents were high achievers tend also to be achievement oriented and to like hard work. Parents typically are a child's first role models. Achievement-oriented parents tend to reinforce achievement behavior by encouraging their children with recognition and praise when they do well.

David C. McClelland has made significant contributions to the study of achievement needs. His findings suggest that the strength of the achievement need in any given situation is dependent on three factors: the expectation of success, the value of the outcomes (rewards and incentives) to the person, and the feeling of personal responsibility for the achievement.[2]

THE NEED FOR COMPETENCE

Some people have acquired the need to do high-quality work. To such individuals, mastery of their jobs and excellence in their task performance are important because

NetNote

The Daily Motivator

http://www.greatday.com/ motivate/

A site dedicated to personal motivation; includes a daily motivation message, archived messages, and links to related sites.

of the personal satisfaction they derive from doing a good job. Managers who have strong **competence** needs tend to be impatient and difficult to work with because they often feel that their associates should share their same high concerns for quality work. Managers with this trait should attempt to recognize the dangers associated with this need and develop and apply adequate organizational behavior skills.

THE NEED FOR POWER

Power is another learned need that is strong in some individuals. Power needs relate to a person's desire to possess control, authority, or influence over others. Individuals whose need for power is low tend to feel uncomfortable and out of place in certain types of occupations, such as law enforcement. Power often accompanies certain types of positions in organizations. A chief executive officer, for example, by the very nature of his or her position in the organizational **hierarchy**, has more power than a first-line supervisor. Some individuals, even when they lack position power, are able to influence others through charismatic authority, the ability to influence others because of personality traits and mannerisms. Chapter 14 discusses charismatic authority in greater depth.

THE HIERARCHY OF NEEDS

One of the best-known contributors to the area of motivational research is Abraham Maslow, who developed the concept of the **hierarchy of needs**.[3] Maslow suggested that human needs can be assigned to various levels, and that each level of need has to be gratified to some extent before the next level assumes importance. Maslow developed a concept of two interrelated hierarchies. Typically the only hierarchy that is discussed is Maslow's basic need hierarchy. This hierarchy distinguishes five levels of human needs, ranging from basic, lower-order needs to social and psychological needs of a higher order. They are the physiologic needs, the safety needs, the belonging needs, status/self-esteem needs, and the self-actualization needs (see Figure 11.2).

Maslow states that these needs are interrelated with other needs that are less well understood (and not often included when his theory is being explained). These needs consist of knowledge needs, understanding needs, and aesthetic needs.[4] Maslow contends that these needs are contemporaneous with the other five needs (they are all working at the same time). Figure 11.2 depicts Maslow's theory; the following sections explain the needs and their relation to motivation.

THE BASIC HIERARCHY

Explanations of Maslow's hierarchy of needs always begin at the bottom of the hierarchy (see Figure 11.2) with the **physiologic needs.** The physiologic needs are the most basic of all needs. They consist of the needs for food, shelter, clothing, water, and **homeostasis** (essentially a need to maintain the body's normal condition).[5] In saying that these are the most basic needs, Maslow means that they are essential to survival. Should you find yourself separated from all civilization, the need to find food, shelter, clothing, and water and to maintain homeostasis would be your sole concern. You would be highly motivated to fulfill these needs. In this situation, the hierarchical nature of these needs would also be demonstrated. When the basic needs are unfulfilled, we do not even realize that there are other needs. So, unfulfilled needs motivate us, and once a need is fulfilled, we become aware of the next need level up in the hierarchy. In the work world, we typically do not try to fulfill

Competence
the state of being adequate or well-qualified; possessing sufficient ability for a task

Power
the ability or capacity to perform or act effectively; strength or force exerted or capable of being exerted

Hierarchy
a series in which each element is graded or ranked

Hierarchy of Needs
a series of needs in which lower needs must be fulfilled (or nearly fulfilled) before the next higher need becomes evident

Physiologic Needs
the needs for food, shelter, clothing, water, and homeostasis

Homeostasis
a need to maintain the body's normal condition

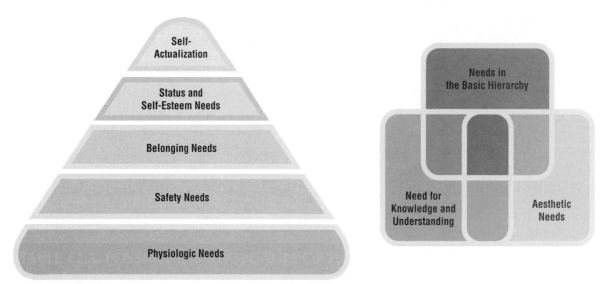

FIGURE 11.2 The categories in Maslow's basic hierarchy of needs are depicted in the left diagram. The right diagram depicts the relationship of Maslow's other needs.

the physiologic needs directly. We do not usually give people food, shelter, clothing, and water; to fulfill these needs, we give people money. The money enables people to purchase those things that meet their physiologic needs. With the physiologic needs fulfilled, or nearly so, we begin to realize the need for safety.

The **safety needs** consist of the need to be safe and secure. Included here would be seeking out stability, freedom, and order, as well as seeking the removal of fear and anxiety.[6] Note that the safety needs include physical safety (freedom from harm from predators or muggers) and mental safety. Mental safety can include feeling free or having job security. In the working environment, the safety needs can be met through the use of safe operating procedures and safety devices such as safety glasses, ear protectors, and steel-toed boots. Mental safety can be addressed by providing a locker where people may secure personal items while at work; by having a guarded parking lot and plant to minimize theft; by providing health, life, and dependent insurance; and by providing job security. Once the security needs are met, the next level of needs will become evident—the belonging needs.

The **belonging needs** consist of the need to be with other people and the need to find a mate.[7] There are few genuine hermits in the world because virtually all people feel the need to be social and mingle, meet, and talk to other people. Some people feel this need more strongly than others, but almost all feel some need here. The strength of the need for a mate can also vary, but most feel something along these lines also. To a degree, it is possible to increase the fulfillment of one side of the belonging need to offset a deficiency in the other side. For example, single people may compensate for a shortage in the meeting of the mate belonging need by increasing contact with friends and increasing the social belonging need fulfillment. Once a person is married, the mate may meet more of the belonging need, and the need for more friends or more contact with friends is diminished. In the work world, the finding-a-mate side of belonging is rarely addressed. Some employers do try to accommodate the social belonging needs by providing for or allowing social interactions. Once the belonging needs are at least somewhat fulfilled, people feel the status and self-esteem needs.

The **status** and **self-esteem needs** are different but occupy the same level on the hierarchy.[8] The status needs can be viewed as an extension of the social belonging

Safety Needs

the need to be safe and secure

Belonging Needs

the need to be with other people and the need to find a mate

Status Needs

the need to have a higher position or standing relative to that of others

Self-Esteem Needs

internal feelings of self-worth

needs. It is as if people first feel the need to be around others (social belonging) and then feel the need to feel better or higher in rank than they (status). Self-esteem needs are internal feelings of self-worth. Self-esteem includes having self-confidence and feeling that one is capable. Self-esteem is derived from earned respect; false or contrived flattery does not produce self-esteem. On the job, status can be conveyed through recognition, a title, awards, promotions, and increased responsibility. Self-esteem can be produced through recognition, achievement, and trust. Some people reach this level of the hierarchy and seem to move no further. For others, once the status and self-esteem needs are fulfilled or even somewhat fulfilled, the need to self-actualize becomes evident.

Self-actualization is probably most succinctly defined in the United States Army's slogan of "Be all that you can be." Self-actualization needs are an individual pushing himself or herself to attain the highest level and to achieve the most that he or she can. Self-actualization involves reaching one's highest potential.[9] You need only look around to see that many people decide it is much easier to grab a beer and the remote control and consider themselves lucky for what they have. Others feel the urge or the call to achieve as much as they possibly can. This may take the form of artistic creation, knowledge gain, discovery, or expertise in anything from parenting, to a spiritual state, to work. The possibility to self-actualize through work can include the work itself, or it may be through education or training. The exact form of the self-actualization is, as with the fulfillment of the other needs, an individual matter.

One reason for the acceptance of this part of Maslow's hierarchy as an explanation for motivation is that Maslow does not specify what exactly is needed to motivate people. Maslow identifies the needs that people feel. Different things satisfy these needs for different people. For example, Maslow identifies a need for status, but he offers different suggestions for how the status need might be fulfilled. Some might fulfill status through a job title, rank in a charitable organization, possessions, family, or the acquisition of money. The amount of status needed by each person varies, as does the item that will bring the status. Remember also that according to the theory, only unfulfilled needs motivate people.

MASLOW'S OTHER NEEDS

The other needs in Maslow's theory are mentioned less often. They consist of the needs for knowledge, understanding, and aesthetics. The **need for knowledge** can be defined as the level of curiosity present in a person or the desire to accumulate facts. It has been considered as a means of achieving the safety need or as a way for intelligent people to self-actualize. However, the desire for knowledge often exceeds that needed to satisfy the safety need, and it is sometimes carried out in spite or in defiance of the need for safety. For others, the quest for knowledge often occurs before reaching the self-actualization level.[10]

The **need for understanding** is essentially an extension of the need for knowledge. The need for understanding involves the search for the relationships between things and between what is known, and it includes the search for meaning.[11] The need for understanding encompasses analysis, organization, and classification of things and knowledge. Once we know something or things, it follows that we would like to know how these things relate to each other and what meaning may be derived from the relationships. In other words, first we know of the tree, then we try to relate one tree to another, and finally we relate trees to soil, earth, and water in order to understand the forest.

The other need that Maslow mentions is the **need for aesthetics.** The aesthetic need is the need to be surrounded by beautiful things. This need is expressed by the

Self-Actualization Needs
an individual pushing himself or herself to attain the highest level and achieve the most that he or she can; reaching one's highest potential

NetNote

Motivation Articles
http://psychclassics.yorku.ca/ Maslow/motivation.htm
Maslow.
http://www.accel-team.com/ human_relations/ hrels_05_herzberg.html
Herzberg.
http://www.envisionsoftware. com/articles/ERG_Theory. html
Alderfer.

Need for Knowledge
the level of curiosity present in a person or the desire to accumulate facts

Need for Understanding
the search for the relationships between things and between what is known, including the search for meaning

Need for Aesthetics
the need to be surrounded by beautiful things that have balance, color, proportion, and good design, and the need to see things through to completion

desire to have and be surrounded by art. It includes the need for balance, color, proportion, and good design in the things around us. The aesthetic need also includes the need for symmetrical design and the need to see things through to completion. According to Maslow, all of these needs are so closely related that it is not possible to separate them. They work together and overlay one another to form a more complete picture of what motivates people to act a certain way.[12]

An Exception to Maslow: Alderfer's ERG Theory of Needs and Motivation   Clayton Alderfer, after observing what he believed to be shortcomings of Maslow's hierarchy of needs concepts, developed a modification of the theory, known as the **ERG theory of needs.** Alderfer's research offers three basic human needs: existence, relatedness, and growth (see Figure 11.3).[13] The first level, **existence needs,** includes physical and material human wants, such as food, water, pay, decent working conditions, and safety-security factors. **Relatedness needs** involve one's relationship with others (being accepted, for example), both on and off the job. The last level, **growth needs,** combines the desires for self-esteem and self-realization.

One distinction between Alderfer's ERG and Maslow's priority-of-needs theories, therefore, is in the former's condensation of the five need levels into three. A more significant difference is that Alderfer's research, as already suggested, doesn't assume that a person climbs the ladder of needs in an order of progression. Instead, hypothesizes Alderfer, any or all three of the levels might be significant at any given time. He also suggests that the less the relatedness needs (relationships with others) are satisfied, the more important the existence needs (physical/material) become, the opposite of Maslow's conclusion. Alderfer differs in another way from Maslow by contending that the less the growth needs (self-esteem, self-realization) are satisfied, the more important relatedness needs become. The burden, therefore, appears to be on you to decide which of the two theories seems to have the greater merit.

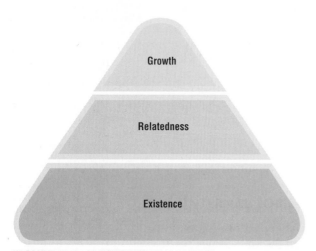

FIGURE 11.3 ALDERFER'S ERG MODEL

HERZBERG'S MOTIVATION–MAINTENANCE MODEL

Frederick Herzberg, a well-known management theorist, is best known for another theory of motivation, the motivation–maintenance model.[14] Herzberg's research indicates that two sets of factors or conditions influence the behavior of individuals in organizations. One set of factors he calls **hygiene or maintenance factors.** Herzberg labels the other set **motivators.** Essentially, hygiene factors are facets of the work environment that need to be present in order to make the job at least minimally acceptable. Motivators are facets that actually give people a reason to grow in their work. Further understanding of the difference between these two sets of factors requires a little time and careful reading. First, according to Herzberg, if the hygiene factors are not adequate, then you will feel dissatisfied with work. However, even if the hygiene factors are adequate, you will simply be not dissatisfied. The hygiene factors operate on a scale ranging from dissatisfaction to no dissatisfaction (see Figure 11.4). Motivators, if adequate, produce real satisfaction, and when the motivators are inadequate, there is no satisfaction (see Figure 11.4). It is important to understand that a state of not being dissatisfied is not the same as being satisfied, and a state of not being satisfied is not the same as being dissatisfied.

One of the best examples for understanding Herzberg's theory is to examine the quality of supervision. For Herzberg, this is a hygiene or maintenance factor. His reasoning is that a poor supervisor can make you unhappy or dissatisfied. However, even having a great supervisor will not make you want to jump out of bed and rush in early just so you can work for him or her. Having a great supervisor will not create feelings of satisfaction or happiness. If you do have a great supervisor, you will simply not feel unhappy. To feel satisfied and happy with work, you would need to have motivator factors fulfilled. A more complete list of the two types of factors may also help in the understanding of this theory.

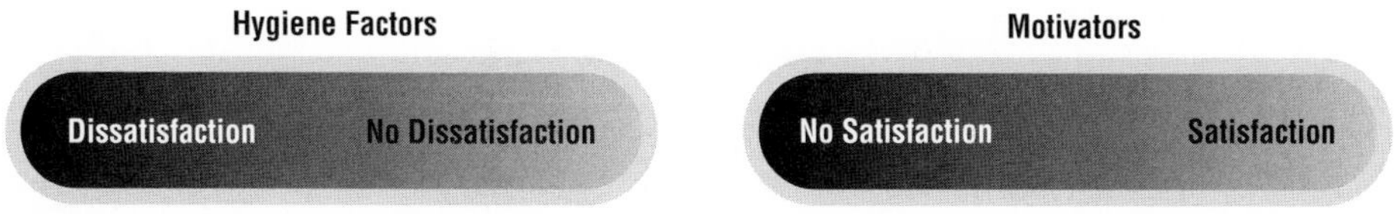

Growth Needs
a combination of the desires for self-esteem and self-realization

Hygiene or Maintenance Factors
facets of the work environment that need to be present in order to make the job at least minimally acceptable

Motivators
facets of the work that actually give people a reason to grow

Hygiene Factors

| Dissatisfaction | No Dissatisfaction |

Motivators

| No Satisfaction | Satisfaction |

FIGURE 11.4 The effect of nonfulfillment (on the left of each scale) and fulfillment (on the right of each scale) of Herzberg's two factors

HYGIENE (MAINTENANCE) FACTORS

First, let's look at the short list of what Herzberg calls maintenance, or hygiene, factors:

1. quality of supervision
2. company rules and policies
3. interpersonal relations with superiors, subordinates, and peers
4. salary and certain types of employee benefits
5. working conditions and job security

Maintenance factors in formal organizations include sick leave, vacation, health and welfare plans, and most other personnel programs. Some managers have convinced themselves that a good employee benefit program will motivate workers. Instead, such programs are usually taken for granted. The main controversy with Herzberg's theory concerns the other half of item 4—money.

Herzberg believes that money is a hygiene factor. This means that money does not motivate and that money does not produce job satisfaction. Herzberg does believe that money is important; he just doesn't believe that it can motivate. He says money only produces movement, but not motivation. He explains that he can get you to move (increase productivity) by offering you more money, but that eventually your productivity will slip back to the previous level. To get you to produce more a subsequent time, you have to be given more money. For example, suppose you make $10 per hour and you make 100 widgets per hour. To get you to make 110 widgets, the company offers you $11. According to Herzberg, eventually your production will slip back to the old comfortable level of 100 per hour. To get you to increase your rate back to 110 widgets per hour, the company has to give you another $1 an hour. Now you are receiving $12 an hour to make 110 widgets per hour, and Herzberg states that you will again eventually slip back to 100 per hour. This is movement, not motivation. According to Herzberg, people should be given an appropriate salary, rather than an hourly wage or a piece rate. Of course, there is still the problem of determining how much is appropriate to maintain people.

You may be surprised to find that working conditions aren't considered motivators. It's probably true that many employees would prefer working in a pleasant environment. But a sparkling new plant seldom substitutes for jobs that people enjoy or for employees' feelings of achievement and recognition. We've all probably seen organizations that function in run-down buildings, yet morale and productivity are high. Herzberg contends that people's attitudes toward their jobs far outweigh the importance of working conditions or environment.

MOTIVATIONAL FACTORS (SATISFIERS)

Now let's take a look at a completely different set of factors. The following list includes what Herzberg calls motivational factors, or satisfiers:

1. achievement
2. recognition
3. the job itself
4. growth and advancement possibilities
5. responsibility
6. feedback

Factors such as these are said to motivate individuals and to produce job satisfaction. Achievement is important to many employees. Is it to you? Achievement means feeling that you've accomplished a goal, that is, that you've finished something that you've started. Some work situations provide this feeling; others, such as assembly-line work, often make feelings of achievement difficult. This is especially true when cycle times (the time needed to complete one task) are as short as 6 seconds or less. One former student working for a food company that prepared institutional meals had a job that repeated every two seconds. His task was to place two slices of white bread on a tray as it passed by on a conveyor belt (later others added meat, condiments, etc., to produce a sandwich). Thirty times a minute the same little task was performed, and he never saw the finished product. Not much sense of achievement here.

Many employees appreciate **recognition.** It gives the employee a feeling of worth and self-esteem. Don't you like to know how you stand in a work situation? When you and other employees know how you are doing, even when the results aren't completely satisfactory, you at least know that your boss is concerned about you. There's a tendency for managers to overlook the need for giving employees recognition and feedback on their performance.[15] Some managers think that it's unnecessary to say anything to an employee when a job has been done well. "Charlie knows he does good work" is a far too typical managerial attitude. Charlie, like most employees, might not be certain what his boss really thinks of his performance without some form of overt recognition.

Recognition
receiving attention or favorable notice

The job itself is a highly important motivating factor. Have you ever thought why some employees are chronically late? In many cases, it's because they dread—either consciously or subconsciously—going to their 9-to-5 jobs. They derive little satisfaction from their monotonous jobs and as a result would like to be able to say, as that defiant country song puts it, "Take this job and shove it!" People who like their jobs tend to be far more motivated to avoid absenteeism and lateness.

Growth and advancement possibilities also serve to motivate. In a sense, these are like the old carrot-and-stick philosophy. Don't you, like many employees, tend to move in directions that help you obtain the carrot, for example, a promotion with more salary? However, managers must keep in mind that if employees never get to taste the carrot but only feel the stick, then their interest in carrots will tend to fade. Motivational tools should never be used to manipulate people. They should be used sincerely, with the employee's as well as the organization's interests in mind.

Responsibility is another factor that motivates many employees. Some people will forgo taking sick leave when they don't feel well out of a sense of responsibility. Others want to take on responsibility for the sense of accomplishment it gives them or from an internal need to see things done right. Even the behavior of some so-called troublemakers in organizations has been modified after they have been given added responsibilities.

Responsibility
being held liable for one's actions in the discharge of a duty

Herzberg believes that the ideal form of **feedback** is inherent to the job. In this way, the person does not have to be told that he or she has done a good job; it is known automatically. For example, when a radiographer examines an X-ray film that was just taken, she or he knows if it is good or if it needs to be repeated. The feedback is instant and inherent.

Feedback
the return of information about the result of a process or activity; an evaluative response

SOME FINAL WORDS ON HERZBERG

Remember that we have been discussing theory. An important consideration to keep in mind is that an employee's perception of a motivational factor is of far greater importance than the manager's perception of it. A factor that merely maintains one person may motivate another.

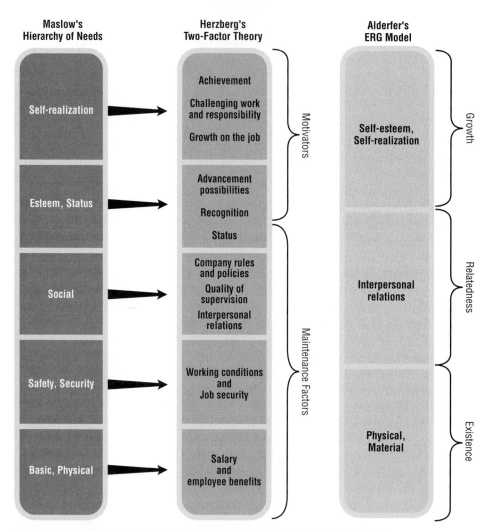

FIGURE 11.5 THE THEORIES OF MASLOW, HERZBERG, AND ALDERFER COMPARED

NetNote

Psychology Today

http://www.psychologytoday. com/articles/pto-20040202- 000002.html

Article on feedback and criticism.

Not every behavioral scientist fully accepts Herzberg's concepts. However, his research does help to reinforce our awareness that some factors in a work environment tend to motivate many employees, and others—even though they seem positive, like paid vacations—have little effect on an employee's motivation and productivity. Finally, see Figure 11.5 for a graphic comparison of the Maslow, Herzberg, and Alderfer theories of motivation.

THE PROCESS OF MOTIVATION

Thus far, we have been discussing motivation by focusing on the perceived internal needs and expected outcomes of the individual, frequently referred to by behavioral scientists as content theories of motivation. Managers, however, cannot always accurately pinpoint an individual's internal needs and expected outcomes. Furthermore, the intensity of needs and perceived outcomes varies widely among people. If you were a manager, imagine, for example, the difficulty you might have trying to measure your employees' need for prestige.

Increasingly popular in recent years is a second set of motivational theories, termed *process theories*, which are concerned with how to relate content variables (human needs and outcomes) to particular actions of the individual. Three major process theories are the reinforcement, expectancy, and equity theories, each of which will be discussed in the following sections.

BEHAVIOR MODIFICATION THROUGH REINFORCEMENT TECHNIQUES

Although some managers shy away from the concept of **behavior modification** because of its appearance of being manipulative, the approach has been increasingly used by managers in numerous firms in recent years. Behavior modification is the influencing of behavior through the use of positive or negative reinforcement techniques.

Behavior Modification
influencing behavior through the use of positive or negative reinforcement techniques

Do you sometimes find yourself repeating behavior that brings pleasure and avoiding behavior that displeases you? To do so is quite natural. In effect, the consequence of certain actions tends to lead to similar actions being repeated (or avoided) in the future. This behavior is termed the *law of effect* and is a major component of what is referred to as reinforcement theory. B. F. Skinner, a well-known behavioral psychologist and researcher in the field of behavior modification, is considered by many to be the father of reinforcement theory.[16]

Managers in the process of motivating workers or anyone attempting to influence others may draw on reinforcement theory for assistance. There are four principal techniques of reinforcement theory: (1) positive reinforcement, (2) escape or avoidance reinforcement, (3) extinction (repeated nonreinforcement), and (4) punishment. Each of these reinforcement methods can be used to influence (but not totally control) human behavior.

POSITIVE REINFORCEMENT

When someone encourages a repetition of certain behavior, he or she is utilizing **positive reinforcement.** We've already learned from the discussion of content theories of motivation that people feel the need for recognition and self-esteem. A manager could link those needs to the process of motivation and positive reinforcement by sincerely praising workers for work well performed. You may use the same technique to influence your manager or peers. For example, if someone asks you your opinion and you want that person to continue to include you in future discussions, you should give him or her an answer.[17]

Positive Reinforcement
encouraging the repetition of behavior

ESCAPE AND AVOIDANCE

Escape and avoidance reinforcement is a somewhat negative technique intended to motivate a person to perform in a favorable manner to escape from, or avoid, a particular situation. For example, Jeffrey is hired and placed in an unpleasant entry-level job. He has been told that if he performs satisfactorily in his job, he is likely to be promoted to a more desirable position within six months. Consequently, he will probably be motivated to do a good job now as a means of avoiding, or escaping from, a position he'd prefer not to have. Escape reinforcement can accomplish the same results as positive reinforcement by concentrating on the avoidance of a negative outcome.

Escape and Avoidance Reinforcement
to elude or stay clear of something

THE STATE OF EXTINCTION

Much of what we've learned thus far about reinforcement theory relates to the concept of conditioned response—the learned or acquired reaction to a particular stimulus. Ivan Petrovich Pavlov, the Russian physiologist, is best known for his contribution to this concept. Pavlov noticed that dogs would salivate when put in front of meat powder. He then rang a bell when putting meat powder before the dogs. Eventually, the dogs associated the sound of the bell with the meat powder, and they would drool just at the sound of the bell. Pavlov carried his experiment one step further. He learned that even though he conditioned the dogs to salivate merely at the ringing of a bell, this response would eventually become extinct if it was not occasionally reinforced.[18]

Extinction
the elimination of a behavior

How does the concept of **extinction** relate to organizational behavior? Consider this example: Carol, a new employee, was constantly making suggestions to her boss, Harold, on her previous job. Harold, following the concept of positive reinforcement, always praised her for presenting ideas, even if they were unusable. Carol was later transferred to a different department where her new boss, Adam, seemed indifferent to her suggestions, seldom uttering much more than something like, "Hmm, that's interesting, Carol. I'll look into it and let you know what I think." However, because Adam never actually followed up with a response, positive or negative, extinction began to affect Carol's flow of fresh, new ideas.

HOW EFFECTIVE IS PUNISHMENT?

Punishment
a penalty imposed for wrongdoing

Punishment is a type of behavior modification that most people would prefer not to experience. It is also the one type that managers tend to dislike having to apply. The basic purpose of punishment reinforcement is to withhold rewards or outcomes from a person because of past undesirable behavior. Theoretically, the person, if aware in advance of the negative consequences associated with punishment, will comply with existing standards. Or, also in theory, people punished for undesirable behavior will avoid such activities in the future.

That's the basic theory behind punishment, but what's the reality? Some now suggest that punishment doesn't always reduce the likelihood of the same response's recurring.[19] Frequently a person's behavior has been positively reinforced prior to the punishment and will continue even if punishment is likely. Also, a by-product of punishment may be the creation of an unpleasant and demotivating working environment accompanied by hostile attitudes toward the boss and organization from which the punishment came. The question arises as to whether punishment really results in desirable behavior.[20] Perhaps punishment should be used only when no other alternatives are available.

Source: DILBERT: © Scott Adams/Dist. by United Features Syndicate, Inc.

A caveat to behavior modification is required, however, because some people believe it is a form of manipulating others. In reality, the process is a form of influencing behaviors. If used to overly control or manipulate others, they may respond in negative and reactive ways.

EXPECTANCY THEORY

Victor Vroom is credited with having popularized expectancy theory. In its original form, Vroom's theory is complex.[21] In its essence, expectancy theory asks two questions of everything that might be used to motivate people. In order to motivate, the answer to both questions must be yes.[22]

The first question that must be asked is: "Does the person want___?" Fill in the blank with the motivator. For example, let us say that an Employee of the Month award is being created, and the prize is an expensive steak dinner. Faria happens to be a vegetarian. So we ask, "Does Faria want an expensive steak dinner?" The answer is no; therefore, there is no motivational effect for Faria. If the award is changed to one extra week of paid vacation, and Faria would want that, then there might, or there might not, be a motivational effect.

To determine if anything that anyone wants will motivate him or her, a second question must be asked: "Does the person think he or she has a fair chance at obtaining___?" Again, fill in the blank with the motivator. If the answer is no, then there is no motivational effect. The answer to both questions must be yes in order for something to motivate a person. To continue our example, if Faria thinks that the award is too difficult to obtain or that someone else has a better chance of getting the award, then there is no motivational effect for Faria. The key word here is *thinks*—if the person *thinks* that he or she cannot obtain the reward because it is too difficult or because of feelings of inadequacy or for whatever reason, then there is no motivational effect. It will not matter whether rewards will be fairly given or not if people don't believe they will be.

Expectancy theory is relatively well accepted for two main reasons. First, it is logical. It makes sense that we cannot motivate people with things they do not want or things they feel they cannot earn. Second, expectancy theory works in conjunction with all other motivational theories. Whether the offer is for money, for recognition (as mentioned by Herzberg), or for status (as identified by Maslow's hierarchy of needs), people must want the motivator and they must believe they have a fair chance of obtaining it in order for it to motivate.

NetNote

**Management by Strengths
A Team-Building Program**

http://www.strengths.com

A site promoting management by strengths. It contains information on team building, employee relations, and morale. You will also find a survey (with results that can be compared to the Myers–Briggs assessment) and links to related Web sites.

THE RELATIONSHIP BETWEEN EQUITY AND MOTIVATION

Employees, of course, want their needs satisfied. But they generally want something else as well. They expect to be treated fairly in the way workloads are assigned and rewards are distributed. Developed by J. Stacy Adams, equity theory, illustrated in Figure 11.6, focuses on the concept of fairness. It looks at the tendency of employees to compare the fairness of what their jobs require them to do (called inputs) with what they receive in exchange for their efforts (called outputs).[23] As with Vroom's theory, equity theory deals with expectations, primarily what people expect to get

Inputs:
Skill
Effort
Performance
Education
Others

Outputs:
Pay and benefits
Recognition
Job satisfaction
Opportunities
Others

Employee

Organization

FIGURE 11.6 THE EQUITY THEORY OF MOTIVATION ASSUMES A BALANCE OF EMPLOYEE INPUTS AND OUTPUTS AS COMPARED TO OTHERS

from their jobs. Employees whose expectations aren't met tend to become dissatisfied, as when they perceive that they are responsible for more tasks than are reflected by the size of their paychecks. Their dissatisfaction can result in lesser motivation or, in some instances, the mere acceptance of things as they are, sort of a resigned "C'est la vie," or "Asi es la vida," attitude.

Employees also expect equity in relation to other employees. For example, an employee may experience a decrease in motivation upon discovering that he or she receives less income for performing comparable tasks. A related theme of the women's movement in recent decades has been "equal pay for equal work." Workers generally do accept differences in pay when others have more seniority with the firm, more experience in the industry, more training, more education, more skills and ability, or when they work a non-prime-time shift (prime time usually meaning the day shift, Mondays through Fridays). Equity, or fair treatment, in work organizations relates not only to pay but also to such factors as vacations, work assignments, and recognition. The elements may be tangible or intangible, external or internal.

Equity theory continues by explaining the comparisons people make in trying to determine if they have equity or not. If they do not have equity, then the theory says that people will take actions designed to bring them to a state of equity between what they put into their work and what they receive in return. The equity state, then, occurs when a person's work inputs (I) equal their work outcomes (O); thus, $I = O$. If the person feels that he or she is putting more into a job than the outcomes or rewards received ($I > O$), then the person will ask for a raise, or work less, or maybe even steal from the company (rationalizing that this is deserved). Equity theory also contends that when people feel they are getting more from their jobs than they are putting into them ($I < O$), then they will feel guilty and they will increase their efforts. Although such people do exist, how many others do you suppose would simply take the money, laugh all the way to the bank, and congratulate themselves on having a pretty good job?

In addition to these three comparisons on an individual level, equity theory says that people make three similar comparisons between themselves and others. According to the theory, people will compare their own inputs/outcomes ratio to the inputs/outcomes ratio of others. The equity state here occurs when an individual's inputs/outcomes ratio is equal to the perceived input/outcome ratios of others, such as coworkers ($I/O_{individual} = I/O_{others}$). Note that the perceived ratio of others may be wrong; the individual may not know the actual ratio, and the perceived ratio may be based on incorrect information or on assumptions. If the individual's input/outcome ratio is perceived to be unjustifiably lower than the input/outcome ratios of others ($I/O_{individual} < I/O_{others}$), then the individual will seek equity. If the individual's ratio is greater than that of others ($I/O_{individual} > I/O_{others}$), then the individual will, according to the theory, feel guilty and work harder. Again, some people might, while others might not care or might try to rationalize the situation.

In other words, we are most comfortable when we feel that what we are receiving from work is roughly equal to what everyone else is receiving from work. This applies whether we and others are receiving money, satisfaction, recognition, responsibility, or any other work derivative. If we feel we are receiving less than others, we will seek to achieve equity. Some may do this by asking for a raise, stealing from the company, decreasing their performance, or quitting. The third possibility is that we might feel we are getting so much more than others that we need to work harder in order to justify the difference. If you felt you were receiving more than others, what would you do?

HUNTER'S INTRINSIC/EXTRINSIC THEORY

Madeline Hunter, known mainly for her work in education, proposes a two-part system of motivation.[24] Hunter adds some new thoughts to motivation and reinforces the theories of others. She does not specify individual motivators, such as money or status, but instead she explains methods that can be used to motivate. The two types of motivation are intrinsic (internal) and extrinsic (external).[25] Of course, if someone's intrinsic motivation is to dig holes, and he or she works as an excavator, then there may be little or no need to be concerned with motivating this person. For those occasions when it is necessary to motivate someone, then one must rely on extrinsic motivation. Extrinsic motivation, according to Hunter, comprises five external factors that can be affected from the outside: level of concern, success, feedback, interest, and feeling tone. These factors may be used individually, or more than one at a time may be used to motivate people to action.

LEVEL OF CONCERN

The first factor, **level of concern,** motivates people by holding them accountable for their actions. For example, if you are told that half of the questions on the next test will cover Hunter's theories, you will be motivated to pay attention to the lecture on Hunter, to take notes, and to study the material. Holding you accountable for knowing the material increases the level of your concern for Hunter, and you learn her theories or flunk your test. You may also be interested intrinsically to learn motivation theory, but if not, level of concern helps provide some motivation. Conversely, if told that you will never be held accountable for knowing Hunter's theories, then only those possessing intrinsic motivation will be moved to learn the material.

When motivating others using level of concern, you must be careful what you ask for because you might get it. For instance, if you measure the arrival times of workers to the second and give rewards for arriving on time and penalties for being late, then you will probably get people to arrive on time. They may do nothing once they are there, but at least they are on time. When you hold people accountable, you are telling them that this particular thing is important to you. When you do not hold people accountable, you are signaling them that something is not important to you.

SUCCESS

A second extrinsic factor is success. Hunter states that people are motivated to perform acts at which they are successful. We tend not to perform acts we are not good at. Consider hobbies or sports that you have tried. You probably continued with

Level of Concern
holding people
accountable for their
actions

those that you were good at and quit those you were not good at. The same may be true of the careers people try and later give up.

An exception to this principle, however, is the period when we are learning. During the learning period, people are willing to continue with activities they are not good at. Eventually, however, people want to see success, or at least some improvement. With improvement, people may continue until they reach a level of success that they deem acceptable. Without some improvement, people tend to quit. Receiving positive feedback can help, however.

FEEDBACK

Feedback on how well one is doing tends to increase motivation and helps during the learning period. Sometimes we tend to give feedback only when something goes wrong—negative feedback. We sometimes figure that people should understand that if nothing is said, their performance is at least acceptable. People need to hear feedback when things are going well and also when they are not going so well. Without positive feedback, self-doubt can convince people that they are not doing well when in fact they are. Feedback is even more important when performance results are not obvious upon the completion of the task. There are additional considerations for feedback to work, however. To be effective, the feedback must be timely and accurate.

Timely feedback is that which occurs soon after the behavior occurs, the sooner the better. This means that, although an annual performance evaluation may be important for other reasons, it is not very effective as a feedback mechanism if it is the only one being used. The feedback must also be accurate. To maintain motivation and performance, people doing the best work must get the highest positive rewards, and people doing the poorest work must receive negative feedback. If people receive the wrong feedback, the entire system looks foolish and will fail. It is also demotivating to give the same feedback to everyone. Everyone cannot be doing the best job (or the worst, either). If everyone receives the same feedback, then the feedback becomes meaningless, or worse. If the better workers are receiving the same feedback as the poorer workers, the better workers may become demotivated and their performance may drop. Why perform well if you earn the same feedback (and rewards) as those doing less well?

INTEREST

Activities that are interesting motivate people to perform them, whereas boring activities demotivate people. Whenever possible, jobs should be made as interesting as possible. When not possible, it may help to rotate jobs, use job sharing, or at least allow for interesting social interactions while the work is being performed.

FEELING TONE

Hunter's last motivational factor is concerned with the tone or feeling imparted on the message used to communicate work to people. Hunter identifies positive, negative, and neutral feeling tones. Essentially, a **positive feeling tone** means asking someone to do something. A **negative feeling tone** involves ordering someone to do something. A **neutral tone** is simply a statement. Consider the difference in the following example. Positive tone: "George, would you please take care of that customer up front?" George doesn't really have a choice, but at least he was asked politely to perform some work. Negative tone: "George, get up there and take care of that customer." This is a direct order. Is George resentful? Recall the communications chapter when thinking about this. Neutral: "There is a customer up front." This is simply a statement, not a request or a command.

NetNote

Psychology Today

http://www.psychologytoday.com/articles/pto-20040308-000001.html

Article on receiving feedback and listening.

Positive Feeling Tone
asking someone to do something

Negative Feeling Tone
ordering someone to do something

Neutral Tone
a statement of fact

SPOT CHECK

11. According to Hunter, holding you accountable for something will motivate you to do that thing. T F
12. Hunter says any feedback, negative or positive, is good feedback. T F
13. Hunter says feedback is not required to be accurate because any feedback is good feedback. T F
14. Asking someone to do something is more motivating that ordering them to. T F
15. During the learning period people need feedback that they are improving so that they don't give up. T F

FYI

Figure out what your needs are and what is needed to fulfill them.

Make sure your job includes most, if not all, of Herzberg's motivators.

Remember that you not only receive reinforcement, you are constantly giving reinforcement; be careful what you reinforce (reinforce what you want to continue).

You can't motivate people by offering them things they don't want.

Be careful what you ask of people; you might get what you ask and only what you ask.

Before you ask for more money, make sure that a lack of money is your problem; money can't make everything acceptable.

Low morale is never the problem; it is a symptom of something else.

Hunter says that the positive tone is the most motivating. A negative tone is a distant second for motivating people. Commanding people to work creates resentment and a reluctance to work in many, although some will perform to spite the boss. A neutral tone does not offend anyone, but it does not motivate anyone either.

TIME, IMPORTANCE, AND MOTIVATION

Two factors that often provide much of the motivation present in the real world are time and importance. Sometimes nothing motivates quite like an impending deadline.[26] The all-nighter, while studying or working, is an all too common effect of an approaching deadline. Some procrastinators seem to require a close deadline in order to work at all. Given ample time to get the job done, they waste time until it is almost, but not quite, too late. For others, there are those times when a lot of work must be done in a small amount of time, which does bring on a focus and a sense of urgency that can get us to move a little faster. Importance can have the same effect.

Importance refers to how important a task is to someone higher up the food chain than you are. If your manager thinks a task is important, you are typically motivated to perform that task, perform it on time, and perform it well.[27] If your manager's manager thinks it is important, you have additional motivation. Conversely, if you know that something is not important to your manager, then you will be less motivated to perform the task. For extra fun, look for tasks that are not only important to your manager and your manager's boss, but that have an immediate deadline as well. With that kind of motivation, who needs caffeine?

THE SPECIAL ROLE OF MONEY AS A MOTIVATOR

Conspicuously absent from our discussion thus far, money has a special place in relation to motivation.[28] First things first: Does money motivate? The answer is, sometimes.[29] Certainly there is an underlying motivational effect from money. Most of us work to earn money in order to purchase the goods and services that we want. To an extent, more money can motivate us to do more. There are times, however, when people dislike their jobs so much that even if they were given a raise, they would work no harder. At other times, people might be satisfied with the amount they are receiving until they find themselves married and wanting a house or expecting a child. Then a new motivation may be upon them. In any case, everyone should be clear about the things money can and cannot do. Money can make a job worth doing to certain people who find the amount acceptable. Money can buy an increase in performance, but this is often limited to a short-term increase (recall what Herzberg said about money). Money cannot compensate for other aspects of the job that are unacceptable, at least not in the long run. There are still times when people quit well-paying jobs because the boss, the social interactions, the working conditions, or the future prospects are less than desirable.

Why do people seem preoccupied with the monetary reward they receive? There are at least five reasons money is of such a concern for people, besides the obvious financial concerns. People ask for money as a reward for working because (1) it is traditional, (2) it is tangible, (3) it is objective, (4) the alternatives are more subjective, and (5) it is symbolic.

MONEY IS TRADITIONAL

The first reason, that money is traditional, has much to do with the way we are raised and with societal expectations. In families and in the media, we often see or hear comments about going in to the boss and asking for a raise. Scenes of people marching in and demanding a raise or of being afraid to ask for a raise reinforce the importance of money and the correctness of asking for more money as a reward. Rarely do you see a portrayal of someone going in to the boss to demand more satisfying work, better working conditions, or some other nonmonetary reward.

MONEY IS TANGIBLE

A second reason people ask for money as a reward is that money is tangible. It is a solid reward that is perceptible to all. Although the psychological rewards of work are important, it is more difficult to show them to the neighbors or to family. Being assigned more interesting work is great for you, but you are about the only one who will know if you received it or not. On the other hand, you will know if you received more money or not, and so will others.

MONEY IS OBJECTIVE

That the receipt of more money is easily knowable and easily measurable demonstrates the objectivity of money. If you ask for more exciting work, you might have difficulty deciding whether the new work really is more exciting and how much more exciting it is. If you earn $10 an hour and get a 10 percent increase, there is no question that this is $1 an hour more. Money has no subjectivity.

ALTERNATIVES TO MONEY ARE OFTEN SUBJECTIVE

A problem with asking for something other than money is that the alternatives are often subjective. People may feel foolish asking for a job with less stress, or more creativity, or more feedback. The amount of each that one should receive is subjective. Instead, many people ask for more money rather than less stress, for example, as compensation. More money may placate them for a short time, but in the long run the problem (too much stress) remains.

MONEY IS SYMBOLIC

The fifth reason people ask for a monetary reward is that money is symbolic. More money represents more success and more achievement, and for some it is an indication of self-worth. For some, money may also be a method for keeping score of how well they are doing. Even though they may not need the money financially, they may need it psychologically, believing that money will solve their problems.

Money, however, does not solve all problems. Here is where an understanding of what money can and cannot do is most important. As Herzberg points out, money is only a short-term satisfier. In many cases, people use it to treat the symptom rather than the problem. To avoid doing this, you need to analyze the situation and try to discover the problem. Once you determine what the problem really is, you must try to determine whether or not money is the solution. For example, if you hate the way the boss treats you, will more money affect the way he or she treats you? Will more money compensate for the undesirable treatment, and if so, for how long? If the problem cannot be solved with money, then you should look for actions to take or outcomes to seek that will.

WHAT THE INDIVIDUAL CAN DO ABOUT MOTIVATION

Most people wait to be motivated by the manager or the organization; Table 11.1 lists what they are most likely to receive as a reward. In terms of getting what you want, this may not be the best strategy.[30] Your manager may not have the time, ability, or desire to ascertain the best motivational methods for you personally. Because

TABLE 11.1 EMPLOYER MOTIVATIONAL REWARDS

Reward	Employers Using Reward
1. Employee recognition program	84%
2. Gift certificate	65%
3. Special event	63%
4. Cash	59%
5. Gift (merchandise)	57%
6. E-mail or printed note	50%
7. Extra training program	47%
8. Travel	21%

Source: Charlotte Huff, "Recognition That Resonates," *Workforce Magazine*, September 11, 2006, pp. 25–27.

you have a direct interest in your own motivation, it may be better for you to take an active role by following this four-step plan:

1. Apply the motivational theories to yourself.
2. Determine how best to fulfill your needs.
3. Prepare to approach your manager.
4. Approach your manager and work together on your motivation.

Remember that the organization will probably have some constraints, and they may not be able to be changed just for you. It may be all right to ask, but remember that to a degree you must work within the system or find another one where you will be happy.

The first step, then, is to apply the motivational theories to yourself and your situation. Analyze your needs. Write down a list of what it is you want or need from work and life. Then determine what it will take to motivate you to achieve these things. Remember, you must know what it is you want before you can go after it.

Not all wants and needs can be fulfilled by work. Therefore, the second step is to differentiate between the needs that work can fulfill and those that will have to be satisfied through other means. For example, if you have a need for increased status but you are working in a flat organization with little chance for promotion, you may decide to try to meet your status needs by rising through the ranks of a volunteer or charitable organization. Keep in mind that many people believe that work should satisfy all of their needs. This is often not possible, so these people end up being frustrated at work and unfulfilled outside of work. Be realistic. If your current job can't satisfy your needs, you must find another job (and perhaps another career) or try to satisfy your needs with something other than employment. Once you have identified needs that can be fulfilled at work, then try to find existing motivators that can apply to you.

The third step is to prepare to meet with the manager. The meeting will go more easily if you are applying existing organizational motivators and rewards (like feedback) to yourself, but it usually doesn't hurt to ask for something different. If you plan to ask for some new motivational method, then you need to describe how this will benefit (1) your work, (2) your manager/employer, and (3) yourself. You must then provide evidence to support your case, and you must lay out your case in a logical, rational manner.

The fourth and last step is to meet with the manager. Present your case in a logical manner and remember that you may not be able to get everything you want all at once. You may have to develop a plan in which you work toward your goal gradually, but at least you will be moving in the direction you wish to go.

MORALE IN ORGANIZATIONS

Morale

employees' attitudes toward either their employing organizations in general or toward specific job factors

We've already learned that needs can influence the motivation of employees. Unsatisfied needs, of course, can adversely affect employee **morale.** It follows that low employee morale can negatively affect productivity and quality management. Much organizational strife is often an indication of sagging morale among employees.

However, unsatisfied needs are merely one category of factors that affect the morale of employees. The remaining section of this chapter discusses the factors that affect morale, reveals the major warning signs of low morale, and explains some common methods for evaluating morale.

Morale Defined

To influence employee morale, a manager must first understand what it is. Morale, however, is an elusive concept, not easy to define, control, or measure, yet exerting a strong influence over the atmosphere of any organization. Morale refers to employees' attitudes toward either their employing organizations in general or toward specific job factors, such as supervision, fellow employees, and financial incentives. It can be ascribed to either the individual or to the group of which he or she is a part. For our purposes, we will define morale as the atmosphere created by the attitudes of the members of an organization. It is influenced by how employees perceive the organization and its objectives in relation to themselves.

Morale and Productivity

Generally speaking, a direct relationship tends to exist between high productivity and high morale.[31] Under conditions of poor morale, favorable output is difficult to sustain for long periods. Profits are usually adversely affected when poor morale reduces productivity. Lower profits can mean fewer wage gains in the future. A full and cumulative circle might then occur because wages can influence morale.

High morale, however, doesn't necessarily cause high productivity; it is merely one, albeit important, influence on total output. For example, a group of workers could be happy as a result of the social relationships that they've developed on the job, but they may be so busy clowning around that their productivity is low. Their morale is high because of the lack of effective leadership. Clearly, for high morale to affect productivity favorably, it must be accompanied by reasonable managerial direction and control.

What Are the Factors That Affect Morale?

The attitudes of employees are significantly influenced by the ways in which they perceive a number of important factors:

1. the organization itself
2. their own activities, both on and off the job
3. the nature of their work
4. their peers
5. their bosses
6. their role expectation
7. their self-concepts
8. the satisfaction of their needs

Let's briefly examine each factor.

The Organization

The organization significantly influences workers' attitudes toward their jobs. For example, the public reputation of the organization, especially if it is unfavorable, can adversely affect the attitudes of employees. An oil company, for instance, that is responsible for a serious oil spill that drastically affected the environment may receive negative publicity damaging to employee morale. Morale can likewise be influenced negatively when a company fails to anticipate market trends and therefore experiences a rapid decline in the demand for its products and in its profitability. The employees of a public agency or school whose reduced public support has caused severe cutbacks in budget and capabilities might also experience poor

There are at least five methods for affecting morale that should be used continuously, which means during bad times as well as good. In fact, continued attention to morale is almost certainly more important during bad times. The factors are communication, recognition and rewards, training, alignment, and leadership.

Communication refers to keeping everyone informed. When people know there are issues but hear nothing about them, they fear the worst and morale declines. People need to be recognized (accurately) for good work and rewarded (with money); if they are not, they can feel unappreciated, and morale and productivity will suffer. Training is another way to show that workers are valued and that management is concerned about keeping people current. Alignment means matching individuals with the goals of the organization by giving everyone a chance to make a meaningful contribution to important projects. Otherwise, people may feel left out and disenfranchised. Leadership refers to showing people that the organization does have a plan and a direction, that it is not foundering. Finally, each of these factors helps to support the others, so that it is not as effective to attend to a couple of them as it is to attend to all five.

Source: Martha Heller, "Six Ways to Boost Morale; If Down Times Have Stalled Your Staff's Productivity and Depressed Its Outlook, Add These Tools to Your Management Arsenal and Watch Them Bounce Back," *CIO*, Nov. 15, 2003, pp. 48–50.

morale. Employees whose companies have been the victims of hostile takeovers may fear that their jobs are in jeopardy and, therefore, experience declining morale. Organizations whose policies, rules, and procedures are perceived as excessively restrictive may develop discontented employees.

EMPLOYEES' ACTIVITIES

Workers are the products of their total environments. The workers' relationships with their families and friends can significantly influence their behavior and attitudes on the job. Most organizations believe that employees should have the right to their own personal lives. However, when their activities off the job affect their performance on the job, managers should have both the responsibility and the prerogative to discuss such activities with employees. Some organizations offer employees counseling on problems ranging from marital difficulties to drug abuse.

THE NATURE OF WORK

Historically, work has tended to become increasingly specialized and routinized, whereas the worker has become progressively better educated. Many behavioral scientists contend that workers' current values and attained levels of education have led them to expect considerably more than just high pay and material prosperity from their work.

Many types of jobs, however, seem to lead to boredom and alienation. A recent investigation by the Institute of Manpower Studies reveals that one of the major reasons people quit their jobs is because of boredom. The study indicates that the following elements led to the feeling that jobs were boring:

1. Employees lacked autonomy and control over the sequence of tasks or pace of work.
2. Employees were not assigned ample responsibility to carry out their jobs adequately.
3. Jobs lacked variety and challenge.
4. Employees' skills were not being fully used.

PEERS

The emergent, or informal, system in an organization can also significantly affect morale. If you're a worker whose previous attitude toward company policies was generally favorable, as a member of a group, your attitude toward a working condition could be swayed by the collective attitudes of your cohorts or union. A condition that formerly didn't disturb you may suddenly have adverse effects on your morale because of the influence of your peers.

LEADERSHIP

Management, from the CEO to first-line supervisors, sets the tone and has the primary responsibility for establishing a healthy organizational climate. Consequently, the actions of managers exert a strong influence over the morale of the workforce. High rates of turnover, for example, often (although not always) indicate ineffective leadership. In later chapters, we will examine some ways in which leaders can improve and maintain morale.

ROLE EXPECTATION

We've already discussed how people tend to assume different roles in different situations. Morale problems often arise when employees have one set of expectations of how their managers should behave, and the managers have another. A concept related to this problem is role expectation, the way in which individuals are mentally set to perceive the behavior of others.

For instance, some managers believe that they will be more effective if they minimize the psychological distance between their associates and themselves. However, if the role expectation of the employees is such that they expect their bosses to keep their distance, attempts at closeness may be difficult if not impossible. Psychological distance is related to feelings of trust, and if a group of employees has a deep-seated distrust of authority, managers will find it difficult to foster closeness and participation. In such an atmosphere, situational thinking and sensitivity are important.

Role expectation can also create morale problems when employees think that rules should apply not only to themselves but also to their bosses. For example, employees would probably think that a rule prohibiting the use of a photocopying machine for personal use should apply equally to everyone. If managers openly use the machine for personal copying but employees cannot, the disregard for organizational rules can create role conflict and discontent among employees, who will think that rules are being applied in a discriminatory fashion.

CONCEPT OF SELF

The self-concept of workers, that is, how they perceive themselves, also tends to influence their attitudes toward organizational environments. For example, individuals who lack self-confidence or who suffer from poor physical or mental health frequently develop morale problems.

PERSONAL NEEDS

How employees' personal needs are satisfied can significantly influence their morale. Paychecks and employee benefits, for example, help to satisfy personal needs. Although increases in pay don't necessarily motivate employees to increase productivity, paychecks can be a source of poor morale, especially when paychecks are compared by employees doing similar work or with those of workers in other firms in the same industry. Employees can become disgruntled when they believe that their paychecks aren't in line with the current industry rates or aren't keeping up with rising prices.

WARNING SIGNS OF LOW MORALE

Morale in organizations is something that managers often take for granted. Morale frequently isn't noticed unless it is poor or until something has gone awry. Far too often, managers do not recognize how badly morale has deteriorated until they are faced with serious crises. Deep organizational scars result from ignoring the warning signs of deteriorating morale.

Perceptive managers are continually on the lookout for clues to the state of morale. Among the more significant warning signs of low morale are absenteeism, tardiness, high turnover, strikes and sabotage, and lack of pride in work. These clues are never problems, however. With low morale in general, these are symptoms of some other problem. Maybe the problem is that the person missing or coming into work late hates the job or the boss, or maybe this person feels trapped in a bad marriage. The real problem may be something the manager or the organization can help with, or it may be something beyond their control, but to remedy the situation, the real problem must be determined. So remember, these are the signs of low morale, and low morale is a sign of some other problem.

EVALUATING MORALE

To improve morale, managers must first attempt to determine what is causing poor morale. In the following section, we will discuss some of the ways in which management can measure morale.

One way to measure morale is to evaluate actual results. Absenteeism and turnover records can provide useful information. For example, during the past four years, the absenteeism rate in your organization rose from 2 to 7 percent. Taken alone, these figures wouldn't be absolute proof that morale had deteriorated. Combined with the results of other techniques of evaluation discussed in the following sections, however, these statistics could give you a fair indication of morale trends and of potential problems.

In some organizations, there are employee counselors whose principal function is to assist employees with their problems and complaints. Counselors are in the position to discover morale problems early. A problem can arise, however, if management regards the counselor as a source of information, and word gets out that he or she is a lapdog or spy of management. Counselors quickly lose effectiveness when they are distrusted.

Another approach to uncovering what bothers people is so obvious that it is often overlooked. Alert managers can usually perceive when someone is behaving

NetNote

CIO

http://www.cio.com/archive/050102/morale.html

Article on morale.

differently simply by observing and listening. A sudden change in the behavior of a particular employee is often a clue that something might be worrying him or her. An increase in the frequency of accidents may also be a sign of a morale problem. Far too frequently, managers don't even listen to the response after they have asked how things are going. Yet one of the most effective means of discovering why people are discontented is to ask them and then listen actively and carefully to their answers.

To explore specific attitudes and opinions of employees in great depth, some managers use morale surveys. Various names have been attached to such surveys, including attitude, opinion, employee, and climate surveys. In general, there are two types of morale survey techniques: interviews and questionnaires. Table 11.2 presents five examples of typical employee attitude survey questions.

In Chapter 9, we discussed some of the most common techniques of interviewing. Two of them—interviews with current employees and exit interviews—can aid in uncovering employee attitudes. The process of interviewing current employees about their attitudes is useful but has its shortcomings. Employees who fear possible reprisals tend to conceal their real opinions and, instead, answer questions according to what they think the boss would like to hear.

The exit interview explores the attitudes of employees who leave the organization. It helps the interviewer to find out the employee's attitudes toward the organization and especially why he or she might be dissatisfied with the organization. This approach also has its limitations because some employees fear that honesty may cost them a favorable letter of recommendation. The interview approach, however, does have the advantage over the questionnaires of permitting greater interviewer sensitivity toward and interaction with respondents.

Some organizations employ a postexit questionnaire in lieu of, or in addition to, an exit interview. This type of questionnaire is thought to elicit more objective responses because it is mailed to the employee some time after his or her termination. Because emotions have probably subsided and the former employee is likely to be firmly entrenched in another job, the postexit interview responses tend to be more honest. Not requiring the identity of the respondent tends to elicit even more candor.

Attitude surveys can be a useful management tool when conducted properly and regularly. If improperly administered, surveys can cause employees to feel suspicious or distrustful of management, and they will not answer the questions candidly. A final important point: Supervisors must be told the purpose and value of surveys. Because supervisors will be administering the surveys, they can make or break the effort.

TABLE 11.2 SAMPLE EMPLOYEE ATTITUDE SURVEY QUESTIONS

	Strongly Agree	Somewhat Agree	Do Not Know	Somewhat Disagree	Strongly Disagree
1. If one of my good friends were offered a job here, I would say take the job—this is a good place to work.	❑	❑	❑	❑	❑
2. Employees in this organization are treated with respect.	❑	❑	❑	❑	❑
3. I agree with the changes made here during the past year.	❑	❑	❑	❑	❑
4. I think management could do much more to make my work more satisfying.	❑	❑	❑	❑	❑
5. Management should trust the workers to do the work instead of supervising so closely.	❑	❑	❑	❑	❑

SUMMARY

In this chapter, we discovered the importance of needs and motivation and their relationship to morale. An understanding of human needs is especially important to managers, who have the vital responsibility of establishing an environment that not only motivates others but also helps to maintain their morale in a positive fashion. Employees and individuals in family and social situations can also benefit from an understanding of needs and motivational concepts.

Felt needs create tensions that motivate a person to make an effort to reduce or eliminate the tensions. Some needs are somewhat basic and internal to the individual, such as the physical need for food. Others are cultural and learned, such as approval, achievement, competence, and power.

Theories of motivation include Maslow's hierarchy, or levels-of-needs concept, Alderfer's ERG theory, and Herzberg's motivation–maintenance model, each of which is considered a content theory of motivation. We also examined process theories of motivation, such as reinforcement, expectancy, and equity theories. Madeline Hunter, although primarily concerned with educational motivation, adds to the theories that attempt to explain how all of us are motivated.

Managers should guard against the tendency to assume that the same factors will motivate all individuals. Motivational influences are highly personal. Each employee in an organization is unique and will thus respond uniquely to specific motivational attempts.

Morale, a condition related to the attitudes of employees, can be influenced by factors both on and off the job. Managers should continually be on the lookout for the warning signs of poor morale to prevent the deterioration of a healthy organizational climate. Among the more important signs of worsening morale are higher rates of absenteeism, tardiness, turnover, strikes and sabotage, and lack of pride in work. Morale can be measured and evaluated in ways ranging from informal observation to formal morale surveys.

CHECKING FOR UNDERSTANDING

1. Why does a need typically have to be recognized before it will motivate?

2. In your opinion, what is the distinction between a need and a want?

3. Why is an understanding of the process of motivation important?

4. Can we "learn" to need something? Explain.

5. List and explain the five levels of needs that Maslow indicated exist in human beings, plus the three related areas in his theory.

6. How does Alderfer's ERG theory of needs and motivation differ from Maslow's theory?

7. Explain why, according to Herzberg's two-factor model, maintenance factors do not necessarily motivate workers.

8. Why did Herzberg categorize working conditions as a maintenance, rather than a motivating, factor?

9. List and describe the five extrinsic factors in Hunter's theory of motivation.

10. Explain the differences among positive, escape, extinction, and punishment types of reinforcement techniques.

11. What are the dangers associated with the use of punishment as a reinforcement technique?

12. Why is the timing of reinforcement techniques important?

13. What is a major difference between Vroom's expectancy theory of motivation and those of Maslow and Herzberg?

14. According to equity theory, what sort of equity do employees want?

15. What are some possible exceptions to the generalization that productivity tends to follow morale?

SELF-ASSESSMENT

Part 1

Complete the motivation questions by marking one motivation level that applies to you (Highly Motivating, Somewhat Motivating, or Not Motivating) for each item. Then rank the items from 1 to 20, 1 being the factor that motivates you the most.

Part 2

1. Explain your results. Why did you rank each item the way you did? Why do some items not motivate you?

2. Explain how you want a manager to motivate you.

3. What would you do to motivate others if you were a manager? (*Hint:* Think about why you were asked to complete Part 1.)

Rank	Highly Motivating	Somewhat Motivating	Not Motivating
___ 1. Money (salary)	_____	_____	_____
___ 2. Piece-rate pay	_____	_____	_____
___ 3. Bonus	_____	_____	_____
___ 4. Annual raise	_____	_____	_____
___ 5. Paid health insurance	_____	_____	_____
___ 6. Paid life insurance	_____	_____	_____
___ 7. Status job title	_____	_____	_____
___ 8. Learning on the job	_____	_____	_____
___ 9. Achievement	_____	_____	_____
___ 10. Promotions	_____	_____	_____
___ 11. Recognition	_____	_____	_____
___ 12. Feedback	_____	_____	_____
___ 13. Success	_____	_____	_____
___ 14. Responsibility	_____	_____	_____
___ 15. Autonomy	_____	_____	_____
___ 16. Setting own goals	_____	_____	_____
___ 17. Interesting work	_____	_____	_____
___ 18. Positive feeling tone	_____	_____	_____
___ 19. Being held accountable	_____	_____	_____
___ 20. A deadline	_____	_____	_____

SKILL BUILD 11

"I tell ya, it's brutal out there, brutal. Why, I don't get no reverence, no reverence at all. The other day I told a worker I needed a break. He said, 'where do want it, the legs or the face?' They're a brutal bunch, I tell ya," Mehmood said as he entered the manager's lounge.

"One of my people told me he'd rather take up housekeeping with a rattlesnake than come to work," Nancy sympathized.

"What are we going to do?" Pam asked. "I always make sure I ask rather than order my people to do things, and I try to tell them when they do well, rather than yell at them when they do something wrong. Then yesterday I told Aricel, you know she's been here for over five years, I told her she did her last job really well. She told me that when she wanted my opinion she would beat it out of me!"

Skill Question 1. Pam talks about using two different theories. What theory or part of a theory is she talking about first?

Skill Question 2. According to the theory, is what Pam is using supposed to motivate people?

Skill Question 3. What theory or part of a theory is she talking about second—the one she describes and then uses the Aricel incident as an example of?

Skill Question 4. According to the theory, is what Pam is using supposed to motivate people?

"It's motivation," Mehmood explained. "Let me give you a couple of examples. Alice. She has no one. Her family is far away, she just got to town; this is her first job. I put her on the demo team, and she is doing better than ever. Why? She feels a part of a group, and that's what she needed. Then there is Damani. Damani the bookworm. This guy is like a walking encyclopedia, got facts coming out his ears; not that they are all related to one another, but give him credit, everything interests him. So, I put him in research. He does great and loves it because he has whatever that need is, that need to, like, read the whole library. That's what we need to do for everyone."

Skill Question 5. Mehmood needs your help. What theory or part of a theory is he using for Alice?

Skill Question 6. What theory or part of a theory is Mehmood using for Alice and for Damani? (*Hint:* The theory or part of a theory he uses on Alice is *not* the same one he uses for Damani.)

Skill Question 7. Explain whether or not the theories he is using for Alice and Damani are correct for them.

"Mehmood, are you nuts? We can't get that involved with each and every person. You know how long that will take? And what if we don't have the ideal spot for each person?" Nancy said. "We need some general things that affect everyone. We need supervisors who are nice to people. We need to revise the work rules so they don't sound so formal. Then we need to work on the look of this place. That's what will motivate these people."

Skill Question 8. Now Nancy needs your help. What theory or part of a theory is she talking about using when she disagrees with Mehmood?

Skill Question 9. According to the theory, is what Nancy mentions supposed to motivate people?

Skill Question 10. What effect will the things Nancy talks about have on people's satisfaction, if any?

"No way, Nancy," Mehmood said, "we have to hold them accountable for everything. Match them up to what they like but hold them strictly accountable. That's motivating."

Skill Question 11. What theory or part of a theory is Mehmood using when he disagrees with Nancy?

Skill Question 12. Is this going to motivate (according to the theories in the chapter)? How?

"Nancy, I don't think what you are talking about will motivate either. I'm thinking the workers need recognition, achievement, feedback, success, those kinds of things," Olivia said, finally joining the conversation.

Skill Question 13. Olivia needs you to help her. What theory or part of a theory is she talking about using when she disagrees with Nancy? (*Hint:* She and Nancy talk about different parts of the same theory.)

Skill Question 14. According to the theory, is what Olivia mentions supposed to motivate people?

Skill Question 15. What effect will the things Olivia talks about have on people's satisfaction, if any?

"How will that work? We have to let people know what matters most to us. Once they know what we think is absolutely critical, they'll come around, they'll perform," Nancy said.

Skill Question 16. What theory or part of a theory is Nancy talking about using when she disagrees with Olivia? Can this motivate, and if so, how?

"I don't know. I just don't know. Maybe we're all wrong. I mean, they complain, they have lousy attitudes, but productivity is the same. Maybe it's not a motivation problem at all," Olivia said.

Skill Question 17. Is the problem these four managers are talking about really motivation, or does some other chapter concept better fit this situation? If you think the problem is motivation, explain why. If you think some other chapter concept applies better, name it and explain why. If the problem is motivation, list motivation ideas that will help. If the problem is something other than motivation, describe what can be done to help with that.

APPLICATIONS

11.1 INDIVIDUAL INDUCEMENTS

You have just taken over a new area with six workers. Three have just completed their projects and need new assignments. Three are in the middle of their projects but are not performing well. You have been brought in to motivate them. You decide to handle the three that need new assignments first—Toni, Donna, and Sunil.

Toni is a temp worker barely getting by. She had a full-time job at another firm with 11 years' seniority when the founder retired and liquidated the assets. Donna is at the highest pay grade in the department and has the highest title—Senior Project Leader. She lives very comfortably and likes to read in many varied areas and create art in her spare time, and would quit and do that full-time if she could. Sunil is easily bored with committees and bureaucracy. He comes in every day ready to take charge. He likes to work and to get things done and then move to the next job.

The three projects to be assigned are the Abruzzi Project, the Regional Extensions Project, and the Tyler Bid. The Abruzzi Project involves product development for a new line of stores selling, essentially, gadgets. The products are not new; many, like the calculator and the digital camera, have been around for a while. Abruzzi stores will sell these and other items with unique designs. The Regional Extensions Project involves using one work crew to construct four regional offices for your company, one per year for the next 4 years. The Tyler Bid is not a sure thing yet. A proposal needs to be worked up for what could become the Tyler Project, and your firm has an excellent chance of winning the bid, resulting in the need for someone to commit to follow through and stay with the project for the next 8 to 10 years.

The three workers with ongoing projects are Scott, Kendra, and Carmella. All are underperforming. Scott claims (with some justification) that he has worked far harder than everyone else in the department for the past 7 years and now he is just "doing what they have been doing"—average. He was given his project because of his work history, and now he is the furthest behind. Kendra is looking for a promotion and a raise after her project is complete but doesn't seem to be working very hard to get it. Kendra thinks the other five people in your department plus about two dozen people outside the department all want the one promotion. You know that no one outside the department is interested or has a chance, and inside the department only Toni would want and need the work. As for Carmella, she has had a succession of short-lived bosses, none of whom took much notice of her. As she explains it, "Nothing bad happens to me if my projects are a little late and nothing good happens if I'm finished on time or early."

QUESTIONS

1. Name specific motivation theories (or parts of motivation theories) that should be applied to Toni, Donna, and Sunil, and explain why the selected theory for each should work.

2. Whom will you assign to each of the new projects? Match the project to the motivation needed by each person and explain how each project will meet each person's motivational needs.

3. What motivation theory is Scott employing or using to explain his current performance? How can this same theory be used to motivate Scott?

4. What motivation theory explains Kendra's situation, and how can that same theory be used to motivate her now?

5. What motivation theory explains Carmella's situation, and how can that same theory be used to motivate her now?

11.2 "GIVE US MORE MONEY!"

Productivity had fallen to a new low among the 20 mechanics in Etienne White's department. She knew that part of the problem was due to the high employee turnover experienced among her workers. Several of her staff were new to the company, replacing mechanics who had quit. Even among the remaining well-trained workers who had been with the company for some time, absenteeism was high, and people didn't seem to put out their best effort.

Six months ago, Etienne decided to do something about her group's productivity problems. Etienne, a recent college graduate, decided to institute some of the motivational techniques she had learned in her organizational behavior and supervision classes. First, she started competition among the workers that would yield recognition to high achievers. She decided to allow the workers to take more responsibility for the jobs the department had to handle, reasoning that this would induce the workers to show greater pride in their work. She also developed a new training program that would allow the mechanics to advance in their skill levels. But as Etienne reviewed the last month's production figures, she had to admit that the results were poor.

Etienne had encouraged her subordinates to make suggestions for improving the department's performance, but with little success. When she tried to pin one worker down, the mechanic responded angrily at Etienne personally. Most of the workers just shrugged their shoulders and evaded the issue. Finally, Jeff Coluntuno, one of Etienne's better workers, told her, "If I told you what I really think about this place, you'd probably fire me on the spot." This gave Etienne the idea of instituting an anonymous suggestion box. She told her workers that they should feel free to make any suggestions they wanted without fear of reprisal.

A week later, as Etienne opened the box, she was again disappointed. Only four of her mechanics had bothered to make suggestions. They were as follows:

"The pay here is lousy. If you want us to do a better job, pay us a living wage."

"We have to pay for our own health insurance benefits here, and I, for one, can't afford it. Dick, who left here for another job, gets free health insurance where he works now."

"The shop is cold all winter. If we close things up and try to get warm, there's no ventilation. How can a guy work when he can't breathe?"

"I don't give a hoot for your contests and classes! I have a family to feed and look after!"

QUESTIONS

1. Why do you think Etienne White's ideas were unsuccessful?

2. Did she perceive the workers' needs in the same way that they themselves did? White was attempting to use which needs as motivators? Which needs were most important to the mechanics?

3. What would you do in this situation? Which motivation theories would you use and why?

NET-WORK

David Brent interviewed for a performance appraisal; now how do you motivate him?

http://www.youtube.com/watch?v=4JaMqb96_TU

Ergonomics in the Workplace

http://www.youtube.com/watch?v=mhwA3o16YFg

PERSONAL POINTS

1. How deeply do you feel the need for achievement?

2. What are your social needs in the workplace, and what would you do if those needs could not be met at work?

3. How important is status to you and why?

4. How do you really feel about money? How much do you *really* need? Would you stay at a well-paying job that you hated? Why or why not?

5. How does your current (or did a previous) workplace affect your morale? What would improve your morale?

EXPERIENTIAL EXERCISE

What Do You Need?

This exercise is designed to help you understand Maslow's motivational theory and to recognize how priorities of needs differ among various individuals.

INSTRUCTIONS

1. Read the following story and then determine the order in which you would make your requests.

2. Form a small group of about five participants and attempt to reach a group consensus on the "correct" order in which requests should be made. Attempt to convince others in your group of your point of view.

3. How did the outcome—the group's ranking—compare with Maslow's hierarchy?

4. How do you account for the differences among individual group members regarding their initial ranking of needs?

STORY

You are sailing with a crew of five from San Francisco, California, to Sydney, Australia. Your boat sinks during a turbulent storm, and you are the sole survivor. You are rescued by a wealthy and eccentric recluse named Isolando, who lives on a small island with a small group of his followers. Because the island is un-charted, there is little chance of your being rescued. Isolando, who discovered the island 10 years earlier with his followers, informs you that you are welcome to his island and all your needs and wants will be satisfied—all you have to do is request what you want. Below are listed five types of requests you may make. Rank them in the order in which you would make them.

Your Requests	Group's Requests	
_____	_____	Companionship of others
_____	_____	The ability to determine your goals and strive to achieve them
_____	_____	Food, drink, shelter
_____	_____	Recognition and attention from others
_____	_____	A set of guidelines describing how life on the island is structured

SPOT CHECK ANSWERS

1. T
2. T
3. F
4. F
5. F
6. F
7. F
8. T
9. F
10. T
11. T
12. F
13. F
14. T
15. T
16. T
17. F
18. F
19. F
20. T

12 | Job Satisfaction and the Quality of Work Life

You can't build a reputation on what you're going to do..

Henry Ford

The return from your work must be the satisfaction which that work brings you and the world's need of that work..

William Edward Burghardt Du Bois

In order that people be happy in their work, these three things are needed: They must be fit for it. They must not do too much of it. And they must have a sense of success in it..

John Ruskin

GOALS

The main goal of this chapter is to make you aware of the factors that constitute job satisfaction. There is much more to feeling satisfied about your job than simply liking the work, and too few people understand this. Knowing what contributes to job satisfaction and the quality of your work will help with your current and future jobs.

OBJECTIVES

When you finish this chapter, you should be able to:

- Define and describe quality of work life.
- List and explain the common features of quality of work life.
- List and describe the 14 factors that can impact and improve the quality of work life.
- Explain the effects the work and social environments can have on the quality of work life.
- Describe innovative ways to work.
- Explain work trends that can affect the quality of work life.
- List and explain the external factors affecting job satisfaction.
- List and explain the internal factors affecting job satisfaction.
- List and explain the individual factors affecting job satisfaction.

INTRODUCTION

Previous generations toiled; the current generation chooses a career path. Admittedly this is a generalization; however, it does serve to illustrate differences in the quality of work life from past to present. That the quality of work life is even discussed also illustrates the differences. To be more specific, consider the plight of earlier generations as compared with the situation today.

For the vast majority of people in the past, work began at or before dawn and continued until dusk. Most lived in a subsistence-level economy. In other words, you worked in order to survive, or you died. There was little distinction between work and nonwork time. Work consumed most of your day, so there was little nonwork time. The work being done, as just mentioned, was essentially toil.

Toil, continuous labor or strenuous work, best describes the quality of work life for workers of the past. Before the Industrial Revolution, most people were farmers or crafts workers using muscle power to shape wood, stone, iron, or dirt. People generally relied on themselves for providing for their needs, or they bartered what they produced for what they needed. Often, little or nothing was left after providing for basic needs. There was little hope that conditions would change.

Immediately after the Industrial Revolution, however, work conditions changed dramatically, but the quality of work life changed little. After the Industrial Revolution, people came together in large numbers to work for others for a wage. As seen in Chapter 1, a greater distinction between work and nonwork time was made. Although the workday was often long, there was now a time when people were off work or not working. Within the workday, however, conditions had not changed much. The work was physically difficult and not mentally challenging. For all intents and purposes, people, like machines, were perceived simply as a means of production—to be discarded when broken, to be replaced when used up. As the work world became more sophisticated and as managers and workers became more educated, the quality of work life improved. Today, workers expect more from a job than just providing a means of support; today, many people expect work to be meaningful. Many of the best and brightest people expect work to be challenging, and growth to be limited only by a person's own abilities.[1] Today, both managers and workers are challenged to provide and to find a high level of quality in work life.

GREATER CONCERNS OVER THE QUALITY OF WORK LIFE

A fairly large proportion of today's workforce has attained higher levels of education than at any time in U.S. history. Rising levels of expectation typically accompany increased achievements in education. Yet many observers believe that the quality of jobs will decline steadily as newer positions offer employees less challenge and less ego satisfaction than existed in jobs that are being phased out. Thus, enormous challenges face today's managers—and workers. The challenges come from needs and motivation, shifting trends in jobs, and a trend toward **outsourcing** work. These challenges make the topic of quality of work life (QWL)—how effectively the job environment meets the personal needs and values of employees—important to you as a potential manager or worker. Why? Worker expectations that aren't fulfilled can cause job dissatisfaction and a weakening of the work ethic.

Outsourcing
hiring people from outside a company to perform work that had been performed from inside the company

NEEDS AND MOTIVATION

We learned earlier about needs and motivation. Employees, of course, aren't like robots—that is, mechanical objects—whose only human trait is caring about their paychecks. Most employees have a strong need for self-esteem and a sense of belonging. Without such satisfactions, many employees become bored, disgruntled, alienated, and sometimes even destructive. Both blue- and white-collar workers often feel alienated from their jobs. These feelings tend to result in increased alcohol and drug abuse, mental illness, shoddy work, lower productivity, pilferage, and sabotage.

SHIFTING TRENDS IN JOBS

Many manufacturing jobs are being lost today due to automation, downsizing, and relocation to other countries where costs are lower. Although some of these jobs had a high level of monotony and lower quality of work life, many offered good pay, good benefits, and a reasonable level of job security. On the other hand, many of the jobs being created (in service and other areas) are just as monotonous and have a lower quality of work life with low pay and few, if any, benefits. Many are part-time positions, and many of the new positions are for temps.[2] Many of the new jobs are in areas that are currently not unionized. These factors can make the task of finding a job equal to the standards of the previous generation difficult. Finding a job with a higher quality of work life is possible, but it is much more arduous a task than in the past. Much of the employment picture is going to change dramatically in the next 10 to 15 years as the bulk of the Baby Boom generation reaches retirement age. As noted in earlier chapters, large numbers of jobs may go unfilled as a result of these retirements.

One might ask why employers bother to hire anyone at all, and some have (also see *Doonesbury* cartoon). In fact, employers as far back as the 1700s asked the same thing. What they learned, often the hard way, was that when they used nonemployee workers, employee theft was rampant. Controlling productivity, quality, and completion time were also difficult. This was partly due to the nonemployee workers' lack of loyalty and partly due to uncertainty. Because these workers were never certain when the work might end, they would make multiple commitments, some of which they could keep and some they could not. Eventually, employers decided it was better to hire people they could supervise and who committed to their firm and, in exchange, the workers gained job security.[3]

TREND TOWARD A 24/7 WORKFORCE

One of the newer trends is the increase in the need for more and more firms to have staff available 24 hours per day, seven days per week, due partially to the increasing use of the Internet. The difficulty in finding staff for all hours of the day and night is compounded by increasing worker demands for quality of life—not just greater quality of work life, but a better balance between work life and personal time. Add in the generally low level of unemployment, and 24/7 staffing has been a difficult challenge for many firms to meet. As a result, some have been experimenting with shifts up to 12 hours long, adding stimulation to the work environment (stronger lighting, music, the scent of lemon or rosemary), allowing short naps and workouts, and schedules allowing three or four consecutive days off.[4]

TREND TOWARD OUTSOURCING WORK

Possibly the most significant threat to the quality of work life is the trend toward outsourcing and downsizing. Starting in the mid-1980s and continuing today, the outsourcing trend is the result of a number of developments. Increased global competition, computer developments (especially home PCs, laptops, and advances in management information systems), telecommuting, the cost of fringe benefits, and other factors led to the idea of moving certain work outside a company. Outsourcing started by moving some work from one company to another in the same country. Now outsourcing is more often associated with moving work to other countries. Much attention has been given to jobs going to India, China, and the Philippines, but Ireland, Argentina, and Canada have also seen work come their way.[5] Firms tend to release "excess" workers, but sometimes they hire back their own former employees as independent contractors (also referred to as consultants or temps) and pay them a similar dollar wage. The employer saves money by not providing expensive fringe benefits (especially medical benefits). In addition, the employer eliminates much of the support services needed by a larger workforce (such as managers, for instance).

Although not always a successful strategy, the trend toward downsizing continues.[6] What, then, is the threat to the quality of work life? The threat comes in the creation of a large corps of temp workers—workers with virtually no job security, workers living from job to job and not knowing where that next job will come from. **Temps** must constantly look for their next assignment in a world where the ability to sell oneself may be more important than having done the previous job well. The stress, uncertainty, and lack of fringe benefits (especially medical benefits) could take a heavy toll on people forced to work this way.

The human toll from downsizing and outsourcing is felt not only by those who leave but also by those who stay. While some jobs are shifted to the outside, others are shifted to the remaining workers. The added responsibility increases the pace or the hours worked and increases stress and resentment. The downsizing itself creates fear in those who were not forced out. Thus their quality of work life declines also.

The underlying assumption behind the forceful creation of legions of temp workers seems to be that workers have no voice in the quality of their work lives. Indeed, articles written on downsizing have an upper-management, this-is-what-is-best-for-our-bottom-line sound to them. The message is that the company will release people and will then contract them back for less cost—and that is that. Or is it? There was an earlier time when company leaders extracted more and more from workers for less and less pay. That was a time when workers had virtually no voice, no power. Actually, individual workers had little power, but there is power in numbers. Workers eventually found a way to gain a voice and power—through unions. Although union membership has been declining for a number of years, conditions may be suitable for a resurgence of unionism. This time, however, it could be with the white-collar temps and technical workers. Although temps make up only 2 percent of the workforce, they represent 20 percent of all new jobs. Even at 2 percent of the workforce, temps are over 2 million strong.[7] If they feel the situation is unacceptable, and if unions want to try to stop their declining memberships, then conditions may be right for a most interesting development in the working environment.

Temps
temporary workers; independent agents working for a company for a short time

WHAT INFLUENCES THE QUALITY OF WORK LIFE?

As discussed in Chapter 1, the quality of equipment, tools, and other technical and material factors influences the productivity of an organization. Also affecting productivity is the quality of work life (QWL). Of course, a factor that enhances

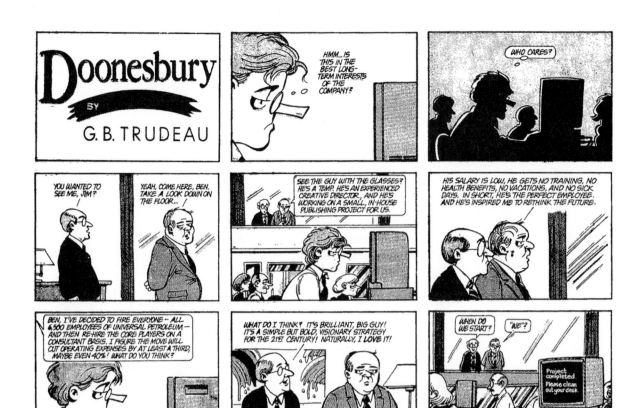

one worker's QWL might have little effect on another worker's QWL. Some common features, however, tend to directly influence the QWL in most organizations.

Eight major categories that together make up the QWL have been suggested:[8]

1. **Adequate and fair compensation.** Is the employee's paycheck sufficient for maintaining a reasonable standard of living? Is the wage or salary comparable to amounts received by others in similar positions?

2. **Safe and healthy working conditions.** Is the work environment relatively free from excessive hazards that could cause employees injury or illness?

3. **Opportunity for developing and using human capacity.** How does the job relate to the employee's self-esteem? Does it permit the employee to use and develop his or her skills and knowledge? Does the worker feel involved and challenged?

4. **Opportunity for continued growth and security.** Are there opportunities for advancement, or is the job perceived as a path to nowhere? Does the job provide the employee with employment and income security?

5. **A feeling of belonging.** Does the worker feel a part of a team or, instead, isolated from the group? Are fellow employees supportive of each other or in a state of continual conflict? Is the work environment relatively free from destructive prejudice?

6. **Employee rights.** What sort of rights does the employee have? What are the standards of personal privacy, attitudes toward dissent, equity in the distribution of rewards, and access to grievance procedures?

7. Work and total life space. How does the job affect the employee's personal life roles, such as his or her relationship with family? Are overtime demands, travel requirements, and transfers perceived as excessive?

8. Social relevance of work life. Does the employee perceive that the organization is socially responsible? Does the organization produce a product or service that contributes to the employee's pride? Or does the organization engage in unethical activities? What are the organization's employment practices? Are they fair? How does the organization dispose of wastes?

Robert Levering, a labor and business writer, identifies these three additional factors:[9]

- trusting the people in the organization
- being able to take pride in the work being done
- having coworkers who are enjoyable to work with

IMPROVING THE QUALITY OF WORK LIFE

Managers and workers have an interest in improving the quality of work life. Many managers believe that improving the quality of work life will increase productivity. Even if productivity remains the same, if the quality of work life can be improved with no detrimental effect to the firm, why not do it? And although productivity might not change, turnover might decrease, the firm might be able to attract better workers more easily, or morale might improve. The interest workers have in improving the quality of work life is even more obvious. If people are miserable 8 hours a day at work, they will be miserable the other 16 hours at home. Improving the QWL can improve a person's entire life.

Given the interest in QWL and the challenges to QWL, in what ways can improvements be made? There are 14 main ways, with some additional possibilities for the future. The current methods for improving the quality of work life are:

- job enrichment
- job enlargement
- vertical and horizontal loading
- manipulating core job dimensions
- job rotation
- cross-training
- feedback and reinforcement
- well pay and floating holidays
- empowerment
- child and elder care
- changes to the work environment and social environment
- ergonomic changes
- wellness programs
- aesthetics and personalization

Of course, many firms elect to use several of these methods in combination.

JOB ENRICHMENT

Job enrichment is a general term for improving the QWL that has a variety of forms. Job enrichment frequently involves greater use of factors that are intended to motivate the worker rather than only maintain a satisfied feeling toward the job.

Job Enrichment
adding depth (increasing difficulty) to a job to increase motivation and interest in performing the job

(Remember Herzberg's motivation–maintenance model?) Basically, job enrichment is a form of changing or improving a job so that a worker is likely to be more motivated. It provides the employee with the opportunity for greater recognition, achievement, growth, and responsibility, the lack of which can cause worker alienation. In short, job enrichment involves modifying jobs so that they appeal more to employees' higher-order needs. An example of job enrichment would be to allow secretaries to sign their own outgoing letters and to be responsible for content and quality.

Another way of explaining job enrichment is in terms of job depth. Enriching a job means to add depth to a job. For example, a production worker's job might consist of the assembly of a circuit board. After assembly, the board is sent to a tester to see if it works properly and is then sent to a third person for assembly with other boards. To enrich this job, depth could be added by training production workers to test their own boards and then assemble them with the other boards. Notice that the difficulty level of the job has increased rather than just increasing the number of tasks (see Job Enlargement, next). Also, the production worker is not being thrown into a more difficult job and expected to learn the job on his or her own. The worker is given the training needed to perform the new job. With this new production job, the job of the tester can also be enriched by assembling boards rather than just testing, thus changing the job of tester to that of production worker, as we now have no need for separate testers.

JOB ENLARGEMENT

Job enlargement generally means that tasks are added to a job. With job enrichment, the additions to the job are of greater difficulty than the tasks of the original job. With job enlargement, tasks are added that are roughly the same difficulty level as those in the original job. Let's look at three workers in a mortgage brokerage, each of whom verifies a different portion of a credit application. One verifies all the employment data, one investigates credit history, and one verifies assets and cash balances. All these tasks are at approximately the same level of difficulty. Job enlargement would consist of having each worker completely verify every third application as opposed to the current job in which each works on one-third of every application. In the initial job, there is not as much of a sense of satisfaction for completing a whole unit (in this case a unit being one application). Consider, however, that there will probably be negligible benefit from enlarging a job that involves screwing one lug nut on a wheel to one in which the worker screws on five lug nuts.

VERTICAL AND HORIZONTAL LOADING

Vertical and horizontal loading are methods of accomplishing job enrichment and job enlargement. As you can observe in Figure 12.1, **vertical loading** involves enriching the work itself by pulling down responsibilities from above and pushing certain tasks of a job down to a lower job classification. In other words, a manager analyzes what he or she currently does for the employees that could be delegated to the employees themselves. Are there tasks performed by employees when the manager is absent that they could do regularly? Could workers be empowered with more responsibility for deciding how things are to be done? Should certain tasks be pushed down to a lower job classification? How could the employees be made to feel more accountable for their actions? Could some controls be removed without removing accountability?

Horizontal loading actually enlarges the job by pushing earlier work stages into it and pulling later work stages into it. Could certain tasks that precede the work be

Job Enlargement
adding tasks at the same level of difficulty to a job

Vertical Loading
job enrichment by pulling down responsibilities from above and pushing tasks down to a lower level

Horizontal Loading
job enlargement by pushing tasks into earlier work stages or pulling tasks into later work stages

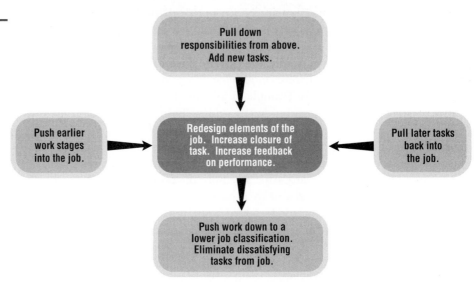

FIGURE 12.1 ENRICHING WORK THROUGH VERTICAL AND HORIZONTAL LOADING

made a basic part of the job for the purpose of making the work more meaningful and responsible and less monotonous?

MANIPULATING CORE JOB DIMENSIONS

What are the principal factors that tend to enrich jobs? J. Richard Hackman and Greg R. Oldham have identified five factors, termed *core job dimensions*, that they believe are essential ingredients of any job if the benefits of job enrichment are to be derived (see Table 12.1).[10] A brief discussion of each follows.

Task Variety A significant core dimension of an enriched job is **task variety.** Basically, this dimension enables employees to perform a wide assortment of operations requiring both thinking and doing types of activities.

Task Identity A second core dimension relates to performing an entire task and is referred to as **task identity.** A job designed with this factor in mind allows the employee to have a more complete job with which he or she can identify rather than a minute, repetitive job that seems to have little relationship to a whole. A later section of this chapter discusses the whole job concept.

Task Significance Many people like to feel that the job they perform has an impact on others. They want to believe that their job is important and makes some contribution to the company and society. When a job offers this dimension, it is said to have **task significance.**

Autonomy Many employees like to feel responsible for their actions. They prefer to have the freedom to make decisions, even when there is a chance of failure. Jobs that empower their holders with the right to make a variety of decisions without first having to consult a higher authority are said to have the **autonomy** dimension.

Task Variety
the different tasks in a job; the degree to which job tasks are different from one another

Task Identity
completing an entire unit or subunit (as opposed to performing one of many tasks required to complete a unit or subunit)

Task Significance
the belief that the work is important

Autonomy
freedom to make decisions; the ability to work without supervision; the level of control people have over their work

TABLE 12.1 THE CORE DIMENSIONS OF JOBS

Factors that tend to enrich jobs include:

1. Task variety—performing a variety of operations and procedures

2. Task identity—completing an entire piece of work

3. Task significance—believing that the work is important to others

4. Autonomy—controlling decision-making opportunities

5. Feedback—receiving information regarding level and quality of performance

Feedback   "How am I doing?" is a question that many employees want answered. The **feedback** dimension exists in jobs where employees consistently receive information on how they are performing. Feedback includes constructive criticism as well as praise. An ideal time for employees to receive feedback is during their formal performance appraisal interview. The interview session also provides the manager with the opportunity to guide the employee toward establishing new goals and improving or modifying future performance.

JOB ROTATION

Job rotation involves workers' switching tasks at regular intervals. Many managers believe that providing employees with a variety of work experiences can help reduce boredom. For example, the job of operating a telephone switchboard can be monotonous, as can the job of receptionist. Rather than assign one person to each task for an entire day, the jobs could be rotated. One person could work the switchboard for two hours and then work as a receptionist for two hours. After lunch, the pattern is repeated. For even greater effectiveness in job rotation, a lesson could be taken from stress-management principles.

Stress can often be managed by employing contrasting or alternating tasks. Tasks can be roughly divided into physical and mental and further divided into highly physical and less physical and those requiring high mental concentration and less mental concentration. The contrast principle states that alternating the types of tasks that are being completed may reduce stress. For example, it is more stressful to perform one task requiring a large amount of physical activity followed by another highly physical activity. A better contrast would be a highly physical task followed by a less physical task. Better yet, follow a highly physical task with one requiring less mental concentration. Using contrast to reduce stress may also work with job rotation and boredom.

Examples of using contrast with job rotation might be found in a warehouse. The job of physically moving items might be contrasted with taking inventory or entering the moves into a computer database. In a hospital or office, the job of medical transcriptionist or word processor might be contrasted with filing or even transporting patients. In an auto repair shop, the job of scheduling appointments and releasing repaired vehicles might be alternated with the actual repairing of vehicles. In a hotel, the check-in clerks might rotate with the porters to reduce stress and boredom. In addition to providing employees with variety, job rotation can provide broader knowledge and greater understanding of the organization's functions and greater respect and appreciation for coworkers.

Feedback
information received by workers regarding the level and quality of performance

Job Rotation
moving people to different jobs on the same organizational level for short times

There can be a downside to job rotation, however. A potential disadvantage is that some people may feel less commitment to specific positions, an attitude which, in some instances, can encourage job hopping. For many employees, though, the benefits of job rotation tend to outweigh any disadvantages.

CROSS-TRAINING

Cross-Training
teaching workers more than one job; multiskilling

Some firms maintain planned programs of **cross-training** (or multiskilling) production workers so that they can easily rotate from one position to another. Cross-trained workers sometimes receive increased pay as compensation for adding to their skill set. Cross-trained employees have been found to have an improved understanding of the entire production process, which can increase quality and decrease the defect rate.[11]

FEEDBACK AND REINFORCEMENT

Too often the only feedback received from work occurs when something goes wrong, and the only reinforcement is negative. Even though virtually everyone prefers praise and recognition, and a diverse group has recommended this approach, negative feedback and recognition continue. It is often possible, however, to change this situation in ways that cost very little to the company but hold large rewards. Drawing from the recommendations of people ranging from management's Frederick Herzberg to education's Madeline Hunter, we can outline the requirements for a feedback and positive-reinforcement system. For maximum benefit, the feedback must be:

- accurate
- frequent
- timely
- integral with the task
- self-evident

To increase the QWL even more, positive reinforcement should also be used. An ideal feedback and reinforcement system must be accurate. People will have no respect for a system that fails to recognize those doing the best work, and they will always know whether or not the system is working. The optimum system will also have frequent feedback. People want to know how they are doing. They must be told much more frequently than once a year at their annual reviews, however. How frequent the feedback should be is different for different jobs, but quarterly is probably a minimum. Hourly, or at least daily, is certainly appropriate for many. Understanding how this may be achieved is probably easier after describing timely, integral, and especially, self-evident feedback.

NetNote

WAHM.com
The Online Magazine for Work at Home Moms

http://www.wahm.com

A site for work-at-home women.

SPOT CHECK

1. Job enrichment involves adding depth to a job. T F
2. With job enlargement, tasks are added that are at a much greater difficulty level as those in the original job. T F
3. Task variety involves performing a multiplicity of operations and procedures. T F
4. Task identity is recognizing that your work is important. T F
5. Task significance involves completing an entire piece of work or at least a significant portion. T F

Feedback is timely when it occurs soon after the event that triggers the feedback. For example, if a manager witnesses a worker going beyond the call of duty to assist a coworker or client, it is best to give the worker the feedback immediately. The longer the manager waits, the less effective the feedback becomes. This is also true of those times when negative feedback or punishment is legitimately called for. Creating a feedback and reinforcement system that is accurate, frequent, and timely is relatively easy compared with designing one that is also integral and self-evident.

Feedback is integral with a job when it occurs as a natural part of the process. For example, when assembling an electric motor, integral feedback is possible if the assembly worker tests the motor and it works. In addition to being integral, the ideal feedback system is self-evident. To be self-evident, the workers must be trained to do their own inspection, and the success of the work must be obvious to all. A radiographer receives feedback that is integral and self-evident when she or he views the digital image or develops the film. When the image is displayed or the X-ray film emerges from the developer, everyone knows if the film is acceptable or not. Even the patient knows as the radiographer returns to make another exposure or to release the patient from the department. It is difficult to make feedback this integral and self-evident for all jobs. When it is impossible, then accurate, frequent, timely feedback should come from the manager.

Feedback from a manager can be given in a variety of ways. Although rewards can be used, a manager may also use words, favorable gestures (a thumbs-up), favorable glances and nods, and a smile. A manager can also give feedback through listening. A manager can stop, listen, and give more eye contact than he or she is receiving in order to deliver positive feedback.

WELL PAY AND FLOATING HOLIDAYS

Excessive employee absenteeism can be a serious problem for many employers. As a means of discouraging absenteeism and tardiness, some organizations provide an extra reward through a program of **well pay** for those who do show up for work as expected. Under this proposal, workers who put in a given number of days without being absent or late are given an extra day off.[12]

Another method for improving the quality of work life that is a little different from well pay is the **floating holiday**. A floating holiday is paid time off that employees can take whenever they want within a certain time. For example, Sherman Hospital in Elgin, Illinois, allows a fall, winter, and spring floating holiday, plus the employee's birthday as paid time off. Each floating holiday must be taken within a three-month period, and the birthday holiday can be taken up to one month before or after an employee's birthday. Essentially, these holidays acknowledge that people need an occasional mental-health day that can be taken on short notice.

EMPOWERMENT

Empowerment is an often-heard term that relates directly to the free-reign approach to leadership. Basically, empowerment is providing employees with higher degrees of involvement and greater authority to make decisions on their own. Empowerment does not always have to be used at the expense of control because varying degrees of empowerment are possible. Managers should not be afraid to empower their employees with the right to make high-risk decisions. Delegation, as we've learned, can aid employees in their growth and

Well Pay
a reward in the form of a scheduled day off with pay in return for not taking an unscheduled day off within a certain time

Floating Holiday
one day off with pay, scheduled on short notice, within a certain time

Empowerment
providing employees with higher degrees of involvement and greater authority to make decisions

People are living longer, but many need assistance. Companies are starting to realize this and some are making an effort to provide elder care.
Source: Courtesy of PhotoEdit/Spencer Grant.

development, improve their QWL, and, especially important, free the manager for other important tasks.

CHILD AND ELDER CARE

Off-the-job concerns can certainly affect an employee's on-the-job morale, and small children are a major concern of today's employees. A large proportion of the workforce requires some sort of child-care facilities for their small children. An increasing number of organizations have begun to recognize that establishing on-site child-care centers has improved employee morale, reduced absenteeism and lateness, and reduced turnover. Alternatives to such on-site centers are financial aid for child care, maternity/paternity leave for expectant and/or new parents, and flexible work hours to allow for the care of a sick child. Johnson & Johnson is at the forefront of a growing movement among U.S. companies to provide better support for employees with family problems.[13]

Elder care is caring for older people, typically relatives. Care may extend to elderly people who live in their own homes, those who live in the homes of their children, or those who reside in nursing homes. Some elderly people just need someone to talk to or simply need a ride to the supermarket. Others suffer from debilitating conditions such as Alzheimer's disease or are too frail or infirm to care for themselves. Elder care can be especially demanding as one watches a parent or other close relative decline and regress. Possibly the greatest stress is placed on those with both child-care and elder-care responsibilities.

CHANGES TO THE WORK ENVIRONMENT AND THE SOCIAL ENVIRONMENT

Some managers improve the QWL of employees by modifying the work environment. This activity is a broad one and could be applied together with all of our suggestions for improving jobs. Wherever possible, teams or work groups should be used. Smaller groups tend to be more cohesive than larger ones. Team members are usually more productive when they can participate in choosing compatible workmates for their groups. With effective leadership, teams tend to improve work standards and accept new processes more readily. Further, many employees like teamwork because it provides for more variety of tasks as compared with repetitive jobs on typical assembly lines.[14] Workers generally prefer some degree of social contact with other employees. The opportunity for conversation, therefore, tends to enhance morale, especially on repetitive jobs that don't require much mental concentration. Also, music can be an effective morale builder in some circumstances, but the captive audience—the workers—should participate in determining the types of music to be played.

Regular rest breaks have been known for some time to have beneficial effects on productivity. Some firms have recently introduced voluntary exercise breaks, which can be a healthy source of enjoyment, especially for workers whose jobs don't require much in the way of physical exertion.

ERGONOMIC CHANGES

With the increasing use of computers, and with worker safety and productivity a continuing concern, the science of **ergonomics** is receiving more attention. Essentially, ergonomics attempts to improve human–machine interfaces to reduce stress or to increase safety or productivity, or all three. Examples include redesigning the handles of tools (such as channel locks and pliers) for fatigue reduction, providing computer monitors and glare screens to reduce eyestrain, providing ergonomically designed computer keyboards, and installing proper lighting and ventilation.[15] Designing ergonomically is not always easy: Knowledge of human anatomy and physiology, engineering, electronics, and mechanics must be combined with knowledge of the work that is being done.

The increased use of computers has spread concerns for ergonomics in recent years. It is estimated that more than 50 million people work with video display terminals (VDTs).[16] VDTs, or computer monitors, are those glare-producing screens for personal computers and workstations. As a result of their use, there are now complaints of monitors causing headaches, deteriorating eyesight, and even miscarriages.

Another ergonomic concern from increased computer usage is carpal tunnel syndrome (CTS). The carpal tunnel, or carpal canal, is actually a concave area on the palm (anterior) side of the wrist. The tunnel is formed by the eight carpal (wrist) bones and contains tendons, nerves, and blood vessels. Carpal tunnel syndrome is a repetitive stress injury that can be brought on by typing on a computer keyboard. CTS has long been common in manufacturing, food processing, health services, and crafts. It is characterized by tingling, numbness, or pain, especially in the thumb. Reports of these symptoms are increasing.

CTS now accounts for more than one-half of all work-related injuries. As a result, pressure has been exerted by concerned groups to encourage the redesign of jobs (maybe job rotation?) and the redesign of equipment to reduce the number of incidents of CTS.

WELLNESS PROGRAMS

Many organizations are realizing the dollars-and-cents value of fitness programs to them and their employees. An increasing number of firms now refer to their fitness programs as wellness programs because they have discovered that physically fit employees generally have better attitudes toward their jobs, are more productive, have lower absentee rates, are in better control of their weight, experience less stress, enjoy reduced chances of heart attacks, and have an enhanced sense of well-being.[17]

AESTHETICS AND PERSONALIZATION

As noted in Chapter 1, the physical work environment can have a significant effect on people. Changes in the existing work environment can often be made to improve the quality of work life. Changing

Ergonomics
equipment design intended to maximize productivity by reducing operator fatigue and discomfort; biotechnology or human engineering

The International Style, championed by Mies Van Der Rohe, who declared that "less is more." Although some may appreciate the straightforward functionality of the glass-box style, others would argue that the aesthetics of this building could be improved.

Source: Courtesy of Rockefeller Center, Inc./Hans Knopf.

colors, saturation of color, color coding, and the addition of decoration and art can all be used to improve the aesthetic quality of the physical environment.

Color has been shown to influence people.[18] It can be used in the work environment to send a message or simply to act as a background. Using dark red around fire alarms and equipment is an example of using color to send a message, as is using yellow to alert people that an area is dangerous. Color can also be used as background, as when pastels are selected for walls to deemphasize an area. To improve quality of work life, certain colors, such as red and yellow, may be reserved for special areas. Other colors may be assigned to specific departments. Here the change in color would support signage informing customers, clients, and workers that they had entered a different area. For example, all employee-only areas might be painted in different shades of blue, whereas shades of brown and tan are used in customer or client areas.

An **aesthetic** work environment in general can improve the QWL in conjunction with the use of color. Employing aesthetics may mean that the design will vary from the purely functional and utilitarian glass boxes of Mies Van Der Rohe's International Style. Some architects have demonstrated that aesthetics and function are not wholly incompatible. Of course, aesthetics would include incorporating art, pictures, and murals into the workplace.

Finally, personalization may be allowed to enhance a work area, independent of color usage and aesthetics. Although some companies rigidly control the amount of personalization permitted, with some allowing none at all, it is sometimes difficult to understand the reasoning. As mentioned earlier in this chapter, people want to take pride in their work. People will often take a certain amount of ownership for their work. Allowing personalization is one way for people to say, "This is my work area, I'm proud of my work, and I am declaring my pride to everyone by bringing in personal items and pictures." Controlling everything, from the pictures on the wall to the color of the wall and the style of the furniture, is often an example of **micromanagement**. The message in this overcontrol is that individuals do not matter. To avoid sending a wrong message, managers should carefully consider the reasons for limiting personalization. Is there a good, solid safety, productivity, or customer communication reason for limiting personalization? If so, explain to everyone why limiting personalization is necessary. If a manager is just trying to exercise his or her power and control over people, then the price in terms of lower morale and lower QWL may well be too high to justify the action.

DOES QWL HAVE ITS LIMITATIONS?

Most managerial programs, such as QWL and job enrichment, have their positive attributes along with certain limitations. For example, at least five limitations are inherent in job enrichment (see Table 12.2).[19]

Furthermore, not all employees necessarily want their jobs enriched. Some individuals, for example, believe that they don't want added responsibility. Their attitude is something like, "I do an adequate job. All I want is my paycheck, thank you!" Managers can't really force something "good" like job enrichment on employees if their needs and attitudes are not in harmony with such programs.

We examined individual differences when we discussed needs and motivation. Each employee differs, as you recall, in the intensity of his or her achievement and security needs. Also, some employees don't feel

Aesthetics
the nature of what is artistically beautiful or pleasing

Micromanagement
excessive concern over even the smallest details; overcontrol

Other architects have shown that aesthetic design can be compatible with business buildings.
Source: Courtesy of The Stock Connection/Jim Pickerell.

TABLE 12.2 LIMITS OF JOB ENRICHMENT

1. Applicable only where workers are and feel underutilized

2. Not all workers feel frustrated

3. Some workers don't desire greater challenge

4. Some workers distrust management's expansion of their tasks

5. Not a substitute for unpleasant working conditions or poor benefits

a strong need for interpersonal relations. Some employees prefer simpler, not more complex, tasks. Nor, as we learned from our study of perception, will every employee perceive job enrichment programs in the same light. Some may distrust management's efforts along such lines.

INNOVATIVE WAYS TO WORK

Because of the changing nature of workers and technology, as well as management's desire to improve productivity and morale, many organizations in recent years have experimented with a wide variety of work-related innovations. Some of the more common approaches include:

- production-based compensation plans
- flextime
- flexplace
- compressed workweek
- contingent employment
- job sharing

Some managers are proud of their successes with certain programs, whereas others have quickly abandoned similar programs because of the belief that they were not accomplishing certain objectives. Regardless of some of these bad experiences, there are various additional modern techniques intended to improve the quality of work life that will be discussed here.

PRODUCTION-BASED COMPENSATION PLANS

A rapidly expanding technique for improving the quality of work life of employees is gainsharing. Also termed **production-based compensation plans,** gainsharing plans are defined as organizational change programs of employee involvement, with an organization-wide financial formula.

In simple terms, gainsharing involves providing employees with periodic cash bonuses for developing ways in which the organization can enjoy cost savings. The payouts are related to financial cost-saving formulas and vary widely among organizations, ranging from 20 percent to as high as 100 percent of the value of the cost savings. Payout typically is made to employees on a monthly basis. In a gainsharing plan, the employer attempts to communicate the state of the business clearly to employees, asks for employee ideas, and seeks to solve problems related to such factors as product quality and productivity jointly.

Production-Based
Compensation Plan
periodic cash bonuses
given to employees
having cost-saving ideas;
gainsharing

The image of flexplace working—comfortable surroundings, commuting time saved, and coworker interruptions reduced.

Source: Courtesy of Getty Images, Inc.–Image Bank/Steve Niedorf Photography.

Many organizations—large and small, manufacturing and service—have found that gainsharing results in cost reductions, along with fewer grievances, improved morale, and a better work climate. Gainsharing programs have also brought about improved labor–management cooperation as a result of labor and management working closer together.[20]

FLEXTIME

Flextime
allowing workers to begin their normal workday at whatever time they wish, often within a predetermined window

Can you imagine showing up for work at almost any time you want and leaving your job early or late, depending on your own personal desires? Alternative work schedules, known by a variety of names, including **flextime,** flexible working hours, and glide time, exist in many firms throughout the world. A West German aerospace firm first introduced the variable-working-hour concept in 1967. Today, 68 percent of workers report that they are allowed to change their work hours; 24 percent are allowed to do so on a daily basis.[21]

Basically, flexibility eliminates the 9-to-5 syndrome faced by many employees and enables them to enjoy hours that more closely match their personal lifestyles. Workers must still work a preestablished number of hours, say, 40 hours per week or 80 hours over a two-week period. But the major difference between flextime and a conventional system of work hours is that flextime gives employees the freedom to choose, within certain limitations and usually with advance notice given to their supervisors, what times they begin and end their jobs each day.

Flextime is not feasible for all workers, however. If, for example, all the workers on an assembly line are required to run the line, it would not be feasible to have some start at 8:00 A.M. and leave at 4:30 P.M. while others start at 10:00 A.M. and leave at 6:30 P.M. It may not be feasible for workers to arrive at one time and their supervisor at a much different time. In general, it is impractical to allow flextime in any situation where other people are depending on workers to be on the job at a certain time, as in opening a store or any of the other numerous service facilities in our modern economy.

Benefits   What are the benefits of flextime? For one thing, it tends to reduce traffic congestion during rush hours in crowded urban areas, which in itself makes going to and returning from a job less hectic for the worker. But the benefits are more far-reaching than the mere alteration of traffic patterns. Individuals under flextime can take care of family and other personal affairs more easily, which tends to reduce absenteeism and tardiness in organizations. For example, employees with children can arrange their hours to coincide with baby-sitting or school requirements, and employees who are morning people can start work at a time when they are likely to be more productive.

Disadvantages   Flextime is not without its shortcomings. Some firms have found that flextime requires a more elaborate record-keeping system for keeping track of employee working hours, which tends to increase administrative costs. Some supervisors have also complained about greater difficulty in coordinating employees who start at varying times. Also, morale problems could increase, rather than decrease, in organizations in which some employees are not permitted to participate in the program because of the nature of their jobs. In general, however, many firms have found that flextime has improved morale, increased productivity, and given employees a greater sense of control over their own lives. Table 12.3 summarizes the main types of flextime programs.

TABLE 12.3 MAJOR TYPES OF FLEXTIME PROGRAMS

1. Daily flextime, fixed lunch, and core time	The employee works a full number of hours each day, typically 8.
2. Daily flextime, flexible lunch	The same as type 1, but the employee has more choice regarding lunch.
3. Weekly flextime	Employees have to work the core hours each day, but do not work a fixed number of hours per day. Instead, they must work a fixed number of hours per week.
4. Monthly flextime	This is similar to type 3, except the employee must work a certain number of hours per month, rather than per week

The reality of flexplace for many—isolation from the organization and work while trying to provide day care or trying to avoid other distractions.

Source: Courtesy of PhotoLibrary.com.

Flexplace
allowing regular employees (full- or part-time) to work at home or at another location away from the company

Flexplace

Flexplace, or telecommuting, involves allowing employees to work at home (or some other location) instead of in an office or plant. Personal computers, laptops, the Internet, and advanced telecommunications allow millions of people to work partially or completely at home. Flexplace working was growing in the late 1990s but has cooled somewhat since the turn of the century. This is partly due to the job situation. In the 1990s, business was booming and jobs were plentiful. This meant a shortage of workspace and a shortage of workers. Workers could demand and receive perks like a flexplace arrangement, which also helped with the lack of office space. When the economy slowed at the start of the new century, some people were laid off, reversing the situation. Although telecommuting is not suited to all jobs or work styles, some employers are still allowing it.

Advantages   Flexplace offers a number of advantages, especially when computers are used. It can help to resolve problems associated with occasional labor shortages, as in periods when there is a tight supply of programmers and data analysts. It can also give more people, such as individuals with disabilities or those with small children, the opportunity to work. A work-at-home parent can be present when the kids get home from school. Employees also have less supervision, lower work-related expenses, and more flexibility. The cost of their workspace at home is tax deductible. Employers require less office space, thus reducing overhead costs. Productivity and accuracy have also been found to be higher among flexplace employees.

Some firms require that their work-at-home employees work set hours, such as 9:00 A.M. to 5:00 P.M. Others provide their flexplace employees with a combination of regular and flexible hours. For example, an employee may have regular hours from 9:00 A.M. to 11:30 A.M. and from 2:00 P.M. to 4:30 P.M., with an additional three hours of work to be done at the convenience of the employee. The only requirement may be that the work be submitted by the opening of the office the next day.

Disadvantages   Working at home does have some disadvantages. Company loyalty may be lacking in the employee who telecommutes rather than actually commutes to a company location where he or she has interaction with other employees and a boss. Work-at-home employees have less opportunity to take part in discussions and meetings with other employees, thus stunting their political growth within the company. Employees at home must develop self-discipline if they are not to be distracted by family demands, gardening projects, or fatigue. Supervisors sometimes resist managing invisible workers. Trust of employees is essential for flexplace to succeed.

Union officials are somewhat skeptical of the programs. They envision the likelihood of exploitation, with violations of child-labor, overtime, and minimum-wage legislation. A home worker's children, for example, could be stuffing envelopes in violation of child-labor laws. Union leaders further find that isolated workers are more difficult and expensive to organize.

Of course, flexplace can't be readily adapted to all types of jobs. It's especially suited to those tasks requiring computer terminals. Nor do all employees want to work at home. Some people work as much for the social interaction they receive on the job as they do for the money. Perhaps flexplace should be applied only when both the employee and the boss want it and when the work does not require the presence of a supervisor.

FLEXIBLE BENEFITS

A growing number of organizations now offer employees a cafeteria-style benefit program (also termed a flexible benefit plan), in which employees can pick and choose a combination of insurance and other options best suited to their personal desires and individual and family situations. In a flexible benefit plan, there typically is a core range of benefits in addition to salary, including a contribution to a retirement plan. Employees can then select options up to the value of a set allowance. Benefits might include such alternatives as child-care assistance or legal fees.[22]

Many employees with grown children, for example, may feel less of a need for life insurance than those with younger children. Others may prefer dental insurance over full medical insurance. Many employees like the feeling of being free to make their own choices among several benefit options. An inherent danger, however, is that some employees with specific benefit needs may not recognize those needs at the time they select their benefits.

COMPRESSED WORKWEEK

Somewhere along the evolution of modern working, the norm became five 8-hour days. Considered full-time, the 5/40 week was almost universal. With other flexibility entering the workplace, it is not surprising to see full-time work hours change also. One of the most common modifications is the 4/40 workweek. The four 10-hour days of this **compressed workweek** can be advantageous for managers and workers.

In some situations, managers may see the advantages of a compressed workweek when they need workers for more than one traditional 8-hour shift, but less than two full shifts. Or managers may need some 8-hour and some 10-hour workers to provide continuity during a **shift change.** There have even been cases of workweeks compressed to two 16-hour days with pay for 40 hours when coverage was needed for two weekend shifts per day. The main advantage to workers is the three-day weekend that comes with the 4/40 arrangement. The three days off, if they are consecutive, can seem like having another week to yourself because it seems that you are off as much as you work. There are, however, concerns with the compressed workweek as well.

One of the main concerns for compressed workweeks is fatigue. Productivity may suffer when adding 2 hours to every day for jobs with high physical or mental demands. Safety may also be a concern. For many jobs, an extra 2 hours is not a burden, but some compressed workweeks involve three 13-hour days, or three 12-hour days and a 4-hour day. Adding 4 to 5 hours a day is asking a lot of almost anyone when it is permanent. The Chevron Corporation offers a compromise between the longer days and the three-day weekends. Chevron's compressed workweek consists of eight 9-hour days and one 8-hour day worked over a **fortnight.** This gives the worker one two-day weekend and one three-day weekend. The Chevron variation also has the added benefit of allowing virtually all employees to participate because the extra hour is relatively easy to handle. The Chevron idea also helps with the other major concern with compressed workweeks—problems with scheduling nonwork activities.[23]

The compressed workweek can cause problems with nonwork activities in addition to on-the-job concerns. A large number of workers are parents without partners or are part of a dual-income family. These workers often have outside-the-job responsibilities ranging from getting children to day care, school, and related

NetNote

SLOWLANE.com
The Online Resource for Stay at Home Dads.

http://www.slowlane.com

A site for work-at-home men.

Compressed Workweek
scheduling full-time jobs for fewer than 5 days per week or fewer than 10 days in a fortnight

Shift Change
the period between one work shift's leaving and the next's being ready for work

Fortnight
2 weeks; 14 nights

TABLE 12.4 POSSIBLE ADVANTAGES OF THE COMPRESSED WORKWEEK

1. Increased productivity (because of less warm-up and cool-down time)

2. Higher morale (because of more time for outside activities)

3. Less absenteeism (because personal matters can be attended to on the extra day off)

4. Enhanced recruiting (many potential employees find the prospects of 4/40 attractive)

5. Lower costs for the employee (less needs to be spent on gasoline, tolls, etc.)

6. Possible reduction in the need for overtime

TABLE 12.5 POSSIBLE DISADVANTAGES OF THE COMPRESSED WORKWEEK

1. Employee fatigue (10 hours may be too long for some without additional rest breaks)

2. For working parents, possible child-care problems (care may be needed for 11 to 12 hours for each 10-hour workday)

3. Concern that the 4/40 approach will lead to employee and union demands for a 4/32, thus increasing the cost of operations

4. Concern that employees are likely to socialize more on the job because the workday is longer

activities to taking care of elderly relatives. It can be difficult, if not impossible, to arrange to have children at day care for 12 hours (10 hours at work and a 1-hour commute each way) or more. It is also difficult to have children in school and then transported to after-school care, and then to take them home, have dinner, complete homework, and have everyone in bed on time. Then they must do it again the next day! A summary of additional advantages and disadvantages of the compressed workweek is provided in Tables 12.4 and 12.5.[24]

CONTINGENT EMPLOYMENT

Contingent Workers
nonpermanent workers; temporary, leased, or consultant workers

Discussed at the beginning of this chapter, **contingent workers**, or temps, are a growing trend. In the past, temporary work was uncommon for executives. However, the organizational trend toward downsizing and restructuring during the late 1980s and early 1990s resulted in an increasing number of managers who had been laid off and were able to acquire only part-time work. In fact, a new breed of temporary employment agency for "flexecutives"—managers and professionals— now exists. But the agencies don't like the term temp, preferring, instead, the more professional sounding interim assignments.

Is the use of part-timers good or bad? The answer to this simplistic question depends on the values of the person answering it. The good-siders contend that part-time and temporary work is highly desirable for individuals who either don't want or don't need full-time work, such as retirees, parents, and those with other interests. We know that people work for a variety of reasons, money being only one of them. Some individuals have a variety of personal interests, such as reading, writing, and bicycling, that are difficult to pursue when a person is locked into a 9-to-5 job. A part-time position, or temporary assignments obtained through agencies such as Manpower, enables a fairly large segment of U.S. society to meet such personal needs.

Other proponents of part-time and temporary work are employers who contend that their use enables organizations to be more flexible in hiring. For example, employers can more easily meet the short-term need for additional production workers or temporary fill-ins for vacationing employees without hiring new full-time employees who would be difficult to discharge if the work volume subsided. Further, the use of part-time and temporary workers has proven a way to avoid layoffs and the negative publicity they sometimes generate in the community.

What's the other side of the story? The detractors argue that company loyalty is practically nonexistent among part-time and temporary workers. Critics add that company productivity suffers because a firm's productivity is affected by the employee's lack of experience with the employing firm. Part-time and temp employees, it is also argued, suffer because they typically receive lower wages and get no medical insurance, retirement benefits, or job security from their positions. However, as more companies seek to use temp workers, and unemployment in general remains low, temp workers are now starting to demand and receive better treatment. This includes health insurance, retirement programs, and time off for vacations and holidays.[25]

JOB SHARING

Another novel idea that has caught on in some occupations and is likely to become more common in the future is a practice referred to as **job sharing,** or twinning.[26]

Job Sharing
two workers dividing
one job

REALITY CHECK

Flexible Work Arrangements

Convincing a manager to allow you to have some type of flexible work arrangement is somewhat more difficult in a slower economy that produces more office space and fewer jobs. With plenty of room for the workers that remain, some managers return to older ways—wanting to see workers in their chairs. It is still possible to get flexible arrangements, but there are more involved guidelines now.

First, you have to ask for the flexible arrangement and you have to overcome the attitude that somehow you will be doing less work if you are allowed to work in some flexible way. The best way to do this is to show how the company will benefit. If the company will neither benefit nor lose from the situation, then you need to prove that your work or customer services will not suffer.

Next, you have to work out the mechanics of the flexible arrangement, especially for meetings, communications, informal information, and your workday. What will you do if your new situation involves being gone during meetings? It is best if you figure out how to attend anyway, either in person or through teleconferencing. You will also need to communicate with coworkers and managers. It is not a good idea to call or e-mail them every few minutes. It is better to establish certain hours when you will definitely be available and regular conference-call times. Maybe the most difficult task is keeping in touch with the informal organization, which can adopt an "out of sight, out of mind" attitude toward telecommuters. Try to find a few key people who will keep you informed informally. Finally, since the impression that you really aren't working is still present, some flexplace workers feel so guilty that they end up putting in far more hours than if they came in every day. Put in your fair share, but beyond that establish boundaries so that you are not working during regular leisure times.

Sources: Jennifer Reingold, "There's No Place (to Work) Like Home," *Fast Company*, November 2000, p. 76; Elizabeth Brewster, "Work Schedules Lose Flexibility," *Chicago Tribune*, December 2003, sec. 6, p 5.

Under this system, two workers divide one full-time job. Not only are the hours split, but so are salary and fringe benefits. Job sharing is available mostly at the clerical level. Most companies do not permit supervisors to share jobs because of the problem of having people report to two bosses.

Those who especially favor the job-sharing concept are mothers and fathers who want to spend more time with their families or on other interests without losing income. Others who lean toward job sharing are older people who want to retire gradually, those with physical limitations, and students.

Although job sharing has the drawback of doubling an employer's training and personnel costs, the overall benefits seem to outweigh any disadvantages. For one thing, employers can more easily achieve affirmative action hiring goals by tapping labor markets previously inaccessible. Another major advantage, according to some studies, is that part-time workers tend to approach their work with far more energy and enthusiasm and put in more than a half-day's work in a half-day's time. Absenteeism also tends to be reduced because one of the job sharers can cover for the other in the event of illness or other emergencies.

Job sharing has become increasingly prevalent in such fields as teaching, library and laboratory work, the professions, and government. Some states, such as Wisconsin and Massachusetts, encourage job sharing among government employees.

JOB SATISFACTION

How do you like your job? The answer to this question is probably the way most people view quality of work life. The end result of quality of work life is the overall satisfaction one receives from a job. The factors affecting quality of work life have been presented, but there are others that affect job satisfaction. The factors affecting job satisfaction can be divided into three main areas: internal factors, external factors, and individual factors (see Table 12.6).

INTERNAL JOB SATISFACTION FACTORS

Six job satisfaction factors are inherent in the work itself. They are:

- the work
- job variety
- task specialization

SPOT CHECK

6. Empowerment is providing employees with more involvement and more personal decision-making authority. T F
7. The goal of ergonomics is to increase productivity. T F
8. Personalization refers to being allowed to enhance your work area as you would like. T F
9. Flextime is feasible for all workers if management would just allow it. T F
10. Having a compressed workweek means you can work whatever hours you wish as long as you work a total of 40 hours. T F

TABLE 12.6 JOB SATISFACTION FACTORS

Job Satisfaction Factors	Description
Internal Factors	
The work	Effect of a person's current job at a particular company
Job variety	Number of skills and depth of knowledge required
Task specialization	The number of different tasks someone performs
Autonomy	Freedom to control your own work
Goal determination	Freedom to set your own goals and success criteria
Feedback and recognition	Private and public notice concerning job performance
External Factors	
Achievement	Success in completing tasks
Role ambiguity and role conflict	Knowing your work roles and agreement between roles
Opportunity	Future prospects with current and other employers
Job security	Assurances of continued employment
Social interactions	Quality and quantity of interactions with others
Supervision	Quality of management
Organizational culture	Effect of the organization's climate or environment
Work schedules	Match between work schedule and the worker's schedule
Seniority	Length of time a person has held a position
Compensation	Monetary rewards and the role of money
Individual Factors	
Commitment	The care in selection of and personal dedication to a job
Expectations	What people believe they will receive in return for work
Job involvement	How important a job is in someone's life
Effort/reward ratio	The balance between the amount worked and the rewards received
Influence of coworkers	Issues that coworkers feel are important
Comparisons	How your job rates with the jobs of friends and relatives
Opinions of others	How prestigious others feel your job is
Personal outlook	Your view of yourself and life in general
Age	How old someone is

- autonomy
- goal determination
- feedback and recognition

These factors are closely associated with the job itself and are the most difficult to alter without leaving the job.

The Work   The prime factor in job satisfaction is the work itself. It is difficult, if not impossible, to have job satisfaction if you hate the work you are doing. However, sometimes people claim to hate their job when in fact they just hate doing the job for their current employer. These people actually like the work; they just don't like the people they are currently doing it for. Others may dislike some aspect of their job. To avoid unnecessary career changes, it is important for you to distinguish between disliking the work and disliking your current employer.

Job Variety   Job satisfaction generally increases as the number of skills used in performing a job increases.[27] Additionally, job satisfaction generally increases as the amount of knowledge needed to perform a job increases.[28] These two factors, re-

Job Variety

the required skills and
quantity of knowledge
needed to perform a job

quired skills and quantity of knowledge, combine to form **job variety.** The opposite of job variety is task specialization.

Task Specialization   When taken to an extreme, task specialization can create jobs with few tasks that repeat every five or ten seconds. It is easy to see how jobs with such low job variety would provide little job satisfaction for some people. Other people, however, can accept limited job variety. What is an acceptable level of job variety is something that must often be left to each individual.

Autonomy   Autonomy refers to the level of control people have over their work.[29] The more freedom people have over the pace of their work and the methods they may employ to perform it, the more autonomy they have. As autonomy, or freedom, increases, so does job satisfaction. The need for autonomy is sometimes felt more strongly in people trying to fulfill the higher needs on Maslow's hierarchy of needs.[30] These higher-level needs would include the need for status and self-esteem, self-actualization, and knowledge.

Goal Determination

the freedom people have
to establish their own
work goals and to
determine their own
criteria for success

Goal Determination   **Goal determination** refers to the freedom people have to establish their own work goals and to determine their own criteria for success. Increased freedom to determine goals and success criteria can lead to increased job satisfaction.[31] Freedom to determine goals may not increase job satisfaction, but in most cases having clear, explicit goals is better than having vague ones.[32] Increased job satisfaction may also come from having goals determined and meeting them, as well as having the freedom to set those goals.

Recognition

noticeable
acknowledgment of
performance; it is
received less often but
carries greater
significance than
feedback

Feedback and Recognition   In this context, **recognition** can be differentiated from feedback by frequency and significance. Recognition is received from a manager, and it is received less often but carries greater significance than feedback. Recognition might be an employee-of-the-month award, whereas feedback may be as simple as a "Good job" from a manager. Feedback may also be inherent in the work. As an example, when a repair person fixes something and makes it work once again, the success is obvious when the item again functions. Instantaneous, direct feedback like this that is inherent in the work is the ideal form of feedback. This also points to some other facets of feedback that must be present if the feedback is to increase job satisfaction.

To maximize the effect on job satisfaction, feedback must be accurate, timely, and frequent.[33] To be accurate, the people doing a good job must know they are doing a good job. However, the people not doing a good job must know how they are performing also. If workers are all told they are doing well, the effect on motivation and job satisfaction can be negative. First, if all are told they are doing well when some are not, then the value of the feedback decreases. Second, if all are told they are doing well when some are not, then the ones who are performing well may allow their performance to slip. Why should they try harder if everyone receives the same feedback regardless of performance?

Recognition for a job well done can lead to increased job satisfaction.[34] Conversely, lack of recognition for a job well done can lead to dissatisfaction. For many people, receiving recognition in front of others can be more satisfying than receiving recognition from a manager in private. Recognition may take many forms, ranging from a public acknowledgment of one's contribution, to an outstanding service or employee-of-the-month or -year award, to a promotion. No matter what the recognition, as with feedback, the recognition must be accurately awarded. The value of the recognition may fall to zero if the undeserving receive it. Recognition does not have to be as timely or as frequent as feedback.

Internal factors, most closely linked to the work itself, are not the only factors affecting job satisfaction. Many years ago it was believed that the job was the sole factor in job satisfaction. We now know that external job factors and individual factors can have an effect on job satisfaction equal to or greater than the work itself.

EXTERNAL JOB SATISFACTION FACTORS

The external job satisfaction factors are related to the work or to the working environment. Those related to the work itself are either easier to separate from the work than the internal factors or they are easier to change. They include:

- achievement
- role ambiguity and role conflict
- opportunity
- job security
- social interactions
- supervision
- organizational culture
- work schedules
- seniority
- compensation

These factors are listed here roughly in order of descending control a worker has over them. At the beginning of the list are those that workers have more control over; at the end are those workers generally have less control over.

Achievement   **Achievement** refers to a person's success on the job. The general belief is that high achievers on the job have high job satisfaction. There are some, like the behavioral managers, who believe that job satisfaction leads to high achievement. The reverse of this situation may be even more important. People who are unsuccessful on the job have little, if any, job satisfaction.[35] Therefore, the cure for low job satisfaction may be to increase job performance. Training, education, increased effort, or improved equipment may be the way to improve achievement and job satisfaction.

Role Ambiguity and Role Conflict   It is difficult for people to have high job satisfaction when they are unsure what their job entails. Not knowing what your job is or what your place is in the organization is referred to as **role ambiguity.** Clarifying the tasks that define your job and your place in the organization (in terms of authority and responsibility) can reduce role ambiguity. Reducing role ambiguity can lead to increased job satisfaction.[36]

It is possible for people to have minimal role ambiguity but to have conflicts with their role. A person may know what his or her job is and what his or her role in the organization is, but there might be conflicts between the parts of his or her role. Increased **role conflict** leads to lower job satisfaction.[37] An example of role conflict occurs all too often when someone is given the responsibility for completing a task without being given the authority needed to do so. Other examples

NetNote

Job Satisfaction with Your Present Job

http://stress.about.com/od/ workplacestress/a/ jobsatisfaction.htm

Maybe you don't have to change jobs to find satisfaction.

Achievement
the success a person has on the job

Role Ambiguity
not knowing what your job is or what your place is in the organization

Role Conflict
when job roles interfere with one another

NetNote

Job Satisfaction

http://www.humanlinks.com/ orgsn/job_satisfaction.htm

Test your job satisfaction.

include conflict between getting the job done fast and getting the job done right, or getting the job done correctly even if it means redoing it and not wasting materials or other assets.

Opportunity

future prospects with a current employer or with another employer

Opportunity   Many people may have more job satisfaction when they believe that their future prospects are good.[38] These future prospects may mean the **opportunity** for advancement and growth with their current employer or the chance of finding work with another employer. If people feel they have fewer opportunities with their current employer than they would like, then their job satisfaction may decrease. Note that we are dealing with people's feelings here: "If people feel they have fewer opportunities." They may in fact have chances for advancement, but if they don't think they do, their job satisfaction suffers anyway. Not only must people think they have good future prospects with their employer, they must think that they have a fair chance of obtaining the future prospects. The same is generally true with opportunities with other companies.

If people believe there are outside job opportunities, their job satisfaction may increase or decrease and is also dependent on whether or not they feel they have a fair chance at obtaining the outside opportunities. Job satisfaction may decrease if there are outside job opportunities, especially if those jobs are perceived to be better. A feeling of the grass being greener on the other side can arise, leading to less satisfaction with the current job. Conversely, if the conditions at the outside jobs are perceived to be poorer than at one's current position (less pay, farther away, less-desirable work hours), then job satisfaction may actually increase. Note that, once again, it is the perception that is important. Actual conditions may be worse, but if someone perceives or believes them to be better, then satisfaction with the current job can be affected.

Job Security

the assurance of continued future employment

Job Security   Job security, an example of Frederick Herzberg's hygiene factors, may affect job satisfaction more when it is not present than when it is.[39] When **job security**, the assurance of employment continuing in the future, is absent, there may be less job satisfaction. When present, job security may be taken for granted. Job security itself is affected by intrinsic and extrinsic factors.

Some employers strive to offer job security; in other cases, job security is an integral part of the employer's culture. However, it sometimes appears that there are fewer and fewer of these employers in today's work environment. For years, IBM, AT&T, and public utilities were known for essentially offering employment for life. Recently, both IBM and AT&T have had large layoffs, and even some utilities have become leaner. Although employment-for-life firms may be difficult to find, many firms still offer significant job security for those who continue to learn, who are flexible and adaptable, and whose work adds real value to the firm. Still, seen earlier in this chapter, there is a large threat to job security, with some believing it will eventually become extinct. Additional intrinsic threats to job security and job satisfaction can originate with individual managers and the firm's performance.

Through their behavior, individual managers may decrease job security and therefore decrease job satisfaction. Constantly reminding people that they are easily replaced, valueless, and disposable company assets decreases job security and satisfaction. Eliminating high-paid workers simply to reduce salary expense, laying off workers instantly if work slows down even slightly, and firing workers just before they become vested in the retirement plan are all actions that decrease job security. Poor performance or a poor financial condition of the firm can also reduce job security and satisfaction because the threat of a merger or the collapse of the firm appears more likely. There are also extrinsic factors, in addition to these intrinsic factors, that can have a negative impact on job security.

The main extrinsic job-security factors involve the economic and political-legal environments that businesses operate in. If economic times in general are poor (recession), sales may decline and layoffs may appear more imminent. The political-legal environment may also affect the condition of the firm and the job security of those working for the firm. If an industry is suddenly regulated or deregulated, the action may create a conservative sentiment among management, and talk may begin about laying people off. Or the political environment may change so that a main supplier in a foreign country may be forbidden to trade with the company, putting it in a weakened position and creating a knee-jerk wave of layoffs in order to save money. In any event, whether due to intrinsic or extrinsic factors, low job security leads to lower job satisfaction.

Social Interactions   Whether using anecdotal evidence or the work of Frederick Herzberg, Abraham Maslow, and others, we see the importance of **social interactions** at work.[40] Sometimes work is the main source of social interactions for people. When the social interactions are not as desired, job satisfaction can decrease. These social interactions are complex entities, the value to the individual being affected by the quantity of interactions, physical and mental isolation, and the quality of the interactions. As the quantity of social interactions increases, job satisfaction may increase. The quantity of social interactions is affected by physical and mental isolation. Physical isolation means that the work site is so remote that few other workers are in the area or that the workers in the area are isolated by the working conditions. Working conditions that prevent communication because the equipment separates workers or the noise level is high can create conditions of physical isolation. The very nature of the work may prevent social interaction, thereby creating mental isolation. This may occur when the concentration level required to perform the work is so high that it prevents communication. When physical and mental isolation increase, the quantity of social interactions decrease, and job satisfaction may decrease.

The quality of social interactions also affects job satisfaction. This quality factor is more subjective, yet it is very powerful. People have stayed at jobs they might otherwise have left because they felt the quality of the social interactions was so high that this outweighed numerous other negative aspects of the job. Conversely, some people have left jobs when they liked the work but disliked the quality of their social contacts on the job. Although volumes could be written, there are two things that can be done that might improve the quality of social interactions.

The quality of social interactions can be affected by the respect you earn from coworkers and by your treatment of coworkers. The best way to earn the respect of your coworkers is through job knowledge and performance. Both job knowledge and performance are required, however. Some people may know how to perform a job, but they are too lazy to actually do it. When coworkers respect you because of your job knowledge and performance, they will want to interact with you. This will increase the quantity of social interactions. You will also attract the best coworkers. Interactions with them can increase the quality of your social

Social Interactions
communicating with others

411

During the routine self-introductions at the start of a management class, an older student explained why he was taking the course. After 30 years with a heavy-equipment manufacturer, he and many others were laid off—not because of the quality or the quantity of their work, but because the company was taken over and the new owners needed to downsize for financial reasons. With the layoff, this student lost everything—his job, his security, his retirement—everything. He said, however, that the thing that made him angriest was that the new owners and the layoffs took away his friends. He lost some who had been his friends for 30 years. He said he tried to keep in touch, but most lived in other towns, and many moved to other states to find work. Of course, the loss of his income and retirement bothered him, but he said by going to school, learning new skills, and working hard, he was confident he could replace the money. He was not so sure he could replace his friends.

interactions as well. In addition, social interactions are affected by your treatment of others.

The general rule that should be followed regarding the treatment of others is not new and is not a secret. It is, unfortunately, not applied often enough. It is "Do unto others as you would have them do unto you." Treating others the way you want to be treated is not always easy. It is tempting to let our darker sides take over, to vent our anger or frustration at others. Too often, what goes around comes around—if you treat others poorly, they will have no reason to treat you well. If you endeavor to treat everyone with respect and civility, then more often than not, you will be treated the same way. People can retaliate in many ways for your poor treatment of them. Delaying action on your requests or being unable to do that rush job of yours can hurt you when you need help. Finally, proper treatment must be extended to everyone. Too often people think that only bosses, and maybe peers, need to be treated well, and that those considered beneath a person do not deserve or require respect. This is far from the truth because virtually everyone in the organization has some power. If you doubt this, consider what work life would be if the trash were never taken out, the cafeteria tables never washed, or the washrooms never scrubbed. Treat everyone well so that every work and social interaction is of the highest quality, and your job satisfaction should increase significantly.

Supervision
the managing or overseeing of someone

Supervision Frederick Herzberg identifies the quality of **supervision** as a hygiene factor. This means that when the quality of supervision is poor, a worker can become dissatisfied.[41] When the quality is good, the worker is not dissatisfied (this does not mean that he or she is satisfied, however). In other words, a bad boss might make you miserable, but even a great boss won't make you jump out of bed in the morning because you can't wait to get to work for him or her. This may seem like a factor that you have little or no control over, but that may not be the case. Sometimes managers do not manage because of the way they are, but because of the way people force them to manage.

The way a manager acts often has as much or more to do with the subordinates than with the manager. Some people are lazy, untrustworthy, or unreliable. This may make an otherwise behavioral manager act as an authoritarian toward this

<table>
<tr><td colspan="1">FYI</td></tr>
</table>

FYI

When considering a job, look at more than the pay; consider the quality of your work life.

Before changing jobs, explore changing a QWL factor so you are comfortable staying.

During a job search, consider the newer benefits, like elder care; will you need them and are they available?

Think about ergonomic concerns before you develop symptoms.

Analyze current or potential jobs on all internal and external job satisfaction factors that are important to you.

If you have doubts or concerns about your current job or career, assess the impact of the individual job satisfaction factors.

If you are having problems at work, don't automatically look for more money as the answer. Consider the many job satisfaction factors and note that few involve money.

If you are not satisfied with your job, be sure to find and work on the problem and not the symptoms.

one person. Workers who perform their jobs, are on time, treat the manager with respect, and can be trusted to do the job without constant supervision may receive completely different treatment. All you need to do is decide how you are going to act and then do it. When you have earned the trust and respect of your manager, the quality of supervision may improve as the manager responds to this desirable situation.

Organizational Culture   The overall **organizational culture** and management style can increase or decrease job satisfaction. A manager may choose to use a classical or behavioral style of management. A subordinate may force a manager to use a classical style or may allow the manager to use a behavioral style. Or the organization's culture or climate may be classical or behavioral. In fact, many organizations have a classical, bureaucratic, or authoritarian culture.[42] Although job satisfaction is often higher in nonbureaucratic organizations, much depends on the individual.[43] An individual needing close, classical supervision or not needing or wanting responsibility may not feel satisfied in a behavioral, employee-empowerment firm. An individual needing or wanting more freedom, more responsibility, or more autonomy may not be satisfied in a classical management atmosphere where these characteristics are in short supply. The important point here is that people should try to match their needs to a company that can meet those needs, thereby increasing job satisfaction.

Work Schedules   It is possible for **work schedules** to increase job satisfaction.[44] Compressed workweeks and flextime (described earlier in this chapter) may increase job satisfaction by allowing for a better interface between someone's personal life and work life. Job satisfaction can also be positively influenced by allowing a subordinate's input into the work schedule or by allowing workers to trade days with other workers. Some managers even go so far as to post a blank schedule with

Organizational Culture
the collective beliefs, values, and attitudes of the organization

Work Schedules
the days and times an individual works

a statement that five workers are needed on Monday and Wednesday and four on Tuesday, and so forth, and allowing people to sign up for whatever days they want and whatever days they can negotiate with coworkers. Sometimes the work schedule is like one of Herzberg's hygiene factors. A bad schedule may make a worker feel dissatisfied, whereas a good or a normal schedule may make him or her not dissatisfied (which is not the same as being satisfied).

Seniority
the time spent working the same job or working for the same employer

Seniority Seniority affects job satisfaction differently for different people.[45] Sometimes satisfaction increases as people learn to perform more proficiently. For others, satisfaction decreases due to boredom or due to the realization that their goals and careers are not advancing as they had hoped. For those with lower job satisfaction due to seniority, many choose to leave the position they are in. They may leave by seeking a promotion, by requesting a transfer, or by looking for a job with another employer. Some job changes are acceptable to potential employers, such as those in the advertising industry, but frequent changes, holding jobs for only a few months, and not staying at even one employer for a respectable amount of time (one to two years) can be perceived quite negatively.

Compensation Ask most people why they work, and they probably say that it is for the money. Of course, money is an important reason for working, but there are many other reasons people work.[46] Still, it is important to understand the special role money plays in the work. For instance, money can satisfy two needs on Maslow's hierarchy—physiologic and status. A certain amount is needed to satisfy the physiologic needs. After the basic needs of food, shelter, water, and clothing are met, the remainder is mostly a matter of status or convenience. Does a family of four need five TVs? Does anyone need a widescreen TV? Who needs a $40,000 sports car or luxury car to drive to work? Does anyone need an Armani suit to wear to the office? The purpose here, though, is not to pass judgment on the rationality of status purchases. The purpose is to simply differentiate between purchases for physiologic needs and purchases for status. Both require money, and in this way money provides satisfaction. However, if a certain amount of money will satisfy these needs, will more money provide more satisfaction? Many people would say that more money does provide more satisfaction. These people would feel justified in asking for more money to increase their job satisfaction or to make up for job dissatisfaction. This may not be the correct course of action in all cases.

A QUESTION OF ETHICS

Seniority and Higher Pay

Usually increasing pay accompanies increasing seniority. Most companies promote the salary scale as an incentive for employees to stay. It is not all that uncommon, however, for some companies to want to jettison more senior employees because they "cost too much." Is it ethical to use higher pay to entice workers to stay with a firm and then when they do just that let them go to save money?

Craft an argument that this is unethical, then look at this from a manager's point of view and design an argument that supports releasing senior workers for monetary reasons. Are there reasons other than trying to retain employees to pay more senior workers more money, and what are they? If releasing more-senior and higher-paid workers saves a company money, what, if anything, does the company also lose?

People sometimes ask for more money when a lack of money is not the problem. To understand the role money plays, we must examine why this is so. First, people generally accept money as suitable **compensation** when other factors that contribute to job satisfaction are absent. Second, money is viewed as suitable compensation when there are undesirable aspects to a job. When the job is dangerous, extra pay is often given. Third, money seems to have a palliative effect, at least for a short time. A palliative effect means that money removes pain, but does not cure the situation. Placating people with money is often effective for only a short time. In order to keep them happy, more money must be given at certain intervals. Eventually, no amount of money can compensate for the basic unbearableness of or dissatisfaction with the job. Sometimes people accept the money because they are dissatisfied but never realize that the satisfaction is temporary because the money does not change or remove the source of the dissatisfaction.

A fourth reason people ask for money is that money is tangible and objective, and a fifth reason is that, in many ways, asking for money it is easier than asking for something else. Money can be touched, counted, spent, and measured. In other situations it may be difficult or impossible, due to the nature of the work, to give a person work that is more interesting within the confines of the current job.

The sixth and last reason people may ask for money is that money is symbolic. To many people, money signifies success and achievement. For some people, it increases their sense of self-worth or symbolizes their achieving some goal they set for themselves. Although money may contribute in some positive way, money does not solve all problems.

Money does not solve everything because quite often money treats a symptom and not the problem. Treating a symptom leaves the underlying problem to return and contribute to dissatisfaction again and again. To avoid this problem, people must determine what the problem is. Once the factor or factors that are causing the dissatisfaction are identified, then it must be determined whether money can solve the problem or not. Often, something other than money is needed. For example, maybe a particular person has far too much work and therefore not enough time. More money will not solve this problem. What might be needed is more equipment, or faster equipment, or additional training, or an assistant. Just giving the person more money might compensate him or her for the short term, but it will not add any hours to the day or reduce the number of tasks. Therefore, in order to maximize satisfaction, people need to know the factors that contribute to job satisfaction, they need to identify exactly which ones are causing any dissatisfaction, and they need to take actions that will eliminate the problem rather than simply mask the problem temporarily. This may involve looking at the external job-satisfaction factors, the internal factors, or the individual factors.

Compensation
the money, benefits, and rewards of employment

INDIVIDUAL JOB SATISFACTION FACTORS

Of the three groups of factors affecting job satisfaction, the individual factors have the least to do with the actual job. The individual factors mainly concern a person and the person's family and network of friends. There are nine individual job satisfaction factors:

- commitment
- expectations

SPOT CHECK

11. Autonomy is the freedom to control your own work. T F
12. Good goal determination is when your manager establishes your work goals for you. T F
13. The effect the organization's climate or environment has on someone's job satisfaction is referred to as an external factor of organizational culture. T F
14. Work as a source of social interactions refers to nonwork activities only, like having a company softball team. T F
15. Having good future job prospects is important, but this is not a part of job satisfaction. T F

- job involvement
- effort/reward ratio
- influence of coworkers
- comparisons
- opinions of others
- personal outlook
- age

Although these factors can greatly affect how someone feels about his or her job, many of these consist of opinions. Opinions can be changed by facts and information. So although these factors can have a great influence on job satisfaction, the individual has more control over them and can effect change if it is needed.

Commitment   The more carefully someone has researched, selected, and prepared for a job, the more likely that person is to be satisfied with the job.[47] If the actions of researching, selecting, and preparing for the job are highly visible to friends and family, then the person is more likely to be satisfied with the job and less likely to admit to any dissatisfaction. The greater the **commitment** the person has made to a job, the bigger the mistake would appear to be if the person said he or she was wrong in selecting it. For a few people, this means that they may stay in an unsatisfying job, unwilling to look foolish or unable to admit to a mistake.

Expectations   People believe that their jobs should fulfill certain needs. These beliefs, or **expectations**, concerning a job's ability to fulfill needs may be realistic or unrealistic.[48] People who expect work to fulfill all of their needs are probably being unrealistic. Using Maslow's hierarchy of needs as an example, it is reasonable for work to fulfill physiologic needs, and some or most of the safety needs, but only some of the belonging needs. Expecting work to provide all of one's needs for belonging would include fulfillment of the social and the individual aspects. Expecting the individual needs for a mate or date to come from one's workplace is not only unrealistic, it is asking for trouble. Even expecting work to provide all of one's social contacts is expecting too much. The important thing here is to determine what one's job can and cannot reasonably provide.

In analyzing a job, four lists could be created. One would include all of your needs. A second would contain those needs that can realistically be fulfilled by

Commitment

how carefully someone has researched, selected, and prepared for a job

Expectations

the needs people believe a job can fulfill

work. A third would be a list of needs that your current job could fulfill, and a fourth would be those needs that your current job is fulfilling. A comparison of the first and second lists would show areas that need fulfillment through activities outside of work. A comparison of the second and third lists might indicate the need for a job change. If work can fulfill certain needs but your current job does not, then maybe it is time to look for a new employer or a new career. Finally, comparing the third and fourth lists might help set objectives for your current job. For example, if a promotion could fulfill your need for status, then maybe it is time to work toward earning that promotion.

When work cannot fulfill some of one's needs, many people turn to areas outside of work. Here, many people seek fulfillment through family and community or volunteer organizations. The fulfillment of some of people's other needs helps explain why so many people volunteer to work for no pay.

Job Involvement   **Job involvement** refers to how important a person's job is in his or her life.[49] The more involved a person is in his or her job, the more satisfaction he or she generally feels.[50] It is possible, however, to become overinvolved in a job. Overinvolvement (becoming a workaholic) can be identified when work becomes so pervasive as to affect one's personal life negatively.[51] At this point, one might need to determine whether work is part of the overall solution or part of the problem.

Job Involvement
how important a person's job is in his or her life

Effort/Reward Ratio   People compare the rewards they receive from work to the effort they put into work partially to determine job satisfaction.[52] If the ratio between the two is heavy on the effort side, then people generally feel less satisfied because they feel they are putting more into their work than they are getting out of it. People will also compare their **effort/reward ratio** to the ratio of others. If they believe their ratio is less than their coworkers' ratios, then they will feel less satisfied because they will feel that they are getting less out of their jobs for the effort they

Effort/Reward Ratio
the comparison of the rewards someone receives from his or her work to the effort he or she puts into the work

---

REALITY CHECK
Dissatisfaction

Being unable to analyze your job situation to determine the cause of any dissatisfaction could cause you to leave a career when all that is needed is a change of working conditions or a change of employer. Following these six steps may help pinpoint any problems and indicate a course of action.

1. Analyze the internal, external, and individual job satisfaction factors. You may wish to use the Job Satisfaction Inventory at the end of the chapter.
2. Identify the factor or factors creating the most dissatisfaction.
3. Determine whether the factor can be altered within the context of your current job.

4. Determine how best to accomplish altering the factor. Consider the material in most of the rest of this book, especially the organization's cultural and political climates.
5. Act to accomplish the needed change.
6. If change is not possible or fails, try to determine whether you would truly be more satisfied with a different employer or a different career. If a drastic change is needed, try to ensure that the new employer or new career not only provides satisfaction with the factors you just identified but also provides satisfaction in areas that are good in your current job. It doesn't do much good to leave a career that had autonomy but no social interaction for one that has social interaction but no autonomy.

put in than their coworkers. In all of this analysis, people look at total rewards from work, not just monetary compensation. Also, we are once again dealing with people's perceptions of effort and reward, which may be real or imaginary.

Influence of Coworkers
the importance coworkers place on certain issues and the degree to which they discuss these issues

Influence of Coworkers   The importance coworkers place on certain issues affects the importance an individual places on those issues; this **influence of coworkers** in turn may affect job satisfaction.[53] For instance, coworkers can influence your thinking if they constantly grumble about the state of the equipment. You may also feel that this is important and will tend to agree that the equipment is substandard. Or if coworkers constantly talk about what a great place you work in, then you will also tend to think that the place is good, and your job satisfaction will increase.

Comparisons
the comparisons people make between their jobs and how satisfied they are with them and the jobs of friends, relatives, and neighbors

Comparisons   People make **comparisons** between their jobs and how satisfied they are with them and the jobs of friends, relatives, and neighbors.[54] A person who is a middle manager may feel quite satisfied if his or her family members and neighbors all have lower-status, lower-paying jobs. This same middle manager might feel less satisfaction if his or her family and neighbors are CEOs and doctors. Here, each job has relative worth, rather than absolute worth.

Opinions of Others
the opinions others have of the status and desirability of someone else's job

Opinions of Others   The **opinions of others** concerning your job also affect your job satisfaction. If other people, especially people whom you admire and respect, believe that you have a good job, then you will typically feel more satisfied than if the people around you think you have a lousy job.[55] This also applies to the way society views entire professions. If society generally regards your profession as valuable and of higher status, then you will be more satisfied than if society feels your job is of low status and worth.

Personal Outlook   A person's general outlook on life is another factor that influences job satisfaction. A person with high self-esteem, with confidence in his or her abilities, and with a positive outlook on life is more likely to have high job satisfaction than someone with a negative attitude.[56]

Age   Job satisfaction typically increases with age.[57] Older workers have more work experience, they understand better which needs work can and cannot satisfy, and overall they have a more realistic view of work and life. Younger workers have comparatively few or no job experiences with which to compare their current jobs. Because of this, they are more likely to substitute the opinions of other people, their own beliefs about other people's jobs, and their own idealistic views of what work should be for their lack of experience. These opinions and beliefs are less applicable than their own experiences and can cause younger workers to feel less satisfaction than they would if they had their own experiences to draw on.

All of these factors combine to produce the single feeling known as job satisfaction. The complexity of the interactions of these 25 different factors yields a much different view of job satisfaction and the quality of work life than one might originally think. To the uninitiated, job satisfaction might seem to be simple to ascertain. One need only ask another, "How much do you like your job?" This might receive a simple answer, such as "Not at all" or "Very much," but we know that two dozen items have to be factored into this simple answer. So although we may get a simple answer, the influences leading to that answer are very complicated.

SPOT CHECK

16. Commitment refers to how strongly people believe that their jobs should fulfill certain of their needs. T F
17. Expectations involves what people think a job will do for them after they have carefully researched, selected, and prepared for that job. T F
18. Job involvement refers to how often a person thinks about work when not at work. T F
19. Opinions of others refers to being influenced when coworkers constantly grumble about what a bad company you all work for. T F
20. Job satisfaction typically decreases with the age of the worker. T F

SUMMARY

Not all attempts at job enrichment, job enlargement, and innovative programs are successful. Some failures, however, are self-imposed. The ways in which new programs are introduced are as important as the programs themselves. Problems can develop when programs are poorly introduced or ill timed as a result of the differing perceptions of organizational members. For instance, senior management may initiate a program that it believes will satisfy and motivate the workers. However, if the employees skeptically perceive the change as a management gimmick, the program is unlikely to succeed. Nor are all workers alike; some may not respond to programs in which others thrive.

Imaginative managers can develop many more innovations to make jobs more interesting, including temporary transfers and special projects. To be successful, however, job enrichment must have the support of senior management and likewise be accepted by workers at all levels. Considerable education of supervisors and employees is essential if programs are to succeed. Stumbling blocks exist when supervisors fear that such programs may threaten their own decision-making authority. Programs viewed by employees as deceptive management schemes designed solely to increase their workloads or reduce the number of employees are also unlikely to succeed. A climate of trust and understanding is essential for the effective use of morale-building techniques.

A major quality-oriented concern of managers today is that of initiating programs for improving the quality

of work life (QWL). These programs include vertical and horizontal loading, job enlargement, job rotation and cross-training, entry-level assignments, consistent positive reinforcement, well pay, building responsibility into jobs, child-care assistance, modifying the work environment, designing the workplace ergonomically, and wellness programs. Most jobs have five core dimensions that are essential for job enrichment: task variety, task identity, task significance, autonomy, and feedback.

In addition, there are a number of innovative ways to work, including gainsharing, flexible working hours, the compressed workweek, flexplace, contingent employment, job sharing, and flexible benefits.

Essential to the success of any or all of the programs that may be developed is acceptance by both workers and management, along with a climate of trust and understanding between them.

Job satisfaction is a complex concept. Over 20 factors combine to create the feeling of satisfaction or dissatisfaction in people. Some of these factors are inherent in the job, whereas others are outside of work. Some are more controllable by the individual, whereas others are beyond the individual's control. Finally, some people expect work to satisfy all of their needs, and when this does not happen, they become dissatisfied with their jobs rather than seeking a job, career, or outside activity that will fulfill the needs that their current job cannot satisfy.

CHECKING FOR UNDERSTANDING

1. What is meant by quality of work life? Define and describe it.

2. What are the common features of quality of work life?

3. List and describe the 14 factors that can impact and improve the quality of work life.

4. Explain the effects the work environment can have on the quality of work life.

5. Explain the effects the social environment can have on the quality of work life.

6. Describe the current innovative ways to work.

7. Explain the current work trends that can affect the quality of work life.

8. List and explain the external factors affecting job satisfaction.

9. List and explain the internal factors affecting job satisfaction.

10. List and explain the individual factors affecting job satisfaction.

SELF-ASSESSMENT

In general, are you satisfied with your current job? Complete the following Job Satisfaction Inventory for your current job.

Job Satisfaction Inventory

1. The number of skills I use in performing my job is relatively. . . Very High   High   Average   Low   Very Low

2. The depth of knowledge required for my job is relatively. . . Very High   High   Average   Low   Very Low

3. The amount of freedom I have to perform my job the way I want is. . . Very High   High   Average   Low   Very Low

4. The amount of freedom I have to perform my job at the pace I want is. . . Very High   High   Average   Low   Very Low

5. The freedom I have to set my own goals is. . . Very High   High   Average   Low   Very Low

6. The freedom I have to determine how successful I am is. . . Very High   High   Average   Low   Very Low

7. The amount of feedback I receive from performing my job tasks is. . . Very High   High   Average   Low   Very Low

8. The amount of feedback I receive from my immediate supervisor is. . . Very High   High   Average   Low   Very Low

9. The amount of public recognition I receive from doing my job well is. . . Very High   High   Average   Low   Very Low

10. The amount of public recognition that it is possible to receive from my employer is. . . Very High   High   Average   Low   Very Low

11. My ability to complete my work tasks is. . . Very High   High   Average   Low   Very Low

12. My roles at work are very clear to me. Very High   High   Average   Low   Very Low

13. There is little conflict among the different roles I play at work. Very High   High   Average   Low   Very Low

14. I could easily transfer to another position of my choosing. Very High   High   Average   Low   Very Low

15. There are opportunities for advancement with my current employer. Very High   High   Average Low   Very Low

16. I could find work with other employers with little trouble. Very High   High   Average   Low   Very Low

17. I have reasonable job security. Very High   High   Average   Low   Very Low

18. The quantity of social interactions on the job is acceptable to me. Very High   High   Average   Low   Very Low

19. The quality of social interactions on the job is acceptable to me. Very High   High   Average   Low   Very Low

20. My boss is a good manager. Very High   High   Average   Low   Very Low

21. The overall working environment at my current employer is agreeable to me. Very High   High   Average   Low   Very Low

22. My work schedule fits well with the rest of my life. Very High   High   Average   Low   Very Low

23. I have been with my current employer for a number of years. Very High   High   Average   Low   Very Low

24. I am fairly satisfied with my level of overall compensation. Very High   High   Average   Low   Very Low

25. I carefully researched and selected my current career. Very High   High   Average   Low   Very Low

26. I carefully researched and selected my current employer. Very High   High   Average   Low   Very Low

27. I am very committed to my career. Very High   High   Average   Low   Very Low

28. I am very committed to my current job. Very High   High   Average   Low   Very Low

29. My expectations about my current job match the reality of it. Very High   High   Average   Low   Very Low

30. Work is an important part of my life. Very High   High   Average   Low   Very Low

31. The amount of effort I put into work matches what I get in return. Very High   High   Average   Low   Very Low

32. In comparison with my friends, I feel I have a pretty good job. Very High   High   Average   Low   Very Low

33. In comparison with my immediate family, I feel I have a pretty good job. Very High   High   Average   Low   Very Low

34. In comparison with my relatives, I feel I have a pretty good job. Very High   High   Average   Low   Very Low

35. My friends think I have a good job. Very High   High   Average   Low   Very Low

36. My immediate family thinks I have a good job. Very High   High   Average   Low   Very Low

37. My relatives think I have a good job. Very High   High   Average   Low   Very Low

38. Overall, I have confidence in myself. Very High   High   Average   Low   Very Low

39. My view of life, in general, is positive. Very High   High   Average   Low   Very Low

40. I have a high level of self-esteem. Very High   High   Average   Low   Very Low

Score 5 points for every Very High answer, 4 points for every High, 3 for every Average, 2 for every Low, and 1 for every Very Low. Total your score. A score of 181–200 indicates an extremely satisfying job, 141–180 a highly satisfying job, 101–140 a satisfying job, 61–100 a less satisfying job, and 40–60 a job that you consider not very satisfying.

SKILL BUILD 12

Audrey, Bushra, Carlos, Jake, and Saqib have been friends since the start of high school. Audrey, Carlos, and Saqib are working now, but Bushra and Jake are still in college. They are sitting around one evening at Audrey's house.

"Guys, what makes a job good? You know, like, not talking about the money, I mean, gratifying, you know?" Bushra asked.

"I know two things about my job that make it good," Audrey said. "My boss tells me how I'm doing, good or bad, at least once a day. Usually more. And the other thing is we can earn bonuses every three months based on how well we do individually. You get money and a nameplate on the Employee Honor Wall for everyone to see. If you get four quarterly awards in a row, the smaller nameplates are replaced by a big one and you get an extra bonus."

Skill Question 1. In talking about her job, is Audrey really talking about one internal job satisfaction factor or two? Name the factor or factors and define each. If two factors are involved, explain the differences between them.

"Wait a minute, you said there are two things you like. Isn't your boss telling you how you're doing and the awards basically the same thing?" Carlos asked.

"No, I think they are different, but I don't know what each is called," Audrey replied.

"Bushra, why do you ask this?" Saqib said.

"Well, I just want my job, when I do finish school, to do it all for me. I know the money will be there, but I want the work to make me feel good, like I'm doing something. So that at the end of the day I feel like I'm accomplishing something and not just putting my time in," Bushra answered.

Skill Question 2. What two individual job satisfaction factors is Bushra talking about with her job? Name and define them in your own words.

"Okay, then, I'll tell you the best things about my job are that I'm around people. I mostly make the rounds of clients I know in the morning. Then I see a few new ones in the early afternoon and then back to the office with the gang for the team meetings. It suits me perfectly. I'm out there, I'm networking, I got connections and, you know, I'm in pretty good where I am, I mean the place basically has to close before I'm out of a job, and at the rate we're going that ain't gonna happen. So the being around people is great and then not having to really worry about not working, those are the two best things with my job," Carlos said.

Skill Question 3. Now looking at Carlos's job, how many external job satisfaction factors is he describing? Define each in your own words and explain if each factor would tend to increase job satisfaction for everyone

as it has for Carlos or whether there is some personal preference involved with each.

"Well, *you* may have it good, but I'm not so sure about my job. For one, I gotta go soon because they put me on the midnight shift," Saqib said.

"Oh, no way!" Audrey said, "I got the pizza dude coming."

"Sorry, but I have to, and I'm not happy about it either. You guys know I have never been a late-night person. I get up early, and I'm ready to go. This is really tough. I've had to stay up all night on my days off because I can't keep changing when I sleep. Plus the people I'm working with are not great. They slack every chance they get. It's starting to rub off on me and I don't like it, but what can I do?" Saqib said.

Skill Question 4. Saqib seems to have an external job satisfaction factor and an individual job satisfaction factor involved with his job. Name them both, identify which is the external and which the individual, and define each in your own words.

Skill Question 5. For this question you will need to draw on what you remember from previous chapters. Let's say Saqib stays on this shift and has the same colleagues, what does he risk if he does *not* go along with their slacking? Do you recommend that he go with the crowd here or that he *not* slack off, and why?

"Well, don't go along with them, man," Jake said.

"What are they pushing you to do?" Audrey asked.

"Sleep on the job. The rule is if you sleep on nights and are lying down, you are fired because they figure that the laying down makes it intentional. If you are sitting and sleeping, they figure that was accidental, so you don't get fired if you are caught. But these guys have all these elaborate ways of getting comfortable while sitting, so they are deliberately sleeping but they make it look accidental. I mean, it's all kind of involved and really designed to not do work. They like to leave stuff go for the day shift so there's more to it, but that is an example. Anyway, I gotta go and catch an hour of sleep before I go in. See you guys later," Saqib said, and he got up and left.

"Wow, see, that's why I asked," Bushra said. "Saqib is making good money, but that situation does not sound gratifying."

"Is that your new word—gratifying? That's the second time you used it tonight. You got a word-a-day calendar or what?" Jake said.

"Hey, you're in college, too, so you should know that word," Bushra replied.

"I'm just saying. Anyway, I'm not having problems. I know it. I spent three years investigating being an oceanographer. I looked at the top 12 schools, spent time at Wood's Hole Oceanographic Institute. I interned at two of the top employers. I'm putting forth effort, and it will yield results," Jake said.

"Yeah, dude, you did do it right, no doubts there. That will be a great job," Carlos said.

"Everyone I talked to feels the same, Jake. They all say you made the right choice," Audrey added. Jake had to admit that all this support did reinforce his feelings about the job.

Skill Question 6. Jake's situation involves two individual job satisfaction factors. What are they? Define them.

Skill Question 7. It is five years later, Jake is an oceanographer, and he hates it. It is nothing like he thought it would be. This group is back together. Based on the chapter materials, what is he likely to say about his job now?

Bushra said, "It's great for you, Jake, but when I look at what I'm doing and what you're doing I feel, I don't know, like maybe I made the wrong choice. Especially when I see how Audrey and Carlos feel, it really affects how I feel about what I chose."

"Well, I don't see how that can be," Jake said. "How can what others feel about their work affect how you feel about yours?"

"I don't know, but I think it kind of does," Bushra said.

Skill Question 8. Help Jake with the statement he makes to Bushra in the second-to-last paragraph. Who is right? Support your answer.

APPLICATIONS

12.1 THE SATISFACTION ANALYSIS

You have been brought in as a consultant to assess a group of 10 workers.

Alyss is the company's sexual harassment officer. There has never been a sexual harassment complaint at the company. Alyss certainly has no problem with that, but she does have a master's degree in human resources and feels she could handle much more. Her boss really believes in specialization even though she only needs about an hour a week to do her job well.

Boris is a morning person. Left on his own, he is up at 5:00 A.M. and ready for work at 6:00 A.M.; at 9:00 P.M. he is ready to sleep where he stands. Boris starts work at 4:00 P.M. and is off at 11:30. He took the afternoon shift in the production department years ago for the extra 50 cents an hour pay but has been unhappy ever since.

Carmen handles customer complaints, which seem to come in waves. It's either feast or famine; either there is nothing to do or there is a line of people and the phone is ringing off the hook. Carmen is sure this is the cause of her ulcer.

Derek has been with the company for 26 years. He has been through almost every department, but that was mostly during his early years. He has been in the same position for 17 years and has turned down numerous transfers and promotions during that time. He's not at all interested in retiring.

Evelyn thought she had a pretty good job as a brand manager for the company's best-selling product, but at her 10-year college reunion she found out what her three best friends are doing. One is the chief operating officer of one of the top 100 companies in the United States. Another was just appointed first-chair cellist for the Chicago Symphony Orchestra. The third is going to the Winter Olympics on the U.S. ski team.

Fred is a new sales representative and is putting in about 60 hours per week. Fred doesn't mind the hours—he is more than willing to work—but all sales reps work on commission, and Fred just can't seem to close a sale. He does great up until then but is reluctant to ask for an order. The lack of strong results is almost enough to depress him.

Gamini is starting to doubt himself. He likes his job as the company recycling collector. It doesn't pay much, but his needs are simple. Collecting the tons of paper and pounds of aluminum cans and plastic water bottles each month makes Gamini feel he is helping the environment, but the other employees think he is crazy. They tell him it is demeaning work and that he is just a slightly glorified garbage collector.

Hope is a client specialist. It is her job to care for visiting clients. As they come from many countries, they have varying needs, which she handles, and by the time they leave, they are all close friends with Hope. She couldn't dream of a better job for her.

Indira is the last COBOL programmer for the company and is worried because there is talk about getting rid of the mainframe. She hasn't seen or heard of another job programming in COBOL since Y2K. She liked COBOL so well that she never paid any attention to the newer programming languages.

Josh is the company artist. He paints murals and custom paintings for employees to improve the aesthetics. This is his third artist-in-residence job in the last two years. Recently, company profits have declined, and the company does not seem to be able to increase prices.

QUESTIONS

1. What job satisfaction factor is best associated with each of these workers, and what supports your position?

2. You have seven opportunities for changing the quality of work life at this company: an employee appreciation award (with personal parking space for one year), job rotation, job enlargement, a daytime assembly supervisor position, advanced job training, outplacement services, and tuition reimbursement. Who gets these (one per person) and why?

3. Three people will not have their quality of work life changed, two because no change is needed and one because you have nothing that would affect the problem. Who are these three? Which two need no change and why? Which one cannot be changed by you and why not?

12.2 THE CHILD-CARE DILEMMA

Bobbie Ann Clark burst through the front door of Medcheck, Inc., out of breath, her coat half unbuttoned, and her uncombed hair flying in all directions. She glanced frantically at the clock—it read 10:35—as she punched one of the four flashing buttons on her ringing desk telephone. "Rene is going to have my head when she finds out I got to work late again," Bobbie thought as she took a call from an annoyed nursing-home manager who had been trying to reach her since 9:00 A.M. Rene Demetris, Bobbie Ann's supervisor, watched Bobbie's whirlwind entrance with dismay. Bobbie Ann was a valued employee at Medcheck, a 50-person firm that reviewed medical claims forms for insurance companies to see that the charges submitted for reimbursement were reasonable and customary. Bobbie Ann examined claims fairly and thoroughly and, until recently, had the lowest error rate in the company. Moreover, she was adept both at handling telephone inquiries from insurers and health-care providers and at working with complex computer programs.

During the past couple of months, however, Bobbie Ann's behavior on the job had changed. She frequently arrived at work late or departed early, and her lunch breaks were stretching into the middle of the afternoon. Rene had also learned that Bobbie had agreements with several colleagues to cover for her absences by, in effect, splitting her work. It seemed to Rene that Bobbie Ann was trying to set her own hours, which did not conform to Medcheck's official 9-to-5 workday. Clearly, the time had come for a talk. Rene asked Bobbie Ann to join her in her office.

"It all began when the baby-sitter quit," Bobbie answered with a sigh when Rene asked about the erratic comings and goings.

"First, I tried placing my son, Buddy, in a day-care center, but the only center that had room for him closes promptly at 5:30 P.M., and I couldn't get there in time to pick him up. That's why I was leaving the office early for a while. I knew I couldn't keep that up, though, so I made arrangements with a woman who watches four or five children at her house. The problem was that she lives way over in Brookdale; by the time I drove there to leave Buddy and headed back to Medcheck, it was already 9:00 A.M.

"When I realized that plan wasn't going to work out, either, I started to look for a new baby-sitter to stay with Buddy at home. The phone calls and interviews meant that I had to take extra-long lunch hours. Now I have a new baby-sitter, one Buddy and I like very much, but she has two children of her own in school, and they both came down with the flu last week. She's had to stay home with them while they're sick, and for days I've had to spend half the morning running Buddy around to whichever friend or relative could look after him for a few hours.

"Rene, I like it here at Medcheck, and I want to do a good job and follow company rules. But I love my son, too, and I want to do what's right for him. I'm at my wit's end with child-care problems. I firmly believe that a more flexible work schedule or some other alternative way of doing things is the only solution."

Rene promised that she would think about what Bobbie Ann had said—and she did, most of the day and all evening. Many of Rene's friends had similar difficulties. Moreover, Rene knew that as a single mother, Bobbie Ann needed to keep her full-time job and had less support to fall back on when problems arose. Rene was fully sympathetic. Still, she wondered what might happen if she allowed Bobbie a flexible work arrangement of some kind. How, for example, would Bobbie's coworkers react? Would it be fair to the men in the company? How would it affect the way she supervised employees? Could she sell the idea of flexibility to Medcheck's management? Rene went to sleep that night unsure what to do.

QUESTIONS

1. What would you do if you were in Rene Demetris's place? Explain the pros and cons of your decision.

2. If you were in favor of a flexible work arrangement in this case, what arguments would you use to persuade top management to adopt it? If you were not in favor of such an arrangement, what arguments would you use to support your position?

3. Is fairness an issue in flextime and similar arrangements? Explain.

4. How might Rene's supervisory methods and style have to change if Bobbie Ann, and perhaps a number of her coworkers, adopted flextime, job sharing, telecommuting, or other nontraditional ways of working?

NET-WORK

What job satisfaction factors can you identify?
http://www.youtube.com/watch?v=yBK02O1Oewc

How does this advice fit with the motivation theories in the chapter?
http://www.youtube.com/watch?v=32vKgi1Le5k

PERSONAL POINTS

1. How do you feel about temp work? While you might not prefer being a temp worker, what would you do to cope if you found that you really needed to be a temp worker due to your previous job's being outsourced or because you were trying to start a new career?

2. How do you feel about empowerment? If your current employer said you were being empowered, what would you take that to mean and would you welcome it or would you prefer not to be empowered and why?

3. How much personalization do you think should be allowed at work and why? Do you think personalization is so important that employers should provide money to each worker to personalize his or her area? Why or why not?

What limits should be placed on personalization in the workplace.?

4. Assume you are going to be job sharing. Who would you job share with? What characteristics would you want your job-share partner to have?

5. Looking at all of the job-satisfaction factors, which will be most important to you in your next job? How will you determine which job has the greatest number of these or which job has them to the greatest degree?

EXPERIENTIAL EXERCISE

Each student should review the following list and select the six most important to him or her (the "a" items), the six least important (the "c" items), and the six remaining ("b" items). Groups should be formed (4–6 members each if possible). Each group, should then review the individual lists and compile a new list that all group members agree to consisting of six "a" items and three "b" items. Groups should have a rationale for the inclusion of these nine items on their respective lists and a rationale for the exclusion of the remaining nine items. The group results may then be compared and the highest-rated criteria for the class determined.

1. The Work
   a. A job you love
   b. A job that is just okay
   c. A job you hate

2. Job Variety
   a. Many skills and much knowledge needed
   b. Some skills and knowledge needed
   c. Few skills and little knowledge needed

3. Autonomy
   a. Complete freedom to control your work
   b. Some freedom to control your work
   c. No freedom to control your work

4. Goal Determination
   a. Complete freedom to set your own goals
   b. Some freedom to set your own goals
   c. No freedom to set your own goals

5. Feedback and Recognition
   a. Abundant amounts of both
   b. Some of each
   c. Almost none of either

6. Achievement
   a. High achievement
   b. Moderate achievement
   c. Low achievement

7. Role Ambiguity and Role Conflict
   a. Low ambiguity and conflict
   b. Some ambiguity and conflict
   c. High ambiguity and conflict

8. Opportunity
   a. Great future job prospects
   b. Moderate future job prospects
   c. Poor future job prospects

9. Job Security
   a. Job for life
   b. Fair job security
   c. High chance of being let go

10. Social Interactions
    a. Many quality interactions
    b. Some moderate-quality interactions
    c. No interactions

11. Supervision
    a. Highly skilled managers
    b. Average managers
    c. Malicious managers

12. Work Schedules
    a. Your ideal schedule
    b. A schedule that is just okay
    c. The opposite of your ideal schedule

13. Compensation
    a. High compensation
    b. Adequate compensation
    c. Below-average compensation

14. Effort/Reward Ratio
    a. Rewards exceed efforts
    b. Rewards equal efforts
    c. Efforts exceed rewards

15. Influence of Coworkers
    a. Coworkers tell you this is a great place to work
    b. Coworkers say little
    c. Coworkers tell you this is a terrible place to work

EXPERIENTIAL EXERCISE (Continued)

16. Comparisons
    a. Friends and relatives say you have a great job
    b. Friends and relatives say little about your job
    c. Friends and relatives say you have a terrible job

17. Opinion of Others
    a. Others feel your job is highly prestigious
    b. Others feel your job has average prestige
    c. Others feel your job has no prestige

18. Seniority
    a. High seniority
    b. Average seniority
    c. Low seniority

SPOT CHECK ANSWERS

1. T
2. F
3. T
4. F
5. F
6. T
7. F
8. T
9. F
10. F
11. T
12. F
13. T
14. F
15. F
16. F
17. F
18. F
19. F
20. F

13 | The Dynamics of Change

If we don't change, we don't grow. If we don't grow, we aren't really living.

Gail Sheehy

A long habit of not thinking a thing wrong gives it a superficial appearance of being right.

Thomas Paine

This is the way we have always done it.

Anonymous

GOALS

The goals of this chapter include the examination of change from the perspective of someone introducing or implementing change (a manager, team leader, or other change agent) and from the perspective of someone who is obligated to change.

OBJECTIVES

When you finish this chapter, you should be able to:

- Explain the importance of anticipating the need for change.
- List and describe the major causes of employee resistance to change.
- List and describe how resistance to change is shown.
- Explain the three-step and six-step processes for change.
- Describe the benefits of participating in change.
- Explain the methods for accomplishing change.
- List and explain six methods for coping with change.

INTRODUCTION

Western culture has only one constant—that things will change. Yet people resist change. Introducing and administering change is probably one of the most difficult and challenging tasks people face. Change is also one of the most important tasks people face because conditions in the world of work seldom remain static. Even the ancient Greek philosopher Heraclitus once said, "There is nothing permanent except change." This chapter will introduce you to some of the principal challenges associated with any attempt to modify processes within organizations. This chapter is divided into six major sections:

1. the effects of change
2. the tendency to resist change
3. how resistance to change is shown
4. change management
5. methods of accomplishing change
6. coping with change

THE EFFECTS OF CHANGE

Unfortunately, change often occurs only after managers recognize that conditions are in a state of crisis. A more rational and usually far less costly approach is for leaders to attempt to anticipate the need for change and to develop creative innovations before serious problems evolve.

THE NEED FOR ANTICIPATION

Far too frequently, managers in organizations haven't set aside the time necessary for analyzing changing conditions or attitudes and have suddenly found themselves in the middle of severe complications. Managers, as we have noted, must learn to delegate routine matters so that they have time for planning necessary changes. The conditions that lead to poor morale can then be anticipated and prevented.

There is something of a paradox between the need for continuity and the necessity for change in organizations. For example, customers and employees usually prefer feelings of continuity in their lives because such feelings enable them to have faith that events in the future will unfold in a predictable manner. Customers hope that a continued supply of materials at comparable prices will be available. Employees want their paychecks to be secure so that they will be able to continue to purchase the items they want and need.

However, in the real world, conditions seldom remain static. Change is a basic part of any entity's existence. Work environments are continually modified. New production processes are regularly introduced. Organizational restructuring sometimes occurs. These are the types of activities that tend to upset some aspects of an organization's **equilibrium** and continuity.

Whenever possible, the need to change with the times (or even before) should be anticipated, and management should attempt to implement these changes before the crisis state is reached. Otherwise, serious organizational behavior difficulties can result.

Equilibrium
a stable, balanced, unchanging system

WHY PEOPLE RESIST CHANGE

Regardless of our attitudes toward change, the likelihood of our having any success in preventing it is negligible. A safe prediction is that change will continue to take place all around us. Perhaps more rational than the attempt to prevent the unpreventable, therefore, would be the attempt to learn more about the change so that we can deal more adequately with its effects.

Why do so many individuals tend to fear and resist change? In the next section we will attempt to answer this question by examining some of the factors that commonly retard or obstruct the introduction of change. These factors are listed in Table 13.1.

PERSONAL ATTITUDES AND PERSONAL IMPACT

Change, of course, doesn't affect everyone in the same way. How individuals respond to particular changes is significantly influenced by their personal attitudes. Some individuals thrive on change, whereas others react negatively to the mildest modification, even when it is beneficial. In general, people operate in a state of equilibrium. When this equilibrium is upset, there is a tendency to resist the change.[1]

Sometimes individuals balk at change because they don't want to exert what they feel to be the extra effort necessary to learn new things. For example, Lois, an IT manager, wants to surprise her friend Richard by loading the Linux operating system into his desktop computer. Lois believes that Linux surpasses Windows XP in advanced features. However, Richard, who feels completely confident and comfortable with the existing version of Windows, may not be at all happy about his friend's attempt to improve his world of bits and bytes.

Some organizational changes require employees to move to a different community. Having to uproot one's family can influence an employee's morale, especially in the case of dual-career families—households in which both spouses have well-established positions with organizations. The wife or husband may have to give up her or his job to enable the other spouse to accept the new position. Furthermore, children must transfer to new schools, and the entire family must leave its friends behind and cultivate new acquaintances. To some, such situations are exciting and challenging; to others, they are threatening.

TABLE 13.1 MAJOR FACTORS THAT OBSTRUCT THE INTRODUCTION OF CHANGE

Personal attitudes	Financial reasons
Alterations in the informal organization	Inertia
Lack of recognition of need	Fear of the unknown
Lack of trust	Revenge
Surprise	Poor timing
Poor approach	Misunderstanding
Absent benefit	Insufficient need
Phariseeism	

FINANCIAL REASONS

Workers may not work for bread alone, but a major cause of their resistance to change is the fear of losing their jobs, their primary source of income.[2] For example, when new and more efficient processes are introduced or senior management announces plans for organizational restructuring, workers sometimes perceive the changes as a threat to their jobs.

In some instances, employees feel so threatened by changes that they attempt to sabotage new processes or products. There are situations, however, when an employee's fears are unfounded. In such cases, employee resistance to change can be lessened if managers introduce the change with greater sensitivity. Effective ways to introduce and manage change will be discussed later in this chapter.

ALTERATIONS IN THE INFORMAL ORGANIZATION

A result of change that is easily overlooked by managers is its effect on the social lives of employees.[3] For example, say you work in the human resources department of an organization and have been responsible for training new employees for the past three years. The head of your department has decided to rotate work assignments among the various department members to "enrich" their jobs. You've been assigned to a position that consists of issuing parking permits and keys, assigning lockers, and making certain that the coffee-break areas are amply stocked with supplies.

Some department members might welcome the change. However, many of your personal friends were aware of your previous responsibilities, and you perceive the change as a reduction of your status, that is, the perceived social ranking that you feel you have relative to your fellow employees. Sometimes seemingly insignificant changes can affect the self-esteem of employees or their standing with their coworkers, families, and friends. A person's self-image can be threatened by certain changes.

Other types of changes can break up established patterns of social interaction or conversation on the job. A change from bench work to assembly-line production, for example, might result in the elimination of an informal communication system among the employees. Taking away one's on-the-job friends may be more devastating to some than changing the job or the equipment. Some workers claim that, for them, one of the most important reasons for coming to work is to see people they like. Changing the relationships through hirings, firings, and transfers can seriously impact job satisfaction and productivity.

INERTIA

Inertia

the tendency for a moving body to continue moving and a body at rest to remain at rest

In physics, **inertia** is the tendency for a moving body to continue moving and the tendency for a body at rest to remain at rest. Work habit, policies, and procedures have inertia—they have a momentum of their own. Because established policies tend to remain in effect on their own, to effect change, the old policies must be stopped and the new policies must be given momentum.[4] Otherwise, people tend to continue in the manner to which they have become accustomed. They form habits—those activities that we perform unconsciously as a result of frequent repetition—because habits can make life less threatening and more comfortable. Sometimes, however, we become so accustomed to doing things in a particular manner that we fail to recognize that there may be better ways.

LACK OF RECOGNITION OF NEED

Sometimes people are so preoccupied with day-to-day pressures that they don't see a gradual deterioration of certain conditions, such as employee morale, and therefore don't recognize the need for modifying existing conditions until after a crisis has erupted. In other words, there is a **lack of recognition of need**. The same is true of the "sudden" aging of someone we have not seen for a long time. Upon seeing the person again, we find the person looks so much older. This person may not have noticed because he or she has seen himself or herself in the mirror every day, and the gradual change has been almost insignificant. Over time, though, the effects build. You see the person and compare him or her with the way he or she looked 10 years ago, and "suddenly" you notice how old the person looks. To avoid this situation, we must stop periodically to take measure of the situation in order to better notice how much change has occurred.

Lack of Recognition of Need
preoccupation that prevents people from noticing a gradual deterioration of conditions

FEAR OF THE UNKNOWN

Fear of the unknown is one of humanity's greatest fears and is a basic cause of resistance to change.[5] Change begets uncertainty, an uncomfortable situation, to say the least. The past is known and familiar. Change is strange. We are not certain of what it will bring, and quite often the anticipation of an event is worse than the actual experience. The uncertainty sometimes creates pressure to prevent change.

Fear of the Unknown
fear from not knowing what the future will bring

Employees often fear change because they don't understand how the change might affect them; they fear, quite naturally, the uncertainty associated with the change. For example, the cost-cutting efforts by General Motors created many uncertainties in the minds of its employees in 1992. The company's head at the time, Robert Stempel, announced in mid-1992 that additional plant closings would take place, but he refused to name any plant or say exactly when the plants would be closed. Fourteen of the twenty-one GM plants, were already scheduled to be closed and 74,000 employees cut by 1995, but the closure of at least four more assembly plants was yet to be announced. A few months later, Stempel himself was sacked by a boardroom coup because of the directors' impatience with his slowness in carrying out restructuring plans. The directors decided in late 1992 to eliminate a total of 120,000 jobs during the decade.[6] Imagine how employees in the remaining plants probably felt, wondering how the company's restructuring activities would affect their own jobs. Job security became a major issue to GM's employees in the 1990s.

NetNote

12Manage: Rigor and Relevance in Management

http://www.12manage.com/ i_co.html

Numerous links to organizational change information.

The fear of uncertainty can also create difficulty in making decisions involving risks. There is a human tendency to prefer the certainty of misery over the uncertainty of pleasure. For example, some people will remain in undesirable situations that are familiar to them rather than risk changes that fail to provide them with a guaranteed result.

Insurance companies have capitalized on the fear of the unknown and the desire to reduce uncertainty. A businessperson who buys a building, for example, acquires a risk. There's the chance, or fear, that the building may be destroyed by fire or some other peril. The payment of a certain number of dollars—the insurance premium—transfers the burden of risk to the insurance company. In the event of fire, the businessperson is reimbursed for roughly the amount of the loss. Thus, the fear of uncertainty has been reduced.

LACK OF TRUST

Resistance to change is likely to be significant in work environments where employees don't trust their managers. Conversely, managers are not likely to ask for employee participation in effecting change if they don't trust their subordinates. Classical managers, who, if you remember, inherently do not trust their workers and believe that workers do not want to be involved, routinely make decisions themselves, again increasing the chances for resistance to change.

Revenge
a desire to retaliate for a real or imagined past wrong

Surprise
sudden, abrupt change; change without warning

Poor Timing
change that coincides with, but is the reciprocal of, other events

REVENGE

Workers may resist change out of **revenge**.[7] When workers perceive that management has wronged them in the past or that a manager has not trusted or supported them, they may feel that resisting change is a justified form of payback. Here also may be the time that a person seeks a return to equity (see Chapter 11) when an imbalance is perceived. Herzberg has discussed a whole "revenge psychology" whereby people feel that they have been so grievously wronged that they not only resist change (in addition to taking other measures) but also pass on the story of the perceived wrong. Sometimes none of the people who were originally wronged are still at work, yet people still say things like, "Remember the time management. . . ." Herzberg claims that some actions by managers can create a "remembered pain" that can never be removed.[8] Management's only choice here is never to betray the trust or act in any way that could create a revenge psychology in the first place.

A GLOBAL GLANCE

The Change Heard round the World

Change is not a phenomenon limited to individuals and organizations. Change is occurring on a planetary scale. Global changes do eventually affect individual organizations and individuals; to avoid being taken by complete surprise, you must keep an eye on the large changes and estimate the potential impact for you and your firm. For most organizations, the lead change is globalization itself. Almost every company is either in the global marketplace or affected by foreign firms entering its domestic markets. The result is not just increased competition. Increased participation in the global economy of emerging nations and currently industrialized nations can introduce a large amount of idle production capability. This makes it difficult for firms to raise prices, even to cover basic cost increases, which require a 3 to 4 percent price increase per year. Adding to the problem is the maturation of the largest world economies. Growth in the United States in the 1980s and 1990s has been the slowest ever. Even if the economy did accelerate at a higher rate (which the Federal Reserve would probably never permit), plenty of foreign firms are ready to take a piece of the pie. Much of the push behind downsizing results from this change in global competition—if you can't raise prices or increase sales, you have to cut costs to stay afloat.

Are there other choices? Some have been proposed but are not yet proven. These include other cost controls (streamlining or outsourcing clerical or distribution functions), increasing flexibility (in purchasing or employee-compensation methods), more careful selection of markets, and keeping an eye on external changes.

Source: Adapted from Lawrence Chimerine, "The New Economic Realities in Business," *Management Review*, January 1997, pp. 12–17.

SURPRISE

A birthday is an acceptable time for a **surprise**; a surprise is less well accepted when it involves working conditions. When a change is suddenly thrust upon people and takes them by surprise, they will usually resist it more than if change is introduced gradually.[9] People may resist making the change in order to take more time to learn about it and to ascertain its effect on them. It is also apparent that people are not involved in the change process when they are taken by surprise by the change. Generally change is more readily accepted by people who are involved in the process, which is another reason to avoid foisting sudden changes on subordinates.[10]

POOR TIMING

The timing of change in relation to other events also may increase resistance to the change.[11] **Poor timing** may be caused by events within the company, by related events outside the company, or by events occurring in someone's personal life. For example, bringing in a young manager from outside the firm at the same time that all of the equipment and procedures are being updated may increase resistance to both changes. One always has to wonder about firms that lay people off right before Christmas. On a personal level, changing a parent's start time just as his or her child begins school thereby preventing the parent from driving the child to kindergarten can increase resistance to the new schedule. Managers should consider other events that are occurring at the same time that a major change is proposed or implemented and avoid poor timing, if possible.

POOR APPROACH

The approach used in presenting a change can increase resistance to the change if people dislike the approach.[12] A **poor approach** to change can be caused either by the way change is communicated or by the communication channel that is selected. Sending an e-mail message or a memo to someone, for example, may not be as effective as delivering the change message in person. An approach may also be considered poor if the person delivering the change message is already disliked. Finally, the words used to explain the change may cause the approach to be poor. Telling a workforce that there will be no raises or bonuses this year and that everyone will have to increase productivity in order to boost the stock dividend may be a poor approach, because the workforce will assume the real objective is to make the stockholders wealthier. However, explaining that the change is needed so that the dividend can be increased in order to increase the stock price and avoid a hostile takeover, a liquidation of the firm, and the firing of everyone may generate more cooperation for the change.

Poor Approach
using an inadequate or inappropriate approach to change

MISUNDERSTANDING

If people do not understand a change, they tend to resist it.[13] The **misunderstanding** may be over the intent of the change. People may misunderstand the motive behind the change, as when they feel that the change is a personal criticism of their performance.[14] Sometimes they just don't understand why a change was needed. It isn't so much that they disagree with the change as that as they just weren't told why the change was needed, or they didn't comprehend the reasoning.

Misunderstanding
when people do not understand a change or its explanation

ABSENT BENEFITS

When people resist change because of absent benefits, they are really saying that there is nothing in the change for them. When a change is absent benefits, it means that the change or the change agent has provided no incentive for the people to change.[15] In actuality, there may be benefits in the new change, but they may not be obvious, or they may not have been explained. Some people may feel this way about recycling paper or soft-drink cans at work. If no immediate benefit is seen, some may not bother. If, however, the long-term environmental benefits are explained, then these people may comply.

NetNote

ChangingMinds.org

http://changingminds.org/ disciplines/ change_management/ resistance_change/ resistance_change.htm

Information on resistance to change.

INSUFFICIENT NEED

People sometimes resist change if they feel that there is insufficient need for the change.[16] The need may or may not be evident in these situations. It is easier to understand resisting a change when no need for the change is seen. Sometimes, the need is seen, but it may not seem large enough to warrant any change or the amount of change being proposed. For example, saving $100 a month on rent by moving a successful 60-person office operation 50 miles from the city to the suburbs may be met with resistance. The need to save $100 when the organization is already profitable may seem an insufficient reason to relocate, print new letterhead, and force some people to drive farther.

PHARISEEISM

Phariseeism

the hypocritical adherence to the letter of the law while missing the spirit of the law

Phariseeism is the hypocritical adherence to the letter of the law while missing the spirit of the law. Here, people are told to change or that the change is beneficial, but the reality of the change has not been revealed.[17] In communicating the change, no one has mentioned who will receive the praise, the recognition, the promotions, or the real benefits of the change. For example, suppose a computer services manager wants all departments to use the same brand of computer, stating that servicing will be easier and money will be saved even though the computers being recommended will replace computers from other manufacturers. The departments don't see the need for uniformity and resist the change. What the computer services manager doesn't reveal is that he or she wants the change because the new vendor will also support the Internet servers the manager knows nothing about. Everyone else is supposed to conform while the computer services manager reaps all the benefits.

HOW RESISTANCE TO CHANGE IS SHOWN

Now that we know why people resist change, we will examine how people show their resistance to change. There are six main methods by which people demonstrate resistance:

- absenteeism
- decreased productivity
- regression
- resignation
- transfer
- sabotage

Note that outright refusal to change is not on the list. People do not usually openly refuse to change, probably because this would be a highly visible act that carries too much risk. Instead of refusing and taking the risk of being disciplined or fired, most people choose a less obvious and less confrontational method of protesting a change.

ABSENTEEISM

Instead of changing, people may try to escape the change by calling in sick or arriving late to work.[18] Through their absence, people are not trying to have the change reversed as much as they are trying to avoid the change or delay its implementation. For example, given a new boss, people may be absent or late in order to escape having to deal with or work for the new manager. **Absenteeism** is a more complex phenomenon, however. First, it has causes other than just change, some of which are related to work and others that are not. Second, absenteeism affects not only the employer or the boss; it affects coworkers who must perform the extra work left by a person or persons who are not at work. Third, there is also an effect on the person who is absent. By trying to escape the change rather than trying to cope with it, the resister creates stress by not facing the change. This stress can be even greater than the stress of adapting to the change.

Absenteeism
missing work without a valid reason

DECREASED PRODUCTIVITY

Decreased productivity differs from other ways people show resistance to change in that it is aimed at reversing the change, and it has some chance of working. This tactic involves people who deliberately slow down so that productivity declines.[19] The thinking behind this tactic is that the manager will notice after the change that productivity is lower than it was before the change without seeing that the decline was artificial. The underlying hope is that if the manager notices the decline, he or she will blame the drop on the latest change, decide that the change is failing, and return conditions to the way they were before the change. There are no statistics on how well this works because if it is done properly, managers will never realize that it was done—and workers certainly won't admit to it.

Decreased Productivity
a deliberate slowing of the pace of work so that productivity declines, and the decline is attributed to a recent change

REGRESSION

Regression is a relatively simple method of showing resistance to change. Here, to resist change, people regress their behavior and understanding to the level of a new, untrained worker.[20] People who display regression are essentially saying, "If things change, you [the manager] will have to tell me how to work under this change and how to do all the rest of my job too." The behavior is not uncommon, even though it is rather childish to pretend that one change has somehow caused people to forget how to do everything. Some people, however, use regression to make the change as painful as possible, hoping the manager will give up or return to the old ways.

Regression
workers pretending to have forgotten their skills so that they perform at the level of new, untrained workers

RESIGNATION

Resigning, the ultimate escape mechanism, is also a method for coping with unacceptable change.[21] **Resignation** may be a poor choice for a resister because he or she may suffer more than the employer, and if the change is later rescinded, he or she will not be there. Resignation should never be used without careful consideration. A person must consider the availability of other jobs and his or her own financial needs before quitting. It can also be more difficult to go from being unemployed to employed than it is to go from being employed in one job directly to being employed in another job. On the other hand, if the change truly is unacceptable, then it may be better to leave a situation than to stay and be miserable. One might, however, be able to transfer rather than resign.

Resignation
quitting one's job

Sabotage
deliberate acts to harm
an organization or to
destroy assets

TRANSFER

A request for a **transfer** to another department in the same company may be caused by change or some other factor.[22] Like resignation, transferring can be an escape mechanism if the person is unwilling to confront the change, or it can be a coping mechanism when the person really cannot cope with or accept the change. Transferring carries less financial worry and risk than resignation, and a transfer can help a firm retain valuable people.

SABOTAGE

Sabotage can be considered the severest form of resistance to change because it is risky, damaging, and typically illegal.[23] Sabotage is a deliberate act to harm the organization. The sabotage can be subtle—sometimes so subtle that it goes undetected. At other times, it can cause significant damage to the company and to innocent workers also. People who choose sabotage generally feel that they have been greatly wronged by the boss or the organization. They typically feel that they are justified in their actions, so sabotage may just be an example of equity theory taken to an extreme. Of course, sabotage can never be condoned; it can be costly, and it can negatively affect many innocent people, such as coworkers and customers. Still, incidences of sabotage are more frequent than one might initially suspect.

CHANGE MANAGEMENT

Before turning to the crux of the matter—effectively introducing change—the need for change should be examined. There is great pressure for constant change. Numerous quality efforts, such as TQM and Six Sigma, leadership books, and common belief state that change must be constant, best practices adopted, everything reengineered. There are times, however, when change for change's sake should not be adopted.

THE ALLURE AND PERIL OF CHANGE

The allure of change is the chance for improvement, but the peril is lost time and wasted effort. Therefore, make change carefully. With the constant pressure to make change, it should not be surprising that some suggest change for reasons other than improvement. These other reasons may include suggesting a change for one's personal gain, although sometimes the proponents of pseudochange really believe they are trying to help.[24] All proposed change should be examined carefully.

Careful review will help separate pseudochange from legitimate change. The first area to examine is the problem the change will allegedly solve. Determine whether there really is a problem and if the problem is big enough to require the proposed solution. Never spend more time and effort on making change than not making change is costing you. You could count, tag, and track every paper clip, but that would take more time and money than the cost for the lost paper clips, so it make no sense to do it. Demand proof of the problem. If there is only one person emphatically insisting it is a problem, then that is almost certainly insufficient proof. Look also at who would benefit most from the change, the organization or the reputation of the person proposing the change. Even if the organization appears to be the main beneficiary, there is more to be determined.

The organization must not only benefit from a proposed change, but it must benefit enough to make the effort worthwhile. The pros and cons of all significant changes must be listed, and the costs must be calculated. All changes have a cost in time and money. To agree to a change without determining the cost is like buying a product without knowing the price. In addition to determining the cost, you must determine the payoff (for example, lower spending or greater service or productivity). Then, what are the odds of receiving the payoff? Only about half of reengineering efforts realize their payoffs, so ask if you would make the change if it earned only half its payoff (the payoff times a 50% chance of earning it based on the typical reengineering result).[25] Or, would you make the change if it ended up costing twice as much? What if both happened, the change cost twice as much and earned half of what was projected? You might also ask what you would do if you had to reverse the change completely.

Since many changes seem to create a need for other changes, try to determine if the proposal is likely to create a cascade effect where one change requires another and another and another. For example, it might seem like a good idea for a beverage maker to change from ounces to milliliters in order to save money with a Chinese bottle and can supplier. However, the different containers would mean the filling machine would have to be changed, the labels changed, the cartons and boxes changed, the price, cost, and profit recalculated or changed, vending machines modified, and so on. The idea's real costs, once all is considered might make it less attractive or even prohibitive.

There are separate concerns if the change proposal is coming from someone new to the organization. If a new person suggests a change is suddenly needed, consider that he or she may just be reselling what was done at his or her last job. You should ask why this wasn't a problem before this person arrived. Has this person learned enough about the present organization's culture to know whether the change will fit? Maybe the new person is trying to change the current organization as a way of resisting change—resisting the change he or she should make by learning the existing procedures and culture.

We've already learned that many individuals have a tendency to resist change, even if they are not new to an organization and avoiding the effort needed to adapt. Therefore, change management—that is, the manner in which managers introduce change, regardless of how ideal their intentions may be—largely determines the success of their efforts. By understanding and applying some basic concepts, managers can improve their track records. Some of the important considerations for leaders to keep in mind when introducing change are cited in Table 13.2.

TABLE 13.2 GUIDELINES THAT ASSIST IN THE INTRODUCTION OF CHANGE

Recognize the three-step nature of the change process.
Stress the usefulness of the change.
Be empathetic toward the feelings of those affected.
Make certain that employees understand the nature and purpose of the change.
Allow for employee participation when possible.
Stress benefits.
Provide economic guarantees when possible.
Consider timing.
Introduce the change gradually when possible.
Introduce the change on a trial basis.

CHANGE AS A THREE-STEP PROCESS

We've already examined how established habits tend to affect the manner in which individuals react to new things. A way to gain a better insight into what people go through when changing is to view the activity as a three-step process: (1) unfreezing, (2) changing, and (3) refreezing.[26]

Unfreezing   As described earlier in this chapter, activities have momentum. It is easier to change an activity if the old way is stopped before the new way is started. The first step in the change process, therefore, should be **unfreezing**—discarding old ideas and habits in order to learn new ones. This significant step is often overlooked when attempting to introduce change. People are likely to resist change until they are willing to unfreeze certain thought and activity patterns. Later sections will discuss in more detail specific techniques that can be employed to assist in the unfreezing step.

Changing   The next step in the process is **changing**—learning new ideas and habits so that the desired behavior can be employed. People will be less willing to change and quite naturally tend to resist the unfreezing process if they are unfamiliar with the new alternatives. As will be seen in the section on accomplishing change, some methods introduce change gradually, and some abruptly. In either case, the change must be introduced; people can't use what they don't know.

Refreezing   The third step in the change process is **refreezing**—the attempt to apply regularly what one has learned. People can learn new ideas, methods, and systems. If they don't consciously apply them on a regular basis, however, they may soon forget them. Some TQM efforts have failed because TQM was introduced and explained but not maintained. There must be continuous attention to the change until it has been completely and thoroughly instituted. The remaining portion of this section provides some useful suggestions for applying the change process.

LARGER SCALE CHANGE—A SIX-STEP PROCESS

For change on the scale of an entire strategic business unit or an entire organization, an expanded process may be necessary, as large-scale change is more difficult to accomplish. These six steps may be needed when a large number of people or departments are involved:

1. Determine the necessity
2. Find the movers and shakers

Unfreezing

discarding old ideas and habits in order to learn new ones

Changing

learning new ideas and habits so that the desired behavior can be employed

---

Refreezing

regularly applying what one has learned

NetNote

Ezine Articles

http://ezinearticles.com/?Coping-with-Change:-Develop-Your-Personal-Strategy&id=51313

Change and coping strategies.

SPOT CHECK

6. When workers call in sick when they are well or when they arrive late to work, it is because they are resisting change. T F
7. Resigning is an acceptable method for coping with change, from the company's point of view. T F
8. Transferring can be a way someone copes with change that lets the company keep a good worker. T F
9. People should learn an organization's culture before proposing change. T F
10. Unfreezing is needed to counteract inertia. T F

3. Communicate the postchange vision and change plan
4. Clear the path
5. Find the good and give the feedback
6. Follow through

Typically a process like this needs to start at the top, but to succeed on a large scale, many other people must be involved, so participation is required every step of the way.

Determine the Necessity   In order to succeed, these questions must be answered: Why is *a* change needed? Why is *this* change needed? Why now? Why me?[27] The change originators, typically top management, must engage in some selling and some persuasion for large-scale changes to occur, to occur smoothly, and to benefit the organization. Ordering large-scale change may get compliance but often will not get cooperation or yield benefits due not only to resistance but also to resentment. The need for, and importance of, the change must be developed, and in the third step it must be widely communicated.

Find the Movers and Shakers   Due to the participation required and the number of people ultimately involved in large-scale change, supporters of the change must be located. The supporters must not only believe in the change, but they must also command the resources (human, financial, material, or informational; see also Chapter 8) needed to make the change happen. The movers and shakers of the organization, the leaders and others who can and will have to make the change happen, need to be recruited to the cause.[28]

Communicate the Postchange Vision and Change Plan   The change originators and the movers and shakers are the change agents. They must now develop the plan for how the change will occur. An overall strategy must be devised along with specific tactics. The timing, costs, and other people involved must be taken into consideration. A vision of the postchange organization must be devised and widely disseminated.[29] The question of how the organization will be different after the change is made must be presented in order for the rest of the organization to make the change happen. For example, if the change agents say the company must become more "customer centered," they must explain what that means and how things will be different after everyone becomes customer centered. Comments like "Who says we aren't customer centered?" and "But what do I *do* to be customer centered?" indicate that the postchange vision has not been communicated or has not been understood.

Clear the Path   This is much like the unfreezing portion of the three-step change model. Here, barriers and resistance are removed.[30] Anything that will block the change needs to be addressed. Old forms need to be thrown out, and old procedures stopped. Established habits need to be broken. This step may also require restating the postchange vision or recruiting new supporters who are hesitant or skeptical.

Find the Good and Give the Feedback   General supporters can be encouraged by hearing about areas where the change is starting to yield benefits.[31] Even the change agents can benefit from some positive feedback. For skeptics, late adopters, and others who are holding back, information on the benefits and advantages the change is providing can be invaluable in getting them to join in the effort. Whether to maintain the effort or to get the last of the resistors moving, this step should not be skipped or underrated.

Follow Through   This last step involves ensuring complete implementation, which means getting everyone to persevere and see the job through to completion.[32] Change agents cannot afford to become complacent, distracted, or tired of the endeavor lest the change collapse and fail. Follow through, then, is verifying that the change has been accomplished. Subsequently, after the change has been assimilated, the refreezing process must be completed, and the change, with all of its policies and procedures, locked in and acculturated.[33]

THE CHANGE MUST BE USEFUL

Any leader attempting to introduce change into the organizational environment should make special efforts to see that affected individuals understand its utility. Workers who see no valid reason for a new situation will tend to resist it. A crucial element in the introduction of change is the communication of why the change is taking place along with what is being changed and how it is changing. This communication will counteract the feeling that change has occurred just for the sake of change rather than for any logical reason.

MANAGEMENT SHOULD BE EMPATHETIC

A manager's perception of change in a particular work situation is not as important as the workers' perception of it. Managers should strive to employ empathy by asking themselves, "How might my subordinates view and react to this change?"

Here's an example of a situation in which an owner of a manufacturing facility—let's call him Sean—overlooked the need for putting himself in the shoes of his employees. After attending a management seminar that included a segment on the benefits of flexible working hours to both employees and employers, Sean decided to initiate such a program at his plant. He assumed that his employees would be grateful for their newly found freedom to determine their own working hours.

A QUESTION OF ETHICS

Not Exactly What One Would Call Country-Club Management

During the early 1990s, things weren't going very well for many companies in the United States. Sales and profits were down, and layoffs were up. Firms were getting leaner and meaner in many instances, with many employees feeling less secure about the future of their careers. Some observers of the organizational scene thought that many employees were beginning to believe that being ethical was becoming too risky. Some employees felt that they were placed in positions where it was too dangerous to just say no to their bosses. What developed was a condition that consultant Barbara Ley Toffler calls the "move it" syndrome. This condition exists when the boss tells a subordinate to "move it—just get it done, meet the deadline, don't ask for more money, time, or people, just do it!"

The boss doesn't necessarily come right out and tell the employee to be unethical, but frequently the lack of ethics has crept in because of the pressure to move it or lose it; that is, "if you don't get the job done, we'll find someone else who will!" Some observers believe that this type of pressure has caused typically honest people just trying to hold their jobs to cross over ethical boundaries.

For example, someone who is told that he or she must finish a project in two weeks that normally takes four weeks might feel compelled to stretch the usual standards of acceptable behavior.

QUESTIONS

You have a good job and a promising career and your boss gives you an order that you know is impossible to achieve ethically. What are the risks in refusing your boss? What are the risks or consequences to obeying him or her and having to act unethically?

Instead, the employees perceived the change differently. They thought that the new program meant they would have to be working irregular hours in the future, such as early mornings and weekends. The employees complained to their union officials, and an unnecessary conflict was created.

THE CHANGE MUST BE UNDERSTOOD BY THOSE AFFECTED

In Chapter 3, we discussed methods for ensuring more effective communication throughout organizations. As we discovered, any modification of the work environment tends to upset the equilibrium of those affected. Consequently, clear and effective communication of any change and its probable effects is essential if the workforce is to accept it. Many changes are likely to be resisted, naturally, but if changes are not understood by those affected, the chance of resistance increases considerably.[34]

For example, suppose you work for a company that manufactures audiological support devices (hearing aids). As a result of the rapidly increasing number of older people in the United States, sales in your organization have been outstanding during the past three years and are expected to continue at a similar brisk rate. Your plant, situated in New Bedford, Massachusetts, is currently operating at the limit of its capacity. Output, however, has not been able to keep pace with current and anticipated demand.

You and the other managers of the organization decide to open another plant in Oakland, California, thus having production and marketing operations close to two major population centers. Because the expansion doesn't directly affect workers at the New Bedford plant, no official announcement is made to the employees there. However, rumors start flying throughout the New Bedford plant. The employees believe the purpose of the new Oakland plant is to replace the existing facility, not merely supplement it. Morale rapidly takes a nosedive, and the union representatives call for a strike. Considerable damage is done to the morale of the employees before the facts of the move are made known.

Without understanding, people are likely to resist a new system even if it is simpler. We already learned about the unwillingness of many Americans to learn and use the metric system of measurement. You can see, therefore, that when the reasons for an impending change aren't made clear by managers, distorted interpretations of its purpose and effect can easily result. Resistance to the change often develops because of a misunderstanding.

EMPLOYEES SHOULD PARTICIPATE WHEN POSSIBLE

When change is necessary, the use of participation can be especially helpful because it often cultivates greater commitment on the part of the participants. Employees tend to be happier to see self-imposed innovations succeed than those that they feel have been forced upon them.

Ideas developed by the entire group (the supervisor and his or her workers) working together are frequently more effective and creative than those developed by one-person rule. Managers should therefore encourage subordinates to air their feelings, positive or negative, about proposed changes. Changes generally seem much less threatening when employees can discuss them openly.

BENEFITS SHOULD BE STRESSED

"What's in it for me?" may seem like a selfish question, but it is likely to be on the minds of workers about to be subject to organizational change. A new process, for example, may be useful because it reduces labor, but how are the people who had

NetNote

Holland and Davis, Inc.

http://www.hdinc.com/

Site includes tips on managing change and a list of change workshops and events.

previously provided the labor likely to be better off? Might they not perceive the laborsaving process as a threat to their economic security? Do you recall the need for security in Maslow's level-of-needs concept? To optimize the acceptance of change, managers should try hard to show how the people affected by the change may benefit.

PROVIDE ECONOMIC GUARANTEES WHEN POSSIBLE

In some instances, it might be possible to provide employees with economic guarantees as a means of increasing their willingness to adapt to new ideas and processes. For example, some organizations have developed formal no-layoff policies guaranteeing that no employee will lose his or her job as a result of the introduction of labor-saving equipment. Such economic guarantees tend to reduce opposition to new technology.

Another example relates to the resistance some employees might have toward being asked to relocate to another city. Guaranteeing the employee reimbursement for all expenses incurred as a result of the move, including assisting with the sale of his or her house, will often reduce some of the potential resistance to the change. Such economic guarantees may seem expensive for an organization, yet they may save money through reduced turnover of existing employees.

THE PROBLEM OF TIMING

The question of timing is as important in managerial activities as it is in athletics. Leaders should attempt to choose a good time for the initiation of any change. There is no one perfect time to introduce a modification into the work environment, but the best time is likely to be influenced by the current organizational culture, the nature of the change itself, and the type of industry involved.

AVOID TOO MUCH TOO SOON

Some years back, author Alvin Toffler introduced the term *future shock* into the American language. Toffler defined the term as "the dizzying disorientation brought about by the premature arrival of the future."[35] The concept of future shock applies to organizations as well. Gradual change is more likely to be accepted than excessively rapid change, because individuals need ample time to become accustomed to new situations. Managers should guard against the tendency to introduce too much change too fast for employees to absorb and accept.

FYI

Look for the good in changes.
Never underestimate people's dedication to resisting change.
When making change, reduce fear and uncertainty.
When making change, gather support and let people know what's in it for them.
To change, old procedures must be stopped so new ones can begin.
Plan for large change carefully.
Never use manipulation to make change.

Change for the sake of change or change because other organizations are changing seems more prevalent than ever. There is a definite price to be paid and a limit to the amount of change that organizations can endure. Too many changes made all at once or successively can cause people to become uncertain as to which change to make or adhere to, and it can cause them to become cynical or to even ignore the changes.[36] Continuous change also distracts people from routine but vital tasks. Prior to introducing another change, these questions should be asked: Is this change really necessary? Is it necessary now? Is it too soon after the last change? Will another change be one too many?

METHODS OF ACCOMPLISHING CHANGE

There are eight main methods for accomplishing change in organizations:

- directives
- participation
- trial period
- new-person method
- training
- organizational development (OD)
- management by objectives (MBO)
- manipulation

The directive, new-person, and manipulation methods are more consistent with classical management theories. The participation, trial period, OD, and MBO methods are more consistent with the theories of behavioral management. Change by training might be used by either classical or behavioral managers.

DIRECTIVES

Making changes using a **directive** or direct order means that the manager makes the decision to change, the manager decides the details of the change and the timing, and the change is posted or the commands issued.[37] The worker's role in the change is to implement the change. Orders are often given in writing in the belief that if everyone receives the same words, then everyone will receive the same message. Issuing an order is the preferred method of authoritarian, classical managers, although a behavioral manager might make minor changes by directive for the sake of expediency. For example, even a behavioral manager may use a directive in order to institute a new safety procedure. Change by directive can create resentment among subordinates, and it can increase resistance to change.

Directive
a direct order initiating changes

Participation
change that involves the manager and the workers

Trial Period
change is implemented for a limited time and then evaluated for its effectiveness

New-Person Method
change made by bringing in a new manager

Training
making change by teaching people to use new methods

PARTICIPATION

Change by **participation** is at the opposite end of the spectrum from change by directive. Used by many behavioral managers, participative change involves the manager and the subordinates. Here, subordinates work with the manager on what will be changed and how it will be changed as well as on implementation of the change.[38] The belief is that better changes will be made when additional viewpoints are included and that the implementation of the changes will be easier and better accepted by subordinates if they are part of the process. Participative change is also the perfect complement to the teamwork that is popular now.

TRIAL PERIODS

Another method of change that is often easier for people to accept is the **trial period.** With a trial period, the change is implemented for a limited time and then is evaluated for its effectiveness.[39] If the change works, it is implemented permanently. If it fails, the situation returns to the way it was, or a different change is tried. If the change is partially successful, it is modified and tried again. In order to use this method effectively, and in order for the change to receive a fair trial, the workers must be convinced that the trial period is legitimate. The mere awareness that something new is not being unilaterally forced on employees often makes their accepting it easier. If, however, the workers suspect that the trial change will be made permanent regardless of the outcome and without modification, then the trial period becomes a manipulative method for making change. Possibly the best way to convince people that the trial period is really only a test is for managers to have modified or discarded failed changes in the past. For workers, it is best to give the trial full implementation and to report results accurately, even if the change works. In this way, managers are reinforced to use trial periods again with other changes. The trial period is also one of the few methods that can work with other methods. A trial period could be used with a directive in an attempt to gain better acceptance, or a trial period could be used with participative change. If the change fails, then the group would reconvene and try again.

THE NEW-PERSON METHOD

One of the more often used methods of change is the **new-person method.** With this method, change is made by bringing in a new manager.[40] The underlying idea here is that subordinates expect a new person to make changes, so change can be made by getting a new person.[41] Of course, in order to bring in a new manager, the current one must be moved or fired, creating the unattractive potential for adequate managers to be replaced simply to facilitate a change. For example, if top management decides to downsize, then a new manager, a hatchet person, may be brought in to clear out the dead wood.

TRAINING

Training in order to bring about change is a simple concept to explain. To make change, people can be trained to use the new methods.[42] The change occurs with the learning of the new ways. This can also make the change easier for people to accept because it reduces the fear and uncertainty that accompany many changes. Although the use of training to make changes may seem logical when skills are involved, training can also introduce other changes. Training people to work in teams introduces them to new skills, but it also paves the way for organizational change. Existing functional departments might be dissolved in favor of cross-functional teams.

ORGANIZATIONAL DEVELOPMENT

Another approach to organizational change that has received considerable attention from managers is **organizational development** (OD), a term that has become something of a catchall. This process applies many of the concepts and techniques that have been developed in such varied behavioral fields as employee relations, sociology, anthropology, management training, organizational behavior, and clinical psychology. Total quality management could be considered an application of the OD process.

In a nutshell, OD is a group problem-solving process intended to bring about planned and orderly change for the purpose of improving the effectiveness of the entire culture of an organization.[43] Activities referred to as interventions are intended to aid organizational members in adapting to rapidly changing technology. Virtually any organizational problem can be a job for an OD practitioner, also known as a change agent or OD consultant, who attempts to diagnose specific problems, provide feedback to organizational members related to his or her findings, and then assist them in developing strategies and interventions for improving the total organization.

The OD Process   A key executive learns of a specific problem with productivity in the organization. An OD specialist, a member of an outside consulting firm or an in-house consultant who is assigned to a human resource department, is called in. The need for an organizational diagnosis or organizational analysis to uncover the causes of the productivity problem is identified. The OD specialist investigates the cultural aspects or norms that seem to work to the detriment of the organization's formal objectives.

The OD specialist attempts to diagnose the organization's sagging productivity through the use of surveys, personal interviews, and direct observation. Most OD practitioners attempt to remain detached during the entire process. They usually perceive their role more as a facilitator, guide, or coach than as a person imposing new systems on the organization.

After analyzing the gathered information, feedback concerning the diagnosed findings is provided to management. Possibly the workers' morale is low because they have little opportunity to share in decision making. The OD specialist and the management group members then attempt to decide which aspect of the problem demands priority attention. Guided by the practitioner, the group attempts to agree on strategies for dealing with the problem.

Remember that the OD specialist typically doesn't impose personal strategies on the organization. However, he or she does provide the tools intended to assist the group in developing its own solutions. For example, the practitioner may present short lectures or exercises related to team building, management by objectives, or other methods for modifying less desirable behavior. In some cases, new training and development programs grow out of these sessions.

THE USE OF **MBO** TO EFFECT CHANGE

Many employees fail to live up to the expectations of their bosses. Why is this? Frequently, it's because employees feel left in the dark. They're not the least bit clear on what managers expect from them, that is, what changes in their

> **Organizational Development**
> a group problem-solving process intended to bring about planned and orderly change for the purpose of improving the effectiveness of the entire culture of an organization

447

Management by Objectives

managers and subordinates mutually establish objectives and develop specific plans for their accomplishment

RIO

responsibilities, indicators, and objectives

behavior and activities are necessary to meet their bosses' standards. We saw in Chapter 3 that ineffective communication can cause organizational problems and conflict. For a manager to communicate organizational objectives to employees so that employees understand and accept them and are willing to change their behavior is far from simple.

To overcome some of these difficulties and to facilitate employee acceptance of the need for change, an approach related to participative management termed **management by objectives** (MBO) may be used. Sometimes referred to as results management, MBO's major focus is on involving managers and their subordinates jointly in developing specific goals and objectives. Naturally, estimates of future results must fit into the overall scheme of the organization's goals and objectives.

Establishing objectives mutually, of course, isn't enough. A formalized MBO approach also involves developing specific plans for accomplishing the goals, which are either agreed upon and accepted by the manager or modified by the mutual agreement of the manager and his or her subordinates. The expected results that are agreed upon then become a guide for future employee performance.

Some managers prefer to explain the MBO procedure in an understandable fashion that they refer to as the **RIO** process, illustrated in Figure 13.1. Using this technique, for example, a middle manager and a first-line supervisor could jointly develop lists of the specific areas of supervisory responsibilities, which represent the *R* in the RIO acronym. The *I* in RIO symbolizes indicators, which are documented existing conditions, such as the number of lost-time injuries in the supervisor's department. Both persons then mutually agree on measurable objectives—the *O* in RIO.

The MBO and RIO processes require managers to provide employees with periodic feedback. The manager should meet regularly with employees to tell them whether progress has been made and whether objectives need modifying. One of the key advantages of MBO is that it creates a situation in which employees tend to feel greater involvement with their work. This participative approach to management also helps employees develop more positive attitudes toward their jobs because they are able to participate in decision making that affects them directly. Of course, MBO is unlikely to succeed in a climate of distrust or when a manager fails to recognize and consider subordinates' needs in relation to the established objectives.

When applying the MBO process, a major challenge for the manager is to make certain that employees understand what constitutes realistic objectives. Statements such as "I will work harder during the forthcoming year" or "I will perform better on my job" describe desirable outcomes but are too vague to meet the basic requirements for sound objectives. Table 13.3 lists the essential ingredients of sound objectives used in the MBO process.

MANIPULATION

Change by manipulation cannot be recommended because it is unethical and because of the high risk that goes with it. Change by manipulation involves someone's pretending to use participative decision making when this person is really deceiving the participants. In the common form the manipulator would call a meeting and ask people to brainstorm ideas or solutions to a problem. The brainstorming session is to make the group members feel that they are providing their

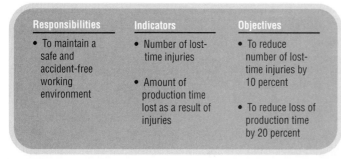

FIGURE 13.1 An example of the use of the RIO process with MBO

TABLE 13.3 BASIC REQUIREMENTS FOR ESTABLISHING SOUND OBJECTIVES IN THE MBO PROCESS

Objectives should	Examples
Contain a verb (an action)	Vague goal—I will perform better on my job.
Be specific and measurable	Objective—I will attend five advanced
Be realistic and practical	training sessions and increase my
Be attainable within a definite	productivity by 10%, with no loss of
time period	quality, by the end of the current quarter.

TABLE 13.4 COPING STRATEGIES FOR CHANGE

Acceptance	Look for the good in the change.
Learning	Thoroughly acquaint yourself with the change.
Participation	Take part in the change.
Support and assistance	Learn and use the change, then teach others.
Utilization	Use the change.
Negotiation	Try to change the change.

input and that they are involved in an important decision. The manipulator listens to all the ideas and waits for someone to suggest the option the manipulator has already decided on, or the manipulator may even guide the group toward what he or she wants. Once someone suggests the idea the manipulator picked before even calling the meeting, the manipulator declares the idea the best, thanks everyone for their efforts, and ends the meeting.

That change by manipulation is unethical because it gives people the false impression they are involved and important should be enough to convince people not to use it. Some, however, are still attracted to it, feeling that if they use it they will be able to claim to be participatory while still getting to make all the decisions themselves. This is taking a large risk. Once the manipulator is found out, and eventually he or she usually is, all trust has been destroyed forever. Once people find out they have been manipulated and used they will never believe or support the manipulator again and may even actively seek the manipulator's removal.

COPING WITH CHANGE

Six strategies can be employed when trying to cope with change: acceptance, learning, participation, support and assistance, utilization, and negotiation. These are summarized in Table 13.4.[44]

Acceptance The first strategy you might try is **acceptance**—to receive the change and regard it as fact. Sometimes accepting the change is easy, as when the color of your paycheck is changed from blue to green. When there is more substantial change, many people think of all the negative aspects, rather than simply

Acceptance

to receive the change
and regard it as fact

449

accepting the change.[45] In order for the change to be accepted, this strategy needs to be reversed. Rather than listing the negative aspects, you should look for the positive ones. There is almost always something good about any change. Looking for the good helps you to become familiar with the change, and this can turn what appeared to be a liability into an asset. At the very least, change breaks the monotony of the same old routine. If you can find nothing good about a change, then it may be time to become more familiar with it.

Learning
becoming thoroughly familiar with a change

Learning **Learning** about a change—becoming thoroughly familiar with it—can increase your understanding of it.[46] Because fear of the unknown is one of our greatest fears, a way not to fear a change is to learn about it so that it becomes known.[47] In addition to removing fear, learning about a change can help you find the positive aspects in it. In learning about a change, remember to ask questions of your manager or someone else knowledgeable about the change. If you are reluctant to ask questions of your manager for fear of looking stupid, you may be tempted to ask a coworker who knows a little or less than you. It is better to ask the manager and receive correct information than to act on incorrect or incomplete information from a colleague. Remember, managers do not expect you to understand a change thoroughly in the beginning, so you will not look foolish if you ask questions immediately. However, you may look foolish if you wait or do the wrong thing first and then go back with questions.

Participation Taking part in the decision-making process that leads to a change is an excellent way to cope with the change.[48] Not only will you be participating in the decision, but you can also help to shape the change itself. Of course, it is then difficult not to accept a change that you had a hand in designing. Still, if opportunities for participation in change decisions arise, it may be wise to participate right from the beginning. Plus, participation provides a head start toward utilization.

Support and Assistance
advocating the change to other people and teaching them the change, its benefits, and how to implement the change

Support and Assistance **Support and assistance** refers to your advocating the change to other people and teaching them about the change, about its benefits, and about its implementation.[49] Support and assistance requires you to use most of the coping strategies explained up to this point. In order to advocate change to others and teach them how to use the change, you must (1) accept the change, (2) learn about it, and (3) be able to utilize it. It is also helpful, though not required, to have participated in the decision to make the change.

Utilization
to use or implement change

Utilization Another way to cope with change is to use or implement the change.[50] **Utilization** is especially effective with new procedures or equipment.[51] Using a new piece of equipment or using a new software package enables you to cope and accept the change by actually experiencing the change and by removing any fear of the unknown. Utilizing the change is also an effective way of unfreezing the old methods as the new methods complement or replace the old way.

Negotiation
changing part of the change

Negotiation The final coping strategy for change is for those occasions when (1) you cannot cope with parts of the change and (2) it is possible to change those parts. **Negotiation** involves changing part of the change.[52] For example, suppose everyone has been given a new starting time of 8:00 A.M. However, traffic from your home is so heavy at this time that what is normally a 20-minute drive now takes 35 minutes. You may try to negotiate to start at 9:00 A.M., when traffic is

16. The trial period method of change can only work if the employees believe it is legitimate. T F
17. Training helps with implementing change; learning about it helps with coping. T F
18. Important changes should be made by manipulation. T F
19. Thinking of all the negative aspects, rather than simply accepting the change, is one way to effectively cope. T F
20. Utilizing a change is an effective way of unfreezing the old methods. T F

lighter, pointing out that you will now be staying until 5:30 P.M., and you can cover for the afternoon shift while the others go to dinner.

In coping with change, remember that change is inevitable and that it is rarely beneficial to fight change, especially modernization. In many cases, resisting change can place you at a disadvantage when compared with adaptable coworkers. Resist learning about the new computer system, and you become less valuable and more expendable. Resisting change for a long time and then catching up can be significantly more difficult, and you may be the main one to suffer. Similarly, failing to cope with change may affect you and no one else. As you seethe with rage, you are the one with the headache and the ulcer; few others, if any, will be bothered by your inability to cope. For your sake, it is quite often better to learn to cope with change than to learn to resist change.

SUMMARY

Managers need to introduce change before conditions in the organization deteriorate to the crisis stage. They must realize, however, that change affects different individuals in different ways and that people generally tend to resist changes. The reasons for such resistance are numerous, ranging from personal attitudes to habits to fear of change itself. Alert and cautious managers and change agents should attempt to familiarize themselves with the major causes of resistance and with methods to reduce resistance so they can manage change more effectively and beneficially for both management and workers. Careful attention should be paid to the unfreezing, changing, and refreezing processes of change and when to use the three-step or six-step change process.

The smoothness (or friction) with which managers introduce change is influenced significantly by their awareness and application of specific behavioral concepts. Some methods, such as directives and training, may be perfectly acceptable in one situation and totally unacceptable in another. For instance, participation or a trial period may be more appropriate than issuing a directive when you are working with highly educated and independent-minded individuals. For example, the use of employee participation in planning changes tends to achieve greater commitment on the part of the participants. The techniques of organizational development (OD) can assist managers who plan to initiate changes. Tools that can assist in effecting change and gaining greater acceptance of new ideas, processes, and goals include participation, trial periods, explaining why change is needed, and management by objectives (MBO).

Introducing change is one concern for you; coping with change is another. To thrive and survive in most, if not all, organizations you will need to be able to cope with changes. Methods for coping range from complete acceptance to negotiating a change in the change. It may not always be possible to use one of these two methods. You may, at times, need to learn as much about a change as possible or actively participate in a change, teach others about the change, or thoroughly implement the change.

CHECKING FOR UNDERSTANDING

1. How does the concept of future shock relate to organizational change?

2. How do personal attitudes influence attempts by managers to introduce change?

3. List some of your own experiences that might cause you to resist certain types of change.

4. How would your attitude toward a new laborsaving process differ if you were working part-time instead of full-time?

5. What sort of changes in your job might affect your self-esteem and the esteem in which your family and friends hold you?

6. Why are habits once established so difficult to break?

7. What causes some people to hold steadfastly to myths?

8. Outline the three-step and six-step change processes.

9. Assume that you're a manager in a firm that plans to move to a new building in the suburbs. Outline some major considerations for effecting this change with a minimum of friction among employees.

10. Why might some workers view as threatening your decision to enrich their jobs?

11. What are some of the principal benefits derived from the application of the management-by-objectives process? How does the RIO process relate to MBO?

SELF-ASSESSMENT

Answer each of the following questions about change as they relate to your work life. Answer SA when you Strongly Agree, A when you Agree, N when you are neutral or not sure, D when you disagree, and SD when you strongly disagree.

1. I look forward to change.   SA   A   N   D   SD

2. Once I learn something I stay with it for as long as possible.   SA   A   N   D   SD

3. Using outdated technology bothers me.   SA   A   N   D   SD

4. Change scares me. SA   A   N   D   SD

5. I enjoy learning new methods of performing my job. SA   A   N   D   SD

6. There is no good time to change.   SA   A   N   D   SD

7. I trust that change is for the best.   SA   A   N   D   SD

8. I'll go slowly learning a change to get back at management for all the bad things they have done to me.   SA   A   N   D   SD

9. I want to be part of change decisions.   SA   A   N   D   SD

10. I don't see why things always have to be changing. SA   A   N   D   SD

11. I like to be the first one with something new.   SA   A   N   D   SD

12. If it's not broken, don't change it.   SA   A   N   D   SD

13. Change is progress.   SA   A   N   D   SD

14. I've never seen a change that did me any good.   SA   A   N   D   SD

15. Just because it works doesn't mean it can't be made to be better.   SA   A   N   D   SD

16. If a change meant seeing less of my friends at work, I would consider quitting.   SA   A   N   D   SD

17. When change comes, I just go with it.   SA   A   N   D   SD

18. Change is a hassle that I would prefer not to have to deal with.   SA   A   N   D   SD

19. Change will happen anyway, so I don't fight it.
SA A N D SD

20. As soon as I get good at something, they change it, and I just don't understand that; we should stick with what we know. SA A N D SD

For all odd-numbered items score 2 for every SA, 1 for very A, 0 for every N, −1 for every D, and −2 for every SD.

For all even-numbered items score −2 for every SA, −1 for very A, 0 for every N, −1 for every D, and −2 for every SD. Total your score. A score of 31–40 indicates that you embrace change, 11–30 indicates that you value change, 10–−10 shows you are ambivalent toward change, −11–−30 indicates discomfort with change, and −31–−40 indicates you dislike change.

SKILL BUILD 13

Nikolai Tekla switched on the department-wide intercom and 3 managers, 12 supervisors, and 107 workers stopped everything to listen to their chief information officer.

Skill Question 1. Why might Tekla's action cause resistance to change (which resistance-to-change factor is this an example of)?

"Your attention please, just for a moment. I have good news. As I have mentioned a number of times before, I have been working on a new system to replace the 11-volume procedure manual that you all refer to on a daily basis. As your CIO I have taken it upon myself to make this decision: Over the next month we will switch from the current printed manual to an Internet-based manual accessible through the new iMac computers you will all be receiving at your work stations," Tekla said.

Skill Question 2. What method of accomplishing change is Tekla using?

Tekla continued, "Believe it or not, this will actually save money, as the multiple printings of the manual each year were getting extremely expensive. I'm sure you all have computers at home and will figure out these Macs on your own. You can keep the printed manuals until you do. In nine months I'll check in to see how things are going. That is all."

Skill Question 3. What was the first step of the three-step change management process that was *not* attended to in this situation?

Skill Question 4. What should have been done that would have addressed this step, and why would this have been difficult to do?

After the stunned silence ended, everyone started talking at once. Many said they would keep using the print manuals as long as possible.

Skill Question 5. Which resistance-to-change factor is this?

Some were scared that they wouldn't be able to figure out the computers or that it would mean there would be layoffs or that productivity would have to increase, and some weren't sure what they were uneasy about.

Skill Question 6. Which resistance-to-change factor is this?

Others threw down their phones and pencils and said that if this was the way things were, they were going to act like it was day one, like they knew nothing and would have to be shown everything all over again.

Skill Question 7. What one method of resistance to change is shown here?

Some of the respected high-seniority people said they were against it, the print manuals were working okay, so what was the point in switching? Many of these people said they would be very reluctant to start new ways of doing things.

Skill Question 8. Which resistance-to-change factor is this?

Some of the supervisors and even a couple of managers said they didn't quite get how things would work because now while one person was on the phone, two others would be looking up the information in the manuals for him or her.

Skill Question 9. Which resistance-to-change factor is this?

With this new system would each and every person get a computer? The supervisors and managers didn't think that was needed or affordable. And then what? Was someone going to be on the phone, and two people would look things up on the computers, or just one, or just the person on the phone? They just didn't get how things were supposed to work.

Skill Question 10. This company really needs your help with this change. Look at each step in the larger scale change model, in order. Which one or ones were addressed here, and which one or ones were not?

Skill Question 11. What should these workers do now to cope with this change?

APPLICATIONS

13.1 THE PRECISION PARAMETER COMPANY

The Precision Parameter Company is an electronics firm whose general offices are located in Sunnyvale, California. The firm has separate divisions located in Annandale, Virginia, and Tempe, Arizona, each involved with similar activities and employing approximately 175 to 200 people. The company is principally a manufacturer of components for electronics equipment, such as computer chips that turn personal computers into videophones.

Mary Levin, an in-house organizational development practitioner, recently analyzed statistical data from each manufacturing unit and discovered a wide discrepancy between the activities of the Tempe plant and those of its Annandale counterpart. Levin discovered that at the Tempe plant:

1. The rate of employee turnover was nearly double.
2. The incidence of accidents on the job was 35 percent higher.
3. Absenteeism was three times higher.
4. There was 65 percent more tardiness.

Levin asked the plant managers of both locations to supply her with production figures and discovered that the Tempe plant also had:

1. Lower levels of production
2. Higher levels of wasted materials and customer-rejected products

Levin decided to call the two plant managers, Charles Drocco of Annandale and Jim Albritton of Tempe, to Sunnyvale for a conference. The following conversation took place during the meeting.

Levin: Gentlemen, each of us here is interested in furthering the goals and objectives of the Precision Parameter Company. I want you to know that I haven't called this meeting to criticize anyone, merely to uncover some information so that we can improve our operations at all of our locations in the future.

I personally feel that people are one of our most important resources. I also feel that we might be able to do a more effective job of managing if we know more about the attitudes of our employees at the production level, and so. . .

Albritton: Ms. Levin, with all due respect to you, Ma'am, I know exactly what you're gonna say. I've been through sessions like this before with "OverDose" specialists and, well, they're all just about alike. They sit up there smugly in their office towers dreaming up new ideas. You're gonna tell me that my division isn't operating as efficiently as Charles's, aren't you? Well, I wanna tell you this. His situation is completely different from mine. You can't get the same types of employees in Tempe that you get in Virginia. They're all either young people who have lost the good, old-fashioned work ethic that we all used to have, or they're old and ready to retire, rock back and forth in their chairs, and bask in the warm Arizona sun. I know those production employees. Heck, I used to be one of 'em myself. All they're interested in is their paychecks.

Levin: Jim, there certainly is the possibility that employment conditions are different in your area, but I want to assure you that I'm not here to criticize. Nothing is perfect, but perhaps we three can put our heads together and come up with some ideas on how we might improve things.

What I'd like is for us to attempt to develop materials that we might incorporate into an employee attitude survey. If we can find out what our employees like and don't like about working for Precision, then perhaps we'll be in a better position to manage more effectively and to retain valuable employees. Let's give it a good, positive effort. What do you say?

QUESTIONS

1. What is your reaction to the way in which Mary Levin conducted the meeting?

2. What do Jim Albritton's statements reveal about his attitude toward workers in his plant? In what ways might he be contributing to the poor results at the Tempe plant?

3. Assume that you are Mary Levin. What broad areas of employee concern would you include in an attitude survey? Develop a list of survey questions that could apply to each of these broad categories.

4. How can the information uncovered in the survey help the managers improve working conditions?

13.2 MODERNIZING CHANGE

Bernard "Bernie" Prentiss and his sister Emma took over the operation of A Step Up—Custom Stairbuilders four months ago from their father, who retired to Hawaii. Bernie is upset because he ordered and had installed three computer-controlled lathes for turning their own balusters and four computer-controlled saws for cutting treads and risers, but they are not being used. Both Bernie and Emma are a little stumped for an answer because both the lathes and the saws use the same teams as the old machines—three people for each lathe and two for each saw. Bernie called together the upper managers, which in addition to Emma and himself include Carlos Lopez, sales manager; Kelly Wilde, the accountant; and Clyde Bressett, production and installation manager.

Bernie: I'm trying to modernize this place, and it's not happening, and I want to know why it isn't and how we can get it done. What is with these people? Carlos, you and Stan Hall have been here for nearly 30 years. Have you talked to him? Why won't he get his team on the new lathes?

Carlos: I did talk to him. He said he could run his old machine blindfolded, and since he is 62 he says he would prefer to just keep on doing things the way he always has until he retires. He said maybe the youngsters would like to try the "new-fangled" gizmos.

Bernie: *Youngsters!* All the young workers are installers, and they are waiting for the old production guys to retire! We have no young production people.

Clyde: I heard a bunch of those guys said they would quit before they used the new machines. And I know why Joe Tashinski won't want to use them, even though I think he has a little home version of the saw of his own.

Bernie: He knows how but won't! Why?

Clyde: He might not know the new machines perfect, but he has an idea. He won't because he is still mad at your dad for not giving him my job when we were both up for it.

Emma: But that was over 10 years ago!

Clyde: Eleven. And Rich Pearson told me he's real nervous around those machines. Says he doesn't know what they are thinking or what they might do next. Said if he can't take it apart and see how it works, he doesn't trust it.

Kelly: Oh, this is ridiculous. Bernie, you and Emma just go in there and tell those people they will use that equipment—orders from the top!

Emma: We can't do that. They don't know how. We need to bring someone in to show them exactly how to work this stuff.

Clyde: What do we do when they all quit like they said they would? We are coming up on the busy season and would never get enough replacements in time. I say we get them together and lay it out like the old stuff is breaking, maybe break a few ourselves, then let them come to our decision.

Carlos: You mean trick them? No. I don't think they will leave either. They have too many years, in and other than home building, the economy is not good. Where would they go? I say we get rid of the supervisors—there aren't too many—and we bring up some young installers. Let them make the change; workers will expect it anyway.

Clyde: What about the order forms? We are still using the old ones. We throw those out and use the computer set-up order forms. It would take them forever to get the measurements off those and written up for the old machines. Then they would have to use the new ones.

Carlos: But our contractors all use the old forms. We could lose their business if we try to make them switch. We need to keep both. We use old forms with existing contractors and new computer forms with new ones.

Emma: Almost all of our business is from current customers. It will take years before we use the new equipment that way.

Bernie: Well, we need to decide on something, even if it takes all night.

QUESTIONS

1. This situation includes five different resistance-to-change factors. Four are impeding this change, and one is being left alone and so is not contributing to resistance. List all five, identify the four that will impede change and the one that will not, and support your answer with information from the case.

2. Bernie and Emma failed to unfreeze the existing situation. Describe this failure as it is revealed in the case.

3. Clyde, Carlos, Emma, and Kelly each propose a different change method. What does each of them suggest? Support your answer with information from the case.

4. Of the four change methods proposed at the meeting, which one should they choose and why should they use it?

NET-WORK

Should you change jobs?

http://www.youtube.com/watch?v=trhAs0qk4yE

You should change jobs

http://www.youtube.com/watch?v=M1owcncKCHg&mode=related&search=

PERSONAL POINTS

1. When you find out a change is imminent, do you prepare to change or do you prepare excuses for not changing? Why?

2. If you are facing change and fear of the unknown, what do you do to relieve your uncertainty? What should you do?

3. If people do not understand a change, what do you do to clarify the change and the reasons for the change? What should you do?

4. Have you ever quit a job or thought about quitting as an escape mechanism to avoid

a change? If you quit, how were you better off? If you just thought about it, were you better off not quitting and why or why not?

5. If you question proposed changes, is it an attempt to avoid the change or are you questioning what seems like a pseudochange? How can you tell the difference? How can you question pseudochange without making it seem like resistance to change?

EXPERIENTIAL EXERCISE

Is This Change Really Necessary?

Analyze conditions on your job and develop some ideas for a change that is long overdue. Carefully answer the questions that follow related to your proposed change. If you currently do not work or lack ample authority to carry out such changes, answer the questions based on the hypothetical assumption that you do have a job and do have sufficient authority.

If you have the opportunity, before actually carrying out the change, gather in groups of five students who have also performed this exercise. Each person then takes a turn at presenting his or her proposed change to the other group members, who then provide feedback and a constructive analysis of the proposal.

Nature of Change

1. How will this change improve the operation of the company and the quality of work life of the employees?

2. Has the change been thoroughly thought out, and is it the best of the alternatives available?

3. Does the change represent an emotional overreaction, or is it a necessary new direction? Explain.

4. Why is this change necessary?

5. Who will be affected by the change?

6. What are the long-range consequences of the change?

7. Is the change consistent with your personal and organizational philosophy?

SPOT CHECK ANSWERS

1. T
2. T
3. T
4. F
5. F
6. F
7. F
8. T
9. T
10. T
11. T
12. T
13. F
14. T
15. T
16. T
17. T
18. F
19. F
20. T

14 | Leadership

No institution can possibly survive if it needs geniuses or supermen to manage it. It must be organized in such a way as to be able to get along under a leadership composed of average human beings.

Peter Drucker

You do not lead by hitting people over the head—that's assault, not leadership.

Dwight Eisenhower

To lead people, give them a reason to follow you and the freedom to do so.

Michael Drafke

GOALS

The main goal of this chapter is to introduce you to the concept of leadership. Today more than ever, leaders are found outside the ranks of management. No matter what your position, you may be called upon to lead a group, small or large. This chapter will demonstrate how you can begin to develop the necessary skills.

OBJECTIVES

When you finish this chapter, you should be able to:

▶ Define leadership.

▶ Differentiate among authority, responsibility, and accountability.

▶ Explain where power comes from.

▶ Differentiate between leadership and management.

▶ List the traits and behavior sets of leaders.

▶ Define and differentiate between transformation and contingency leadership methods.

▶ Differentiate between Theory X and Theory Y leaders.

▶ Compare the major styles of leadership.

▶ Describe the Vroom–Yetton continuum of manager–subordinate involvement.

▶ Identify the skills that are fundamental for effective management.

▶ List methods for building trust.

▶ Summarize four ways in which managers can improve their leadership skills.

INTRODUCTION

You are in a room with five other people who were chosen at random to work on a problem. No one seems to know what to do, what the exact problem is, how long the group has to work, or how to even begin. You soon find that you are emerging as the only person willing to take charge. You find that you are able to influence the other members of the group in certain ways. Your group, therefore, is an organization, albeit a tiny one, from which a leader has evolved.

Organizations, even small ones, tend to develop leaders, that is, people who influence others. Can you imagine how difficult the fulfillment of organizational goals would be if there were no specified individuals with the authority and responsibility to plan, organize, coordinate, lead, and control their activities?

THE FUNCTIONS AND CHARACTERISTICS OF LEADERSHIP

Perhaps we'd better attach a meaning to the term *leadership*, which has no simple definition applicable to all situations. As you will shortly discover, a variety of leadership styles may be applied effectively to different situations.

LEADERSHIP DEFINED

Leadership
the ability to influence the activities of others, through the process of communication, toward the attainment of a goal

Leadership has been described as "the ability to influence the activities of others, through the process of communication, toward the attainment of a goal."[1] This definition might strike you at first as being somewhat manipulative, but think carefully about your own behavior. To accomplish some of your personal goals, don't you regularly try to influence the behavior of others to accomplish something specific? Basically, the attempt to influence behavior is a key element of leadership. Your objectives don't have to be insidious or negative when leadership techniques are being employed.

Also, note the word *communication* in the definition. Direction takes place through communication, and leadership requires you to provide others with direction. Your associates are unlikely to comply if you can't communicate your plans, as outstanding as they may be.

THE DIFFERENCE BETWEEN LEADERSHIP AND MANAGEMENT

It is perhaps not obvious that there are differences between leadership and management, although these terms are frequently used interchangeably. Leadership deals directly with people and their behavior; it's only one aspect of management. Management, a broader concept, includes the activity of leadership but may also involve nonbehavioral functions that don't directly or immediately affect others. Management is concerned with global issues, such as keeping the organization running, and works well with hierarchies; leadership involves the initiation of actions and expediting change. Ultimately, management is a process of planning, organizing, coordinating, leading, and controlling the activities of others.

Leadership is concerned with gaining the voluntary participation of others, while management combines leadership and motivation in the directing function and also adds the planning, controlling, and organizing functions.[2] Leadership is concerned with moving people toward a vision, but management is grounded more in the present. Leadership involves creatively inspiring people when management is more focused on rational productivity. Leadership is more about getting people excited, up out of their chairs and moving, and management is more about getting the job done on a daily basis. Leaders may or may not manage, and managers may or may not lead. Managers usually should lead; a manager who does not lead may be called an administrator (someone who ensures the workers have what is needed so they can get the job done). Administrators are more often found in professional bureaucracies such as law, medical, architectural firms, and colleges.

FORMAL LEADERSHIP

A person may be either promoted or transferred to a position of **formal leadership** from within an organization or may be recruited specifically for the particular position from a source outside the organization. To ensure the future availability of leaders from within the organization, management development or succession programs are often provided.

The formal leadership of an organization can generally be discovered by looking at a company's organization chart. Organization charts are formal documents that serve as guides to authority relationships established in organizations. They also show official titles that have been assigned to managers.

Time out for some clarification of terms. Three words used regularly around work organizations and related to leadership are *authority, responsibility*, and *accountability*. Each term is significant to the formal organization but has a distinct meaning.

Authority is the right or power delegated to people in an organization to make decisions, act, and direct others to act. It is also sometimes referred to as empowerment (a term to be discussed in greater detail later). For example, a supervisor might have the authority to schedule the work of others, determine who works overtime, approve vacation schedules, and authorize certain purchases. Authority, therefore, is something that is passed down—that is assigned or delegated—to people by their bosses.

Responsibility, on the other hand, is not a right; it is a duty. It is the obligation someone has to perform assigned work or to make certain that someone else performs it in a prescribed way. The plural form, *responsibilities*, usually refers to the specific tasks or duties that have been assigned to an employee to perform.

Accountability is the answerability of an employee to his or her boss. Bosses, of course, are answerable to their own bosses. (The term *accountability* is sometimes used interchangeably with *responsibility*.)

Try to visualize that authority and accountability flow in different directions. As you can observe in the simplified organization chart in Figure 14.1, authority flows downward from the president to the workers. For example, Ms. Ton, the company president, has delegated to Mr. Gonzales, the plant manager, the right to make decisions necessary to run the plant. Furthermore, Ton has assigned Gonzales the responsibility to operate the plant in a profitable manner. Gonzales later delegates work-scheduling duties to a supervisor, Ms. Steinberg, who has organized her department into a team. She has empowered the workers in her team to conduct scheduling activities on their own. Keep in mind that accountability flows upward. Therefore, the workers are accountable to Steinberg for the results they achieve with their scheduling activities. Steinberg is accountable to the plant manager, Gonzales, for the results related to the scheduling activities in her department. Gonzales is accountable to Ton for the overall results achieved in the plant.

Formal Leadership

leadership arising from an organization to accomplish organizational objectives

---

Authority

the right or power delegated to people in an organization to make decisions, act, and direct others to act

---

Responsibility

the obligation someone has to perform assigned work or to make certain that someone else performs it in a prescribed way

---

Accountability

the answerability of an employee to his or her boss

Power

the ability to command resources

Personal Power

an individual's power

Institutional Power

power from an organization

Charisma

the power and ability developed by some individuals to influence and win the devotion and respect of others; the power that emanates from a special quality of personal magnetism or charm that some individuals appear to possess

Expert Power

power from knowledge

Coercive Personal Power

power from the threat of physical harm

Coercive Institutional Power

power from nonphysical threats

Reward Power

power from the ability to give people things that they want

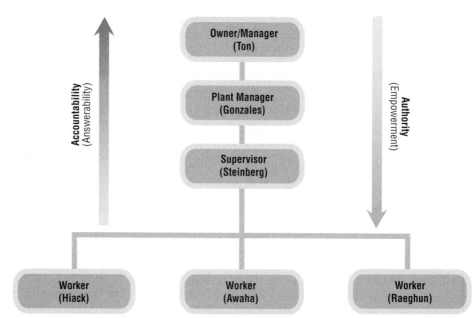

FIGURE 14.1 ACCOUNTABILITY FLOWS UPWARD; AUTHORITY FLOWS DOWNWARD

POWER

Power is the ability to command resources. Recall in the chapter on understanding management that there are four general resources: people, supplies and materials, money, and information. The more of these one controls, the more power one has. Power comes from two sources: personal power and institutional power. **Personal power** originates with the individual, while **institutional power** comes from organizations (although ultimately it comes from laws that give owners the right to control their resources; the owners may then delegate that right to others, typically managers). Both personal and institutional power have three sources, and while some people have personal power and others institutional, it is quite common for people to have both.

Personal power can be divided into charismatic, expert, and coercive power.[3] Charismatic personal power (sometimes called referent power) obviously comes from someone having **charisma**—the power and ability developed by some individuals to influence and win the devotion and respect of others. It is the power that emanates from a special quality of personal magnetism or charm that some individuals appear to possess. **Expert power** comes from knowledge. In organizations, this most commonly comes from job knowledge resulting from education or experience or both, but even trivia experts can derive some expert power from what they know. **Coercive personal power** is threat-based power that comes from the possibility of someone's doing others physical harm. A few people in organizations might try this, but it is not common even though media coverage of the extremes of workplace violence receives much attention.

Institutional power also has three parts: coercive, reward, and legitimate.[4] **Coercive institutional power** is threat-based, like coercive personal power, but coercive institutional threats are not physical. This coercive power is centered on punishment or the threat of punishment and might involve firing or suspending someone, giving the person unpleasant work or undesired hours, withholding a raise or bonus, or just threatening to take any of these actions. **Reward power** is much the opposite—the ability to give, rather than withhold, things people want. This might include something as small as giving someone the break time he or she wishes and may range up to the ability to give people raises, promotions, transfers, or even the initial job itself. Finally, legitimate power is essentially authority. **Legitimate power** is derived from one's position in the organization. It is commonly accepted that, at least as far as this one dimension of power is concerned, those near the apex of the organization chart have more power than those at the base.

Having power from any of these six sources is different from using power. The first thing one should keep in mind is this: Power can only be used on those who allow it to be. In other words, no one can make anyone do anything he or she doesn't agree to. In the most extreme, if someone is pointing a gun at you, and you are willing to take a chance on, or pay the price of, being shot, you can't be made to do anything you don't want to do. Granted that is a rare occurrence, but if a manager tells a worker to do something, and that worker is willing to take any situation to the limit of being fired, the manager will be unable to make the worker do anything the worker does not want to do. The manager will have no power over such a worker. Knowing this, where is the real power in any organization?

A second thing to keep in mind about power is that it should never be abused. Abuse of power is a quick way to get others to refuse to let the abuser use his or her power over them. To avoid abusing power, it is best to use one's power only when it is necessary. Some people seem to like to use their power because they can, but the wise person uses power only when it is required. In situations where using power is not absolutely necessary, the wise person uses leadership to accomplish goals.

HOW IMPORTANT ARE LEADERS?

A preoccupation with the topic of leadership has become noticeable in the business press in recent years. Some management authorities have contended that the United States has not a shortage of management but, instead, a shortage of leaders in contemporary organizations. They also contend that corporate America has been on the receiving end of an onslaught of challenging changes, such as global competition, takeover threats, rapid technological change, revolution in management–labor relationships, and fears that the United States is declining as an international economic powerhouse. Such factors, it has been argued, have greatly increased the need for corporations to evolve and adapt. As a result, the need for unusually creative leaders to deal with these challenges has become significant.[5]

WHAT MAKES PEOPLE LEADERS?

Neither the titles that some individuals have been assigned nor their positions on formal organization charts are what make some individuals leaders. To function as leaders, they must have an emotional appeal that instills in other people the desire to follow them. Leaders will be able to lead only when they can effectively influence people over extended periods of time. Many famous titular heads of countries have fallen or have been forced to resign after losing their ability to influence others effectively, especially after losing the confidence of their public. Leaders everywhere are much more likely to retain the support of their followers when their behavior sets a good example.

The behavior set that is present in many leaders includes the following:[6]

- confidence
- honesty

Legitimate Power power from one's position in an organization

NetNote

Organizational Power

http://www.geocities.com/ Athens/Forum/1650/ htmlpower.html

Detailed article on power.

DILBERT

Source: DILBERT: © Scott Adams/Dist. by United Features Syndicate, Inc.

- assertiveness
- enthusiasm
- self-awareness
- extroversion
- intelligence
- initiative
- achievement
- decisiveness

Although the primary responsibility of leaders is to achieve the objectives of their organizations, they are less likely to do so if they don't also meet the needs of their followers. Even in military organizations, where the formal organization can be extremely significant, we can find numerous examples of designated leaders who have lost their ability to influence their subordinates effectively. There are historic examples of second lieutenants, for example, who have shouted "Charge!" at the tops of their lungs as they rushed frantically up a hill, but the gold-plated bars on their neatly laundered battle dress didn't guarantee that their troops would follow; sometimes they didn't.

CHARISMATIC LEADERS

Some people are able to influence others substantially, at least in the short run, as a result of their having what is termed *charismatic authority*. Individuals with charisma may be designated formally as leaders, or they may completely lack any formal authority within the organization. They are people who enjoy power and influence over others because of their ability to inspire personal trust and confidence. Followers tend to identify with them.

SPOT CHECK

1. Leadership is defined as arranging resources to achieve organizational goals. T F
2. Responsibility is the answerability of an employee to his or her boss. T F
3. Power is the right to make decisions, act, and direct others to act. T F
4. Expert power is derived from one's position in an organization. T F
5. Legitimate power is derived from one's position in the organization. T F

Both John F. Kennedy and Ronald Reagan were charismatic leaders. President Kennedy especially seemed to have the ability to inspire the youth of the United States during his short tenure as president (although he tended not to be perceived in the same charismatic manner by much of the business community). President Reagan, with his special type of personal magnetism, was able to retain his popularity through far more of a second term than were most of his predecessors. Sometimes referred to as "the great communicator," Ronald Reagan greatly enhanced his public image through his polished ability to communicate.

TRANSFORMATIONAL LEADERS

Transformational leaders are defined by their accomplishments.[7] Achievements are looked at instead of individual characteristics. The changes a leader brings about would be an example of a transformation. This type of leader would help others achieve goals and earn rewards by explaining the larger view of the organization so others could understand it and their role in realizing it. Recalling Maslow's hierarchy, the transformational leader would help people to reach self-actualization.

The types of activities transformational leaders are associated with include creating an imperative for immediate change. They also take the long view, however, as when they make a commitment to excellence. With a long-term view they also take a broad view of the organization's goals and accomplishments. The broad and long-term views are then combined into a vision. The vision must then not only be communicated, but also must inspire others. To this end, the transformational leader typically uses charisma, but it is used as one of several tools, rather than as the main or only tool.

CONTINGENCY AND SITUATIONAL LEADERS

There are several contingency or situational leadership methods with at least one shared element—each believes that the leadership may need to change depending on the situation one is faced with. One method believes that the leader himself or herself might need to be changed depending on the situation; at least two others propose that it is possible to keep the same leader, but that person would have to lead differently. The three methods described here are: Fred Fielder's contingency theory, the Hershey-Blanchard situational model, and Robert House's path–goal theory.

465

Fielder's Contingency Theory Fielder believes that each leader has a style that cannot really be changed. Fielder's theory, then, is to find the style of each leader and assign that leader to a situation that needs or matches that style.[8] Employing Fielder's theory starts with leaders' completing the "least preferred coworker" assessment. This evaluates how well or how poorly they would work with the coworker they like the least. If the assessment shows that they would actually work fairly well even with the person they like least, then they are relationship motivated. If they do not have a very complimentary view of the person they like least, then they are classified as task motivated.

Assigning the leader is a little more complicated even when his or her classification is known. According to Fielder, the leader's performance is related to how favorable the situation is with regard to relations, tasks, and the leader's power. In a situation where there are good relations and structured tasks and where the leader can exert control, a task-motivated leader should do well. Here, the task leader just needs to provide direction and vision. A task-motivated leader should also do well, however, in a situation with poor relationships and tasks that are not structured and where the leader has little positional power. Here a strong task leader can bring order. The relationship leaders are suited for the middle—between the extremes—where favorable and unfavorable elements are present and only moderate control is needed.[9] Since Fielder believes leaders cannot change their methods, when a situation doesn't match the leader, a new person needs to be brought in.

Hershey–Blanchard Situational Model This model differs significantly from Fielder's in that it contends that leaders can change their leadership methods. It goes on to prescribe the method that is needed for each situation. The model first requires the leader to examine the followers and essentially assess their ableness and willingness. Their ableness refers to their education, training, and capability of performing their work. Their willingness refers to how agreeable they are to accepting responsibility for their actions. Those who are highly willing can work autonomously; those who are unwilling can't or won't work autonomously. The two possibilities for those two factors create four possible situations, each needing a different leadership style.[10]

Followers who are unable and unwilling will require a classical, Theory X leader (which some might say is a manager rather than a leader; see the following section). These followers can't do the work because they have little or no training, education, and experience, nor are they willing to work autonomously (and they couldn't, even if they wished to). They need to be shown *the* way and supervised closely. Those who are unable but willing to work on their own need a trainer/coach style of leadership. They need to be shown how and then have their confidence built up so they can work independently. One might face this situation with educated workers or professionals learning new skills; they want to do the work, but the skill is too new for this, so instruction and practice are needed.

Those who are able but unwilling need a participatory, Theory Y leader (see the following section). An example might be a group of able workers facing a change they do not relish making. They need someone who will involve them in the change process so they stop resisting and become willing. The last situation involves those who are able and willing. This calls for inspirational leadership, a leader who will provide the spark, direction, and vision to keep the followers moving ahead.

Path-Goal Theory Robert House's theory also includes the idea that a manager can and should adapt his or her leadership style to the circumstances. Path–goal theory is similar to the expectancy theory of motivation (see Chapter 11). Path–goal theory starts by stating that a leader should determine the path people need to follow in order to achieve organizational and personal goals. Then the leader should determine what rewards each person would want to receive when the goals are reached and provide those rewards. The leader also selects one of four styles to use to facilitate achieving goals.[11]

The four leader styles in path–goal theory are the directive, supportive, participative, and achieving.[12] The directive style is essentially classical Theory X management/leadership (see the following section). The supportive style is used with highly stressful, frustrating work lacking in job satisfaction or with followers who lack confidence. The supportive leader provides assistance, empathy, and encouragement. The participative style is basically the behavioral, Theory Y, group-decision-making style (see the next section). The achieving style is used with autonomous workers. The leaders set lofty goals that require followers to constantly maximize their efforts to improve and produce. This style works well with those who desire and respond to new challenges.

TRADITIONAL LEADERSHIP

The perceptual tests we examined in Chapter 2 showed us that our perception is not always accurate. Perceiving drawings and photographs, however, is often far less hazardous than perceiving human beings. Have you ever noticed that some managers tend to perceive their employees in positive or favorable ways and others in negative or suspicious ways? If you were a manager, how would you perceive the people who worked with you? Read through the following sets of statements labeled "Theory X Attitudes" and "Theory Y Attitudes," which describe management attitudes devised by Douglas McGregor. Which of the two sets of attitudes seem to fit your conceptual scheme toward others?

Theory X Attitudes

1. Most employees dislike work and will avoid it whenever they can.
2. Because most people dislike work, they have to be pushed, closely supervised, and threatened with punishment to get them to help achieve the objectives of the organization.
3. Most people are basically lazy, have little ambition, prefer to avoid responsibility, and desire security as a major goal.
4. The typical worker is self-centered and has little concern for organizational goals.

Theory Y Attitudes

1. Most people find work as natural as play or rest, and their attitude toward work is related to their experiences with it.
2. People don't have to be threatened with punishment to be motivated to help an organization accomplish its goals. They will be somewhat self-directed when they are able to relate to the objectives of the organization.
3. Within a favorable organizational culture, the average person learns not only to accept but also to seek responsibility.
4. A large part of our working force has the ability to exercise imagination and creativity on the job.

With which set of statements did you feel more in agreement: X or Y? Would you personally be considered an X-rated or a Y-rated person if you were a manager? Read on for a better understanding of the implications of X and Y types of attitudes.

X AND Y LABELS

Don't be confused by the letters X and Y, which are merely labels assigned by Professor Douglas McGregor to two general ways in which workers may be perceived by managers.[13] Theory X, as you may have discerned, takes a somewhat negative view of humanity. Theory Y, in contrast, begins with the premise that workers will do far more than is expected of them if treated like human beings and permitted to experience personal satisfaction on the job. Theory Y does not represent the extreme backslapping managers who bend over backward to be regarded as nice guys.

If your set of attitudes falls into Theory X, you fit into the pattern of the more traditional manager/leader. Theory Y, however, is the result of newer and more positive assumptions that many managers/leaders have developed in recent years. An increasing number of leaders have discarded the traditional attitudes. Because your beliefs significantly influence the way you work with and through people, as well as their feelings of motivation, an understanding of the two views is important.

DERIVED-X THEORY

Many managers believe (or at least hope) that their approach to leadership is the correct one. Many managers are sincerely interested in adopting a more positive stance in their managerial activities, but, unfortunately, their previous experiences have caused them to develop an attitude that we'll call Derived X, or the "I've been burned" theory. The following illustration should make this theory clear: A single person falls deeply in love but soon thereafter is abandoned and deeply hurt. The individual who has been ditched may have had optimistic and positive attitudes about love, but if such disappointing experiences recur regularly, the person may shift to a Theory X position in future relationships.

REALITY CHECK

Leadership Paradoxes

If being a leader were easy, everyone would do it. One of the more difficult aspects involves handling three leadership paradoxes. The first paradox concerns those opposing your leadership. In order to lead, it is often necessary to allow everyone to provide input, including those who oppose your leadership. Typically they oppose you because they have something to lose if your leadership involves changes, and that something is often power. So how do you allow everyone to have input but keep skeptics, critics, and cynics at bay? One answer is to draw any opponents into the process while keeping them separate from one another. In this way, the group or groups exert peer pressure to bring them along to your (and their) way of thinking.

The second paradox involves your vision as a leader. While you wish to move rapidly forward toward your vision, others can get bogged down in the details. You may say "Go forward," while others ask "How?" The result is, you wish to go toward your vision, but you feel you can't until you explain how. If you stop to explain all the details of how, you will never move toward your vision. The recommendation is not for you as leader to provide the detail; instead, you establish methods to measure how your people are progressing toward the vision—they will have to manage the details in order to progress.

The third paradox involves leading change—people who are afraid of change will only change when they feel safe, but they mostly feel safe when they don't have to change. To overcome this paradox, it helps to give them enough authority and responsibility to take ownership of their work and to provide them with a complete understanding of what is expected of them.

Source: Adapted from Thomas Stewart, "How to Lead a Revolution," *Fortune,* November 28, 1994, p. 57.

The same holds true for managers who might try to maintain optimistic and positive attitudes toward subordinates but are "burned" in the process. The following is a list of attitudes that can be derived from negative experiences with employees:

Derived X (the "I've been burned" theory)

1. I want to feel that people are conscientious and find work a natural activity, but I've been burned too many times by some of my employees.
2. I've given my subordinates the chance to make decisions and to assume responsibility, but I've been burned too many times. They've simply taken advantage of me.
3. I've tried to create an atmosphere of growth and development for my subordinates by giving them the freedom to make mistakes and to fail, but I've been burned too many times. They haven't grown and developed; they've merely made mistakes and failed.
4. I've tried to get workers to participate in planning activities for achieving organizational goals, but I've been burned too many times. They're more interested in paydays than in accomplishing organizational goals.

If you find yourself shifting from a Y position to a Derived X, you could probably benefit from an attempt to analyze your own situation thoroughly. Could present notions about your subordinates possibly cause your shifting attitude? Are you truly concerned about your employees, and are you really trying to do something for them, or is your concern merely lip service? Remember that you're likely to be judged more by your behavior than by your words.

Of course, a manager must be realistic. You're likely to be burned occasionally. Undoubtedly, some workers aren't self-directed and self-controlled. Some workers do prefer security to responsibility. Some employees prefer to seek satisfaction during their leisure time and view their jobs as merely the means to non-work-related ends. But in spite of these realities, try to retain a certain degree of sensitivity. Be realistic in your feelings but sensitive in your behavior. You must have a certain amount of trust in subordinates; you can't search all workers as they leave the premises each day. Few people want to work in an atmosphere of suspicion.

Traditional Leadership   Have you ever had a boss who was a negative leader? This type of boss attempts to motivate through fear and believes that workers must be forced to cooperate and produce, mainly because "People are just no damn good!" Managers who exercise negative or **traditional leadership**, a more traditional approach toward subordinates, tend to engage in excessively close supervision and find it difficult to delegate work. As a result, much of their time is spent putting out fires and checking the work of subordinates instead of carrying out essential management functions such as planning, organizing, coordinating, leading, and controlling. In contrast, current standards of leadership include influencing human behavior in an uncertain world.[14]

Traditional Leadership
leadership through fear and intimidation

Fear and Motivation   Workers who operate in an aura of fear may be productive in the short run, but in the long run their morale is likely to be adversely affected, to the predictable detriment of the quantity and quality of their output. Often, subordinates who work under negative leaders devote much of their time to trying to protect themselves from the boss by keeping unnecessary records in case they must prove later that "It wasn't my mistake, Boss!" Workers on the receiving end of negative motivation may appear to be cooperative but are often searching for the opportunity to put one over on their supervisors. Turnover ratios of company personnel tend to be considerably higher in organizations in which the climate is filled with tension and fear, thus substantially increasing the training and operative costs of the work unit.

Behavioral Leadership
the application of
positive techniques of
leadership

Behavioral Leadership   Modern managers have learned that the application of more positive techniques of leadership is more effective with subordinates. **Behavioral leadership** assumes that most people will want to do good work if shown the reasons for their efforts. Such managers attempt to increase, rather than decrease, the satisfaction of their subordinates. Being positive doesn't mean that you're soft in your application of discipline. You can be positive and still be firm in your application of company policies and rules. An important point, however, for the positive leader is to treat employees with fairness and respect.

Positive leaders attempt to explain why a job is to be done rather than to coerce a person into doing it. Effective leaders soon learn that a positive approach results in the expenditure of even less time and involvement because their subordinates feel that they can use their own initiative without the fear of failure and the need for covering up mistakes.

You might be productive for both a positive and a negative leader, but to whom would you be most likely to say, "Take this job and shove it!" if a better opportunity came your way? From whom would you be most likely to get more job satisfaction over the long run? When you become a leader, will you recall these concepts? Keep in mind that concepts not applied are quickly forgotten. Some further suggestions for effective leadership can be viewed in Table 14.1.[15]

TABLE 14.1 A DOZEN GUIDELINES TO EFFECTIVE LEADERSHIP

1. Trust your subordinates. You can't expect them to go all out for you if they think you don't believe in them.

2. Know when to step in. Leading means you have to be present sometimes. You must strike a balance between dominating the team and abandoning the team.

3. Develop a vision. Some executives, suspicions to the contrary, realize that planning for the long term pays off. People want to follow someone who knows where he or she is going.

4. Keep your cool. The best leaders show their mettle under fire.

5. Encourage risk. Nothing demoralizes the troops like knowing that the slightest failure could jeopardize their entire career.

6. Be an expert. From boardroom to mail room, everyone had better understand that you know what you're talking about.

7. When you don't know something, admit it; promise to find out; keep that promise.

8. Invite dissent. Your people aren't giving you their best or learning how to lead if they are afraid to speak up.

9. Share power. The world is more complex, so you will need the help of others. To receive their help, give some of your power. Sharing power also shows trust and is needed in order to delegate work.

10. Simplify. You need to see the big picture in order to set a course, communicate it, and maintain it. Keep the details at bay.

11. Know your limitations and know when to say no to more assignments.

12. Learn to learn on the job. Constantly learn from each situation, whether it is a success or failure (in either case, learn why the result occurred).

STYLES OF LEADERSHIP

Designating leaders as positive or negative is one way of classifying leadership. Another way is to classify leadership styles by the philosophy of the leaders. Three styles can be distinguished: autocratic, participative, and free rein.

As a potential leader in organizational situations, you may have already recognized the value of encouraging employees to participate in making some of the decisions that affect the achievement of organizational goals. However, you will probably find that your approach must, at times, be decisive and direct and that you cannot always afford the time that the participative approach to leadership requires.

A MAJOR PROBLEM

Many leaders face the problem of balancing the two values of participation and decisiveness. What sort of leader do you as an employee prefer? One who tells you what to do? One who asks for your opinions and advice? Or one who presents you with a task and permits you to perform the job without direct supervision?

There isn't one approach to leadership that neatly fits every situation. Before we can decide when to use a particular style of leadership, we should explore some of the major characteristics of the three principal forms, as illustrated in Figure 14.2.

Autocratic Style
authoritarian leadership; leadership whereby others are simply told how to follow

AUTOCRATIC STYLE

Managers who employ the authoritarian or **autocratic style** of leadership could be termed *tellers*. Autocratic leaders usually feel that they know what they want and tend to express those wants as direct orders to their associates. Autocratic leaders usually keep decisions and controls to themselves because they have assumed full responsibility for decision making. Autocratic leaders usually structure the entire work situation for their workers, who merely follow orders.

Autocratic Pros Although in general the autocratic form of leadership is looked upon as negative, once again things are not all black or white in the real world of organizations. Many autocratic

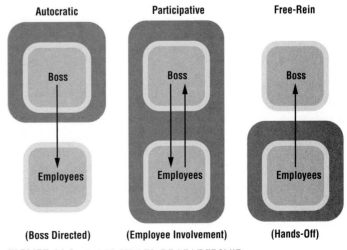

FIGURE 14.2 THREE STYLES OF LEADERSHIP

leaders have been successful in accomplishing goals. To be successful, however, autocratic leaders must have broad and diversified backgrounds. They must also have employees who expect and want their leaders to give them strong direction. Workers who are either somewhat submissive or prefer not to be responsible for participating in planning and decision making tend to respond positively to boss-centered leadership. Also, employees whose job responsibilities are not clearly defined or who lack sufficient knowledge and training to perform their jobs without assistance often welcome more directive leadership.

Some leaders are what is referred to as benevolent autocrats. Such leaders still retain absolute decision-making power, but they attempt to provide positive rewards to employees who follow their directives. These leaders also tend to be supportive of their employees. Some employees respond favorably to benevolent autocratic leadership.

In some situations, a manager may have little choice but to apply autocratic leadership. For example, during an emergency or crisis, there is rarely sufficient time to assemble the group for a question-and-answer session. If the building were burning, it's doubtful that an effective manager would say to his or her employees, "People, we've got a problem. The entire second floor of our factory is engulfed in flames. The ceiling of this room should collapse within five minutes. What are your suggestions regarding the resolution of this problem?" Instead, the manager would probably shout, "Hey! The building's on fire! Everybody get the heck out of here right now!" It is doubtful that even so autocratic an approach would evoke much resistance from employees.

The autocratic approach might also be used during an emergency occasioned by the breakdown of machinery with which the manager is familiar. Time being extremely critical in such situations, the manager might well use a directive approach to leadership.

And the Cons?   The autocratic style of leadership is typically more X-oriented because managers who use this approach frequently feel that the individual employee lacks the capability of providing constructive input. Autocratic leadership has the potential for creating problems of both morale and production in the long run. It also fails to develop the workers' commitment to the objectives of the organization. Employees on the receiving end of autocratic leadership frequently lack information about their functions and fear using their own initiative in their work. Furthermore, individual growth and development are far more difficult to attain within an autocratic framework.

PARTICIPATIVE STYLE: INVOLVING EMPLOYEES

Employee involvement (EI) is actually a newer term for another approach to leadership termed *behavioral, democratic,* or **participative leadership**. Leaning toward a Y-oriented approach to leadership, this style assumes that individual members of a group who take part personally in the decision-making process will be more likely, as a result, to have a far greater commitment to the objectives and goals of the organization.

The participative approach doesn't necessarily assume that leaders make no decisions. On the contrary, leaders should understand in advance what the mission and objectives of the organization are so they can draw upon the knowledge of the members of the work group.

Effective managers who use the participative approach in planning, effecting change, or resolving problems will customarily meet with affected workers and

Participative Leadership

leadership involving individual members of a group taking part in the decision-making process inform them fully of the problems, needs, and objectives of the organization. Then the participative manager will ask for the group's ideas about implementing the change.

Professors John R. Turney and Stanley L. Cohen contend that a certain degree of structure is necessary even when the participative style of management is employed.[16] They cite the example of a manager of an engineering design group who, during an open staff meeting, asked for employee assistance in planning a reorganization. After discussing his plans and objectives for change, he asked the employees to think about the implications of the change for a week or so and then let him know their concerns and recommendations. The manager received no response whatsoever.

The manager still believed in a participative approach but realized that after such a dismal response, he had better change his tactics. He then asked each department to appoint a representative. He conferred with each representative to outline what reorganization issues needed to be worked on and what sort of information would aid him. He also requested that they meet for two hours a week for three weeks and then present their findings in four weeks. The manager discovered that by structuring the participation process, he could obtain a large assortment of helpful ideas needed for the reorganization.

The Pros of Participative Leadership   The participative approach tends to be extremely effective in numerous situations. Workers like to feel that their ideas are important and tend to feel considerably more committed to changes and decision making in which they have participated. Workers also develop greater feelings of self-esteem when they feel that they have been trusted to make competent decisions. Often the combined knowledge and experience of the members of a group exceed those of the leader. Furthermore, problems worked on collectively often give birth to new ideas created as a result of the interpersonal exchange.

On the other hand, consider an inexperienced manager who is contemplating a change in the production process. Human beings tend to resist change, even when a new situation is easier or more efficient. There is no labor law, however, that requires this manager to do any more than merely notify workers of their new duties as a result of the change. If this direct, nonparticipative approach is followed, what might be the reaction of the workers? In many industrial situations where change has been forced upon others, the equilibrium of the group members has been so upset that excessive conflict has developed, made manifest by such activities as wildcat strikes, boycotts, slowdowns, and so on. Might there not be more effective ways to develop group commitment to organizational objectives?

The Cons of Participative Leadership   The participative approach makes certain assumptions that when false can result in complications for the organization. For example, this approach assumes a considerable commonality of interest between the managers and their employees. However, in any group, some individuals may be genuinely uninterested in their jobs, especially those who perceive their position merely as means to other, more satisfying ends. Therefore, they prefer not to expend any energy on participative decision making. Furthermore, employees in the organization must be receptive to the participative approach. Some workers might perceive the managers as ill qualified if they have to consult with the "lowly" workers. Other employees might perceive the participative approach as an attempt to manipulate them.

The participative approach also assumes that workers have the necessary knowledge and skill to participate in the decision-making process. If knowledge and skill are lacking, managers may find that they must either be bound by bad decisions or override the decisions of the group, thus detracting from the participative approach. Some managers feel uncomfortable using a participative style, especially those leaders who haven't developed an open climate of trust and confidence in their work groups. Other managers hesitate to use participative leadership for fear that control over their followers will be lost. However, participation by workers often eliminates feelings of hostility and opposition and, instead, creates a climate of cooperative attitudes that tends to enhance managers' influence over their employees. Often managers wish to exercise a power over their employees that they don't really have. Through participation, managers do give up some of their authority, but they gain far more control by using positive forces within the group.

Participation: It's a Matter of Degree   Another way of looking at leadership styles relates to the degree to which a manager is willing to share decision-making and problem-solving activities with associates. A model developed by professors Vroom and Yetton shows various styles of leadership ranging from no participation from employees, to the leader's carrying out alternatives that were generated by the group.[17] Table 14.2 shows the various leadership possibilities on a continuum, with styles ranging from style I to style V. As in our previous discussion of leadership styles, the Vroom–Yetton model also calls for a situational, or contingency, approach. The best style of leadership, according to Vroom and Yetton, depends on the answers that a manager might find to a number of questions, such as:

1. How critical to the success of the activity is acceptance of the manager's decision by employees?
2. Is conflict among employees likely to result from the manager's decision?
3. Does the manager have enough data and information to make an effective decision on his or her own?
4. Do associates have enough data and information to make a useful contribution to the decision-making process?
5. Do associates relate to the goals associated with the decisions that must be made?
6. Is the definition of the problem clear to all involved with the decision-making process?

TABLE 14.2 THE VROOM–YETTON CONTINUUM OF MANAGER–EMPLOYEE INVOLVEMENT

I	II	III	IV	V
The manager solves the problem and makes the decision alone.	The manager gathers information from employees but actually makes the decision alone.	The manager shares the problem with each employee but actually makes the decision alone.	The manager shares the problem with employees as a group but actually makes the decision alone.	The manager shares the problem with employees as a group; the group generates and evaluates alternatives; and the manager implements the decision developed by the group.

FREE-REIN STYLE

Another approach to leadership is called laissez-faire or **free-rein leadership**. This approach does not mean total absence of leadership. It does mean the absence of direct leadership. The free-rein leader, of course, should work through organizational goals. However, with this approach, a task is presented to group members who ordinarily work out their own techniques for accomplishing those goals within the framework of organizational objectives and policy. The leader acts principally as a liaison between outside sources and the group and ascertains what necessary resources are available to them.

Free-Rein Leadership
also called laissez-faire leadership; an absence of direct leadership; group members work out their own techniques for accomplishing goals

Would a Theory Y manager always use a free-rein style of leadership? You might think so at first glance, but it's not necessarily so. Managers still need to work with employees to establish objectives that are in harmony with organizational goals. Employees, even when under a Theory Y manager, are seldom free to engage in any type of activity they might want.

In some instances, a free-rein approach to leadership degenerates into chaos. In others, the absence of direct leadership is appropriate. For example, the director of a science laboratory or medical clinic doesn't have to be involved in every decision made by the scientists or doctors. Such professionals usually have the knowledge and skill to accomplish their tasks without direct supervision. The director might present a task to a scientist who would then decide how to accomplish the organizational goals.

Free rein is also often found in educational settings. A dean seldom tells professors how to perform their jobs. The dean might tell them what subjects they are to teach; the professors themselves generally decide the methods of carrying out the objectives of the institution.

Empowerment is another often-heard term these days that relates directly to the free-rein approach to leadership. Basically, empowerment is providing employees with higher degrees of involvement and greater authority to make decisions on their own. Professors David Bowen and Edward Lawler suggest that applying the concept to the workplace does not mean adopting an either/or approach to empowerment versus control. They point out that there are degrees of empowerment, which increase as additional knowledge, information, power, and rewards are pushed down the organization. Despite feelings of reticence among some managers about giving up some of their power, the trend toward empowering employees seems to be increasing among U.S. corporations.[18]

WHICH IS THE BEST STYLE OF LEADERSHIP?

As you may have determined from our discussion, there isn't necessarily one best style of leadership. In some instances, employees should be encouraged to participate in making some of the decisions that affect the achievement of the organization's goals. In other cases, however, a decisive and direct approach is preferred because of time pressures or the nature of the work group. The best style of leadership for a given situation depends on three important factors:

1. the situation
2. the type of followers
3. the type of leader

To be an effective leader, therefore, you may need to tailor your style to fit these variables.

A leader's conduct during an emergency, for example, might also vary substantially from his or her conduct under normal working conditions. Furthermore, leaders may sometimes use positive and at other times negative techniques of leadership. Effective leaders may find that in some situations an autocratic form of direction is most effective, whereas in other situations, participative or even free-rein approaches are useful. Some leaders are designated as such by the formal organization; others develop their influence over members of their groups naturally and informally because of such characteristics as age, seniority, knowledge, education, and popularity.

In practice, research has found five general leadership styles for CEOs. The five facets of CEO leadership include strategic, human resources, expertise, procedures, and change styles. In the strategic style, the CEO delegates day-to-day operations and concentrates on the grand strategy, vision, and plan for the company's future. With the human resource style, the CEO becomes personally involved in the evolution of as many managers and workers as possible. Careful attention to developing human resources within the company and watching and guiding careers is designed to ensure that everyone is working for the company's best interests. In the expertise style, effort is concentrated on developing the organization's technical knowledge. This expertise gives the organization its competitive advantage. The CEO's job is to focus the expertise and ensure that it spreads throughout the organization. With the procedures style, a CEO leads by establishing rules, controls, and organizational values. Here, the financial and cultural controls are seen as the best way to achieve an advantage over the competition. In the fifth style, the CEO functions as a change agent, and the change is continuous and made on a large scale. It has also been found that although CEOs may use parts of all five styles, they typically employ just one or two of these for the majority of the time.[19]

SHOULD LEADERS GET CLOSE TO THEIR ASSOCIATES?

A situation that some leaders find difficult is that of deciding how friendly or close they should be to their associates. *Psychological distance* is the term used to denote the mental attitudes of supervisors toward their employees from the standpoint of the closeness of the working relationship. The greater the psychological distance, the more remote the managers are from their employees.

For example, believing that familiarity breeds contempt, some managers avoid becoming close to their employees, contending that too much closeness leads to loss of respect and control. Other leaders try extremely hard to be one of the gang with their employees. Still others attempt to strike some sort of balance between the two extremes.

Which approach is best? There isn't complete agreement, but the more modern approach to management suggests that a minimum (but not complete elimination) of psychological distance is the most effective. The important factor is that supervisors should be genuinely interested in their personnel and operate in a manner that achieves intended objectives.

Managers who aren't afraid to get to know their associates as human beings and who are seen as human beings themselves actually tend to gain respect and control. Managers who are willing to be close to some of their employees must be careful, of course, that all their employees are treated fairly and without favoritism. Managers will lose a substantial degree of effectiveness if associates think that all an employee needs to do to obtain special favors is to be a friend to the boss. To be close to employees requires a reasonable amount of confidence, not only in yourself but also in your employees.

NetNote

LeadershipNow

http://www.leadershipnow.com/

Articles and information on leadership.

It is one thing to talk about the importance of leadership and developing leaders, but how is this put into practice? Some companies have found success in developing special leadership programs while others have found value in providing leadership training for a wide range of employees.

Entertainment Arts (EA), a popular video and computer game manufacturer, found that 66 percent of internally trained leaders were promoted, and their turnover rate was half that of non-leadership-trained groups. EA, however, found it needed two distinct types of leaders. It needed special leadership training for its business employees (marketers, production managers, distributors) but a much different type of leadership training for the creative employees who conceived the worlds and characters of its games. Both programs have provided a large return on investment for the company.

Fujitsu Transactions and Unisys also have internal leadership programs, but both have stressed training many employees rather than a select few. These firms believe that more employee leaders improve customer relations and that when workers and managers attend leadership training, managers are more likely to use their newly acquired leadership skills. Fujitsu does not allow worker-leaders to do whatever they wish; they are held accountable for their leadership efforts. Unisys found that by training a variety of people, discussions of leadership continued long after the training because many more people had something in common to discuss.

The lesson to be learned from these companies is that leaders are not likely to appear out of the masses on their own, so companies must actively work to develop leaders. These examples also show that if you put forth effort, you can get results.

Sources: Maryann Hammers, "High Scores in the Leadership Game," *Workforce Management*, December 2003, pp. 55–56; Sarah Fister Gale, "Leaders Are the Only Differentiator," *Workforce*, October 2002, p. 83; Sarah Fister Gale, "A Culture of Leadership," *Workforce*, October 2002, p. 84.

Supervisors should, however, guard against appearing to be excessively familiar, which can sometimes lead to problems when discipline is to be administered or less-pleasant tasks assigned. Extreme remoteness, on the other hand, can create artificial barriers between managers and workers and result in less-effective interaction and communication. Once again, leaders should attempt to use situational thinking and develop the ability to know which approach enables them to accomplish specific organizational goals while satisfying employees' social needs.

SOME FINAL CONCLUSIONS ON THE BEST STYLE OF LEADERSHIP

From our discussion of leadership, we should realize that a major difference in styles of leadership is in the amount of decision making done by the leader. The autocratic leader need not be a dictator or a marine drill sergeant, but can be a Theory Y type of leader who has followers who require more direction. A participative leader shares decision making with the workers but also reserves final decision-making authority. A free-rein leader allows workers to make decisions and serves mainly as a resource person for empowered associates.

LEADERSHIP AS A SKILL

Some people seem to have a knack for leading others, but fortunately most good leaders are not born but made.[20] Effective leadership, as with good listening habits, is an activity that is usually developed. A competent leader requires skill and knowledge, neither of which is necessarily inborn; they are acquired and developed, honed and perfected. In general, anyone with managerial aspirations should attempt to develop the following: technical skills, human resource management skills, conceptual skills, and trust-building skills.

TECHNICAL SKILLS

Technical Skills
the knowledge and ability necessary to perform the particular task or type of activity required by your job

A potential leader should have **technical skills**—the knowledge and ability to perform the particular task or type of activity required by the job. If you are a computer salesperson, you must certainly have the technical knowledge to decide which types of hardware and software are best suited to the specific needs of your customers. After you become a sales manager, you'll still need the technical knowledge necessary for training your sales force and resolving technical problems. However, if you move into management, you are likely to have less need for technical skills than when you were an operating employee. You will tend to lean more on your subordinates for technical assistance. The amount of technical knowledge necessary for a managerial position depends principally on the nature of the managerial position.

HUMAN RESOURCE MANAGEMENT SKILLS

Human Resource Management Skills
the behavioral skills of being able to work effectively with and through people

If you become a manager with an office-equipment firm, technical skills are likely to be useful but will be less important than **human resource management skills**—the behavioral skills of being able to work effectively with and through people. We've already discussed a number of attributes that are essential for competent leaders, such as perceptual, communication, listening, empathetic, and motivational skills. The ability to plan, interview, coordinate, and control are also necessary managerial skills.

For example, proficient managers are more likely to perceive subtle changes in the behavior of their employees, changes that could cause serious problems if not dealt with immediately. Moreover, skilled managers are able to communicate orally, in writing, and by electronic means, such as by computer modems or fax machines, with fewer misunderstandings. The most significant reason many leaders and managers fail to achieve their organizational objectives is not necessarily that they lack technical skills, but that they lack human resource management (people-oriented) skills.

CONCEPTUAL SKILLS

Conceptual Skills
the ability to think abstractly and see relationships between seemingly disparate entities; the ability to see the big picture

Administrative or **conceptual skills** become increasingly important as individuals move into management. These skills entail the ability to conceptualize, that is, to think abstractly and see relationships between seemingly disparate entities. Many leaders need the ability to analyze current problems and anticipate and prevent future ones. They must often plan for longer time periods. They must also be able to plan and coordinate the overall operations of an organization and its personnel. Senior executives of multinational corporations may have to judge the effects of currency fluctuations on future profits and decide whether to shift funds from one country to another as a hedge against value loss. All of these activities require the ability to think abstractly.

In summary, therefore, human resource management skills are important, regardless of your managerial level in an organization. Figure 14.3 shows how, as you rise, the importance of technical skills diminishes and that of conceptual skills increases.

A challenge experienced by many individuals who come up through the ranks is making the transition from an operating employee with highly developed technical skills to a manager who suddenly needs a high degree of human relations and conceptual skills. Learning as much as you can about management processes and techniques before you become a manager can ease any transitional difficulty you might experience.

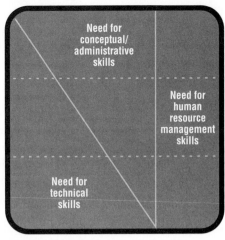

Senior Management

Need for conceptual/ administrative skills

Middle Management

Need for human resource management skills

Supervisory Management

Need for technical skills

FIGURE 14.3 MANAGERS NEED THREE TYPES OF SKILLS: TECHNICAL, HUMAN RESOURCE MANAGEMENT, AND CONCEPTUAL/ADMINISTRATIVE
Technical skills become less important and conceptual ones more important as managers rise within the organization.

TRUST-BUILDING SKILLS

Leadership is built upon **trust**, the willingness of someone to be vulnerable to the actions of another.[21] People will not follow someone they do not trust. As vital as trust is, it is in serious trouble today. In recent years downsizing, outsourcing, and the most serious of ethical failures have shaken the trust that the majority of employees had in management and their organization's leaders.[22] It is not just headline-grabbing events that undermine trust, however. Ineptitude, aimlessness, and a vague or unstated mission all contribute.[23] A lack of trust not only weakens or disables leadership, but it also decreases productivity, thus costing organizations money.[24] It is also not just a one-time downsizing that erodes trust but the combination of many small management or leadership actions over time. While trust can be lost slowly or quickly, it can only be built slowly.

Seven elements are needed to build trust: ability, honesty, integrity, openness, responsiveness, concern, and benevolence. In general, all seven must be present to build trust in an individual. When all, or almost all, of the leaders in a firm possess individual trust, then there is organizational trust. **Organizational trust** is the belief that the organization will help, or at least not hurt, the individuals in the organization.[25]

In building trust, **ability** refers to possessing the technical skills mentioned earlier in the chapter. People have little trust for someone who holds a position but does not have the required technical skills and cannot perform the required functions.[26]

Honesty includes telling the truth, but goes further. **Honesty** means saying exactly what you mean and then doing what you say.[27] It means your actions follow your words, that you never make a promise you do not intend to keep, and that you don't make a commitment unless you will follow through. One has to be consistent in this, though. Keeping one promise is not enough to be considered reliably honest.

Integrity means being incorruptible. Of course that includes not doing anything illegal or unethical, but it also means not violating a confidence, not spreading rumors, and not being susceptible to pressure to do something wrong or unjust.[28] While having integrity means not accepting undue influence, openness is needed in order to receive positive inputs.

Openness runs two ways; you need to be open to listening to others but also open to telling people exactly where you stand.[29] **Openness** requires that you go out among people and communicate. It also requires communicating both the good news and the bad news.[30] It would destroy trust for people to find out you had withheld bad news from them. Letting people know what you think reduces their doubt and

Trust
the willingness of someone to be vulnerable to the actions of another

Organizational Trust
the belief that the organization will help, or at least not hurt, the individuals in the organization

Ability
possessing technical skills

Honesty
saying exactly what you mean and then doing what you say

Integrity
being incorruptible

Openness
going out among people and communicating

Responsiveness
giving feedback

Concern
being sensitive to the
needs of others

Benevolence
the desire to do good

NetNote

Coping.org site

*http://www.coping.org/
growth/trust.htm*

Building trust, mainly for
people who have difficulty
trusting others.

provides them with a sense of direction. This does not mean that you tell everything you know (as you must maintain your integrity), but everything you tell must be the truth (to maintain your honesty).

Responsiveness means to give feedback. When asked a question or presented with a concern, a trust-building leader responds. Hiding from situations, not getting involved, or remaining silent (not returning calls or e-mails) may seem tempting when the subject is unpleasant, but these are not the actions of a leader, and avoiding issues works to destroy trust.[31]

Concern means being sensitive to the needs of others and can be related back to the definitions of individual and organizational trust. If trusting means to be open to the actions of others—and those actions should help others—then to build trust a leader has to listen to what others need and provide for those needs.[32] So if a worker is to trust a manager, the manager needs to consider and look out for the interests of the worker.

Finally, building trust requires **benevolence**, which is the desire to do good.[33] It is being kind, even when giving criticism or correcting behavior. Benevolent criticism is not meant to hurt, to belittle, to insult, or to be cruel; it is meant to help people improve. Being benevolent does not mean being weak or ignoring wrongdoing, as you still need to be open. When confronting someone, it means assisting the person to do things correctly without being nasty toward him or her.

DEVELOPMENT OF LEADERSHIP SKILLS

Skill in leadership doesn't usually develop by accident; it can be acquired and perfected by trial and error, formal education, on-the-job experience, and supplemental reading. Whatever techniques are used to develop leadership skills, potential leaders develop best in a growth atmosphere that allows them the freedom to make mistakes.

TRIAL AND ERROR

As with any skills, leadership skills can be developed with ordinary practice and through trial and error on the job. Although many highly skilled leaders achieved their positions and developed their abilities in such a random fashion, more systematic approaches are currently used. Let's turn to some other ways in which leadership skills can be developed far more rapidly and with much less happenstance.

FORMAL EDUCATION

Formalized education can make your work and personal experiences more meaningful and your trials less filled with error. Courses in human relations, organizational behavior, management, personnel management, business, and the liberal arts frequently enable individuals to advance more rapidly in organizations.

ON-THE-JOB EXPERIENCE

Reading about leadership and observing managers can certainly give you insights on how to be an effective leader. However, these activities cannot substitute for actual on-the-job experience. Well-organized firms usually have formalized management development programs designed to assist and accelerate the development of the skills of employees with apparent managerial potential. Some organizations have discovered the hard way that they had failed to groom anyone for unexpectedly vacated managerial positions. Other, more farsighted firms have initiated formal company programs in which existing leaders help to develop new leaders.[34]

Assessment centers are used by some organizations to help decide which employees possess management potential. They also help determine the training and development needs of specific employees. An assessment center isn't a place; it's a method. A group of employees is given a variety of simulated job experiences, tasks related to their future success as managers. Trained observers watch and evaluate how the participants handle themselves and then write a report summarizing the participants' strengths, weaknesses, and probable success as managers.

Coaching is another widely used on-the-job technique that provides potential managers with useful experiences and helps them develop necessary skills. Typically, an experienced and skilled person, usually a manager, is assigned to a lesser-skilled employee. As with athletic teams, the coach is responsible for developing the employee. Coaching is considered a fairly effective management development tool because of the close and regular contact an employee has with a manager who provides continual feedback on the employee's progress. Coaching should really be an ongoing aspect of any manager-employee relationship and needn't be a formalized program.

Understudy assignments are related to coaching but differ in this manner: The lesser-skilled employee is assigned to an experienced manager and is groomed to take over the manager's job. Some organizations have formal policies indicating that managers cannot be eligible for promotions unless they have developed someone to take over their positions. For example, Alfred P. Sloan, Jr., while head of General Motors, believed that a primary duty of any executive is to develop a successor, preferably one more capable than himself or herself. Not all organizations seem to agree, however. Many companies have acquired the reputation of enlisting the service of executive headhunters who raid other corporations to fill senior-level executive positions. However, such organizations are the exception, not the rule, and the majority of managerial and supervisory positions are not senior level. Consequently, the policy of internal management development programs and promotion from within continues to retain considerable merit.

We touched on only a few of the on-the-job experiences that assist in developing managers here. Other types include job rotation and horizontal promotions intended to provide more diversified experiences for potential managers. The

FYI

Lead, follow, or get out of everyone else's way.

Give people a reason to follow you.

Only use power when you have to.

Explain how you envision things will be. If you can't communicate your ideas, people can't follow you.

You can't lead from behind your people.

There can't be leaders without followers. Know when to be each.

People have to trust you to follow you; you have to trust them for them to trust you.

Don't rely on one leadership style for all occasions; use the right tool for the job.

SPOT CHECK

11. The autocratic style of leadership is authoritarian. T F
12. Laissez-faire or free-rein leadership is the absence of direct leadership. T F
13. Integrity means telling the truth. T F
14. Concern is the desire to do good. T F
15. In building trust, ability refers to possessing the technical skills. T F

techniques available are limited only by the imagination and creativity of those who are responsible for management development programs.

SUPPLEMENTAL READING

Not all organizations have formalized management development programs, the smaller ones especially may not have such programs. Regardless of what provisions have been made by an organization for human resource development, the major burden of the development of managerial skills rests on individual organizational members themselves.

One way for potential and current managers to maintain their acquired educations is to continue reading regularly after their formal training and classroom education have ceased. Some organizations today even provide their managers with "reading breaks," said to be far more healthful than coffee and cigarette breaks. Publications such as *Business Week*, *The Wall Street Journal*, and *Fortune* frequently present case histories of firms, knowledge of which can often assist managers in their own organizational activities. Each year, numerous books on businesses and economics are published, and a growing number of Web sites contain leadership information. Well-rounded managers, however, will attempt to supplement their acquired educations by reading books other than those related only to business or government.

THE NEED FOR A SUPPORTIVE ORGANIZATIONAL CULTURE

As is the case with people, organizations are unique. Likewise, each has a set of values. As mentioned in Chapter 1, the values that influence the environment in which people work are called the organizational culture. An organization's culture is what influences how leaders and other employees function. Some organizations provide employees with a supportive environment in which they have plenty of opportunities to participate and make decisions, and others are restrictive and tend to suppress creative talent.[35]

Employees are better able to develop leadership skills when their own leaders provide a positive organizational culture, or atmosphere, for growth.[36] To develop into leaders, individuals must first learn to make decisions. In an organizational culture that fosters growth, associates are given decision-making responsibility and a reasonable amount of freedom to carry out that responsibility. Not all employees have the opportunity to make decisions, however. The value systems of some organizations don't allow employees the freedom to fail. Certainly, employees shouldn't make an excessive number of mistakes, but some employees seldom feel free to make decisions because of the probable consequences of their mistakes.

Managers, in a sense, are teachers. One of their chief responsibilities is to educate, train, and assist others. If managers want to create a culture that encourages initiative and decision making in their employees, they should be cautious when handling the mistakes made by conscientious employees.

SUMMARY

The term *leadership* has no catchall meaning but can be described as the ability to influence the activities of others, through the process of communication, toward the attainment of a goal. Accountability accompanied by authority (empowerment) enables leaders and other organizational personnel to make decisions and carry out their responsibilities more effectively.

Management, which includes the activity of leadership, is a broader concept and may include nonbehavioral activities. Managers and leaders derive power from two sources: personal power and institutional power. Leadership directly affects the behavior of individuals in organizations.

Leaders are not true leaders unless they have an emotional appeal, that is, they must have both followers and the ability to influence people over extended periods of time. Some individuals seem to possess a special charm, power, and ability to influence and win the devotion and respect of others, known as charisma.

Leaders may be classified according to their attitudes toward associates as positive (Theory Y) or negative (Theory X) and by their style of leadership, autocratic, participative, or free-rein. Many leaders are more likely to be selective in their perception of associates (Selective X–Y). Leaders who feel they've been burned by associates may develop an attitude termed Derived X. The best type of leadership in a given situation depends on three major factors: the leader, the followers, and the situation.

We saw that transformational leaders are defined by their achievements. Fielder believes that leaders have a style and that can't be changed. According to Fielder, one should find the style of each leader, then assign that person to a matching situation. The Hershey–Blanchard situational model differs from Fielder's, contending that leaders can change their leadership methods and that they should change for each situation. Path–goal theory also says that a manager can change; it is similar to the expectancy theory of motivation.

Professors Vroom and Yetton developed a model that shows various styles of leadership, ranging from no participation drawn from associates, to the leader's carrying out alternatives generated by the group members.

Leadership is built upon trust, and trust is built upon ability, honesty, integrity, openness, responsiveness, concern, and benevolence. To be effective, leaders also need three major skills: technical, human resource management, and conceptual skills. Leadership skills can be developed through trial and error, formal education, on-the-job experiences, and supplemental reading.

Managers, in a sense, are educators and trainers; they therefore have the responsibility to groom others for leadership positions. Individuals tend to develop leadership traits more rapidly in a supportive organizational culture that gives them a reasonable amount of freedom to carry out their assigned responsibilities.

CHECKING FOR UNDERSTANDING

1. What is the major distinction between leadership and management?

2. How do the terms *accountability*, *authority*, and *responsibility* differ in meaning?

3. What helps to determine whether a person is an effective leader?

4. How might charisma be misused?

5. What tends to cause a person to adopt a Derived X approach? How might this condition be avoided?

6. What are some of the probable consequences of workers' operating in an aura of fear?

7. Describe the circumstances in which the three major styles of leadership might be used effectively. Which would you use and why?

8. Is an autocratic style of leadership always counterproductive? Explain.

9. Describe the five styles of leadership related to employee participation developed by professors

Vroom and Yetton. Give examples of when you might use each of the approaches.

10. Why do technical skills become less important as a person rises in the organizational hierarchy?

11. What are the two main sources of power and the three subtypes of each?

12. What is the path–goal theory of leadership and what motivational theory is it related to?

13. What is the Hershey–Blanchard model of leadership?

14. What is the Fielder theory of leadership?

15. What can someone do to build trust?

SELF-ASSESSMENT

Answer each of the following questions in relation to your work life. Answer SA for those you Strongly Agree with, A for those you Agree with, D for those you Disagree with, and SD for those you Strongly Disagree with.

1. I believe in my ability to lead others.   SA   A   D   SD

2. People I work with would say I am truthful truthful.   SA   A   D   SD

3. I am an active advocate for myself and those I represent.   SA   A   D   SD

4. I am an optimistic and fervent proponent of causes I believe in.   SA   A   D   SD

5. I know my abilities.   SA   A   D   SD

6. I know my limitations.   SA   A   D   SD

7. I compensate for my limitations.   SA   A   D   SD

8. People say I'm outgoing.   SA   A   D   SD

9. People say I possess an above average or greater intellect.   SA   A   D   SD

10. When something needs to be done I have the drive to see that it gets started.   SA   A   D   SD

11. My aim is to get things done, to see them through to completion.   SA   A   D   SD

12. Once I make up my mind, I am determined to carry out my decision to a successful conclusion.   SA   A   D   SD

Score 4 points for every SA, 3 for every A, 2 for every D, and 1 for every SD answer. A score of 36–48 indicates you may be a leader, 25–35 indicates you may be a leader or a follower, and 12–24 indicates you may need more work to be a leader or you may be a good follower.

SKILL BUILD 14

Jiajang Xu entered Tom Watson's office where Tom was talking casually with a peer, Nena Rezoga.

"Tom," Jiajing started, "Have you found a new leader for the Bernese team? They asked five weeks ago and recently have been e-mailing me every two or three days."

"I been giving some thought to Casey, Casey Neustrom," Tom replied in his Texas drawl.

"What sort of leader is he?" Jiajing asked.

"What *kind* of leader is he? I don't rightly know what you mean," Tom said.

"What style does he use? He must have a style. How else will he lead?" Jiajing said.

"Well heck, he knows that area inside and out. Knows it like the back of his hand. That gives him power. Plus I'll promote him. Make him a Level 7 technician. That's two levels higher than anyone else on that team. That's more power. Why, time I get done with him, the boy'll be drippin' with power," Tom explained.

Skill Question 1. Tom, Jiajing, and even Nena could use your help. What kind of power does Tom say Casey already possesses? What kind of power does Tom say he will give Casey?

"I do not believe that power alone is sufficient. He must be trained as a leader and must follow some theory or method. Must he not?" Jiajing said.

"I think I remember reading that all people have a certain way of leading and that what must be done is to find a team that needs the leader's way and put the two together," Nena said.

Skill Question 2. What leadership theory is it that Nena must have read about? Define that theory in your own words. Do you agree or disagree with this theory and why?

"This team is our best. Together they have more education than any other team, more experience, too. They have just completed the latest training and have had the best success record. I think this is why they clamor for a leader. They can do it; they just need support and especially direction, someone to inject enthusiasm and vision into the group. They are most anxious to have someone who can rouse them to achieve the most that they are able to," Jiajing said.

Skill Question 3. When Jiajing describes the Bernese team, her description seems to fit which contingency and situational leadership theory? According to this theory, what type of leader does the Bernese team need and why?

"Aw, shucks, I never had any of that, and I turned out fine," Tom said. "Who needs a buncha rah-rah? Casey won't need to lead that bunch. All's he needs to do is throw the work into their room; they'll tear right into it. His biggest job will be to talk to the teams that he works with and smooth things out for his people."

Skill Question 4. What leadership style does Tom believe in? Does this seem appropriate to the Bernese team and why or why not?

"I am uneasy about sending this man with no apparent leader style or training, but if this is your choice we will see how he works out," Jiajing said.

Skill Question 5. What are the other two things that should go with the power Casey has and was given? From what you can determine from the information

provided, has Casey been given these other two things? Should he have been given them and why or why not?

Three weeks later, Nena came to Tom's office.

"Tom, I thought I would warn you. I think there is a problem with the Bernese team and Casey Neustrom," Nena said.

""What? I ain't heard nuthin'. What makes you say that?" Tom replied, alarmed.

"I just happened to have lunch with a couple of the team members on Monday, and then Wednesday I ran into Casey, also at lunch. From what I have put together from the team, Casey, and even from a couple of my people who sometimes work with the Bernese team, Casey seems to have told them about the 4 percent raises, but he neglected to mention that their new project requires them to work late and come in almost every Saturday. Seems he shows up at the cubes about 10 minutes before the typical end of the day and hands out a couple of hours of work to each team member—work that must be done before they leave. He doesn't tell them they need to come in Saturday until late Friday afternoon," Nena explained.

"Aw, bull feathers. Well, at least he's talking to them—some," Tom said.

"Actually, that may be the limit of their conversations. From what I heard, when they ask how things are going, he has no real reply. He doesn't say they are doing bad, but also doesn't say they are doing well. When they bring up things they are worried about, he has said he will take care of them, but he told me himself that he intends to do nothing. As he put it, 'problems that come up by themselves, can go away by themselves,' and once in a while this is true, but you can't promise to handle something and then not; at least I don't think you should. What will you do?" Nena asked.

"Jeez, girl, I don't know. I tooted Casey's horn to Jiajing, and now it looks like I'm goin' to get gored with it," Tom said dejectedly.

Skill Questions 6–9. Examine the trust factors and how Casey handled his team. He has a problem with four trust factors. Which are they (number them 6, 7, 8, and 9). For each, explain what Casey did wrong and what he should have done.

Skill Question 10. Will Casey still be able to lead this team? Why or why not?

APPLICATIONS

14.1 HELP FOR HENRY

Henry Richards looked at his three-month evaluation for the tenth time and was having a hard time believing it. The appraisal, from virtually everyone in the company, was not good. What really baffled Henry was how low he was rated on leadership and trust. On his job skills he was at the top of the ratings; seems no one doubted or had any complaints with his talent as chief financial officer. Of course he knew he was good at that because no one had noticed that he paid himself double one month to get the down payment on his Porsche. He paid it all back in the next two months with a little extra cash that Slite-of-Hande Accounting gave him to be selected as the company's auditor, and no one was the wiser. But low ratings in leadership? He graduated at the top of his seminar group at the Leader Furnace, graduated "Fully Forged." He doubled productivity in his department on a weekly basis—wasn't that leadership enough? That burned out three of his eight department heads, but that was their problem; they were weak. When he was hired, it was with the understanding that he would update the financial information systems software. He never did, but who was going to notice that? He always made his daily rounds, however. He talked to every main contact in the company every day and all "fringe" people every week. He was rated good at communicating, and he always got back to people. One of his primary rules was e-mails returned the same day, phone calls returned in an hour, walk-ins dealt with immediately. And this was the thanks he got! Well, he'd make them pay. He didn't know how yet, but someone was going to suffer for this.

QUESTIONS

1. Evaluate Henry on the trust factors. Is he doing anything right in regard to trust? If so, identify the factors, define them, and show how he is doing them right with examples of his behavior.

2. If he did some things related to trust correctly, why was he still rated low in trust in general?

3. Is he doing anything wrong in regard to trust? If so, identify the factors, define them, and show how he is doing them wrong with examples of his behavior.

4. If Henry is doing anything wrong in regard to trust, make suggestions for how he should change.

5. Why was Henry rated low in leadership and trust, that is, why wasn't he just rated low in trust?

14.2 BANKING ON A SOLUTION AT THE DATA CENTER

Fourth Interstate Bancorp has a computer center in Rapid City, South Dakota, that is the size of a typical city block. The facility handles a large proportion of the data-processing operations for Fourth Interstate's 154-branch network in five western states. The employees have been assigned specialized duties in the particular sections of the data center in which they work. Using the latest computer equipment, the different sections handle such tasks as processing credit card accounts, servicing mortgage loans, inputting and updating customer information files (CIFs), and generating reports.

A number of problems have developed in recent months. For example, almost every day some sections are extremely overloaded with work, while employees in other sections are sitting around with little to do. When the workload is excessive in some sections, employees tend to become harried and tense, a situation that has led to a fairly high number of complaints within the bank. On numerous occasions, CIFs were updated with incorrect information, and reports have been coming out late or incomplete.

QUESTIONS

1. If you were the data-center manager for Fourth Interstate Bancorp, what would you do to resolve the problems?

2. What style of leadership would you apply? Why?

NET-WORK

The need for leadership

http://www.youtube.com/watch?v=KpbTmSa_9t4

A leader speaks: JFK—leadership and the result

http://www.youtube.com/watch?v=Kza-iTe2100

A leader's vision: MLK "I Have A Dream" excerpt

http://www.youtube.com/watch?v=dgheL67IYzw&mode= related&search=

A negative leader: Paul Parducci #4

http://www.youtube.com/watch?v=Gddmq0EJrkg&mode= related&search=

PERSONAL POINTS

1. What is your interest in or desire for a formal leadership role?

2. How would you use authority at work if you had it?

3. How much expert power do you now possess? If you needed to increase your expert power, how would you do so?

4. Which styles of leadership have you experienced? Which have you preferred and why? Which did you not like and why?

5. If you need to acquire additional leadership skill, how will you do this?

EXPERIENTIAL EXERCISE

What Do You Assume?

This exercise is intended to help you become more aware of the assumptions you make about others and their attitudes. Ten sets of statements follow. Read each set. Then assign a weight from 0 to 10 to each statement in the set based on the relative strength of your belief in each statement. The points assigned for each pair must total 10. For example, in set 1, the strength of your belief in the *a* statement might indicate a weight of 7, and in the *b* statement a weight of 3, for a total of 10. Be as open and honest as you can. Try not to respond as you think things are or should be. This exercise is not a test. There are no right and wrong answers. The exercise is designed to aid you in learning more about yourself and the assumptions that you make about others.

1a. It's only human nature for people to do as little work as they can get away with. X _____

b. When people avoid work, it's usually because their work has lost its meaning. Y _____

2a. If employees have access to more information than they need to do their immediate tasks, they will usually misuse it. X _____

b. If employees have access to any information they want, they tend to have better attitudes and behave more responsibly. Y _____

3a. One problem in asking for employees' ideas is that their perspective is too limited for their sugg- estions to be of much practical value. X _____

b. Asking employees for their ideas broadens their perspective and results in the development of useful suggestions. Y _____

4a. If people don't use much imagination and ingenuity on the job, it's probably because relatively few people have much of either. X _____

b. The more knowledge and freedom a person has regarding the job, the fewer controls are needed to ensure satisfactory performance. Y _____

EXPERIENTIAL EXERCISE (Continued)

What Do You Assume?

5a. People tend to lower their standards if they are not punished for their misbehavior and mistakes. X _____

b. People tend to raise their standards if they are accountable for their own behavior and for correcting their own mistakes. Y _____

6a. It's better to withhold unfavorable news because most employees want to hear only the good news. X _____

b. It's better to give people both good and bad news because most employees want the whole story, no matter how painful. Y _____

7a. Because a supervisor is entitled to more respect than those below him or her in the organization, it weakens his or her prestige to admit that a subordinate was right and he or she was wrong. X _____

b. Because people at all levels are entitled to equal respect, a supervisor's prestige is increased when he or she supports this principle by admitting that a subordinate was right and he or she was wrong. Y _____

8a. If you give people enough money to feel secure, concern for such intangibles as responsibility and recognition will be less. X _____

b. If given interesting and challenging work, people are less likely to complain about such things as pay and supplemental benefits. Y _____

9a. If people are allowed to set their own goals and standards of performance, they tend to set them lower than their manager would. X _____

b. If people are allowed to set their own goals and standards of performance, they tend to set them higher than their manager would. Y _____

10a. The more knowledge and freedom a person has regarding the job, the more controls are needed to keep him or her in line. X _____

b. The more knowledge and freedom a person has regarding the job, the fewer controls are needed to ensure satisfactory performance. Y _____

Instructions

Subtract the smaller number in each set from the larger number. If the net amount relates to the X statement, indicate the value by drawing a small dot above the corresponding number on the X side of the continuum below. If the net amount relates to the Y statement, indicate the value by drawing a dot on the Y side of the continuum. For example, if in set 1 your X response was 7 and your Y response was 3, your net amount would be 4 related to the X statement. You would then place a dot over the corresponding number (in this case, 4) on the X side of the continuum.

The validity of this exercise depends largely on your ability to respond accurately to the statements. If most of your dots are clustered on the right (Y) side of the continuum, the chances are fairly good that your assumptions about other people in general lean toward the positive. If, on the other hand, most of your dots are clustered on the left (X) side of the continuum, you could probably benefit from determining ways to improve your attitudes toward and assumptions about others.

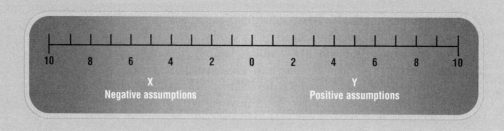

SPOT CHECK ANSWERS

1. F
2. F
3. F
4. F
5. T
6. T
7. T
8. T
9. T
10. T
11. T
12. T
13. F
14. F
15. T

15 | Stress

Some stress is important; too much is deadly.

Patricia King

The problem is not stress. Rather, it is how we react to stress. Emotions—not events—cause stress-related events.

Michael Morrison

GOALS

The goals of this chapter are to introduce the topics of stress and stress management to show the effects stress can have on you and to present an overview of the main methods used in coping with stress.

OBJECTIVES

When you finish this chapter, you should be able to:

▶ Define stress and stressors.
▶ Define and differentiate eustress and distress and mental and physical stress.
▶ Define, differentiate, and explain the flight and fight responses.
▶ List and define causes of stress.
▶ List and explain the reactions to work-related distress.
▶ Diagram and explain the three stages of stress.

▶ Explain the relationship between frustration and stress.
▶ Identify burnout and explain its causes and cures.
▶ Explain how you might cause distress in your associates.
▶ Identify signs of substance abuse.
▶ Identify recommendations for general stress management.
▶ Identify methods for managing career-related stress.

INTRODUCTION

Pressures, demands, and changes—these all exist in a person's environment and often result in a condition called **stress**. There seems to be no shortage of stress these days in people's lives, both on and off the job. Stress-causing events can happen with little warning, even when people are seeking pleasure. We are never going to remove stress completely from our lives, nor should we try. It is not the stress itself as much as the way you meet the stress that counts.[1] This statement suggests that the way we manage our stress determines how it affects us. In this chapter, we will discuss the nature of stress; typical reactions to stress, including burnout; and various proven techniques for managing stress.

THE NATURE OF STRESS

It's important to realize that not all stress is harmful; in fact, people need stress in order to survive.[2] The complete absence of stress (sensory deprivation) leads to death. The trick, however, is to get more of the right kind of stress and to control your reactions to any bad stress you do receive. What exactly is stress? Dr. Hans Selye, a pioneer in stress research, defines stress as a body's nonspecific response to a demand.[3] Furthermore, a **stressor** is anything that produces a demand on an organism.[4] In differentiating between types of stress, Selye identified two types, each with two variations: distress and eustress.

When most people speak of stress, they are referring to harmful or disease-producing stress. This is called **distress**.[5] Some stress is beneficial and necessary. This is called **eustress** (pronounced you-stress).[6] There are two variations to distress and eustress, however. Each type of stress has a physical and mental variant. There are **physical distress** and **mental distress**, and **physical eustress** and **mental eustress**. Whether an activity generates distress or eustress depends on the situation. We don't know whether being chased will result in distress or eustress until we know the context. Being chased as part of a sport or game causes physical eustress, whereas being chased by a mugger causes physical distress. Similarly, reading a magazine may produce mental eustress, whereas reading five chapters for the first time 20 minutes before the final exam may create mental distress. The type of stress is important, but our response to the stressor is also important.

OUR BASIC RESPONSES

We have only two basic and ancient responses to stress—fight or flight. Of the two, the **fight response** is the more powerful. With the fight response, the individual goes on full alert to defend himself or herself. Pulse, blood pressure, and breathing increase markedly, and adrenaline is released.[7] The digestive system is shut down as blood is diverted from internal organs to the skeletal muscles, and the body prepares for an all-out defense.[8] This system served us well when there were many physical threats in the environment. Today, however, the need for this response is rare. Unfortunately, with a conscious effort, we may react in the same way to mental distress. The world now is filled with mental distress, and the severe response that was designed for physical distress is more harmful than helpful.

Our other basic response to stress is the **flight response**. Less drastic, the flight response prepares us to escape distress rather than to battle it. Pulse, blood pressure, and breathing do not increase as much as with the fight response; fewer and different hormones are released. Less strain is placed on the nervous system, and consequently, there is less strain on the organism.[9] Although individuals have their own tolerance levels for stress, eventually a response is chosen. Effecting control over the responses selected can be the key to coping with distress and living a healthier life.

Our ancient ancestors had little or no choice in how they would respond to stress. It is possible for us to control our response, however. Choosing to respond to distress with a fight response is termed a **catatoxic reaction**, whereas choosing a flight response is a **syntoxic response**.[10] Choosing a syntoxic response is preferable to choosing a catatoxic response for all but life-threatening stress. It is especially important to strive to react in a syntoxic manner today because most of our stress is mental rather than physical. The problem with selecting a catatoxic response to emotional distress is that all of your body systems are placed in a high state of readiness as if you were about to fight to the death. Eventually, given a number of catatoxic responses, the increased blood pressure, heart rate, hormonal release, and rate of gastric secretions take their toll—on you. Headache, ulcers, irritable bowel syndrome, and other maladies up to and including heart attacks can be produced, and you suffer, not the person you are mad at.[11] Syntoxic responses to distress can drastically reduce these effects. Developing a syntoxic response is not easy, however.

It is possible to develop a syntoxic response to distress, but for most people, significant effort will have to be expended in order to do so.[12] Specifically, a syntoxic response means that you do not become irritated, angry, or upset. You control your response so that you do not become agitated. How do you do this? The first step is to decide that you can and will change. A conscious effort must also be maintained in order to accomplish this. Second, you must realize and accept that losing your temper and losing control is bad for you. Third, you must do whatever you can not to lose control or become upset when facing distress. This may mean counting to 10 (or 100!) or walking away and taking a time-out. Or you might have to rationalize with yourself. For instance, you may have to say to yourself, "I don't need him," or "Her opinion doesn't matter to me," or anything else you can tell yourself to keep from placing all your systems on alert. Fourth, it may be helpful to perform a self-analysis to identify which circumstances upset you. You should first find out what pushes your buttons so you can work to disconnect those buttons. For example, if rushing through heavy traffic drives you crazy, find other transportation, find a different route to work, or leave earlier. If a certain coworker irritates you, then discover what specifically upsets you about him or her and address it or do what you can to avoid him or her. If it seems to be life in general that is overstressing you, then follow some of the general stress-reduction suggestions discussed later in this chapter.

Flight Response
the body's escapist defense response; preparation to flee distress

Catatoxic Reaction
choosing a fight response to distress; choosing to become upset

Syntoxic Response
choosing a flight response; choosing to cope with stress by not becoming upset

---

SPOT CHECK

1. Eustress is disease-producing stress. T F
2. A flight response is a syntoxic response. T F
3. Being chased as part of a game of football produces physical eustress. T F
4. For almost all situations, a syntoxic response is preferable to a catatoxic response. T F
5. You cannot choose the response, catatoxic or syntoxic, that you will have to a stressor. T F

CAUSES OF STRESS

Many factors in life can cause stress; here, we are mainly concerned with work-related stressors. Tables 15.1 and 15.2 summarize work and nonwork stressors. Seven general work-related factors contribute to stress either individually or in combinations. These factors include:

- quantitative demands
- qualitative demands
- work-pace control
- participation
- work shift
- work roles
- the accumulation of factors

QUANTITATIVE DEMANDS

Quantitative Demand Distress

distress produced from the amount of work demanded, the time allotted to complete work, repetition, or the amount of concentration required

Quantitative demand distress can be produced by the amount of work demanded, the time allotted to complete work, repetition, and concentration.[13] The amount of work demanded from someone can cause distress if it exceeds the person's capabilities. Sometimes a person might be able to manage a high workload for a short time before the effects of stress are seen. If the high demands continue, the distress will take its toll. Distress can also be caused by a decrease in the time allotted to complete a regular quantity of work. Work that is highly repetitious can produce distress from the boredom created by performing the same tasks over and over. Jobs requiring a high degree of concentration can also contribute to or cause distress.

TABLE 15.1 CAREER-RELATED CAUSES OF STRESS

Performance anxiety (e.g., caused by new job or promotion)	Insecurity (regarding job responsibility, future, etc.)
Poor planning or goal setting	Lack of needs satisfaction
Unclear job requirements	Misunderstanding and ineffective communication
Little recognition of performance	
Insufficient authority to make decisions	Formal performance appraisals
Peer pressure	Working conditions
Conflict with others	Equipment
Excessive work demands	Organizational politics
Underuse of skills	Inconsistent managers
Work overload or underload	Unsupportive boss
Low morale	Receiving criticism in front of others
	Rapid change

TABLE 15.2 OFF-THE-JOB CAUSES OF STRESS

Family problems	Automobile problems
Financial difficulties	Neighbors
Poor health	Current events
Substance abuse (alcohol, cigarettes, or hard drugs)	Insomnia (can also be a result of stress)
Traffic violations	Home-maintenance problems

QUALITATIVE DEMANDS

Qualitative demand distress can result from job content that is too narrow for the individual.[14] Narrowness of a job's content refers to autonomy, opportunities to solve problems, and opportunities to use one's creativity. A lack of autonomy (the freedom to be self-supervising) can cause distress when someone desires to be free from, and is capable of working without, supervision. Insufficient opportunity for a person to apply his or her problem-solving skills or creativity may cause distress if he or she feels confined or overrestricted given his or her abilities.

WORK-PACE CONTROL

Long lines of customers, piles of work marked "Urgent," and assembly lines can all cause distress if workers cannot control the pace of the work themselves.[15] Some workers have a limited amount of control over the pace of their work, and others have virtually no control. For example, even with a long line of customers, a bank teller has some control because he or she can service each customer slowly or quickly. Workers on many assembly lines have no control over the pace of work because the next piece is coming down the line as work is performed on the current one. As control over the pace decreases, frustration and **work-pace-control distress** can increase. This is especially true as the work pace approaches the limits of a worker's capabilities.

PARTICIPATION

Participation distress affects those workers who wish to contribute to the social or the work environment.[16] People who are prevented from participating in the decision-making process or in the information or work flow can feel mental distress. Separation from the social environment, for example, when people are physically isolated from others or are temporarily separated, as when working the night shift or weekends only, can also cause mental distress.[17]

WORK SHIFT

The shift a person works can produce physical distress, mental distress, or both.[18] **Work-shift distress** can be caused by a failure to adjust to a work shift. This is most common when a person works a **swing shift**, which is a rotating work shift, for example, working the day shift for a week, the afternoon shift for a week, the night shift for a week, and then back to the day shift. Physical distress can also result from a day person's working nights or a night person's working days. For some people, mental distress can result from working a shift other than Monday through Friday because much of society is geared toward people on this schedule. However, this shift or any other may cause mental distress if it differs greatly from the shift of family and friends. If friends and family all work the afternoon shift but you work days, this may cause mental distress if you miss holidays and family gatherings.

WORK ROLES

Role ambiguity and role conflict can cause a form of mental distress—**work-role distress**. Role conflict can occur when people are given contradictory instructions, when they are asked to violate their ethics or the law, when they feel they must exceed their authority in order to accomplish tasks, or when they feel responsible for events that cannot be controlled.[19] Role ambiguity can result from an inaccurate,

---

Qualitative Demand Distress

distress caused by a mismatch between an individual and his or her job content

Work-Pace-Control Distress

distress from a worker's lack of control over the pace of work

Participation Distress

distress from a lack of participation for workers who wish to contribute to the social or working environment

Work-Shift Distress

physical or mental distress, or both, caused by any failure to adjust to a work shift

Swing Shift

rotating work shift, e.g., working the day shift for a week, the afternoon shift for a week, the night shift for a week, and then back to the day shift

Work-Role Distress

distress caused by work-role ambiguity or role conflict

nonexistent, or uncommunicated job description; a rapidly changing work environment; or changes in the informal organization.[20]

ACCUMULATION OF FACTORS

Chronic stress, the accumulation of effects that go unnoticed on a daily basis, can cause psychological and physiologic problems.[21] Such long-term stress may arise from the Peter Principle (being overpromoted), being underpromoted, having your ambitions impeded, or a lack of job security. These factors may not produce effects for years, but eventually, if not attended to, they can.

REACTIONS TO WORK-RELATED DISTRESS

There are three general categories of reactions to work-induced distress: affective, behavioral, and physical. Affective reactions are those that are emotional in nature. Behavioral reactions manifest themselves in our actions. Physical reactions produce physiologic changes. A person feeling distress may exhibit reactions in one, two, or all three of these categories. In addition, a person may exhibit more than one reaction from the same category.

Affective Reactions **Affective reactions** are subjective rather than objective, arising from emotions rather than from conscious thoughts.[22] Anger, probably the most common of the affective reactions, includes hostility, aggression, and fear. Although affective reactions are often expressed through yelling, fighting, depression, or even physical abuse, physical illness can result if emotions are repressed.[23] Work-related distress should not be used as an excuse to explode and vent your anger on innocent clients, customers, managers, subordinates, or peers. It may be necessary to employ alternative release mechanisms or stress management (described later).

REALITY CHECK

Small Releases for Small Stressors

Maybe you're doing a pretty good job of handling stress, or maybe you just have a few small stressors disturbing you. You don't need to read a lot of books on stress management, you don't need the employee assistance program, and you certainly don't need a shrink. Is there anything for someone who just needs a little help? The answer is yes. At least five techniques will help you with those low levels of distress.

1. Take a break. People take breaks for physical stress but sometimes forget to do so when subjected to mental distress. Take a few minutes to get up and move around, check the radio for news, or visit a favorite Web site.

2. Talk about those things that are stressful. If you can't talk to a friend or spouse, then it is sometimes helpful to keep a journal.

3. Play music. Find something relaxing, something you can work to, and play that in the background. On the way home from work, turn off the all-news station and the talk-radio station and listen to a music station, a tape, or a CD.

4. Take time to get organized and plan your activities. Sometimes this is more important when you are less busy. Busy people have little choice; their schedule dictates when and for how long they will work on something. When you are less busy, it is easier to procrastinate and often more important to plan.

5. Compress your worrying. If you find yourself worrying throughout the day, designate 20 or 30 minutes each day for worrying. You should exhaust your capacity for worrying in this amount of time and will then be free to concentrate on other matters.

Source: Adapted from Bob Condor, "Discharge the Anxiety with Some of These Stress-Busting Techniques," *Chicago Tribune*, November 6, 1996, sec. 5, p. 9.

Behavioral Reactions   There are three categories of **behavioral reactions** to distress: substance abuse, active behaviors, and passive behaviors.[24] Substance abuse is such a large topic that it will be discussed later in this chapter.

Active behavioral reactions to work distress typically involve some form of escape, which often results in a decline in the quantity of work. This may be a work slowdown or an avoidance of some tasks altogether. Escape could entail coming in late (tardiness) or missing a whole day of work (absenteeism). Both of these behaviors could also be caused by other factors, however. If the distress is perceived to be great enough, then the escapist behavior might be to transfer to a new department or even to resign from the firm. Each of these behaviors is an attempt to reduce the amount of distress by avoiding the stressors.

Passive behavioral reactions to stress are more likely to affect the quality, instead of the quantity, of work. Motivation may decline, or people may become uninterested in correcting errors. Instead of being interested in work, people can become indifferent toward it. Apathy, lethargy, and a lack of curiosity about the job can develop. Rather than being escapist, these attitudes are defeatist, a surrendering to the distress rather than attempting to cope with it.

Accidents may increase and participation may decrease as a result of passive behavioral reactions to distress. A person uninterested in work may become careless and suffer more injuries on the job as a result. It is also easy to understand how an apathetic worker would also be apathetic about participating in the company's formal and informal organizations.

Physical Reactions   The **physical reactions** to distress are often more consciously associated with distress than are the affective or behavioral reactions. Physical reactions to stress can cause anatomical and physiological changes. For introductory purposes, these reactions can be divided into those manifested in the gastrointestinal system, in the circulatory system, and in other systems.

Reactions to distress can occur at virtually any point along the length of the gastrointestinal tract.[25] Dryness of the mouth and throat can be caused by physical or mental distress, and there can be an increase in the production of gastric juices in the stomach. An increase in gastric acids may upset the stomach or produce ulcers of the stomach or duodenum (the first segment of the small intestine). The stomach, small intestine, and large intestine are all susceptible to distress-induced spasms that can lead to conditions such as irritable bowel syndrome.

Circulatory system disturbances caused by distress can vary in severity and length. Temporary increases in the heart rate are possible and are typically limited in overall detrimental effect. Blood moves to skeletal muscles from internal organs such as the intestines and also from the hands in preparation for a fight response.[26] An increase in blood pressure, on the other hand, can occur with little noticeable effect, can last for many years, and can be quite damaging. The cardiovascular system exhibits both types of characteristics. Heart disease may pass unnoticed for a long time and then manifest itself in either a mild or a severe heart attack. An alarming number of patients do not survive their first heart attack, which contributes to heart disease being one of the leading causes of death in the United States.[27]

Other systems affected by distress range from the muscular system to the nervous system. For example, the brain releases cortisol and adrenaline—stress hormones.[28] While the senses reach a level of heightened awareness, the muscles tense. The result is preparedness for a fight or flight response, or with today's lack of escape valves, it can cause one of the most common modern reactions to distress—the headache.

Behavioral Reactions
changes in a person's actions as a result of stress

Active Behavioral Reactions
escapist activities

Passive Behavioral Reactions
a decrease in activity; apathy or lethargy

Physical Reactions
anatomical and physiological changes caused by stress

SPOT CHECK

6. Quantitative demand distress can result from job content that is too narrow for the individual. T F
7. Qualitative demand distress can be produced by the amount of work demanded, the time allotted to complete work, repetition, and concentration. T F
8. Participation distress affects those workers who do not wish to contribute to the social or the work environment. T F
9. Work-shift distress can be caused by a limited amount of control over the pace of the work. T F
10. Active behavioral reactions to work distress typically involve some form of escape. T F

THE THREE STAGES OF STRESS

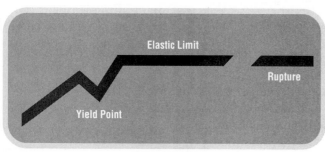

FIGURE 15.1 THE THREE STAGES OF STRESS
Yield point represents a slight change from normal behavior. Elastic limit represents a danger zone that results in greater change in normal behavior. Rupture results in severe mental and physical damage (nervous breakdown).

Source: Adapted from Jere E. Yates, *Managing Stress* (New York: American Management Association, 1979), p. 23.

Yield Point

the first stress stage that reveals itself as a slight change from normal behavior

Elastic Limit

a warning stage that tells us when we are near our stress threshold

Rupture Point

a nervous breakdown; a stress reaction that can cause severe and permanent mental and physical damage if we don't manage our stress properly

The human mind and body are a lot like a metal spring. A spring has a certain tolerance for stress. It can be strained up to certain limits (depending on its strength and construction), and then will return to its original shape. We are much like a spring; we can be pressured up to certain limits, and generally we will rebound. Dr. Jere E. Yates points out that there are actually three different stages, or points, that humans can experience with stress. As you can see in Figure 15.1, the first, the **yield point**, is the stage that reveals itself as a slight change from normal behavior. We will reach this point from time to time. The next stage—an extremely critical point—is called our **elastic limit**. Yates has described this point as an early-warning device that tells us when we are near our stress threshold. We can function reasonably well between our yield point elastic limit and can function for a while at our elastic limit. However, if pressed beyond our elastic limit, we will not rebound easily. Once we go beyond our elastic limit, we may reach our **rupture point**, which can cause some severe and permanent mental and physical damage if we don't manage our stress properly. We'll discover shortly some of the methods that can be used for preventing or reducing the harmful effects of distress.[29]

FRUSTRATION: ANOTHER RESPONSE TO STRESS

You have undoubtedly experienced **frustration**, the feeling of insecurity and dissatisfaction arising from unresolved problems or unsatisfied needs and wants, from time to time. Perhaps someone of whom you were quite fond has rejected you. Or maybe you were turned down for a job you wanted. Or you may have been bypassed for a particular job promotion to which you had anxiously aspired. Problems often arise when the needs of organizational members, either on or off the job, go unsatisfied for a long time.

WITH A LITTLE HELP FROM YOUR MIND

The mind, either consciously or subconsciously, generally attempts to cause behavior designed to help the frustrated person adjust to an unresolved situation, a type of behavior termed an **adjustive reaction** or defense mechanism. Some adjustive reactions are positively directed, whereas others may be negative.

Some frustrations may result in mild adjustive reactions; other reactions may be extreme and emotional. The intensity of a particular adjustment generally depends on two factors: the type of frustration activity and the previous experience of the frustrated person. Psychologists have developed a variety of terms to describe the numerous types of adjustive reactions to frustration.

REACTIONS TO FRUSTRATION

An understanding of psychological concepts, such as adjustive reactions, certainly won't enable you to lie on your cozy, make-believe psychiatrist's couch, skillfully playing the role of a psychotherapist while sensitively treating your own complex mental problems or those of others. Any person with chronic or severe problems should seek professional assistance. However, an awareness of the major adjustive reactions, or defense mechanisms, may enable you to deal more effectively with the relatively normal stresses and strains of everyday living that can affect both you and others in your organization. When you recognize some of the adjustive responses in others, you should be able to empathize with them more fully and understand behavior that previously might have made you angry, frustrated, or disappointed.

The adjustive reactions with which we'll be primarily concerned are:

- rationalization
- compensation
- negativism
- resignation
- repression
- pseudostupidity
- obsessive thinking
- displacement
- conversion

RATIONALIZATION

"Shoot, I didn't really want that crummy promotion anyhow. Besides, that job will be nothing but problems for the geek who got it. Actually, I'm darn lucky I didn't get it." This psychological adjustive reaction is termed **rationalization**, which exists when an individual attempts to give plausible (rational)—but not necessarily true—explanations for specific and often undesirable behavior.

Another example of rationalization is provided by the person who says, "Everybody else cheats on exams, expense accounts, income taxes, and in politics; so why shouldn't I?" But does everybody else cheat? Not likely, but such a belief is a defense mechanism that tends to make the person feel that his or her behavior is more acceptable. Even if you believe that the ethical values of an increasing number of individuals have deteriorated, should you follow suit? In effect, the person who attempts to justify behavior that he or she feels is undesirable—either consciously or subconsciously—is engaging in rationalization.

Frustration
the feeling of insecurity and dissatisfaction arising from unresolved problems or unsatisfied needs and wants

Adjustive Reaction
defense mechanism people employ in order to attempt to cope with stress

Rationalization
giving plausible, but not necessarily true, explanations for specific and often undesirable behavior

COMPENSATION

You've probably heard of people with physical limitations who went on to achievements far beyond the capabilities of many individuals without similar challenges. Well-known examples are Franklin D. Roosevelt, Ray Charles, Stevie Wonder, and Stephen Hawking, the almost totally paralyzed, speechless, and wheelchair-bound physicist and author of the best-selling book, *A Brief History of Time*. In reality, many organizational members who strive with unusual zeal to attain certain self-imposed goals are exhibiting a form of adjustive reaction. We are referring to the concept of **compensation** when we discuss a situation in which individuals with feelings of inadequacy—either real or imagined—exert extra effort in an attempt to overcome the insecure feelings.

Some forms of compensation may be quite beneficial, or positive, whereas others are harmful, or negative. Positive compensation might be found in a person whose child died from a birth defect and who expends an inordinate amount of energy on helping children with physical or intellectual challenges. Employees who feel that their abilities are inferior to those of coworkers may work particularly hard on certain projects to prove that they can do as well. Often, students who lack a certain degree of confidence but who labor with extra vigor on their projects prepare the best college term papers. The best students seldom seem to feel that they have expended sufficient time on assignments.

Some people may react in a negative fashion because of their feelings of inadequacy. They may become aggressive, pushy, overcritical, and sometimes even power hungry. Some historians believe that Napoleon's ambitious military conquests may have been related to feelings of inadequacy brought about by his short stature.

NEGATIVISM

The promotion on TV of many products is directed toward the normal insecurities most people tend to have, such as the fear of rejection by others ("Drink this or you won't be cool!"). Many high achievers are driven by a fear of failure that makes them insecure. One of the unfortunate by-products of some people's insecurities can be termed **negativism**, the subconscious resistance to other people or objects. Take, for example, the hypothetical case of a supervisor named Hattie Ferndowner, whose ideas at a particular supervisors' meeting had been totally rejected. Hattie originally thought that her proposals were good, but as a result of their rejection, she felt disappointed and frustrated. A reasonably secure and well-adjusted person might have either attempted to analyze the rejection of the ideas or merely dismissed the situation from his or her mind and gone on to other important matters. Hattie, however, returned to her department and for the rest of the day caustically picked apart nearly everything that her subordinates did. At the end of the day, Hattie regretted her actions even though she didn't fully understand the reasons for her negative behavior. In one sense, Hattie was not only "belittling"; she also was "being little."

RESIGNATION

"You can't fire me, J.B. You know why? Because I quit, that's why!" This statement to J.B. is the ultimate in **resignation** by an organizational member but is only one of various types. The psychological term *resignation* generally refers to a deep-seated, extremely intense type of frustration sometimes experienced by individuals. The condition may be long lasting or temporary. Resignation can be defined as the state of giving up or withdrawing from one's involvement with a particular situation.

Compensation
the exertion of extra effort in an attempt to overcome a deficiency

Negativism
the subconscious resistance to other people or objects

Resignation
the state of giving up or withdrawing from one's involvement with a particular situation

An example with which students might identify concerns a 10-page term paper due only two days from now. Let's say that you've already done all of the necessary background reading and research, but you are finding it extremely difficult to put it all together. The excessive noise coming from a nearby room doesn't help a bit; it only tears apart any ideas flowing through your head. You've sat in front of your laptop for two hours, but you've produced only two paragraphs, both of which provide you with no personal satisfaction—and they'll probably please your professor even less! Finally, in disgust, you shout, "To heck with it! I'll bang this darn thing out tomorrow night," and out the door you go. Your decision to stop working and to do a less than adequate job tomorrow evening is a form of resignation.

You might have adjusted more positively to the situation. You might have asked the people in the next room to be quieter, or you might have attempted to change your environment by going to a library or to another room. Sometimes, however, the act of resignation appears, at least temporarily, to be the easy way out, but it neither gets your tasks completed nor provides you with a feeling of achievement.

REPRESSION

"Oops! I'm sorry, boss, but I completely forgot to tell you about the Purdy Upsett Company. That big order they placed a while back, you remember? Well they canceled it last week."

This example of a lost account illustrates that a person may "forget" something, especially something psychologically disturbing, because of the sense of anxiety or guilt that it might arouse. When individuals unknowingly exclude certain experiences or feelings from their consciousness, they are experiencing an adjustive reaction called **repression**.

Not all repression is necessarily negative. The human mind is a miraculous instrument whose tendency to repress the unpleasant aspects of many experiences is often beneficial. For example, years after a vacation, family members may remember the events that gave them pleasure, but they tend to repress, or forget, the less pleasant parts, such as the flat tire when they had no spare, the high prices at the gas stations, the biting mosquitoes, and the upset stomachs.

People who have experienced many tragedies during their lives, such as accidents or the unexpected deaths of loved ones, often appear later not to be excessively disturbed by the events. Nevertheless, they may have been profoundly affected by the experiences when they occurred. The mind tends to repress unpleasant events, and the individual who continually focuses on distressing past experiences often finds little enjoyment in the present.

Repression
unknowingly excluding certain experiences or feelings from one's consciousness

PSEUDOSTUPIDITY

In some cases the act of forgetting, instead of being the unconscious repression of events, is intentional and used as a means of avoiding certain types of activities. Referred to as **pseudostupidity**, it is exhibited by some individuals who consciously attempt to give the impression of being forgetful or inept. Let's look at the case of Fred. He's frustrated at what he perceives to be an excessive workload. He's also sick and tired of attending all those company meetings that do nothing, he feels, but waste his time. In general, he's considered to be a competent employee, but everyone around him is well aware of his "absentmindedness." They actually expect him to forget—which, in reality, is his goal. However, there are certain things that Fred never forgets, such as who borrowed lunch money from him!

Pseudostupidity
intentionally forgetting something as a means of avoiding it

Obsessive Thinking
enlarging problems out
of all realistic proportion

NetNote

Steven Burns, M.D.

http://www.teachhealth.com/

A stress, depression, and anxiety site with links to other sites.

Displacement
the psychological process
of redirecting pent-up
feelings toward objects
other than the main
source of the frustration

Conversion
a psychological process
whereby emotional
frustrations are expressed
in bodily symptoms of
pain or malfunction

OBSESSIVE THINKING

Another adjustive reaction is **obsessive thinking**. The term refers to the behavior of a person who enlarges out of all realistic proportion specific problems or situations that he or she has experienced. For example, individuals employed in dull, monotonous jobs requiring little in the way of active thinking or concentration may continually mull over personal or company problems in their minds. Perhaps the particular problems are not especially grave, but the obsession with them can create an exaggerated effect, making the problems appear gigantic.

A mind that is kept occupied, however, has little opportunity for obsessive thinking. If the job could be redesigned, or if the person could be allowed to talk with other employees, the chances for obsessive thinking might be diminished.

DISPLACEMENT

What personal motives might have caused the following immoderate (to say the least) types of behavior?

- A disgruntled employee shot four supervisors Friday at a battery plant, police said.
- An airline passenger was arrested after putting his hands around the throat of a flight attendant who spilled a drink on him, officials said.
- A disgruntled employee opened fire Monday in the factory where he worked, killing three colleagues, police said.

We all react to frustration, but one hopes our reactions are far less psychotic than the examples just cited. The incidents seem more like fiction than truth, but each appeared as an opening sentence in a newspaper article. These events could have been extreme examples of **displacement**, the psychological process of redirecting pent-up feelings toward objects other than the main source of the frustration.

When a particular situation affects a person's feelings of security, he or she may react by lashing out verbally (or, as we have seen, physically) at others. Prejudice toward other groups is often the result of an individual's own insecurities and can be a form of displacement. Scapegoating—blaming others for one's own problems or insecurities—is also a type of displacement. Some of our negative reactions to others may really be our own psyches telling us (and others) something about ourselves. Remember: When Clarence talks about Suzie, we may learn a lot about Clarence and very little about Suzie. People who are reasonably well-adjusted and secure tend to perceive positive traits in others. Unfortunately, those who are insecure and fail to accept their shortcomings tend to perceive others in a negative light.

CONVERSION

The mind and the body are inextricably related and significantly affect each other. A healthy body tends to facilitate the existence of a healthy mind, and healthy mental attitudes often make for healthier bodies. Some bodily disorders, for example, are psychosomatic in origin; they are physical symptoms of inner mental conflict. The term **conversion** is used to symbolize a psychological process whereby emotional frustrations are expressed in bodily symptoms of pain or malfunction.

For example, suppose Walter, an unusually conscientious employee with your organization, was assigned the responsibility of presenting a detailed forecast of his department's production for the next six months at a meeting next Monday. Walter's cousins, whom he has not seen for five years, unexpectedly dropped in for the entire weekend on the way to their annual vacation. As a result of the surprise visit, Walter was unable to complete his project on time. Instead of explaining to his boss why he had not completed the task, Walter developed a painful headache and called in sick on the morning of his scheduled presentation. The pain may have been real to Walter, but it could have been caused by his mental frustrations. Many aches and pains result primarily from anxieties.

BURNOUT: THE DISEASE OF HIGH ACHIEVERS

Have you ever noticed what typically occurs when you've run a machine too long and too hard? It may burn out. High achievers sometimes do the same to themselves: They run themselves too long and too hard. A similar phenomenon often occurs—a condition psychologists refer to as **burnout**, the complete exhausting of a person's physical and intellectual resources caused by excessive efforts to attain certain unrealistic, job-related goals.

WHO ARE CANDIDATES FOR BURNOUT?

Burnout candidates tend to be people with extremely high aspirations. They are typically idealistic and self-motivated high achievers. They usually start projects with a high degree of enthusiasm. Even though their schedules tend to be jam-packed with projects, they still have difficulty saying no to new opportunities or tasks that come their way. They also tend to do more than their share of work when working on team projects.[30]

WHAT ARE THE SYMPTOMS OF BURNOUT?

The goals that burnout candidates set for themselves tend to be unrealistic and unattainable. As a result, such individuals usually become frustrated and lose much of their earlier enthusiasm. They tend to become apathetic toward their jobs and develop feelings of wanting to get away from it all—the flight syndrome discussed earlier. Individuals suffering from burnout frequently feel that they are working harder and harder and accomplishing less and less. They also tend to feel tired much of the time. In addition, they are likely to feel irritable, develop aches and pains, pull away from friends and loved ones, and lose their sense of humor. Table 15.3 summarizes some of the major symptoms of burnout.

Burnout
the complete exhausting of a person's physical and intellectual resources caused by excessive efforts to attain certain unrealistic, job-related goals

TABLE 15.3 SYMPTOMS OF BURNOUT

Individuals experiencing burnout have the tendency to:

1. Become apathetic toward their work responsibilities
2. Engage in the flight syndrome
3. Feel that they are working harder and accomplishing less
4. Feel irritable
5. Develop physical pain
6. Withdraw from friends and loved ones
7. Lose their sense of humor
8. Feel tired much of the time
9. Consume greater quantities of alcohol than in the past

WHAT IS THE CURE FOR BURNOUT?

If not "cured" in time, burnout victims frequently find their stress-related problems compounded. Their unhappiness with their stressful situations may lead to divorce, the abuse of drugs, nervous breakdowns, and even fatal strokes. Assuming that you are a high-achieving person, what can you personally do to prevent your catching the burnout disease or at least to reduce its negative effects? The sections that follow provide some useful suggestions for dealing with pressure and stress. Carefully study them (along with the guidelines you will see listed in Table 15.4) and you may be able to help yourself develop immunity to the disease. In addition, you might want to reflect on the words of humorist Ken Hubbard, who said, "Do not take life too seriously; you will never get out of it alive."[31]

CAUSING ASSOCIATES TO BECOME DISTRESSED

So far, we've discussed the various ways to manage stress related to your own career and personal life. If you are a manager, you may, at times, be guilty of creating stress in others, such as associates in your organization who are accountable to you. They

TABLE 15.4 GUIDELINES FOR AVOIDING EMPLOYEE TENSION AND STRESS

1. Don't set impossibly high goals in the mistaken belief that they will make employees try more earnestly.
2. Don't criticize employees for not spending enough time at their desks getting work done after you've called frequent, lengthy meetings.
3. Don't put employees on the spot, especially in front of others. Give them time to research answers to your questions.
4. Don't continually take employees off one project to work on others, requiring them to juggle numerous projects at the same time. Often it is better to allow them to concentrate and finish one project at a time.
5. Don't involve the entire staff in every problem or crisis, especially when some of the individuals can do nothing to alleviate the difficulty.
6. Don't bring up employees' past mistakes when you are correcting them for a current mistake.

may encounter some of the same types of stressors that you periodically experience. Try to be sensitive to any observable symptoms of stress in your associates, such as chronic headaches or continual tiredness.

Because employees tend to follow as they are led, you should attempt to set a good example for your associates. If you look unsettled and fraught with pressure and act in a short-tempered manner, you may cause your associates to behave in a similar way. Table 15.4 lists six guidelines for avoiding employee tension and stress.[32]

THE WRONG WAY TO MANAGE DISTRESS: SUBSTANCE ABUSE

Substance abuse has emerged in recent decades as a major concern both on and off the job. Although reasons vary, substance abuse can occur when people use substances to try to manage or reduce distress. Here, a general overview of the nature and extent of the problems of alcohol and drug abuse are presented.

WHAT CONSTITUTES A DRINKING PROBLEM?

We should be clear about what is generally meant by a drinking problem. In all cases related to alcohol abuse, a common factor is the unfavorable effect alcohol has on the health or well-being of the drinker and his or her associates. In general:

- Alcoholics are absent from work two to four times more often than nonalcoholics.
- On-the-job accidents for alcoholics are two to four times more frequent than for nonalcoholics. Off-the-job accidents are four to six times more numerous.
- Sickness and accident benefits paid out for alcoholics are three times greater than for the average nonalcoholic.
- Alcoholics file four times more grievances than nonalcoholics.

DRUG ABUSE

Drug abuse, or drug addiction, exists when the taking of drugs, whether prescribed or nonprescribed, legal or illegal, causes difficulties in any area of an individual's life. Years ago, the stereotype of the drug user was either a glazed-eyed musician frantically beating his sticks on the tight skin of a drum or a person who dwelled in a ghetto. Mass publicity on drug abuse has long since caused that stereotype to fade from view; now in some circles drug use is almost seen as fashionable. The drugs of choice and people's attitudes toward them may constantly change, but the problem of drug abuse appears to be continuing unabated.

RECOGNIZING ALCOHOL AND DRUG ABUSE IN THE WORKPLACE

Pinpointing the specific symptoms of alcohol and drug abuse problems is not a simple task. A supervisor's main responsibility, therefore, should not necessarily be uncovering evidence of dependency on alcohol and drugs but instead being observant for declining job performance. Yet there are certain behavioral patterns that some excessive users of alcohol and drugs display. These patterns can sometimes be spotted through simple observation. Increasingly, however, employers are taking more aggressive steps to ferret out substance abuse among their workforces. A growing number of companies, especially large ones with more than 5,000 employees and those in businesses with the potential to affect public health or safety (e.g., transportation companies, utilities, hazardous-materials handlers), are adopting drug-testing programs.

The signs of alcohol dependency, unfortunately, do not always become manifest until the middle or late stages of the problem. The earlier treatment begins, naturally, the easier it will be. A person can experience some isolated incidents of drinking problems without necessarily being an alcoholic. However, alcohol abuse usually results in declining job performance.

Drug dependency also produces observable changes in work performance. The signs of drug dependency, however, are not always obvious. Some managers have mistaken an employee's euphoric appearance for the "look of love." Some of the symptoms associated with alcoholism could also be related to drug dependency.

DRUGS AND THE WORKPLACE

The owner of a small family-run business in the Midwest took a walk through his plant one day. He didn't know what to do with the suspicious-looking packet of white powder he found on his way through the building, so he called in the local police to take a look. An investigation revealed a ring of cocaine dealers operating out of the company's facilities. They were moving the drug inside the stuffed animals manufactured there.

ORGANIZATIONAL APPROACHES TO ALCOHOL AND DRUG ABUSE

NetNote

Substance and Alcohol Abuse

http://alcoholism.about.com/

Articles, self-tests, and other information.

Until relatively recently, most managers seemed not to want to recognize that alcohol and drug abuse were organizational behavior problems in need of their attention. When cases did become known, they were often covered up until the worker could no longer function effectively on the job and had to be dismissed, which did little to correct the individual's problem. At long last, however, most authorities recognize that alcoholism and drug addiction are treatable diseases and therefore require medical attention or therapy, as do other diseases.

An increasing number of organizations, private and public, have taken an active interest in attempting to reduce the prevalence of these two costly afflictions by developing employee assistance programs that offer help for alcoholism, drug abuse, and other behavioral problems and chronic illness. Many corporations have established in-house employee assistance programs. Many executives believe that their businesses have actually saved money as a result of investing in such programs.

THE NATURE OF COMPANY PROGRAMS

Organizations with established programs have attempted to steer clear of the traditional solutions of firing the person with a drinking or drug problem, giving sermons on the evils of excessive consumption of alcohol, or calling in the police. Instead, modern organizations have concentrated on counseling people to seek treatment, generally with an outside agency, while keeping them on the job. Although sympathetic understanding of the problem is conveyed, the employee is told that deterioration of work habits, absenteeism, or other troubles created by alcohol or drug abuse will not be tolerated indefinitely. Typical programs, therefore, deal with three principal stages: detection, treatment, and rehabilitation.

The words *alcoholic* and *drug addict* have disagreeable and frightening connotations to most people. Company managers involved with the establishment of employee assistance programs (EAPs) need to be concerned with semantics when determining what to call their plans. A key problem, therefore, is how to eliminate the stigma of such programs.

As we've already mentioned, the programs shouldn't be considered as something separate and apart from other medical and counseling services. Some employee relations directors believe that calling something an alcohol program gives it the kiss of death. Some organizations use broad titles such as "Employee Counseling Service" or "Employee Assistance Program," preferring not to stress solely the problems of alcohol and drug dependency. These programs frequently include assistance in a variety of other areas, such as self-identity, health, marriage, and financial difficulties. Some firms even prefer to avoid any stigma that might be associated with the words *counseling* or *therapy*. To make it easier for employees to get advice on drug programs, some companies, such as Xerox, have established toll-free numbers that workers and their families can call to get advice on drug problems. These services guarantee privacy to employees. The hotline counselors attempt to encourage employees to seek help through EAPs or local clinical programs.

STRESS MANAGEMENT

The previous discussion might lead you to believe that the world, especially the work world, is filled with nothing but bad stress. However, there is eustress in the world, even at work! Table 15.5 compares and contrasts distress and eustress. When examining these signs, remember that these are general signs of stress; they may or may not be caused by work factors.

STRESS-MANAGEMENT RECOMMENDATIONS

This discussion is not meant to replace professional help for serious distress; rather, the purpose here is to demonstrate that there are strategies for stress management and to provide examples of that help. Some elements of work can minimize distress; they have been discussed in previous chapters. They include the design of the working environment and work equipment; proper sound, light, and ventilation conditions;

TABLE 15.5 CONTRASTING DISTRESS AND EUSTRESS

Signs of Distress	Signs of Eustress
Insomnia and other sleep disturbances	Job satisfaction
Asthma and other breathing problems	Positive attitude toward work and life
Skin rashes	Willingness to listen to others
Anorexia or other eating disturbances	Responsiveness to others
Nausea	Empathy toward customers and coworkers
Ulcers	Smiling
Small or large intestine spasm	Sense of humor
Increased heart rate or blood pressure	Application of knowledge
Headache, neckache, backache	Creativity
Dry mouth or throat	High level of productivity

proper safety precautions and procedures; adequate safety equipment; task variety; worker autonomy; opportunities for social contacts; and opportunities for personal development.[33]

Some factors should be avoided, if at all possible, in order to reduce distress. These include a mechanically or automatically controlled work pace; rapid and repetitive motions; inflexible work methods; high level of concentration combined with a controlled pace; tasks requiring little knowledge, initiative, or responsibility; autocratic supervision; and high levels of noise or other hazards.[34]

Distress is sometimes caused by managers or coworkers. If so, take action to reduce or eliminate situations causing large amounts of distress. This may require you to employ conflict-management techniques, time management, or professional stress-management methods. However, one of the first steps involves reading this book. Studying the behavior of people in organizations can help you explain and understand actions that might annoy others who do not have the benefit of this knowledge.

Some stress-management techniques can be used on and off the job. Four main steps are involved: (1) identify stressors, (2) differentiate distressors to identify those causing the most distress, (3) resolve to yourself to do something about stress management, (4) actually take action to manage stress. This last step includes getting training or professional help in stress management, when necessary.[35]

Of the after-work stress-management techniques, some can be implemented without special training or professional assistance. In the long run, it is important for people to have outside activities—activities other than work. Many people look to work to solve all of their needs. When this does not happen, they may feel distress. It is unlikely, however, that work can completely satisfy all needs. People must analyze their needs, find out which ones can and cannot be satisfied by work, and look for alternative satisfiers for unsatisfied needs causing significant distress. Other nonwork stress-reduction techniques include hobbies, entertainment, and time for play.[36]

Eustress produced by exercise can also help to negate the effects of distress.[37] Relaxation and meditation techniques may also help, but these are beyond the scope of this book. Biofeedback may also help, but special equipment and professional help are required.[38] For the most severe cases, a stress-management expert, psychologist, or psychiatrist may need to be consulted.[39]

MANAGING STRESS WITH FAITH

Faith
a belief or allegiance that does not require logical proof or material evidence

The word **faith** has many meanings. To some, faith is a belief, trust in, and loyalty to God, or a belief in the traditional doctrines of a formal religion. To others, it may be an absolute allegiance to something concrete, such as one's country, or to something abstract, such as the symbolic meanings of the U.S. flag or the phrase "family values." Other types of faith that individuals may have are in themselves, in humanity, or in their own futures. Without the existence of some positive beliefs, a person has little to look forward to. People who lose all or most of their faith often turn to negative, and frequently destructive, styles of behavior.

For example, individuals who lose faith are thus aimless and pessimistic about the future. They may abuse alcohol or drugs, they may believe that violence and theft are reasonable, or they may develop negative attitudes about almost everything, including xenophobic attitudes toward immigrants. They may develop a tendency to make wisecracks during serious situations, or they may develop an unhealthy "Who cares? What difference does it make?" philosophy.

ESTABLISH ETHICAL VALUES

Unethical practices can be an unnecessary stressor. If you continually engage in unethical practices with others, say, your associates, your organization, or members of the general public, two principal problems might confront you. The first is the added stress you create for yourself caused by your own conscience, and the second is the tendency to assume that others are as unethical in their dealings as you are, which is not necessarily the case. Ethical values and behavior can eliminate most, if not all, of these stressors.

IDEALISM

Those who retain hope while half-submerged in a sea of despair are sometimes accused of being cockeyed idealists. But isn't **idealism** likely to be a far more positive and constructive approach than **pessimism?**

Optimism and faith in humanity do not necessarily imply **naïveté**. On the contrary, psychological studies point out that hopeful people are more likely to overcome barriers, that hope plays a significant role in giving people a measurable advantage in areas such as academic achievement, withstanding stress on the job, and coping with tragic illness. Dr. Charles R. Snyder, who devised a scale to assess a person's hope, contends that hope is not merely the feeling that everything will turn out all right. Instead, Snyder asserts, "Having hope means believing you have both the will and the way to accomplish your goals."[40]

MANAGING CAREER-RELATED STRESS

In this section, we examine the nature of work-related stress, followed by some specific suggestions that can aid you in coping with career-related stress, as listed in Table 15.6.

DEVELOP READILY ATTAINABLE GOALS

One activity that can assist you in reducing career-related stress is the development of readily attainable short-range goals. Flexible long-range goals, such as the desire to be a corporate executive, an office manager, a lawyer, or a physician, can be beneficial because they tend to give you a sense of direction. However, relatively easily attained short-range goals are just as important because they tend to provide you with periodic feelings of accomplishment. For example, your plans may include the

Idealism
the act or practice of envisioning things in an ideal form

Pessimism
the tendency to expect the worst

Optimism
a tendency to expect the best

Naïveté
a lack of worldliness and sophistication; being simple, credulous, or ingenuous

NetNote

Reducing tension

http://stress.about.com/od/ tensiontamers/ Tension_Tamers_How_To_ Feel_Better_Right_Now.htm

Stress-management ideas.

TABLE 15.6 SELECTED GUIDELINES FOR MANAGING CAREER-RELATED STRESS

Develop readily attainable goals.
Select a satisfying occupation.
Have faith in yourself and seek opportunities.
Contrast stressful activities.
Take the workaholic cure—learn how to unwind.
Take stock of yourself—analyze your feelings that may be causing stress.
Don't succumb to Parkinson's law.
Don't succumb to Kossen's law.

The same circumstances may cause distress for some but not for others. Much of the difference lies in how people react to situations. In addition to the specific situations discussed in the chapter, a major factor is the degree of control one feels over a situation. Less control leads to greater distress. Contrary to what many people believe, it is not long work hours that necessarily increase stress; it is lack of control over the work that produces distress. Some people work very long hours with no ill effects because they feel in control of the situation and the hours. Middle management, on the other hand, contains much distress for many because of the perception of having less control from trying to please upper management and frontline workers. Also distressful for many is inheriting a bad situation. The feeling of lack of control comes from not having caused the situation but still having to handle it.

The way you view and react to any situation can have a great effect on whether it is distressful to you. The more you fight, complain about, refuse to address, or exaggerate the negative in the situation, the more distressful it becomes. Focusing too much on the short term ("look how terrible this has made my week") also contributes to distress. Alternatives to inflating the distress exist. First, take a long-term view. Consider whether getting angry at something now will hurt your future prospects. Second, is there a way that handling something distressful now may produce opportunities or benefits in the future? Look for the benefit in handling the circumstances. One benefit that may be overlooked is the chance to rescue the situation and be the hero. Third, focus on what you can control and don't be consumed by things you can't control. If something is truly out of your hands, then let it be. Fretting about it isn't going to bring you control over it. Fourth, if something is still distressful and it isn't going away all at once, then start to reduce it by making small changes; enough small reductions will eventually add up to a large one.

Sources: Cheryl Dahle, "Don't Get Mad—Get Over It!" *Fast Company*, February 1999, p. 190; Lauren Heist, "Cease and De-Stress," *Fast Company*, May 2000; Anni Layne Rodgers, "How to Stress Less—And Smarter," *Fast Company*, September 2001.

acquisition of a bachelor's or master's degree in business administration. Short-range goals could include the satisfactory completion of each college course in which you have enrolled along the way, as well as a two-year associate's degree. Working toward the two-year degree, for example, could enable you to feel the satisfaction of accomplishment and even provide stimulation for your long-run efforts.

Too frequently, however, we tend to wish away our lives, often in segments. Some young people while in high school may wish those years away so that they can be free from what they feel is their drudgery. If they serve in the military, those years are often wished away. If they begin apprenticeship training in a trade, they tend to wish those months or years away. If they are in occupational positions with promotional possibilities, they may go on wishing their time away. Some people awaken one day, look at their aging faces in the mirror, and suddenly realize that they have wished away substantial portions of their irreversible lives.

SELECT A SATISFYING OCCUPATION

An important consideration, especially for a younger person, is the choice of occupation. If you have the opportunity to take a wide variety of college courses, you may, as a result, tap previously unknown interests. When you discover a particular field that excites you, interview individuals who work in the occupation. Ask them open questions and attempt to uncover their true feelings about their occupations. You might ask them such questions as "What do you like least (most) about your position?" Wait for answers, listen carefully, and you may discover relevant and useful information. The first step toward maintaining a positive attitude in a work situation is to choose a field that truly interests you.

Some individuals who have had one opportunity after another slip away, or who have felt certain barriers to be insurmountable, may develop an "I don't care" attitude and give up. This attitude is understandable; however, such people might close their despondent eyes to real opportunity when it comes along. As anthropologist Ashley Montague said, "The deepest personal defeat suffered by human beings is constituted by the difference between what one was capable of becoming and what one has in fact become."

We learned that a person's expectations of an event or certain types of behavior can actually cause the event to occur. The concept could be modified to relate to a person's expectations or belief in himself or herself, something that we'll call an inner-directed Pygmalion effect. Far too frequently, many people develop a defeatist attitude that becomes deeply cemented into their subconscious. They have become programmed to believe that they will never do some of the things that others have done.

The negative, inner-directed Pygmalion—that is, the pessimistic person—often passes up opportunities that come very near. You can do numerous things, however, to make your job seem more interesting, challenging, and satisfying, and less stressful. For example, periodically you might analyze the methods currently being used on your job to determine how they might be improved, which is far more satisfying than mere criticism with little positive action. You might enter company slogan or name-a-product contests. You might volunteer for special projects or temporary assignments. Company publications usually need interesting material. Perhaps you have the latent interest and ability to apply some of your inactive literary talents to writing an article. You might be amazed at how such efforts help to satisfy your higher-order needs. The major point, regardless of the activity you choose, is that there are infinite ways you can make your own job and life more interesting and less stressful if you seek out fresh, realistic opportunities and convince yourself that you can accomplish those things.

EMPLOY CONTRAST

Another technique for managing stress is to contrast stressful activities. This means contrasting mental and physical stress, eustress and distress. For example, studying a textbook may create a mild form of mental distress. This should be contrasted with activities that create either mental eustress (reading a magazine) or physical eustress (walking) for 10 minutes every hour. For contrast to help, you need to avoid simply changing activities. Studying calculus for 30 minutes and then studying genetics for 30 minutes is not contrast because both activities can engender mental distress. Likewise, working on a spreadsheet and then taking a break to work on presentation graphics is not contrast. Working on a spreadsheet and surfing the Web for fun is an example of contrast. The same principles apply to physical distress. The key to minimizing net distress effects is balance—not to overtax any one area.[41] Mix physical and mental activities, and mix eustress in with distress.

WORKAHOLICS

Have you ever found that you tend to create some of your own tensions and pressures? Many individuals do. They are unable to relax even when they have some spare time. They tend to fill up every available moment of their waking hours with work activities. They are in a continual struggle against time and frequently have a false sense of urgency. They are punctual people and are enraged at anyone who is late. They frequently do several things simultaneously. They gulp down meals. They drink too fast. They drive too fast and too close to the cars in front of them, and they are continually irritated at the driver who cruises along at the speed limit. They are, in effect, work addicts. People with these characteristics are what cardiologists Meyer Friedman and Ray Roseman have labeled type A personalities.[42]

A type A personality may be useful in rising up an organizational ladder to higher management positions. However, Friedman and Roseman believe that people, in order to cope more effectively with life's innumerable pressures and frustrations, should learn to turn off A periodically and become type B personalities. Type B people may have some of the same characteristics as type As, but Bs are less likely to have characteristics that are chronic, incessant, or constantly overdone. They ordinarily attempt to enjoy a reasonable amount of leisure. Many individuals, however, find the use of their spare time extremely difficult. For example, a surprisingly large number of managers and professional people in organizations suffer from an affliction believed to be worse in some respects than excessive drinking. Its name? Work addiction, often called workaholism. Some persons apparently overwork for the same reason that alcoholics overdrink: to escape (they hope) from frustration.

Workaholic

a person who tends to fill every available moment with work activities

There are parallels between the alcoholic and the type A **workaholic**. Both crave their activities—excessive drinking for one and excessive work activity for the other. Both develop a capacity—some alcoholics "enjoy" an at least 18-drink day, whereas some managers regularly work an 18-hour day. Both can develop withdrawal symptoms: The alcoholic develops tensions and anxieties without his or her beverage; the person addicted to work often develops tensions and anxieties on weekends or vacations.

Perhaps burying oneself in work is an activity similar to flight. Work may serve to shield the work addict from other, less-satisfying activities. Many people in organizations are hard workers, but the major difference between them and the type A work addict is that the addict feels guilty when not working; the hard worker does not. Type A individuals, especially when their goals are unrealistic, are often ripe candidates for burnout, a condition previously discussed.

Any obsessive-compulsive worker should attempt to learn how to enjoy leisure. Some psychologists believe that workaholics need help just as alcoholics do. Both must first recognize that they have problems. Both engage in destructive behavioral patterns that have to be unlearned so that their energies can be channeled into more positive directions.

Type A work addiction can lead to trouble. For example, it can lead to dreadful careers, destructive family relationships, drug and alcohol abuse, and even early death. Without work, the work addict starts coming unglued. There might be a little workaholic in each of us. Wouldn't you prefer, however, to try to recognize the warning signs of addiction and cope with them before it's too late? If you are an obsessive-compulsive worker and not really deriving the satisfaction from living that you would like, examine the guidelines in Table 15.6 and consider whether they might help you maintain or develop the faith and hope that we have been discussing.

TAKE STOCK OF YOURSELF

We all feel nervous, anxious, and tense from time to time. Turmoil in one's life can be exhausting and make coping with work and personal responsibilities extremely difficult. H. Randall Hicks, M.D., suggests that when experiencing anxiety, a person can take some immediate steps to deal with the problem. Dr. Hicks suggests, "Find a quiet space in your home and sit down with your thoughts. Write down the things you think may be causing your nervousness. Put them in rank order and write down a plan of how you can effectively deal with them." Dr. Hicks also recommends talking out your feelings with someone you trust; taking a long, soothing bath; going for a walk; doing a physical workout; or getting lost in a novel. "These activities can give you a sense of control," explains Dr. Hicks. "They can dissipate some of your stress and they can divert your mind from troubling thoughts."[43]

Your computer can also provide you with therapeutic value when you feel stressed about something. The mere act of inputting your frustrations and feelings into your nonjudgmental word-processing system (or writing them by hand) can provide release of tension and solutions to problems as effectively as would a visit to a therapist or doctor.

BREAK THE LAW OF PARKINSON

Have you ever noticed before embarking on a vacation or business trip that you were concerned about not having enough time to pack your luggage? If you've taken trips regularly, you may have noticed that the preparations for them tend to expand to fill your available time. If you have three days to prepare, you may spend much of those three days getting ready, whereas if you have only a half-hour's advance notice, you still manage to pack in time.

Were you ever amazed at how fast you readied yourself for work or school on mornings on which you overslept? Some people ordinarily allow about two hours in which to ready themselves; yet 20 minutes will suffice when they oversleep.

The point of the previous examples is expressed by C. Northcote Parkinson in his famous **Parkinson's law**, which states that work expands to fill the time available for its completion.[44] Although individuals differ, many people work far more efficiently when they are pressed for time. When individuals have excessive amounts of time, they often find less important tasks or time wasters to do. According to an old adage with a grain or two of truth in it, "If you want something done right, then give the task to a busy person."

An intelligent use of time, accompanied by adequate planning and the establishment of objectives, can enable you to break Parkinson's law not only with impunity but also with the rewards of accomplishment. These feelings of accomplishment tend to reduce feelings of stress and tension that usually accompany many tasks. To combat Parkinson's peril, however, you must be willing to overcome some of your deep-seated habits.

BREAK KOSSEN'S LAW

Let's assume that you're well aware of the stresses that can develop when you fail to organize. You know about the pitfalls of Parkinson's law, so you carefully plan your activities right down to the month, the week, the day, the hour—even the minute. You don't look for additional work to fill any gaps in your time; in fact, you feel that you don't even have any time gaps! Unfortunately, you may find that your sophisticated and highly developed state of organization hasn't really reduced your stress level much. Additional activities, tasks, responsibilities, and interruptions seem to come your way. This particular stumbling block is termed **Kossen's law**.

There are ways, however, to break Kossen's law. One way is to allow for surprise factors, which are those unexpected interruptions that continually upset the

Parkinson's Law
work expands to fill the time available for its completion

Kossen's Law
regardless of your state of organization, new tasks and interruptions will seek you out, thereby expanding your responsibilities, commitments, and workload

513

well-structured plans that people have made. However, should you really be surprised when your boss or one of your employees develops the urgent need to discuss something with you? Should you really be surprised when one of your customers has an unscheduled, serious problem that demands your immediate attention? Should you really be surprised when you didn't allow for an unexpected traffic jam, and the rush-hour traffic has you tense and upset because you have an important appointment on the other side of town? Overscheduling your activities—not allowing for the unexpected—can cause you to experience continual frustration and stress. To avoid the disquieting effects of Kossen's law, allow a reasonable amount of slack time for those not-so-surprising surprise factors that never seem to be out of sight for long.

What can you do if you are asked to take on new tasks and responsibilities that you know can't be comfortably worked into your already crammed schedule? Be honest with the person. Point out that you would sincerely like to help but that your present commitments prevent you from doing a satisfactory job on the project. You could also indicate that, rather than do a lousy job, you'd rather not take on any additional responsibilities at this time. In some instances, you might maintain a better personal image with the requester if you indicate that you'd like to give the request some careful consideration before deciding. Then, within two or three days, contact the requester and indicate that your present schedule doesn't allow you to

SPOT CHECK

16. Focusing too much on how bad last week was can contribute to distress. T F

17. An example of how you should contrast stressful activities would be reading a Windows system operating manual and then reading *Fortune* magazine. T F

18. Workaholics have failed to select a satisfying occupation. T F

19. Parkinson's law states that regardless of your state of organization, new tasks and interruptions will seek you out, thereby expanding your responsibilities, commitments, and workload. T F

20. Kossen's law states that work expands to fill the time available for its completion. T F

take on any additional responsibilities. Don't let too much time elapse, however, between the request and your response. If you do, you might begin to develop guilt feelings that could interfere with your normal work activities.

Of course, as we'll learn in the following chapter, like it or not, you should consider the political implications of your turning down a new task or opportunity. Your career path might be damaged in some instances if you fail to make certain adjustments in your schedule to show your boss that you are willing to accept additional assignments.

SUMMARY

In this chapter, we explored the nature of stress and the effects that it can have on individuals. We looked at stress from different standpoints, eustress (positive) and distress (negative), career-related and off-the-job stress, and how to avoid causing stress in associates.

We also examined some of the main types of reactions that individuals may experience in their attempts to adjust to everyday stresses and frustrations. Adjustive reactions range from the normal, mild kinds to the psychotic extreme. Some high achievers are like machines that have been run too long and too hard—they sometimes burn out. We examined some of the typical symptoms and cures for the condition of burnout. We have also seen a desperate and negative attempt to cope with distress—substance abuse.

Faith in oneself, in humanity, and in the future are essential if individuals are to derive personal satisfaction from living. Individuals with little faith or hope tend to be restless in their behavior, changing schools, jobs, addresses, and mates with excessive frequency. The search for utopia is difficult because many of the problems from which individuals are attempting to escape tend to follow them to each destination.

We further inspected some useful methods for living with and managing stress. We examined how friends and counselors can help us when we are approaching or have passed through our stress threshold. Finally, we analyzed some of the essential ingredients of those nebulous concepts, happiness and success.

We customarily spend much of our lives in work situations. Consequently, the choice of a satisfying occupation, as well as an enjoyable personal life imbued with a variety of interests, can aid us in achieving a more satisfying existence and in maintaining a reasonable degree of faith and hope in both the present and the future.

CHECKING FOR UNDERSTANDING

1. What is the difference between eustress and distress?

2. Define stressor.

3. Explain the significance of the terms *yield point*, *elastic limit*, and *rupture point* as they relate to stress.

4. Do you think that the defense mechanism of rationalization is beneficial or harmful to the person who experiences it? Explain.

5. What are some individual behaviors that could indicate that a person has a drinking problem?

6. Define *alcoholic* and *social drinker* and differentiate between them.

7. What's meant by the "stigma of alcohol or drug programs"? How might such stigmas be overcome?

8. What is your own personal definition of *faith?* Could a person have faith and yet not believe in a formalized religion? Explain.

9. What is the difference between type A and type B personalities? Which one do you think you are? Which is better? Why?

10. What tends to cause burnout? What can be done to combat or prevent burnout?

11. How can a person try to break Parkinson's law?

12. Describe Kossen's law. How might its implications be avoided?

13. If forced waiting frustrates you, how might you develop a situation in which it is not necessary for you to wait?

14. Explain the concept of contrast in combating distress.

15. What is a workaholic?

SELF-ASSESSMENT

Answer each of the following questions in relation to your work environment. Select SA for each statement with which you Strongly Agree, A for those with which you Agree, D for those with which you Disagree, and SD for those with which you Strongly Disagree.

1. When faced with distress my first inclination is to struggle against and resist it.   SA   A   D   SD

2. I am comfortable with the amount of work I am typically expected to produce.   SA   A   D   SD

3. I have as much freedom and control over my work as I desire.   SA   A   D   SD

4. My work requires more creativity than I can deliver.   SA   A   D   SD

5. I have very limited control over the pace of my work.   SA   A   D   SD

6. I am as involved with the social activities at work as I care to be.   SA   A   D   SD

7. I am quite clear as to what work roles I am expected to fulfill.   SA   A   D   SD

8. The hours of the day that I work are suitable to me.   SA   A   D   SD

9. My work roles clash with each other.   SA   A   D   SD

10. My total distress is right at the limit of what I can tolerate.   SA   A   D   SD

For items 1, 4, 5, 9, and 10, score 4 for every SA, 3 for every A, 2 for every D, and 1 for every SD. For items 2, 3, 6, 7, and 8, score 1 for every SA, 2 for every A, 3 for every D, and 4 for every SD. A score of 10–20 indicates a lower level of work distress. A score of 21–30 indicates a moderate level of work distress that the more simple stress-reduction methods may help. A score of 31–40 indicates higher levels of work distress that may need more involved stress-management methods.

SKILL BUILD 15

"I am not taking this lying down! I don't know what I'm going to do, but it's something. They're sending me out there alone! Me! I *hate* working alone! I took this job because I thought I would be working Main Office with everyone else. I want to be here! Do you know how many birthday sing-alongs I organized? How about getting the bowling team together? Oh, and Late-Night Thursdays. I organized that. That was *my* idea. It isn't fair. I actually feel sick to my stomach over this. Couldn't even touch Julie's Tofu Tuesday dish, and I was the one who got people to start Tofu Tuesday. I am, like, *totally* upset and bummed," Anuja lamented.

Skill Question 1. What basic stress response does Anuja exhibit?

Skill Question 2. What is the term for the cause of Anuja's distress?

Skill Question 3. What type of reaction to work-related distress is Anuja exhibiting?

"Tell it to someone who cares, baby," Bernice said.

"*What* is your problem?" Anuja said accusingly.

"At least you're still on days, permanent. I got switched too. I'm now the 'cover girl'—I get to work a week of days, then a week of afternoons, then a week of nights, then a week of days, then a week of afternoons, then a week of nights, then a week of . . ."

Skill Question 4. What is the term for the cause of Bernice's distress, and why does she have this distress (where does it come from)?

"All right, I get it already," interrupted Anuja. "At least you're still working, right?"

"Wrong," Bernice replied, "I'm not working. Oh, I'm coming in, but I'm not doing anything. I just don't care anymore. I gave them three good years, and this is what I get? Forget it. I'm just going to wander around like I have someplace to go. Maybe I'll get lucky, and they'll fire me, and then I'll just get worker's comp. Yeah, some time off with worker's comp will even things out. I mean, they put me on a schedule like that, and they don't deserve any work from me. It's an even trade—I come in on the crummy shift, so I get to reduce my workload."

Skill Question 5. What type of reaction to work-related distress is Bernice exhibiting?

Skill Question 6. What reaction to frustration does Bernice employ?

Just then Calvin Hobbes came crashing through the door, picked up an empty pop can, threw it against the wall, and when it didn't bank off the wall and into the garbage can, he kicked the garbage can nearly across the room. Anuja and Bernice looked at each other and then back at Calvin.

"Looks like you could join our misery club—if you weren't so violent," Bernice said to Calvin.

"I am not violent; I am mad. There's a difference. And when I get mad at least I take it out on inanimate objects and not on people!" Calvin replied.

Skill Question 7. What reaction to frustration is Calvin talking about employing?

"Is that a threat?" Anuja asked.

"No, I'm talking about that idiot of a boss I have. He just got back from two weeks vacation, and I, and three other people, had lists, honest to goodness lists, of questions. So he's back, so we started asking. Then he gets all mad, says he needs a little time to readjust. For what? He was *back!* He's been here for nine years. At least we let him hang his coat up," Calvin explained. "So, he gets all mad, and he blames me, and then he takes my team away from me. Says I used poor judgment in asking a question the minute after he walks in the door. So, I throw a can and kick a can, big deal. You won't have to worry about it anymore though because I'll show him; I'm quitting. That'll teach him a lesson!"

Skill Question 8. What reaction to frustration is Calvin talking about employing?

Skill Question 9. How should Anuja manage her career-related stress?

Skill Question 10. How should Bernice manage her career-related stress?

Skill Question 11. How should Calvin manage his career-related stress? Also, think back on previous chapters; is there some other action Calvin should consider given how he was treated?

APPLICATIONS

15.1 THE RAT RACE

Quentin hasn't felt like doing much of anything lately. He has been really fed up with most things these days. He dreads Monday morning, so he has been taking a lot of sick leave (typically every other Monday) and spending nearly the whole day in bed. Man, what a waste, but it's one heck of a lot better than going to that dull office in town. He hasn't been feeling too well lately, with terrible headaches most of the time. He and his wife, Gladys, tried moving to Surreptitious Valley to get away from the city. All that really did was give Quentin a 1-hour commute each way, as work is 30 miles from his house. Every night he complains to Gladys, "Back and forth, back and forth, every day on the same highway." And his boss—what a jerk. He makes the pointy-haired boss in *Dilbert* look like a genius. Now the company is thinking of restructuring, and nobody's sure if they're going to be working or not a month from now. The only real pleasure Quentin feels he gets these days is drinking beer and watching the games on TV on the weekends.

QUESTIONS

1. What do you think is troubling Quentin?

2. What adjustive reactions discussed in the chapter does Quentin appear to be experiencing?

3. How might Quentin improve his attitude?

15.2 STRESS AND THE SALESPERSON

It's all Andrea can think of—the oil, the oil, the oil. That and the president. The president is fighting terrorism. That's good. That threatens Middle East oil. That's bad. The company I work for imports products from China, and business is increasing. That's good. But if the oil exports slow from the terrorism thing, then the ships can't get products across the Pacific, and I won't have anything to sell, and then I have no money, and why do I all of sudden have to have my territory taken away, and now I have to cover the city? Sales might be better there. That's good. There might not be enough oil. That's bad. It's the president's fault!

Well, I won't take the new territory! Look how many customers I would have. More than triple what I have now. Can I set up my own sales call, like now? Nooooo! Brad Fredricks, the city sales manager, tells the entire salesforce where to go, and when. I'd like to tell him where to . . . well that's it! I hate it, I hate it, I *hate* it! I couldn't even sleep the last week. I thought it all over

and, and I hate it! I hate it, and my stomach hurts. My head hurts too.

I'll quit. No, I'll *threaten* to quit. Right! No! I'll tell them I can't do it. If they want me to go to a new territory with their appointments, then I don't know how to do nothin'! Maybe I forgot how to call on customers when it isn't on my schedule. And look at this traffic!

"Hey pal, I only got two nerves left and you're getting on both of them!"

"If there isn't any oil, why do we need a president? And why do I have to make more sales calls in the morning than the afternoon. Stupid Brad. I'm not a morning person. More calls, more morning calls . . . got to think of something oil, I mean something else. I am *not* taking this! I'm telling Brad I quit. I don't need more money. This isn't my fault. Ooh, I'm ready to explode here because I won't be able to pay my bills because of the oil, in the city, with the schedule I have to use that I don't want to, and I'll quit or scream or both!"

QUESTIONS

1. What general type of distress does Andrea have here and what type of general reaction has she chosen? Support your answer.

2. What are the two causes of her distress? Support your answer.

3. What two kinds of reactions to work-related distress is Andrea exhibiting? Support your answer.

4. Where is Andrea in the three stages of stress, and what stage is coming next?

5. Andrea seems a little frustrated. What four stress responses to this frustration are seen here? Cite supporting examples from Andrea's thoughts.

PERSONAL POINTS

1. What work-related stressors do you face or have you faced?

2. How do you react to work-induced distress?

3. How do you react to frustration in general and at work?

4. What are your strategies for stress management?

5. How do you manage career-related stress?

EXPERIENTIAL EXERCISE

Are You a Candidate for Burnout?

Answer yes or no to the following statements. Your answers should be considered general responses.

Yes	No	
____	____	1. I feel really tired most of the time.
____	____	2. I even feel tired after I have had seven or more hours of sleep.
____	____	3. I am much less patient and more short-tempered with my associates than I used to be.
____	____	4. I seldom feel that I am meeting my deadlines.
____	____	5. I am not exercising regularly nor spending as much time on hobbies as I did in the past.
____	____	6. I am spending much less time with my family and friends than I did in the past.
____	____	7. I seldom feel that I have accomplished enough work.
____	____	8. I seldom feel that I have time to relax.
____	____	9. I am drinking or taking drugs more than I did in the past.
____	____	10. I generally become quite annoyed when the automobile in front of me is traveling too slowly and I can't pass.

Instructions

Count the number of yes responses. If you have five or more yes responses, you are a potential candidate for burnout. If you have eight or more, the chances are that you already feel burned out much of the time. If so, review the concepts in Chapter 15 and try your best to apply them to your own life.

ARE YOU AN "A" OR A "B"?

Instructions

Print the number of your choice in the space after the item. Add the numbers when you are finished.

1. Do you ever have trouble finding time to get your hair cut or styled? Never (1); occasionally (10); almost always (12). _____

2. Your everyday life is filled mostly by problems needing solutions (34); challenges needing to be met (37); a rather predictable routine of events (3); not enough to keep you interested or busy (13). _____

3. How often do you actually put words in a person's mouth in order to speed things up? Frequently (9); occasionally (10); almost never (1). _____

4. If you tell your spouse or a friend that you will meet somewhere at a definite time, how often do you arrive late? Once in a while (18); rarely (18); never (3). _____

5. When you have to wait in line at the post office, a restaurant, or a store, what do you do? Accept it calmly (2); feel impatient but don't show it (10); feel so impatient that someone can tell you are restless (12); refuse to wait in line, and find ways to avoid such delays (12). _____

6. How do you feel about competition on the job or in outside activities? Prefer to avoid it (1); accept it because it is a necessary evil (6); enjoy it because it's stimulating (13). _____

EXPERIENTIAL EXERCISE (Continued)

Are You a Candidate for Burnout?

7. How was your temper when you were younger? Fiery and hard to control (5); strong but controllable (26); no problem (26); I almost never got angry (32).

8. Would people you know well agree that you tend to get irritated easily? Definitely yes (4); probably yes (11); probably no (21); definitely no (11).

9. Would people you know well agree that you have less energy than most people? Definitely yes (4); probably yes (16); probably no (11); definitely no (13).

10. Would people you know agree that you enjoy a contest (competition) and try hard to win? Definitely yes (16); probably no (10); definitely no (1).

11. When you are in a group, how often do other people look to you for leadership? Rarely (0); about as often as they look to others (3); more often than they look to others (5).

12. How much schooling did you receive? High school graduate (11); trade or business school (13); some college (18); graduated from a four-year college (36); postgraduate work (38).

13. When you were in school, were you an officer of any group, such as student council, glee club, 4-H club, or sorority or fraternity, or captain of an athletic team? No (3); yes, I held one such position (23); yes, I held two or more such positions (33).

14. How often do your daily activities motivate you to work harder? Less often than most people's activities (1); about average (9); more often than most people's activities (17).

15. Do you ever keep two jobs moving forward at the same time by shifting back and forth rapidly from one to the other? Never (2); yes, but only in emergencies (17); yes, regularly (36).

16. How often do you make yourself written lists to help you remember what needs to be done? Never (1); occasionally (5); frequently (9).

17. Do you ever set deadlines, goals, or quotas for yourself at home? No (1); yes, but only occasionally (6); yes, once a week or more (12).

18. When you have to work against a deadline, what is the quality of your work? Better (20); worse (2); the same (8).

19. If you were looking for a job, which would you rather take? A job with somewhat higher pay but less prestige and challenge (2); a job with more prestige and challenge, but somewhat lower pay (29).

20. After you have been away from your normal daily schedule for a week or more (such as a vacation), you want to stay away longer if possible (0); feel about ready to return to your normal daily activities (2); feel impatient for the vacation to end so you can get back to your regular schedule (3).

_____ TOTAL. A raw score of 253 or more indicates you're a type A personality. A score of 252 or less indicates you're a type B. Remember: This is only one measurement of type A and type B behaviors.

SPOT CHECK ANSWERS

1. F
2. T
3. T
4. T
5. F
6. F
7. F
8. F
9. F
10. T
11. T
12. T
13. F
14. F
15. T
16. T
17. F
18. F
19. F
20. F

16 | Challenges and Opportunities

The ablest administrators do not merely draw logical conclusions from the array of facts of the past which their expert assistants bring to them; they have a vision of the future.

Mary Parker Follett

It is not in the still calm of life . . . that great challenges are formed. . . . Great necessities call out great virtues.

Abigail Adams

GOALS

The goal of this chapter is to present the major challenges facing organizations today that were not mentioned in the previous chapters. These challenges may also be viewed as opportunities for the astute individual.

OBJECTIVES

When you finish this chapter, you should be able to:

- Recognize the increased concern of organizations for global organizational behavior issues.
- Explain the need to understand differences in customs among different cultures and list examples of variations in customs.
- List examples of differences in communication, workforces, and labor laws among other cultures and countries.
- Identify methods for reducing the effects of culture shock and repatriation related to foreign job assignments.
- Explain the importance of multicultural issues to organizations.
- Differentiate between prejudice and discrimination.
- Describe and list examples of discrimination laws.
- Describe the challenges facing women in today's workplace.
- Define and explain the significance of a "mommy track."
- Define sexual harassment.
- List measures that address workplace violence.
- Describe the problems older workers face.
- Differentiate between myths and facts concerning older workers.
- Describe the problems workers with disabilities face.
- Describe laws affecting workers with disabilities.

CHALLENGES AND OPPORTUNITIES

In many ways, organizations are facing the greatest challenges ever to their cultures and to understanding behavior within them. In some ways, organizational behavior and culture were easier to comprehend when employees were all of the same type. It was also grossly unfair to only employ people of only one type. Today we are at the beginning of a period of inclusion, a period in which workers of every type are being integrated into the workforce. Although this is a great challenge, it is also a great opportunity. The opportunity to have problems assailed by people from a wide variety of backgrounds—the indigenous, foreigners, men, women, the able, the challenged, the young and the old, and those from a variety of cultures—can be realized if all of us are willing to surrender any limiting beliefs from the past and to acknowledge that every individual has the potential to make a useful contribution. We need only to make the effort and take the time to look beyond any differences and to include everyone fairly. To start along this path, we must first know and understand the major issues involved.

UNDERSTANDING GLOBAL ORGANIZATIONAL BEHAVIOR

As more U.S. firms become global in their operations, more of them will require managers and workers who are global in their outlook. The concepts that you have already studied in this text will have to be adapted to what could be termed *global organizational behavior*. Such OB concepts as communication, motivation, leadership, morale, and adaptation to change are especially important to managers of global operations. The ability to apply OB concepts to other cultures is becoming increasingly important for American managers.

ORGANIZATIONAL CULTURES IN A GLOBAL ENVIRONMENT

As we learned earlier, each organization has its own distinct culture. Culture is important in establishing and maintaining the value of its members. A significant challenge faced by American global managers is determining how to blend established American organizational cultures with those that exist in other nations.[1] The task is not easy (see Table 16.1). However, it is less difficult after Americans learn what significant types of differences exist in various regions of the world. It is beyond the scope of this text to cover each cultural difference that exists in each region of every country. The following discussion is intended to reveal some of the factors that vary among peoples of the world. Keep in mind, however, the dangers of generalizing about any culture. Each nation has wide variations within it. Merely

TABLE 16.1 SELECTED FACTORS THAT INFLUENCE THE CULTURE AND OPERATIONS OF GLOBAL ORGANIZATIONS

Customs	Labor laws
Language and communication styles	Standards of ethics
Attitudes toward time	Political climate
The workforce	Variations in foreign exchange rates
Differences in pay scales	

travel through Sweden and Italy, and you will soon discover that not all Swedes are blond nor Italians brunette.

DIFFERENCES IN CUSTOMS

"What's wrong with these people? Don't they know that the way we do it in America is much better than the way they do it? And why do they keep asking me, 'Which one, North, South, or Central?' when I say I'm from America? Those other people aren't Americans; they're Canadians, Salvadorans, or Peruvians—not Americans." Some U.S. citizens receive a rude cultural awakening when they first hit the shores of a foreign land. When they encounter the different **customs**, or practices, there, many of them experience something known as **culture shock**, a state of confusion and anxiety that can affect individuals when they are first exposed to an unfamiliar culture. They find no round-the-clock convenience stores, few—if any—laundromats, and high-speed driving habits that are often stress inducing. Americans, of course, aren't the only people afflicted with culture shock. Japanese managers and their families who have moved to the United States have also experienced this malady. Some Japanese firms have even established separate schools for the children of Japanese employees located in the United States.

Up to the First Floor   Confusion is somewhat natural at first for transplanted **expatriates** of any nationality. To add to their bewilderment, new arrivals find things much different from the way they were back home. For example, they may discover that in some countries the first floor is not synonymous with the ground floor, or lobby, as it typically is in the United States. In many countries, such as France, Italy, and Spain, what an American perceives as the second floor is considered the first.

Time Zones a Hassle   Merely coping with differences in time zones can be a hurdle. For example, American managerial expatriates are often on the phone calling corporate headquarters in the United States just after midnight or right before dawn. However, with the advent of sophisticated fax machines and e-mail, messages can now be stored and scheduled to transmit at any future date and time to take advantage of international time differences and low rates.

Foreign Expatriates in the United States   In the last 25 years a number of foreign companies began or expanded their operations in the United States. And just like American managers abroad, foreign expatriates working in the United States have adjustments to make. Some of them working for the first time in the United States feel uncomfortable in the American environment. For example, Japanese managers attending an American classroom training environment need encouragement before they will readily speak out. Many Japanese believe it to be impolite to be as outspoken as their American counterparts in training sessions. Hispanic transplants, too, have their differences. For example, they tend to feel it is impolite to start a business meeting before engaging in a certain amount of relaxed small talk. American managers, on the other hand, are more likely to want to start the business discussion immediately.

DIFFERENCES IN LANGUAGE AND COMMUNICATION STYLES

Communication and language are areas where significant differences exist among cultures. Such factors as conversational styles vary substantially in different countries.

Customs

practices followed by people of a group or region

Culture Shock

a state of confusion and anxiety that can affect individuals when they are first exposed to an unfamiliar culture

Expatriates

people who live and work in a country other than their native country

For example, Latins, especially some South Americans, tend to speak mere millimeters away from the faces of their listeners. Non-Latins often feel uncomfortable in such situations. Latins also tend to touch each other more than do many Americans and northern Europeans. (People from Italy, France, Spain, and Portugal are also considered to be Latins.)

Words also have different meanings in different cultures, and it is important to have a complete knowledge of slang and idiomatic expressions. Possibly the most famous example of what can happen when words are misunderstood occurred when GM went to sell its Nova automobile in Mexico. GM found that the name in Spanish essentially sounded like the words for "no go," which didn't help sales. Parker Pen Company managers' faces also turned a bright red after their company blitzed Latin America with an advertising campaign that—much to their chagrin—used the Spanish word *embarazar* for the English word embarrass, implying that its new ink would help to prevent pregnancies.[2] Some common names for U.S. products, such as the Fig Newton cookie or the fanny pack worn by skiers, joggers, and tourists, are considered obscene words in Germany and Great Britain, respectively.

DIFFERENCES IN ATTITUDES TOWARD TIME

Attitudes toward time vary among cultures. Americans tend to be relatively punctual for business engagements. Swiss businesspeople usually expect you to be precisely on time for an appointment. The spectrum shifts markedly in some cultures, however, where businesspeople may not even show up for the first or second appointment. When they finally do appear, they convey the impression that punctuality was not one of their priorities. Such persons may have expected you to wait for them for one-half to a full hour. These illustrations are not intended to be critical nor presented as rights and wrongs; they are merely intended to illustrate cultural differences. You will save yourself considerable stress and aggravation if you learn and attempt to accept the attitudes and customs of nationals in the countries where you may work. Expecting everything to be just as it is back home is unrealistic.

DIFFERENCES IN THE WORKFORCE

The global workforce is anything but homogeneous. Employees' attitudes and value systems vary greatly in a wide variety of important ways. One of these ways is productivity. Few firms can compete effectively on a global basis unless productivity, the level of output per employee, is comparable to that of their competitors. In some cultures, managers and employees alike are interested primarily in getting the job done, with little concern for how long it takes or how productive their efforts are. Such relaxed attitudes probably don't lead to burnout, but they also don't do much to assist the bottom lines of global concerns.

DIFFERENCES IN LABOR LAWS

Labor laws related to such factors as vacations, family leave, compensation, discharge, and taxation also differ considerably from country to country. Managers are expected to conform to the regulations of the countries in which they operate. Each country varies in the ease or difficulty with which employees can be lawfully discharged. For example, job security tends to be more assured in many European countries than it generally is for employees in the United States.

The degree of worker participation in managerial decision making also varies among countries. In some nations, **codetermination**, worker representation on the

Codetermination

worker representation on a company's board of directors and participation in decision making

Yes, things can be quite different in other countries. The best advice that can be given someone bound for an assignment in another country is to do as much research and reading as possible on the customs of that country. If at all possible, talk to someone from the country you are going to who is here. Go to the library and read all you can on the culture and customs.

Use the World Wide Web to contact people in the other country and learn all you can. It is not possible to be overprepared. Here are just a few randomly selected examples of differences that can be found abroad. Business cards are more important in many other countries than they are here. In Europe, South America, and Africa, they are often considered to be a condensed resume. In Britain, Germany, and the Netherlands, long-established firms are given additional respect, so the founding date of older firms should appear on the business card. In Japan, business cards are exchanged immediately after the introductions and bows. The card is scrutinized, especially for your title. All of the cards are then displayed on the conference table, in order of rank, for reference during the meeting.

Gift giving varies considerably throughout the world. The Japanese give gifts on many occasions, so be prepared, but allow them to initiate the custom. On the other hand, gift giving is rare in Western Europe. The continents of Africa and South America provide a wide variety of cultures and differences, so each country must be studied independently. For example, Spanish is spoken in most South American countries, except for Brazil, where Portuguese is the national language. Africa can be divided into three general regions: the mainly Arabic north, the middle countries, and South Africa.

Food can be vastly different, as can dining customs. Wine is a source of great national pride in France and Italy, and it is a part of all fine dining in these two countries. It would be inappropriate to ask for water, milk, or a soft drink, but you might be able to request a sparkling water if you explain that you are really not allowed to drink any alcohol.

The time to conduct business also varies. In Latin America, punctuality is not overly emphasized, whereas in Germany it is an absolute requirement. Saturday is the Israeli holy day, whereas Friday is the holy day in Arab countries. It would be considered quite rude to try to conduct business on those days.

Even the building that business is conducted in may be subject to local custom. In China, a master of feng shui is consulted so that all buildings are situated and designed for good fortune and to avoid evil spirits.

Finally, people from other countries often feel that Americans are too loud and gesture too much. In general, we need to be more reserved when overseas and to follow the cues of our hosts. When communicating with those from other countries, be more formal than you usually would be, be respectful of other cultures rather than judgmental, and be very clear in what you say. Do not use slang, abbreviations, or humor; choose your words carefully. Often a valuable strategy for making a good impression is to talk less and listen more to show your interest in people from other countries and cultures.

Sources: Adapted from Marjorie Whigham-Desir, "Business Etiquette Overseas: The Finer Points to Doing Business," *Black Enterprise*, October 31, 1995, pp. 142–144; Sondra Snowdon, "Business Protocol: Your Passport for Gaining the Global Edge," *Los Angeles Business Journal*, April 25, 1994, pp. 5A–8A; Barbara Ettore, "Letitia Baldridge: Arbiter of Business Manners and Mores," *Management Review*, April 1992, pp. 50–55; Roger Axtell, *Do's and Taboo's around the World*, 2nd ed. (New York: John Wiley & Sons, 1990); Scot Ober, *Fundamentals of Contemporary Business Communication*, 2nd ed. (Boston: Houghton Mifflin, 2007) pp. 27–28.

board of directors, is legally required. German firms provide an interesting example of codetermination. German managers are generally noted for their more authoritarian approach to leadership in comparison with their American or Japanese counterparts, yet workers are, by law, entitled to have representatives serve on the executive committees of large corporations. Worker representatives are also elected to serve on management committees. Worker representatives are expected to make managerial decisions that are in the best interest of the organization and the workers. As a result of codetermination, labor strife in Germany has typically been substantially less than in the past. (Codetermination continues to be voluntary in the United States but is likely to be utilized to a greater extent in the future.)

Managers of global firms are responsible for complying with the various labor laws that exist in their host countries. Learning, absorbing, and adapting to the various differences that exist among different countries can be a frustrating experience at times. Many European countries are more accustomed than the United States to regulated employment and labor relations and have more comprehensive social benefits. In some instances, legislation and practices in other countries differ greatly from those in the United States.[3]

DIFFERENCES IN ETHICAL STANDARDS

American managers conducting business abroad sometimes find themselves on the horns of a dilemma. They contend that the bribing of foreign officials and business-people to acquire sales contracts is standard practice in some countries and that such activities are considered financial favors by locals, not unlike giving a hairdresser a tip in appreciation for a job well done. Some American managers contend that they must engage in situational ethics, the application of moral standards that relate to the attitudes and laws in a particular social and cultural environment. However, to American government officials, the offering of financial favors, that is, **bribes**, to foreign officials and businesspeople to acquire or maintain business is illegal.

DIFFERENCES IN POLITICAL CLIMATE

The political climate of a nation has a considerable effect on expatriates and other employees in an organization. Certain types of events can be disrupting to business activity. For example, the U.S. government has in the past sometimes imposed **sanctions** on countries. Sanctions are coercive measures adopted against a country whose behavior is considered unacceptable.

EASING THE TRANSITION FOR INNOCENTS ABROAD

A cultural leveling effect has been taking place throughout the world as a result of increased international travel, global satellite TV, shortwave radio, popular music, and films. Worldwide communication now takes place with ease through direct-dial portable telephone systems, palmtop computers with built-in modems, and fax machines. Yet, in spite of such leveling trends, there remain specific cultural differences that make adjustment for the expatriate a continual challenge. Certain practices, however, can ease the transition for innocents abroad. These include:

- selecting the right people for the right place
- allowing orientation visits
- providing training opportunities
- using foreign nationals

SELECTING THE RIGHT PEOPLE FOR THE RIGHT PLACE

As with any position, sound selections for assignments overseas or across borders are essential.[4] The "my country, right or wrong" type of individual usually doesn't adapt well to foreign environments. Some Americans abroad have damaged both their company's and their country's image by conveying an attitude of cultural arrogance,

Bribes

things such as money or favors offered to a person in a position of trust to influence that person's views or conduct

Sanctions

coercive measures adopted usually by several nations acting together against a nation violating international law

a concept similar to the ethnocentric trait discussed earlier. As with **ethnocentrism**, cultural arrogance exists when a person conveys the attitude that his or her own culture is superior to another's.

Some employees do not function well in a foreign environment. The right people should, of course, be competent in their specialty. In addition, people should be selected on the basis of their desire to work and live in a foreign culture. Whenever possible, people with knowledge of a foreign language or those who have already traveled or lived in other countries, especially the host country, should be seriously considered. The attitudes of the employee's spouse and children toward living in a foreign country should also be taken into account because the employee's family often makes or breaks the assignment.

The right place depends on the employee's willingness and ability to adapt to the foreign environment. Some firms attempt to make the American employee's first assignment easier to adapt to by sending him or her to a country that closely reflects the employee's own cultural background.

ALLOWING ORIENTATION VISITS

An employee's adjustment to a first assignment in a foreign country can be facilitated and apprehensions reduced if he or she can make one or two orientation visits to the new location before actually assuming job responsibilities. Levi Strauss International, for example, allows its managers to spend some time in the new environment, arranging housing for their families and schools for their children. Some companies also assume the responsibility of disposing of the employee's U.S. housing if desired.

PROVIDING TRAINING OPPORTUNITIES

Cross-cultural training for employees soon to be assigned to foreign countries is essential if they are to get off to a good start. Many firms believe that involving employees' spouses in certain aspects of training programs allows for easier adjustment.

Some companies provide their soon-to-become ex-pats and their spouses with orientation related to the customs and cultural differences in the host country. Employees should learn as much as they can in advance about the host country's laws, business practices, and customs. They should also be familiar with the U.S. laws that affect global operations. Some global companies provide opportunities for their employees to take an intensive course in the host country's language. Kai Lindholst, a director with Egon Zehnder, a management recruiting firm, believes that "languages are important, especially a working knowledge of French and Spanish, and perhaps even Portuguese, for working overseas."[5]

USING FOREIGN NATIONALS

Knowing all the ins and outs of a foreign culture is difficult for American managers. Natives of a particular country, of course, tend to have a much greater sense of their own lands than do managers sent from the United States. Many U.S. firms, therefore, hire a substantial number of local people, either as full-time employees or as part-time consultants. The nationals should be immersed in the corporate culture of the U.S. company as well. U.S. firms operating abroad sometimes send their foreign managers to the United States to gain a greater awareness of the company's domestic corporate culture.

Ethnocentrism
belief in the superiority of one's own ethnic group

REPATRIATION: RETURNING HOME

"I had no idea going back home would be such a shock!" These are words that may be difficult to appreciate if you have not spent considerable time living in another culture. Once expatriates adjust to their new environments, however, they often grow to appreciate the best of both worlds.

Repatriation
bringing an employee back to his or her home country

Repatriation, bringing an employee back to the home country, may require considerable adjustment. After returning home, the employee sometimes discovers that something is missing from the American culture. Certain extras on which they became somewhat dependent, such as a chauffeur, maid, or premium pay, are not provided in the domestic assignment. Their hometown and circle of friends may also be different. "Things just don't seem the same at home anymore" is a common attitude of repatriates. In some cases, things were never as the employee idealized while in the overseas post.

COMPANY GUIDANCE AND COUNSELING

To ease the transition of returning home, some firms provide their employees with counseling, which should begin before the repatriation actually takes place. Candid communication with the repatriates is also important. Returning employees want, and are entitled to know, what their new job assignments will be; in which direction their careers are now headed; and how their promotional opportunities have been affected by their stint overseas. A repatriation agreement that spells out in advance specifically what the new job assignment will be can also help to reduce anxiety.

MULTICULTURALISM AND DIVERSITY

Multicultural
relating to or including several cultures

Americans today live and work in a society that is more **multicultural** than ever before.[6] The Bureau of Labor Statistics (BLS) projects even greater diversity in the near future. For instance, the BLS concludes that by 2014 nearly 16 percent of the workforce will be Hispanic, 5 percent will be Asian, and 12 percent will be Black (up from 13 percent, 4.3 percent, and 11.3 percent in 2004). Most observers of the U.S. scene would agree that progress has been made in the area of civil rights and in the more equitable treatment of minorities and women—individuals who have received unfair treatment, especially in employment, in the past.

Here we explore some of the principal organizational behavior problems concerning people who receive different treatment for reasons unrelated to their employment

---

SPOT CHECK

1. An expatriate is someone who no longer believes in the values of his or her native country. T F
2. Attitudes toward time are the same among different cultures; strict punctuality is required by all. T F
3. Codetermination is legally required in some countries. T F
4. Ethnocentrism is the belief that one's own ethnic group is superior to all others. T F
5. Repatriation rarely requires adjustment by the employee or the company. T F

---

situations. Different treatment is a more polite way of saying discrimination. Some individuals are treated differently principally because they're part of a special employment group. In our diverse society, although much progress has been made in recent decades, there still remain considerable **prejudice** and discrimination toward these groups. A word seldom used in the past, **xenophobia**, has become commonplace in newspapers in recent years. Xenophobia is an unreasonable fear or hatred of foreigners or people who are different.

We will investigate the nature of prejudice and **discrimination** and discuss two broad groups that have been on the receiving end of both—ethnic minorities and women. We'll then examine some of the problems these groups face in organizations and offer suggestions to those who supervise them. Finally, we'll look specifically at the principal problems facing ethnic minorities and women managers.

THE NATURE OF PREJUDICE AND DISCRIMINATION

If someone were to ask you if you were prejudiced, how would you respond? Regardless of your answer, the chances are that you have some prejudices; virtually everybody has. Discriminating against human beings is, however, quite another matter. The issues of prejudice and discrimination have always been emotional ones, and your own background and experiences will influence your perception of them. Let's now turn to these two important topics by first defining them.

WHAT IS THE DIFFERENCE BETWEEN PREJUDICE AND DISCRIMINATION?

Prejudice is related to attitudes. It is basically an internal phenomenon that entails the act of prejudging, or making judgments based on insufficient evidence. If you understand and are reasonably well acquainted with something or someone, in effect you are not prejudging. Discrimination is the result of prejudice and is external. It is

Prejudice
an adverse judgment or opinion formed beforehand or without knowledge or examination of the facts; irrational suspicion or hatred of a particular group, race, or religion

Xenophobia
an unreasonable fear or hatred of foreigners or people who are different

Discrimination
the ability to make fine distinctions or to differentiate; unfair treatment or consideration based on class or category rather than on individual merit; partiality or prejudice

REALITY CHECK

Is Diversity Required?

Some companies, such as Hoechst Celanese, Xerox, Avon, AT&T, IBM, and Levi Strauss, are committed to diversity at all levels of the organization even though there are no real-world studies proving that a diverse workforce improves a company's performance. These companies believe that the need for diversity is obvious. Their customers are a diverse group. U.S. Labor Department studies, such as *Workforce 2000*, predict that white males will constitute less than half (45 percent) of the workforce soon, so diversity is coming one way or another. Other firms, such as Maybelline, point out that one does not need to be a member of a certain group in order to comprehend the product and service needs of that group. Maybelline is not against diversity; it simply does not track it. Still, academic research indicates that diverse groups may view issues from a broader perspective, and they may create solutions that a homogeneous group will not. In the end, although there may be no proof that diversity is better for a company, there is also no one claiming that it is bad for companies. As diversity seems to be on the way, there may be advantages for firms who commit to it early, have the support of the CEO, and make diversity an objective having equal weight with customer satisfaction, profitability, and safety.

Source: Faye Rice, "How to Make Diversity Pay," *Fortune*, August 8, 1994, pp. 79–80; Nancy Lockwood, "Workplace Diversity: Leveraging the Power of Difference for Competitive Advantage," *HRMagazine*, June 2005.

an action directed either against or in favor of something or someone. Attitudes can cause prejudice, which may then lead to discrimination.

In many of our daily activities, we make prejudgments about situations and people. In the real world of work, decisions must be made or organizations couldn't function. The pressures of time often don't permit the exploration of all available evidence. However, when we make judgments based on less than complete data, we should leave a margin for error in case the results differ from our expectations. We should at least attempt to withhold our judgments until after we've examined the best available evidence.

PREJUDICE: AN ACQUIRED HABIT

According to most studies, prejudice toward other human beings is not an inborn response but a learned one. In short, we learn from others to use the mental shortcut of prejudice. As children, we go through stages referred to by psychologists as the modeling-identification-socialization process, and it is during this process that prejudice can be acquired.

Parents are believed to be the major teachers of prejudice, especially because their influence is greatest during the modeling stage, the period when children are under five years old. Modeling is a process in which young children imitate others, usually their parents.

As children grow older and attend school, they tend to be influenced by their peers. During this stage they identify with, not just imitate, their models, frequently the parent of the same sex. After children are nine years old, however, the parental ties begin to wear thin, and others begin to exert strong influence on their values. Peer acceptance, for example, tends to become all-important. At this stage, socialization has taken place. The role of parents is extremely significant in shaping the values of their offspring because, according to many child psychologists, our attitudes are strongly developed during the first five or six years of life. Parents can therefore be effective teachers of prejudice. Yet by their words and actions, parents can also teach their children to grow up in harmony with people of different races and backgrounds rather than to use prejudice as a means of resolving their own personal problems and feelings of insecurity.

REALITY CHECK

Best Companies for Minorities—and Performance

Not only is diversity a good idea morally, it also pays in the performance of a company's stock. A positive correlation exists between the efforts made toward having minority employees and a firm's stock exceeding the performance of the broad-based Standard and Poor's 500 index. Some believe that diverse groups make better decisions and this is why performance is good. Others attribute successes to minority company members being better at reaching minority markets. While many companies strive to include minorities, the top 10 according to *Fortune* magazine are:

McDonald's	U.S. Postal Service
Fannie Mae	Pepsi
Sempra Energy	Southern California
Union Bank of	Edison
California	
Denny's	Freddie Mac
	PNM Resource

Source: Cora Daniles, "The 50 Best Companies for Minorities," *Fortune*, June 28, 2004.

PREJUDICE IN FAVOR OF A GROUP

Prejudice isn't always directed against others; it can favor a particular group. Sometimes people who belong to the same political party, have attended the same university, or belong to the same religious faith develop positive prejudgments about each other. These prejudices, too, may well be inaccurate, and managers should guard against succumbing to the "old school tie" and "old boy network" forms of prejudice, as well as to negative prejudices, when interviewing applicants for positions.

PREVENTIVE PREJUDICE

Individuals sometimes engage in an activity toward others that can be termed *preventive prejudice*, which means that they prejudge the intentions of others and thus react first on the basis of an often-unfounded belief that an action is going to be taken against them.

Here's an organizational behavior example of preventive prejudice: Jordan's job performance has not been up to acceptable standards in recent months. Jordan is actually considered to be quite a capable employee, but he is unfamiliar with some complex equipment that the company recently acquired. As a result, Jordan has made a number of mistakes in attempting to operate it. Jordan's boss, Ed, recently commented about the quality of Jordan's work and indicated that he soon would be taking some action related to it. Jordan prejudged Ed's remarks to mean that Ed intended to fire him. Jordan decided that he would not wait for Ed to discharge him—he would quit first. Thus, Jordan's prejudgment caused him to react to what he believed would be an action, which was not based on reality. All that Ed had decided to do about the performance problem was to send Jordan to a training program sponsored by the equipment's manufacturer.

THE "OPPRESSED MAJORITY"

Who is on the receiving end of discrimination in the United States? One could argue that there really is no such thing as prejudice against a minority in the United States because, collectively, all those who have been discriminated against have added up to a majority. Furthermore, the population growth of so-called minorities is increasing at a much more rapid rate than that of Caucasians.[7] The terms *minority* and *majority*, however, aren't as important as the fact that numerous people in American society have been, and in many cases still are, discriminated against in employment as a result of the prejudiced attitudes of some members of organizations.

The list of groups who have been on the short end of the employment stick is appallingly long and includes a wide variety of culturally diverse people. Almost anyone could find himself or herself on the receiving end of prejudice and discrimination.

IT'S THE LAW

Organizational members should be aware of the various employment laws that affect the workplace today. The U.S. Congress has passed some significant laws in recent decades. Special employment groups affected by such legislation are sometimes referred to as protected classes of workers.

In 1963, Congress approved an important law—the Equal Pay Act—forbidding sex discrimination in wage scales and attempting to guarantee that women doing the same work as men would be paid the same. (The act applied, however, only to employers covered by the Fair Labor Standards Act of 1935 and did not apply to women—or men—in administrative, professional, or executive positions.)

One of the most significant acts of Congress is the Civil Rights Act of 1964, whose Title VII provides for equal employment opportunities. The act prohibits employers, labor unions, and employment agencies from discriminating against people on the basis of color, religion, sex, or national origin. The act also established the Equal Employment Opportunity Commission. The EEOC, as it is typically called, is responsible for regulating employment practices of organizations under civil rights acts. Most federal contracts also have clauses requiring "acceptable" proportions of minority employees. Many firms are monitored by the Office of Federal Contract Compliance to ensure that they have adequate minority representation.

Legislation alone can't alter the feelings of hatred and xenophobia that some individuals have for others, but it can help to create a climate that makes the unfair treatment of human beings more difficult.

RELIGIOUS BELIEFS

A further challenge exists for employers in regard to days of worship and religious holidays of a small minority of a company's employees. Civil rights legislation also extends to those with different religious beliefs. Not only is it unlawful to discriminate against employees regarding conditions of employment, but civil rights legislation also requires that employers make reasonable accommodation for employees to practice their religion. Employers may allow such employees a flexible work schedule or provide other accommodations to enable them to practice their religion. However, employers are not required to make accommodations that would place undue hardship on the company or on other employees.

LEGAL DISCRIMINATION IN EXCEPTIONAL CASES

Did you know that discrimination is legal in certain situations? Section 703 of the Civil Rights Act of 1964 exempts certain employment practices from the scope of Title VII enforcement. The major exceptions are the bona fide occupational qualification (BFOQ) exception, the testing requirement exception, and the seniority exception. We'll briefly look at each of these.

BONA FIDE OCCUPATIONAL QUALIFICATION (BFOQ) EXCEPTION

According to Section 703(e) of Title VII, it is legal for an employer to discriminate against employees in hiring practices on the basis of their religion, sex, or national origin "in those instances where religion, sex, or national origin is a bona fide occupational qualification (BFOQ) reasonably necessary to the normal operation of a particular enterprise."

Can you think of an example in which the BFOQ clause might be applied? Here's an interesting actual case: A Supreme Court ruling upheld as a BFOQ a requirement that all guards be male in a male maximum security correctional facility in Alabama. The Court argued that female guards would not be practicable because 20 percent of the inmates were convicted sex offenders and would create an excessive threat to the security of female guards. Can you think of any other BFOQ examples?

FYI

Learn about different cultures.

Welcome those from other cultures.

Respectfully explain to people from other countries how things are done here.

The keys to working abroad are preparation, education, and advice from people who are from there or have been there.

Focus on what people can do, not on what they can't do.

Focus on what you can do, not on what you can't do.

Age, weight, height, gender, color, nationality, and disabilities mean nothing. Only performance matters.

Before you can determine performance, you have to give people a chance.

THE TESTING REQUIREMENT EXCEPTION

Here's another important exception to Title VII: Section 703(h) of the Civil Rights Act of 1964 authorizes the use of professionally developed ability tests if they are not "designed, intended, or used to discriminate." For example, a commercially developed typing test or math ability test can be used, as long as the wording of the materials or the usage of the results does not discriminate against any group.

SENIORITY SYSTEM EXCEPTION

Another exception to the Civil Rights Act of 1964 can be found in Section 703(h). Organizations that have seniority systems provide a degree of security to employees who have been employed for longer periods of time. A seniority system refers to "a set of rules that ensure workers with longer years of continuous service for an employer a priority claim to a job over others with fewer years of service."

Seniority systems have occasionally discriminated against minorities in organizations that had to lay off people during periods of declining economic activity, or recessions. "Last hired, first fired" describes the condition that has affected minorities during such declines. The courts have generally ruled that this exception to the Civil Rights Act of 1964 is legal as long as the intent of the seniority provision was not to discriminate against minorities, women, or various ethnic groups.

REVERSE DISCRIMINATION: AN ORGANIZATIONAL DILEMMA

A young evening-session student named John was enrolled in a course on organizational behavior and once complained during a class discussion that he was being discriminated against in his efforts to become a firefighter. John, who was white, said that the city fire department had an **affirmative action** hiring program that favored minorities. John groused, "Why should I suffer for something I had nothing to do with?"

Affirmative Action

a program designed to create greater equity in employment

OFFSETTING PAST INEQUITIES THROUGH PROPORTIONAL EMPLOYMENT

John's plight is not an uncommon one. Although affirmative action programs (AAPs) have as their objectives the creation of greater equity in employment, they have sometimes led to reverse discrimination. The challenge associated with an AAP is how to offset past inequities. In order to achieve a workforce that is more representative of the surrounding community, many civil rights proponents advocate a program of proportional employment, hiring practices that attempt to match the percentages of particular groups in the local workforce. If, for example, the local workforce is 10 percent Hispanic, then a firm's proportional employment goal would be 10 percent Hispanic employees.

THE CHALLENGES FACING WOMEN IN THE WORKPLACE

Most observers of economic history would probably agree that the lives of many women have traditionally been filled with challenges. For many years, a primarily male-dominated society seemed to believe that a woman's place was in the home. That view appears to have faded to a great extent. Blatant female stereotyping appears also to have diminished to some degree.

THE EFFECTS OF CULTURALIZATION ON VALUES TOWARD WOMEN

We've already discussed the effect that our past experiences—our culturalization—have had on our perception and values. In the same way that we are what we eat, psychologically our attitudes are conditioned by the nourishment that our minds absorb.

Although there have been substantial changes in the use of sexual stereotypes in grade-school primers, a large proportion of American adults were raised on a reading diet of little girls compartmentalized into inferior roles. These stereotypes were perpetuated by high schools not permitting young women to attend automobile mechanics, wood shop, and other trade classes. Many young women were instead encouraged to concentrate on courses in home economics.

FAST TRACK VERSUS MOMMY TRACK

Mommy Track

a career path for women who want to combine career and children, typically involving fewer promotions and raises

Glass Ceiling

a level to which mommy trackers are allowed to advance in which they can see the upper levels that they will never be permitted to reach

In recent years, some companies have established secondary tracks that distinguish between women who want to dedicate themselves to the job and those who want to combine career and children. The practice is often referred to as the **mommy track**.[8] The concept was popularized by Felice Schwartz, a women's rights advocate, who points out that too many employers give manager moms only two options: full-time work or no work at all. Schwartz says that instead, companies should offer flexible working hours, part-time jobs, and job sharing for working mothers. However, some employers turned this into a way to perpetuate a **glass ceiling** philosophy. Some fear that employers will not take mommy trackers as seriously as other employees.

Today the glass ceiling has not been completely eliminated. After more than 40 years of struggling against the mommy track, the glass ceiling, and especially discriminatory pay, women are trying a new approach—suing their employers and winning some multimillion dollar settlements.[9] Still, many women do not wish to give up having children, even though doing so is often viewed as necessary to climb to the highest levels.[10]

To eliminate the combined effects of the mommy track and glass ceiling, companies can make work schedules more flexible, allow individuality in how people advance in their careers, strive to retain women, and ensure that women are represented in all areas of the firm, including sales and other line departments. Companies can also seek women with entrepreneurial skills as these skills are often an indicator of later business success; women-owned family businesses are almost twice as productive as those owned by men.[11] Finally, companies need to ensure that women have the skills and opportunities to rise to senior management and board levels, even if they take time out for a family. Some companies implement baby-to-work programs. With these programs, either parent is allowed to bring an infant to work, with some allowing the baby to sleep next to the parent's desk.[12]

SPOT CHECK

6. Xenophobia is an unreasonable fear or hatred of foreigners or people who are different. T F
7. The Equal Employment Opportunity Act forbids gender discrimination in wage scales. T F
8. Title VII of the Fair Labor Standards Act of 1935 prohibits employers, labor unions, and employment agencies from discriminating against people on the basis of color, religion, sex, or national origin. T F
9. Bona fide occupational qualifications (BFOQs) are prohibited because they discriminate. T F
10. The effect of the mommy track is that it limits the career advancement of mothers. T F

CHALLENGES FACING EVERYONE IN THE WORKPLACE

There are three challenges facing everyone in the workplace that have either been of concern recently or soon will be. Sexual harassment came to the forefront in the early 1990s, and while it is often thought of as men harassing women, it can include women harassing men or people of the same gender harassing each other. Workplace violence, the severest cases of which are also often headline news, is another challenge faced by all. The third challenge here is that of a predicted labor-force shortage following the retirement of the Baby Boom generation.

SEXUAL HARASSMENT

The Equal Employment Opportunity Commission (EEOC) defines sexual harassment as "Unwelcome sexual advances, requests for sexual favors, and other verbal or physical conduct of a sexual nature that constitutes sexual harassment when submission to or rejection of this conduct explicitly or implicitly affects an individual's employment, unreasonably interferes with an individual's work performance or creates an intimidating, hostile or offensive work environment." Sexual harassment comes under Title VII of the Civil Rights Act of 1964, and problems continue to this day. Even though there have been increased efforts in the past decade to educate people, there are still too many who have not altered their behavior. While all types of sexual harassment continue, possibly the most difficult for organizations to define is the "hostile work environment," as that is still somewhat vague.

As a result of such court cases are *Faragher v. City of Boca Raton* and *Booker v. Budget-Rent-A-Car* in 1998, and *Mikels v. City of Durham*, in 1999, management's role in sexual-harassment claims is becoming clearer. Management must devise a sexual-harassment policy, distribute and communicate the policy, and train managers. Maybe most importantly, management must respond to sexual-harassment complaints. Complaints must be investigated, not dismissed out of hand. When a complaint is found to be valid, action must be taken. The courts have shown that they are even more unhappy with sexual harassment that has been ignored and allowed to continue.

Individuals also have responsibilities in cases of sexual harassment, the first of which is to tell the harasser to stop. Some actions may not constitute sexual harassment if they occur only once. Repeating the behavior after being told to stop may make that action sexual harassment. For example, if someone tells a slightly sexual joke once, that may not be sexual harassment. If he or she is told to stop but then continues, that could be a violation. The second responsibility for the individual is to report instances of repeated or severe sexual harassment. Managers cannot be everywhere, and they can't address a situation they don't know about.[13]

WORKPLACE VIOLENCE

The FBI reports that the most common forms of workplace violence involve minor assault, domestic violence that has been brought to work, and threats of violence, rather than front-page, multiple homicides at work. All organizations should have a workplace-violence program aimed at prevention. However, a 2005 survey conducted by the Department of Labor's Bureau of Labor Statistics showed that 5 percent of employers had a workplace-violence incident, and the incident had a negative impact on workers in about 33 percent of the cases. Of the firms

NetNote

EEOC

http://www.eeoc.gov/facts/fs-sex.html

Sexual-harassment information.

experiencing violence, 9 percent had no policy or program. The programs that should exist should include a statement of the employer's antiviolence policy, specific methods for handling threats, a response team for violent incidents, a training program, and consistent enforcement of behavior standards.

Workplace-violence policies should describe the employer's standards for acceptable behavior along with a commitment to a safe workplace. Employer and employee responsibilities regarding harassment, threats, and violent behavior should be described. The policy should clearly state that not only physical violence but also threats, bullying, harassment, and weapons possession will not be tolerated. Once written, the policies need to be communicated to all managers and employees, along with relevant training.[14]

There are also preventive measures management can take, including preemployment screening. The screening should be used to identify potentially violent people before they are hired, but must adhere to privacy protections and antidiscrimination laws. It is best to have all workplace-violence policies reviewed by a labor lawyer specializing in this area. While background checks can be expensive and time-consuming, they may be necessary given the level of concern for violence in the workplace today.[15]

THE WORKER SHORTAGE

A development related to older workers may present one of the greatest challenges to organizations in the coming years, even though it doesn't take long to explain what it is. The Baby Boomers are starting to retire. While many people fret about downsizing and outsourcing, fewer are concerned about the Boomer retirement. Yet this may lead to a massive labor shortage—a shortage of 8 million or more workers in the United States by 2010.[16] This may increase wages (as supply goes down, price goes up), increase demand for older workers to delay retirement, increase the temptation to outsource jobs overseas, or increase the desire to increase immigration. Organizations should begin to prepare for this shortage now before finding a crisis exists in the next decade.

OLDER WORKERS

Who are considered to be the older workers in the United States? Age, of course, is relative. Few people 40 years old consider themselves to be old or older. The older worker, however, is officially defined by the Age Discrimination in Employment Act of 1967, as amended in 1978 and 1986, as age 40 and over. The official age of an older person is not as significant as the specific problems that many individuals experience merely as a result of their own advancing ages. Managers must recognize that, as another special employment group, older workers are protected by legislation and, as a result, are legally entitled to employment, proper placement based on physical limitations, adequate training, fair pay, impartial consideration for available promotions, and retirement assistance.

THE PROBLEM OF JOB LOSS FOR THE AGING

There is an expression often uttered by older workers that stresses part of their plight: "Too old to rehire and too young to retire."

The problems of older workers are often disguised by unemployment statistics, which show that unemployment rates tend to decrease with age. This condition is

NetNote

Workplace violence

http://www.fbi.gov/page2/ march04/violence030104. htm

FBI site on workplace violence.

http://www.workplace-violence-hq.com/

Workplace violence headquarters.

not surprising because older people generally have more seniority and thus are usually the last to be laid off. However, once out of work, individuals over 40 are likely to remain unemployed much longer than their younger coworkers. In fact, the likelihood of long-term unemployment actually tends to increase with age. From the age of 40, many unemployed workers often find job hunting a nightmare.

Older women share the same unemployment problems that older men do—and then some. Older women face even greater barriers after age 40 than men do. Their unemployment rates are one-third higher than men's. Older women remain out of work longer than older men; income is lower for older women.

When older persons, especially those over 50 years old, lose their jobs, they have difficulty finding others. A large proportion of workers who were not covered by employer-sponsored retirement plans or who had pensions in companies that went bankrupt face potential financial problems when they retire. They also face personal problems, including loneliness, loss of purpose, housing difficulties, failing health, and fear of death. The aging often find it difficult to secure employment because of biased attitudes of some employers. Table 16.2 cites some of the more common myths and realities associated with the employment of older workers. Each of these is summarized in the section that follows.

There is a new trend for older workers, but it may be a good news–bad news situation. The bad news is that many older workers find the need to continue working even after retirement; the good news is that many of them are finding work. More workers 55 to 64 years old are employed now, and this trend is likely to continue as lawsuits, employer needs, and a coming worker shortage create more openings for knowledgeable, experienced workers.[17]

INCREASED COSTS OF EMPLOYEE BENEFITS

An attitude toward the aging often expressed by employers is that operating costs rise when older workers are hired because of the increased expense for health and retirement plans. Not all employers, however, agree that costs necessarily rise; some contend that any increased cost in benefits is more than offset by savings in turnover and training costs, plus not having to pay retirement costs until later.

FEWER WORKING YEARS

Another cause of age bias is the assumption that younger people potentially have more years remaining with a company; that is, a 25-year-old could potentially be

TABLE 16.2 MYTHS AND REALITIES ASSOCIATED WITH THE EMPLOYMENT OF OLDER WORKERS

Myths	Realities
They cost more in employee benefits.	They may actually reduce total costs, especially related to turnover and training.
They have fewer working years left.	They tend to remain on the job longer than younger workers.
They are physically too weak for certain jobs.	They vary significantly in their physical capabilities, as do younger workers.
They have higher rates of absenteeism.	Documented facts show that they have better attendance than younger workers.
They are old rather than older.	People age at varying rates.

with an organization for 40 years, whereas a person age 50 would ordinarily have only 10 to 15 years remaining at the most.

However, studies have consistently indicated that turnover rates are actually higher among people 25 to 34 years old than among those over 50 years old. Younger people often feel that they have less to lose by changing jobs, or even careers, early in their working years. The older individual is far more likely than a younger one to finish out his or her career with a company. Furthermore, the average time that all individuals have held their jobs is only between 3 and 4 years. In light of this information, 10 years is a fairly long time for a company to have the potential of a mature, trainable person, and that assumes that at 50 the person becomes unable to work. Usually, such is not the case.

PHYSICALLY TOO WEAK

Another attitude that has worked to the detriment of older employees is the belief that older workers are physically weaker than younger ones. Although this contention is often true, exceptions are numerous. Many members of society, including medical doctors, try to force aging persons into a preconceived role. After all, aren't old people supposed to be sick much of the time? There's a story, for example, of the man of 104 who, when he complained of a stiff knee, was told, "After all, you can't expect to be agile," and replied, "My left knee's 104, too, but that doesn't hurt."

On occasions when an older employee has not had sufficient muscular strength for a specific job, some concerned managers have either reassigned the person to a different job within the organization or redesigned the job to enable a physically weaker person to perform it.

HIGHER RATES OF ABSENTEEISM

There is also the belief that older employees have higher rates of absenteeism, another myth refuted by many managers. Studies have consistently shown that older people have a substantially lower absenteeism record than younger ones. The tight job market and aging of the workforce has increased the value of older workers even more. The best companies are now scrambling to attract, train, and retain older workers.[18]

ASSISTING THE OLDER WORKER

As with any organizational behavior challenge, managers must develop a high degree of sensitivity to and understanding of the problems of aging employees. Ours has been, and will continue to be in the foreseeable future, a work-oriented society, which in itself can place psychological stress on under- and unemployed middle-age and older persons.

OLDER RATHER THAN OLD

We know that people age at different rates. Some employers perceive applicants for employment as old when, in reality, they've merely lived more years than some people; that is, they are older. Other employers have begun to recognize the value of hiring the older worker. Partially as a result of a shortage of willing teenage help, Kentucky Fried Chicken and the McDonald's Corporation hire older workers. Other firms recruiting older workers include Chevron, Monsanto, Prudential, and GE Information Services.[19]

NetNote

Senior Employment Program

http://www.sremploy.org/

This site contains information on senior employment programs, training, and job referrals.

SPOT CHECK

11. Only a request for sex is considered to be legitimate sexual harassment. T F
12. Unfortunately there are no effective preventive measures to reduce workplace violence. T F
13. There is predicted to be a significant worker shortage in United States by 2010. T F
14. The Age Discrimination in Employment Act of 1967 defines older workers as age 50 and up. T F
15. Documentation shows that older workers have better attendance than younger workers. T F

LEGISLATION FOR THE OLDER WORKER

The older worker in the future, instead of being pressured to take early retirement, is likely to be encouraged to work longer or begin a second career after retirement in light of the impending shortage of skilled labor predicted for upcoming decades.[20]

The passage of the Age Discrimination in Employment Act reflects this greater awareness of the aging process. With current population trends, larger proportions of the total U.S. population are likely to be included under the act in the future. The basic provisions of the act are these:

1. Private employers of 20 or more persons and federal, state, and local governments, regardless of the number of employees, may no longer refuse to hire qualified workers over 40.
2. Employers may no longer fire employees in this age group because of age alone or discriminate against them in terms of salary, seniority, and other job conditions.
3. Employment agencies may no longer refuse to refer workers in this age group to prospective employers nor try to classify them on the basis of age.
4. Labor unions with 25 or more members may no longer exclude those over age 40 from membership or refuse to refer older members to employers simply because of their age.
5. Help wanted advertisements may no longer include age specifications.
6. All organizations obligated under the act must post in conspicuous places the rights of employees or union members related to the act.

THE CHALLENGES FACING PEOPLE WITH DISABILITIES

People with physical and intellectual challenges used to be given little, if any, treatment in most texts on organizational behavior. Perhaps little was written about their employment problems for the same reasons that so-called normal people tend not to look at another person's disabilities. Have you ever felt self-conscious when your eyes met those of a person whose face was scarred or mutilated? Perhaps we also tend to develop the same uncomfortable feelings when discussing the topic of persons with disabilities.

Many employers, for reasons that we shall examine, are afraid to hire persons with physical or intellectual disabilities. Many Americans have met with unfortunate

TABLE 16.3 PRINCIPAL CAUSES OF PHYSICAL AND MENTAL DISABILITIES

Congenital problems	Birth injury
Accidents	Cultural or environmental deprivation
Disease	The aging process

accidents and may have to spend their entire lives in wheelchairs. Still others have become disfigured as a result of fires. Some were born with impaired vision or other disabilities. For many challenged persons, regardless of their condition, entry into the job market has been as difficult as for minority groups in the past.

People with disabilities continually encounter other forms of discrimination, such as those caused by architectural, transportation, and communication barriers and overprotective rules and policies. Unfortunately, people with disabilities, as a group, have long occupied an inferior status in American society and have been severely disadvantaged vocationally, economically, and educationally. Physical and mental challenges can result from a variety of causes. The principal ones are listed in Table 16.3.

IT'S THE LAW

Two principal laws assist **individuals with disabilities**. The first, the Rehabilitation Act of 1973 (amended in 1980), is aimed at the public sector and affects all federally assisted programs and activities. The act introduced a new philosophy of hiring people with disabilities in the United States. It finally extended the concept of affirmative action to those with disabilities. Section 503 of the law states that firms with government contracts in excess of $2,500 have significant responsibilities to people with disabilities. The law requires that efforts be made to select **qualified individuals with disabilities**. It also requires employers to attempt to make sure that their supervisors and coworkers will accept workers with disabilities and that workers with disabilities receive promotional opportunities. In addition, accommodations are to be made by employers so that individuals with disabilities will not face insurmountable obstacles.

Section 504 of the act requires that organizations receiving government grants (as opposed to contracts in Section 503) must also adopt nondiscrimination policies related to workers with disabilities. An additional part of the act (originally controversial because of the cost of implementing it) is the provision that requires providing physical access for individuals with disabilities to public schools, colleges, community health and welfare facilities, and public transportation and housing. However, it doesn't require that every building or part of a building be accessible, only the program as a whole. The act allows any person with physical or intellectual challenges who has been discriminated against to file a complaint with a regional office for civil rights.

Another significant law, the Americans with Disabilities Act of 1990 (ADA), broadens the scope of the Rehabilitation Act by requiring that private, as well as public, employers provide persons with disabilities the same protection against discrimination as is provided by other civil rights legislation (see Table 16.4).[21] The EEOC is responsible for implementing the intent of the ADA. For businesses, the ADA provides an area for concern not so much from the intent of the law but from its wording. Businesses must make reasonable accommodations in order to employ persons with disabilities but not so much as to cause undue hardship on the firm.

NetNote

U.S. Department of Justice, ADA Home Page

http://www.usdoj.gov/crt/ada/

Americans with Disabilities Act information on the Web.

Individuals with Disabilities

people who have a physical or mental impairment that substantially limits one or more of the major life activities

---

Qualified Individuals with Disabilities

individuals who, with or without reasonable accommodation, are capable of performing the essential functions of the employment position

---

TABLE 16.4 MAJOR PROVISIONS OF THE AMERICANS WITH DISABILITIES ACT OF 1990

Bans discrimination against persons with disabilities or with conditions that might be considered as limiting or causing negative public reactions.
Requires employers, including unions, to modify the workplace and employment tests to accommodate persons with disabilities.
Ensures that employees and dependents with disabilities have health insurance.
Protects employees who are recovering from illness or drug dependency.

These four words—reasonable accommodations and undue hardship—create a vagueness for businesses trying in good faith to implement the law.

WHO ARE INDIVIDUALS WITH DISABILITIES?

Accurate statistics on the number of persons with disabilities are scarce. However, estimates by the U.S. Department of Health and Human Services places the number of Americans with one or more disabilities at about 43 million, and this number is increasing as the population as a whole grows older. One in eight Americans is believed to have some sort of physical or intellectual disability.

When we use the expression "individuals with disabilities," to whom are we referring? The U.S. Department of Labor Employment Standards Administration defines an individual with disabilities as "any person who has a physical or mental impairment that substantially limits one or more of the major life activities of such individual, has a record of such an impairment, or is regarded as having such an impairment." Most persons with disabilities, however, are capable of working and are referred to as qualified individuals with disabilities, individuals who, with or without reasonable accommodation, are capable of performing the essential functions of the employment position. Table 16.5 cites the types of persons considered to have disabilities under the Rehabilitation Act of 1973 that was expanded in scope by the Americans with Disabilities Act of 1990.

COMMON ATTITUDES TOWARD THE PHYSICALLY AND INTELLECTUALLY CHALLENGED

Employers have given state departments of rehabilitation an assortment of excuses for not hiring people with disabilities. Among the more common defenses offered are that insurance costs will rise and that people with disabilities are offensive to the public. Let's take a look at both of these reasons.

TABLE 16.5 INDIVIDUALS LEGALLY CONSIDERED TO HAVE DISABILITIES

Sensory disabilities (vision, hearing, deaf/blind, speech)
Motor problems (loss of limb, paralysis)
Neurological malfunction (mental retardation, mental illness, heart disease)
General body system malfunctions (allergies, diabetes, heart disease)
Multiple limitations (multiple sclerosis, cerebral palsy, muscular dystrophy)
Dependency on alcohol and drugs (when they do not pose a direct threat to property or the safety of others in the workplace)
Disease or infection (when it does not pose a health or safety risk to themselves or coworkers)

INCREASED INSURANCE COSTS

According to representatives at the California State Department of Vocational Rehabilitation, a frequent excuse given by employers for not hiring individuals with disabilities is that their workers' compensation insurance premium costs will rise. Insurance rates, however, bear no relationship to the hiring of people with disabilities. Rates are determined by the nature of the industry and the accident experience of the individual firm.

OFFENSIVE TO THE PUBLIC

Some employers shy away from conferring positions on individuals with disabilities for fear that the person's appearance will be offensive to the public. When thinking about those with disabilities, far too many employers seem to have the image of the person who is armless, legless, and wheelchair bound. However, there are degrees of disability; most are not as severe or as highly visible as these. Even those with severe disabilities are not necessarily a public relations liability. On the contrary, employers who have the reputation for being concerned about people often enjoy an enhanced public image.

In the past, individuals with disabilities were sometimes called handicapped, a word with unfavorable connotations to many people. Unfortunately, the word often conjures up an image of a person who is wheelchair bound and incapable of doing any type of work. In reality, however, most people who were considered handicapped had no desire—or need—to be charity cases. Frequently, they were able and willing workers who had been deprived of opportunities because of misunderstanding and bias. In reality, most individuals considered handicapped are merely persons with physical or intellectual challenges or, to use another politically correct term, differently abled. Besides, don't we all have to face physical and intellectual challenges of some sort on our jobs?

Actually, the proportion of total jobs that require people with unimpaired faculties is declining. Of course, good health, youth, and the use of all limbs and senses are unquestionably desirable. But for many jobs available today, demands are changing. Industrial, manual types of jobs are becoming less available, whereas the proportion of jobs in the service, professional, and technical occupations has increased.[22]

Many recent high-tech developments have also opened up new career opportunities for persons with physical challenges. For example, individuals with hearing impairments can use the Telecommunication Device for the Deaf (TDD), which allows a person with a hearing impairment to communicate over the telephone with someone who has the same device at the other end. Another example of newer technology: computers with voice synthesizers that convert text into speech and actually "read" text aloud to workers with vision impairments.

Numerous companies have attempted to accommodate individuals with disabilities. Texas Instruments, for example, enabled someone with almost no hearing capability to obtain a surgically implanted device that allows him to function like a hearing person both in person and on the telephone. GTE-Michigan worked out a method for magnifying the letters and numbers on the computer screen of an employee with a visual impairment so that words and phone numbers appear two inches high. AT&T has installed hands-free telephones for employees with motor disabilities. IBM has provided sight-impaired employees with talking computers and Braille printers.

A SOCIAL RESPONSIBILITY

NetNote

The National Forum on People's Differences

http://www.yforum.com/

Diversity questions answered. At this site you may ask any question about people who are different from you and receive a straightforward answer.

One of the stated goals of the U.S. Congress is to provide equal employment opportunities for all U.S. citizens. Sometimes the individuals who need the most assistance tend to be overlooked. Both private and public resources are needed to provide the necessary rehabilitation for persons with disabilities so that they, too, may have lives as full as their abilities will permit. The major types of assistance needed by individuals with disabilities include medical examinations and treatment, guidance counseling, training, and placement.

In the short run, legislation such as the Rehabilitation Act and the ADA place additional demands on the energies and time of today's managers, as well as on the purse strings of society. However, the long-term benefits to society as a whole are likely to be substantial. The hiring of people with disabilities can enable another group to participate in the mainstream of U.S. economic activity. Persons previously unemployed can become taxpayers rather than welfare recipients. Further, people with disabilities can help to offset the nation's shrinking labor pool of qualified workers. Probably most important is that hiring people with disabilities enables them to develop a feeling of contribution and self-respect. Productive work is usually far more satisfying for people with disabilities than enforced idleness. If we ever feel that it's just too costly to aid individuals such as those with physical and intellectual challenges, we ought to remind ourselves that there but for fate go we.

SUMMARY

Many managers of firms throughout the world believe that operating on a global basis is essential to ensure their survival in the highly competitive world of business today. Opportunities continue to exist throughout the rapidly changing world in spite of economic crises and tribal conflicts in many regions. An understanding of global organizational behavior and how cultures differ is essential for employees of global concerns.

A number of factors influence the culture and operations of global organizations. These include customs, language and communication styles, attitudes toward time, the workforce, differences in pay scales, labor laws, standards of ethics, and political climate. Although a

cultural leveling has occurred throughout the world, there remain numerous differences in various regions and countries. The transition from working in a home country to working abroad can be eased by effective selection and assignments, orientation visits, adequate training, the use of foreign nationals, and providing expatriates with extras to enable them to satisfy their needs.

Repatriation may also require adjustment. Providing counseling, along with a repatriation agreement that clarifies future job assignments, can ease the shock of returning home after an extended stint abroad.

The word *prejudice* means to prejudge. A prejudgment is an attitude usually based on insufficient facts or no facts at all. As mainstream Americans have learned more about the similarities, as well as the differences, between minority Americans and themselves, many of their fears and uncertainties have become allayed. Likewise, minorities and women must continue to prepare themselves for opportunities that may open up for them in the future.

Many organizations have experienced gratifying results with their affirmative action programs and greater concern for gender equity. Not only have women and ethnic minorities generally been satisfactory workers, but through increased exposure to women and minorities, other employees have also found that much of their prejudice had been based on ignorance and a lack of understanding.

Many myths, based on tradition and custom, have long surrounded women in the workplace. When women were typically limited to lower-level jobs, a rapid turnover of female employees was inevitable. Women are now being given more responsible positions in which they are interested in staying, which contributes toward stability of employment. Today a larger proportion of women in the workforce work to support completely, or in part, themselves and their families. In addition, greater numbers of women in the workforce have more education and responsibilities than ever before.

All workers face some common problems: sexual harassment, workplace violence, and a projected worker shortage. Organizations should have policies for each of these, but there is an individual impact, too.

CHECKING FOR UNDERSTANDING

1. Why is it important for organizational members to understand differences in customs among different cultures?

2. How do labor laws differ among other cultures and countries?

3. What methods can be used to reduce the effects of culture shock and repatriation from foreign job assignments?

4. In what ways are multicultural issues important to organizations?

5. Differentiate between prejudice and discrimination.

6. List and describe examples of discrimination laws.

7. Describe the challenges facing women in today's workplace.

8. Define sexual harassment.

9. What are individuals responsible for in cases of alleged sexual harassment?

10. What measure can be taken to help prevent workplace violence?

11. Why is a worker shortage predicted?

12. List and describe the problems older workers face.

13. List and differentiate between myths and facts concerning older workers.

14. What problems can workers with disabilities face in the workplace?

15. What laws affect workers with disabilities?

SELF-ASSESSMENT

Answer SA if you Strongly Agree with the statement, A if you Agree, N if you are Neutral or undecided, D if you Disagree, and SD if you Strongly Disagree.

1. I am not comfortable working with people from other countries. SA A N D SD

2. The majority not only rules, it is always right. SA A N D SD

3. Increasing diversity benefits us all. SA A N D SD

4. My country, love it or leave it. SA A N D SD

5. Women must choose between career and family just as men have had to.   SA   A   N   SD

6. I am interested in other cultures.   SA   A   N   D   SD

7. Older workers need legal protection because they just can't keep up with the young.   SA   A   N   D   SD

8. Men should be paid more than women for the same work because men support families.   SA   A   N   D   SD

9. Older workers are valuable for their accumulated experience.   SA   A   N   D   SD

10. I am not comfortable working with people who have disabilities.   SA   A   N   SD

For items 1, 2, 4, 5, 7, 8, and 10, score 2 points for each SD answer, 1 for each D, 0 for each N, −1 for each A, and −2 for each SA. For items 3, 6, and 9, score 2 points for each SA answer, 1 for each A, 0 for each N, −1 for each D, and −2 for each SD. A score of 6–20 indicates a fairly positive attitude toward diversity, a score of 5−−5 indicates a less positive attitude toward diversity, and a score of −6−−20 indicates additional reading on or exposure to diversity may be beneficial.

SKILL BUILD 16

Magicbox Electronics recently sold its aged assembly plant in Antediluvia, Maine, in order to combine its operations with its two-week-old facility in Neuville, Quebec. A transition team has been formed with Alonso, Janet, and Rishima from the Antediluvia branch and Conrad, Lanying, and Pramod from Neuville. The group needs your help, and you will need to draw on course materials from every chapter (including focus boxes) for your answers. The first 15 questions refer to Chapters 1 through 15, *in order*. Questions 16 through 20 all refer to Chapter 16.

"All right, let's get this going and over with, I have important things to do," Conrad started gruffly.

"Excuse me, sir, but I think this is most important," Rishima responded.

"Yeah, well, you would, coming from the junkyard. This is our place, and it's going to be up to you to fit in—the few that we do take," Conrad said.

"What do you mean 'the few'? Our instructions were clear. Select the skills needed most and the best from either location," Alonso said.

"Skills!" Conrad said with mock surprise. "You said skills, plural. People only need one skill because they are only getting one task each. You Yanks have a lot to learn."

"I am hardly a 'Yank,' as I am from India, but no matter, what you propose sounds quite boring, doing only one thing all of the time," Rishima replied.

"Boring or not, that's the Neuville way. Unless you think you have something better," Conrad challenged.

"Actually, I think I have a better idea, an idea where people have an assortment of things to do, but the name for that escapes me at the moment. I'm sure it would increase motivation and interest in the overall work," Janet said.

Skill Question 1. Help Janet out. What concept is she referring to? How will it affect motivation and interest, if at all?

"I think we are getting way ahead of ourselves here," Pramod said. "We are talking about working conditions, and we don't even know how many people will be staying or leaving."

"We don't?" Lanying said, sounding confused.

"No, we don't," Pramod replied, "and I'm sure that should be the first step in resolving this problem."

"I don't agree with that at all," Conrad said. "I don't want no artificial limits placed on this. I don't want a quota so's we start takin' people that aren't good just to reach a certain number."

"But we don't want to tell some that they can transfer only to find out they can't," Pramod countered.

"Look, we ain't got time for that. We take only the best qualified, sort the rest out later."

Skill Question 2. What is Pramod referring to? Who is right, Pramod or Conrad, and why?

"So are you saying that you would rather get this done quickly than get it done right?" Alonso asked.

"Did you hear those words come out of my mouth? Are you saying that I want us to be wrong?" Conrad replied.

"Are you saying I'm putting words in your mouth?" Alonso asked, his voice rising.

"You sayin' I don't understand you?" Conrad shot back, and at this point they both stood up.

"Gentlemen!" Lanying said, looking both shocked and surprised. "I think you both are trying to use the proper technique, but it doesn't seem to be working."

"What technique?" they said simultaneously but without talking their eyes off each other.

"You have both upset me so that I can't recall the name, but we had better try something else," Lanying said.

Skill Question 3. To what technique does Lanying refer? Explain what it is in your own words. What is the purpose of this technique?

Conrad and Alonso both sat down and after a minute Conrad said, "Can't we just get to it? Look, it ain't that hard." He picked up an HR folder and read, "Fred Reogers, 19 years old, with the company five months. Too young and not enough seniority to be worth anything. Gone. End of story. Next."

Skill Question 4. What term describes what Conrad just did? Is it a good idea or a bad idea and why?

"Um, you know, I don't want to rush this, but I must be in my office in 90 minutes because then it will be 3:00 P.M. on an even-numbered day," Janet announced.

"Why is three o'clock on an even-numbered day important?" Rishima asked.

"That's phone time. My voice mail tells everyone who calls me that no matter what I will return their calls by between three and four on every even-numbered day. I really need this to keep up. Don't you all to this?" Janet said.

Everyone shook theirs heads no.

"I don't do this, but maybe I should. What is it called?" Rachima asked.

"Get back to her later; let's get moving," Conrad insisted.

Skill Question 5. What does Rashima need to get back to Janet about, and what exactly is it?

"Whether you have to leave soon or not, I am still bothered by this one-person, one-task idea, that just sounds incredibly tedious," Janet said.

"Hey, too bad. If some don't like it, they don't have to transfer. Why make things harder for our people," Conrad said.

"I'm not talking about giving people harder work. I think we just give them different things to do. Different, not more difficult," Janet replied.

"Yeah, isn't there some management idea along the same lines?" Alonso asked.

Skill Question 6. Is Alonso right? If so, what is this idea, and what is it supposed to do for people? If Alonso is wrong, and there is nothing like this, is there something else you can suggest they use?

"No . . .," Conrad started, but was interrupted by Pramod.

"Now, Conrad, wait. We can at least talk to the bosses to see if this might work on an individual basis. They would have to agree, though."

"Bosses?" Rashima said, surprised. "Do you mean to say that each worker has more than one boss?"

"Well, sort of. Each worker has a supervisor and each supervisor has a manager," Lanying explained.

"So what I meant," continued Pramod, "was that if the manager agreed in general and then the supervisor agreed for each individual, then maybe we could try this."

"So each worker really just has the supervisor to deal with?" Rashima said.

"Correct. Is that a problem?" Pramod asked.

Skill Question 7. Is this a problem? Is there a management principle that covers this? If so, what is it, and is it being applied properly?

"That reminds me of something," Alonso interjected. "What happens about assigning people to supervisors?"

"Oh, that'll just work itself out naturally," Conrad replied.

"Naturally? What does that mean? Will workers just wander around until they 'naturally' find a supervisor? How would they decide? Isn't that something management should do?"

"Whatever, I just don't think it's a big deal. Trust me, if they show up to work, someone will tell them what to do, and if not, they'll group themselves," Conrad said.

"Well, they might group themselves, but they might not be in the groups that are best for the company. I don't think we leave it to chance," Alonso said.

Skill Question 8. Is Alonso right in that assigning the transferred workers to supervisors is something management should do, and if so, why? What are all the main management purposes?

Skill Question 9. What is Conrad talking about when he says workers might group themselves? Is there anything like this in orgranizations? Why would people do this? Should they be allowed to do this, as Conrad describes, and why or why not?

"I have to agree with Alonso," Lanying said. "My first time as a groups leader I thought I was being nice, let all the teams form on their own. Total disaster. Some people got left out for various reasons, some teams were too small, one was way, way too big. The entire project failed, and it wasn't cheap and couldn't be hidden. I had actually started cleaning my desk out, I was so sure I would be fired."

"I remember that," Janet said. "Your teams were supposed to develop a line of household battery testers. Radio Shed ended up beating us to market by a year. How did you ever come back from that?"

"It wasn't easy," Lanying explained. "First I analyzed the situation. Letting teams form themselves wasn't the only mistake I made, but it was the biggest. I made a list of everything I did wrong, typed it up, and kept it in the top drawer of my desk. Every day for years I looked at that list first thing in the morning and last thing at night. I made sure I never did any of those things again.

"Next, I took on several projects no one wanted. Including heading up the Unified Fund charity drive. I did everything I could so each project met its goals and a few exceeded them."

"So you were a superstar?" Alonso asked.

"Not at all, but I did turn in respectable performances, and everything I did was on time or a little early. I never gave anyone a reason to complain about my effort."

"And that was it?" Janet said, doubting it was.

"Well, no. I made sure I didn't hide. I wasn't defiant, but I didn't lower my eyes every time a manager walked by. That was hard as I was definitely embarrassed. What was even harder was trying to let my manager know how I was doing without looking like I was bragging. I kept her informed, and I made sure others got credit when it was due, but I made sure I got credit when I deserved it. With time, I think they viewed that first mistake as an exception and something I had learned from. Whatever it was, I'm still here today.

Skill Question 10. Is this really how one should try to come back from a mistake? If not, what should Lanying have done? Were there steps she should have followed? List and explain them and describe what she did that was incorrect. If she did do what she was supposed to, were there steps to the process she followed? List and explain them and describe whether she followed them correctly or not.

"Well that's a lovely story, but can we get back to the job at hand?" Conrad said condescendingly. "You're as bad as my subordinates. Only thing gets them moving is money, and the only thing that keeps them in line is the belief they might lose that money."

Skill Question 11. What style of management is this? What assumption about workers do managers who use this style make? What do these managers believe will motivate workers?

"You're not serious," Rashima asked, stunned.

"Darn tootin'. I say what goes. I dictate everything, from the pictures on the walls to the carpets on the floors. Nothing happens I don't approve of," Conrad explained.

"Aren't you in charge of marketing?" Rashima asked.

"That's exactly right. I'm large and in charge. I'm known throughout the area for my successful clear-desk policy."

"Clear desk?" Rashima said.

"Yes, ma'am. No one is allowed any of that silly, personal bric-a-brac. All desktops are clear at all times except for what you're workin' on, and at the end of the day everything must be off the top of every desk. If you were wise, you would take charge of every aspect of what your people do from the moment they walk in up to the point they walk out. I even give them suggested lunch menus, and it ain't smart not to pick one of my options. That goes down in your permanent record," Conrad explained, beaming.

Skill Question 12. What term describes how Conrad is running the Marketing Department? Define it in your words. Does this seem like a good idea or a bad idea and why (you might look beyond Chapter 12 for this answer)?

"I'll tell you right now all of our people are used to having a fair amount of leeway to personalize their space," Alonso said.

"It has improved a lot of attitudes and reduced turnover, with no loss of productivity; there was even a slight gain after this was introduced," Janet added.

"A gain?" Conrad said, raising both eyebrows. He paused to think a bit and then said, "Well, I can't just change everything. What worked for you might not work here."

"What if you allowed some personalization for a month or two to see what would happen? If it doesn't work, go back to the old way. Or try something else," Janet suggested.

"I don't know, is that legit? To give it a shot while telling people if it don't work we'll change back or change to something else?" Conrad asked, sounding doubtful.

Skill Question 13. Is what Janet suggested a real way to conduct change? If so, does it have a name, can you describe it in your own words, is it generally a well-regarded way to try to make change, and why?

"Whatever," Conrad said. "Now, can we *please* get to the matter at hand? What about the Antediluvia research and development team. They . . ."

"All come over," Alonso said. "As a group. They are fantastic. They are go-getters. Each one is top-notch, and when they get an assignment, they attack it. They're work animals, I tell ya. All they need is the right leader."

Skill Question 14. What kind of leader does the R & D team need, seeing as they are described as capable and eager? What leadership theory would this leader be applying, and what would he or she need to provide for this team?

"*Forget it!*" Conrad yelled. "We ain't takin' a whole group of anything, and I don't care how blasted great they are. We're here to cut, and cuttin' is what we will do!"

Rishima looked at the fuming Conrad and said calmly, "You know, you have resisted virtually everything said and done here today. Must you react in such a way? I know your outbursts and negativity are not good for us, but certainly they are not good for you either. Can't you find another way?"

Skill Question 15. Is there another way Conrad could react? If so, what is it called and how would you describe it? Is there a name for how Conrad is currently reacting, and if so, what is it? Is it good for him to act the way he does, or bad, or doesn't it matter, and why?

"*Fine.* I'll shut up if it will get things moving," Conrad said.

After a long silence Pramod said, "Well. Maybe we can next consider Sonja Ramstein?"

"Has anyone seen her new baby? She is just adorable," Janet proclaimed.

"She just had a baby? She'll miss a lot of work. We'll get more mileage out of someone without a kid," Conrad stated flatly.

The rest of the group stared at Conrad.

"What?" he said, surprised, "I was calm wasn't I?"

"You can't be serious about not transferring her just because she has a baby, can you?" Janet asked, astounded.

"No, of course not," Conrad replied. "I just meant we have to be careful where we put her. No sense putting her on the fast path to upper management when she has already made her choice. Supervisor. Maybe. But no more that that."

Skill Question 16. What is Conrad trying to do with Sonja? What assumption is he making about her?

"Oh, this is too much!" Janet said, and the others nodded in agreement.

"Fine, fine. I'm just trying to look out for the company," Conrad said defensively.

"Then you agree that she comes with no limitations?" Rishima said.

"Fine," Conrad said. "Let's move on." He opened another folder and said, "What's this David something-or-other? Why does it say 'access adaptations'?"

"David is in a wheelchair, and he needs a ramp access if there are stairs, and his worktable needs to be lowered a few inches. I forget exactly how many. It's probably in the file there," Alonso answered.

Conrad closed the file and said, "Well, we won't have to worry about that."

"Why?" Alonso asked, dubious, "Is the building already prepared?"

"No, and we won't be needing to prepare anything," Conrad said. "This is a brand-new building. A new start. I can't see, when we don't have positions for everyone anyway, taking on someone who is not working up to standard. I can't see cobbling up a makeshift ramp on a new building and sawing the legs off of brand-new tables either."

Skill Question 17. What assumption is Conrad making about David, and is it a legitimate concern? Should the modifications David needs be made?

"For your information, David is our top electronics assembler," Alonso replied in a calm but stern tone. "He doesn't need to walk for that; he has the strongest arms I have ever seen, and he is very fast and accurate. We are privileged to have him, wheelchair or not."

"Well, seems like, according to you people, I just can't get anything right today. Guess I'll just make a note not to exclude anyone for any reason."

"That's not it exactly," Lanying said. "We don't have to just take anyone off the street, but you have to have proper reasons that are directly related to the job. There is an odd-sounding term for that, I think, but I can't think of it right now."

Skill Question 18. Is there a term for what Lanying is talking about? If so, what is it and how would you describe it in your own words?

"How about this for a 'proper reason': We don't take anyone over 55 because they only have 10 years left to work, and these people are sick a lot?" Conrad asked.

Skill Question 19. Now what group is Conrad making assumptions about? Is he right, and why or why not?

"Would you not hire some 25-year-old if you thought he or she was only going to stay 10 years, because a lot of them don't," Pramod said. "I'd be willing to bet more 55-year-olds stay 10 years than 25-year-olds."

"I'm just about to give up here," Conrad said, "but this next guy scares me. He was suspended for threatening a coworker once, for threatening a supervisor once, and for getting in a fistfight with coworkers twice. We can't take this guy, and why hasn't he been let go?"

The other five looked at each other and nodded. Rishima spoke for all of them. "We agree we do not want him, but he was allowed to stay because we had no policy for dealing with this. We really need to write one."

On this they all finally agreed.

Skill Question 20. What policy did they not have here that they needed? In writing one, what should it include in order to be comprehensive?

APPLICATIONS

16.1 LOYALTY OR EFFICIENCY?

Joe Morales, a department head with the Phaseout Supply Company, currently finds himself in an uncomfortable position. He recently attended a meeting of all department heads that was conducted by the executive vice president, Paula Pickwick. The department heads were informed at the meeting that a slowdown in the demand for Phaseout's products required that the company be restructured and a number of employees be laid off. Ms. Pickwick told each department head that personnel budgets would have to be reduced by 15 percent.

Eunice Brown, another department head, shared Joe's dismay. While in the photocopying room, she saw Joe and complained, "You know what this means, don't you? Pickwick is going after the older workers. It would have been a lot easier if she had said to cut five workers, rather than laying off people based on a percent of budget. I know that the only way to cut my department's personnel

budget by 15 percent and still come close to meeting my departmental goals is to lay off the employees at the top of the pay range. I think Pickwick's idea is ridiculous!"

After Joe had looked over his own personnel budget, he could see that Eunice was right. To meet the targeted percentage reduction in his department, he had two main options. The first option would be to discharge Laura Sohoni, age 48, and Lewis O'Brien, age 55, both senior employees at the top of the pay range. Joe's second option was to discharge his five lowest-paid employees, each of whom was unmarried and had joined the company within the last 2 years. Joe also had to consider that the nature of the work in his department was changing. Later this year his department was converting to computerized workstations, which would require additional training for the employees. Joe had already gotten some clues of potential resistance from some of the older employees, who resented the proposed changes. Most of the younger employees, however, had learned something about computers in school and had little in the way of computer phobia. As Joe analyzed his data again and again, he wondered how Laura, a widow and head of a household with three children, would survive if she lost her job. Laura had been with Phaseout for about 6 years, which was an insufficient amount of time for her profit-sharing retirement fund with Phaseout to be fully vested. At least Lewis, who had been with the company for 20 years, would be eligible to collect early retirement pay. Joe found himself almost wishing that the company had a union contract that would automatically make the decision for him—one that would require the less-senior employees to be laid off first. Joe felt, however, that he had to deal with the realities of the situation. He convinced himself that he really had only one choice if he was to reduce the personnel budget by 15 percent and still meet his department's goals. He decided to lay off Laura and Lewis.

QUESTIONS

1. Do you think that age discrimination is an issue in this incident? Explain.

2. What would you do if you were in Joe's position?

16.2 THE DISABLED PHOTOGRAPHY-LAB WORKER

When Kelly Darby was 15 years old, she was a passenger in a car that was involved in a serious accident. Her injury required the amputation of her left leg. Kelly was fitted with an artificial appliance that enables her to function nearly as well as anyone else under most circumstances. She is currently 23 years old, married, and the mother of a two-year-old daughter. Kelly enjoys physical activity and spends weekends with her family bicycle riding and working in her vegetable garden. Kelly, a high school graduate, learned about a year ago that there was a department of rehabilitation near her home where she could obtain assistance and training designed to aid her in preparing for a career position. For a number of years, she has had a strong interest in photography, and she was able to obtain training in printing and processing techniques through the department.

About two months ago, the department obtained a job for Kelly at the Color-Rite Photo Laboratory. Kelly was overjoyed with the opportunity and felt quite fortu-nate to be offered a job in an area in which she had interest. Her major hope, however, was that her coworkers would treat her as they would any other worker.

Unfortunately, Kelly's wishes have not come true. Most of her fellow employees seem to feel sorry for her and continually refuse to allow her to carry darkroom equipment or packages of photographic materials. Kelly has attempted to convey to her coworkers that she can carry whatever they can, but the other employees refuse to heed her requests.

Recently, Kelly has become quite moody on the job. She sometimes feels that she is being treated as if she is helpless or "some kind of a freak." Kelly has started getting into conflicts with the other employees in areas that do not relate to her disability. Today, Kelly has felt especially depressed and believes that she has had it with her job. She has decided that she will tell her supervisor, Habib, that she intends to leave her job with Color-Rite.

QUESTIONS

1. What do you think is the major problem in this case?

2. If you were Habib, what would you do about the situation?

16.3 "BUT WE NEVER NEEDED A POLICY BEFORE!"

Suman Patel addressed her department heads Siu Key, Kathleen O'Malley, and Jean-François Milain.

"I have heard of two different instances of poor behavior—behavior we have never had here before," Suman said. "Three of our female crane operators were overheard saying in their change room that some of the men have suggested that they could earn extra money as, how shall I say it, ladies of the evening. Never have I heard of something like this, and I will not have it in my company."

"Actually, I know the men you are referring to, and they have been saying that for some time; you just haven't heard of it. It comes to nothing," Jean-François said.

"You have known and have done nothing!" Kathleen exclaimed.

"The women, they have not complained to me. I just hear some man talk," Jean-Francois replied.

"Well, something must be done about that and about the day and afternoon security guards. They nearly fought over the condition one left for the other in the guard shack," Suman said.

"Again, a long-standing tradition between those two. They are both just macho types, and Joe only pulled a knife on Bob once," Jean-François said.

"What! We don't give them guns or knives. They are mostly there to guard the workers' cars from vandals. This must stop immediately!" Suman said.

"With respect," Siu said, "We have no policies against these things. At my brother's company there are policies for both sexual harassment and workplace violence."

"Siu, then you take the lead on this and get someone to write these for us," Suman said.

Siu has recruited you to answer a couple of questions and write these policies.

QUESTIONS

1. What should the female crane operators and Jean-François have done differently in this situation and why?

2. What should the sexual-harassment policy address?

3. What should the workplace-violence policy address?

4. Write both policies.

NET-WORK

Is this diversity?

http://www.youtube.com/watch?v=tVjXbFOW0Kc&mode=related&search=

Silver Entrepreneurs—starting a business after retirement

http://www.youtube.com/watch?v=_3adA1dZ02Q

PERSONAL POINTS

1. What do you know about your company's global competitors? What do you know of the cultural and communication differences of your company's global competitors?

2. What are your feelings about working with women? What are your feelings about working with men? Are there any differences in your feelings, and if so, what are they and why do think you have them?

3. How would you feel about having a work partner who had a disability? What changes would have to be made in order to keep your current job if you were suddenly injured so that could use your arms but needed to use a wheelchair? How would you feel if others refused to work with you or your employer refused to make the needed changes?

4. How do you feel about people bringing their religious beliefs into the workplace? How do you feel if they were the same beliefs as yours? What if they are significantly different from yours?

5. How do you feel about working with people who are significantly older or younger than you are? Are your feelings different than they are for working with people the same age as you, and why or why not?

EXPERIENTIAL EXERCISE

A Cultural Quiz

Answer the following statements either generally yes or generally no.

PART I

Generally Yes	Generally No	
____	____	1. enjoy eating foods that some people consider weird.
____	____	2. I have friends from a variety of ethnic backgrounds.
____	____	3. I can converse in at least one foreign language.
____	____	4. I have traveled to a foreign country at least once.

EXPERIENTIAL EXERCISE (Continued)

A Cultural Quiz

_____   _____ 5. I can visualize myself retiring in
                  a foreign country.

_____   _____ 6. I can imagine myself living
                  without television.

PART II

Generally   _Generally_
Yes   _No_

_____   _____ 1. I believe that foreigners, like the
                  Japanese, should not be allowed
                  to buy U.S. companies and real
                  estate.

_____   _____ 2. I believe that French people
                  generally do not like Ameri-
                  cans.

_____   _____ 3. I believe that Yankee ingenuity
                  is, and always will be, the best
                  in the entire world.

_____   _____ 4. I believe that soccer matches
                  could never seem as exciting as
                  American football games.

_____   _____ 5. The Japanese could never have
                  developed all those fancy
                  electronic gadgets unless they
                  had copied all of America's
                  products.

_____   _____ 6. I believe it is important for me
                  to spend significant amounts of
                  time with people of my own re-
                  ligious, ethnic, racial, and na-
                  tional background.

Total generally yes responses, Part I: _____

Total generally no responses, Part II: _____

Key: Get together with four or five other members of your class. Compare your answers. How many of your responses in Part I were generally yes? How many of your responses in Part II were generally no? If you answered five in Part I generally yes and five in Part II generally no, you might be a favorable candidate for an overseas assignment with a global company because of your apparent adaptable attitudes toward different things and cultures. This exercise is not definitive. There are far more factors that would influence the success of an overseas assignment than are inherent in these statements.

SPOT CHECK ANSWERS

1. F
2. F
3. T
4. T
5. F
6. T
7. F
8. F
9. F
10. T
11. F
12. F
13. T
14. F
15. T
16. T
17. F
18. T
19. F
20. F

NOTES

CHAPTER 1

1. Frederick W. Taylor, *The Principles of Scientific Management* (New York: Harper and Brothers, 1911).
2. Brenda Paik Sunoo, "Union Membership Slipping," *Workforce,* June 1998, p. 19.
3. Michael McCoby and Katherine Terzi, "What Happened to the Work Ethic?" in *The Work Ethic in Business,* ed. W. Michael Hoffman and Thomas Wyly Oelgeschlager (Cambridge, MA: Gunn and Hain, 1981), pp. 31–32.
4. Henry Smith and John Wakeley, *Psychology of Industrial Behavior,* 3rd ed. (New York: McGraw-Hill, 1972), p. 38.
5. Douglas McGregor, *The Human Side of Enterprise* (New York: McGraw-Hill, 1960).
6. Michael Cherington, *The Work Ethic: Working Values and Values That Work* (New York: AMACOM, 1980), p. 20.
7. Julie Fintel, ed., "The Work Ethic," *Keying In,* National Business Education Association, January 1997, p. 3.
8. Max Weber, *The Theory of Social and Economic Organization,* trans. A. M. Henderson and T. Parsons (New York: Free Press, 1947), p. 329.
9. Abbas J. Ali, Thomas Falcone, and A. A. Azim, "Work Ethic in the USA and Canada," *Journal of Management Development,* June 1995, pp. 26–35.
10. McCoby and Terzi, p. 34.
11. Brian O'Reilly, "Is Your Company Asking Too Much?" *Fortune,* March 12, 1990, pp. 38–46.
12. "Psycho Bosses from Hell," *Fortune,* October 18, 1993, pp. 128–129.
13. Jim Harris and Joan Brannick, *Finding and Keeping Great Employees* (New York: AMACOM, 1999), p. 161.
14. Brian O'Reilly, "What Companies and Employees Owe One Another," *Fortune,* June 13, 1994, p. 44.
15. Keith H. Hammonds, "Balancing Work and Family," *Business Week,* September 16, 1996, pp. 74–80.
16. Kenneth Labich, "Kissing Off Corporate America," *Fortune,* February 20, 1995, p. 44.
17. Thomas J. Smith, "Is It Too Cold in Here?" *Call Center Magazine,* September 2003, pp. 8–9.
18. Don Graf, *Basic Building Data,* 3rd ed. (New York: Van Nostrand Reinhold, 1985), p. 172.
19. Jay Heizer and Barry Render, *Principles of Operations Management,* 5th ed. (Upper Saddle River, NJ: Pearson Prentice Hall, 2004), p. 379.
20. Peter A. Andersen, *Nonverbal Communication: Forms and Functions* (Mountain View, CA: Mayfield Publishing, 1999), p. 59.
21. F. H. Mahnke and R. H. Mahnke, *Color and Light in Man-Made Environments* (New York: Van Nostrand Reinhold, 1987), p. 204.
22. Robert Heller and Tim Hindle, *Essential Manager's Manual* (New York: DK Publishing, 1998).
23. Mahnke and Mahnke, p. 157.
24. David C. Alexander and Babur Mustafa Pulat, *Industrial Ergonomics* (Norcross, GA: Industrial Engineering and Management Press, 1985), p. 84.
25. Heizer and Render, p. 379; Robert D. Ramsey, "Managing Noise in the Workplace," *Supervision,* September 1996, pp. 3–6.
26. Alexander and Pulat, p. 140; Bjarne W. Olesen and Thomas Madsen, "Measurements of the Physical Parameters of the Thermal Environment," *Ergonomics,* January 1995, pp. 138–154.
27. Pierre Goumain, *High-Technology Workplaces* (New York: Van Nostrand Reinhold, 1989), p. 36.
28. Graf, p. 170.
29. Andersen, pp. 59–60.
30. Beverly Russell, "Ad Agency Offices," *Interiors,* June 1995, pp. 72–78.
31. Brenda Paik Sunoo, "Redesign for a Better Work Environment," *Workforce,* February 2000, pp. 39–46.
32. Heizer and Render, pp. 257, 332.
33. Jack Meredith, *The Management of Operations: A Conceptual Emphasis,* 4th ed. (New York: John Wiley & Sons, 1992), p. 341.
34. Meredith, pp. 338–339.
35. Meredith, p. 279.
36. Ziva Freiman, "Hype vs. Reality: The Changing Workplace," *Progressive Architecture,* March 1994, pp. 48–55, 89–90.
37. Lauren Goldstein, "Whatever Space Works for You," *Fortune,* July 20, 2000, pp. 269–270.
38. Michelle Conlin, "Is Your Office Killing You?" *Business Week,* June 5, 2000, pp. 114–128.
39. Ryan McCarthy, "Your Office May Be Innocent," *Inc. Magazine,* July 2006, p. 24.

40. Steven Brown and Thomas Leigh, "A New Look at Psychological Climate and Its Relationship to Job Involvement, Effort, and Performance," *Journal of Applied Psychology,* August 1996, pp. 358–369.

41. Douglas McGregor, *The Human Side of Enterprise* (New York: McGraw-Hill, 1960), p. 29; Gigi Hirsch, "A Dysfunctional System May Be Adding to Your Stress," *American Medical News,* November 4, 1996, pp. 40–42.

42. Frederick Herzberg, *Work and the Nature of Man* (Cleveland, OH: World, 1966), p. 36.

43. Herzberg, p. 49.

44. Herzberg, p. 74.

45. McGregor, p. 74.

46. McGregor, p. 53.

47. W. J. Rothwell and Hercules Kazanas, *Strategic Human Resource Development* (Englewood Cliffs, NJ: Prentice Hall, 1989), p. 453.

48. Rothwell and Kazanas, p. 449.

49. Rothwell and Kazanas, pp. 452–453.

50. Herzberg, p. 51.

51. K. Lloyd, *Jerks at Work* (Franklin Lakes, NJ: Career Press, 1999), p. 73.

52. Lynne Andersson and Christine Pearson, "Tit for Tat? The Spiraling Effect of Incivility in the Workplace," *Academy of Management Review,* July 1999, pp. 452–454.

53. Lloyd, p. 77.

54. Barbara Buchholz, "Irritation Situation," *Chicago Tribune,* March 26, 2003, sec. 6, p. 1.

55. Lloyd, p. 72.

56. Christopher Davis, "Office Poison. (Toxic Coworkers.)," *Pittsburgh Business Times,* April 27, 2001, p. 19.

57. Lloyd, p. 70.

58. James Carlopio and Dianne Gardner, "Perceptions of Work and Workplace: Mediators of the Relationship between Job Level and Employee Reactions," *Journal of Occupational and Organizational Psychology,* December 1995, pp. 321–326.

CHAPTER 2

1. Stephen Robbins and Mary Coulter, *Management,* 8th ed. (Upper Saddle River, NJ: Pearson Prentice Hall, 2005), p. 357.

2. Eric Mankowski and Robert Wyer, "Cognitive Processes in Perception of Social Support," *Personality and Social Psychology Bulletin,* September 1996, pp. 894–906.

3. Carey Ryan, Charles M. Judd, and Bernadette Park, "Effects of Racial Stereotypes on Judgments of Individuals," *Journal of Experimental Social Psychology,* January 1996, pp. 71–104; Jennifer Laabs, "Does Image Matter?" *Personnel Journal,* December 1995, pp. 48–58.

4. David Dunning and Andrew Hayes, "Evidence of Egocentric Comparison in Social Judgment," *Journal of Personality and Social Psychology,* August 1996, pp. 213–230.

5. Gary Haitzel, "Avoiding Evaluation Errors," *NASSP Bulletin,* January 1995, pp. 40–51.

6. Clare Morris, "Seven Simple Tools for Problem Solving," *Financial Times,* May 31, 1996, p. 12.

7. Ryan Mark, "Customized Management: Walk Your Own Path," *Organizations and People,* August 1996, pp. 15–18.

8. Gary Kirby and Jeffery Goodpaster. *Thinking*, 3rd ed. (Upper Saddle River, NJ: Pearson Prentice Hall, 2002), p. 123–127.

9. David Myers, *Psychology*, 5th ed. (New York: Worth Publishers, 1998), p. 307.

10. "Bad Things Come to Those Who Wait," *Chicago Tribune,* June 25, 2006, sec. 6, p. 1.

11. Hara Estroff Marano, "Getting Out from Under: Don't Wait for Your Workload to Overwhelm You. Waiting Until the Last Minute Can Do You In," *Psychology Today,* March/April 2006.

12. Gary Kirby and Jeffery Goodpaster, p. 37.

13. Gary Kirby and Jeffery Goodpaster, p. 37.

14. Gary Kirby and Jeffery Goodpaster, p. 37.

15. David Myers, p. 308.

16. Gary Kirby and Jeffery Goodpaster, p. 37.

17. Marta Mooney, "Deming's Real Legacy: An Easier Way to Manage Knowledge," *National Productivity Review,* Summer 1996, pp. 1–9.

18. "Finding Ways to Keep the Juices Flowing," *Nation's Business,* October 1995, p. 12.

19. Debbie A. Shirley and Janice Langan-Fox, "Intuition: A Review of the Literature," *Psychological Reports,* October 1996, pp. 563–585.

20. Robbins and Coulter, p. 141.

21. Robbins and Coulter, pp. 148–150.

22. Robbins and Coulter, p. 151.

23. Jim Frederick, "Creativity—Cut Restrictive Rules. The End of Eureka!" *Working Woman,* February 1997, pp. 38–43.

24. Alan Rosenspan, "The Care and Feeding of Creative," *Direct Marketing,* January 1997, pp. 18–23.

CHAPTER 3

1. Stephen Robbins and Mary Coulter, *Management,* 8th ed. (Upper Saddle River, NJ: Pearson Prentice Hall, 2005), pp. 360–362.

2. "The 1999 Doublespeak Awards," *A Review of General Semantics,* Winter 1999–2000.

3. William Lutz, "Nothing in Life Is Certain except Negative Patient Care Outcome and Revenue Enhancement," *Journal of Adolescent & Adult Literacy,* November 2000, pp. 320–324.

4. Ron Grossman, "It's the Jargon, Stupid—and It Doesn't Belong in Business," *Chicago Tribune*, February 11, 2007, sec. 2, p. 5.

5. Ronald B. Adler and George Rodman, *Understanding Human Communication,* 3rd ed. (New York: Holt, Rinehart and Winston, 1988), pp. 109–111; Miles Patterson, "Evolution and Nonverbal Behavior: Functions and Mediating Processes," *Journal of Nonverbal Behavior,* Fall 2003, pp. 201–208.

6. Anne Beall, "Body Language Speaks," *Communication World,* March/April 2004, pp. 18–20.

7. Julius Fast, *Subtext* (New York: Viking Penguin, 1991), p. 63.

8. Peter A. Andersen, *Nonverbal Communication: Forms and Functions* (Mountain View, CA: Mayfield Publishing, 1999), p. 40.

9. Michael Marriot, "Looking Out from behind a Game Face (New York City Metropolis Prompts Inhabitants to Keep a Distance from One Another)," *New York Times,* November 10, 1996, p. 22.

10. Fast, p. 62.

11. Fast, p. 63.

12. Nicolas Guéguen and Céline Jacob, "Direct Look versus Evasive Glance and Compliance with a Request," *Journal of Social Psychology,* June 2002.

13. "More Than Words Can Say: How Body Language Affects Your Ability to Communicate," *American Salesman,* April 1996, pp. 24–26.

14. Fast, p. 63.

15. Jacquelyn Lynn, "First Impressions: You Can't Do Them Over," *Commercial Law Bulletin,* July/August 2001, pp. 32–33.

16. Fast, p. 62.

17. "More Than Words Can Say," pp. 24–26.

18. Fast, p. 64.

19. Adler and Rodman, p. 114.

20. "More Than Words Can Say," pp. 24–26.

21. Fast, p. 65.

22. Sharon Begley, "Gesturing as You Talk Can Help You Take a Load Off Your Mind," *Wall Street Journal,* November 14, 2003, p. B1.

23. Fast, p. 73.

24. Fast, p. 77.

25. Fast, p. 70.

26. Fast, p. 73.

27. Fast, p. 49.

28. Freda Sathré-Eldon, Ray W. Olson, and Clarissa Whitney, *Let's Talk,* 3rd ed. (Glenview, IL: Scott, Foresman, 1981), p. 65.

29. Fast, p. 49.

30. Fast, p. 50.

31. Fast, p. 51.

32. Adler and Rodman, pp. 118–119.

33. Fast, p. 52.

34. Adler and Rodman, p. 119.

35. Adler and Rodman, p. 119.

36. Fast, pp. 52–53.

37. Fast, p. 71.

38. Fast, p. 71.

39. Mark L. Knapp, *Essentials of Nonverbal Communications* (New York: Holt, Rinehart and Winston, 1980), p. 74.

40. Martin Remland, Tricia Jones, and Heidi Brinkman, "Interpersonal Distance, Body Orientation, and Touch: Effects of Culture, Gender, and Age," *Journal of Social Psychology,* September 1995, pp. 281–297; Andersen, pp. 44–45.

41. Richard D. Lewis, "Space at a Premium," *Management Today,* September 1996, pp. 105–106.

42. Andersen, pp. 57–58.

43. Albert Merabian, *Nonverbal Communication* (Chicago: Aldine-Atherton, 1972), p. 45.

44. Fast, p. 85.

45. Fast, p. 85.

46. Merabian, p. 86.

47. Fast, p. 66.

48. Fast, p. 66.

49. Nancy Briton and Judith Hall, "Beliefs about Female and Male Nonverbal Communication," *Sex Roles: A Journal of Research,* September 1995, pp. 79–90.

50. Deborah Tannen, *Talking from 9 to 5* (New York: William Morrow, 1994), p. 13.

51. Deborah Tannen, *You Just Don't Understand* (New York: Ballantine Books, 1990), p. 43.

52. Tannen, p. 62.

53. John Gray, *Men Are from Mars, Women Are from Venus* (New York: HarperCollins, 1992), p. 17.

54. Gray, p. 20.

55. Gray, p. 16.

56. Tannen, *Talking from 9 to 5,* p. 40.

57. Gray, p. 17.

58. Gray, p. 69.

59. Gray, p. 29.

60. Gray, p. 43.

61. Tannen, *Talking from 9 to 5,* p. 67.

62. Gray, p. 60.

63. Tannen, *You Just Don't Understand,* p. 43.

64. Tannen, *You Just Don't Understand,* p. 49.

65. Gray, p. 48.

66. Tannen, *You Just Don't Understand,* p. 59; Gray, p. 22.

67. Gray, p. 23.

68. Gray, p. 25.

69. Gray, p. 15.

70. Tannen, *Talking from 9 to 5,* p. 22.

71. Gray, p. 60.

72. Tannen, *Talking from 9 to 5,* p. 22.

73. Tannen, *Talking from 9 to 5,* p. 41.

74. Tannen, *Talking from 9 to 5,* p. 66.

75. Gray, p. 29.

76. Gray, p. 117.

77. Gray, p. 60.
78. Gray, p. 31.
79. Gray, pp. 60–61.
80. Mark Peters, "The Math on Miss Motor Mouth," *Psychology Today*, March/April 2007, p. 21.
81. Catherine New, "Take Me to Your Leader," *Psychology Today*, March/April 2007, p. 15.
82. Gray, p. 62.
83. Gray, p. 67.

CHAPTER 4

1. John Galvin, "Cheating, Lying, Stealing," *Smart Business,* June 2000, pp. 86–99.
2. Rita Kowalski, Joel Harmon, and Dan Kowalski, "Reducing Workplace Stress and Aggression," *Human Resource Planning,* no. 2, 2003, pp. 39–53.
3. Peter A. Andersen, *Nonverbal Communication: Forms and Functions* (Mountain View, CA: Mayfield Publishing, 1999), pp. 283–285.
4. Julius Fast, *Subtext* (New York: Viking Penguin, 1991), pp. 129–131.
5. Susan Dellinger and Barbara Deanne, *Communicating Effectively* (Radnor, PA: Chilton, 1980), p. 38; Tom Dossenbach, "Are We Really Listening?" *Wood & Wood Products,* June 1999, pp. 53–54.
6. Freda Sathré-Eldon, Ray W. Olson, and Clarissa Whitney, *Let's Talk,* 3rd ed. (Glenview, IL: Scott, Foresman, 1981), p. 13.
7. Dellinger and Deanne, p. 185.
8. Sathré-Eldon, p. 14.
9. Deborah Tannen, "The Power of Talk: Who Gets Heard and Why," *Harvard Business Review,* September/October 1995, pp. 138–148.
10. Paul M. Litwick, "Nix Negativity Now," *Canadian Manager,* Spring 1996, pp. 17–18.
11. Deborah Weider-Hatfield and John D. Hatfield, "Relationships among Conflict Management Styles, Levels of Conflict, and Reactions to Work," *Journal of Social Psychology,* January 1995, pp. 687–698.
12. Thomas K. Capozzoli, "Conflict Resolution," *Supervision,* December 1995, pp. 3–6.
13. Michael B. Coyle, "Quality Interpersonal Communications: Resolving Conflicts Successfully," *Manage,* January 1994, pp. 4–6.
14. Lee Harrisberger, *Succeeding: How to Become an Outstanding Professional* (New York: Macmillan, 1994), pp. 216–222; Jerry Wisinski, "What to Do about Conflicts," *Supervisory Management,* March 1995, p. 11; Litwick, p. 17.
15. Ted Pollock, "Mind Your Own Business: Conflict Management," *Supervision,* November 1996, pp. 21–24.
16. Roger Fisher, Elizabeth Kopelman, and Andrea Kupfer Schneider, *Beyond Machiavelli* (New York: Penguin, 1996), p. 33.
17. Fisher, Kopelman, and Schneider, p. 43.
18. Fisher, Kopelman, and Schneider, p. 75.
19. Fisher, Kopelman, and Schneider, p. 74.
20. Fisher, Kopelman, and Schneider, p. 76.
21. Fisher, Kopelman, and Schneider, p. 77.
22. Fisher, Kopelman, and Schneider, p. 78.
23. Fisher, Kopelman, and Schneider, p. 80.
24. Fisher, Kopelman, and Schneider, p. 81.
25. Fisher, Kopelman, and Schneider, p. 78.

CHAPTER 5

1. Charlene Marmer Solomon, "Stressed to the Limit," *Workforce,* September 1999, pp. 48–54.
2. Jennifer Laabs, "Overload," *Workforce,* January 1999, pp. 30–37.
3. John Galvin, "Cheating, Lying, Stealing," *Smart Business,* June 2000, pp. 86–99.
4. Andy Meisler, "Little White Lies Yield Red Ink for Corporate Recruiters," *Workforce Management,* November 2003, pp. 89–90.
5. Nantaporn Makawatsakul and Brian Kleiner, "The Effect of Downsizing on Morale and Attrition," *Management Research News* 26, 2003, p. 52.
6. Shoshana Zuboff, "Behind the Scandals: Men at Work," *Fast Company,* February 2004, p. 93.
7. Louis Lavelle, Jessi Hempel, and Diane Brady, "Executive Pay," *Business Week,* April 19, 2004, pp. 106–118.
8. Zuboff, p. 93.
9. Julia Cosgrove and Susann Rutledge, "Heiress in Handcuffs," *Business Week,* November 24, 2003, pp. 32–40.
10. Curtis Verschoor, "Toward a Corporation with Conscience," *Strategic Finance,* January 2004, pp. 20, 22.
11. Verschoor, pp. 20, 22.
12. Andy Serwer, "Dirty Rotten Numbers," *Fortune,* February 18, 2002, pp. 74–78.
13. Serwer, pp. 74–78.
14. Justin Fox, "Can We Trust Them Now?" *Fortune,* February 18, 2003, p. 97.
15. Faith Arner and Lauren Young, "Can This Man Save Putnam?" *Business Week,* April 19, 2004, pp. 100–105.
16. Linda Trevino and Katherine Nelson, *Managing Business Ethics,* 3rd ed. (Hoboken, NJ: John Wiley & Sons, 2004), p. 163.
17. Trevino and Nelson, p. 23.
18. Amey Stone, "Putting Teeth in Corporate Ethics Codes," *Business Week,* February 19, 2004.
19. Stone.
20. Louis Lavelle and Amy Borrus, "Ethics 101 for CEOs," *Business Week,* January 26, 2004.

21. Barbara Ley Toffler, "Five Ways to Jump-Start Your Company's Ethics," *Fast Company,* October 2003, p. 36.

22. Stone.

23. Toffler, p. 36.

24. Wendy Zellner, "What Was Don Carty Thinking?" *Business Week,* April 25, 2003.

25. Trevino and Nelson, p. 295.

26. Toffler, p. 36.

27. Trevino and Nelson, p. 281.

28. Verschoor, pp. 20, 22.

29. Trevino and Nelson, p. 277.

30. W. M. Greenfield, "In the Name of Corporate Social Responsibility," *Business Horizons,* January/February 2004, pp. 19–28.

31. Maryann Hammers, "Babies Deliver a Loyal Workforce," *Workforce,* April 2003, p. 52; John Sullivan, "Why You Need Workforce Planning," *Workforce,* November 2002, pp. 46–50.

32. George White, "Taco Bell Rushes to Set Example in City Hit by Riots," *Los Angeles Times,* June 10, 1992, p. D1.

33. Frank Edward Allen, "Big U.S. Corporations Form Alliance to Spur Recycling," *Wall Street Journal,* September 4, 1992, p. 7.

34. Spencer E. Ante, "The Secret behind Those Profit Jumps," *Business Week,* December 8, 2003.

35. Neil Brandon and Brian H. Kleiner, "Etiquette for Managers," *Agency Sales Magazine,* April 1994, pp. 36–41.

36. "Call on Employees for Telephone Etiquette: Politeness Can Pay Off," *Profit-Building Strategies,* February 1993, pp. 6–8.

37. Michael Packard, "Telephone Courtesy Sets the Tone of Customer Relations," *RVBusiness,* May 1993, pp. 23–24.

38. "Call on Employees for Telephone Etiquette," pp. 6–8.

39. Brandon and Kleiner, pp. 36–41.

40. Steve Ditlea, "Future Manners," *Omni,* pp. 55–58.

41. Brandon and Kleiner, pp. 36–41.

42. Barbara Pachter and Marjorie Brody, *Complete Business Etiquette Handbook* (Englewood Cliffs, NJ: Prentice Hall, 1995), pp. 122, 129.

43. Charles Lauer, "Calling for Some Manners," *Modern Healthcare,* February 16, 2004, p. 24.

44. Lynn Hayes, "Learning to Love Your Phone," *Lodging Hospitality,* November 1994, p. 34.

45. "Workplace Developments Create New Office Etiquette Dilemmas," *Supervision,* September 1995, p. 9.

46. James Mackey, "Improper Use of Firm's Voice Mail System Could Cost Customers," *Houston Business Journal,* October 7–13, 1994, pp. 27, 33.

47. Steve Ditlea, *Omni,* pp. 55–58.

48. Robert D. Ramsey, "Voice Mail Etiquette," *Supervision,* March 1996, pp. 11–13.

49. Dana Nigro, "Manners Matter," *Meetings and Conventions,* June 1995, pp. 76–80.

50. Ramsey, pp. 11–13.

51. Ditlea, pp. 55–58.

52. Michele Marchetti, "Barbarians at the Buffet," *Successful Meetings,* May 2003, pp. 56–60.

53. Lauer, p. 24.

54. Ditlea, pp. 55–58.

55. Pachter and Brody, p. 84.

56. Julia Fintel, ed., "Business Etiquette," *Keying In,* January 1996, pp. 1–8.

57. Pachter and Brody, p. 83.

58. Teresa A. Daniel, "Electronic and Voice Mail Monitoring of Employees: A Practice Approach," *Employment Relations Today,* Summer 1995, pp. 1–11.

59. "Workplace Developments Create New Office Etiquette Dilemmas," p. 9.

60. Emily Huling, "Mind Your P's and Q's," *Rough Notes,* February 2003, pp. 43, 64.

61. Huling, p. 43.

62. Jennifer Reese, "The Decline of Office Manners," *Fortune,* May 13, 1993, pp. 20–22; "Call on Employees for Telephone Etiquette," *Fortune,* May 13, 1993, pp. 20–22.

63. Huling, p. 64.

64. Pachter and Brody, pp. 163, 159, 177.

65. Pachter and Brody, p. 177.

66. Sue Potton, "Videoconferencing Etiquette," *Meetings and Conventions,* November 1995, p. 26.

67. John T. Molloy, *New Dress for Success* (New York: Warner Books, 1988), pp. 42–43.

68. Alan Flusser, *Style and the Man* (New York: HarperCollins, 1996), p. 62.

69. Laura Egodigwe, "Here Come the Suits," *Black Enterprise,* March 2003, p. 59.

70. Nora Wood and Tina Benitez, "Does the Suit Fit?" *Incentive,* April 2003, pp. 31–35.

71. Flusser, p. 68; Molloy, *New Dress for Success,* pp. 106, 110–113.

72. Wood and Benitez, pp. 31–35; Flusser, pp. 36, 41, 44, 60.

73. John Fetto, "Dress Code," *American Demographics,* May 2002, p. 13.

74. Ryan Underwood, "They Look Marvelous!" *Fast Company,* November 2003, p. 50.

75. John T. Molloy, *The Woman's Dress for Success Book* (New York: Warner Books, 1978), p. 51.

76. Underwood, p. 50.

77. Esther Wachs Book, "The Style of Power," *Fortune,* November 11, 1996, pp. 96–104.

78. Molloy, *The Woman's Dress for Success Book,* pp. 79–80.

79. "View from the Experts," *Woman's Wear Daily,* September 20, 1995, p. 14.

80. Molloy, *The Woman's Dress for Success Book,* pp. 86–88, 94.
81. Egodigwe, p. 59.
82. Fintel, pp. 1–8.
83. Pachter and Brody, pp. 49–51.
84. Helen Wilkie, "What's the Message of Your Manners?" *Canadian Manager,* Fall 2002, pp. 26, 29.
85. Pachter and Brody, p. 67.
86. Brandon and Kleiner, pp. 36–41; Pachter and Brody, p. 70.
87. Fintel, pp. 1–8.
88. Brandon and Kleiner, pp. 36–41.
89. Fintel, pp. 1–8.
90. Pachter and Brody, pp. 201, 213.
91. Fintel, pp. 1–8.
92. Rhonda Reynolds, "Avoiding the Looks That Kill Careers," *Black Enterprise,* June 1995, pp. 281–288.
93. Fintel, pp. 1–8.
94. Andy Cohen, "Manners Matter," *Sales & Marketing Management,* October 2003, pp. 32–37.
95. Fintel, pp. 1–8; Pachter and Brody, p. 212; Reynolds, pp. 281–288.
96. Michael Adams, "Charm Schools: Your Salespeople Are Tough, Taut, Competitive. But a Few Lessons in Etiquette May Help Them Sell Even Better," *Sales & Marketing Management,* April 1996, pp. 72–76.
97. Pachter and Brody, p. 209.
98. Pachter and Brody, p. 212; Fintel, pp. 1–8.
99. Pachter and Brody, p. 201; Fintel, pp. 1–8.
100. Pachter and Brody, p. 201; Fintel, pp. 1–8; Brandon and Kleiner, pp. 36–41.
101. Carla D'Nan Bass, "Manners Matter," *Chicago Tribune,* April 2, 2000, sec. 6, p. 3; Pachter and Brody, p. 153; Daniel Janal, "How Do I Thank Thee? With a Note, of Course," *Compute,* p. 84; Brandon and Kleiner, pp. 36–41.
102. Kate Murphy, "Corporate Gifts: What's Naughty or Nice," *Business Week,* December 11, 1995, p. 122; Roberta Maynard, "Tips for Choosing Corporate Gifts," *Nation's Business,* January 1996, p. 21; Suzie Amer, "Corporate Giving," *Successful Meetings,* December 2003, p. 23.
103. Penelope Trunk, "You Will Attend the Christmas Party. And You Will Like It." *Business 2.0,* December 2002/January 2003, p. 158.
104. Pamela Kruger, "Can You Ask Your Boss to Put Out a Cigarette?" *Redbook,* March 1995, pp. 49, 52.
105. Pachter and Brody, p. 97.
106. Kruger, p. 49.

CHAPTER 6

1. Joel G. Lewin III, *Every Employee's Guide to the Law* (New York: Pantheon, 1993), pp. 52–53.
2. William B. Gould IV, *A Primer on American Labor Law,* 3rd ed. (Cambridge, MA: MIT Press, 1993), p. 115.
3. William Bridges, "The End of the Job," *Fortune,* September 19, 1994, pp. 62–74.
4. Eamonn Fingleton, *Blindside: Why Japan Is Still on Track to Overtake the U.S. by the Year 2000* (Boston: Houghton Mifflin, 1995).
5. Brian O'Reilly, "The New Deal: What Companies and Employees Owe One Another," *Fortune,* June 13, 1994, pp. 44–52.
6. Fingleton, p. 120.
7. Fingleton, pp. 120–122.
8. Patricia Braus, "What Workers Want," *American Demographics,* August 1992, pp. 30–37.
9. Alan Deutschman, "Information Technology," *Fortune,* July 11, 1994, pp. 88–98.
10. Jason Greer, Thomas Buttross, and George Schmelze, "Using Telecommuting to Improve the Bottom Line," *Strategic Finance,* April 2002, pp. 46–50.
11. Denise Laframboise, Rodney Nelson, and Jason Schmaltz, "Managing Resistance to Change in Workplace Accommodation Projects," *Journal of Facilities Management,* February 2003, pp. 306–321.
12. Julie Cohen Mason, "The Death of 9 to 5?" *Management Review,* January 1993, pp. 14–18.
13. Jaclyn Fierman, "It's 2 A.M., Let's Go to Work," *Fortune,* August 21, 1995, pp. 82–88.
14. Keith Hammonds, Kevin Kelly, and Karen Thurston, "The New World of Work," *Business Week,* October 17, 1994, pp. 76–87.
15. Hammonds, Kelly, and Thurston, pp. 84–85.
16. Bernard Wysocki Jr., "High-Tech Nomads Write New Program for Future of Work," *Wall Street Journal,* August 19, 1996, p. 11.
17. Karen Danziger, "Career Plans Key to Keeping Best People," *Internet Week,* January 29, 2001, p. 69.
18. Carol Kleiman, "Knowledge Worker: Another Way to Say Guaranteed Job," *Chicago Tribune,* July 14, 1996, sec. 6, p. 1.
19. Thomas A. Stewart, "Your Company's Most Valuable Asset: Intellectual Capital," *Fortune,* October 3, 1994, pp. 68–74.
20. Chuck Lucier and Jan Dyer Torsileri, "Steal This Idea!" *Strategy + Business,* no. 20, Third Quarter, 2000, pp. 21–24.
21. Alan Farnham, "Are You Smart Enough to Keep Your Job?" *Fortune,* January 15, 1996, pp. 34–48.
22. Stewart, p. 68.
23. Farnham, "Are You Smart Enough," pp. 35–36.
24. Anthony Carnevale and others, "Skills Employers Want," *Training and Development Journal,* October 1988, pp. 23–30; Arno Penzias, "Putting the Idiot in Idiot Savant," *Fortune,* January 15, 1996, p. 46.
25. Penzias, p. 46.

26. Thomas Stewart, "Planning a Career in a World without Managers," *Fortune,* March 20, 1995, pp. 72–73.

27. Penzias, p. 48.

28. Alan Farnham, "Out of College, What's Next," *Fortune,* July 12, 1993, p. 60.

29. Louis S. Richman, "The New Worker Elite," *Fortune,* August 22, 1994, pp. 56–66.

30. Ronald Henkoff, "Winning the New Career Game," *Fortune,* July 12, 1993, pp. 46–49.

31. Farnham, "Out of College," pp. 59–60.

32. Farnham, "Out of College," pp. 60–61.

33. Farnham, "Out of College," pp. 60–61.

34. Stratford Sherman, "A Brave New Darwinian Workplace," *Fortune,* January 25, 1993, pp. 50–56.

35. Henkoff, p. 46.

36. Stewart, "Planning a Career," p. 72.

37. Eugenie Allen, "Dodging the Downsizers: Some Employees Know How to Make Themselves Invaluable," *Working Women,* May 1996, pp. 65–66.

38. Danziger, p. 69.

39. Farnham, "Are You Smart Enough," p. 36.

40. Kimberly Baytos and Brian Kleiner, "New Developments in Job Design," *Business Credit,* February 1995, pp. 22–26.

41. Celestine Ntuen and Evi Park, "Effects of Task Difficulty on Pilot Workload," *Computers and Industrial Engineering,* October 1996, pp. 487–489.

42. Baytos and Kleiner, pp. 22–26.

43. Baytos and Kleiner, pp. 22–26.

44. John A. Uzzi, "Work Effectiveness," *Manager's Magazine,* October 1995, pp. 23–25.

45. "Job Sharing: Widely Offered, Little Used," *Training,* November 1994, p. 12.

46. Max Weber, *The Theory of Social and Economic Organizations,* trans. A. M. Henderson and T. Parsons (New York: Free Press, 1947), p. 331.

47. Dan Rafter, "Ganging Up," *Chicago Tribune,* March 26, 2000, sec. 6, p. 3.

48. Jennifer Merritt, "Improv at the Interview," *Business Week,* February 3, 2003, p. 63.

49. Arthur Bell and Dayle Smith, *Interviewing for Success* (Upper Saddle River, NJ: Pearson Prentice Hall, 2004), pp. 7–16.

50. Shirleen Holt, "'Parachute' Arises Again as Best Seller," *Chicago Tribune,* November 20, 2002, sec. 6, p. 3.

51. Gary Hartzel, "Avoiding Evaluation Errors: Fairness in Appraising Employer Fairness," *NASSP Bulletin,* January 1995, pp. 40–51.

52. Alison Hardingham, "How Metaphors Throw Light on Training Issues," *People Management,* January 23, 1997, p. 49.

53. Hartzel, pp. 40–51.

54. Hartzel, pp. 40–51.

55. Donna Deeprose, "Seven Deadly Sins of Performance Appraisals," *Supervisory Management,* January 1994, pp. 7–8.

56. George Strauss and Leonard R. Sayles, *Behavioral Strategies for Managers* (Englewood Cliffs, NJ: Prentice Hall, 1980), p. 272.

57. Sal Divita, "Job Evaluations Often Focus on Personalities, Not Performance," *Marketing News,* January 3, 1994, pp. 21–23; Brian Knutson, "Facial Expressions of Emotion Influence Interpersonal Trait Inferences," *Journal of Nonverbal Behavior,* Fall 1996, pp. 165–183.

58. Mahmoud Nourayi and Frank Daroca, "Performance Evaluations and Measurement Issues," *Journal of Managerial Issues,* Summer 1996, pp. 206–218.

59. Elissa L. Perry, Carol T. Kulik, and Anne C. Bourhis, "Moderating Effects of Personal and Contextual Factors in Age Discrimination," *Journal of Applied Psychology,* December 1996, pp. 628–647; Stan Gibson, "Everyone but Me Is Biased," *PC Week,* July 19, 1999, p. 78.

60. Joanne Cleaver, "Time to Rev Up: Find a Path to a Winning Job Evaluation," *Chicago Tribune,* February 26, 2003, sec. 6, p. 1.

61. Cleaver, p. 4.

62. Ronald Henkoff, "So, You Want to Change Your Job," *Fortune,* January 15, 1996, pp. 52–56.

63. Marshall Loeb, "What to Do If You Get Fired," *Fortune,* January 15, 1996, pp. 77–78.

64. Katherine Sopranos, "Heeding the Signs," *Chicago Tribune,* March 22, 1998, sec. 6, pp. 1–3.

65. Gloria Dunn, "What to Do after You've Lost Your Job," *Workforce Extra,* April 1999, pp. 2–3.

66. William Bridges, "The End of the Job," *Fortune,* September 19, 1994, pp. 62–74; Henkoff, "So, You Want to Change Your Job," pp. 52–54.

67. Henkoff, "So, You Want to Change Your Job," p. 54.

CHAPTER 7

1. Henri Fayol, *General and Industrial Management,* rev. Irwin Gray (Belmont, CA: David S. Lake Publishers, 1987), p. 62.

2. Fayol, pp. 79–83.

3. Kenneth Meier and John Bohte, "Span of Control and Public Organizations: Implementing Luther Gulick's Research Design," *Public Administration Review* 63, no. 1, January/February 2003, pp. 61–70.

4. Stephen Robbins and Mary Coulter, *Management,* 8th ed. (Upper Saddle River, NJ: Pearson Prentice Hall, 2005), p. 244.

5. Richard Daft, *Organizational Theory and Design,* 8th ed. (Mason, OH: South-Western, 2004), pp. 99–100.

6. Peter Drucker, *The Practice of Management* (New York: HarperBusiness, 1993), p. 208; Peter F. Drucker, *Management: Tasks, Responsibilities, Practices* (New York: HarperBusiness, 1993), p. 520.

7. Tom Peters, *Liberation Management* (New York: Knopf, 1992), p. 285.

8. Michael Goold and Andrew Campbell, "Making Matrix Structures Work: Creating Clarity on Unit Roles and Responsibility," *European Management Journal,* no. 3, June 2003, p. 351.

9. Daft, pp. 110–114.

10. Daft, pp. 113–114.

11. Peter Senge and others, *The Fifth Discipline Fieldbook: Strategies and Tools for Building a Learning Organization* (New York: Doubleday, 1994), p. 49.

12. Gene Calvert, Sandra Mobley, and Lisa Marshall, "Grasping the Learning Organization," *Training and Development,* June 1994, pp. 38–43.

13. Senge and others, pp. 25–27.

14. Neal McChristy, "Creating a Learning Organization," *Office Solutions,* February 2002, pp. 26–29.

15. Calvert, Mobley, and Marshall, p. 41.

16. Thomas Stewart, "The Invisible Key to Success," *Fortune,* August 5, 1996, pp. 173–177.

17. Stewart, p. 175.

18. Daft, pp. 209–210.

19. Peters, p. 259.

20. Peters, pp. 62–71.

21. Peters, p. 14.

22. Peters, p. 9.

23. John A. Byrne, "Congratulations. You're Moving to a New Pepperoni," *Business Week,* December 20, 1993, pp. 80–81; Raymond Miles and Charles C. Snow, "The New Network Firm: A Spherical Structure Built on a Human Investment Philosophy," *Organizational Dynamics,* pp. 5–18.

24. Byrne, "Congratulations," pp. 80–81.

25. John A. Byrne, "Management's New Gurus," *Business Week,* August 31, 1992, pp. 44–52; Stephen Campbell and Brian Kleiner, "New Developments in Re-engineering Organizations," *Management Research News,* no. 3/4, 2001, pp. 5–8.

26. Tom Pope, "Core Competencies: Only Do What You Really Know," *The Non-profit Times,* November 1, 2002, pp. 49–51.

27. Bernard Baumohl, "When Downsizing Becomes 'Dumbsizing'" *Time,* March 15, 1993, p. 55.

28. Areil Mishra and Karen Mishra, "Mutual Trust in Downsizing," *Human Resource Management,* Summer 1994, p. 264; Sarah J. Freeman, "Organizational Downsizing as Convergence or Reorientation," *Human Management,* Summer 1994, pp. 213–237; Stephen Franklin, "Downsizing Realities Revealed," *Chicago Tribune,* October 23, 1995, sec. 4, p. 11.

29. "The Downside of Downsizing," *Psychology Today,* September–October 1993, p. 21; Ronald Henkoff, "Getting Beyond Downsizing," *Fortune,* January 10, 1994, pp. 58–62; Julie Connelly, "Have We Become Mad Dogs in the Office?" *Fortune,* November 28, 1994, pp. 197–199.

30. Mishra and Mishra, p. 264.

CHAPTER 8

1. Michael W. Drafke, *Working in Health Care: What You Need to Know to Succeed,* 2nd ed. (Philadelphia: F. A. Davis, 2002), p. 64.

2. Stephen Robbins and Mary Coulter, *Management,* 8th ed. (Upper Saddle River, NJ: Pearson Prentice Hall, 2005), pp. 139–40.

3. Peter Hess and Julie Siciliano, *Management: Responsibility for Performance* (New York: McGraw-Hill, 1996), p. 112.

4. R. W. Griffin, *Management,* 4th ed. (Boston: Houghton Mifflin, 1993), p. 213.

5. James W. Dean Jr. and Mark P. Sharfman, "The Relationship between Procedural Rationality and Political Behavior in Strategic Decision Making," *Decision Sciences,* November–December 1993, pp. 1069–1083.

6. Griffin, p. 410.

7. Ramon Aldag and Timothy Stearns, *Management,* 2nd ed. (Cincinnati, OH: South-Western, 1991), p. 340.

8. Griffin, p. 410; E. N. Chapman, *Supervisor's Survival Kit,* 6th ed. (New York: Macmillan, 1993), p. 214.

9. Griffin, p. 44.

10. Robbins and Coulter, p. 149.

11. David J. McLaughlin, "Strengthening Executive Decision Making," *Human Resource Management,* Fall 1995, pp. 443–462.

12. John M. Ivancevich, Peter Lorenzi, and Steven Skinner, *Management: Quality and Competitiveness,* 2nd ed. (Chicago: Irwin, 1997), p. 123.

13. Gwen Ortmeyer, "Making Better Decisions Faster," *Management Review,* June 1996, pp. 53–57.

14. Hess and Siciliano, p. 106.

15. Helga Drummond, "Giving It a Week and Then Another Week," *Personnel Review,* February 1997, p. 99.

16. Donald Mosley, Leon Megginson, and Paul Pietri, *Supervisory Management—The Art of Working with and through People,* 2nd ed. (Cincinnati, OH: South-Western, 1989), p. 71.

17. Ivancevich, Lorenzi, and Skinner, p. 128.

18. Rajagopal Raghunathan and Michel Tuan Pham, "All Negative Moods Are Not Equal: Motivational Influences of Anxiety and Sadness on Decision Making," *Organizational Behavior & Human Decision*

Processes, July 1999, pp. 56–57; Nigel Howard, "The Role of Emotions in Multi-Organizational Decision-Making," *Journal of the Operational Research Society,* June 1993, pp. 613–623.

19. T. S. Bateman and C. P. Zeithaml, *Management: Function and Strategy,* 2nd ed. (Homewood, IL: Irwin, 1993), p. 102.
20. Griffin, p. 214.
21. Robbins and Coulter, p. 149; Ortmeyer, pp. 53–57.
22. Bateman and Zeithaml, p. 88.
23. Mosley, Megginson, and Pietri, p. 69.
24. Robbins and Coulter, pp. 144–145.
25. Bateman and Zeithaml, p. 88.
26. Mosley, Megginson, and Pietri, p. 72.
27. Bateman and Zeithaml, p. 96.
28. L. W. Rue and L. L. Byars, *Supervision,* 4th ed. (Homewood, IL: Irwin, 1993), p. 37.
29. Darren McCabe, "The Best Laid Schemes of TQM: Strategy, Politics, and Power," *Industrial Relations Journal,* March 1996, pp. 28–39.
30. Hess and Siciliano, p. 113.
31. Robbins and Coulter, p. 30.
32. Robbins and Coulter, p. 30.
33. Robbins and Coulter, p. 30.
34. Robbins and Coulter, pp. 28–31; Peter F. Drucker, *Management: Tasks, Responsibilities, Practices* (New York: HarperCollins, 1993), p. 384.
35. T. Shawn Taylor, "Fear Factor Drives Workers in Tough Times," *Chicago Tribune,* March 19, 2003, sec. 6, p. 1.
36. Robbins and Coulter, p. 33–34.
37. Gus Tyler, "The Work Ethic: A Union View," *It Comes with the Territory,* ed. A. R. Gini and T. J. Sullivan (New York: Random House, 1989), p. 128.
38. Terry L. Paulson, *They Shoot Managers, Don't They?* (Berkeley, CA: Ten Speed Press, 1991), p. 4.
39. Oren Harari, "Ten Reasons TQM Doesn't Work," *Management Review,* January 1997, pp. 37–44.
40. John G. Watson and Appa Rao Korukonda, "The TQM Jungle: A Dialectical Analysis," *International Journal of Quality and Reliability Management,* September–October 1995, pp. 100–110.
41. John Wareham, "A Short History of Executive Incompetence," *Across the Board,* July–August 1995, pp. 49–50; Shari Caudron, "Building Better Bosses," *Workforce,* May 2000, pp. 33–39.
42. Shari Caudron, "The Boss from Hell: Coping with a Bad Boss," *Industry Week,* September 4, 1995, pp. 12–17; Gillian Flynn, "Stop Toxic Managers before They Stop You," *Workforce,* August 1999, pp. 40–46.
43. Wareham, pp. 49–50.
44. John A. Byrne, "The Craze for Consultants," *Business Week,* July 24, 1994, pp. 60–66.
45. John A. Byrne, "Keeping Cool in Front of the Consultants," *Business Week,* July 24, 1994, p. 66.

46. Caudron, pp. 12–14.
47. Caudron, pp. 14–15.
48. Caudron, p. 15; Brian Dumaine, "America's Toughest Bosses," *Fortune,* October 18, 1993, pp. 38–50.
49. Caudron, p. 14.
50. Gillian Flynn, "Eight Toxic-Manager Behaviors—and the Cultures That Nurture Them," *Workforce,* August 1999, p. 44.
51. Caudron, p. 15.
52. Caudron, pp. 14–15.
53. Caudron, p. 15.
54. Paul Kaihla, "Getting Inside the Boss's Head," *Business 2.0,* November 2003, pp. 49–51.
55. Caudron, p. 15; Dumaine, pp. 40, 48.
56. Dumaine, pp. 40, 41, 44, 48.
57. "The Bully Rulebook: How to Deal with Jerks," *Inc. Magazine,* February 2007, pp. 43–44.
58. Dumaine, p. 44.
59. Dumaine, p. 48.
60. Dumaine, pp. 41–43.
61. Dumaine, p. 42.
62. Caudron, p. 15.
63. Caudron, pp. 15–16.
64. Caudron, p. 17.
65. Caudron, p. 17.
66. Susan Oakland and Alister Ostell, "Measuring Coping: A Review and Critique," *Human Relations,* February 1996, pp. 131–156.
67. Caudron, pp. 17–18; Dumaine, p. 50.
68. Jay T. Knippen, Thad Green, and Kurt Sutton, "Modifying Behavior in the Chain of Command," *Security Management,* May 1993, pp. 24–26.
69. John A. Byrne, "A Tour Guide to Management Meccas," *Business Week,* September 18, 1995, pp. 124–125.
70. Donald Mosley, Paul Pietri, and Leon Megginson, *Management: Leadership in Action,* 5th ed. (New York: HarperCollins, 1996), p. 63.
71. Christopher Farrell, Michael Mandel, and Joseph Weber, "Riding High: Corporate America Now Has an Edge over Its Global Rivals," *Business Week,* October 9, 1995, pp. 134–146.
72. Peggy Simonsen, "Do Your Managers Have the Right Stuff?" *Workforce,* August 1999, pp. 47–52.
73. Robert Levering and Milton Moskowitz, "The 100 Best Companies to Work For," *Fortune,* January 10, 2000, pp. 82–110.
74. Russel Mitchell and Michael Oneal, "Managing by Values," *Business Week,* August 1, 1994, pp. 46–52.
75. Levering and Moskowitz, pp. 82–110.
76. Mosley, Pietri, and Megginson, p. 372.
77. Michael A. Verespej, "Managee-Managers," *Industry Week,* May 16, 1994, p. 30; Gerald White, "Employee Turnover: The Hidden Drain on Profits," *HR Focus,* January 1995, pp. 15–18.
78. White, pp. 16–17; Levering, p. 36.

79. Byrne, pp. 127–128.
80. Mitchell and Oneal, p. 50.
81. Verespej, p. 30; Mitchell and Oneal, p. 47.
82. Mosley, Pietri, and Megginson, p. 372; Mitchell and Oneal, p. 47.
83. Mosley, Pietri, and Megginson, pp. 370–371; Verespej, p. 30; Mitchell and Oneal, p. 49.
84. Sara P. Noble, ed., *Managing People: 101 Proven Ideas* (Boston: Goldhirsh Group, 1992), p. 55.
85. Dave Murphy, "Best Bosses Ask Right Questions for Success," *Chicago Tribune,* November 25, 2002, sec. 4, p. 4.
86. Mitchell and Oneal, p. 47; Peter F. Drucker, *The Practice of Management* (New York: HarperCollins, 1993), p. 370.
87. Mitchell and Oneal, pp. 48–49.
88. "The Top Managers of 1995," *Business Week,* January 8, 1996, pp. 50–63.

CHAPTER 9

1. Gerard Egan, "The Shadow Side," *Management Today,* September 1993, pp. 32–39.
2. Egan, pp. 32–39.
3. Richard Daft, *Management,* 6th ed. (Mason, OH: Thomson South-Western, 2003), p. 503.
4. Mark A. Frohman, "Do Teams . . . But Do Them Right," *Industry Week,* April 3, 1995, p. 22.
5. Solomon E. Asch, *Group Dynamics: Research and Theory,* 2nd ed., ed. Darwin Cartwright and Alvin Zander (New York: Harper & Row, 1960), pp. 188–200.
6. John Ivancevich, Peter Lorenzi, and Steven Skinner, *Management: Quality and Competitiveness* (Chicago: Irwin, 1997), pp. 300–301.
7. Randy Hodson, "Group Relations at Work: Solidarity, Conflict, and Relations with Management," *Work and Occupations,* November 1997, pp. 430–431.
8. Hodson, pp. 449–451.
9. Ivancevich, p. 302.
10. U.S. Bureau of Labor Statistics, *Occupational Outlook Quarterly,* Winter 2003–2004.
11. Patricia Karathanos and Anthony Auriemmo, "Care and Feeding of the Organizational Grapevine," *Industrial Management,* March–April 1999, pp. 26–30.
12. Keith Davis and John Newstrom, *Human Behavior at Work,* 8th ed. (New York: McGraw-Hill, 1989), p. 375.
13. Stephen Robbins and Mary Coulter, *Management,* 8th ed. (Upper Saddle River, NJ: Pearson Prentice Hall, 2005), pp. 268–269.
14. Robbins and Coulter, p. 378.
15. Christopher P. Neck and Charles C. Manz, "From Groupthink to Teamthink: Toward the Creation of Constructive Thought Patterns in Self-Managing Work Teams," *Human Relations* 47, no. 8, 1994, pp. 929–949.
16. Barbara Pachter and Marjorie Brody, *Complete Business Etiquette Handbook* (Englewood Cliffs, NJ: Prentice Hall, 1995), p. 159.
17. Patrick Sauer, "What Time Is the Next Meeting?" *Inc.,* May 2004, pp. 70–78, 112.
18. Frohman, pp. 21–24.
19. Frohman, p. 22.
20. Donald Mosley, Paul Pietri, and Leon Megginson, *Management: Leadership in Action* (New York: HarperCollins, 1996), p. 459.
21. John Beck and Neil Yeager, "Moving beyond Team Myths," *Training and Development,* March 1996, pp. 51–55.
22. Beck and Yeager, p. 54.
23. Beck and Yeager, p. 54.
24. Frohman, p. 22.
25. Ed Hopkins, "Effective Teams: Camels of a Different Color?" *Training and Development,* December 1994, pp. 35–37.
26. Frohman, p. 22.
27. Hopkins, p. 36.
28. Beck and Yeager, p. 55.
29. Beck and Yeager, p. 55.
30. Hopkins, p. 36.
31. Beck and Yeager, p. 55.
32. Hopkins, p. 55.
33. Hopkins, p. 55.
34. Hopkins, p. 55.
35. Tracy E. Benson, "A Braver New World?" *Industry Week,* August 3, 1992, pp. 48–54.
36. Susan G. Cohen and Gerald E. Ledford Jr., "The Effectiveness of Self-Managing Teams: A Quasi-Experiment," *Human Relations,* January 1994, pp. 13–44.
37. Hopkins, p. 55.

CHAPTER 10

1. From an address delivered by Robert N. Hilkert, while first president of the Federal Reserve Bank of Philadelphia, at the annual convention of the American Institute of Banking, May 30, 1961, Seattle, WA.
2. T. Shawn Taylor, "Temper Your Temper," *Chicago Tribune,* October 23, 2002, sec. 6, pp. 1, 4.
3. Tracey Schubert, "Stop Bad Vibes Rising," *New Zealand Management,* September 2000, pp. 32–35.
4. Casey Hawley, *100 + Tactics for Office Politics* (Barron's: Hauppauge, NY, 2001), p. 34.
5. Paul Falcone, "When Employees Have a 'Tude," *HRMagazine,* June 2001, pp. 189–194.
6. Hawley, p. 36.

7. Sarah Cliffe, "What a Star—What a Jerk," *Harvard Business Review,* September 2001, pp. 37–40.

8. Marilyn Moats Kennedy, "The Politics of Mean," *Across the Board,* September 1992, pp. 9–10.

9. Hawley, p. 93.

10. Hawley, p. 97.

11. Katherine Sopranos, "The Eyes Have It: In Today's Technology-Driven Workplace, Privacy Is NOT On the List of Benefits," *Chicago Tribune,* March 5, 2000, sec. 6, pp. 1, 7.

12. Sheila Anne Feeney, "Love Hurts," *Workforce Management,* February 2004, pp. 36–40.

13. Daniel S. Hamermesh and Jeff E. Biddle, "Beauty and the Labor Market," *American Economic Review,* December 1994, pp. 1174–1195.

14. Timothy Noak, "How to Reduce Deaths from Tobacco? Duh. Take the Toxic Stuff out of Cigarettes" *(Outlook, 1997), U.S. News and World Report,* December 30, 1996, pp. 66–68.

15. David M. Katz, "Indoor-Air Perils Called 'Silent Crisis,' " *National Underwriters Property and Casualty—Risk and Benefits Management,* January 20, 1997, pp. 1–4.

16. "Nation-wide Class-Action Seeks Compensation for Flight Attendants Suffering from Medical Conditions Caused by Exposure to Second-Hand Cigarette Smoke," *PR Newswire,* February 25, 1997; John M. Bragg, "Lower Mortality Stimulates Older Age Market," *National Underwriter Life and Health— Financial Services Edition,* September 18, 1995, pp. 11–13.

17. Ellen Alderman and Caroline Kennedy, "Privacy," *Across the Board,* March 1996, pp. 32–35.

18. Jeffery Mello, "Personality Screening in Employment: Balancing Information Gathering and the Law," *Labor Law Journal,* October 1995, pp. 622–626.

19. Fred E. Inbau, "Integrity Tests and the Law," *Security Management,* January 1994, pp. 34–41.

20. "Your Company, AIDS, and the Law," *Training and Development,* January 1994, pp. 48–50.

21. Steve Schmitt, "Privacy and Employees," *Credit Union Executive,* January–February 1996, pp. 38–43.

22. Samaul Greengard, "Privacy: Entitlement or Illusion?" *Personnel Journal,* May 1996, pp. 74–83; Michael Prince, "Privacy Lacking in the Office," *Business Insurance,* September 23, 1996.

23. Jeffrey Pfeffer, *Managing with Power* (Boston: Harvard Business School Press, 1992).

24. Rob Norton, "New Thinking on the Causes—and Costs—of Yes Men (and Women)," *Fortune,* November 28, 1994, p. 31.

25. Rebecca A. Thacker and Sandy J. Wayne, "An Examination of the Relationship between Upward Influence Tactics and Assessments of Promotability," *Journal of Management* 21, no. 4, 1995, pp. 739–756.

26. Sandy Wayne and others, "The Role of Upward Influence Tactics in Human Resource Decisions," *Personnel Psychology,* Winter 1997, pp. 979–1006.

27. G. Marwell and D. R. Schmitt, "Dimensions of Compliance-Gaining Behavior: An Empirical Analysis," *Sociometry* 30, 1967, pp. 350–364.

28. Asha Rao, Stuart Schmidt, and Lynda Murray, "Upward Impression Management: Goals, Influence Strategies, and Consequences," *Human Relations,* February 1995, pp. 147–168.

29. John Maslyn, Steven Farmer, and Donald Fedor, "Failed Upward Influence Attempts: Predicting the Nature of Subordinate Persistence in Pursuit of Organizational Goals," *Group & Organization Management,* December 1996, pp. 461–480.

30. Thacker and Wayne, pp. 739–756.

31. Daniel Cable and Timothy Judge, "Managers' Upward Influence Tactic Strategies: The Role of Manager Personality and Supervisor Leadership Style," *Journal of Organizational Behavior,* March 2003, pp. 197–214.

32. Richard Ringer and R. Wayne Boss, "Hospital Professionals' Use of Upward Influence Tactics," *Journal of Managerial Issues,* Spring 2000, pp. 92–108.

33. Wayne and others, pp. 979–1006.

34. Marwell and Schmitt, pp. 350–364.

35. Steven Farmer and others, "Putting Upward Influence Strategies in Context," *Journal of Organizational Behavior,* January 1997, pp. 17–42.

36. Lisa Skolnick, "Buttering Up the Boss," *Chicago Tribune,* October 1, 2003, sec. 6, pp. 1, 4.

37. Steven Appelbaum and Brent Hughes, "Ingratiation as a Political Tactic: Effects within the Organization," *Management Decision* 36, no. 2, 1998, p. 85; Thacker and Wayne, pp. 739–756.

38. Farmer and others, pp. 17–42.

39. Wayne and others, pp. 979–1006; Maslyn, Farmer, and Fedor, pp. 461–480.

40. Farmer and others, pp. 17–42.

41. Maslyn, Farmer, and Fedor, pp. 461–480.

42. Rao, Schmidt, and Murray, pp. 147–168.

43. Robert Bramson, *What Your Boss Doesn't Tell You Until It Is Too Late* (New York: Fireside, 1996), pp. 17–20.

44. Robert McGarvey, "More Power to Them," *Entrepreneur,* February 1995, pp. 73–75.

45. Andrew J. DuBrin, *Reengineering Survival Guide* (Cincinnati, OH: Thomson Executive Press, 1996), p. 182.

46. McGarvey, p. 73.

47. McGarvey, p. 74.

48. David Holzman, "When Workers Run the Show," *Working Woman,* August 1993, p. 381.

49. McGarvey, pp. 74–75.
50. Colette Frayne and J. Michael Geringer, "Self-Management Training for Joint Venture General Managers," *Human Resource Planning,* December 1992, pp. 69–86.
51. DuBrin, p. 182.
52. Holzman, p. 40.
53. John M. Ivancevich, Peter Lorenzi, and Steven Skinner, *Management: Quality and Competitiveness* (Chicago: Irwin, 1997), p. 355.
54. Frayne and Geringer, pp. 69–86.
55. Ivancevich, p. 356.
56. Brian Dumaine, "Who Needs a Boss?" *Fortune,* May 7, 1990, pp. 52–58.
57. Tracy Bensen, "A Brave New World?" *Industry Week,* August 3, 1992, pp. 48–54.
58. Peter Drucker, *Management: Tasks, Responsibilities, Practices* (New York: HarperCollins, 1993), p. 441.
59. Stephen Robbins and Mary Coulter, *Management,* 8th ed. (Upper Saddle River, NJ: Pearson Prentice Hall, 2005), pp. 353–354.
60. Ivancevich, p. 356.
61. Frayne and Geringer, p. 75.
62. Ivancevich, p. 356.
63. Ivancevich, pp. 356–357; Frayne and Geringer, p. 76.
64. Frayne and Geringer, p. 77.
65. McGarvey, p. 74.
66. Holzman, p. 73.
67. Michael A. Carter, "Quit Empowering Me and Let Me Do My Job," *Supervision,* September 1995, pp. 6–9.
68. McGarvey, p. 75.
69. Holzman, p. 73.
70. Carter, p. 6.
71. McGarvey, p. 73.
72. Holzman, p. 73; Tom Gegax, "Eight Steps to Managing Yourself," *Modern Tire Dealer,* September 15, 1992, pp. 50–52.
73. Dumaine, pp. 52–58.
74. Holzman, p. 73.
75. Hyrum W. Smith, "The 10 Natural Laws of Successful Time and Life Management," *Warner Books,* 1994, p. 26.
76. Frank J. Lucco, "Effective Time Management," *Appraisal Journal,* October 1994, pp. 580–586.
77. Therese Hoff Macan, "Time Management: Test of a Process Model," *Journal of Applied Psychology* 79, no. 3, 1994, pp. 381–391.
78. Teri Lammers, "The Custom-Made Day Planner," *Inc.,* February 1992, pp. 61–63.
79. Lucco, p. 581.
80. Lucco, p. 582.
81. Lynn Harris, "Find Your Own Time Zone," *Working Woman,* November 1994, pp. S1–3.
82. Roy Alexander, "Starving Out the Time Gobblers," *Supervisory Management,* February 1993, p. 8.
83. Terry L. Paulson, *They Shoot Managers, Don't They?* (Berkeley, CA: Ten Speed Press, 1991), p. 49.
84. Alexander, p. 8.
85. Franklin J. Stein, "Finding Management Time," *Supervisory Management,* February 1993, p. 7.
86. Alexander, p. 8.
87. James E. Brill, "Not Enough Hours," *American Bar Association Journal,* June 1992, p. 98.
88. Brill, p. 98.
89. Lynn Harris, "Discipline Your Desk," *Working Women,* November 1994, p. 8.
90. Brill, p. 98.
91. Harris, "Discipline Your Desk," p. 8.

CHAPTER 11

1. Research by D. P. Crowne and D. Marlowe, in *The Approval Motive: Studies in Evaluative Dependence* (New York: John Wiley & Sons, 1964), as reported in and adapted from Gardner Lindzey, Calvin S. Hall, and Richard F. Thompson, *Psychology* (New York: Worth, 1975), p. 354.
2. David C. McClelland, *The Achieving Society* (New York: Van Nostrand, 1961).
3. Abraham H. Maslow, *Motivation and Personality* (New York: Harper & Row, 1954).
4. Abraham H. Maslow, *Motivation and Personality,* 3rd ed. (New York: Harper & Row, 1970), pp. 23–25.
5. Maslow, 3rd ed., pp. 23–25.
6. Maslow, 3rd ed., p. 18.
7. Maslow, 3rd ed., pp. 20–21.
8. Maslow, 3rd ed., pp. 21–22.
9. Maslow, 3rd ed., pp. 22–23.
10. Maslow, 3rd ed., pp. 23–26.
11. Maslow, 3rd ed., p. 25.
12. Maslow, 3rd ed., pp. 25–26.
13. Richard L. Daft, *Management,* 6th ed. (Mason, OH: Thomson South-Western, 2003), pp. 531–532.
14. Frederick Herzberg, *Work and the Nature of Man* (Cleveland, OH: World Publishing, 1966).
15. Brenda Paik Sunoo, "Praise and Thanks—You Can't Give Enough," *Workforce,* April 1999, pp. 56–60.
16. B. F. Skinner, *About Behaviorism* (New York: Knopf, 1974).
17. B. F. Skinner, *Beyond Freedom and Dignity* (New York: Alfred A. Knopf, 1984), pp. 34–35.
18. Marilyn B. Gilbert and Thomas F. Gilbert, "What Skinner Gave Us," *Training,* September 1991, pp. 42–47.
19. Gilbert and Gilbert, pp. 42–47.
20. Patrick Frimary and Alan Poling, "Making Life Easier with Effort: Basic Findings and Applied Research on

Response Effort," *Journal of Applied Behavioral Analysis,* Winter 1995, pp. 583–591.

21. Ken Snead and Adrian Harrell, "An Application of Expectancy Theory to Explain a Manager's Intention to Use a Decision Support System," *Decision Science,* July–August 1994, pp. 499–514.

22. Stephen Robbins and Mary Coulter, *Management,* 8th ed. (Upper Saddle River, NJ: Pearson Prentice Hall, 2005), p. 405.

23. Robbins and Coulter, pp. 403–404.

24. Madeline Hunter, "Motivation Theory for Teachers," *Hunter Enterprises* (Los Angeles: 1996), pp. 11–32.

25. Sylvie Richer and Robert Vallerand, "Supervisors' Interactional Styles and Subordinates' Intrinsic and Extrinsic Motivation," *Journal of Social Psychology,* 135, no. 6, 1995, pp. 707–722.

26. Ted Pollock, "A Personal File of Stimulating Ideas, Little Known Facts, and Daily Problem Solvers," *Supervision,* November 1995, pp. 21–24.

27. Steven Appelbaum, "Self-Efficacy as a Mediator of Goal Setting and Performance: Some Human Resource Applications," *Journal of Managerial Psychology,* March 1996, pp. 33–48.

28. Robbins and Coulter, p. 298; John M. Ivancevich, Peter Lorenzi, and Steven Skinner, *Management: Quality and Competitiveness,* 2nd ed. (Chicago: Irwin, 1997), pp. 277–279.

29. Adrian Furnham, Bruce Kirkcaldy, and Richard Lynn, "National Attitudes to Competitiveness, Money, and Work among Young People: First, Second, and Third World Differences," *Human Relations* 47, no. 1, 1994, pp. 119–132.

30. Robert Bramson, *What Your Boss Doesn't Tell You Until It Is Too Late: How to Correct Behavior That Is Holding You Back* (New York: Fireside, 1996), pp. 79–96.

31. Linda Grant, "Happy Workers, High Returns," *Fortune,* January 12, 1998, p. 81.

CHAPTER 12

1. Charlene Marmer Solomon, "Workers Want a Life! Do Managers Care?" *Workforce,* August 1999, pp. 54–58.

2. "Lifetime Employment Relic of Past," *Chicago Tribune,* August 21, 1995, pp. 1, 8.

3. John Purcell, "A Good Question. (On Being a 'Good' Employer)," *People Management,* April 17, 1997, pp. 40–43.

4. Dayton Fandray, "Eight Days a Week," *Workforce,* September 2000, pp. 34–42.

5. Owen Thomas, "The Outsourcing Solution," *Business 2.0,* September 2003, pp. 159–160.

6. Bernard Baumohl, "When Downsizing Becomes 'Dumbsizing,'" *Time,* March 15, 1993.

7. "Lifetime Employment Relic of Past," pp. 1, 8.

8. Richard E. Walton, "Criteria for Quality of Working Life," in *The Quality of Working Life,* vol. 1, ed. Louis E. Davis and Albert B. Cherns (New York: Free Press, 1975), pp. 91–97; Ian Wylie, "Danger: Toxic Firms at Work (Companies That Treat Employees Badly)," *The Guardian,* May 15, 1999, p. 3; Ann Vincola Caela Farren, "Life Balance Makes for Better Workers," *HR Focus,* April 1999, p. 13.

9. Robert Levering, *A Great Place to Work: What Makes Some Employers So Good (and Most So Bad)* (New York: Random House, 1988), p. 26.

10. Stephen Robbins and Mary Coulter, *Management,* 8th ed. (Upper Saddle River, NJ: Pearson Prentice Hall, 2005), pp. 401–403.

11. Muneto Ozaki, "Labor Relations and Work Organizations in Industrialized Countries," *International Labor Review,* January–February 1996, pp. 37–59.

12. "Banks That Pay Days," *HR Magazine,* April 1995, p. 26.

13. Carol Kleiman, "Fel-Pro Does It Right," *Chicago Tribune,* October 27, 1996, sec. 6, p. 1.

14. Anthony R. Montebello and Victor R. Buzzotta, "Work Teams That Work," *Training & Development,* March 1993, pp. 59–65.

15. Mark Hanson and David Sysar, "Making the Right Moves—Implementing Effective Ergonomic Management," *Risk Management,* February 1997, pp. 50–54.

16. Bob Baker, "Computers Bring Stress, Job Isolation," *Contra Costa Times,* June 23, 1991, p. C1.

17. Roberta Maynard, "A Wellness Program's Bottom Line Benefits," *Nation's Business,* January 1997, pp. 9–10.

18. J. R. Meredith, *The Management of Operations,* 4th ed. (New York: John Wiley & Sons, 1992), p. 341.

19. Robbins and Coulter, p. 401.

20. Helen Richardson, "Get Your Piece of the Pie," *Transportation and Distribution,* January 1997, pp. S2–7.

21. Rebecca Gardyn, "Who's the Boss?" *American Demographics,* September 2000, pp. 53–58.

22. Charles Fishman, "Moving toward a Balanced Work Life," *Workforce,* March 2000, pp. 38–42.

23. As related to Stan Kossen by Donald Ledwith, a manager with Chevron Corporation.

24. Kathy Bergen, "Timely Exercise: Compact Schedules Help Workers Stretch," *Chicago Tribune,* March 2, 1997, sec. 5, pp. 1, 6.

25. Linda Davidson, "Temp Workers Want a Better Deal," *Workforce,* October 1999, pp. 44–50.

26. Susan Berfield, "Two for the Cubicle; Sharing a Job Is Always Dicey. How One Pair Has Made It Work for 15 Years. *Business Week,* July 24, 2006, p. 88.

27. John Ivancevich, Peter Lorenzi, and Steven Skinner, *Management: Quality and Competitiveness,* 2nd ed. (Chicago: Irwin, 1997), p. 251.

28. Simon S. K. Lam, "Quality Management and Job Satisfaction," *International Journal of Quality and Reliability Management,* April 1995, pp. 72–79.

29. Robbins and Coulter, pp. 401–402.

30. M. M. Gruneberg, *Understanding Job Satisfaction* (New York: John Wiley & Sons, 1979), p. 45.

31. Levering, pp. 108–110.

32. Leslie A. Wilk and William K. Redmon, "The Effects of Feedback and Goal Setting on the Productivity and Satisfaction of University Admissions Staff," *Journal of Organizational Behavior Management,* Winter 1998, pp. 45–65.

33. Wilk and Redmon, pp. 45–65.

34. Linda Davidson, "The Power of Personal Recognition," *Workforce,* July 1999, pp. 44–49.

35. Lawson K. Savery, "The Congruence between the Importance of Job Satisfaction and the Perceived Level of Achievement," *Journal of Management Development,* June 1996, pp. 18–28.

36. Carrie S. McCleese and Lillian T. Eby. "Reactions to Job Content Plateaus: Examining Role Ambiguity and Hierarchical Plateaus as Moderators," *Career Development Quarterly*, September 2006, pp. 64–77.

37. Richard Daft, *Management,* 6th ed. (Mason, OH: Thomson South-Western, 2003) pp. 503–504; Ivancevich, Lorenzi, and Skinner, p. 300.

38. Samuel Greengard and Wood Kinnard, "The Key to Your Career May Be a Job Change," *Personnel Journal,* October 1995, pp. 100–106.

39. Keith Hammonds, Wendy Zellner, and Richard Melcher, "Writing a New Social Contract," *Business Week,* March 11, 1996, pp. 60–61.

40. Ricky Griffin, *Fundamentals of Management* (Boston: Houghton Mifflin, 1997), p. 341.

41. Stephan Crow and Sandra Hartman, "Can't Get No Satisfaction," *Leadership and Organizational Development Journal,* April 1995, pp. 34–39.

42. C. Argyris, "Personality and Organization Theory Revisited," *Administrative Science Quarterly,* 1973, pp. 141–167.

43. Jesse Beeler, James Hunton, and Bensen Wise, "A Survey Report of Job Satisfaction and Job Involvement among Governmental and Public Auditors," *Government Accountants Journal,* Winter 1997, pp. 26–32.

44. Bergen, p. 6.

45. Michael Tremblay, Alain Roger, and Jean-Marie Toulouse, "Career Plateau and Work Attitudes: An Empirical Study of Managers," *Human Relations,* March 1995, pp. 221–238.

46. A. R. Gini and T. J. Sullivan, *It Comes with the Territory: An Inquiry Concerning Work and the Person* (New York: Random House, 1989), p. 17.

47. Diane Dodd-McCue and Gail Wright, "Men, Women, and Attitudinal Commitment: The Effect of Workplace Experiences and Socialization," *Human Relations,* August 1996, pp. 1065–1092.

48. Timothy Judge and others, "An Empirical Investigation of the Predictors of Executive Career Success," *Personnel Psychology,* Autumn 1995, pp. 485–520.

49. Beeler, Hunton, and Wise, pp. 26–32.

50. Tod Morris, "Employee Satisfaction: Maximizing the Return on Human Capital," *CMA—The Management Accounting Magazine,* December 1995, pp. 15–18.

51. Sharon Lund O'Neil and Elwood Chapman, *Your Attitude Is Showing,* 10th ed. (Upper Saddle River, NJ: Prentice Hall, 2002), p. 106.

52. Ivancevich, Lorenzi, and Skinner, pp. 323–324.

53. Dodd-McCue and Wright, pp. 1065–1092.

54. Gary Adams, Lynda King, and Diane King, "Relationship of Job and Family Involvement, Family Social Support, and Work-Family Conflict with Job and Life Satisfaction," *Journal of Applied Psychology,* August 1996, pp. 411–421.

55. Adams, King, and King, pp. 411–421.

56. John Wareham, "The Desperately Unhappy Executive," *Across the Nation,* January 1997, pp. 49–51.

57. Andrew Clark, Andrew Oswald, and Peter Warr, "Is Job Satisfaction U-Shaped in Age?" *Journal of Occupational and Organizational Psychology,* March 1996, pp. 57–81.

CHAPTER 13

1. Andrew J. DuBrin, *Reengineering Survival Guide: Managing and Surviving in the Changing Workplace* (Cincinnati, OH: Thomson Executive Press, 1996), p. 89.

2. Max Messmer, "Helping Employees Adapt to Change," *National Public Accountant,* July 2003, p. 30.

3. Denise Laframboise, Rodney Nelson, and Jason Schmaltz, "Managing Resistance to Change in Workplace Accommodation Projects," *Journal of Facilities Management,* February 2003, pp. 306–321.

4. Paul Strebel, "Choosing the Right Change Path," *Financial Times,* February 9, 1996, pp. S5–8.

5. Audrey Pihulyk, "Embrace Change," *Canadian Manager,* Winter 2003, pp. 27–28.

6. "GM Says It May Announce More Plant Closings in '92," *Wall Street Journal Europe,* August 13, 1992, p. 3; William McWhirter, "What Went Wrong?" *Time International,* November 9, 1992, pp. 40–46.

7. Robert A. Luke Jr., "Managing Change," *Supervisory Management,* October 1992, p. 10.

8. Frederick Herzberg, *Work and the Nature of Man* (Cleveland, OH: World Publishing, 1966).

9. John Zimmerman, "The Principle of Managing Change," *HR Focus,* February 1995, pp. 15–17.

10. Robert Kreitner, *Foundations of Management* (Boston: Houghton Mifflin, 2005) p. 393; Dan F. Kennedy, "Re-Engineering—The Small Local Exchange Carrier," *Telecommunications,* November 1995, pp. 57–61.

11. Donald L. Kirkpatrick, "Riding the Winds of Change," *Training and Development,* February 1993, pp. 29–32.

12. Kreitner, p. 392.

13. Suzanne Koudsi, "Actually, It Is Like Brain Surgery," *Fortune,* March 20, 2000, pp. 223–224.

14. Kirkpatrick, p. 31.

15. "Scaling the Wall of Resistance," *Training and Development,* October 1995, pp. 15–19.

16. "Scaling the Wall of Resistance," pp. 15–19.

17. Anne B. Fisher, "Making Change Stick," *Fortune,* April 17, 1995, pp. 121–127.

18. Jim Clark and Richard Kounce, "Engaging Organizational Survivors," *Training and Development,* August 1995, pp. 22–31.

19. Ronald Recardo, "Process Re-Engineering in a Finance Division," *Journal for Quality and Participation,* June 1994, pp. 70–73.

20. John Mariotti, "Troubled by Resistance to Change? Don't Fight It. First, Try to Understand It," *Industry Week,* October 7, 1996, pp. 30–31.

21. Leon Rubis, "Playing by the Books," *HR Magazine,* May 1995, pp. 38–46.

22. Ramon Aldag and Timothy Stearns, *Management,* 2nd ed. (Cincinnati, OH: Southwestern, 1991), p. 313.

23. Jennifer Laabs, "Employee Sabotage: Don't Be a Target," *Workforce,* July 1999, pp. 33–42.

24. G. Neil Karn and Donna Highfill, "The Dark Side of Change," *Across the Board*, March/April 2004, pp. 39–41.

25. G. Neil Karn and Donna Highfill, pp. 39–41.

26. Gregory Iskat and Jay Liebowitz, "What to Do When Employees Resist Change," *Supervision,* August 2003, pp. 12–14.

27. John Kotter, *The Heart of Change* (Boston: Harvard Business School Press, 2002), p. 15.

28. Kotter, p. 37.

29. Kotter, pp. 61, 83.

30. Kotter, p. 103.

31. Kotter, p. 125.

32. Kotter, p. 143.

33. Kotter, p. 161.

34. Jennifer Laabs, "Paving the Way to Profitability," *Workforce,* March 2000, pp. 66–70.

35. Alvin Toffler, *Future Shock* (New York: Random House, Bantam Books, 1970), p. 11.

36. Eric Abrahamson, "Avoiding Repetitive Change Syndrome," *MIT Sloan Management Review,* Winter 2004, pp. 93–95.

37. Rick Maurer, "Using Resistance to Build Support for Change," *Journal for Quality and Participation,* June 1996, pp. 56–64.

38. Richard Daft, *Management,* 6th ed. (Mason, OH: Thomson South-Western, 2003), p. 385.

39. Mark Clifford, "On the Rocks," *Far Eastern Economic Review*, March 3, 1994, pp. 60–61.

40. Stephen Robbins and Mary Coulter, *Management,* 8th ed. (Upper Saddle River, NJ: Pearson Prentice Hall, 2005), pp. 322–323.

41. Eliza Collins and Mary Anne Devanna, *The Portable MBA* (New York: John Wiley & Sons, 1990), p. 41.

42. Collins and Devanna, p. 41.

43. Robbins and Coulter, p. 318.

44. Michael W. Drafke, *Working in Health Care: What You Need to Know to Succeed,* 2nd ed. (Philadelphia: F. A. Davis, 2002), pp. 141–142.

45. Elwood Chapman and Cliff Goodwin, *Supervisor's Survival Kit,* 9th ed. (Upper Saddle River, NJ: Prentice Hall, 2002), p. 232.

46. Robbins and Coulter, p. 320.

47. Robbins and Coulter, p. 319.

48. Robbins and Coulter, p. 320.

49. Kreitner, p. 394.

50. Mariotti, pp. 30–31.

51. T. S. Bateman and C. P. Zeithaml, *Management: Function and Strategy,* 3rd ed. (Chicago: Irwin, 1996), p. 636.

52. Robbins and Coulter, p. 320; Leonard Marcus, "A Negotiation Toolbox: An Approach for Each Situation," *American Medical News,* January 6, 1997, pp. 39–40.

CHAPTER 14

1. Stephen Robbins and Mary Coulter, *Management,* 8th ed. (Upper Saddle River, NJ: Pearson Prentice Hall, 2005), p. 422.

2. Andrew DuBrin, *Leadership,* 5th ed. (New York: Houghton-Mifflin: 2007), pp. 4–5.

3. Charles Greer and W. Richard Plunkett, *Supervision: Diversity and Teams in the Workplace,* 10th ed. (Upper Saddle River, NJ: Prentice Hall, 2003), p. 76.

4. Robbins and Coulter, pp. 436–438.

5. Ian Wylie, "Is Management a Dead Duck? It's a Leading Question," *Guardian,* March 1, 1997, pp. HRII–IV.

6. DuBrin, pp. 33–47; Robbins and Coulter, p. 423; "The Top 25 Managers of the Year," *Business Week,* January 10, 2000, pp. 60–78; "The Top

Entrepreneurs," *Business Week,* January 10, 2000, pp. 80–82.

7. DuBrin, pp. 83–87.
8. DuBrin, pp. 138–143.
9. Richard Daft, *Management,* 6th ed. (Mason, OH: Thomson South-Western, 2003), pp. 525.
10. DuBrin, pp. 145–149.
11. DuBrin, pp. 143–145.
12. Robbins and Coulter, p. 431.
13. Douglas McGregor, *The Human Side of Enterprise* (New York: McGraw-Hill, 1960), pp. 34–57.
14. Stratford Sherman, "How Tomorrow's Best Leaders Are Learning Their Stuff," *Fortune,* November 27, 1995, p. 90.
15. Susan Caminiti, "What Team Leaders Need to Know," *Fortune,* February 20, 1995, pp. 93–100.
16. John R. Turney and Stanley L. Cohen, "Participative Management: What Is the Right Level? Need for Structure," *Management Review,* October 1980, p. 69.
17. Victor Vroom and Philip Yetton, *Leadership and Decision Making* (Pittsburgh, PA: University of Pittsburgh Press, 1973).
18. Andrew J. DuBrin, *Reengineering Survival Guide* (Cincinnati, OH: Thompson Executive Press, 1996), pp. 175–203.
19. Charles M. Farkas and Philippe De Backer, "There Are Only Five Ways to Lead," *Fortune,* January 15, 1996, pp. 109–112.
20. Ronald Heifetz and Donald Laurie, "The Work of Leadership," *Harvard Business Review,* January–February 1997, pp. 124–135.
21. Hwee Hoon Tan and Christy S. F. Tan, "Toward the Differentiation of Trust in Supervisor and Trust in Organization," *Genetic, Social, and General Psychology Monographs,* May 2000, pp. 241–256.
22. Samuel Greengard, "What's in Store for 2004," *Workforce Management,* December 2003, pp. 34–40.
23. Shari Caudron, "Rebuilding Employee Trust," *Workforce,* October 2002, pp. 28–34.
24. Caudron, pp. 28–34.
25. Tan and Tan, p. 248.
26. Tan and Tan, p. 251.
27. Caudron, pp. 28–34.
28. Tan and Tan, p. 254.
29. Bill Breen and Cheryl Dahle, "Trust for a Change: How Building Trust Can Facilitate Change," *Fast Company,* December 1999, p. 398.
30. Shari Caudron, "Rebuilding Trust through Communication," *Workforce,* October 2002, p. 30.
31. Hyler Bracey, *Building Trust* (Taylorsville, GA: HB Artworks, 2002), p. 23.
32. Bracey, pp. 9, 43.
33. Tan and Tan, p. 254.
34. Randall Richards, "Lending a Hand to the Leaders of Tomorrow," *Association Management,* January 1997, pp. 35–38.
35. Emmett C. Murphy, *Leadership I.Q.* (New York: John Wiley & Sons, 1996), p. 28.
36. Perry Pascarella, "Executive Role: Leading through Change," *Management Review,* January 1997, pp. 22–24.

CHAPTER 15

1. Cheryl Dahle, "Don't Get Mad—Get Over It!" *Fast Company,* February 1999, p. 190; John M. Kelly, "Get a Grip on Stress," *HR Magazine,* February 1997, pp. 51–55.
2. Hans Selye, *Stress without Distress* (New York: Harper & Row, 1987), p. 8.
3. Max E. Douglas, "Creating Eustress in the Workplace: A Supervisor's Role," *Supervision,* October 1996, pp. 6–10.
4. C. L. Cooper and S. Cartwright, "Healthy Mind; Healthy Organization—A Proactive Approach to Occupational Stress," *Human Relations,* April 1994, pp. 455–472.
5. Selye, *Stress without Distress,* p. 18.
6. Hans Selye, *The Stress of Life* (New York: McGraw-Hill, 1976), p. 74.
7. Clive Coukson, "How Stress Can Make You Ill," *Financial Times,* October 7, 1995, p. WIT2.
8. Selye, *Stress of Life,* p. 408.
9. David Concar, "Act Now, Think Later (Nonconscious Affect of the Human Emotional Psyche)," *New Scientist,* April 27, 1996, pp. S20–22.
10. Selye, *Stress without Distress,* p. 41.
11. Lauren Heist, "Cease and De-Stress," *Fast Company,* May 2000.
12. Selye, *Stress without Distress,* p. 41.
13. Jennifer Laabs, "Overload," *Workforce,* January 1999, pp. 30–37.
14. Katherine Yung, "New Corporate Climate: Faster, Better, Cheaper," *Chicago Tribune,* April 6, 2004, sec. 3, p. 4.
15. Shari Caudron, "On the Contrary, Job Stress Is in Job Design," *Workforce,* September 1998, pp. 21–23.
16. Caudron, pp. 21–23.
17. Thomas Li-Ping and Robert Fuller, "Corporate Downsizing: What Managers Can Do to Lessen the Negative Effects of Layoffs," *SAM Advanced Management Journal,* Autumn 1995, pp. 12–17.
18. Peggy Westfall, "Too Tired to Work? Fatigue from Ineffective Work Scheduling," *Safety and Health,* September 1996, pp. 74–77.
19. David Antonioni, "Practicing Conflict Management Can Reduce Organizational Stress," *Industrial Management,* September–October 1995, pp. 7–9.

20. Charlene Marmer Solomon, "Stressed to the Limit," *Workforce,* September 1999, pp. 48–54.

21. Ben Fletcher, *Work, Stress, Disease, and Life Expectancy* (New York: John Wiley & Sons, 1991), pp. 83–98.

22. Michael O'Driscoll and Cary Cooper, "Coping with Work Related Stress," *Journal of Occupational and Organizational Psychology,* December 1994, pp. 343–355.

23. Concar, p. S21.

24. Michelle Cottle, "Working 9 to 5," *Washington Monthly,* January–February 1997, pp. 40–43.

25. Catherine Kedjidjian, "How to Combat Workplace Stress," *Safety and Health,* April 1995, pp. 36–41.

26. Bob Condor, "Life Is a Stress Test," *Chicago Tribune,* November 6, 1996, sec. 5, pp. 1, 9.

27. Kedjidjian, pp. 36–41.

28. Condor, p. 9.

29. Jere E. Yates, *Managing Stress* (New York: American Management Association, 1979), pp. 23–24.

30. Price Pritchett, *A Survival Guide to the Stress of Organization Change* (Dallas, TX: Pritchett & Associates, 1995).

31. Michael Hudson, "Job Burnout: Cause and Cure," *American Business,* February 1981, p. 22.

32. Adapted from F. J. McGuigan, director of the Institute for Stress Management at United States International University, as reported in "Inefficient Bosses May Contribute to Employee Stress Disorders," *Contra Costa Times/Business,* February 10, 1989, p. 50.

33. Afzalur Rahim, "Stress, Strain, and Their Moderators," *Journal of Small Business Management,* January 1996, pp. 46–59.

34. Fletcher, pp. 197–215.

35. Stewart Wolf and Albert Finestone, eds., *Occupational Stress* (Littleton, MA: PSG Publishing, 1986), p. 162.

36. Anita Bodnar, Carolyn Marshall, and Saba Bahouth, "Identifying the Relationship between Work and Non-Work Stress among Bank Managers," *Psychological Reports,* December 1995, pp. 771–778.

37. Barron Maberry, " 'Good God, It's Morning.' How to Make Stress Work for You," *Trial,* January 1996, pp. 70–73.

38. Michael A. Wanko, "Cut Stress Now," *Education Digest,* March 1995, pp. 40–42.

39. William Umikes, "Psycho-Cybernetics: The Proactive Approach to Stress Management," *Medical Laboratory Observer,* November 1994, pp. 28–31.

40. "Hopeful People More Likely to Overcome Barriers, Study Says," *New York Times,* December 23, 1991, p. 27.

41. Laabs, p. 36.

42. Meyer Friedman and Ray H. Roseman, *Type A Behavior and Your Heart* (Greenwich, CT: Fawcett Publications, 1974); Cathy Trost, "Like Mother, Like Baby, Type-A Study Says," *Wall Street Journal,* March 6–7, 1992, p. 4.

43. Ellen Michaud and Lila L. Anastas, *Listen to Your Body* (Emmaus, PA: Rodale Press, 1988), pp. 263–265.

44. C. Northcote Parkinson, *Parkinson's Law* (Cambridge, MA: Riverside Press, 1957), pp. 2–12.

CHAPTER 16

1. Lee Gardenswartz and Anita Rowe, "Cross-Cultural Awareness," *HR Magazine,* March 2001, pp. 139–40.

2. Stan Kossen, *Creative Selling Today,* 3rd ed. (New York: HarperCollins, 1989), p. 447.

3. Robert Robinson and Geralyn McClure Franklin, "Walking a Tightrope: Employment Rights of Foreign Nationals in the Workplace," *Business and Social Review* 107, no. 4, 2002, pp. 489–500.

4. Albert C. Bersticker, "International Strategy That Works: Lessons from Seven Decades of Global Competition," *Industry Week,* October 21, 1996, p. 96B.

5. Charlene Marmer Solomon, "Unhappy Trails," *Workforce,* August 2000, pp. 36–41.

6. Richard Bucher, *Diversity Consciousness* (Upper Saddle River, NJ: Pearson Prentice Hall, 2004) p. 2.

7. Bucher, p. 3.

8. Meg Lundstrom, "The New Mommy Track: Chief Executive, Cook, and Bottle Washer," *Business Week,* December 2, 1999.

9. Betsy Morris, "How Corporate America Is Betraying Women," *Fortune,* January 10, 2005, p. 64.

10. Laura Tyson, "What Holds Women Back: New Views," *Business Week,* October 27, 2003.

11. Nadine Heintz and Bobbie Gossage, "Five Ideas to Watch," *Inc.,* December 2003, p. 27.

12. Carol Kleiman, "Baby-to-work Policy Nurtures Loyalty," *Chicago Tribune,* January 19, 2004, sec. 4, p. 4.

13. Karen Klein, "Your Invitation to a Hot Date in Court," *Business Week,* February 19, 2004.

14. Eugene Rugala and Arnold Isaacs, eds., "Violence in the Workplace: Preventing It; Managing It," *Federal Bureau of Investigation,* March 1, 2004.

15. Todd Henneman "Ignoring Signs of Violence Can Be a Fatal, Costly Mistake," *Workforce Management,* February 27, 2006, pp. 10–11.

16. Patricia O'Connell, "Ready for a Worker Shortage?" *Business Week,* March 22, 2004.

17. Jonathon Petersom, "U.S. Looking for Ways to Retain Older Workers," *Chicago Tribune,* March 5, 2007, sec. 3, pp. 1, 4.

18. "Turning Boomers into Boomerangs," *The Economist,* February 18, 2006, pp. 65–67.

19. Jennifer Reingold and Diane Brady, "Brain Drain," *Fortune,* September 20, 1999, pp. 112–126.

20. Karen Schwartz, "Old Pros," *Chicago Tribune,* November 28, 1999, sec. 6, pp. 1, 7.

21. Barbara Sullivan, "Final Do's, Don'ts for Disabilities Act," *Chicago Tribune,* October 19, 1995, sec. 3, p. 1; Pamela Mendels, "ADA Landmarks Ahead," *Business Week,* October 25, 2001; Suzanne Robitaille, "The ADA's Next Step: Cyberspace," *Business Week,* July 25, 2003.

22. Brenda G. Russell, "Adaptable Workplaces," *Chicago Tribune,* January 30, 2000, sec. 6, pp. 1, 7.

INDEX